STILL THE LAW OF THE LAND?

STILL THE LAW OF THE LAND?

Essays on Changing Interpretations of the Constitution

Joseph S. McNamara,
Executive Editor

Lissa Roche,
General Editor

Hillsdale College Press
Hillsdale, Michigan

Hillsdale College Press

Books by the Hillsdale College Press include: volumes by George Roche, president of Hillsdale College; *Champions of Freedom* series on economics; *The Christian Vision* series; *Scorpions in a Bottle: Dangerous Ideas About the United States and the Soviet Union; Political and Economic Pluralism in the Third World;* and other works.

STILL THE LAW OF THE LAND? ESSAYS ON CHANGING INTER-PRETATIONS OF THE CONSTITUTION

© 1987 by the Hillsdale College Press
Hillsdale, Michigan 49242

Printed in the United States of America

First Printing 1987
Library of Congress Catalog Number: 86-081686
ISBN 0-916308-92-8

Cover photo by Neil Slavin Studio

Contents

Contributors

Edward J. Erler

Holding the department chair in political science at California State University—San Bernardino, Edward Erler is also an associate editor of *Interpretation: A Journal of Political Philosophy*, and a contributing editor to *Benchmark*. He frequently lectures on the Constitution and legal-political theory and is the author of *Equality, Natural Rights and the Rule of Law* (1984) as well as articles in *The Modern Schoolman, The Claremont Journal of Public Affairs, Political Science Reviewer, Polity, The Georgia Law Review, The Claremont Review of Books, The Harvard Salient,* and *The Encyclopaedia of the American Constitution,* and chapters in a number of standard texts on constitutional history.

Lino A. Graglia

Lino A. Graglia is the Rex G. Baker and Edna Heflin Baker Professor of Constitutional Law at the University of Texas at Austin. A former attorney for the U.S. Department of Justice and previously in private practice in Washington, D.C. and New York, Professor Graglia has been at the University since 1966. His writings include *Disaster by Decree: The Supreme Court Decisions on Race and the Schools* (1976) and *The Supreme Court's Busing Decisions: A Study of*

Government by Judiciary (1978). He is a frequent contributor to law reviews and major journals of opinion.

Stephen J. Markman
Stephen Markman currently serves as assistant attorney general of the United States. Prior to this appointment, he was chief counsel of the Senate Subcommittee on the Constitution. Mr. Markman is a graduate of Duke University and the University of Cincinnati School of Law as well as a member of the Michigan and Supreme Court bars. He is a frequent contributor to academic and popular journals on legal and constitutional issues and co-author of *The 1982 Amendments to the Voting Rights Act: Legislative History* (1983).

Edwin Meese III
Edwin Meese became the 75th attorney general of the United States on February 25, 1985. For four years prior to that, he held the cabinet-level position of counselor to the president. During Reagan's years as governor of California, Mr. Meese served as his executive assistant and chief of staff (1969-74), and as his secretary of legal affairs (1967-68). Attorney General Meese has also been a deputy district attorney in Alameda, California, a professor of law at the University of San Diego, a director of the Center for Criminal Justice Policy and Management, and a vice president for Rohr Industries, an aerospace and transportation company.

Avi Nelson
For the past twelve years, Avi Nelson, known to many for his regular appearances on the PBS series, *The Advocates*, has been a prominent figure in the Boston media, an unusual circumstance considering the fact that he holds master's degrees in business administration from Cornell and in physics from Harvard. Mr. Nelson is the president of WMFP

Television in the Lawrence-Boston area, and editorial director of CBS affiliate WEEI. He also serves as an on-the-air analyst for WCVB Channel 5 news, as well as a panelist for the channel's weekly public affairs program, *Five on Five*.

Charles E. Rice

A professor of law at the University of Notre Dame, Charles Rice has also been a professor at Fordham University and New York University as well as a practicing lawyer in New York. He is currently a member of the Education Appeal Board for the Department of Education, and co-editor of the *American Journal of Jurisprudence*. Among his books are *Freedom of Association* (1962); *The Supreme Court and Public Prayer* (1962); *The Vanishing Right to Live* (1969); *Authority and Rebellion* (1971); *Beyond Abortion: The Theory and Practice of the Secular State* (1979), and *Reagan and the Courts' Prospects for Reform* (1980, 1982).

Glen E. Thurow

The author of *Abraham Lincoln and American Political Religion* (1976); co-author of *American Government: Origins, Institutions, and Public Policy* (1984); and co-editor of *Statesmanship and Rhetoric* (1984), Glen Thurow also has over fifty articles, reviews and papers to his credit. He is chairman and director of the graduate program in the department of politics at the University of Dallas, having taught previously at the University of Virginia, the University of Georgia, State University of New York—Buffalo, Bucknell University, and Harvard.

J. Clifford Wallace

J. Clifford Wallace is a judge of the United States Court of Appeals for the Ninth Circuit. Formerly a district judge and a San Diego lawyer, Judge Wallace has held numerous positions as an officer of state and local bar associations and legal committees. He has taught at Brigham Young University, the University of San Diego and California Western School of Law. He is the author of more than a dozen law review essays and a special study commissioned by the Chief Justice of the United States on the future of the judiciary. He travels frequently in Europe, the Middle East and the Far East as a lecturer and consultant to foreign judiciaries.

Foreword

The commemoration of the bicentennial of the United States Constitution should be an occasion of festivity tempered by solemn gratitude for the gift our Founding Fathers bequeathed to us. But if the Constitution is to survive as something more than an abstract symbol—a parchment counterpart of the Statue of Liberty—the celebration must also be the occasion for broadened public awareness of the principles of constitutional government. For the anniversary comes at a time of grave crisis in our constitutional history.

The federal judiciary, originally designed as part of a carefully balanced mechanism in which it shared guardianship of the Constitution with the executive, the two houses of Congress, and the state governments, has gradually taken sole custody unto itself, proclaiming that its decisions and not the Constitution are the supreme law of the land. What is even more dangerous, the Supreme Court has, during the last two or three decades, become progressively more blatant in disregarding the Constitution and arriving at decisions on the basis of the justices' ideological predilections in regard to "social progress" and "human dignity." These usurpations are compatible neither with the idea of constitutional government nor with the ideal of a government of laws.

All the essays in this volume are, in one way or another, addressed to this problem, its ramifications, and its implications. They are the product of long, deep, and careful research and reflection; but, though they are appropriately cast in the muted tones of scholarship, collectively they sound an alarm bell in the night. Every thinking and public-spirited American can learn from their message. For two centuries the Constitution has provided the American people with a framework of limited government, designed for liberty. It is up to us to preserve that framework for our posterity, even as the Founders created it for theirs.

Forrest McDonald
Department of History
University of Alabama

Introduction

In less than a year, the people of the United States will celebrate the two hundredth anniversary of their Constitution.
The approaching bicentennial finds Americans of all political
persuasions united in the belief that this ancient document is
the surest guardian of their liberties and way of life. Nonetheless, the interpretations of its provisions are as controversial today as they were in Washington's first term. Some
Americans believe that the Constitution requires a wall of
separation between church and state, while others see governmental assistance to religion generally, although not to
any preferred sect, compatible with religious liberty. Some
see "the equal protection of the laws" as requiring affirmative
action by the government on behalf of minorities, while
others see the same constitutional provision as forbidding
this practice. Some regard the First Amendment's guarantee
of freedom of speech as absolute, while others would quali-
fy or limit its exercise.

At the highest level of thinking about the Constitution,
opinion is also divided. The dominant school of constitutional jurisprudence, legal realism, or noninterpretivism,
holds that the Constitution is merely a procedural document
containing no principles beyond the procedures themselves.
According to this school of thought, the aim of the Constitu-

tion is not to inform American political life with any ethical norms, nor to shape public policy in terms of any set of values. Rather, America should be regarded as a pluralist society, containing a number of equally valid value systems, each struggling for the means of expressing itself. Constitutional procedures merely set the rules of the competition. In short, the Constitution is seen as wholly indifferent to the end results produced by constitutional procedures. John Hart Ely, a leading proponent of this view, has characterized the Constitution as neutral with respect to substantive values, concerned only with procedural fairness.

Over the past two decades, however, another school of constitutional interpretation has arisen, contending that this doctrine is not consistent with the Founders' beliefs. This newer scholarship, which presents itself as a revival of an older, more authentic tradition, holds that the authors of the Constitution believed that its provisions were informed by the "Laws of Nature and of Nature's God," and gave expression to immutable principles of justice. The dominant, value-free school of thought answers these criticisms by pointing out that the Constitution is a living document, that it must evolve over time, and that an important step in its evolution has been its escape from the confinements of the natural law thinking which characterized the Founders.

All of the essays here, with the exception of Lino A. Graglia's *How the Constitution Disappeared*, were originally presented at Hillsdale College. In March of 1986, Hillsdale College's Center for Constructive Alternatives (CCA) sponsored a week-long seminar in order to ask, "Who is right, the interpretivists or their critics, the modern legal realists?" If the Constitution is to be understood as consistent with human liberty and dignity, must it also be understood as grounded in immutable principle, or must the natural-right framework of interpretation be discarded as outmoded and unduly restrictive? If the Framers were wrong, should we take steps to reform the Constitution? If they were right and still present superior claims to understanding constitutionalism and the rule of law, then should steps be taken to restore the original understanding of their work?

The March CCA, entitled "The Authority of the Constitution: Procedural or Ethical?" paid particular attention to the interpretation of the First and Fourteenth Amendments to the Constitution. The former provides for freedom of speech, press, assembly, and religion, and the latter guarantees the equal protection of the laws to all citizens. Controversies surrounding the interpretation of these portions of the Constitution are key to understanding the issues between the modern constitutional scholars and their natural-law critics, because it has largely been through the adjudication of cases concerning these amendments that the realists' canons of constitutional interpretation have come to assume their present dominance.

Special appreciation is extended to Dr. Thomas F. Payne of the political science department at Hillsdale College for his help in preparing the introduction to this volume, and to Mrs. Patricia DuBois for her assistance in compiling and typing all of the essays included here.

Whose Constitution?
An Inquiry into the Limits
of Constitutional Interpretation

J. Clifford Wallace

Next year we will celebrate the two hundredth anniversary of our Constitution. This remarkable document has structured our government and secured our liberty as we have developed from thirteen fledgling colonies into a mature and strong democracy. Without doubt, the Constitution is one of the grandest political achievements of the modern world.

In spite of this marvelous record, we will celebrate our nation's charter in the midst of a hotly contested debate on the continuing role that it should have in our society. Two schools of constitutional jurisprudence are engaged in a long-running battle. Some contend that the outcome of this conflict may well determine whether the Constitution remains our vital organic document or whether it instead becomes a curious historical relic. The competing positions in this constitutional battle are often summarized by a variety of labels: judicial restraint versus judicial activism, strict construction versus loose construction, positivism versus natural law, conservative versus liberal, interpretivism versus noninterpretivism. In large measure, these labels alone add little assistance in analyzing a complex problem. Ultimately what is at stake, however, as the title suggests, is whose constitution will govern this country. Will it be the written document drafted by the Framers, ratified by the people, and passed down, with amendments, to us? Or will it be an illusive parchment upon which modern-day judges may freely engrave their own political and sociological preferences?

In this essay, I intend to outline and defend a constitutional jurisprudence of judicial restraint.[1] My primary purpose is to suggest that a key principle of judicial restraint—namely, interpretivism—is required by our constitutional plan. I will also explore how practitioners of judicial restraint should resolve the tension that can arise in our current state of constitutional law between interpretivism and a second important principle, respect for precedent. Finally, these two themes will be applied to the central question of whether the authority of the Constitution is procedural or ethical.

Interpretivism and Noninterpretivism

What is the difference between interpretivism and noninterpretivism? This question is important because I believe interpretivism is the cornerstone of a constitutional jurisprudence of judicial restraint. By "interpretivism," I mean the principle that judges, in resolving constitutional questions, should rely on the express provisions of the Constitution or upon those norms that are clearly implicit in its text.[2] Under an interpretivist approach, the original intention of the Framers is the controlling guide for constitutional interpretation. This does not mean, of course, that judges may apply a constitutional provision only to situations specifically contemplated by the Framers. Rather, it simply requires that when considering whether to invalidate the work of the political branches, the judges do so from a starting point fairly discoverable in the Constitution.[3] By contrast, under noninterpretive review, judges may freely rest their decisions on value judgments that admittedly are not supported by, and may even contravene, the text of the Constitution and the intent of the Framers.[4]

I believe that the Constitution itself envisions and requires interpretivist review. To explore this thesis, we should first examine the Constitution as a political and historical document. I hope that you have read the Constitution recently. If you have, I am sure that you were struck by how procedural and technical its provisions are. Perhaps on first reading it may have been something of a disappointment to you. In contrast to the fiery eloquence of the Declaration of Independence, the Constitution may seem dry or even dull. This difference in style, of course, reflects the very different functions of the two documents. The Declaration of Independence is an indictment of the reign of King George III. In a flamboyant tone, it is brilliantly crafted to persuade the world of the justice of our fight for independence. The Constitution, by contrast, establishes the basic set of rules for the nation. Its genius lies deeper, in its skillful design of a government structure that would best ensure liberty and democracy.

The primary mechanism by which the Constitution aims to protect liberty and democracy is the dispersion of government power. Recognizing that concentrated power poses the threat of tyranny, the Framers divided authority between the states and the federal government. In addition they created three separate and co-equal branches of the federal government in a system of checks and balances.

The Framers were also aware, of course, that liberty and democracy can come into conflict. The Constitution therefore strikes a careful balance between democratic rule and minority rights. Its republican, representative features are designed to channel and refine cruder majoritarian impulses. In addition, the Constitution's specific individual protections, especially in the Bill of Rights, guarantee against certain majority intrusions. Beyond these guarantees, the Constitution places its trust in the democratic process— the voice of the people expressed through their freely elected representatives.

Professor Raoul Berger argues persuasively in his book *Government by Judiciary* that the Constitution "was written against a background of interpretive presuppositions that assured the Framers their design would be effectuated."[5] The importance of that statement may escape us today when it is easy to take for granted that the Constitution is a written document. But for the Framers, the fact that the Constitution was in writing was not merely incidental. They recognized that a written constitution provides the most stable basis for the rule of law, upon which liberty and justice ultimately depend.

As Thomas Jefferson observed, "Our peculiar security is in the possession of a written constitution. Let us not make it a blank paper by construction."[6] Chief Justice Marshall, in *Marbury* v. *Madison*, the very case establishing the power of judicial review, emphasized constraints imposed by the written text and the judicial duty to respect these constraints in all cases raising constitutional questions.[7]

Moreover, the Framers recognized the importance of interpreting the Constitution according to their original intent. In Madison's words, if "the sense in which the Constitution was accepted and ratified by the Nation . . . be not the guide in expounding it, there can be no security for a consistent and stable government, [nor] for a faithful exercise of its powers."[8] Similarly, Jefferson as president acknowledged his duty to administer the Constitution "according to the safe and honest meaning contemplated by the plain understanding of the people at the time of its adoption—a meaning to be found in the explanations of those who advocated . . . it."[9] It seems clear, therefore, that the leading Framers were interpretivists and believed that the constitutional questions should be reviewed by that approach.

Leaving the critical history of the importance of interpretivism to the Founders, I would now like to consider whether interpretivism is necessary to effectuate the constitutional plan. The essential starting point is that the Constitution established a separation of powers to protect our freedom. Because freedom is fundamental, so too is the separation of powers. But separation of powers becomes a meaningless slogan if judges may confer constitutional status on whichever rights they happen to deem important, regardless of a textual basis. In effect, under noninterpretive review, the judiciary functions as a superlegislature beyond the check of the other two branches. Noninterpretivist review also disregards the Constitution's careful allocation of most decisions to the democratic process, allowing the legislature to make decisions deemed best for society. Ultimately, noninterpretivist review reduces our written Constitution to insignificance and threatens to impose a tyranny of the judiciary.

Important prudential considerations also weigh heavily in favor of interpretivist review. The rule of law is fundamental in our society. To be effective, it cannot be tossed to and fro by each new sociological wind. Because it is rooted in written text, interpretivist review promotes the stability and predictability essential to the rule of law. By contrast, noninterpretivist review presents an infinitely variable array of possibilities. The Constitution would vary with each judge's conception of what is important. To demonstrate the wide variety of tests that could be applied, let us briefly look at the writings of legal academics who advocate noninterpretivism. Assume each is a judge deciding the same constitutional issue. One professor seeks to "cement[ ] a union between the distributional patterns of the modern welfare state and the federal constitution." Another "would guarantee a whole range of nontextually based rights against government to ensure 'the dignity of full membership in society.'" Yet a third argues that the courts should give "concrete meaning and application" to those values that "give our society an identity and inner coherence [and] its distinctive public morality." Another professor sees the court as having a "prophetic" role in developing moral standards in a "dialectical relationship" with Congress, from which he sees emerging a "more mature" political morality. One professor even urges that the court apply the contractarian moral theory of Professor Rawls's *A Theory of Justice* to constitutional questions. [10] One can easily see the fatal vagueness and subjectiveness of this approach: each judge would apply his or her own separate and diverse personal values in interpreting the same constitutional question. When the anchor is lost, we drift at sea.

Another prudential argument against noninterpretivism is that judges are not particularly well suited to make judgments of broad social policy. We judges decide cases on the basis of a limited record that largely represents the efforts of the parties to the litigation. Legislators, with their committees, hearings, and more direct role in the political process, are much better equipped institutionally to decide what is best for society.

But are there arguments in favor of noninterpretivism? Let us consider several assertions commonly put forth by proponents. One argument asserts that certain constitutional provisions invite judges to import into the constitutional decision process value judgments derived from outside the Constitution. Most commonly, advocates of this view rely on the due process clause of the Fifth and Fourteenth Amendments. It is true that courts have interpreted the due process clause to authorize broad review of the substantive merits of legislation. But is that what the draftsmen had in mind? Some constitutional scholars make a strong argument that the clause, consistent with its plain language, was intended to have a limited procedural meaning. [11]

A second argument asserts that the meaning of the constitutional text and the intention of the Framers cannot be ascertained with sufficient precision to guide constitutional decision making. I readily acknowledge that interpretivism will not always provide easy answers to difficult constitutional questions. The judicial role will always involve the exercise of discretion. The strength of interpretivism is that it channels and constrains this discretion in a manner consistent with the Constitution. While it does not necessarily ensure a correct result, it helpfully excludes from consideration entire ranges of improper judicial responses.

Third, some have suggested that the Fourteenth Amendment effected such a fundamental revision in the nature of our government that the intentions of the original Framers are scarcely any longer relevant. It is, of course, true that federal judges have seized upon the Fourteenth Amendment as a vehicle to restructure federal/state relations. The argument, however, is not one-sided. Professor Raoul Berger, for example, persuasively demonstrates that the Framers of the Fourteenth Amendment had much more limited objectives. [12] In addition, one reasonable interpretation of the history of this amendment demonstrates that its Framers, rather than intending an expanded role for the federal courts, meant for Congress (under Section 5 of the amendment) to play the primary role in enforcing its provisions. [13] Thus it can be argued that to the extent that the Fourteenth Amendment represented an innovation in the constitutional role of the judiciary, it was by limiting the courts' traditional role in enforcing constitutional rights and by providing added responsibility for the Congress.

Advocates of noninterpretivism also contend that we should have a "living Constitution" rather than be bound by "the dead hand of the Framers." These slogans prove nothing. An interpretivist approach would not constrict government processes; on the contrary, it would ensure that issues are freely subject to the workings of the democratic process. Moreover, to the extent that the Constitution might profit from revision, the amendment process of Article V provides the only constitutional means. Judicial amendment under a noninterpretivist approach is simply an unconstitutional usurpation.

Almost certainly, the greatest support for a noninterpretive approach derives from its perceived capacity to achieve just results. Why quibble over the Constitution, after all, if judges who disregard it nevertheless "do justice"? Such a view is dangerously shortsighted and naive. In the first place, one has no cause to believe that the results of noninterpretivism will generally be "right." Individual judges have widely varying conceptions of what values are important. Noninterpretivists spawned the "conservative" substantive economic due process doctrine in the 1930s as well as the "liberal" decisions of the Warren Court. There is no principled or predictable result in noninterpretivism.

But even if the judge would always be right, the process would be wrong. A benevolent judicial tyranny is nonetheless a tyranny. Our Constitution rests on the faith that democracy is intrinsically valuable. From an instrumental perspective, democracy might at times produce results that are not as desirable as platonic guardians might produce. But the democratic process—our participation in a system of self-government—has transcendental value. Moreover, one must consider the very real danger that an activist judiciary stunts the development of a responsible democracy by removing from it the duty to make difficult decisions. If we are to remain faithful to the values of democracy and liberty, we must insist that courts respect the Constitution's allocation of social decision making to the political branches.

Precedent, Judicial Restraint and the Rule of Law

I emphasized earlier the importance of stability to the rule of law. I return to that theme to consider a second principle of judicial restraint: respect for precedent. Respect for precedent is a principle widely accepted, even if not always faithfully followed. It requires simply that a judge follow prior case law in deciding legal questions. Respect for precedent promotes predictability and uniformity. It constrains a judge's discretion and satisfies the reasonable expectations of the parties. Through its application, citizens can have a better understanding of what the law is and act accordingly. Unfortunately, in the present state of constitutional law, the two principles of judicial restraint that I have outlined can come into conflict. While much of constitutional law is consistent with the principle of interpretivism, a significant portion is not. The question thus arises how a practitioner of judicial restraint should act when respecting precedent would require acceptance of law developed by a noninterpretivist approach.

The answer is easy for a judge in my position, and, indeed, for any judge below the United States Supreme

Court. As a judge on the Ninth Circuit Court of Appeals, I am bound to follow Supreme Court and Ninth Circuit precedent even when I believe it is wrong. There is a distinction, however, between following precedent and extending it. Where existing precedent does not fairly govern a legal question, the principle of interpretivism should guide a judge. For Supreme Court justices, the issue is somewhat different. The Supreme Court is obviously not infallible. Throughout its history, the Court has at times rejected its own precedents. Because the Supreme Court has the ultimate judicial say on what the Constitution means, its justices have a special responsibility to ensure that they are properly expounding constitutional law as well as fostering stability and predictability.

Must Supreme Court advocates of judicial restraint passively accept the errors of activist predecessors? There is little rational basis for doing so. Periodic activist inroads could emasculate fundamental doctrines and undermine the separation of powers. Nevertheless, the values of predictability and uniformity that respect for precedent promotes demand caution in overturning precedent. In my view, a justice should consider overturning a prior decision only when the decision is clearly wrong, has significant effects, and would otherwise be difficult to remedy.

Significantly, constitutional decisions based on a non-interpretivist approach may satisfy these criteria. When judges confer constitutional status on their value judgments without support in the language of the Constitution and the original intention of the Framers, they commit clear error. Because constitutional errors frequently affect the institutional structure of government and the allocation of decisions to the democratic process, they are likely to have important effects. And because constitutional decisions, unlike statutory decisions, cannot be set aside through normal political channels, they will generally meet the third requirement. In sum, then, despite the prudential interests furthered by respect for precedent, advocates of judicial restraint may be justified in seeking to overturn noninterpretivist precedent.

The Procedural and Ethical Authority of the Constitution

Having outlined some thoughts on judicial restraint, it is easier to comment briefly on Hillsdale College's conference theme. Thus the question: How would a person who accepts my jurisprudence of judicial restraint respond to whether the authority of the Constitution is procedural or ethical?

It should be evident by now that I have great difficulty using an appeal to natural law, or to any other general ethical principle, as the primary guide for a judge to interpret the Constitution. I certainly do not dispute the existence of objective moral principles; I have adopted moral and religious principles which govern my private life. My judgment is that America would benefit if each citizen adopted and applied sound ethical or religious principles. But this judgment system answers a different inquiry than whether judges should use their concept of natural law—apparently based on their individual concept of ethical or religious principles—to interpret the Constitution. I see no basis in the Constitution for resting constitutional decision making on one's individual concepts of natural law.

Moreover, in twentieth-century America, it is simply not conceivable that different judges applying their own conceptions of "natural law" could produce a stable and coherent body of constitutional law. The general pitfalls of noninterpretivist approaches would certainly be present if constitutional decisions were to be based upon each individual's concept of a doctrine as ill-defined as "natural law." Thus, I see "natural law" as having the potential of becoming just one of many labels under which judges could enshrine their own subjective preferences as constitutionally mandated.[14]

On the other hand, I believe that the Constitution is heavily procedural. But that admission does not assign me to the "value-free" school of thought. I do not believe that its procedures are divorced from ethical values. On the contrary, the Framers deliberately crafted rules and structures that would secure and promote fundamental values such as liberty and democracy. It is these values that form the philosophical basis of judicial restraint.

Therefore, in answer to the question which the conference posed, whether the authority of the Constitution is procedural or ethical, I suggest it is both—and properly so. A jurisprudence of judicial restraint ensures judicial safeguarding of this constitutional plan. In a very important sense, then, the jurisprudence of judicial restraint guarantees a Constitution that is both procedural and ethical.

Notes

1. I have elsewhere presented various aspects of this jurisprudence. See, e.g., Wallace, "A Two Hundred Year Old Constitution in a Modern Society," 61 *Texas Law Review* (1983), 1575; and "The Jurisprudence of Judicial Restraint: A Return to the Moorings," 50 *George Washington Law Review* (1981), 1.
2. Wallace, *supra* note 1, *Texas Law Review*; John H. Ely, *Democracy and Distrust: A Theory of Judicial Review* (Harvard University Press, 1980), 1.
3. Ely, 2.
4. *Ibid.*, 43-72.
5. Raoul Berger. *Government by Judiciary: The Transformation of the Fourteenth Amendment* (Harvard University Press, 1977), 366.

6. *Ibid.*, 364. Quoting letter to Wilson Cary Nicholas, September 7, 1803.
7. *Marbury* v. *Madison*, 5 U.S. (1 Cranch) 137, 176-80 (1803).
8. *Ibid.* Quoting *The Writings of James Madison.*
9. *Ibid.*, 366-67. Citing Jonathan Elliot, *The Debates in the Several State Conventions on The Adoption of the Federal Constitution.*
10. Monaghan, "Our Perfect Constitution," *New York University Law Review* (1981), 353. Summarizes theories of noninterpretivists.
11. Berger, 193-220.
12. *Ibid.*
13. *Ibid.*, 220-29.
14. On another level, however, natural law may have an important role to play in constitutional decision making. Natural law may have had some influence on the Framers, see, e.g., Berns, "Judicial Review and the Rights and Laws of Nature," 49, *Supreme Court Review* (1982), 76-83; but cf. Ely, 49-50 (natural law had little influence on the Framers); and, Berger, 252 (Framers were deeply committed to positivism). To the extent that natural law is demonstrated to have influenced particular parts of the text, its consideration would be helpful in understanding the Framers' intent. This method of analysis is completely consistent with the interpretivist approach since it is directed to finding the meaning of the document.

The Constitution of Principle

Edward J. Erler

On the eve of the bicentennial of the Constitution, we find ourselves engaged in a vigorous national debate concerning how we are to understand this document. Perhaps this is the most appropriate way to celebrate the Constitution—by renewing the debates that surrounded its framing and ratification. After all, the bicentennial presents that natural occasion for reflection on the origins of our system. Those who were closer to the origins understood better than we do today the primacy of first principles. The young Alexander Hamilton wrote in 1775 that "When the first principles of civil society are violated, and the rights of a whole people are invaded, the common forms of municipal law are not to be regarded. Men may then betake themselves to the law of nature; and, if they but conform their actions, to that standard, all cavils against them, betray either ignorance or dishonesty."[1] This statement linking first principles to natural law was not solely the product of Hamilton's youthful exuberance. Both the Virginia Bill of Rights (1776) and the Massachusetts Bill of Rights (1780) posit "a frequent recurrence to fundamental principles" as the indispensable means of preserving free

15

government. It is this frequent recurrence to first principles which supplies our access to those fundamental questions that reach to the very foundations of our way of life as a people.

"Original Intent" and the Modern Debate

A recent exchange between Attorney General Edwin Meese and Supreme Court Justice William Brennan concerning the issue of constitutional interpretation has reminded us once again of the necessity of recurring to first principles. The attorney general has called for a "jurisprudence based on first principles." He describes this jurisprudence as the attempt to recover the "original intent" of the Framers of the Constitution. Original intent is the only reliable guide for interpretation because, in the attorney general's words, it allows us "to judge policies in light of principles, rather than remold principles in light of policies. . . . A jurisprudence seriously aimed at the explication of original intention would produce defensible principles of government that would not be tainted by ideological predilection."[2]

The attorney general's remarks were prompted by the fact that for more than twenty years the Supreme Court has tended to regard constitutional interpretation as an instrument for remolding society and adapting the Constitution to what it perceives to be evolving standards of law and justice. No doubt he had in mind such cases as *Griswold* v. *Connecticut* (1965) in which the Court created a fundamental right to privacy out of the various "penumbras" and "emanations" of the Constitution, and *Roe* v. *Wade* (1973) which created a right to abortion as a necessary incident of the "fundamental right to privacy" that the Court had earlier found lurking in the Constitution in *Griswold*. Meese has also criticized the Court for its ruling in the 1961 case of *Mapp* v. *Ohio* which gave constitutional status to the judicially created exclusionary rule, and the 1966 *Miranda* case which required police warnings to insure the "voluntariness" of criminal confessions. In perhaps his most acerb comment, Meese ridiculed the Court's recent school prayer decisions, remarking that the Framers of the Constitution would have regarded "as somewhat bizarre" the Court's requirement that the government must maintain an absolute neutrality as to the existence of religion or irreligion in the country. It is Meese's position that the touchstone of constitutional interpretation must be the intention of the Framers of the Constitution. If the Constitution is fundamental law, he argues, its basic precepts cannot be changed by the interpretations of the Supreme Court.

Meese's call for a jurisprudence of original intent was ridiculed by Justice Brennan. Brennan candidly admits that "judicial power resides in the authority to give meaning to the Constitution," but he denies that this meaning can be derived from the original intent of the Framers. He goes further: Even if it were possible to discern original intent, he insists it would be undesirable to bind ourselves by that original understanding. The Constitution, Brennan remarks, represents our evolving aspirations of human dignity, and the "demands of human dignity will never cease to evolve."[3]

Brennan's main complaint, of course, is that an adherence to a jurisprudence of original intent would put constitutional limits on the demands that can be made in the name of "human dignity." These are the demands that have been identified with the expansion of the radical welfare state. According to Justice Brennan, those who propose to adhere to the original intent of the Constitution—the proponents of "facile historicism"—are really establishing "a presumption of resolving textual ambiguities against the claim of constitutional right." This is because "the original document, before addition of any of the amendments, does not speak primarily of the rights of man, but of the abilities and disabilities of government." Although the Constitution did contain some specific prohibitions on government power that protected individual rights (e.g., the prohibition on ex post facto laws, bills of attainder, etc.), it was the Bill of Rights and the Civil War amendments, according to Brennan, that provided the "sparkling vision of the supremacy of the human dignity of every individual." One commentator has expressed this idea by asserting that judges must respect all rights as absolute trumps on the powers of government. [4] Thus the rights contained in the amendments preferred by Justice Brennan are understood as being somehow in opposition to the Constitution, not an attempt to adapt the Constitution in accordance with the original intention of the Framers. In Brennan's view those who call for a jurisprudence of original intention therefore wish to ignore the Bill of Rights as the vehicle for the "transformation of social conditions and [the] evolution of our concepts of human dignity."

What this amounts to, in Brennan's argument, is that those who "would restrict claims of right to the values of 1789 specifically articulated in the Constitution turn a blind eye to social progress and eschew adaptation of overarching principles to changes of social circumstance." In short, this view "expresses antipathy to claims of the minority to rights against the majority." This is true because the original Con-stitution establishes the principles of majority rule—it is the Bill of Rights and the Civil War amendments which provide the countermajoritarian protection for minority and individual rights. And, Brennan quickly adds, it is the role of the Court to provide this countermajoritarian protection by standing as the *virtual representative* for those groups that are said to be permanently isolated from the majoritarian political pro-cess—the so-called "discrete and insular minorities."

It is true that the purpose of republican government is to protect the rights and liberties of all who consent to be governed. Republican government does, however, vest the exercise of sovereign power in the majority of society, and because it does so there is always the possibility that a majority will exercise rule in a manner that Madison described as "adverse to the rights of other citizens, or to the permanent and aggregate interests of the community."[5] In short, there is always the possibility that the majority will become a majority faction. The principal problem of republican government, therefore, is to devise a constitution that will insure that majorities can rule in the interest of the society as a whole, that is, in the public good.

Madison described the aim of republican constitutionalism in this manner: "It is of great importance in a republic, not only to guard the society against the oppression of its rulers; but to guard one part of the society against the injustice of the other part."[6] The first aspect of this is addressed by the separation of powers; the second, and more difficult one, requires an extensive regime with a "multiplicity of interests" designed to militate against the formation of majority faction. In a large, diverse republic, Madison reasoned, it will rarely be in the *interest* of the majority to invade the rights of the minority. Since, in all probability, there will be no permanent class interests in society, it is unlikely that there will be permanent majorities and permanent minorities; the majority will never develop a sense of its own identity and interest *as a majority*. In such a situation, there is less probability that "a majority of the whole will have a common motive to invade the rights of other citizens."[7] Madison spoke in terms of the necessity of producing constitutional majorities—majorities that could exercise power consistent with the public good—as opposed to merely numerical majorities which would rule in terms of their own class status as a majority. By and large, the solution of the Framers has worked remarkably well. American politics has never been dominated by majority factions.

"Qualitative Liberalism" and the Judiciary

But for Justice Brennan—and here a majority of the Supreme Court agrees with him—it is inconceivable that a majority could rule in the interest of the whole of society. He simply assumes that the Framers failed in their task of creating a constitution that would produce constitutional majorities and that the American political process has always been dominated by a "monolithic" majority which has merely sought to aggrandize its own interest at the expense of the various "discrete and insular" minorities in society. In short, Brennan (and a majority of the Court) looks upon the majority as just another special interest group.

This idea rests at the heart of what Allen Matusow, in his recent book *Unraveling America* (1984), has called "qualitative liberalism." In the 1950s qualitative liberalism came to replace the older progressive liberalism. The rapid expansion of the middle classes in the post-World War II era had posed a dilemma for liberal intellectuals: Economic inequality had virtually disappeared as a political issue. As Matusow writes:

> the distinguishing feature of the post-World War II era was its remarkable affluence. . . . Sociologically, increased discretionary income blurred class lines and eased class antagonisms. Gone with the old issues was the old feeling of kinship with the masses. In the thirties, intellectuals had expected politics to be the battleground of ideologies, the focal point of class conflict, the medium

for translating the will of the people into policy. In the fifties "the people" were transformed into that scourge of the age—"mass man."[8]

Liberals discovered that they had been "betrayed" by the people; the people did not want reform, they wanted middle class affluence. It was at this point that liberals discovered "the public interest," and "qualitative liberalism."

For the new liberals, the most distressing characteristic of the newly arrived middle classes was their lack of public spiritedness. Liberals now came to believe that the middle classes had co-opted the majoritarian political process to serve their own selfish ends at the expense of those who were not middle class. Whereas a tenet of liberalism once was that the majority in a pluralist society could safely rule in the interest of the whole, now the majority was seen to be the principal obstacle to the promotion of the public interest. If, therefore, democracy was to work for the common good, the essential task of ruling would have to be given over to a vanguard who could act in the majority's stead, i.e., act in the way that majority would act if it were not corrupted by an overweening sense of its own particular class interest. Qualitative liberalism thus found it necessary to mount an attack upon middle-class selfishness, in a word, to force public spiritedness upon this recalcitrant class. In this way, the new liberalism could demonstrate its own public spiritedness, since it would not be working for its own class interest, but for that of the various discrete and insular minorities in society.

How else can one explain the liberals' anger at the self-satisfaction of the middle classes? The middle classes moved to the suburbs in order to send their children to better schools. The liberals invented busing. The middle classes moved to the suburbs to escape crime. The liberals invented a new kind of judicial activism aimed at protecting criminals.

The middle classes moved to the suburbs for better jobs. The liberals invented affirmative action. Harvey Mansfield, in a parody of one of the "qualitative liberals," writes that "to rediscover the whole, or the public, we must recapture the suburbs for the city." Massive busing, he laconically notes, "would remove an important incentive to escape the city."[9]

The theoretical formulation for the new "qualitative liberalism" appeared somewhat belatedly in John Rawls's *A Theory of Justice* published in 1971. The central tenet of this work is that "all social primary goods—liberty and opportunity, income and wealth and the bases of self-respect—are to be distributed equally unless an unequal distribution of any or all of these goods is to the advantage of the least favored."[10] According to Rawls, an apportionment based on the notion of equal opportunity is unjust because it dispenses rewards based on "unmerited" or "arbitrary" natural inequalities. Justice properly understood requires that "equal opportunity" give way to "fair equal opportunity" to correct this "natural lottery."

Rawls thus provided the justification for the rule of a "new class" of administrators who would use their "superior talents" for the benefit of the "least advantaged." This was the justification for a welfare state ruled by public spirited administrators that qualitative liberalism needed. Hardly anyone can fail to see the extent to which this argument has come to occupy a central position in the attempt to extend the radical welfare state and the extent to which it has influenced the federal courts.

The principal agent of qualitative liberalism is the liberal judiciary, which liberalism itself has cast in the role of virtual representative for discrete and insular minorities. As one enthusiastic proponent of the liberal judiciary has stated it recently, "the task of custodianship has been and should be assigned to a *governing body* that is insulated from political responsibility and unbeholden to self-absorbed and excited majoritarianism."[11] No member of the liberal vanguard has taken up the cudgels against middle class democracy with more ideological fervor than Justice Brennan. He writes that

> We current Justices read the Constitution in the only way that we can: as Twentieth-Century Americans. We look to the history of the time of framing and to the intervening history of interpretation. But the ultimate question must be, what do the words of the text mean in our time . . .? What the constitutional fundamentals meant to the wisdom of other times cannot be their measure to the vision of our time.

And what the Constitution stands for today is "a sublime oration on the dignity of man, a bold commitment by a people to the ideal of libertarian dignity protected through law." And, he further notes, "protection of the human dignity of citizens requires a *much modified* view of the proper relationship of individual and state."

The judiciary must, of course, take the leading role not only in reflecting society's progress, but in forming and articulating the ground for progress. We once thought, for example, that human dignity required the protection of private property rights. Now, according to Brennan, we have come to see that human dignity requires a new kind of property rights—the right to government entitlements. Brennan, of course, would be the first to admit that the language of human dignity is not the language of the Constitution. But what Brennan does recognize is that the language of the Constitution is not as amorphous as the language of human dignity, and thus does not lend itself as readily to the kind of progressive reinterpretation that he insists upon. As Brennan remarks, the striving toward the goal of a "comprehensive definition of the constitutional idea of human dignity" is an "eternal quest," a quest that, we might add, has long ago ceased to pretend that it has anything to do with the Constitution.

Brennan's ultimate vision of constitutional interpretation is revealed in his discussion of capital punishment. Brennan does not argue—as indeed he could not—that the Framers of the Bill of Rights intended to abolish capital punishment when they wrote the proscription against "cruel and unusual punishment" into the Eighth Amendment. After all, both the Fifth Amendment and the Fourteenth Amendment prohibit any person from being "deprived of life, liberty, or property, without due process of law." The clear implication is that individuals *can* be deprived of life *with* due process of law. The Fifth Amendment also speaks of "capital crimes." Capital punishment thus could not have been regarded by the Framers of the Constitution or the Framers of the Bill of Rights as "cruel and unusual punishment." As everyone seems to agree, the Framers were attempting to prohibit the star chamber proceedings that had been a part of English criminal law.

Despite the unequivocal intentions of the Framers in this matter, Brennan remarks: "As I interpret the Constitution, capital punishment is under all circumstances cruel and unusual punishment prohibited by the Eighth and Fourteenth Amendments." While the Constitution is viewed by Brennan as a flexible and mutable instrument to be adapted to evolving standards of civilization, his own ideas on the subject of capital punishment, as he informs us, are "fixed and immutable." These ideas are therefore exempt from the need for progress or "evolving standards." They proceed from a "constitutional vision of human dignity" which, he reminds us, is not shared either by a majority of his fellow citizens or a majority of the Supreme Court. The key to understanding the ban on cruel and unusual punishment, according to Brennan, is recognizing its "fundamental premise that even the most base criminal remains a human being possessed of some potential, at least, for common human dignity." Thus, he continues, "the calculated killing of a human being by the States involved, by its very nature, an absolute denial of the executed person's humanity." The state must therefore "treat its citizens in a manner consistent with their intrinsic worth as human beings . . . so as not to be degrading to the very essence of human dignity."

Even conceding, merely for the sake of argument, that the language of human dignity might be inferred from the Constitution, Brennan is totally mistaken about what constitutes human dignity. He seems never to have considered the fact that a country that honors those who, by their actions, have demonstrated no regard for human dignity is dishonoring human dignity itself. *If* the Constitution stands for the ultimate human dignity of the individual, as Brennan insists, then according honor to those who refuse—by murder, rape, torture or other inhuman acts—to recognize the dignity of others would simply convert the Constitution into a "suicide pact." A society which truly hallows human dignity elevates those who demonstrate a regard for human dignity by honoring the laws and the Constitution, and punishes those who are either incapable or unwilling to recognize the human dignity or human rights of others. From the point of view of constitutional government, the death penalty must be properly regarded as affirming the value that society places on life. Brennan's position makes no sense whether regarded from the original intent of the Framers of the Constitution and the Bill of Rights or from the point of view of the eternal quest for evolving standards of human dignity

Who can by now fail to recognize that the original intent of the Framers, rather than Brennan's amorphous notion of

"human dignity," is the true ground of constitutional government? All constitutional debate must take place within the
context of the intentions of the Framers. But how do we resolve ambiguities? And how do we apply old constitutional
principles to new situations? These, of course, are legitimate
questions. Some parts of the Constitution are unequivocal—
for example, that the president must be thirty-five years of
age. But even this plain dictate of language is questioned by
those who would argue that the Constitution has no original
meaning. After all, this could mean that the Framers only
wanted someone to fill the office of the presidency who had
reached mature years and they hit upon thirty-five years as
being merely indicative of maturity. They may have really
meant that any mature person could hold the office regardless of his exact age. A recent scholar—although I hesitate
to call him such—questioned the meaning of a constitutional
provision that all revenue bills must originate in the House of
Representatives. What could the word "originate" possibly
mean here, he asked. Throwing up his hands, he despaired
of any answer, because, he said, everyone knows that today
revenue bills "originate" in the Office of Management and
Budget. If this analysis is correct then it is only too obvious
that written constitutions are mere absurdities. But, of
course, we are not to take such tergiversations and obfusca-
tions seriously.

   But what about cases where genuine debate is possible
about the precise meaning of the Constitution? Of course,
our first obligation, as Madison reminded us, is to the language of the Constitution itself, and to the sense in which it
was understood by those who ratified it. It is only when the
meaning of the Constitution cannot be discerned from its
plain language that resort to extrinsic aids is warranted. But
even such extrinsic aids as the constitutional convention
debates and *The Federalist Papers*—however authoritative

they may be—do not always supply the arguments to resolve debate. What, for example, does "privileges and immunities" or "due process" mean? What, indeed, does "equal protection of the laws" mean? Brennan's position—a position shared by many ideological liberals—is that since there can be differences of opinion about the intention of the Framers, this very possibility makes the debate about intent meaningless. But if the debate is not about the Framers' intent, what could the debate possibly be about? Any other debate would make written constitutions superfluous—as surely Brennan's interpretation of the Eighth Amendment makes the Constitution superfluous.

The Court has relied on Chief Justice Marshall's famous decision in *Marbury* v. *Madison* (1803) in making its boldest claim to judicial supremacy. Justice Brennan, writing an opinion signed by all the members of the Court in the case of *Cooper* v. *Aaron* (1958), recited what he called "some basic constitutional propositions which are settled doctrine," and which were derived from the arguments of *Marbury*. First is the proposition, contained in Article VI of the Constitution, that the Constitution is the supreme law of the land; second is Marshall's statement that the Constitution is "the fundamental and paramount law of the nation"; third is Marshall's declaration that "it is emphatically the province and duty of the judicial department to say what the law is." Justice Brennan concluded that *Marbury* therefore "declared the basic principle that the federal judiciary is supreme in the exposition of the law of the Constitution, and that principle has ever since been respected by this Court and the country as a permanent and indispensable feature of our constitutional system. It follows that the interpretation of the Fourteenth Amendment enunciated by this Court in the *Brown* case is the supreme law of the land." The defect of Brennan's argument, of course, is that it confounds the Constitution with constitutional law, the Constitution and the Court's interpre-tation of the Constitution.

Marshall did indeed say that the Constitution was "the fundamental and paramount law of the nation," and that any "ordinary legislative acts" "repugnant to the Constitution" were necessarily void. But when Marshall wrote the famous line relied upon by Brennan that "it is emphatically the prov-ince and duty of the judicial department to say what the law is," he was referring not to the Constitution but to "ordinary legislative acts." In order to determine the law's conformity with the Constitution it is first necessary to know what the law is. And once the law is ascertained it is also necessary to determine whether the law is in conformity with the "para-mount law" of the Constitution. This latter, of course, means that "in some cases" the Constitution itself "must be looked into by the judges" in order to determine the particular dis-position of a case. But Marshall was clear that the ability of the Court to interpret the Constitution was incident to the necessity of deciding a law's conformity to the Constitution, and not a general warrant for constitutional interpretation of judicial legislation. Marshall was emphatic in his pronounce-ment that "the province of the Court is, solely, to decide on the rights of individuals."

As Marshall went on to note, "it is apparent that the Framers of the Constitution contemplated that instrument as a rule for the government of courts, as well as of the legisla-ture." And, as he laconically noted in peroration of his argument, "it is also not unworthy of observation, that in declaring what shall be the supreme law of the land, the Constitution itself is first mentioned; and not the laws of the United States generally, but those only which shall be made in pursuance of the Constitution, have that rank." For Mar-shall, Brennan's assertion that the Court's decision in *Brown* was "the supreme law of the land," would indeed make "written constitutions absurd" because it would usurp the "original right" of the people to establish their government on "such principles" which must be "deemed fundamental" and "permanent." If the Supreme Court were indeed to sit as a "continuing constitutional convention" as many have urged, any written constitution would certainly be superfluous since, under the circumstances, there would be no "rule for the government of courts."

First Principles

The key to understanding the original intention of the Framers is in understanding the character of the exercise of the original right by the people. For it is by the exercise of this right that the people establish their constitution on "such principles" as they deem necessary for their safety and happiness. The Framers of our Constitution explicitly sought to put into motion the principles enunciated in the Declaration of Independence, a document which they believed derived its authority from the "Laws of Nature and Nature's God." Madison, for example, said that the Constitution was derived from the "fundamental principles of the revolution," the very source of America's "manly spirit." Thus the Constitution cannot be understood primarily as an historical document; it must be understood as a document embodying the natural law teachings of the Declaration. It is only when the Constitution is read in this light that its intentions become clear and can be articulated in a consistent manner. This is the reason that Abraham Lincoln called the Declaration the "standard maxim" of our political life and the "sheet anchor" of our republicanism.

What the Declaration teaches, above all, is that political life can rest on the ground of political principle; the principle that "all men are created equal" and its necessary concomitant that all legitimate government rests upon the consent of the governed. The idea of equality supplies our access to nature or natural right. Equality—the fact that human beings have no natural rulers—is the unique expression of human nature. Unlike every other species, human beings have the potential to choose their form of government, and it is this human potential for choice—rooted in human nature—that accounts for human freedom *and* rationality. Government based on the consent of the governed was therefore a dictate of the "Laws of Nature and Nature's God." As Jefferson wrote in 1816, republican government (by which he meant those based on the consent of the governed) is the only form of government consistent with natural right. [12] Because the idea of equality is grounded in human nature it necessarily points to nature or natural right. The radical core of the Declaration was the fact that it replaced history with nature as the standard of political right. The Declaration appeals to the natural rights of man, not the historic rights of Englishmen.

Scholars today maintain that the argument of the Declaration is only "an intellectual construction" or "cultural artifact" of the late eighteenth century. The truths that the Framers believed derived from the Laws of Nature were, in fact, only the relative "truths" of that historical epoch. [13] This argument claims to provide an ahistorical insight into the ideas of that time. As such it claims to be something more than an "intellectual construct"; but a genuine insight. But how is this argument exempt? Can any argument claiming the historicity of all thought itself be exempt from historicity? The Framers—unlike most contemporary commentators— were fully conscious of the distinction between historical prescription and natural right. [14]

But insofar as the Constitution allowed the continued existence of slavery, it was only an incomplete expression of the principles of the Declaration of Independence. No matter to what extent the Constitution may have placed the institution of chattel slavery on what Lincoln rightly termed "the road to ultimate extinction," it was still inconsistent with the principled injunctions of the Declaration that all legitimate power must be derived from the consent of the governed. The formal completion of the Constitution—as a complete expression of the principles of the Declaration—did not occur until the Thirteenth and Fourteenth Amendments to the Constitution were ratified. The Thirteenth abolished slavery, and the Fourteenth extended to the newly freed slaves the whole panoply of civil rights that are the necessary incidents of federal citizenship. The proponents of the Fourteenth Amendment were quite explicit about the fact that they regarded that amendment as the principled completion of the regime. Thaddeus Stevens, the leading Radical Republican, made this precise point in a speech urging the adoption of the Fourteenth Amendment before the House of Representatives on May 8, 1866:

> I beg gentlemen to consider the magnitude of the task which was imposed upon the [Joint Committee on Reconstruction].They were expected to suggest a plan for rebuilding a shattered nation. . . . It cannot be denied that this terrible struggle sprang from the vicious principles incorporated into the institutions of our country. Our fathers had been compelled to postpone the principles of their great Declaration, and wait for their full establishment till a more propitious time. That time ought to be present now.[15]

References to the Declaration as organic law were so frequent throughout the debates that one can hardly doubt that the Reconstruction Congress was self-consciously engaged, in some sense, in ratifying a refounding of the regime by embodying in the Constitution the victories that had been won on the battlefields of the Civil War. From this point of view the Civil War must be viewed as the last battle of the Revolutionary War, since only the Reconstruction amendments bring the Constitution into full compliance with the revolutionary principles of the Declaration.

The attorney general recently quoted approvingly a remark of Judge Robert Bork to the effect that "our constitutional liberties arose out of historical experience and out of political, moral, and religious sentiment. They do not rest upon any general theory." It is historical experience, Bork continues, "that gives our rights life, rootedness, and meaning."[16] But if this is indeed true, our liberties have no ground other than our own particular experiences. If then, we had not been a people who had experienced freedom, then we would have no ground to assert a right to freedom. Such a positivistic view of right would undermine any moral ground for the existence of rights or liberties. From this point of view, the only rule of political action that is left is the rule of force.

Meese cites the infamous *Dred Scott* decision (1857) as a "tragic" example of a decision not securely grounded in "the jurisprudence of original intent." In this case, the attorney general asserts, "the Supreme Court under Chief Justice Roger B. Taney read blacks out of the Constitution in order to invalidate Congress's attempt to limit the spread of slavery." The lesson here is the "danger in seeing the Constitution as an empty vessel into which each generation may pour its passion and prejudice."[17] What the attorney general ignores in his citation of *Dred Scott* is the fact that Taney believed that his opinion was derived from the original intent of the Framers of the Constitution, and he attempted a full explication of that original intent to support his conclusion that blacks were never intended to be citizens of the United States. So far from preventing Taney from pouring his passion and prejudice into the law, the doctrine of original intent was the vehicle for Taney to do precisely that. Taney's attempt to uncover the original intent of the Framers rested on purely historicist grounds. One can infer the Framers' intent, Taney reasoned, by examining the experience or practice at the time of the Founding. No state constitution admitted blacks into full citizenship and blacks were everywhere generally accorded second class status or worse. How, then, Taney asserted, could the Framers have intend- ed to include blacks among those whose due process rights were to be protected by the Fifth Amendment? The Fifth Amendment guarantees that no person shall be deprived of life, liberty, or property without due process of law. How are slaves to be regarded?—as property? As human beings themselves deserving of the right to life, liberty, and prop- erty? Taney did not see the tension inherent in the Fifth Amendment; that the Constitution could be read both ways. After all, other provisions of the Constitution give positive protection to slavery—the provision for the continuance of the foreign slave trade for twenty years, the three-fifths com- promise, and the fugitive slave clause. These provisions were all part of the great bundle of compromises that was struck at the constitutional convention. But compromises are not principles—they are departures from principle de- signed to uphold or maintain the principle while at the same time recognizing that necessity might from time to time require some postponement of the operation of the principle. It is the Declaration's principle of equality, a principle that asserts the equality of all members of the human species, that provides the proper gloss on the due process clause. The lit- eral language of the Constitution is inadequate for resolving the question.

It is not enough to intone the necessity of recurring to original intent, as if the Constitution were merely a document of positive law. On these grounds—on the ground of positivism—Taney would be right. Experience and practice had indeed placed blacks "below the level of men."[18] *But experience is not the standard of the Constitution.* The standard of the Constitution, in Madison's words, is "the transcendent Law of Nature and of Nature's God."[19] It is only by reference to this standard that one can declare that all men are created equal and that all men must be accorded due process rights and equal protection of the laws. It is not enough to declare the original intention; it is also necessary to defend the rightness of that intention. Justice Brennan is correct when he remarks that the Constitution embodies a general theory of values. He is wrong, however, about what that theory is. The Constitution does indeed have a "general theory"—it is the theory of the Declaration of Independence. The original intent of the Framers is not to be valued simply because it was the intent of "our" forefathers, and that intent embodies our historical experience—this is indeed "facile historicism." Rather, the original intent of the Framers is to be valued because it embodies the true principles of political order. The ground of legitimate political order is not history or experience, but the laws of nature and nature's God—the rationality of the unaided human intellect. This idea was perfectly expressed by Alexander Hamilton when he remarked that "The sacred rights of mankind are not to be rummaged for, among old parchments, or musty records. They are written, as with a sun beam, in the whole *volume* of human nature, by the hand of divinity itself; and can never be erased or obscured by mortal power."[20] America's claim to be grounded in natural right was its unique claim to greatness. To miss this is to miss the essential point of the Framers' intent.

If it is true that America is uniquely a regime of principle as the Founders believed, then it is necessary for the people of America to rethink periodically those principles by which they constitute themselves as a people. The two hundreth anniversary of the drafting and ratification of the Constitution provides the natural occasion for this essential activity.

Notes

1. "The Farmer Refuted," *The Papers of Alexander Hamilton*, Vol. 1, edited by Harold C. Syrett (Columbia University Press, 1961), 136.
2. Edwin Meese III, "Address Before the District of Columbia Chapter of the Federalist Society," Nov. 15, 1985; "Address Before the American Bar Association," July 9, 1985.
3. William Brennan, "The Constitution of the United States: Contemporary Ratification," Text and Teaching Symposium, Georgetown University, Oct. 12, 1985. Unless otherwise noted, all further quotations from Justice Brennan are from this speech.
4. Sotirios A. Barber, *On What the Constitution Means* (Johns Hopkins University Press, 1984), 35; Edward Erler, "Judicial Enlightenment Run Riot," *Claremont Review of Books*, Vol. 14 (Fall, 1985), 17.
5. *The Federalist* No. 10, edited by Clinton Rossiter (New York: New American Library, 1961), 78.
6. *Ibid.*, No. 51, 323.
7. *Ibid.*, No. 10, 83.
8. Allen Matusow, *The Unraveling of America: A History of Liberalism in the 1960s* (New York: Harper & Row, 1984), 6.
9. Harvey Mansfield, *The Spirit of Liberalism* (Harvard University Press, 1978), 35.
10. John Rawls, *A Theory of Justice* (Cambridge: Belknap Press, 1971), 303.
11. Jesse Choper, *Judicial Review and the National Political Process* (University of Chicago Press, 1980), 68.
12. Letter to John Taylor, May 28, 1816, in Merrill Peterson, ed.,*Jefferson: Collected Works* (Oxford University Press, 1984) 1392.
13. Joyce Appleby, *Capitalism and a New Social Order* (New York University Press, 1984), 101.

14. *See* Edward Erler, *Equality, Natural Rights, and the Rule of Law: The View from the American Founding* (Claremont Institute, 1984).
15. *Congressional Globe*, 39th Cong., 1st Sess., 2459 (1866).
16. "Address Before the American Enterprise Institute," Washington, D.C., Sept. 6, 1985.
17. "Address Before the District of Columbia Chapter of the Federalist Society," Nov. 15, 1985.
18. *The Federalist* No. 43, 277.
19. *Ibid.*, 279.
20. "Farmer Refuted," *Papers*, I, 122.

How The Constitution Disappeared

Lino A. Graglia

Attorney General Edwin Meese's recent statement in a speech to the American Bar Association that judges should interpret the Constitution to mean what it was originally intended to mean probably did not strike most people as controversial. Nevertheless it brought forth immediate denunciation by a sitting Supreme Court Justice as "doctrinaire," "arrogant," and the product of "facile historicism." "It is a view," Justice William J. Brennan, Jr. said in a speech at Georgetown University, "that feigns self-effacing deference to the specific judgments of those who forged our original social compact," but that "in truth . . . is little more than arrogance cloaked as humility" because it is not possible to "gauge accurately the intent of the Framers on application of principle to specific, contemporary questions." [1] The view is not only mistaken, but misguided, Justice Brennan continued, because it would require judges to "turn a blind eye to social progress and eschew adaptation of overarching principles to changes of social circumstance."

This essay originally appeared in the February 1986 issue of *Commentary*.

What Is at Stake?

To state that judges should interpret the Constitution as intended by those who wrote and ratified it ("the Framers") is only to state the basic premise of our political-legal system that the function of judges is to apply, not to make, the law. Indeed, it would be difficult to say what interpretation of a law means if not to determine the intent of the lawmaker. Justice Brennan's angry attack on the obvious as if it were disreputable, soon joined by the attacks of his colleague Justice John Paul Stevens and a legion of media commentators, makes evident that much is at stake in this debate on a seemingly esoteric matter of constitutional interpretation. What is at stake is nothing less than the question of how the country should be governed in regard to basic issues of social policy: whether such issues should be decided by elected representatives of the people, largely on a state-by-state basis, or, as has been the case for the last three decades, primarily by a majority of the nine justices of the United States Supreme Court for the nation as a whole.

The modern era of constitutional law began with the Supreme Court's 1954 decision in *Brown* v. *Board of Education*, holding compulsory school racial segregation and, it soon appeared, all racial discrimination by government, unconstitutional. The undeniable rightness of the decision as a matter of social policy, in effect ending legally imposed second-class citizenship for blacks, and its eventual acceptance by the public and ratification by Congress and the president in the 1964 Civil Rights Act, gained for the Court a status and prestige unprecedented in our history. The moral superiority of decision making by judges to decision making by mere "politicians" seemed evident. The result was to enable the Court to move from its historic role as a brake on social change to a very different role as the primary engine of such change.

In the years since *Brown*, nearly every fundamental change in domestic social policy has been brought about not by the decentralized democratic (or, more accurately, republican) process contemplated by the Constitution, but simply by the Court's decree. The Court has decided, on a national basis and often in opposition to the wishes of a majority of the American people, issues literally of life and death, as in its decisions invalidating virtually all restrictions on abortion and severely restricting the use of capital punishment. It has decided issues of public security and order, as in its decisions greatly expanding the protection of the criminally accused and limiting state power to control street demonstrations and vagrancy, and issues of public morality, as in the decisions disallowing most state controls of pornography, obscenity, and nudity. The Court has both prohibited the states from making provisions for prayer in the schools and disallowed most forms of aid, state or federal, to religious schools. It has required that children be excluded from their neighborhood public schools and bused to more distant schools in order to increase school racial integration; ordered the reapportionment of state and federal legislatures on a "one-man-one-vote" basis; invalidated most of the law of libel and slander; and disallowed nearly all legal distinctions on the basis of sex, illegitimacy, and alienage. The list could easily be extended, but it should be clear that in terms of the issues that determine the nature and quality of life in a society, the Supreme Court has become our most important institution of government.

Since his appointment to the Court by President Eisenhower in 1956, Justice Brennan has participated in all of the Court's major constitutional decisions, has consistently voted in favor of Court intervention in the political process, and has often been a leader on the Court in reaching the decision to intervene. Indeed, he has ordinarily differed with the Court only in that he would often go even farther in disallowing political control of some issues; he would, for example, go farther than the Court has in disallowing state regulation of the distribution of pornographic material and he would prohibit capital punishment in all cases. If the Court has been our most important institution of government for the past three decades, Justice Brennan—although his name is probably unknown to the great majority of his fellow citizens—has surely been our most important government official. To argue that the Supreme Court should confine it-self or be confined to interpreting the Constitution as written is to undermine the basis of this status and challenge the legitimacy of his life's work.

The Power of the Supreme Court

Constitutional law is as a practical matter the product of the exercise of the power of judicial review, the power of judges, and ultimately of Supreme Court justices, to invalidate legislation and other acts of other officials and institutions of government as inconsistent with the Constitution. The central question presented by constitutional law—the only question the great variety of matters dealt with under that rubric have in common—is how, if at all, can such a power in the hands of national officials who are unelected and effectively hold office for life be justified in a system of government supposedly republican in form and federalist in organization? The power was not explicitly provided for in the Constitution and had no precedent in English law— where Parliament, not a court, is said to be supreme—which could well be taken as reason enough to assume that no such power had been granted. Alexander Hamilton argued for the power in *The Federalist* No. 78, however, and Chief Justice John Marshall established it in *Marbury* v. *Madison* in 1803 on the ground that it is inherent in a written constitution that declares itself to be supreme law. The argument is hardly unanswerable—other nations have written constitutions without judicial review—but judicial review limited to interpretation of the Constitution in accordance with the Framers' intent does obviate the problem of policy making by judges.

Constitutional limitations on popular government are undoubtedly undemocratic, even if they were themselves democratically adopted by a supermajority, but the only function of judges in exercising judicial review on the basis of a written constitution with determinate meaning would be the entirely judicial function of enforcing the Constitution as they would any other law. The judges, Hamilton assured the ratifying states, would have neither "force nor will"; able to "take no active resolution whatever" in enforcing the Constitution, their power would be "next to nothing." "Judicial power," Marshall reiterated, "has no existence. Courts are mere instruments of the law, and can will nothing." The notion that a court has "power to overrule or control the action of the people's representatives," Justice Owen Roberts confirmed during the New Deal constitutional crisis, "is a misconception"; the Court's only function in a constitutional case is "to lay the article of the Constitution which is invoked beside the statute which is challenged and to decide whether the latter squares with the former."

Even Justice Brennan purports to recognize what, as he notes, Alexander Bickel called "the counter-majoritarian difficulty" presented by judicial review. "Our commitment to self-governance in a representative democracy must be reconciled," Justice Brennan concedes, "with vesting in electorally unaccountable justices the power to invalidate the expressed desires of representative bodies on the ground of inconsistency with higher law." Supreme Court justices, he acknowledges at the beginning of his speech, echoing Judge Learned Hand, "are not platonic guardians appointed to wield authority according to their personal moral predilections." At several points he even seems to offer the standard justification for judicial review, that the judges merely interpret the written Constitution. He states, for example, that the duty of the judge is to "draw meaning from the text" and "remain faithful to the content" of the Constitution and that "the debate is really a debate about how to read the text, about constraints on what is legitimate interpretation." These statements are consistent with the remainder of his speech, however, only if reading or interpreting a document is considered indistinguishable from composing or rewriting it.

Unfortunately, however, the debate is not about how judges should read or interpret the text of the Constitution, but about whether that is what they should in fact confine themselves to doing in deciding constitutional cases. The view that the duty of judges is to read and interpret the Constitution—to attempt to determine what the Framers intended to say—is precisely the view that Justice Brennan seeks to rebut and derides as uninformed and misguided. The whole point of his speech is that judges should not be confined to that task, for to so confine them would be to give them much too limited a role in our system of government and leave us insufficiently protected from the dangers of majority rule.

Justifying the Exercise of Power

Justice Brennan is far from alone today in his view of the proper role of judges in exercising judicial review and of the essential irrelevance of the Constitution to constitutional law.

It is, indeed, the view taken by most contemporary constitu-tional law scholars, who share the political ideology of the modern-era Supreme Court and see it as their professional duty to legitimize the fruits of that ideology. Because it has become increasingly difficult—in fact, impossible—to justi-fy the Court's controversial decisions as the result of consti-tutional interpretation, the bulk of modern constitutional law scholarship consists of the invention and elaboration of "noninterpretivist" or "non-originalist" theories of judicial review—justfications for a judicial review that is not con-fined to constitutional interpretation in any sense that would effectively restrain judicial choice. Because the product of this review is nonetheless always called "constitutional law" and attributed in some way to the Constitution, the result is the paradox of noninterpretivist constitutional interpretation, constitutional law without the Constitution.

That more and more constitutional scholars, and now a Supreme Court justice, should come to recognize and ac-knowledge that the Supreme Court's constitutional decisions of recent decades cannot be justified on any other basis—that they are not in fact based on the Constitution—can be taken as a hopeful sign. Although the effort today in an increasing flood of books, articles, and speeches is to justify those decisions nonetheless, the inevitable failure of such efforts must, it would seem, eventually cause the enterprise to be abandoned and the fact that they cannot be justified in a system of self-government to be also generally recognized and acknowledged. Justice Brennan has performed a public service by bringing this extremely important and little under-stood issue to greater public attention, conveniently summar-izing the standard arguments for "noninterpretivist" or "non-originalist" review—i.e., what is popularly referred to as "judicial activism"—and stating his own position with un-usual, even if not total, clarity and candor.

Defenders of judicial activism face the dilemma that, on the one hand, judicial policy making cannot be defended as such in our system—the justices, even Justice Brennan must concede, are not authorized to enact their "personal moral predilections" into law and must therefore claim that their decisions derive somehow from the Constitution. On the other hand, it happens that the Constitution is most ill-suited as a basis for substantial judicial policy making by frequent judicial intervention in the political process in the name of protecting individual rights from majority rule. The central difficulty is that although the Constitution does create some individual rights, they are actually rather few, fairly well-defined, and rarely violated. The first task of the defender of judicial activism, therefore, is to dispose of the Constitution as unhelpful, inadequate, or irrelevant to contemporary needs. Reasons must be found why the Constitution cannot be taken to mean what it rather clearly is known to mean—especially when read, as all writings must be, in historical context—or, even better, to have any determinate meaning at all.

After disposing of the Constitution by depriving it of its historic meaning, the next task of defenders of judicial activism is to imagine a much more expansive, elevated, and abstract constitution that, having no specific meaning, can be made to mean anything and serve therefore as simply a mandate for judges to enact their versions of the public good. In response to the objection that the very thinly veiled system of government by judges thus achieved is obviously inconsistent with democracy, the argument is made that the value of democracy is easily overrated and its dangers many. The "very purpose of a Constitution," as Justice Brennan states the standard argument, is to limit democracy by declaring "certain values transcendent, beyond the reach of temporary political majorities." In any event, no real inconsistency with democracy is involved, the argument concludes, because the judges, though unrestrained by the actual text of the Constitution, will continue to be restrained by its principles, the adaptation of which to changing circumstances is the true and indispensable function of judges. Justice Brennan's speech can serve as a textbook illustration of each of these moves.

Justice Brennan's attack on the notion of a constitution with a determinable historic meaning could hardly be more thorough. First of all, he finds that the Court's "sources of potential enlightenment" as to the intended meaning are often "sparse or ambiguous." Even more serious, the search for meaning is likely to be futile in any event because even the Framers, he believes, usually did not know what they meant: "Typically, all that can be gleaned is that the Framers themselves did not agree about the application or meaning of particular constitutional provisions, and hid their differences in cloaks of generality." Then there is the question of "whose intention is relevant—that of the drafters, the congressional disputants, or the ratifiers in the states?" Indeed, there is the most basic question of all, whether the very notion of intent makes sense, "whether the idea of an original intention is a coherent way of thinking about a jointly drafted document drawing its authority from a general assent of the states." It is almost as if the Constitution and its various provisions might have been drafted and adopted with no purpose at all. Finally, there is the problem that "our distance of two centuries cannot but work as a prism refracting all we perceive." For all these reasons, the idea that judicial review is legitimate only if faithful to the intent of the Framers can be held only by "persons who have no familiarity with the historical record."

Justice Brennan has still another, although it would seem unnecessary, nail to put in the coffin of the now demolished Constitution. Should any shred of constitutional meaning somehow survive the many obstacles he sees to finding it, he would accord it little or no value. The world of the Framers is "dead and gone," and it would not do, he believes, to hold the Constitution captive to the "anachronistic views of long-gone generations." "[A]ny static meaning" the Constitution "might have had" in that dead world must, therefore, be of dubious relevance today. In any event, "the genius of the Constitution rests," in his view, not in any such meaning but in "the adaptability of its great principles to cope with current problems and current needs." Strange as it may seem, a writing can be great apart from its meaning and solely by reason of its supposed ability to mean anything.

Most of Justice Brennan's objections regarding the difficulties of constitutional interpretation have some basis, but they could also be made in regard to interpretation of almost any law. For example, one can almost always wish for a clearer or more detailed legislative history, and it is always true that legislators cannot foresee and agree on every possible application of a law. If these difficulties made the effort to determine legislative intent futile, a system of written law would hardly be possible. In any event, from the premise of an unknowable or irrelevant Constitution, the conclusion should follow that judges have no basis or justification for declaring laws unconstitutional, not that they are therefore free to invalidate laws on some other basis and still claim to be interpreting the Constitution.

Most important, whatever the difficulties of legal interpretation, they have little or no relevance to actual constitutional decision making by the Supreme Court because no issue of interpretation, no real dispute about the intended meaning of the Constitution, is ordinarily involved. For example, the Constitution contains no provision mentioning or apparently in any way referring to the authority of the states to regulate the practice of abortion. However one might undertake to defend the Court's abortion decisions, it does not seem possible to argue that they are the result of constitutional interpretation in any non-fanciful sense. As another example, although the Constitution does mention religion, no process that could be called interpretation permits one to go from the Constitution's protection of religious freedom from federal interference to the proposition that the states may not provide for prayer in the schools.

A constitution so devoid of ascertainable meaning or contemporary relevance would seem quite useless as a guide to the solution of any contemporary problem and certainly as a written law enforceable by judges. The judges might as well be told to enforce a document written in an unknown language or, more in keeping with Justice Brennan's view, in disappearing ink. Having effectively eliminated the actual Constitution, however, Justice Brennan proceeds to remedy the loss—judicial activism cannot proceed with no constitution at all—by imagining and substituting a much more impressive, inspiring, and usefully uncertain one.

The Constitution as Written

The constitution of Justice Brennan's vision is undoubtedly a wonderful thing, one of "great" and "overarching" principles and "majestic generalities and ennobling pronouncements [that] are both luminous and obscure." It is nothing less grand than the embodiment of "the aspiration to social justice, brotherhood, and human dignity that brought this nation into being," "a sublime oration on the dignity of man," and "a sparkling vision of the supremacy of the human dignity of every individual." Justice Brennan accurately reflects current constitutional law scholarship, here as throughout his speech, by seeing the Constitution as simply "the lodestar for our aspirations." It is a source of constant wonderment that scholars and judges of otherwise the most secular and rationalist turn of mind can grow mystical when discussing the Constitution.

The temptation is strong, of course, to dismiss Justice Brennan's rapturous statements as mere flights of poetic fancy or utopian ecstasy, obviously not meant as serious descriptions or explanations of the Constitution. The fact remains, however, that this view of the Constitution is the only justification offered by him, or other contemporary defenders of judicial activism, for the Court's assumption and exercise of enormous government power. Fanciful as it may seem, a contitution that is simply the embodiment of "our," or at least his, aspirations accurately describes the constitution he has been enforcing for nearly three decades to override the will of the people of this country on issue after issue. It cannot be too strongly emphasized, therefore, that the Constitution we actually have bears almost no relation to, and is often clearly irreconcilable with, the constitution of Justice Brennan's vision. No more is necessary to rebut all contemporary defenses of judicial activism than that a copy of the Constitution be kept close at hand to demonstrate that the defenders of judicial activism are invariably relying on something else.

Although it may come as something of a disappointment to some, an "aspiration for social justice, brotherhood, and human dignity" happens not to have been what brought this nation, or at least the government founded on the Constitution, into being. The convention to revise the Articles of Confederation was called and the Constitution was drafted and ratified not to provide additional protections for human rights—on the contrary, the stronger national government created by the Constitution was correctly seen as a potential danger to human rights—but almost entirely for commercial purposes. The primary motivating force for the creation of a stronger national government was the felt need of a central authority to remove State-imposed obstacles to interstate trade. How little the Constitution had to do with aspirations for brotherhood or human dignity is perhaps most clearly seen in its several provisions regarding slavery. It provides, for example, that a slave was to be counted as three-fifths of a free person for purposes of representation and that slaves escaping to free states were nonetheless to be returned to their masters. It is not, as Justice Brennan would explain this, that part of the "egalitarianism in America has been more pretension than realized fact," but that there was at the time the Constitution was adopted very little pretension to egalitarianism, as is illustrated by, for example, the widespread use of property qualifications for voting.

Given the original Constitution's limited and mundane purposes, it is not surprising that it provides judges with little to work with for the purpose of advancing their personal notions of social justice. The Constitution is, first of all, a very short document—easily printed, with all twenty-seven amendments and repealed matter, on fewer than twenty pages—and apparently quite simple and straightforward, not at all like a recondite tome in which many things may be found with sufficient study. The original Constitution is almost entirely devoted to outlining the structure of the national government and setting forth the sometimes complicated methods of selection, and the responsibilities, of members of the House of Representatives, senators, the president, and Supreme Court justices. It contains few provisions protecting individual rights from the national government—federalism, i.e., limited national power and a high degree of local autonomy, was considered the principal protection—and even fewer restrictions on the exercise of state power. As to the national government, criminal trials are to be by jury, treason is narrowly defined, the writ of habeas corpus is protected, and bills of attainder and ex-post-facto laws are prohibited. The prohibition of bills of attainder and ex-post-facto laws is repeated as to the states, which are also prohibited from discriminating against citizens of other states. Finally and by far the most important in terms of actual challenges to state laws, the Framers, nicely illustrating their lack of egalitarian pretension, undertook to protect creditors from debtor-relief legislation by prohibiting the states from impairing contract rights.

The first eight of the first ten amendments to the Constitution, the Bill of Rights adopted in 1791, provide additional protections of individual rights, but only against the federal government, not the states, and these, too, are fewer than seems to be generally imagined and certainly fewer than is typical of later declarations of rights, such as in the United Nations Charter. In terms of substantive rights, the First Amendment prohibits Congress from establishing or restricting the free exercise of religion—the main purpose of which was to leave matters of religion to the states—and from abridging the freedom of speech, press, or assembly. In addition, a clause of the Fifth Amendment prohibits the taking of private property without just compensation; the Second Amendment, rarely mentioned by rights enthusiasts, grants a right to bear arms; and the Third Amendment, of little apparent contemporary significance, protects against the forced quartering of troops in private homes. The Seventh Amendment, requiring jury trials in civil cases involving more than twenty dollars, is hard to see today as other than an unnecessary inconvenience. The remaining provisions (search and seizure, grand-jury indictment, double jeopardy, privilege against self-incrimination, due process, jury trial, right to counsel and to confront adverse witnesses, and cruel and unusual punishment) are related to criminal procedure.

Additional protections of individual rights are provided by the post-Civil War Amendments. The Thirteenth Amendment prohibits slavery and the Fifteenth prohibits denial of the right to vote on grounds of race. The great bulk of constitutional litigation concerns state laws and nearly all of that litigation purports to be based on a single sentence of the Fourteenth Amendment and, indeed, on one or the other of two pairs of words, "due process" and "equal protection." If the Constitution is the embodiment of our aspirations, it must have become so largely because of those four words. The clear historic purpose of the Fourteenth Amendment, however, was to provide federal protection against certain state discriminations on the basis of race, historically our uniquely intractable problem, but not otherwise to change fundamentally the constitutional scheme. Finally, the Nineteenth Amendment protects the right to vote from denial on grounds of sex, and the Twenty-seventh from denial on grounds of age for persons over eighteen.

The Constitution's protections of individual rights are not only few but also, when read in historical context, fairly clear and definite. State and federal legislators, all of whom are American citizens living in America and generally at least as devoted as judges to American values, have, therefore, little occasion or desire to violate the Constitution. The result is that the enactment of a clearly unconstitutional law is an extremely rare occurrence: the clearest example in our history perhaps is a 1933 Minnesota debtor-relief statute plainly prohibited by the contract clause, although, as it happens, the Supreme Court upheld it by a five-to-four decision. If judicial review were actually confined to enforcing the Constitution as written, it would be a much less potent force than the judicial review argued for and practiced by Justice Brennan.

The Constitution is undoubtedly a great document, the foundation of one of the freest and most prosperous nations in history. It does not detract from that greatness to point out that it is not, however, what Justice Brennan would make of it, a compendium of majestic generalities and ennobling pronouncements luminous and obscure; indeed, its greatness and durability surely derive in large part from the fact that the Framers' aims were much more specific and limited. Far from intending to compose an oration to human dignity, the Framers would have considered that they had failed in their effort to specify and limit the power of the national govern- ment if the effect of the Constitution should be to transfer the focus of human-rights concerns from the state to the national level. The Framers' solution to the problem of protecting human freedom and dignity was to preserve as much as possible, consistent with national commerce and defense requirements, a system of decentralized democratic decision making, with the regulation of social conditions and personal relations left to the states. Justice Brennan's solution means virtually unlimited Supreme Court power to decide basic social issues for the nation as a whole, effectively disen- franchising the people of each state as to those issues, and is directly contrary to the constitutional scheme.

The Right of Self-Government

Judicial review on the basis of a constitution divorced from historical meaning and viewed, instead, as simply "the lode- star for our aspirations" is obviously a prescription for policy making by judges. It should therefore be defended, if at all, as such, free of obfuscating references to "interpre- tation" of the Constitution. The only real question it presents is, why should the American people prefer to have important social-policy issues decided for the whole nation by the Supreme Court—a committee of nine lawyers unelected to and essentially unremovable from office—rather than by the decentralized democratic process? Justice Brennan's answer to this question is, in essence, why not? The argument that judicial interpretation of the Constitution in accordance with the Framers' intent is essential for "depoliticization of the judiciary," he points out, has its own "political underpinnings"; it "in effect establishes a presumption of resolving textual ambiguities against the claim of constitutional right," which involves "a choice no less political than any other."

Justice Brennan is certainly correct that the presumption of constitutionality accorded to challenged acts of government officials has a political basis, but it is surprising that he should find "far from clear what justifies such a presumption." What justifies it is the basic premise of democratic government that public-policy issues are ordinarily to be decided through the electoral process, not by unelected judges; that constitutional restrictions on representative government—even if, unlike judge-made restrictions, they were once democratically adopted—are the exception, not the rule. To refuse to assume the validity of the acts of the electorally responsible officials and institutions of government is to refuse to assume the validity of representative self-government. It has, therefore, from the beginning been considered the bedrock of constitutional litigation that one who would have a court invalidate an act of the political branches must assume the burden of showing its inconsistency with the Constitution, ordinarily a most difficult task. By reversing the presumption of constitutionality, Justice Brennan would simply reject political decision making as the norm and require elected representatives to justify their policy choices to the satisfaction of Supreme Court justices, presumably by showing that those choices contribute to the justices' notion of social progress.

Justice Brennan would justify the judicial supremacy he favors on the not entirely consistent grounds that, on the one hand, the justices are the true voice of the people and, on the other, that the people are in any event not always to be trusted. "When justices interpret the Constitution," Justice

Brennan assures us, "they speak for their community, not for themselves alone" and "with full consciousness that it is, in a very real sense, the community's interpretation that is sought." Apart from the fact that no question of constitutional interpretation is in fact involved in most "constitutional" cases—the judges do not really decide cases by studying the words "due process" or "equal protection"—the community is, of course, fully capable of speaking for itself through the representatives it elects and maintains in office for that purpose. Justice Brennan does not explain why he thinks the community needs or wants unelected judges to speak for it instead or why the judges can be expected better to reflect or express the community's views.

The actual effect of most judicial rulings of unconstitutionality is, of course, not to implement, but to frustrate the community's views. For example, Justice Brennan would disallow capital punishment as constitutionally prohibited despite not only the fact that it is repeatedly provided for in the Constitution, but also the fact that it is favored by a large majority of the American people. In some cases, however, he explains, a justice may perceive the community's "interpretation of the text to have departed so far from its essential meaning" that he "is bound, by a larger constitutional duty to the community, to expose the departure and point toward a different path." On capital punishment, Justice Brennan hopes to "embody a community striving for human dignity for all, although perhaps not yet arrived." Interpreting an aspirational constitution apparently requires prescience as well as a high degree of self-confidence.

The foundation of all defenses of judicial activism, however, is not any fanciful notion that the judges are the true voice of the people, but on the contrary, the conviction that the people and their elected representatives, should not be permitted to have the last word. Rarely has this conviction, common among our intellectual elite, been expressed with more certainty than in Justice Brennan's speech. Judicial acceptance of the "predominant contemporary authority of the elected branches of government" must be rejected, he argues, for the same reason he rejects judicial acceptance of the "transcendent historical authority of the Framers." That reason, it now appears, is not so much that original intent is unknowable or irrelevant as that its acceptance as authoritative would be inconsistent with his notion of "proper judicial interpretation" of the Constitution because it would leave judges with too little to do. "Faith in the majoritarian process," like fidelity to original intent, is objectionable, he is frank to admit, simply because it "counsels restraint." It would, he points out, lead the Court generally to "stay its hand" where "invalidation of a legislature's substantive policy choice" is involved. Justice Brennan's confidence that his university audience shared his suspicion of democracy and distrust of his fellow citizens was such as to put beyond need of argument the unacceptability of a counsel of restraint by Supreme Court Justices in deciding basic issues of social policy.

Legislative supremacy in policy making is derided by Justice Brennan as the "unabashed enshrinement of majority will." "Faith in democracy is one thing," he warns, but "blind faith quite another." "The view that all matters of substantive policy should be resolved through the majoritarian process has appeal," he concedes, but only "under some circumstances," and even as so qualified "it ultimately will not do." It will not do because the majority is simply not to be trusted: to accept the mere approval of "a majority of the legislative body, fairly elected," as superior in public-policy issues would be to "permit the imposition of a social-caste system or wholesale confiscation of property," a situation "our Constitution could not abide." How a people so bereft of good sense, toleration, and foresight as to adopt such policies could have adopted the Constitution in the first place is not explained. Justice Brennan seems to forget that if the Constitution prohibits such things—indeed, if it is an oration to human dignity, as he maintains—it must be because the American people have made it so and therefore, it would seem, can be trusted. It cannot be Justice Brennan's position that political wisdom died with the Framers and that we are therefore fortunate to have their policy judgments to restrain us; he rejects those judgments as unknowable or irrelevant. Like other defenders of judicial activism, however, he seems to view the Constitution not as an actual document produced by actual people but as a metaphysical entity from an extraterrestrial source of greater authority than the mere wishes of a majority of the American people, which source, fortunately, is in effective communication with Supreme Court Justices.

The social-caste system feared by Justice Brennan would probably be prohibited by the post-Civil War amendments, without undue stretching, and confiscation of property by the national government—though not by the states— would be prohibited by the just-compensation clause of the Fifth Amendment. (These constitutional provisions, it may be noted in passing, would operate as impediments to such policies, providing grounds for opposing arguments, even if they were not judicially enforceable.) The real protection against such fears, however—and columnist Anthony Lewis's similar fear that without activist judicial review Oregon might establish the Reverend Sun Myung Moon's Unification Church as the official state religion—is simply the good sense of the American people. No extraordinary degree of confidence in that good sense is necessary in order to believe that these and similarly outrageous policies that are invariably offered as providing an unanswerable justification for judicial activism are so unlikely to be adopted as not to be a matter of serious concern. If they should be a matter of concern nonetheless—if, for example, it is truly feared that the people of some state might establish a church and believed that no state should be free to do so—the appropriate response would be the adoption of a constitutional amendment further limiting self-government in the relevant respects. To grant judges an unlimited power to rewrite the Constitution, Justice Brennan's recommended response would be to avoid largely imaginary dangers of democratic misgovernment by creating a situation in which judicial misgovernment is guaranteed.

Judicial activism is not necessary to protect us from state-established churches, favored by almost no one, but it does operate to deprive the people of each state of the right to decide for themselves such real issues as whether provision should be made for prayer in the public schools. In any event, the issue presented by contemporary judicial activism is not whether majority rule is entirely trustworthy—all government power is obviously dangerous—or even whether certain specific constitutional limitations on majority rule might not be justifiable; the issue is whether freewheeling policy making by Supreme Court justices, totally centralized and undemocratic, is more trustworthy than majority rule.

Defenders of judicial activism invariably match their skepticism about democratic policy making with a firm belief in the possibility and desirability of policy making on the basis of principle. To free judicial review from the constraint of a constitution with a determinate meaning is not to permit unrestrained judicial policy making in constitutional cases, it is argued, for the judges will continue to be constrained by the Constitution's principles, which, like the smile of the Cheshire cat, somehow survive the disappearance of the Constitution's text. According to this argument, judicial activism amounts to nothing more than the adaptation and application of these basic principles to changing circumstances, a necessary task if the Constitution is to remain a "living document" and a contributor rather than an obstacle to the national welfare. Thus, judicial activism is necessary in Justice Brennan's view, as already noted, if we are not to "turn a blind eye to social progress and eschew adaptation of overarching principles to changes of social circumstance" and because the genius of the Constitution rests not in what, if anything, the Framers actually intended to provide, but in the "adaptability of its great principles to cope with current problems and current needs."

The argument that judges are constrained by constitutional principles, even though not by the constitutional text, bears no relation to reality. In the first place, it is not possible to formulate useful constitutional principles apart from or beyond the Constitution's actual provisions. The Constitution protects certain interests to a certain extent, from which fact the only principle to be derived is that the Constitution does just that. An even more basic fallacy is the argument's assumption that the solution of social problems lies in the discovery, adaptation, and application of preexisting principles to new situations. Difficult problems of social choice arise, however, not because of some failure to discern or adapt an applicable principle, but only because we have many principles, many interests we regard as legitimate, and they inevitably come into conflict. Some interests have to be sacrificed or compromised if other interests are to be protected—for example, public demonstrations will have to be regulated at some point in the interest of maintaining public order—and there is no authoritatively established principle, rule, or generality that resolves the conflict. If there were such a principle, the conflict would not present a serious problem, but would be a matter that has already been decided or that anyone can decide who can read and reason. Value judgments have to be made to solve real policy issues, and the meaning of self-government is that they are to be made in accordance with the collective judgment of those who will have to live with the results.

There is also very little basis for Justice Brennan's apparent belief that judicial review confined to the Constitution as written would somehow be incompatible with social progress—unless social progress is simply defined as the enactment of his views. The Constitution does contain several provisions that we would probably be better off without, for example, the Seventh Amendment's requirement of a jury trial in federal civil cases involving more than twenty dollars and the Twenty-second Amendment's limitation of presidents to two terms. Apart from the fact, however, that the Constitution, of course, provides procedures for its amendment—it can be updated if necessary without the Court's help—judicial activism has not generally served to alleviate the undesirable effects of such provisions. In any event, the Constitution's restrictions on self-government are, as already noted, relatively few and rarely such as a legislature might seek to avoid. Rarely if ever will adaptation of the Constitution's overarching principles, if any, be necessary in order to permit a legislature to implement its views of social progress.

Indeed, on the basis of our actual constitutional history—which includes the Supreme Court's disastrous decision that Congress could not prohibit the extension of slavery, helping after the Civil War bring on the decision that Congress could not prohibit racial segregation in public places—it is possible to believe that social progress might go more smoothly without the Court's supposed adaptations of principles. If the Constitution can be said to have an overarching principle, the principle of federalism, of decision making on most social-policy issues at the state level, is surely the best candidate, and that principle is not adapted or updated but violated by the Court's assertion of power to decide such issues. Far from keeping the Constitution a "living document," judicial activism threatens its demise.

Whatever merit Justice Brennan's justifications for judicial activism might have in theory, they do not seem relevant to the judicial activism actually practiced by the Supreme Court for the past three decades. It would be very difficult to justify the Court's major constitutional decisions during this period, and particularly its most controversial decisions, on any of the grounds Justice Brennan suggests. It would not seem possible to argue, for example, that the justices spoke for the community, not for themselves, in reaching their decisions on abortion, busing, criminal procedure, and prayer in the schools. Nor does it seem that any of those decisions can be justified as providing a needed protection from a possible excess of democracy, as merely delaying effectuation of the aberrational enthusiasm of "temporary political majorities" until they could return to their senses. Judicial review may, as Chief Justice Harlan Fiske Stone put this standard rationalization, provide the people with an opportunity for a "sober second thought," but no amount of thought or experience is likely to change the view of the vast majority of the American people that, for example, their children should not be excluded from their neighborhood public schools because of their race or that no new protections of the criminally accused should be invented with the effect of preventing the conviction and punishment of the clearly guilty.

Finally, the contribution of most of the Court's constitutional decisions of recent decades to social progress— for example, its decision that California may not prohibit the parading of vulgarity in its courthouses or that Oklahoma may not impose a higher minimum drinking age on men than on women—is at best debatable. Very few of these decisions, it seems, could be used to illustrate the adaptation of overarching constitutional principles or transcendent constitutional values to changing circumstances. They could probably more easily be used to illustrate that, rather than helping us to cope with current problems and current needs, the Court's constitutional decisions have often been the cause of those problems and needs.

Whatever the merits of the Supreme Court's constitutional decisions of the past three decades, they have, as to the issues decided, deprived us of perhaps the most essential element of the human dignity Justice Brennan is concerned to protect, the right of self-government, which necessarily includes the right to make what others might consider mistakes. It is not the critics of judicial activism but the activist judges who can more properly be charged with being doctrinaire and arrogant, for it is they who presume to know the answers to difficult questions of social policy and to believe that they provide a needed protection from government by the misguided or ignorant. An opponent of judicial activism need not claim to know the answer to so difficult a question of social policy as, say, the extent if any, to which abortion should be restricted to know that it is shameful in a supposedly democratic country that such a question should be answered for all of us by unelected and unaccountable government officials who have no special competence to do so.

Note

1. "The Constitution of the United States: Contemporary Ratification," delivered at a "Text and Teaching Symposium," October 12, 1985. All other quotations from Justice Brennan are taken from this source unless otherwise indicated.

The Moral Foundations of Republican Government

Edwin Meese III

Taking the opportunity to pause and reflect on the roots of our freedom is always an important thing for us to do. But it is especially important now, as we prepare to celebrate the bicentennial of our Constitution. For our Constitution remains, as William Gladstone, the great British statesman once described it, "the most wonderful work ever struck off at a given time by the brain and purpose of man."

Too frequently we view our Constitution primarily from the standpoint of litigation, as little more than a lawyer's brief or a judge's opinion. But it is, as you know, far more than that. Not only is the Constitution fundamental law, it is also the institutional expression of the philosophical foundation of our political order, the basis of our very way of life. George Roche has explained why this is so as clearly as anyone. "The Founding Fathers," he has written,

> derived their principles of limiting government and protecting individual rights from a belief in Natural Law; that is, a belief that God had ordained a

framework of human dignity and responsibility that was to serve as the basis for all human law and as the root assumption behind a written constitution.

During this bicentennial period especially it is crucial that we cast aside the notion that the Constitution is only a litigator's brief or a judge's opinion. Our task is to reawaken public opinion to the fact that our substantive constitutional values have a shape and content that transcend the crucible of litigation.

In order to successfully effect this reawakening, it is necessary to move beyond the current legal debate over jurisprudence. It is, in fact, necessary to move beyond current legal cases and controversies to the political and social milieu of the era in which our Constitution was written. We need to understand the generation of Founders not simply as a historical curiosity. Our obligation is to understand the Founders as they understood themselves.

Now this is no small task. And my remarks are obviously merely an introduction to what is, by any measure, an area of inquiry as intellectually complex as it is politically rich. I would like to offer a few general observations about the moral foundations of the government the Founders designed. In particular, I will argue that the ideas of natural rights and the consent of the governed are essential to understanding the moral character of our civil society. Further I will discuss the institutional forms of the Founders' politics that facilitated the cultivation of virtue in our people—virtues upon which our form of government still depends.

In approaching this subject, we first need to remember that our Founders lived in a time of nearly unparalleled intellectual excitement. They were the true children of the Enlightenment. They sought to bring the new found faith in human reason to bear on practical politics. Hobbes and

Locke, Harrington and Machiavelli, Smith and Montesquieu—these were the teachers of our Founders. These were the authors of celebrated works that had called into question long-prevailing views of human nature and thus of politics. Our nation was created in the light cast by these towering figures. That is what Alexander Hamilton meant in *The Federalist Papers* when he argued that the "science of politics . . . like most other sciences has received great improvement. The efficacy of various principles is now well understood, which were either not known at all, or imperfectly known to the ancients." Our Founders, in many ways, sought to give practical effect to David Hume's desire "that politics may be reduced to a science."

Natural Rights and Consent
of the Governed

What, then, are the moral foundations of our republican form of government? Much of the answer, I believe, can be found in our charter of fundamental principles, the Declaration of Independence. I think it is worth recalling Thomas Jefferson's famous formulation of these first principles. "We hold these truths," he said, "to be self-evident,"

> That all men are created equal, that they are endowed by their Creator with certain inalienable rights, that among these are Life, Liberty, and the pursuit of Happiness. That to secure these rights, Governments are instituted among Men deriving their just powers from the consent of the governed.

Now these rights were neither the result of legal privilege nor the benevolence of some ruling class. They were rights that existed *in nature* before governments or laws were ever formed. As the physical world is governed by natural laws such as gravity, so the political world is governed by other natural laws in the form of natural rights that belong to each individual. These rights, like the laws of gravity, antedated even mankind's recognition of them.

But because these rights were left unsecured by nature, as Jefferson said, governments are instituted among men. Thus there exists in the nature of things a natural standard for judging whether governments are legitimate or not. That standard is whether or not the government rests, in the phrase of the Declaration, upon the consent of the governed. Any political powers not derived from the consent of the governed are, by the laws of nature, illegitimate and hence unjust. Only by such a natural standard can arbitrary power be checked.

"Consent of the governed" is a political concept that is the reciprocal of the idea of equality. Because all men are created equal, nature does not single out who is to govern and who is to be governed. There is no divine right of kings, for example. Consent is the means whereby man's natural equality is made politically operable.

In this theory of government, this philosophy of natural rights and the consent of the governed, we find the most fundamental moral foundation of republican government. For it presupposes a universal moral equality that makes popular government not only politically possible but morally necessary.

However accustomed we have become to ideas of natural rights and the consent of the governed, we should never lose sight that these were, two centuries ago, morally revolutionary ideas. During this bicentennial period we should refresh ourselves as to the truth of these ideas.

Of course, it is one thing to argue that the only legiti-mate foundation of government is the consent of the governed, but it is quite another matter to put this theory into practice. The key here is the Declaration's maxim that in order to secure rights "governments are *instituted* among men" It is then, by the act of choosing, by the political act of constituting a government, that the moral standard of the consent of the governed is given definite shape and formidable weight. But such an act of creation is not easy.

That is what Alexander Hamilton had in mind when he introduced the first essay in *The Federalist Papers* by asking the question of "whether societies of men are really capable or not, of establishing good government from reflection and choice, or whether they are forever destined to depend, for their political constitutions, on accident and force." For after all was said and done, after the Revolution had been won, it remained to be seen whether the glowing rhetoric of the Declaration could actually be made the standard of political practice.

One thing their recent experience with England had taught the Americans was the necessity of a constitution. And not just any sort of constitution would do. The celebrated English Constitution, after all, had allowed what they saw as a gross abuse of political power. That, we must remember, is what most of the Declaration of Independence is about: the long catalogue of abuses the Americans had suffered. This experience with the all-too-malleable English Constitution bolstered their own earlier inclinations—from the Mayflower Compact on—toward a *written* constitution. The one best way to hedge against arbitrary political power was to clearly stake out the lines and limits of the institutions that would wield power. Thus the purpose of our written Constitution was, as Walter Berns has said, to get it in writing.

This belief in a written constitution was the fulfillment of the more basic belief in the moral authority of the consent of the governed. A written constitution, when duly ratified, would stand as the concrete and tangible expression of that fundamental consent. This document would stand as testimony to the Founders' unfaltering faith in (to borrow the late scholar Alexander Bickel's term) the "morality of consent."

The question facing the Americans then became how to devise such a constitution that would, in the language of the Declaration, be "most likely to effect their Safety and Happiness." Indeed, as James Madison would bluntly put it later in *The Federalist Papers,* "A good government implies two things; first, fidelity to the object of government, which is the happiness of the people; second, a knowledge of the means by which that object can be best attained."

After the War for Independence was won, the Americans set about to secure their revolution. The states began to draft their constitutions and the confederation of the states sought to draft a constitution for its purposes. By 1787, one thing had become clear. Popular government was not simply good government. The state governments had, in many instances, proved tyrannical. The national authority under the Articles of Confederation had proved inept. The period between 1776 and 1787 had shown many Americans that they did not yet possess that "knowledge of the means" by which the happiness of the people could best be secured.

By the time the federal convention came together in Philadelphia in May 1787, however, there was a collection of men who had thought through the causes of their present difficulties. They were convinced that the mechanics of republican government could be adjusted in order to defend against charges that it was "inconsistent with the order of society." What was at issue was the very question of the moral basis of the republican form: Could a republic be saved from its own excesses? A sufficient number of Americans believed it could. And they set about to do just that.

These young men of the Enlightenment, these students
of Hobbes and Locke and Montesquieu, believed themselves
capable of devising a republic "of a more perfect structure,"
as Hamilton put it in *The Federalist Papers.* The reason, he
said, was relatively simple:

> The science of politics . . . like most other
> sciences has received great improvement. The effi-
> cacy of various principles is now well understood,
> which were either not known at all, or imperfectly
> known to the ancients. The regular distribution of
> power into distinct departments—the introduction
> of legislative balances and checks—the introduc-
> tion of courts composed of judges holding their
> offices during good behavior—the representation
> of the people in the legislature by deputies of their
> own election—these are either wholly new dis-
> coveries or have made their principal progress
> towards perfection in modern times.

This new science of politics, Hamilton confidently argued,
provided the "powerful means by which the excellencies of
republican government may be retained and its imperfections
lessened or avoided."

Now one of the basic problems of the old political order
was what many began to see as an unhealthy reliance on the
virtue of the people. In many ways, the earlier republicans in
America, those historian Pauline Maier has dubbed the "Old
Revolutionaries," had created their constitutions in light of
their belief that somehow the Americans were a new breed
of man, self-reliant, commonsensical and, above all, civical-
ly virtuous. They had thought themselves uniquely capable
of continuing self-denial and unfaltering devotion to the public good. As a result, the constitutional order they had
created depended to a great degree on "Spartan habits" and
"Roman patriotism." By the mid-1780s it was clear to many

that to love the public and to sacrifice personally for it was proving more easily said than done. Americans, too, it seemed, were corruptible. And this unhappy fact called into question the old assumption that Americans were somehow blessed with exceptional character.

By 1786, Rufus King (later a delegate to the Federal Convention) confessed that:

if the great Body of people are without Virtue, and not governed by any internal Restraints of Conscience, there is but too much room to fear that the Framers' of our constitutions and laws have proceeded on principles that do not exist, and that America, which the Friends of Freedom have looked to as an Asylum when persecuted, will not afford that refuge.

By 1788 Alexander Hamilton was even more pointed in his criticism. In *The Federalist Papers* he argued that Americans were clearly "yet remote from the happy empire of perfect wisdom and perfect virtue." Experience had proved beyond much doubt, he said, that men are by nature "ambitious, vindictive and rapacious." Indeed, Hamilton concluded, the very reason government was necessary was because "the passions of men will not conform to the dictates of reason and justice without constraint."

Hamilton's perspicacious collaborator Madison was even more succinct. "If the impulse and opportunity be suffered to coincide," he wrote in the famous tenth *Federalist Paper,* "we well know that neither moral nor religious motives can be relied on as an adequate control." In what is arguably one of the most famous passages in American political writing, Madison laid the theoretical foundation for the Framers' "novel experiment" in popular government. Reflecting on the institutional contrivances of the new Constitution, Madison, in *The Federalist* No. 51 neatly captured his new theory of republican government. His theory, at its deepest level, relied on a certain understanding of human nature. Thus, he wrote, "what is government itself but the greatest of all reflections on human nature? If men were angels, no government would be necessary. If angels were to govern men, neither external nor internal controuls would be necessary." However, he concluded, "In framing a government which is to be administered by men over men, the great difficult lies in this; you must first enable the government to controul the governed; and in the next place, oblige it to controul itself."

According to Madison the purpose of the Constitution's mechanics—separation of powers, bicameralism, representation, and so forth—was to hedge against an all too predictable human nature. The object was to offset "the defect of better motives." Good intentions were to be replaced by good institutions.

Commerce and Civic Virture

To many, the most shocking feature of the Framers' new science of politics was its bold and nearly unqualified reliance on the power of commerce to make civil society orderly. This was a truly radical step. Commerce, you see, had long been thought to be the primary cause of corruption of the manners and the morals of free people. And private vice, the prevailing belief held, could never produce public virtue.

We take commerce so much for granted that this idea is puzzling to our generation. But to many of the founding generation, commerce produced greed and venality—it brought forth, as its critics said, the worst impulses of mankind. One Anti-Federalist critic of the proposed Constitution summed it up by arguing that such a reliance on commerce would encourage an "excessive fondness for riches and luxury" that would, if left untempered, and unchecked by a concern for public virtue, "totally subvert the government and erect a system of aristocratical or monarchaic tyranny," thereby losing "perhaps forever" the liberties of the people.

The new science of politics of the Constitution was as bold as those Founders who pushed the hardest for it. They were, as one historian has described them, young men of a continental vision. This was the time of Madison and Hamilton and Morris; the day of Adams and Franklin and Lee was quickly passing. They saw more in America than just America. They saw in the founding a great example for all the world. And they believed that commerce was an essential part of this vision.

So it was that these young nationalists rejected the cautious confederalism of the older generation of Founders. Their object was not to secure a confederacy of small and virtuous republics of public spirited citizens. Their object was—in the words of one of their guiding lights, Adam Smith—to establish a "great mercantile republic." Indeed, they sought to establish nothing less than a great republican empire of commerce.

Unleashed, these nationalists believed, the commercial power of self-interest that the Anti-Federalists feared, could be turned to republican advantage. By drawing people together, by making them work together for their private gain, commerce could help to tame human nature. Brutish greed would become a prudent concern for profits. A nation of shopkeepers would not be characterized by crude self-interest but by what Alexis de Tocqueville would later celebrate as "enlightened self-interest." While commerce would surely depend upon human passions, it would also serve to moderate them. Commerce and constitutionalism together would make Americans free and prosperous at home and secure among the nations of the world. America would be, they believed, a new kind of republic in a world itself quite new.

But what of civic virtue? Would there be none? Surely there would have to be, because the new science of politics demanded it. As Madison pointed out in the Virginia ratifying convention, a certain degree of virtue was necessary if our form of civil society was to endure.

As we have seen, the political science of the Founding Fathers did not seek to inculcate virtue in its citizens by the terms of the Constitution. But that document, as I have said, is, morally praiseworthy because it *does* protect natural rights and it *does* rest upon the consent of the governed. Still, the Founders understood the relevance of what I would call the "character question." They knew the oldest question of politics (the one Aristotle asked)—the question of what kind of people does a regime produce, what kind of character do they have—is always important.

Under the new political order of the Constitution, the cultivation of character was left to the states and the private sphere. Through the political principle of federalism, the Framers left to the people in their states sovereignty sufficient to legislate in these areas; state governments could attempt, under this scheme, directly to promote virtue among the people. In addition, family and church and private associations were expected to provide the support for the inculcation of virtue. And, in a curious way, even the thriving commercial republic the Founders envisioned would itself promote a new kind of public virtue. It would, of course, not be virtue in the classical or the Christian sense. Nor would it be the old small republican variety, starkly Spartan in its demands. Rather, it would be what the late Martin Dia-mond accurately described as the "bourgeois virtues"—the virtues of honesty and decency that commerce itself, that business, presupposes.

Moral Foundations

But the question we must ultimately confront is how well has our Founders' constitutional handiwork in this regard fared? I suspect I will shock no one by suggesting that it fared very well for most of our history. For while not overtly concerned with morality, our Constitution, I submit, has produced the frame of government in which America has thrived as one of the most moral nations in the history of the world.

How is it that in America the moral concerns of republican government and the concomitant demand for individual liberty have been maintained in such a steady balance? At its deepest level, popular government—republican government—means a structure of government that not only rests upon the consent of the governed, but more importantly a structure of government wherein public opinion can be expressed and translated into public law and public policy. This is the deepest level precisely because public opinion over important public issues ultimately is a public debate over justice. It is naive to think that people only base their opinions on their conceptions of their narrrow self-interest. Very often public opinion and political debates do reflect deeper concerns—if you will, moral concerns.

It is this venting of the moral concerns of a people that is the very essence of political life. In a popular form of government it is not only legitimate but essential that the people have the opportunity to give full vent to their moral sentiments. Through deliberation, debate, and compromise a public consensus can be formed as to what constitutes the public good. It is this consensus over fundamental values that knits individuals into a community of citizens. And it is this liberty to debate and determine the morality of a community that is an important part of the liberty protected by our Constitution.

The toughest political problems deserve to have full and open public debate. Whether the issue is abortion, school prayer, pornography or aid to parochial schools, the people within their communities and within the several states must be allowed to deliberate over them and reach a consensual judgment.

This is not to say, of course, that the people must be allowed to choose any substantive end a majority prefers at any given moment. That is not good republican government; that is a simplistic notion of popular sovereignty. The political theory of our Constitution rejects such a simplistic theory. As one commentator has observed, "there are certain substantive things, such as slavery, that a democratic people may not choose because those substantive ends would be inconsistent with the fundamental premises that give majorities the right to decide."

But to deny the right—the liberty—of the people to choose certain other substantive ends reduces the American Constitution to moral relativism. In that direction lies the danger, to borrow Abraham Lincoln's phrase, of "blowing out the moral lights around us."

During the past several decades an aggressively secular liberalism often driven by an expansive egalitarian impulse has threatened many of the traditional political and social values the great majority of the American people still embrace. The strong gusts of ideology have indeed threatened to blow out the moral lights around us. This has been the result of our knocking down certain institutional barriers to national political power—in particular, the abandonment of an appreciation for the necessity of the separation of powers, and for the continuing political importance of federalism.

I would argue that the demise of these two institutional arrangements has had a disastrous impact on the moral foundations of republican government. I would further argue that these deleterious developments should be abandoned as the dangerous innovations that they are, for they violate our most fundamental political maxim: that in a system of popular government, the people have the liberty and the legitimate power within certain limits to define the moral, political, and legal content of their public lives. When we allow this principle to be transgressed, we risk severing the necessary link between the people and the polity. Indeed, we cut the moral cord that binds us together in our common belief that we have a vital role to play in deciding how we live our collective lives.

We have an obligation today—a moral obligation—to restore those institutional arrangements that the Founders knew to be essential to the nurturing of public virtue. We have an obligation to restrict the insensitive intrusiveness of the national government in order to allow the most important decisions to be made by the people, not by what Adam Ferguson once called the "clerks and accountants" of a large and distant bureaucracy. We have an obligation to allow the states and communities the maximum freedom possible to structure their politics and infuse them with the moral tone they find most conducive to their happiness. This is, as I say, the moral obligation of our generation.

We may either reassert our right to govern ourselves or we can surrender to the stultifying leviathan of big government. We must restore those structures that will shore up our sagging moral foundations or we risk losing the liberties which rest upon those foundations.

A decade after the adoption of our Constitution, the Anti-Federalist Mercy Warren, with a good bit of melancholy, expressed her fear that in the end, her countrymen might be remembered as having been "too proud for monarchy, . . . too poor for nobility, and . . . too selfish and avaricious for a virtuous republic." While we may not ever be simply a virtuous people, we must surely endeavor to assuage Mercy Warren's fear by recognizing and perpetuating what Madison believed we possess: "sufficient virtue for self-government."

The Jurisprudence of Constitutional Amendments

Stephen J. Markman

There is the story that Daniel Webster, the great American lawyer, was on his last sickbed when he was visited by a friend. The friend said to him, "Well, cheer up Senator, I believe your constitution will pull you through." "Not at all," Webster responded, "my constitution was gone long ago, and I am living on my by-laws now."

Our own age is sadly short of statesmen the stature of the great Webster. But just as he jested in the face of troubles that his personal constitution had failed him, so do many Americans today feel seriously that their organic, political health as a people—the Constitution of the United States—is on its sickbed. And somewhat like Webster, many feel that we live today not so much by virtue of our Constitution, as by its more pastel interpretations.

My topic concerns the amendment process. Were I to limit myself to a simple description of how the Constitution may properly be amended, this would be a very short essay. I would quote the text of Article V, and be done. Instead, however, I would like to focus on a comparatively modern but nonetheless important phenomenon. It is the effort to amend the Constitution not to correct defects in the document's text or structure, but to overturn specific conclusions of the Supreme Court. My thesis is simply that while the history of successful and unsuccessful attempts to amend the Constitution has generally concerned perceived shortcomings in constitutional mechanisms or process, our age is concerned as never before with the *substance* of constitutional law as articulated by the courts. And it will be my argument that the manifold efforts to reverse the substance of Supreme Court pronouncements by constitutional amendment reflects a fundamental problem in contemporary Supreme Court jurisprudence.

Not since ratification of the Bill of Rights has Congress seriously considered so many separate constitutional amendment proposals. Until recently, the states were simultaneously entertaining—for the first time since the Bill of Rights—two proposed amendments to the Constitution (the Equal Rights Amendment and the Washington, D.C. Voting Rights Amendment). In the past several years, Congress has also given serious consideration to proposed amendments on abortion, school prayer, electoral college reform, the line item veto, and the balanced budget. Moreover, the Senate Subcommittee on the Constitution has conducted extensive hearings on diverse amendments relating to forced school busing, affirmative action, congressional pay levels, congressional and presidential tenure, the legislative veto, a system of national referenda, presidential transition periods, and English as an official language of the United States. Still other members have pressed for the consideration of amendments relating to immigration, campaign contributions, capital punishment, and the elimination of lifetime tenure for federal judges.

Generally, such debate and discussion is an important and legitimate part of the legislative process on Capitol Hill. Having served for a number of years as chief counsel to the Subcommittee on the Constitution, I know that that body has always welcomed the opportunity to build an historical record for even those amendments which we most strongly opposed. Let me assure you that after assessing the array of initiatives offered to modify the Framers' handiwork, one appreciates their work of two hundred years ago all the more.

Still, the fact that so many amendments on so many subjects have been introduced suggests that many members of Congress are seriously dissatisfied with the current state of constitutional law. This is cause for deep concern. As Justice Story recognized in his *Commentaries on the Constitution,* a government that is forever changing and change-able is one "bordering upon anarchy and confusion." Certainly, a great nation needs a system of law that is not entirely fixed and inalterable. But the modern proliferation of proposed constitutional amendments may be, I fear, symptomatic of deeper and more fundamental problems within our constitutional jurisprudence.

On reflection, it is probable that the growing array of proposals for constitutional change reflects less any general dissatisfaction with the Constitution than it reflects widespread dissatisfaction with the federal judiciary's treatment of constitutional law. Indeed, what distinguishes many of these amendment proposals is that they seek to re-establish the constitutional principles and values that their proponents believe have been undermined by some recent Court decisions. Unlike most earlier proposed amendments, then, which were essentially *reformative* in character, most recent amendments, at least from the perspective of their sponsors, have been essentially *restorative.*

My purpose is not to defend any of the amendments put forward in recent years; it is instead simply to suggest an explanation for this growth industry. To the extent the federal courts continue to embark upon what former Attorney General Levi has called a "social policy making role," disregarding in the process traditional notions of jurisprudence, I believe that the present surfeit of amendment efforts is likely to continue.

Social Issues and Judicial Activism

Perhaps the best area to begin with in illustrating the problem is the so-called trilogy of "social issues"—abortion, school prayer, and school busing. Putting aside the controversial substance of these issues—and I know that this is not easy to do—what they have in common is that advocates of constitutional amendments addressing these issues believe themselves to be advocating nothing more than a restoration of longstanding, historic interpretations of the Constitution that have only recently been upset by the federal judiciary. It is not necessary to concur with this perception, I believe, to understand its basis.

With respect to abortion, for example, proponents of constitutional change point to the Supreme Court's seminal 1973 decision in *Roe* v. *Wade*. It is beyond dispute that *Roe* overturned, in one fell swoop, the laws on abortion then existing in every state of the union. As a result of this decision, a new regime was created—a regime more permissive of abortion than had been reflected in the considered judgments of the elected representatives of the people in each of the fifty states.

The Supreme Court employed as the constitutional basis for its decision an alleged "right to privacy"—broad enough to include a right to terminate pregnancy—said to be contained in the due process clause of the Fourteenth Amendment. As former Solicitor General Archibald Cox, himself a proponent of legalized abortion, commented about this novel right, "Neither historian, layman, nor lawyer will be persuaded that the details of *Roe* v. *Wade* are part of the Constitution."

When the United States Senate, more than a decade after *Roe* v. *Wade*, split fifty-fifty on a proposed "state's rights" abortion constitutional amendment, most senators who expressed themselves in support of the measure claimed that they were voting to restore a lost status quo. They were not voting to change the Constitution, but to restore a changed Constitution.

A parallel is found in Congress's efforts to propose a school prayer amendment. Until 1962 and the Supreme Court's decisions in *Engel* v. *Vitale* and *Abington* v. *Schempp*, expressions of devotion were a normal part of the daily regimen in the vast majority of public schools in this country. Such expressions were not considered to be in violation of the establishment clause of the First Amendment by the overwhelming number of parents and school districts throughout the nation.

Before these decisions, the First Amendment, at least in the view of proponents of a school prayer amendment, had been generally understood to prohibit the state from pre-ferring any particular church or denomination over others. As the distinguished constitutional scholar, Edward Corwin, wrote more than three decades ago,

> The historical record shows beyond question that the core idea of the "establishment of religion" comprises the idea of preference; [not any mere] act of public authority favorable to religion in gen-eral can be brought under the ban of that phrase without manifest falsification of history.

For most of the nation's history, this view of the establishment clause influenced the development of public policy and
provided for the toleration—and indeed encouragement—of
public school prayer. What emerged abruptly in *Engel* and
Abington, however, was an understanding of the First
Amendment sharply at variance with this notion. In place of
a simple prohibition against the state displaying a preference
for a particular faith or denomination, the Court endorsed the
notion of an absolute and unbreachable "wall of separation"
between church and state. All state encouragement of rever-
ential expression was to be considered unconstitutional, no
matter how neutral the manner in which it was expressed.

The effect of these Supreme Court school prayer decisions was to overturn the laws of more than forty states of
the Union. In literally tens of thousands of jurisdictions
across the country, longstanding policies of student prayer
were transformed overnight from educational and character-
building exercises into First Amendment violations.

As was the case with the abortion amendment, most of
the fifty-six members of the United States Senate who supported President Reagan's proposed school prayer amendment in 1984 believed it was not the Constitution that they
were modifying, but a series of aberrant Court decisions
inconsistent with the permanent Constitution.

In the final element of the social issue trilogy—school
busing—the same pattern emerges. Many, if not most, of
those who support constitutional amendments in such areas
as busing or civil rights policy or affirmative action believe
that the courts have sharply redefined traditional conceptions
of "equal protection of the laws." In the place of the color-
blind notion of equal protection expressed in Justice Harlan's famous dissent in *Plessy* v. *Ferguson* as well as in
Brown v. *Board of Education* and the Civil Rights Act of
1964, we have witnessed the rise over the past two decades

of a radically different notion of equality: The focus on equality of opportunity has shifted to a focus on equality of results, while the idea of discrimination as a wrongfully motivated activity has been transformed into a concept of mere statistical disparity. We have witnessed the tolerance of racial decision making incorporated in *Regents of University of California* v. *Bakke*, the encouragement of reverse discrimination in the private sector in *United Steelworkers* v. *Weber*, and, perhaps most remarkably, the allowance in *Fullilove* v. *Klutznick* of federal grants to classes of individuals having nothing in common more than their pigmentation.

Again, those who propose to amend the Constitution in this area—to restrict, for example, school busing for purposes of securing appropriate racial proportions—are in their judgment reaffirming the traditional equal protection ideal eroded badly by these and other cases. There are other examples—constitutional amendments on capital punishment designed to overturn the high court's line of cases stemming from *Furman* v. *Georgia*; amendments restricting the rights of illegal aliens designed to overturn *Plyler* v. *Doe*; amendments relating to the legislative veto designed to overturn *I. N. S.* v. *Chadha*; and amendments in the area of criminal procedure designed to overturn such decisions as *Miranda* v. *Arizona* and *Mapp* v. *Ohio*. Even constitutional amendments requiring a balanced federal budget may be seen as responding to court decisions that have eroded any serious limitations upon the spending and taxing power of the Congress. What seems to be clear is that those federal court decisions that some would characterize as exercises in "judicial activism"—those decisions in which the court has involved itself in areas outside its traditional bounds, identifying a wealth of new "rights" and entitlements—have generated an increasingly strong reaction by the Congress that often finds expression in the form of constitutional amendments. It is ironic that charges of illicit "tampering with the Constitution" have frequently been leveled against those who have sought to use the Constitution's own explicit amendment mechanism to respond to what they see as change achieved through extra-constitutional means.

Article V and the
Amendment Process

In their wisdom (and in their humility, which for many national political leaders often amounts to much the same thing), the Framers of our Constitution recognized that the "fundamental law" articulated by that document must be susceptible to change in response to unanticipated circumstances. A defect of the Articles of Confederation had been their inflexibility and inability to respond to such changing conditions. Accordingly, because it was to embody the nation's supreme and permanent governing principles, it was necessary for the Constitution to contain a mechanism for self-correction. That authority for fundamental change was established in Article V, setting out procedures for constitutional amendment. James Madison summarized the need for Article V in *The Federalist* No. 43, observing:

> That useful alterations [of the Constitution] will be suggested by experience could not but be foreseen. It was requisite, therefore, that a mode for introducing them should be provided. The mode preferred by the convention seems to be stamped with every mark of propriety. It guards equally against that extreme facility which would render the Constitution too mutable; and that extreme difficulty which might perpetuate its discovered faults. It moreover equally enables the general and the State governments to originate the amendment

of errors as they might be pointed out by the experience on the one side or on the other.

The "mode" of amendment in Article V to which Madison refers provides, of course, for the ratification by three-fourths of the states of proposals committed to them either by the Congress, on a two-thirds vote, or by a convention called on the application of two-thirds of the states. It is a "mode" of amendment which has produced only twenty-six amendments in the history of the Republic, only sixteen having been ratified in the one hundred and ninety-five years since the Bill of Rights. It is also the *sole* mode of amendment permitted by the Constitution. As its provisions seem to make clear, it was the intent of the Framers that their intentions be followed unless changed in accordance with Article V.

Article V of the Constitution—one of the document's great overlooked provisions—contains in microcosm many of the Constitution's greatest animating principles. Perhaps most basically, the existence of Article V as the Constitution's exclusive amending mechanism reaffirms the Preamble's declaration that "We the people" are the ultimate source of governmental power: It was only with the people's consent that our present form of government was adopted, and it is only with their further consent, in the manner that they have set forth in Article V, that this form of government can be altered.

Other principles are also implicit in Article V. Its requirement, as a precondition for change, that there be supermajorities in the both the Congress and the states reflects the Founders' care in balancing majoritarian decision making with the need to protect the rights of minorities. The understanding that state ratification should not be conducted by popular referendum, but through the legislatures or state conventions, reflects the Founders' idea that the democratic will was most appropriately expressed through intermediary, representative institutions rather than in a direct manner. By allowing for either the national or state governments to pro-pose amendments, Article V employs a system of checks and balances that also operates in other constitutional con-texts to separate, oppose, and ultimately limit governmental power. Finally, by vesting ultimate control over the adoption of amendments in the state governments, Article V under-scores the concepts of federalism and dispersed govern-mental power so fundamental to our system.

These principles—separation of powers, checks and balances, majority rule with respect for the rights of minor-ities, republican government, federalism—embody the core purposes of our Constitution. The genius of Article V, therefore, lies in its mandate that changes in the Constitution be brought about only in accordance with the principles that already underlie the Constitution. In this way, amendments may alter the Constitution, but they will be made in accor-dance with the root principles and values set forth in the original document.

The corollary of this proposition, however, is also true; to the extent that constitutional change is rendered in defiance of Article V, through unauthorized means, these broader constitutional values are likely to be undermined. As Elbridge Gerry observed at the founding convention, an attempt to amend the Constitution in "any other way" than through Article V represents a "high crime and misdemean-or" that should bring on appropriate consequences.

While the Framers carefully left open the application of Article V to virtually any substantive or procedural end, they seem to have anticipated that amendments, like the rest of the Constitution generally, would address governmental pro-cesses rather than substantive outcomes. A structure of limit-ed and balanced government had already been devised, with sufficient flexibility in the popular, representative branches to respond to changing exigencies; presumably, therefore, most amendments would speak to the *means* by which this government would act rather than address specific *results*. In *The Federalist* No. 85, Alexander Hamilton announced his "thorough conviction" that any amendments likely to be thought useful "will be applicable to the organization of the government, not to the mass of its powers."

This belief has been largely vindicated by history—at least until recently. Since the Bill of Rights—which can largely be viewed as part of the original text—amendments have primarily adjusted the machinery of constitutional gov- ernment—the Eleventh Amendment fine-tuning federalism; the Twelfth and Seventeenth Amendments altering the pro- cedures of elections; the Twentieth, Twenty-second, and Twenty-fifth Amendments fleshing out the details of repre- sentative government; and the Fourteenth, Fifteenth, Nineteenth, Twenty-third, Twenty-fourth, and Twenty-sixth Amendments working to broaden the franchise.

Contemporary experience, however, has been very dif- ferent. Recent years have witnessed a massive increase in the sheer number of constitutional proposals. More significantly these proposals, by and large, have been very different from those accorded real consideration in the past.

Most of the serious amendment proposals advanced of late *have* had substantive content, aimed at altering specific federal policy outcomes with regard to abortion, prayer, bus- ing, or a balanced budget, for example. Only the Eighteenth Amendment, ushering in Prohibition, and the Twenty-first Amendment, ushering it out, can be compared with the new- ly emergent spawn of single-issue amendments. (Even the so-called "Reconstruction amendments" were directed gener- ally towards expanding and guaranteeing pre-existing rights to previously excluded persons.) What is unique is that this new breed of amendment is not designed (as the Framers primarily envisioned) to adjust "errors" in the Constitution or to perfect the mechanisms of democracy, that is, to *reform* the Constitution; rather, these proposals are intended to *restore* a Constitution modified by means other than Article V.

This novel use of a provision, Article V, generally employed for *procedural* reform, to effect *substantive* change in constitutional doctrine, may be seen as a gauge that something has gone awry. The proponents of recent amendments believe that the Constitution has been modified by the federal judiciary, principally the Supreme Court, sitting as a kind of continuing constitutional convention—a mode of modification clearly not within Article V, and therefore not sanctioned by the Constitution. Many believe the courts have imported into our permanent law notions of government outside the purview of the Framers, but which have been justified by modern judges as changes designed to enable the Constitution to respond to evolving circumstances and maturing needs. As Justice Brennan has opined, "Judges cannot turn a blind eye to social progress."

He and his colleagues, however, have forgotten the wisdom of President George Washington, who admonished in his Farewell Address that:

> If in the opinion of the People, the distribution or modification of the Constitutional powers be in any particular wrong, let it be corrected by an amendment in the way in which the Constitution designates. But, let there be no change by usurpation; for though this, in one instance, may be the instrument of good, it is the customary weapon by which free governments are destroyed.

"Change by Usurpation"

Disregard for the appropriate avenue of constitutional amendment—what Washington called "change by usurpation"—undermines free government because it disregards those fundamental values rooted in the Constitution and reflected within Article V. When federal courts render purportedly "constitutional" decisions not clearly rooted in the constitutional text, it does grievous harm to these fundamental values in at least three important respects.

First, it violates the principle of federalism. To treat an issue—abortion, for example—as being of constitutional dimension is automatically to impose a national, uniform, inflexible, and presumably permanent policy mandate. Matters that, when treated at the local or state level, can be addressed in a variety of ways depending upon the diversity of local or state experience are, when nationalized by non-Article V, court-crafted constitutional amendments, reduced to a single, rigid rule. What is worse is that such judicially "constitutionalized" issues tend to be those that are the most divisive and emotional and complex. Such issues are precisely those *least* susceptible to a single, national solution and *most* in need of experimentation, trial-and-error, and flexible governmental response. Further, once an issue has been "constitutionalized" in this way, those dissatisfied with the Court's resolution are encouraged to constitutionalize and nationalize their own preferred policies through constitutional amendments. Thus, we see perpetuated the treadmill of debate over differing visions of uniform, national public policies.

The second way constitutional "amendments from the judgment seat," in Bentham's terms, upset fundamental constitutional values is through their impact upon the notion of separated powers. Judicial "constitutionalization" of issues not only permanently removes issues from the state to the national level, but once on federal ground transplants them from the legislative to the judicial field. Again, the pragmatic consequences are undesirable. Untempered by the give-and-take and bargaining, negotiation, and compromise inherent in day-to-day legislative process, these issues tend to be resolved through black-and-white solutions, without the occasional shading of reality. Again, these involve difficult public policy issues, those most in need of legislative accommodation and least amenable to absolute, end-of-the-spectrum solutions.

Finally, the tendency toward the "constitutionalization" of public policy issues by the courts can only have the effect of undermining genuine rule by "We the people," imposing as it does rules dictated from above by unelected and largely unaccountable members of the judiciary. These particular "rascals," alone among public officials, are immune to being "thrown out" by a disgruntled citizenry. It is a contemporary fact of life that the Supreme Court, on any given Monday in May or June, routinely issues more pronouncements on important public policies than Congress does in the course of an entire session. It is to belabor the obvious to note that the policies articulated by the court, unlike those of the Congress, bear absolutely no semblance of being the product of a representative or democratic process.

Even where the judicial solution in a given area might be said by some omniscient seer to be "wiser" than what popular officials might have produced (and it is not at all clear that this is generally the case), such decision making entails costs. It engenders frustration and resentment among the "losers"—those whose policy prescriptions have not been adopted by the judges. Further, it breeds a sense of alienation much deeper than that caused by rejection by a legislative majority. When a court bypasses Article V and usurps power that the people in their Constitution properly left with themselves and their elected representatives, it repudiates the notion that, in the words of Hamilton, the "power of the people is superior to" each of the powers of the separate branches of the government.

This alienation, this frustration, has been compounded in recent years because roughly the same group of people is disenfranchised time after time. For want of a better term, we may speak of this class of victims as being often from the middle and the lower middle class, possessing traditional values and without access to public-opinion molding institutions. Their only political power is at the ballot box. They are those for whom the media, by and large, does not speak, and who are without elite legal advocates or spokesmen. They are something distinct from the articulate and involved "new class." They are quite understandably those most frustrated when their one source of public influence is repeatedly wrested from them.

The alienation of these "losers" has increasingly manifested itself not only in constitutional amendments but in resort to a variety of extraordinary efforts for overcoming unpopular constitutional decisions involving means other than the normal amendment route. In an effort to bypass the time-consuming and burdensome Article V process—it is properly hard to amend the Constitution—we have witnessed a growing number of attempts by members of Congress to rely upon constitutional shortcuts.

These shortcuts have taken different forms. Some members have sought, for example, to reverse Supreme Court establishment clause decisions by simply stripping the Court of jurisdiction over this issue under the controversial authority of the provisions of Article III. Others have sought to reverse the decisions on abortion by the simple tack of ignoring them and enacting into law plainly contradictory legislation. Still others have attempted to overturn Court decisions on the meaning of the Fourteenth and Fifteenth Amendments by simply relying upon the enforcement clauses of these amendments as grants of authority to redefine their provisions as well. Recently, under this extremely dangerous theory—showing that conservatives are not the only ones frustrated with the courts—one legislator recently introduced a resolution to read the Equal Rights Amendment into the law through a simple statute.

In addition, we are experiencing a new effort to use the long dormant constitutional convention process for proposing amendments. As you may know, this alternative amendment process has never been used successfully to secure the ratification of an amendment. There are at present, however, twenty states calling for a constitutional amending convention on the subject of abortion, and a remarkable thirty-two states were calling, until lately, for just such a convention for the purposes of proposing a balanced budget constitutional amendment. Only two additional states were needed to trigger the first amending convention in the history of the republic.

It is ironic, by the way, that those individuals most fearful of a constitutional amending convention called into being by the states and most supportive of placing obstacles in its way—a procedure explicitly set forth in Article V—are also those most generally enthusiastic about the need for the courts to interpret the Constitution "creatively" and "innova-tively" and thereby effectively alter the Constitution through a procedure not set forth there, and quite at odds with the values implicit in Article V.

The Constitution as
Fundamental Law

So long as the federal courts persist in their role of pro-ducing "legislation without representation," I anticipate that we are likely to see continuing evidence of strong congressional reaction. I am personally enthusiastic about some of this response—I believe that the constitutional convention mode of amendment has the potential to reinvigorate the institution of federalism generally. About other elements of this response—the growing variety of means of circumventing the processes of the Constitution—I am concerned. My purpose here is not to justify or condemn any particular legislative response, but merely to explain them. If, however, blame is to be meted out, I choose to accord it not merely to those without the patience to pursue traditional Article V amendment procedures, but also to those on the bench, and to their allies in academia and elsewhere, who have created a judicial regime that routinely shortcuts proper means of constitutional revision. Can we reasonably expect that opponents of such wholesale constitutional revision from the bench will continue forever to tolerate such action without responding in kind?

Just as the Tenth Amendment is regarded as the constitutional embodiment of federalism and the First Amendment as the expression of values of free speech and association, Article V of the Constitution is the definitive articulation of the idea that the Constitution is not "written on water"; that its meaning is not to evolve and "mature" over time that judges are not to do "justice," but are to do "justice under law"; that it matters what the Founders intended their work to mean. Article V of the Constitution is the ultimate expression that the Constitution is not a "mere parchment barrier," but that its guarantees and principles are permanent and unchanging in the absence of formal constitutional amendment. It mandates that constitutional intent, unless altered through Article V's exacting process, shall remain the original intent.

Justice Brennan has said that "judicial power resides in the authority to give meaning to the Constitution." It seems to me, however, that the very existence of Article V's exclusive amendment mode demonstrates beyond doubt that our fundamental law was designed to establish certain principles not necessarily dependent on the personal predictions of any platonic guardians, be they British royalty or federal judges. Those principles can constitutionally be altered only in accordance with the prescribed democratic forms.

In closing, I think it fitting to quote from Alexander Hamilton one final time: "A Constitution is, in fact, *and must be regarded by the judges as*, a fundamental law." (emphasis added). Those who applaud extra-constitutional alteration of the document ignore this central premise of the system of government that we have chosen to live by. The values that run so deeply through Article V—the federalist structure designed to disperse power and localize conflict, the need to establish multiple checks on power through a written document; and, most importantly, the understanding that ultimate sovereignty resides with the people—all are principles basic to the Constitution and interwoven throughout its text. The recent surge of efforts to invoke Article V's amendment procedures, I believe, evidences a strong sense that the values embodied in that article and in its surrounding clauses are badly in need of resuscitation.

Federalism in Principle and Practice

Charles E. Rice

The Constitution of the United States is the first instance in all history of the creation of a government possessing only limited powers. The Magna Carta, the Petition of Right, the English Bill of Rights, and all the other previous efforts to restrain government had merely imposed restrictions on the otherwise unlimited power of government. The Framers of the Constitution, however, created a new government that would possess only the powers delegated to it. To be sure, some implied powers were delegated and some of the delegated powers, such as the power to regulate interstate commerce, were subject to elastic interpretation. Nevertheless, the federalism ordained by the Constitution rested upon the essential principle that the federal government was given only the powers delegated and that all other governmental power was reserved to the states. This principle was embodied in the Constitution even before the adoption of the Tenth Amendment. Thus, Article I, Section 1, provides *"All legislative powers herein granted . . . ."* (emphasis added) The

Tenth Amendment merely reaffirmed the principle, as if to say, "And we really mean it."

Various factors have contributed to the erosion of federalism in constitutional theory and practice. The changed character of the economy, the conferral on the federal government by the Sixteenth Amendment of an unlimited power to tax income, the direct election of senators provided by the Seventeenth Amendment, and the effect of four major wars in seven decades are among the most prominent. Here, however, I will focus on a little noticed but decisive reason for the shift in governmental power from the states to Washington in matters affecting basic aspects of local government and community life. Consider a few examples:

When a twelve-year-old girl was shot and killed not long ago in the cross-fire of a gang fight in Chicago's Cabrini-Green Housing project, why were the police unable to respond to the demands of residents and columnists that they search the project, seize all the illegal weapons and arrest their possessors?

When a small midwestern city finds that the newest addition to its downtown business district is a bar featuring totally nude dancing, why are the authorities unable to close the place down?

When a public school teacher responds to the unanimous request of the parents of her kindergarten class by allowing the children to recite the *Romper Room* grace "God is great, God is good, Let us thank Him for our food" before their cookies and milk, why is that teacher subject to injunction as a violator of the First Amendment to the Constitution?

Why are public high schools and colleges required to recognize a homosexual club on the same basis as they recognize other student organizations such as a stamp club or a history honorary society?

Why are unborn human beings killed each year in this country in numbers equivalent to the combined populations of Boston, Denver, and Seattle and the states are unable to do anything effective to prevent it?

Why is a public figure who is financially destroyed by a falsehood published by a newspaper unable to recover a dime unless he proves that the falsehood was published with actual malice?

Incorporation Doctrine

These are questions about which many Americans are concerned. And the answer in each case is that the states and communities are prevented from doing anything because of the incorporation doctrine. This has nothing to do with corporations. It is, rather, an invention of the Supreme Court of the United States by which that Court, contrary to the intent to the Constitution, has succeeded in binding the states uniformly by every requirement of the first eight amendments of the Bill of Rights as those requirements are interpreted by the Supreme Court. These amendments were intended by the first Congress and by the states which approved them to protect the specified rights against invasion by the federal government. The state governments were not bound by those provisions. For protection of their rights against invasion by state governments, the people relied primarily upon state constitutions.

The Fourteenth Amendment and "New" Rights

The Fourteenth Amendment, adopted in 1868, provides that "No State shall . . . abridge the *privileges or immunities* of citizens of the United States; nor shall any State deprive any person of life, liberty, or property, without *due process* of law; nor deny to any person within its jurisdiction the *equal protection* of the laws." (emphasis added) In a line of decisions beginning more than six decades ago, the Supreme Court has held that virtually all of the protections of the first eight amendments of the Bill of Rights are included in the "liberty" protected by the Fourteenth Amendment due process clause and that therefore the states are as fully obliged to comply with them as is the federal government. In the view of the Court, "The Fourteenth Amendment has rendered the legislatures of the states as incompetent as Congress to enact" laws in violation of, for example, the clause of the First Amendment which provides, "Congress shall make no law respecting an establishment of religion."[1]

The Court has interpreted the Bill of Rights so as to include also rights not specified therein; rights arising from its own interpretation which it has proceeded to apply against the states. For example, in 1965 the Supreme Court struck down as unconstitutional a Connecticut law prohibiting the use of contraceptives. But to accomplish this, the Court had to find a right of reproductive privacy in the Bill of Rights so as to hold that the due process clause of the Fourteenth Amendment forbids Connecticut to violate it. Less resource-ful jurists might have said, as Justice Black did in dissent, that the Framers did not have reproductive privacy in mind when they proposed the Bill of Rights and that therefore the Connecticut law did not violate the Fourteenth Amendment. The majority of the Court, however, discovered such a right of privacy in the "penumbras formed by emanations from the Bill of Rights."[2] This ruling was the precursor of *Roe* v. *Wade*[3] in which the Supreme Court held that the unborn child is not a person for purposes of the Fourteenth Amend-ment and that this right of privacy prevents the states from prohibiting abortion. Even in the third trimester, the state cannot prohibit abortion in any case where it is sought for the physical or mental health of the mother. In view of the elasticity of mental health as a criterion, the rulings are thus a warrant for elective abortion at every stage of pregnancy, right up to the time of birth. As a result, every year we kill by legalized abortion more than 1.5 million babies. The point here is not to analyze the abortion issue itself. Rather, the purpose is to discuss the error involved in the Supreme Court's holding that the first eight amendments of the Bill of Rights are strictly applied against the states through the Fourteenth Amendment. This error affects areas as diverse as defamation, school prayer, search and seizure, self-incrimination, capital punishment, pornography, and homosexual activity.

The legislative history of the Fourteenth Amendment demonstrates that the application by the Supreme Court of the Bill of Rights to the states fits Justice Holmes's description, in another context, of "an unconstitutional assumption of powers by courts of the United States which no lapse of time or respectable array of opinion should make us hesitate to correct."[4] In his definitive analysis of that legislative history, Charles Fairman exhaustively analyzes the "mountain of evidence" from the Congressional debates, the state ratifying proceedings and other original sources in support of his conclusion that the proponents and ratifiers of the Fourteenth Amendment did not intend to make the Bill of Rights applicable against the states.[5] He contrasts this "mountain of evidence" with "the few stones and pebbles that made up the theory that the Fourteenth Amendment incorporated Amendments I to VIII."[6]

Nor can it be soundly argued that the Fourteenth Amendment applied some, but not all, of the provisions of the first eight amendments against the states. This selective incorporation theory, as Louis Henkin wrote, "finds no support in the language of the amendment, or in the history of its adoption, and it is truly more difficult to justify than Justice Black's position that the Bill of Rights was wholly incorporated."[7]

In this matter, the Supreme Court prefers its own fictional version to the actual meaning of the Constitution. A central feature of the Constitution is the division of powers between the federal and state governments. The Supreme Court's erroneous application of the Bill of Rights against the states has imposed an artificial uniformity which obliterates that division of powers in important areas. It is also counterproductive in that it frustrates that capacity for innovation and local diversity which is itself a significant safeguard of liberty.

The erroneous application of the Bill of Rights against the states is a major contribution to the congestion on the docket of the Supreme Court itself. Various proposed remedies for that congestion, such as higher standards for counsel and a new intermediate court of appeals, miss the point that an essential cause of the Supreme Court's overload is the Court's own misinterpretation of the Fourteenth Amendment's guarantee of due process of law; the Court interprets that guarantee so as to make every state and local subdivision uniformly subject to the prohibitions contained in the Bill of Rights, for example, in matters of speech, religious expression, admissibility of illegally seized evidence against a criminal defendant and the like. Since the Court mandates one uniform rule in these matters there must be one interpreter which is, of course, the Supreme Court itself. Hence the avalanche of appeals to the Court. The problem is compounded because the Court is wont to invent rights which are not in the Bill of Rights, for example, the right of reproductive privacy which the Court uses as a justification for legalized abortion. In short, the overload of cases is primarily due to the Court's own activism.

A Proper Interpretation
of the Fourteenth Amendment

Respect for the intent of the Constitution requires that the Supreme Court abandon its erroneous doctrine that applies the Bill of Rights against the states. But a proper interpretation of the Fourteenth Amendment would not leave the states free from all federal restraint in the matter of individual rights. The Supreme Court has misconstrued the due process clause of the Fourteenth Amendment so as to bind the states strictly by the Supreme Court's interpretations of the Bill of Rights. But another clause of that amendment, the "privileges or immunities" clause, *was* intended to limit the powers of the states with respect to basic rights, including the rights to life, property, personal security and mobility. Unfortunately, the Supreme Court in the *Slaughterhouse* cases in 1873 interpreted the "privileges or immunities" clause so as to render it ineffectual. Under a proper interpretation of the "privileges or immunities" clause, federal courts would have a limited power to declare state laws unconstitutional on account of their denial of equality in the enjoyment of basic rights. This judicial power would be limited by the power of Congress to enforce the Fourteenth Amendment, a power explicitly conferred by Section 5 of that amendment. And a further check is provided by the power of Congress under Article III, Section 2, to limit the appellate jurisdiction of the Supreme Court as well as the jurisdiction of lower federal courts.

The "privileges or immunities" clause was intended to confirm the constitutionality of the Civil Rights Acts of

1866. The "'fundamental' rights which the Framers were anxious to secure were those described by Blackstone—personal security, freedom to move about and to own property; they had been picked up in the 'privileges and immunities' of Article IV, Section 2; the incidental rights necessary for that protection were 'enumerated' in the Civil Rights Act of 1866; that enumeration, according to the Framers, marked the bounds of the grant; and at length those rights were embodied in the 'privileges or immunities' of the Fourteenth Amendment."[8] The "original design" of the Fourteenth Amendment

> was to make the "privileges or immunities" clause the pivotal provision in order to shield the "fundamental rights" enumerated in the Civil Rights Act from the Black Codes. Intertwined with that enumeration was repeated emphasis on the enjoyment of the "same rights," and "equal benefit of all laws and proceedings for the security of person and property." . . . In lawyer's parlance, the privileges or immunities clause conferred *substantive* rights which were to be secured through the medium of two *adjective* rights: the equal protection clause outlawed statutory, the due process clause judicial, discrimination with respect to those substantive rights.[9]

The underlying concept of the privileges or immunities clause was equality of treatment with respect to basic rights. That clause provided a limited and sufficiently flexible restriction on state action which denied that equality. In the *Slaughterhouse* cases,[10] however, the Supreme Court gave the privileges or immunities clause a restrictive interpretation by holding that it protected only a limited category of privileges of "a citizen of the United States." The privileges or immunities clause was thereby effectively nullified as a significant restraint on state action. Ultimately, of course, the Supreme Court provided that restraint in substantive as well as procedural matters through the due process clause and especially through the incorporation doctrine with which this essay is concerned.

The errors discussed here are fundamental. So are the consequences in terms of the erosion of federalism. And the remedy should likewise be fundamental. What is needed is a reversal of the incorporation doctrine and a reversal of the *Slaughterhouse* cases so as to restore the three clauses of the Fourteenth Amendment—privileges or immunities, equal protection and due process—to their proper functions. The amendment was serviceable as conceived by its Framers. And it can be made serviceable again whether through corrective action by Congress in the exercise of its Section 5 power to enforce the amendment by "appropriate legislation" or through the recovery by the Supreme Court of a sense of its own responsibility to interpret the Constitution rather than to amend it.

Notes

1. *Abington School District* v. *Schempp*, 374 U.S. U.S. 203,215 (1963).
2. *Griswold* v. *Connecticut*, 381 U.S. 479,484 (1965).
3. *Roe* v. *Wade*, 410 U.S. 113 (1973).
4. *Black and White Taxicab Co.* v. *Brown & Yellow Taxicab Co.*, 276 U.S. 518,533 (1928); Justice Holmes dissenting.
5. Charles Fairman, "Does the Fourteenth Amendment Incorporate the Bill of Rights?" 5, *Stanford Law Review*, 134 (1949).
6. *Ibid.*
7. Louis Henkin, "Selective Incorporation in the Fourteenth Amendment," 73, *Yale Law Journal*, 74-77(1963); see also

Raoul Berger, *Death Penalties: The Supreme Courts' Obstacle Course* (Harvard University Press, 1982), 15-16.

8. Raoul Berger, *Government by Judiciary: The Transformation of the Fourteenth Amendment* (Harvard University Press, 1977), 36.

9. *Ibid.*, 208-9.

10. *Slaughterhouse* cases, 83 U.S. (16 Wall.) 36 (1872).

The Declaration of Independence and the Equal Protection of the Laws

Glen E. Thurow

"No State shall . . . deny to any person within its jurisdiction the equal protection of the laws." These words of the Four-teenth Amendment to the Constitution have not only formed the basis of much modern jurisprudence, but they are a cru-cial passage in the current debate over how to interpret the Constitution. The equal protection clause is central to this debate for three reasons: First, it is taken as a prime example of those clauses in the Constitution which are sufficiently general or vague that it is difficult to determine their meaning from the text. What constitutes "equal protection of the laws" for the very different groups which make up America? Second, it is argued that it is equally or more difficult to determine its meaning by examining the legislative history of the Fourteenth Amendment. That history only reveals that the framers of the amendment were not very clear about the meaning of the words they endorsed. Consequently, as the dean of the Stanford Law School, John Hart Ely, has put it, "we are left with a provision whose general concern—

equality—is clear enough but whose content beyond that cannot be derived from anything within its four corners or the known intentions of its framers."[1]

But there is a third even more important reason why this clause is central to the debate over interpreting the Constitution. It seems to speak to the very heart of what we as a democratic nation stand for, and thus its interpretation is critical to our understanding of ourselves and what we are about. It not only addresses the relationship of one race to another under the law, but also seems to speak to other equally important relationships such as those between men and women and between poor and rich. Because the proper character of many of these relationships is a current issue in American politics, the equal protection clause is crucial in today's partisan politics. Because these relationships profoundly affect the character of our life as a nation, the meaning of the equal protection clause is vital to the character and success of our democratic experiment.

I wish to argue that the meaning of the equal protection clause, although general, is far from being vague. Its meaning is quite clear when it is understood in the context of the Constitution as a whole, and this meaning is confirmed by the intention of its Framers. Our current confusion arises because we attempt to give the Fourteenth Amendment an historicist reading, one which sees its original meaning as rooted in the historical circumstances of the time of its adoption and seeks its current meaning in present day opinions and desires. This historicist reading must give way to one that recognizes that, in writing a constitution, men knew that they were not merely legislating for their times but for future generations as well, and understood that the nature of a constitution requires that its clauses announce permanent arrangements and principles rather than the fleeting preoccupations of the moment.

The Meaning of Equal Protection

There are two distinct issues in interpreting the equal protection clause. One is, what does it mean? The other is, who is to enforce its requirements? The first question is the more fundamental one and it is that question I shall address in this paper. Although I shall not examine the answer to the second question, let me only say that I do not think it self-evident that the courts are the principal means by which the Fourteenth Amendment ought to be enforced.

There are some things about the meaning of the equal protection clause that are evident from its wording. First, it is a restriction upon state action, "No state shall . . . ." Second, it applies not only to citizens but to "any person" within the jurisdiction of a state. Third, what is prohibited is that a state may not deny any such person the "equal protection of the laws." This clearly means that the state may not extend the protection of the laws to some people while excluding others.

The difficult interpretive issue arises from the question of the degree to which the Fourteenth Amendment restricts the content of the laws which must apply to all. "Equal protection of the laws" may mean the laws must be enforced for everyone; but it may also mean that protection extended by the law must be equal for all. If it means the latter, we face the difficulty that common sense tells us that many distinctions made by the law in extending protections are quite reasonable while others appear unjust. It is reasonable to distinguish between old people and young people in determining who gets social security benefits; it is unjust to reserve residential areas for the white race only. What distinctions are permissible? In order to answer this question, let us first consider some principles that should guide any interpretation of the Constitution.

How to Interpret the Constitution

One cannot properly interpret the Constitution without remembering what a constitution is. As John Marshall put it, ". . . we must never forget, that it is a constitution we are expounding." A constitution differs from an ordinary law in that it is fundamental and is meant to last forever. It is, therefore, not addressed simply to the immediate situation of its establishment, but to the long future stretching before it. Should its Framers attempt to detail every conceivable circumstance that might arise it would, as Marshall said, "partake of the prolixity of a legal code, and could scarcely be embraced by the human mind."[2] Furthermore, the problem is more than technical. Even if the Framers had had the resources of modern information storage they could not have detailed every circumstance because of their inability to foresee the future, including the vast technological advances with which we are so familiar. Consequently a well-written constitution is one which marks its "great outlines" and "important objects," which establishes the proper constitutional principles while leaving their application in particular circumstances to those whose duty it is to uphold the constitution in times to come.

It should also be recognized that those who wrote our Constitution were well aware of this characteristic. It is why our Constitution speaks of "commerce" instead of "shipping," why it grants Congress the power to "constitute tribunals inferior to the Supreme Court" rather than to specify the number and nature of the inferior courts. And, I think it can be shown that the authors of most of the amendments to the Constitution were similarly aware of the nature of a constitution.

One of the great errors of constitutional interpretation is to forget this characteristic of a constitution. In our time we are led to this neglect by a kind of historicism which reads our Constitution in the light of the particular circumstances and issues of the times in which it was written. It assumes that the Framers were not and could not be speaking in terms of general principles but that they must be reflecting only the parochial views of their times. This historicism has old and not very respectable roots in American constitutional interpretation. One of the earliest and most famous historicist misinterpretations concerned, not the Constitution, but the Declaration of Independence. Nearly a hundred and thirty years ago in the *Dred Scott* case, Chief Justice Taney denied that the Declaration's phrase, "all men are created equal," could possibly mean what it plainly said. Why? Because some of the Framers owned slaves. Hence the Declaration must mean "all white men are created equal."[3] How many of us follow perfectly the principles we nevertheless believe? Taney denied that our principles can be better than our practice. He neglected the possibility, as Lincoln noted, that the authors of the Declaration meant to set up a "standard maxim for free societies" which though never perfectly attained—certainly not in their own day—could be a continuing goal for a free society.

How to Interpret the
Equal Protection Clause

Because the events and circumstances of the passage of the Fourteenth Amendment are so vivid in our national memory and their consequences still so much with us today, there has been an overwhelming temptation to read the Fourteenth Amendment in the light of those circumstances. When the Supreme Court first had occasion to interpret the equal protection clause in the *Slaughterhouse* cases, it predicted, "We doubt very much whether any action of a state not directed by way of discrimination against the Negroes as a class, or on account of their race, will ever be held to come within the purview of this provision." It is so clear that the framers of the Fourteenth Amendment meant somehow to protect the rights of the newly freed slaves that even those who would give the clause a broad meaning today understand the original intention to protect the freedmen. It is for this reason that Ely, as I have already noted, says that the intentions of the framers of the Fourteenth Amendment can give us little guidance, for those framers seemed exclusively preoccupied with how the general words of the clause were to apply to one particular issue, that of the freedmen.

Indeed, in the debates in the House and Senate leading to the passage of the Fourteenth Amendment, the issue which did occupy everyone was that of how to protect the rights of the former slaves. The one occasion on which the discussion touched upon some other application of the clause was most unsatisfactory and unenlightening. In the House debate, Representative Robert Hale of New York, an opponent of the proposed amendment, claimed that the equal protection clause would mean that the states would no longer be free to distinguish between the rights of married women and those of single women or men, as all the states then did. Thaddeus Stevens replied that it would only require that the states treat all married women the same and all unmarried women the same, but it would not require the states to treat married and unmarried women the same. The answer was obviously inadequate and Hale rightly noted that by its reasoning the amendment would only require that all blacks be treated the same, not that they would have to be treated the same as whites. [4] Hale then insisted upon continuing his speech and the issue was dropped. Obviously, there is little in this exchange which would guide one towards an answer to the question of whether the clause allows distinctions between men and women or married and unmarried persons. The supporter (and chief mover) of the amendment, Stevens, maintains that it would, but his reasoning is specious; and the opponent of the measure, Hale, says that it would not, but his statement is a mere assertion not endorsed by anyone else. The intentions of the framers seem a blind alley.

But suppose we look at the clause in a different way. Instead of being mesmerized by the issue of slavery, let us read it as part of the Constitution, assuming that its general language does indeed mean to state a general principle which ought to be read in the light of the Constitution as a whole. Then the debates over its adoption reveal that its framers, however much they were practically concerned with the issue of the freed slave, understood that they were writing a constitution meant to speak to other issues in other days and that they were establishing a general principle of American constitutional government.

In this light, three things are evident from the debate. First, that its supporters did not regard it as establishing a new principle for the Constitution. It is reiterated several times in the debate that the principle that all ought to be equally protected by the laws was not new, that it was indeed the "very foundation of a republican government."[5] Second, it is evident that its supporters thought that what they were doing was not inventing a new principle, but extending its practical effect. They were giving power to Congress to make sure that no state would deny the equal protection of the laws to its citizens. Many indeed believed that even this was not a radical change, but was made necessary only because the Supreme Court had misunderstood the original federal principle in the *Dred Scott* case.[6] Third, the framers of the clause understood its meaning as a fulfillment of the principle of the Declaration of Independence. As Thaddeus Stevens noted, all of the provisions of the first section of the Fourteenth Amendment were "assert-ed, in some form or other, in our Declaration or organic law."[7] Even though the debaters were concerned immediately with the issue of the rights of the freed slaves, they clearly recognized that they were writing a constitution meant to endure beyond the immediate issue, that they were embodying in the Fourteenth Amendment a basic principle of republican government to be understood in the light of the Declaration of Independence.

The Principle of Equal Protection

In order to understand the principle of equal protection it is proper, therefore, to begin with the Declaration of Independence. It is well to remind ourselves of several features of the equality of men as it is proclaimed in the famous phrase, "all men are created equal." The equality proclaimed is not one made by laws or human decree, rather men are *created* equal—they are by nature equal. What does it mean to say that they are by nature equal? It does not mean that they are equal in all respects. The Declaration does not deny that some are stronger than others, some more beautiful, some more intelligent. Rather, as the Declaration explains, it means that they are "endowed by their Creator with certain unalienable rights . . . ." This means that with respect to these rights, no man has the right to tell another what he must do. No one, in other words, is the governor or ruler of another with respect to these rights. Or, as Jefferson put it, "the mass of mankind has not been born with saddles on their backs, or a favored few booted and spurred, ready to ride them legitimately by the grace of God."[8] By nature no man is the ruler of another. All have equal rights.

Yet, although all men possess equal rights, all govern-ment involves inequality, even in a democracy. For government involves some men telling others what they must do. The principle is not different if it is one man or a minority telling the majority what to do, or whether it is a majority telling the minority what it must do. In either case there is a relationship of inequality, of some governing and others being governed. The Declaration implies that although there is nothing in the differences which exist among human beings which would justify this inequality, this inequality is nevertheless necessary. It is necessary because without it our rights, our natural grant to govern ourselves, would be ineffective because we are incapable of defending our rights for ourselves. The insecurity of our rights makes government necessary. It is the purpose of government to secure these rights.

Government, which requires inequality, can only be justified by the consent of all. Because we are rightfully our own governors, we have the right to decide who among us will be given the right to make those common laws which we need in order to secure our rights. Government derives its just powers from the consent of the governed.

This basic principle leads to two corollaries, the first being that consent is not given once and for all, but can be withdrawn. Hence there is a right of revolution, even when a people have consented to a particular government (as the Americans did to British rule prior to 1776). It is but a short step from this to the realization that a continuing measure of consent, by free elections for example, is an appropriate way to both ensure continuing consent and make the government one likely to gain consent.

The second corollary points us toward the rule of law. Precisely because our rights are insecure, it is not sufficient that we give our consent to government. A just government must also be a government which will take as its aim the protection of our rights and one which we can be reasonably confident will restrict itself to that aim. Hence the Declaration leads to the rule of law in which no one can be restricted except in the manner prescribed by the advanced notice of the law, and in whch the law applies equally to all, the governors as well as the governed. These principles make it more difficult for the power of the government to be directed unjustly against some individual or group, or to be designed to favor the ruling group or individual.

The requirement that all men be equally protected by the laws thus reflects the natural equality of all men. It is because men are created equal that they ought to be equally protected by the laws. What distinctions, then, may be made in the law compatible with equal protection? In principle we can say this: All men must be protected in their unalienable rights to life, liberty, and the pursuit of happiness because all are equal in the possession of these rights. However, in those matters in which men are not naturally equal, the law may legitimately make distinctions. It may send smart people to college and prohibit entrance to less talented ones. Classifications that are founded upon relevant natural distinctions are consistent with equal protection; those that extend different protections to groups defined by merely historical or accidental distinctions are contrary to the principle of equal protection.

Affirmative Action and
the New Inequality

The greatest dispute over the meaning of the equal protection clause today is that concerning affirmative action. By affirmative action I mean not any aid to minorities but the position which says that members of certain groups, as a matter of justice, are entitled to privileges under the law denied to others because of the injustice done to that group in the past.

Some claim that the equal protection clause requires affirmative action. To be equally protected by the laws according to this reasoning means that there must be a remedy in the laws for the injury done to a group, and that remedy can only be some compensatory benefit at the expense of the group or groups responsible for the injury. On the other hand, others claim the opposite, that the clause forbids affirmative action because people are treated unequally in affirmative action. A person who has never been injured may receive a benefit simply because of the group to which he belongs; while one who has never committed any injury may be denied a benefit solely because of his group.

Racial distinctions in American law are properly treated as inherently suspect. The standard developed by the Court, that in making such a classification one must show that there is some great societal good to be accomplished and that there is no way of accomplishing it other than a racial classification, seems to be the very standard of Nature itself. The reason, however, is not the one the Court has sometimes used, that classifications cast a stigma upon a particular race. That view leads to the conclusion that laws discriminating against whites are constitutional because people will not take the discrimination as a sign of inferiority of the white race. No stigma, no denial of equal protection. Rather, the reason such classifications are suspect is because there is no natural distinction among the races which justifies them. Discrimination against whites is just as bad in principle as discrimination against blacks. The first Justice Harlan perceived this when he argued in his dissent in the *Plessy* case that the legally required railway car segregation of Louisiana was contrary to the "personal liberty of citizens."[9]

In one sense, affirmative action is clearly a policy of inequality—some people will be given rights denied to others solely because of the group into which they were born, just as in bygone years those born into the aristocracy were given privileges in the law denied to the common people. Yet affirmative action is defended in the name of equality, not inequality. The advantages some groups will get today is justified by the disadvantages they suffered yesterday. These advantages will be at the expense of groups which have had more than their share of advantages, and thus all will be made equal. The end of the new inequality is equality so conceived. Equality is restored through the notion of compensatory justice.

This notion of compensatory justice for groups rests upon the historicism I mentioned earlier. One's identity under the law is determined by the group to which one belongs, and that group is defined by historical circumstances. Blacks are the beneficiaries of affirmative action not because they are black nor even because they are victims of discrimination today, but because they are a group which has been victimized in the past. Their present status in the law is to be determined not by their present condition but by their past condition. The newborn black infant is not equal in the law of affirmative action to the newborn white infant not because of a difference in their nature, but because of a difference in the history of the groups into which they are born. It does not matter whether a particular individual has discriminated against anyone else or whether he has been the victim of discrimination. The past overrules the present.

The view of equality which underlies this policy is one which rejects nature as a standard for political action. The traditional American notion of equality under law means that all have a right to consent to the law and all have a right to be judged under the law in accordance with whether or not one has violated the law. And all must have their rights equally protected. Affirmative action rejects all of these premises. Instead it replaces them with the notion that the object of law is not to protect our rights but to ensure our equality. That equality is determined by sameness rather than by looking to what our nature entitles us. It is a view of equality that in principle destroys liberty.

I can illustrate this point by referring to one of today's leading constitutional law authorities, Professor Laurence Tribe of Harvard. Professor Tribe entitled a recent book *Constitutional Choices*. He wishes to emphasize by this title that we have a wide latitude to make whatever choices we think appropriate about the Constitution—there is no one set of principles or one standard of interpretation to which we may repair. We are constrained neither by the words of the Constitution nor by the nature of man. The consequence is that we can give a new meaning to equality and the equal protection of the laws.

But when the standards of our nature are rejected, the meaning of equality no longer hinges on a recognition of the character of human nature and the differences which exist among men. Nature itself may be judged by another standard. When found wanting, she may be captured and changed. The true meaning of equality then becomes not the protection of the rights of all (and thus the protection of their differences), but the remolding of each in the image of others. According to Professor Tribe, for example, the law should not take account of differences between the sexes except to ensure that these differences do not result in different ways of life. If the consequence of sexual intercourse is motherhood for women, but not motherhood for men, then it is the duty of the law to see that such need not be the consequence for either sex. Equality requires that women not be faced with any consequences of their actions not also faced by men. [10] That this understanding of equality destroys liberty can be seen if the reasoning is transferred to the realm of speech. If the consequence of speaking is ridicule for one man with a squeaky voice and glory for another with a deep one, then the law must ensure that these different consequences do not result—presumably, in this case, by forbidding the good speaker to speak.

It is proper to understand justice in the case of individuals in terms of compensation for past wrongs. If an individual has been injured, it is just that he be compensated to the fairest extent possible. If a black has been unjustly discriminated against by a white, it is proper for the white to be made to compensate him for his injury. However, a just relationship among groups in society cannot be understood in the same way. The same principle of justice applied to groups leaves the result that some who have received no injury will receive compensation and some who have done no injury will be made to pay. Injustice, therefore, cannot be wiped out by such a policy but only be perpetuated in a new guise. In looking at the relationship among groups in society we should rather look to what our common good requires.

The common good under affirmative action appears only in the view that every group ought to be equal to every other. This does not, in fact, establish a common good, but is instead a notion of something like sovereign statehood for individual groups. Different groups are held together, not as parts of one country, but for the sake of getting what they can from other groups. To cut the pie among groups in some particular way may keep the peace, but it does not create a common good.

The change which has occurred in our politics with the change in the understanding of equality can be seen in the difference between Martin Luther King and Jesse Jackson. Martin Luther King spoke in the name of the Declaration's understanding of equality, calling upon all Americans to live up to their belief that everyone is entitled to equal rights. As a consequence, he could form a political movement of whites

as well as blacks, and many whites, not part of the movement themselves, could nevertheless be moved by it. Jesse
Jackson, on the other hand, has sought to form a "Rainbow
Coalition." Of course, there is no white in the rainbow.
Jackson, unlike King, has not called upon both whites and
blacks to live up to the best that is in them. Rather, he has
appealed to the poor, including whites, to recognize that they
are in reality colored. Every group which is in some way
disadvantaged is to unite together in order to demand what is
rightfully theirs from the rest. Farmers, blacks, old people,
the poor, would all be part of one political movement, not
because they share a view of the common good but because
they desire more from the government and the dominant
whites. Where is the common good? The Republicans made
an effective charge against the Democrats in the last election
that they were nothing but a collection of interests. But the
view of equality inherent in affirmative action leaves no common good beyond a collection of interests.

Nonracial Classifications

What does the equal protection clause say about other kinds
of classifications in the law? The traditional standard of the
court has been that if the government has a legitimate aim
and if the classification is related to that aim, then the classification is legitimate, provided that it involves neither a
suspect classification nor a fundamental right. A wide discretion is given to the legislature to select the means it con-
siders most appropriate to gaining its legitimate end. In
recent years, however, this neat division has broken down.
Are there other distinctions like the racial ones that should be
held to a more exacting standard? The distinction most often
mentioned is that made on the basis of sex.

Distinctions based on gender are significantly different from those on the basis of race. This is not only because the alleged oppression of women by men is of an entirely different order than the oppression of blacks by whites, but is also because the distinction between the sexes is not a distinction like that of race which can in principle be ignored. Perform this experiment. Imagine a society in which people were color- or racial-blind so that they could not know which person belonged to which race. There would be no barriers whatever to establishing a perfectly good society among such people. Try the same experiment with sex. Suppose people were sex-blind, so that they could not tell who was male and who female. Here is prime material for a satirist. One simply could not properly perform the most basic tasks of society, beginning with the regeneration of the human population. All of the institutions based upon a recognition of this distinction, such as the family, would be impossible. The distinction between male and female is not simply irrelevant in the way that the distinction between races is in principle irrelevant, in the formation of a good society.

What the proper relationship is between male and female is no easy thing to define; nor is it easy to say what relationship between them is most compatible with republican government. The liberation of women in recent years has certainly achieved many obvious and significant benefits. Yet it cannot be denied that it has also spawned problems that we have yet to adequately face, problems at least partially recognized within the women's movement itself. In making the honor given both men and women turn on their success in the market place, do we not see a significant increase in unedifying, indeed degrading, materialism? Does it not also lead to increased neglect of the children who will be the republican citizens of tomorrow? Will those children have the qualities of mind and character republics require of their citizens? Whatever the particular conclusion reached, the principle of justice involved in making distinctions of gender in the law is clear. The extent that distinctions of rights under the law based upon sex are appropriate recognitions of natural differences between the sexes is the same extent that distinctions are constitutional. To the extent that the distinctions do not reflect such natural differences, they are contrary to the equal protection of the laws. What those differences may be are proper matters for our common deliberation and for the decision of our legislative bodies.

In looking at the equal protection clause of the Fourteenth Amendment, then, we must keep in mind that it is a constitution we are interpreting. A constitution must be read with the presumption that it has been designed to state general principles in order that it might last forever. We must also remember that our Constitution requires us to study our nature in order to know how we are to apply standards that are rooted in and derived from that nature.

Notes

1. John Hart Ely, *Democracy and Distrust: A Theory of Judicial Review* (Harvard University Press, 1980), 31.
2. *McCulloch* v. *Maryland* 4 Wheaton 316 (1819).
3. *Dred Scott* v. *Sandford* 19 How. 393 (1857).
4. Alfred Avins, ed., *The Reconstruction Amendments Debates* (Virginia Commission on Constitutional Government, 1967), 154.
5. *Ibid.*, 217.
6. *Ibid.*, 212.
7. *Ibid.*
8. Andrew A. Lipscomb, ed., *The Writings of Thomas Jefferson,* XVI (Thomas Jefferson Memorial Association, 1903), XVI, 182.
9. *Plessy* v. *Ferguson*, 163 U.S. 537 (1896).
10. Laurence H. Tribe, *Constitutional Choices* (Harvard University Press, 1985), 238-45.

The Layman's Perspective on the Constitution

Avi Nelson

When I was putting together some ideas for this presentation on the Constitution, I asked a recent college graduate, a young professional, about the topic. Her immediate answer was "I don't know anything about it." That may well be a true reflection of the layman's perspective on one of the most important features of democracy.

Ironically, there is also a corresponding lack of knowledge about the layman's perspective itself. I thought that it would be relatively easy to find a few articles, check some poll data; in short, get a feel for public opinion, but no such information in any updated form exists. One researcher at a very prestigious survey firm said, "Quite frankly, there is nobody to hire us to do that because nobody cares." This is unfortunate because the Constitution is clearly written as a governing document and it is written for ordinary people. The wording of the Constitution is quite plain. Its authors did not use high-sounding phrases or technical terms. Thomas Jefferson once described the Constitution as a text of civil instruction, but it appears that we have sadly neglected it.

We can ask three questions: How well do most people understand the Constitution? How are they educated about the Constitution? And how important is it that they be educated or knowledgeable about the Constitution?

The most recent surveys which we may look to were taken in 1944 and 1946. One of these asked:

Question:
What do you know of the Bill of Rights?

Answers:
Never heard of it./I'm not sure I have — 31%
Had heard of it, but could not identify — 36%
Confused, unsatisfactory or incorrect — 12%

That leaves 21 percent of our citizenry who had a reasonably accurate idea of the content. It may be significant that the particular survey firm which used the question, the National Opinion Research Center, has not employed it on any of their subsequent surveys. Perhaps they were discouraged by the results.

There is a general belief in some quarters that the Bill of Rights could not be passed today in any popular referendum. This opinion gained great currency over ten years ago during an event called the People's Bicentennial. (That was the bicentennial of the Declaration of Independence, not the Constitution, of course.) One group of radicals wanted to protest the national celebration of our two hundredth anniversary. Its members frequented supermarkets and parking lots, asking questions such as "Do you think people who want to violently overthrow the government of the United States should be able to say anything they want at any time?" Well, you try accosting someone coming out of the supermarket with that question. Every time, the answer was "No." The radicals chalked that up as opposition to the First Amendment and, by inference, to the entire Bill of Rights.

Many newspapers picked the story up, circulated it, and it persists today. But it is a myth. It is not that the people wouldn't approve of the Bill of Rights; they probably don't know enough about it one way or the other to cast an intelligent vote.

Let us return to the polling data for a moment. In another survey conducted in the 1940s the question was asked: *Which represents your opinion: Our form of government, based on the Constitution, is as near perfect as can be and no important changes should be made.* About two-thirds of the people, 67 percent, agreed with that. Or: *The Constitution has served well but should be thoroughly revised to fit present-day needs.* About 20 percent agreed with that. (Please be aware that throughout this essay, I have paraphrased the questions slightly, but without distorting the meaning or the implication of the results.)

A Historical Perspective

How else are we to get a feel for the layman's perspective? We must use collateral means, beginning with some general speculation about our past. During the 1780s, debate about the formulation and ratification of the Constitution was not limited to the floor of the Constitutional Convention. In every state, the provisions were passionately discussed. It is safe to say that people knew more about the Constitution at that point in our history than at any other time. And, of course, the disagreements among the nation's leaders and the convention delegates mirrored disagreements in the broad American community as well. Thomas Jefferson, who was in France at the time, objected to the Constitution's drafting because it did not have a Bill of Rights. Thomas Paine, also in France, objected because he was against a presidency. He was also concerned about the duration of the Senate terms.

But both of them went along with the proposed document, interestingly enough, because they were encouraged by the prospect of amending it. Like many others, they thought they could iron out the imperfections later. They felt the need to have something to replace the Articles of Confederation as soon as possible. Paine phrased it this way: "Thirteen staves and nary a hoop will not a barrel make." And they pointed out that they would have voted for worse documents just to get something down on paper.

There were, however, deep misgivings about the Constitution. Gouverneur Morris from New York warned, "Give the votes to the people who have no property and they will sell them to the rich who will be able to buy them." Exactly the opposite point of view was expressed by a Massachusetts countryman, Amos Singletary, who said, "These lawyers and men of learning and moneyed men that speak so finely and gloss over matters so smoothly to make us poor illiterate people swallow down the pill expect to get in Congress themselves. They expect to be the managers of this Constitution and get all the power and all the money into their own hands, and then they will swallow up all us little folks, like the great Leviathan." In the end, significantly, the strongest support for the Constitution came from the artisans. Half to two-thirds of the adult males in the cities were tradesmen. They correctly perceived that the Constitution was not only a document of government, but also a document of commerce. At the time, the British were dumping goods in America, commerce was stagnating, the economy was crippled, and there were numerous demands for tariff protection. These artisans saw the benefit of speedily adopting the new Constitution.

To put the public discourse on political affairs into context, one must remember that in the 1780s few printed discussions of issues were circulated. Paine's famous *Common Sense* pamphlet reached only a few hundred thousand people and this was considered an extraordinary accomplishment. Ordinarily, newspapers might reach 5,000 people; pamphlets, 2,000. Mass communication was very limited. But Professor Alfred Young of the University of Northern Illinois has made the observation that by studying accounts of public celebrations we may gauge public interest on many issues.

In celebrating the ratification of the Constitution in 1788, people turned out in unprecedented numbers for parades. In Boston more than 4,000 marchers participated. In New York, 5,000; in Philadelphia, over 5,000; and the artisans were once again in the majority. They marched alphabetically or by trade. They each had floats and they had slogans that went along with them. One group of bakers had a huge "Federal Loaf of Bread." The coopers had a float that depicted 13 staves on a barrel, a fulfillment of Paine's earlier metaphor. Blacksmiths and nailers used the slogan "While Industry Prevails, We Need No Foreign Nails." Chairmakers, who were naturally more interested in exports, responded with the "The Federal States and Union-Bound O'er All The World Our Chairs are Found." The shipbuilders added, "The Federal Ship Will Our Commerce Revive, and Merchants and Shipwrights and Joiners Shall Thrive." The tallow chandlers boasted "The Stars of America—A Light to the World."

After the ratification era, the poetry lapsed and so did our knowledge of the public's view of the Constitution. There were periods, of course, when people would get agitated about a particular issue such as slavery, and when amendments were proposed, people naturally discussed them. But beyond these generalizations, public awareness of the Constitution is a phenomenon we know little about.

In the absence of direct methodology Professor Michael Kammen of Cornell University relies on another interesting technique—the study of language and rhetoric—to assess what the Constitution meant to past generations. Grand descriptions of the Constitution are not formulated by farmers in the fields or men in the street; they are produced by intellectual and political leaders, but in the absence of anything else, they may shed some light on the common view since they were likely to exert some degree of influence on it. In 1774 Thomas Jefferson referred to the yet unwritten document as "the great machine of government." John Quincy Adams used the same image in 1839, and James Russell Lowell revived it in 1888. Throughout the nineteenth century the Constitution was still depicted as a machine, a mechanical device. Over time, however, the image evolved into an organic or living document—those were Holmes's words in 1914. Cardoza said in 1925, "The Constitution has an organic life." And Frankfurter commented as late as 1951, "The Constitution is an organism." During his presidential campaign, Woodrow Wilson put it this way:

> The makers of our Federal Constitution constructed a government as they would have constructed an orrery* to display the laws of nature. Politics in their thought was a variety of mechanics. The Constitution was founded on the law of gravitation. The government was to exist and move by virtue of the efficacy of checks and balances.
>
> The trouble with the theory is that government is not a machine, but a living thing. It falls not into the theory of the universe, but under the theory of organic life. It is accountable to Darwin, not to Newton.

---

*An orrery is an apparatus invented in 1731 showing the relative positions of heavenly bodies in the solar system by using balls moved by wheelwork.

Now there is some significance in this statement. The original construction of the language, of course, predates Darwin. Since the theory of evolution was not known in the 1780s, it is logical that in the eighteenth century men would use the scientific terminology of the day, born of the Industrial Revolution, machinery, and growth. Darwin, in the succeeding century, inspired the use of the biological terms (My suspicion is that even today judges and politicians probably find themselves more comfortable justifying departures from constitutional interpretation when they feel they are advancing a life form, rather than tampering with a machine.)

Still, it is doubtful that the lay public on the farms or in the cities in either century actively debated as to whether the Constitution should be described as a machine or an organism. Their civic education came, as it does now, primarily from textbooks and school. That education may be superficial and even inaccurate. One text published in 1900 presented John Adams and Thomas Jefferson actively involved in the 1787 convention when they happened to be serving as our ministers to Britain and France, respectively, at the time. Admittedly, the Constitution can be a very dry and complicated subject. And the meaning and the intention behind many passages are disputed even by informed and articulate leaders. These disputes often are as old as the Constitution itself. One can hardly expect the public to be fully informed about "loose v. strict construction," "judicial review," "flexible versus unchanging interpretations" and so on.

The Supreme Court, with more recognized authority on the Constitution than any other body, has, historically, chosen not to educate the public. The justices keep their distance from the people almost allowing their roles to be shrouded in mystery. Even the procedures and the internal workings of the Court are not well publicized. The media has also failed to educate the public about such basic features of our government. There is precious little broadcast or written about the Constitution. And I would venture to say from my own experience in the field that most journalists don't know any more about the Constitution than the lay public.

Public Opinion
and the Constitution

Another way of assessing the public's attitude about the Constitution is to ask questions about issues which have constitutional ramifications. *Do you believe in free speech?* Ninety-five percent of the Americans polled answered "yes" to this question on a recent survey. In 1982 the question was reworded to state: *I believe in free speech no matter what views are being expressed.* With that slight change of wording, approval dropped to 85 percent. Then the survey asked: *Would you allow someone to make a speech against churches and religions in your community?* Thirty-four percent answered that question "no," even though the questions were asked back-to-back. *Would you allow someone who has views against churches and religion to teach?* Fifty-one percent answered "no." *Should an admitted communist be allowed to make a speech in your community?* Forty-one percent said "no." *Should somebody who wants to do away with elections and let the military run the country be allowed to make a speech?* Forty-two percent said they would not allow him to make a speech. *Should such a person be allowed to teach?* Fifty-six percent would not allow him to teach. *Should a homosexual be allowed to make a speech in the community?* Thirty-one percent of the respondents said "no," and 41 percent said they would not allow him to teach. All these answers are from people who are self-avowed firm believers in freedom of speech.

There was another study done in 1975 which asked, *Do you think the United States should allow speeches against democracy?* Forty-two percent of the people said "no." Well, clearly at least one-third of the population cannot be accused of being confined by consistency! More likely, however, it is probably evidence of a belief in both the values of religion and free speech. When you ask about them independently, you get strong favorable opinions for both. But when you put them in contest and challenge one to the other, you force people to make a value judgment and some of them will choose to protect religion over freedom of speech and vice versa.

People believe just as strongly in the freedom of the press and still offer contradictory opinions. In a 1985 survey, 17 percent of the people polled said that the media should be regulated by government. In 1957, 39 percent of the people said socialists should not be allowed to publish newspapers. In 1963, people were asked: *Do you think that members of the Communist Party should be allowed to speak on radio?* Sixty-seven percent of the people polled answered "no." And in 1953: *Do you agree newspapers should not be allowed to criticize our form of government?* Forty-two percent of the people agreed that newspapers should not be allowed to criticize our form of government. The layman's view of the First Amendment is multifaceted, to put it charitably. The flip side of this, by the way, is that civil liberties never seem to arouse much concern among the populace. Surveys frequently ask *What is the most worrisome problem facing the nation, facing you, and facing your community?* Never more than one or two percent of the respondents will identify anything having to do with civil liberties. These freedoms are taken for granted and are generally accepted with whatever restrictions accompany them in every era, whether it is during a world war, a cold war, or the present.

There are, however, issues which will rouse public indignation. Recently 81 percent of the populace disagreed with the Supreme Court on the school prayer decision. In 1967, only 47 percent agreed with the statement that the Court was impartial. That shows a fair amount of disenchantment with the Supreme Court of the United States among people who are not actively involved in political issues. In 1969, 54 percent rated the Supreme Court fair or poor; only 33 percent excellent or good. Fifty percent trust the Congress more than they trust the highest court in the land.

Does the federal judiciary reflect your views? In 1981, 77 percent of the public said "no." Ten percent said "yes." *Should the court have its jurisdiction on busing withdrawn?* "Yes," 81 percent; "no," 14 percent. *Should there be a congressional override of the Supreme Court by two-thirds vote?* (In other words, if two-thirds of the Congressmen vote to override a Supreme Court decision, should that constitute an equivalent to a presidential veto?) Fifty-five percent said "yes." Thirty percent said "no." *Should there be a periodic reconfirmation of judges?* Seventy-five percent were in favor of it. They are also in favor of electing federal judges. Here is an interesting note from a 1985 poll: *Who is most responsible for high crime in Texas?* Commanding 28 percent, the number one answer was "the judges!" The number two answer was "lawyers." So they got the spawn as well as the progenitor. (By the way, the third answer was the parole board.) And when asked the question *Is there too much concern for the rights of criminals shown by the courts?,* 70 percent answered "yes." It is evident that the courts have earned very little sympathy and have engendered a fair amount of cynicism.

But here, too, there is no groundswell of support for draconian measures. People are not marching in the streets demanding to overhaul the legal system. They may disagree with the courts and with an intrusive government (73 percent say the government has too much power over citizens), but there seems to be an adaptability quotient. People are willing to accept what goes on and to survive and thrive nonetheless. When one thinks about the difficult conditions under which some other nations' citizens have to endure—privation, corruption, repression, and the like—putting up with some questionable Supreme Court decisions becomes less than a monumental problem.

Concern about the government, the courts, and the Constitution is not new. In the 1920s, two very different senators, Edwin Ladd, a Republican from North Dakota, and Robert Lafollette, a Progressive from Wisconsin, agreed on one statement: "The Constitution is not what its plain terms declare, but what these nine men construe it to be." This sounds like a discussion right out of modern times. And in 1937, a musicial by Kaufman and Hart entitled "I'd Rather Be Right" has the Supreme Court declare the Constitution of the United States unconstitutional. The humor is perhaps more fitting than it should be.

The Public Faith in the Constitution

What we know of public opinion on constitutional issues is diverse at best, confusing and inconsistent at worst. It tells us something about public political philosophy, but it fails to capture an important spirit about the Constitution: the belief in it. Our knowledge about it may be lacking, but the devotion to and the faith in the Constitution is and appears to always have been widespread and deep. Don Devine, the former director of the U.S. Office of Personnel Management, has called the combination "ignorance and consensus," but veneration for the Constitution is genuine and longstanding. It is not faddish, and I don't think it is at all self-destructive. Around the turn of the century, A. Lawrence Lowell, of Harvard University put it this way:

> For a long time the Constitution was regarded as something peculiarly sacred and received an unquestioned homage for reasons quite apart from any virtues of its own. The Constitution was to us what a king has often been to other nations. It was the symbol and pledge of our national existence. The people may not have taken the Constitution to their heads, but they appear to have taken it to their hearts.

A more jaundiced description of this mystical aspect of the Constitution and Constitutional perspective comes from Thurmond Arnold, an administrator in the New Deal. And he writes rather cynically:

> The Constitution became for them (meaning the people) a sort of abracadabra which would cure all disease. Copies of the Constitution, bound together with the Declaration of Independence and Lincoln's Gettysburg Address were distributed in cigar stores. Essays on the Constitution were written by high school students. Incomprehensible speeches on the Constitution were made from every public platform to reverent audiences which knew approximately as much about the history and dialectic of that document as the masses in the Middle Ages knew about the Bible in those days when people were not permitted to read the Bible. The American Liberty League was dedicated to Constitution worship. Like the Bible, the Constitution became the altar whenever our best people met together for tearful solemn purposes, regard-

less of the kind of organization. Teachers in many states were compelled to swear to support the Constitution. No attempt was made to attach a particular meaning to this phrase, yet people thought it had deep and mystical significance and that the saying of the oath constituted a charm aganist evil spirits. The opponents of such oaths became equally excited and equally theological about the great harm this ceremony might do.

I don't think that such cynicism is warranted. But there is something interesting about his allusion to the Bible. Most people's lives have a religious aspect, and they take this quite seriously. This transcends and is not at all diminshed by the inability of people to pass a quiz on the Bible and the same applies to the Constitution.

How important is it that people really be educated and knowledgeable about the Constitution? Maybe it is less important than we might think. Of course, it would be nice if everybody were knowledgeable about the document. But knowledge is no cure for dissension. The debate on the role of the Constitution in our society will go on, regardless of the degree of civic awareness.

The belief in the Constitution is like love of one's country. And just as with the love of country, the feeling is not acquired through a rational deduction but through emotion. It is genuine, powerful, and compelling, nonetheless. Here is a passage from a constitution which may illustrate the point:

> Citizens are equal before the law without distinction of origin, social or property status, race or nationality, sex, education, language, attitude to religion, type and nature of occupation, domicile or other status. The equal rights of citizens are

guaranteed in all fields of economic, political, social and cultural life.

Article: Citizens of different races and nationalities have equal rights. Any direct or indirect limitation of the rights of citizens or establishment of direct or indirect privileges on grounds of race or nationality, and the advocacy of racial or national exclusiveness, hostility, or contempt are punishable by law.

Article: Citizens are guaranteed freedom of conscience (that is the right to profess or not to profess any religion; the church is separated from the state and the school from the church).

Article: Citizens are guaranteed inviolability of the person. No one may be arrested except by a court decision or on the warrant. . . . Citizens are guaranteed inviolability of the home. No one may, without lawful grounds, enter a home against the will of those residing in it.

Article: The privacy of citizens and of their correspondence, telephone conversations, and telegraphic communications, is protected by law.

Article: Respect for the individual and protection of the rights and freedoms of citizens are the duty of all state bodies, public organizations, and officials. Citizens have the right to protection by the courts against encroachments on their honor and reputation, life and health, personal freedom and property.

Now, I venture to say that those words and concepts sound pretty good. If I put them forward to the average man-on-the-street, I would elicit his general support for them. But these passages are not from our Constitution. They are taken from the Constitution of the Union of Soviet Socialist Republics, the most recent and currently governing version adopted in October 1977. If I read these passages or similar ones from our Constitution to ordinary citizens in the Soviet Union, they would perhaps recognize them as somehow connected with constitutional authority, but the meaning given to the words would be very different from the meaning given to the words by Americans. People here *do* have an understanding of what it means to have property rights, of what it means to have individual liberty. They have an appreciation for what democracy is all about, even if they are not precise and cannot cite the appropriate historical references and logical arguments. Their perspective on what freedom in America is about is clear and their suspicion of what "freedom" in the Soviet Union means is also very clear. The layman knows very little about the U.S. Constitution, granted. He knows even less about the Constitution of the U.S.S.R., but he knows full well that he would rather live here than there. That's an appreciation of the Constitution on the most fundamental level.

Constitutional comparisons also give strength to the concern about the intentions of the Founders. I have omitted some of the other articles of the Soviet Union's Constitution and the Preamble which gives the official Russian perspective on what the Bolshevik Founders meant, but that document should demonstrate the importance of not taking words out of context. It also offers a compelling reason why we should be concerned that nine lawyers on a committee called the Supreme Court, unelected and ensconced for life in their office, should be able to determine in broad measure social, economic, and constitutional policy for the United States. Giving too much power to any centralized authority leads to a compromise of individual liberty and ultimately a diminution of the democratic nature of our republic. As Professor Lino A. Graglia of the University of Texas Law School has put it, the Constitution "was not written in disappearing ink." He continues:

> The Framers' solution to the problem of protecting human freedom and dignity was to preserve as much as possible . . . a system of decentralized democratic decision making, with the regulation of social conditions and personal relations left to the states. [Giving] virtually unlimited Supreme Court power to decide basic social issues for the nation as a whole, effectively disenfranchising the people of each state . . . is directly contrary to the constitutional scheme.

I think the American people would agree. I think they would sooner take their chances with the democratic process and a strict interpretation of the Constitution.

From
Needmore
to
Prosperity

From
Needmore
to

Hoosier Place Names
in Folklore & History

Prosperity

Ronald L. Baker

INDIANA UNIVERSITY PRESS   BLOOMINGTON & INDIANAPOLIS

The paper used in this publication meets the
minimum requirements of American National
Standard for Information Sciences—Permanence
of Paper for Printed Library Materials,
ANSI Z39.48-1984.

 ™

Manufactured in the United States of America

Library of Congress Cataloging-in-Publication Data

Baker, Ronald L., date
    From Needmore to Prosperity : Hoosier place
names in folklore and history / Ronald L. Baker.
      p. cm.
    Includes bibliographical references.
    ISBN 0-253-32866-7 (alk. paper). —
ISBN 0-253-20955-2 (pbk. : alk. paper)
    1. Names, Geographical—Indiana. 2. Indiana—
History, Local. 3. Folklore—Indiana. I. Title.
F524.B33 1995
917.72'003—dc20   94-44707

1 2 3 4 5 00 99 98 97 96 95

For my pals, **Flash** and **Moozie**

"I have fallen in love with American names . . ."

Stephen Vincent Benét

CONTENTS

From
Needmore
to
Prosperity

Introduction

Place Names and Cultural Studies

Place-name research in the United States generally is a matter of inquiry into historical records, not a matter of etymological research and linguistic analysis, as place-name research developed in Europe. This book, however, deals with the folklore as well as with the history of the names of populated places in Indiana and is, therefore, a cultural study, rather than strictly an historical study, of Hoosier county and settlement names.

The aim of cultural studies is not merely the compilation of facts to discover a single vision of formal culture, as apparently it was for some nineteenth-century historians. Cultural studies should strive to present the diverse thoughts and feelings of a community, and it does this through an interdisciplinary study of cultural constructions, material as well as verbal, within historical, physical, and social contexts rather than focusing simply on so-called facts.

It is mainly in this sense of the study of culture that folklore contributes to place-name research. Folklore presents other voices and other visions and provides a context for place-name history. Folk legends add flesh to the bare bones of dates and details and contribute to the humanization of the study of place names.

Folklore and History

In the preface to *American Folklore and the Historian*, Richard M. Dorson, who held the title of distinguished professor of both folklore and history at Indiana University, wrote that "recently American historians have begun to turn to folklore as a vital source for black, ethnic, urban, and frontier historical writing. Some of them "actively encourage the marriage of American history and folklore in a manner I can only find heartwarming after years of frosty indifference."[1] Indeed, there has been a "frosty indifference" to the marriage of folklore and history. On one hand, many contemporary folklorists are interested in only the ethnographic present, and, as Dorson noted, these folklorists "provide rich detail for the contemporary settings of folklore but bypass the historical dimension."[2] On the other hand, Dorson also pointed out that "scientific historical method, reverencing the documentary source, gives short shrift to oral tradition."[3] More recently, historian Lawrence W. Levine echoes Dorson's generalization when he writes of "an attitude still plaguing historians."

> Trained to use books, newspapers, diaries, letters, official reports—the written remains of the highly literate portions of society—historians too often neither know what to do with orally transmitted folk materials nor see the need to preserve them. Yet without such preservation and use many of the varied voices that make up any society as large as ours are stilled and we are lulled into the belief that those voices that are recoverable from traditional printed sources are the only ones there were.[4]

Folklore often has been given short shrift by historians partly because popularly folklore is equated with anything considered false or irrational. A dictionary definition of folklore, for example, is "a widely held unsupported specious notion or body of notions,"[5] and an elder historian once told Henry Glassie that "folklore is a pack of damned lies."[6] Thus, anything unsupported and not believed by rational human beings often is called "folklore" or "mythical"; however, folklore, like written history, may be true or false, and even if it is false, it may reveal values and attitudes that are nevertheless accurate.

What's more, some forms of folklore, notably myths and legends, though disparaged by outsiders, are believed to be true by those who pass them along. As old-time folklorist Alexander H. Krappe suggests, what others believe we call "superstition"; and what we believe we call "religion."[7] More directly to the point, Henry Glassie has observed that "viewed from within, from the perspective of the historian at work in a community, all histories are history. Viewed from without, all histories are folk histories, in some measure false and irrelevant. Simply, folk history is what we call other people's history, and if they were snide enough to adopt our terms, folk history is what they would name the history confected in the little community of the academy."[8]

As early as 1908 Sir George Laurence Gomme, one of the founders of the English Folklore Society and the author of *Folk-Lore as an Historical Science,* warned that bad history and fiction cannot be classified as folklore, and Gomme himself attempted to use folklore to reconstruct history.[9] Even Gomme's friends and colleagues in the Folklore Society, however, attacked his approach and countered that so-called facts revealed by traditions could be proved correct only by historical methodology. More recently, methodologies have been proposed by Jan Vansina and others for reconstructing history from oral traditions, and it is generally agreed that oral traditions used as historical sources must be supplemented by other documents and that genres of oral tradition vary in worth as historical sources.[10]

Accordingly, oral traditions sometimes are placed on a continuum according to their historical worth, with oral history at one extreme and oral literature at the other. According to this view, prose genres such as personal experience tales that deal realistically with the past are more reliable as history than more poetic genres such as ballads, which are performed largely for entertainment. As Bill Jansen has shown, though, tellers of personal experience tales often embellish their stories, or give them what his informants called "the treatment." "The treatment," according to Jansen, "includes: individualizing characters; supplying direct discourse, particularly dialogue; supplying rather stereotype contexts, both geographical and psychological; establishing some kind of personal tie between the performer and the narrative performed—the treatment may consist of any or all of the above."[11]

One of Jansen's informants, for example, was nicknamed "Honest John" because of his devotion to plain talk. "Honest John" ended several of his personal experience tales with a variant of the same sentence: "Rose [his wife] and I argued about that all night long, and we actually made up our minds during breakfast just before I went to work—but we never regretted our decision." When Jansen asked "Honest John" if it was true that on several occasions he and his wife sat up all night trying to make up their minds about something, his informant replied, "Well . . . maybe not. I don't know. Maybe it's the best way I know to show it was a difficult decision. . . . And, of course, I want to show that my wife is part of my life and shares in my decisions."[12]

As Jansen points out, even when informants relate what they consider factual accounts of events that they have witnessed or participated in, they "may quite unwittingly apply to those accounts the same techniques of narrative formulation and stylization" that they use when performing what they consider fictional stories.[13]

It may well be, then, that genres of oral literature as well as genres of oral history might be of value in reconstructing history. For instance, there are a number of historical folk songs, and as D. K. Wilgus and Lynwood Montell demonstrate in "Beanie Short: A Civil War Chronicle in Legend and Song," a local folk song along with a body of local legends can be used to reconstruct a hundred-year-old episode in local history that could not have been told if only the standard historical documents and methods were used. Wilgus and Montell point out that "the events that gave rise to the song and legends about Beanie Short, a rebel guerrilla, were never placed in writing—not in newspapers, for there were none, and not in the court records, for guerrilla bands during the Civil War seldom stood trial for their crimes"; however, Wilgus and Montell aptly show "that, with due caution, the investigator can turn profitably to the folk themselves for their history."[14]

Even folk literature from other times and places, like the older ballads in the Child collection, may be of historical worth. As another old-time folklorist, Gordon Gerould, has said, ballads are not just narrative songs; they are records of the past. Gerould, though, is more interested in the folklore that ballads preserve than in any actual dates and details. Ballads, according to Gerould, "embody the experiences . . . and imaginings of the people who have made and sung them";[15] they "reflect not only the opinions and feelings of ordinary folk but their beliefs and customs as well."[16] Even in ballads that are not classified as historical, like the popular romantic tragedy "Lord Thomas and Fair Annet" (Child 73A),[17] we can see, for example, the emergence of class consciousness and conflict in England. In this ballad, Lord Thomas forsakes the aristocratic Fair Annet for a commoner, conventionally called the nut-brown bride, and when the jilted Annet arrives at the wedding and sits beside the bride, the jealous nut-brown bride asks Annet, "And whair gat ye that rose-water, / That does mak yee sae white?" Annet, flaunting her fairness, which she and her Anglo-Norman culture equate with superiority of birth, replies:

> "O I did get the rose-water
>   Whair ye will neir get nane,
> For I did get that very rose-water
>   Into my mither's wame."

This notion of class consciousness and conflict is developed in a variant of another Child ballad, "Lamkin" (Child 93A). In this version of the ballad the mason Lamkin builds a castle for Lord Wearie, who refuses to pay Lamkin when the castle is finished. Lamkin warns Lord Wearie that he will be sorry if he doesn't pay him, and while Wearie is away, with the help of a nurse in the castle, Lamkin kills Lord Wearie's wife and child. When Lamkin asks the nurse if he should kill Lady Wearie, the nurse replies, "O kill her, kill her, Lamkin, / for she ne'er was good to me." Lamkin then asks the nurse for a basin to catch Lady Wearie's heart's blood, for it was believed that allowing aristocratic blood to seep into the floor was an indignity punished by the soul after death. But the nurse replies:

> "There need nae bason, Lamkin,
> lat it run through the floor;
> What better is the heart's blood
> o the rich than o the poor?"

Of course, as Gerould suggests, it is the thirty-eight Robin Hood ballads in the Child collection that really develop "a trustworthy index to the restiveness of the common people under political, economic, and social abuses."[18] According to Child, Robin Hood, as we know him, is not historical but simply a product of the ballad muse, because the best information on Robin Hood comes from the thirty-eight ballads.[19] Contemporary chroniclers did not mention Robin Hood, and later historians who do mention him seem to get their information from the ballads. J. C. Holt, professor of medieval history at the University of Cambridge, points out that

> Robin Hood enjoys a unique distinction. He was accorded in the *Dictionary of National Biography* an article devoted entirely to arguing that he never existed. The author, Sidney Lee, who was also the editor of the dictionary, believed that Robin was purely mythical and tried to write him out of history. Yet obstinately he remains within it. From the first he was believed to be a real historical person.[20]

Holt points out in his prologue that his book on Robin Hood "is about a legend rather than a man."[21] Knowledge of personal legends, though, suggests that there probably was a Robin Hood. We know that more recent legendary outlaws, such as Jesse James and John Dillinger, really lived, and we also know that they didn't do all the things attributed to them in story and song. Most likely there was a Robin Hood, too, but he didn't do all the things attributed to him in the ballads. Stories of other outlaws as well as fabricated adventures probably accumulated around the one central figure, Robin Hood. Though all the incidents in the ballads are not historical facts, the ideals of common people are represented in the ballads of Robin Hood, just as the ideals of knighthood are represented in the legends of King Arthur. As representations of the ideals of common people, the Robin Hood ballads tell us something about social justice in the Middle Ages. Robin Hood was popular because he upheld a natural law and opposed the social law, which at that time was in the hands of outsiders, the Normans, and considered unjust.

In spite of the close relationships between folklore and history, many American place-name historians have had virtually no use at all for folklore. As Robert S. Rudolph says in *Wood County Place Names*, the investigator of place names, among other things, "seeks to illuminate true origins obscured by folk etymologies."[22] Rudolph's view is typical of that of most place-name historians, who have been interested in the factual rather than in the imaginative aspects of place naming, in the historical rather than in the cultural significance of names. Since in popular usage the term *folklore* generally is equated with what is false, place-name researchers seeking the so-called truth about names usually do not knowingly report folklore. Folklorists, on the other hand, generally are interested in the facts of place naming only as a point of departure or frame of reference for the study of place-name legends.[23] Folklorists typically have been interested mainly in unofficial names that don't appear on maps and names that appear in other genres of folklore. Since the nineteenth century, folklorists have been interested in name magic as well.[24]

Influenced by earlier European models, some American place-name researchers have focused on the spelling, pronunciation, origin, and meaning of place names as words, not as names that function regardless of their origin or of what they originally meant, and they have drawn on folklore only if it helps explain origin, history, change, or meaning of a name as a word. But as W. F. H. Nicolaisen has observed, "names . . . survive because they can be meaningful as *names* even if they have become meaningless as *words*."[25] Regardless of its actual origin or meaning, a name serves as "equipment for living," to borrow Kenneth Burke's phrase.[26] By naming the geographical features around them, people are able to manage their environment and bring order to their world, thus contributing to their emotional stability. Since names are so extremely important in human culture, place-name researchers should examine what they mean to all people who know them and use them as well as what they meant at the time of naming.

Several kinds of folklore—including folk speech, folk etymology, nicknames, place-name jokes, folk biography—as well as fieldwork techniques can assist place-name historians in their work. But place-name legends, especially, contribute to place-name research in at least five ways.[27]

First, researchers of place-name facts should understand the nature of place-name legends so they will recognize a legend when they hear one or read one. In their investigations into the origins of names, place-name historians unfamiliar with the nature of folk legends sometimes mistake a folk legend reported in a printed source for historical fact.

Second, researchers of place-name facts should be knowledgeable of place-name legends because sometimes local names are derived from folk legends. Some place-name researchers think the name always comes first and stories arise to explain the name, but sometimes the legend comes first and the physical setting of the legend takes its name from the legend. Thus, not only is folklore created from names, but names also are created from folklore.

Third, researchers of place-name facts should also be interested in place-name legends because local legends can help the place-name researcher find unofficial and variant names that aren't on maps. In and around any community are many local names and variant names that don't appear on maps or in books, but people living in the community know the names and through oral tradition pass them along to others. One problem for place-name researchers not living in the community whose names they are studying is finding these unofficial and variant names to include in their surveys. Usually legends are set very specifically, and many times the names people give places are related to legends set there. Knowing the legends often helps locate and explain hard-to-find variant and informal names.

Fourth, researchers of place-name facts should also collect and report place-name legends because unofficial names and their accompanying legends sometimes serve as a better index of culture than official names and the facts of naming. By studying the unofficial names associated with place-name legends, the place-name researcher can get much closer to actual people living in a community than by studying only official names. Not only is there a lot of local flavor in unofficial names, but along with their accompanying legends they also reveal something about the humor, beliefs, prejudices, and values of the people who applied the names and continue to use them. While official names might praise the "great men" who were generals, governors, senators, or presidents of the United States, local names might celebrate the many anonymous common laborers who played an equally important role in the development of a state and the nation.

Finally, researchers of place-name facts should be aware of place-name legends because some legends are migratory and are attached to several places, where they function to explain local names. An acquaintance with the migratory quality of legends prevents a place-name historian who is looking for historical data from accepting floating stories as fact.

Legends may not be accurate in the details they preserve or fail to preserve, but they reveal other kinds of valuable information. Place-name legends often give place-name researchers and their audiences an impression of the people who live in a place and use its names, whatever the origin of the names might be; and legends, of course, reveal what the names mean to the people. To the folk who pass them on, legends are by no means false. Legends, right or wrong, are believed; they serve as folk history. Moreover, as place-name scholar Robert Rennick warns, often it is "extremely difficult for even the most sophisticated historian to distinguish between fully authenticated truth and local legend and thus to assure the complete accuracy of his data." Rennick aptly advises that for "the more conservative place-name researcher, a rule of thumb might be to accept every account as legend unless he is completely confident about it."[28]

Indiana Place-Name Legends

Most American place names, as H. L. Mencken suggests, are unimaginative names.[29] That is, they are borrowed from the names of other places or from the names of people. In Indiana, though, as in every state, there are imaginative narratives explaining the origins of some of the unimaginative names and most of the unusual names. These fanciful accounts of place naming are legends—stories that natives often believe but that may or may not be factual. Usually, even if these stories had some kernel of truth at their inception, through many years of retelling they have changed and new versions have arisen.

Local pronunciations have inspired some place-name legends, such as those about Hymera and Terre Haute. Terre Haute was pronounced TERRY HUT by some residents, and that gave rise to a local legend that the city was named for a popular tavern, Terry's Hut. In reality, Terre Haute means "high land" and was applied by French settlers to describe the relatively high banks along the Wabash River. Hymera was pronounced HIGH MARY by some Hoosiers living in the area, and three legends are based on this pronunciation. One tale says that the postmaster, John Badders, named the town for his unusually tall adopted daughter, nicknamed "High Mary." Another story states that a woman named Mary worked in the post office, and neighbors passing or entering the post office would wave and call, "Hi, Mary!" More recently, it is said that High Mary was a local prostitute who charged high prices. Although state and local histories report only versions of these legends, Hymera probably was named for the classical city Himera, founded in 648 B.C. on the northern coast of Sicily.

It is not especially unusual that place names honor women, but there are some unusual legendary origins of names commemorating women. Noblesville most likely was named for James Noble, Indiana's first United States senator; however, legends say the name comes from Kathleen or Lavinia Noble, sweetheart of a cofounder of the town, James Polk. Allegedly, Polk built a home for his fiancee in the center of town and planted a vegetable garden in a pattern that spelled out Miss Noble's last name. Much to Polk's dismay, Miss Noble found the garden insulting and broke the engagement; however, the garden remained, and strangers passing through mistook the girl's name in the garden for the name of the community. Although Saratoga apparently was named for Saratoga, New York, according to a local tale it was named for Sara Loller. The story goes that the postmaster was in Albright's general store when Miss Loller, a beautiful redhead, walked in. The postmaster asked her if she would like to have a town named for her, and, of course, she said she would. Storekeeper Albright suggested they add "toga" to her name, so the town was named Saratoga. Galveston probably is a transfer name from Texas, but a local legend provides a more imaginative origin. After James Carter laid out the town in 1852, he was gazing out a window contemplating a name for the new town when a girl with a vest on passed before him, which suggested the name.

Several Indiana place names supposedly were chosen randomly from books, especially from the Bible, suggesting a form of bibliomancy. Throughout Europe the Bible, sometimes opened with a golden needle, was used for divination or advice. One place name allegedly selected from the Bible is Jasper. A local tradition holds that the oldest woman in the community opened the Bible and put her finger on the word *jasper*. Although Orland probably is a transfer name, a local legend maintains that the postmaster opened a hymn book and selected the name from the title of the first hymn he saw. Secular books, especially geography books, might also be used to randomly select place names in legendary accounts. Supposedly, the name of one Hoosier village was taken from a geography book when a pin stuck in the book pierced the word *Zulu* on a page about Africa.

Quite a few Indiana place names, according to legends, have their origin in various remarks, sayings, and exclamations. For instance, Birdseye supposedly got its name from a statement made by Reverend "Bird" Johnson, who was invited to help select the post office site. After surveying several possible locations, he finally decided, "This spot suits Bird's eye to a T-y-tee." Although Onward probably is a commendatory name, a local anecdote explains that the name comes from a remark repeated by loafers when leaving a general store: "I must now plug onward." According to tradition, Daylight received its name from a statement made by a railroad engineer. Each evening when he dropped off a construction crew, the engineer said, "I'll pick you men up at day-light."

Exclamations inspired the naming of several Hoosier communities, according to legends. Mohawk probably was named for the Iroquois tribe, but a local story says there was a flight of hawks overhead and residents who looked up called, "Mo' [more] hawks, mo' hawks!" Eureka allegedly received its name when settlers were looking for a tract of land opposite French Island on the Ohio River. A watchman sighted the island at dawn and cried, "Eureka!" Roann perhaps was named for Roanne, France; however, a local legend says that once during a flood a girl named Ann attempted to row a boat ashore, but a swift current kept carrying her downstream. Her father, watching help-lessly, called, "Row, Ann! Row, Ann!" Although Hobart was named for Hobart Earle, brother of the founder, according to a local legend, the city was named for a command given a horse. A man in a buggy pulled up in front of an old country store and called, "Ho, Bart!"

Utterances by drunks, foreigners, and Native Americans who had trouble with the English language also became names of Hoosier com-munities, according to local legends. Eugene, probably stemming from a Christian name, is explained only by legend. A town drunk frequently called "Oh, Jane!" for his wife, but because of his drunkenness the cry sounded like "Eu, Jene!" Tampico, founded in 1840, no doubt was named for the Mexican seaport, but an elderly Bloomington informant gives another explanation:

I heard this about 60 years ago. In the early days Tampico was called "Pico." It was the trading point for the German settlement ten miles east of Brownstown. Well, one of these old Germans that got his English pronunciation fouled up when he got excited or mad, went to Pico to get some large spikes to use in building his barn. After driving all the way to Pico, he was told that they had no spikes that large. He became very angry and cried, "Well, tam [damn] Pico, anyhow; I will trade in Brownstown." After that, they started calling Pico "Tampico."[30]

Stereotyped notions of how Native Americans handle the English language especially contributed to place-name legends. Auburn is a transfer name from England via New York, but a local legend has it that a group of Indians were sitting around a campfire when one Indian stuck his finger in the fire and exclaimed, "Ah, burn!" Although Merom was named for the biblical lake, a local anecdote explains that the town was named for a remark repeated by Indians who came to town for liquor and said, "Me, rum!" Tecumseh was named for the famous Shawnee chief who attempted to unite the western Indian tribes. His name means "going across" or "crossing over," apparently referring to a meteor. According to local legend, though, the chief's name was Tee: "There was this band of Indians that had a powwow where the town is now. The chief's name was Tee. A couple of warriors went through the woods and found this huge river. They ran back shouting, 'Tee, come see! Tee, come see!' So that's how Tecumseh got its name."

Place names often are descriptive, and while place-name legends recognize this principle of place naming, the stories are not always accurate. Bloomfield, for example, was named for Bloomfield, New Jersey, but according to a legend, early settlers saw blooming fields there. Bloomington may have been named for an early settler, William Bloom; however, a similar local legend says the name comes from blooming flowers that impressed a group of pioneers. Smartsburg perhaps was named for a pioneer physician, Dr. Smart, although a local tradition explains that the name is descriptive of smartweed growing along a nearby creek. Wilders, formerly called Wilders Crossing, Wilders Junction, and Wilders Station, probably comes from a family name, but a legend maintains the community was so named from its location in the wilderness. Although Lacy apparently honors a local family, a traditional account says the name comes from small lace caps worn to church by women of a religious sect. Greencastle was named for Greencastle, Pennsylvania, the former home of the earliest settler. According to legend, though, the first settler built his house on posts that sprouted after the house was constructed, so he called his house his "green castle." Cayuga was named for the lake in New York, but one legend says the name is descriptive of the sound of Model T Ford horns.

Some related legendary accounts of naming are descriptive of incidents that allegedly occurred in the communities. One of Indiana's most colorful place names, Gnaw Bone, is explained by several legends, some about early settlers or soldiers who were snowed in and when help arrived were nearly starved and gnawing on bones. An educated guess, actually no more than a folk legend of the sophisticated, is that the community was named by French settlers for Narbonne, France. When another celebrated Hoosier community, Santa Claus, was founded, the suggested name was Santa Fe; however, since there already was a Santa Fe in Indiana, someone jokingly suggested Santa Claus as an alternate name, and it was accepted. Naturally, there are several legends about the origin of the name. One legend explains that when the town was founded on Christmas Eve, the German settlers held a meeting to select a name. After several names were suggested and each was rejected, the door of the meetinghouse swung open, and in walked a man in a Santa Claus suit. One of the settlers suggested they name the community Santa Claus, and since by this time they were all pretty drunk, they did.

According to local legends, two Indiana communities, Story and Gasburg, were named for storytelling. Although Story probably was named for one of its first settlers, Dr. Story, a traditional account maintains the name commemorates storytelling sessions held at a general store. Gasburg is explained only by legend. Supposedly, an early settler, Gideon Johnson, was regarded as the windiest man in the county and was well known for his tall tales. Because of his "gas" the village was named "Gas Burgh."

Some settlements are named for nearby streams, and several streams in Indiana allegedly were named for men who fell into them. Nineveh Creek appears to have a biblical name, but according to local legends it was first called Nineveh's Defeat because Ninevah Berry fell into the stream and nearly drowned while carrying a deer's carcass across it. Beanblossom Creek is explained by several legends. One story goes that General Tipton named the stream for a soldier named Bean Blossom who nearly drowned in it. Other traditional accounts say that Bean Blossom was an Indian or a horse thief who fell in the stream and nearly drowned. Actually, the name is a translation of a Miami name for the stream. Jack's Defeat Creek, too, is explained by several legends, frequently involving Jack Storm, who fell into the creek for one reason or another. One legend says simply that Jack Storm's horse got mired in the mud as Jack attempted to cross the creek on horseback. Another tale tells about Jack and another young man who were courting the same girl. On his way to the girl's house when the stream was flooding, Jack went far out of his way to cross at a shallow spot. In the meantime, the rival suitor forded the flooding stream at the usual spot, got to the girl's house before Jack, and won the girl.

Place names often come from the names of people, but usually not from the kind of people commemorated in legends about the naming of Bono, Buddha, and Francisco. According to a local legend, Bono was named for a French settler who was chased out of town; however, it seems more likely that the name honors the Bono brothers, early settlers. A legend says Francisco was named for a Spanish laborer who was fired from his job on the Wabash and Erie Canal. After he was fired, he built a shack and became the first settler. Buddha is explained by a couple of legends, one stating that Buddha was named for a tramp passing through the settlement and the other holding that a traveling salesman suggested the name. Buddha may have been named for Buda, one of the two cities now forming Budapest, Hungary.

Frequently in place-name legendry, names considered unusual are said to be Native American names. Somerset, for example, is a transfer name from England, although a local tradition says the village was named for a Native American chief. Radnor, too, is thought to be a Native American name, but probably it is a transfer name from Wales via Pennsylvania. Indian maidens are involved in several Hoosier place-name legends. Nappanee was named for Napanee, Ontario; however, one legend says the name means "mud" or "knee-deep-in-mud," and the community received its name because an Indian maiden was found there knee deep in mud. Another legend says early settlers found an Indian maiden napping on her knees, so they called the place "Nap-on-knee." Mishawaka comes from a Potawatomi word meaning "country of dead trees," although a local legend has the name honoring a Native American princess who died in 1818. Thorntown is the English translation of the name of a Native American village once there, but a popular tale tells of an Indian princess who was denied her sweetheart because her father had promised her to someone else. Heartbroken, she ran off through the brush and fell on a thorn, which pierced her heart and killed her.

Place-name legends may be a lot more fanciful than factual, but they provide the student of culture with information on what the names mean to the people who use them and sometimes offer a better index of culture than do sober factual accounts. What's more, these legends indicate that when factual information on place naming has been forgotten or is unavailable, people will invent etiological stories, which, of course, reveals the widespread human interest in place names and their meanings.

Telling place-name legends enables Hoosier folk to form a closer bond with their region and helps them situate themselves in history, which, like Glassie's folk in Ballymenone, they conceive of as spatial, not temporal. "In Ballymenone," Glassie writes, "history is arranged spatially. Events are less part of a temporal chain than they are rooted eternally in specific places. In the academy, time dominates. Events are subsumed to causative sequence."[31] He adds: "If folk history is organized spatially, we understand why it is unsteady about dates and loose in its handling of causative sequences."[32] Since folk history is rooted more in space than in time, place-name legends offer a rich field of study for both the regional folklorist and the local historian, for the folk's own history is inseparable from the names they give to the places they know. As Scott Russell Sanders so aptly shows, there is a geography of the mind as well as a geography of the earth:

> other narrative threads, some weak and some tough, connect me to every place I have known. Thus the Mahoning River, long-since dammed, still runs in me, because, one winter dawn while checking muskrat traps, I slipped into the chill current and nearly drowned. A field of wildflowers blooms in me because a woman who lived there alone in a cabin once filled my palm with seeds. In memory, a forest I have not seen for twenty years still murmurs with the voice of my father naming trees, a pasture gleams under the hooves of horses, a beach dimples under the footsteps of my wife. I am bound to the earth by a web of stories, just as I am bound to the creation by the very substance and rhythms of my flesh. By keeping the stories fresh, I keep the places themselves alive in my imagination. Living in me, borne in mind, these places make up the landscape on which I stand with familiarity and pleasure, the landscape over which I walk even when my feet are still.[33]

Who's a Hoosier?

Probably the best-known place-name legends in Indiana are about the origin of Hoosier, the nickname of the state. In *The Hoosiers*, published in 1900, Meredith Nicholson, considered "the dean of Hoosier writers,"[34] says that "in many quarters" there is an assumption "that the Hoosier Commonwealth is in some way set apart from her neighbors by reason of the uncouthness and ignorance of the inhabitants; and the word 'Hoosier' has perhaps been unfortunate as applied to Indianians in that it has sometimes been taken as a synonym for boorishness and illiteracy." Nicholson countered that "the Indiana husbandmen, even in the pioneer period, differed little or not at all from the settlers in other territorial divisions of the West and Southwest; and the early Indiana town folk were the peers of any of their fellows of the urban class in the Ohio Valley."[35]

As Nicholson suggests, apparently for a good many people who were not born or raised in Indiana, the nickname *Hoosier* has been a derogatory epithet, denoting a person who is unpolished and uneducated. This negative stereotype about people living in Indiana appeared frequently in nineteenth-century travel literature and chapbooks. For instance, in 1824 the Englishman Captain William Blane wrote that "the Western Americans, and particularly those in Indiana, are more rough and unpolished in their manners than those of any country I ever travelled in."[36] But another traveler through northern Indiana, C. F. Hoffman, wrote in 1833 that "I am now in the land of the *Hooshiers,* and find that long-haired race much more civilized than some of their Western neighbors are willing to represent them. The term 'Hooshier,' like that of Yankee, or Buckeye, first applied contemptuously, has now become a *soubriquet* that bears nothing invidious with it to the ear of an Indianian."[37]

About this same time, hack writers who had never visited Indiana and had never seen an actual Hoosier continued to portray Hoosiers as subhuman in popular literature. For instance, Hoosiers are mentioned in several almanacs supposedly written by Davy Crockett and his heirs and published between 1835 and 1856. In one of these almanacs, Crockett, himself rough and boisterous, gives the following account of a Hoosier:

> Now the Hoosiers are a different class o' human natur altogether. They are half taller an' bristles, an' so all-sweaten fat and round, that when they go to bed they roll about like a cider barrel in a cellar, an' therefor they're always obleeged to have a nigger each side on 'em to keep 'em still; an' when they wake up, they have to fasten down their cheeks before they can open their eyes. A Hoosier can eat a hog, tail, fur and all, and in the fall of the year, the bristles come out on him so splendifferous thick that

he has a regular nateral tippet about his throat, an' a nateral hogskin cap on his head. I once had one of these half-starved critters to work on my plantation—till one hot day come, an' if he didn't spill his hull self, nails, hair and all, into my hay wagon, then cut me up for shoe greasers; an' arter we cooled it, thar he was a complete cake o' hog fat, an' thar was enough on him to grease all the harnesses and wagons for a hull year.[38]

In his 1942 article, "The Hoosier as an American Folk-Type," Richard Lyle Power demonstrates that this kind of nineteenth-century popular literature nourished the Hoosier stereotype. He says that "a fertile source of Hoosier stories is the humorous bi-monthly periodical *Yankee Notions, or Whittlings from Jonathan's Jack-Knife,* which ran through fifteen volumes from 1852 to 1866 . . ."[39] According to Power, "While other states than Indiana provided the putative settings for rustic anecdotes—Arkansas, Missouri, Tennessee, Kentucky, each supplying two or three instances per volume—Indiana was distinguished not only by more frequent mention but by more extravagant literary treatment."[40] Power speculates that the "Hoosier story," "a crude sort of newspaper feature" found in nineteenth-century popular periodicals, appears "to be a journalistic innovation intended to ridicule a type of culture which was antithetical to that of the Yankees."[41]

These Hoosier stories written by anonymous writers, according to Power, generally deride "a way of life derived directly from the South."[42] Frequently they depict a country bumpkin or numskull "amid sophisticated surroundings and grandeur; his first experience with steamers, street cars, or trains; and the Hoosier at the circus, at fisticuffs, or on the stage." They also brought together "stock characters: the Hoosier with the Yankee, the Irishman, the Frenchman, the Jewish peddler, or the dandy." The Hoosier "was pictured as making a ridiculous public wager with Dan Marble, the circus man, or as impudently heckling Jenny Lind during one of her performances."[43] Power observes, however, that

withal, the literary traffickers in the Hoosier folk-type did not drive too hard a bargain with the figure they purveyed. No weakling, his roistering courage in physical encounter belied his supposedly debilitating environment. The Hoosier's sense of humor salted many a story. Although the Hoosier might be "green to the highest degree of verdancy, ignorant and awkward, and attired in the acme of flashy bad taste," he was likely to prove "quite as sharp as city folks . . ."

Notwithstanding the slatternly, swamp-bred women prescribed by legend as the mates of the ungainly males, it seems possible that the writings of these local-colorists dealt more charitably with its people than with Indiana as a place. Along with the extreme rurality and illiteracy imputed to Indiana the unwary reader of mid-century was encouraged to believe that barter economy, wildcat finances and bank notes, disorderly and ignorant legislators, unenlightened public policy, and easy divorce chronically emphasized the state's lapses from social orthodoxy. . . .[44]

A series of letters about *Hoosier* published in the *Wall Street Journal* in 1987 clearly illustrates persistent folk traditions, both stereotypes and legends, about Hoosiers in American popular culture.[45] On January 27, 1987, the newspaper ran a front-page article on the popularity of President Ronald Reagan in Indiana. One native of Clarksville, Indiana, speaking for most residents of the state, wrote a letter to the editor, which was printed on February 9. He did not argue with the main point of the article but did object to being called an "Indianian." He surmised that the essay "was surely written by a 'New Yorkian' who did not realize that people from Indiana prefer to be called Hoosiers rather than Indianians!"

In another letter to the editor (February 24), a New Yorker wondered why "Indianians prefer to be called Hoosiers," because, he claimed, "Hoosier derives from the pejorative hoojee or hoojin, meaning a dirty person, a tramp." The New Yorker probably found his derivation of the word in the World Publishing Company's dictionary, *Webster's New World Dictionary of the American Language*, issued in 1964, which stated that the word probably comes from the dialectical word *hoosier,* meaning "mountaineer"—an extension of *hoojee, hoojin*, "dirty person, tramp." The editors of *Webster's New World Dictionary* justified this etymological guess by noting that "southern Indiana was largely settled by Kentucky mountaineers."[46] As my wise freshman English teacher told his class one day when he disagreed with a dictionary definition of a word in *Walden,* "Dictionaries aren't written by God!" If the editors of *Webster's New World Dictionary* were right, then vagrant Kentuckians, not native Indianians, would be the real Hoosiers, since Indiana, without mountains, does not have any homegrown mountaineers.

On March 18, letter writers from Virginia, Wisconsin, and California, as well as a letter writer from Indiana, replied to the New Yorker's claim that a Hoosier is a dirty tramp. Naturally the letter writer from Indiana "immediately took offense at the supposed derivation of the word Hoosier as 'a dirty person, a tramp,'" and cited versions of two common legends concerning the origin of the nickname:

When Indiana was the Wild West, settlers and Indians often took vengeance on each other by cutting off the ears of their enemies. These ears were often worn on belts and found later on dead warriors. A standing joke was made with the phrase 'Whose ear?' which was quickly picked up by the residents of Indiana as their nickname. Other folklore speculates the phrase "who's 'er'" when company knocked at the log cabin door is the origin.[47]

The Virginian also reported a version of the "Whose ear?" legend "to settle the burning question of the etymology of Hoosiers." His source was Phog Allen, legendary basketball coach of the University of Kansas Jayhawks. Quoting a paragraph concerning the invention of the football helmet from Allen's 1947 book, *Coach Phog Allen's Sports Stories*, the Virginian wrote: "It was particularly popular with Indiana players who practiced in the sand-dune country. When scrimmaging, these Indiana boys would grind their opponents' heads into the earth with disastrous results. After scrimmage, players would go about picking up the loose ears of their opponents and saying, 'Whose ears?' Ever since, Indiana teams have been known as Hoosiers."

A better-known variant of the "Whose ear?" legend maintains that there was a lot of fighting in early Indiana taverns, and the frontiersmen scratched, gouged, and bit—often biting off noses and ears. Frequently following a fight a settler found an ear on the sawdust floor of a tavern and asked, "Whose ear?"[48] This subtype of the "Whose ear?" origin legend was the favorite account of the "Hoosier Poet," James Whitcomb Riley,[49] and is one of several versions still collectible in the Indiana oral tradition, as the following text illustrates:

> When my dad was running for office, this man was telling me how the name Hoosier came about. He said that when the state capital was in Corydon, there was a tavern that most of the people went to, and there was a jar on the bar that had an ear in it, and when strangers came in, they would ask, "Whose ear?" In time, this phrase became popular and was eventually shortened to Hoosier for a nickname for people that came from around there.[50]

Defending his fellow midwesterners, the letter writer from Wisconsin said that if the New Yorker "would spend a little time with some native Hoosiers from the rolling limestone hill country, he would find them neither dirty persons nor tramps—quite the contrary." This Wisconsin Badger reported a version of another common legend concerning the origin of Hoosier: "One popular theory is that the word stems from 'husher,' which refers to one who could hush another with his fists."

One of the earliest versions of that legend was collected in Indiana in the 1930s by WPA fieldworkers:

> Early in 1819 many squatters, principally from Kentucky, had built cabins and had made some improvements on a part of the public domain. Some

of these squatters hastened back to Kentucky to tell their friends that the country was now opened for settlement and to insist on coming to the "New Purchase." They gave such glowing accounts of the soil, fine timber, abundance of wild game, and the level country that they were deemed by some who heard them as extremely visionary.

Many of their listeners were the Pennsylvania Dutch, who had always lived in a mountainous region. They were especially incredulous. After listening to what they regarded as exaggerations, they would turn away and say to others, "Well, he is a hoosher"—meaning a husher, a silencer.

This epithet became proverbial until all who returned from Indiana were facetiously called "hooshers." This, my Kentucky parents told me, was the origin of the name "Hoosier," as it was pronounced later.[51]

In the March 26 issue of the *Wall Street Journal,* a Hoosier from Nappanee, Indiana, acknowledged that it "is generally agreed upon" that "Hoosier once denoted a crude, rustic, backwoodsy character." Referring to the "husher" legend, he also attributed a trickster quality to Hoosier:

> "Husher" was a word Pittsburgh boatmen (unsavory characters on their own), who brought dirty coal barges down the Ohio River in the 1820s, hurled at rival Indiana boatmen. It stuck, as the term came into use along the lazy streams that percolated through Indiana country, to Indianians in general.
>
> As it began to lose its sneering connotation (as did Methodist, Quaker, Yankee) it also lost its original pronunciation. Husher (as in push-er) became Hoosier.
>
> In his journal, under the date of July 14, 1827, a Black Creek schoolmaster related how a squatter in Wabash country, fearing land-grabbers might take the land he hadn't paid for, spread a false alarm about Indians. While the populace fussed about preparing for the worst—throwing up fortifications, and inspecting shooting irons—he slipped up to Crawfordsville and made everything legal-like. "There is a Yankee trick for you," he concluded his yarn, "done up by a Hoosier!"[52]

The "husher" origin legend has been popular in and out of Indiana, probably because a version of it appears in John Russell Bartlett's 1838 *Dictionary of Americanisms;*[53] however, as Jacob Dunn points out, "Nobody had ever produced any evidence of the use of the word 'husher' as here indicated. It is not found in any dictionary of any kind—not even Bartlett's."[54] Nevertheless, the "husher" legend remains popular in Hoosier folk tradition, as the following version collected in Terre Haute in May 1968 attests:

> The way I heard it was that the people that first came to Indiana Territory were pretty rough. They settled down on the Ohio River and worked flatboats and stuff. They were really big and tough. I guess that the south, near the river, was a rough place to live and there used to be lots of fights,

guys getting killed and things. Well, from what I hear, those guys that worked on the river loved to get in and mix it up. They were so big and strong that any fight they got into they usually won. I guess the word they used to describe them was "husher" 'cause they quieted things down so well. I guess that it somehow got changed to "Hoosier," but it means the same thing.[55]

The "husher" legend nearly always is associated with flatboatmen on the Ohio River. Accepting some truth in this account and citing an article in the Piqua, Ohio, *Courier and Enquirer* of February 17, 1838, a celebrated historian of the Midwest, R. Carlyle Buley, reports that "more likely the sobriquet [*Hoosier*] was one of many used by the Ohio River boatmen to designate a real man, a word equivalent to 'ripstaver,' 'scrouger,' 'snorter,' 'bulger,' 'hoover,' 'screamer,' 'roarer,' etc., words which never attained later respectable standing." Buley writes that "by some caprice the term came to be confined solely to those boatmen who lived on the Indian[a] shore and then to those on the Indiana stretch and finally to Indianans."[56]

As Mencken points out, "The earlier American etymologists all sought to connect the term [*Hoosier*] with some idea of ruffianism. . . ."[57] Accordingly, a legend related to the "husher" type agrees that early settlers or Ohio River boatmen were vicious fighters, but they were called "hussars" because they fought like those European soldiers. Dunn traces the various forms of this legend to Colonel John Jacob Lehmanowsky, who served under Napoleon and then in Indiana before becoming a celebrated lecturer on the Napoleonic wars.[58] A pioneer preacher, Aaron Wood, preserved the following version of this legend:

> The name "hoosier" originated as follows: When the young men of the Indiana side of the Ohio river went to Louisville, the Kentucky men boasted over them, calling them "New Purchase Greenies," claiming to be a superior race, composed of half horse, half alligator, and tipped off with snapping turtle. These taunts produced fights in the market house and streets of Louisville. On one occasion a stout bully from Indiana was victor in a fist fight, and having heard Colonel Lehmanowsky lecture on the "Wars of Europe," who always gave martial prowess to the German Hussars in the fight, pronouncing hussars "hoosiers" the Indianian, when the Kentuckian cried "enough," jumped up and said: "I am a Hoosier," and hence the Indianians were called by that name. This was its true origin. I was in the State when it occurred.[59]

According to the most widely held legendary account of the origin of *Hoosier*—also popularized by Bartlett in his 1838 *Dictionary of Americanisms* and already quoted from the March 18 *Wall Street Journal*—pioneers in Indiana greeted visitors at the doors of their log cabins by calling out, "Who's 'ere [there]?" Of nine versions in the Indiana State University Folklore Archives, one collected in Terre Haute in May 1968 goes:

> Now, I'm not sure about this, but this is the way I had it explained to me. I think one of my grade school teachers told us. It is kind of dumb, but here it is anyway. Well, anyway, it seems that the first people to settle in Indiana came up from the south. They couldn't speak too clearly, had an accent or something, so everything they said came out with a drawl. Well, I guess that when someone would come to their cabin door and should knock on it, the owner of the cabin would holler out "Who's there?" but with that southern twang, it would come out something like "hoosier."[60]

Another legendary account of the origin of *Hoosier* collected in Indianapolis in December 1971 (also from the ISU Folklore Archives) appears to be a blend of the "Whose ear?" and the "Who's there?" legend types: "Another man told me that the nickname Hoosier came from the question 'Who's here?' that people would yell whenever they came into a tavern."

Versions of the related "Who's your . . . ?" Hoosier origin legends are almost as popular as versions of the "Whose there?" type. Versions in the ISU Folklore Archives ask, "Who's your ma?" or "Who's your pa?" or "Who's your daddy?" or "Who's your state?" or "Who's your neighbor?" or, as in the following account, collected at Turkey Run State Park in July 1972, "Who's your friend?":

> I do know how we people from Indiana came to be called Hoosiers. We were talking about the early days in history here, of how we prospered because of commercial interest that began to develop after the [Civil] war was finally ended. And this young captain had acquired his grant from the U.S. Army, or government, and in due time he began to prosper by the fact that he had built the grain mill and pork processing plant. They had a tannery, and they did some weaving. They had all of these things, and their business was so good that they had to look for different outlets. So at this time they began to search for places to sell. And, of course, the natural [place] was in the South because the South didn't have a lot of the things that we had at this time. So here came an era of the flat-boat. They'd build a flatboat and send tons of material south. And these flatboats were generally built of the tulip tree, a large tree growing in our area. And they were not only used for the boat, but upon arrival there, they would sell the cargo and, along with that, the boat. And, of course, they would have to tread their way back north. Many people, of course, were lost on the way down because of severe weather and so forth. The story that we hear around here was that these traders that would go south were friendly, sociable people, but they were not always welcomed with open arms in being transit, of course. But once they were

there and established in the community in the South, why, they were welcome. And they were accepted and taken into the homes and given a night's lodging of a week, if necessary. If they had a friend along, they had to account for him and identify him. And maybe at a late hour they'd say, "Well, there are two of us here." They'd say, well, "Who's your friend?" And here is where we have heard that the word "Hoosier" originally started.[61]

According to some explanations, *Hoosier* comes from a non-English language. The *Wall Street Journal* of March 26 included a letter to the editor from a New Yorker, who wrote that Hoosier "is, of course, a corruption of the French *huissier,* a minor magistrate in 18th-century Vincennes, the administrative center of the French colony that was to become Indiana. . . . Hoosier was first used to describe the magistrate, then any Frenchman, and finally any non-Indian. As Americans settled in Indiana, the name was applied to them and so it has remained to this day." Another non-English-language origin theory holds "Hoosier" comes from the French *houssières,* "bushy places." Another explanation is that the nickname is Native American, coming from *hoosa,* an alleged Indian word for maize. One legend dealing with a Native American origin of *Hoosier,* collected in Terre Haute in May 1968, goes:

> Sure, I know why we are called "Hoosiers." I thought everybody knew that. My mother told me that it is an old Indian word. See, the first people to come to Indiana were terrible liars and braggers. The one thing they had going for them was they could raise corn. I guess they talked a lot about what great farmers they were, especially about the corn. Anyway, lots of people got tired of hearing them brag, so they hung this Indian word, hoosier, on them. I guess it means one who brags a lot.[62]

Other accounts say that *Hoosier* comes from English or American folk speech. Some say the word comes from *huzza,* an exclamation of either early settlers who gained a victory over marauders from a neighboring state or flatboatmen who for some reason commonly jumped up and yelled "huzza."[63] Another explanation suggests that *Hoosier* comes from an English dialectical word, *hoose,* for a disease caused by roundworms.[64] Apparently this disease in the throats of calves caused the animals' hair to turn back and gave their eyes a wild look, as, it is said, Indiana frontiersmen in their coonskin caps appeared to others. A version of this legend collected in Mount Vernon in April 1963 goes:

> "Hoosier" was at one time a slang word in the South referring to a "jay" or "hayseed." The term originated from England, where "hoose" was a common name for a disease of calves. This disease causes the calves' hair

to turn back, and it gives them a wild, staring look. The coonskin caps which the pioneer men and boys wore made their hair lay funny, and the homemade whiskey produced the wild-eyed look. Thus, the word "hoosier" was used to describe these early pioneers, and then it was later applied to all Indiana folk.[65]

The letter writer from California in the March 18 *Wall Street Journal* gave still another account of the English dialect origin of *Hoosier*, writing that "the present-day meaning of Hoosier in Indiana was used as far back as 1829. The word comes from the Cumberland dialect word 'hoozer,' meaning anything unusually large." This letter writer probably was influenced directly or indirectly by Dunn, who as early as 1907 was convinced that *hoosier* "must be an old English dialect or slang word," citing *hoozer*, "something big, monstrous," in Wright's *English Dialect Dictionary* as support.[66] Dunn argued that in the United States *hoosier* became a southern dialect word "signifying a rough or uncouth person, before it was applied to Indiana."[67]

In "Word Magic, or Would You Want Your Daughter to Marry a Hoosier?" Raven McDavid corroborates Dunn's work. Field records for the Linguistic Atlas of the Middle and South Atlantic States reveal that in some southern states *Hoosier* has been a derogatory epithet connoting uncouthness and is synonymous with *hick, hayseed,* and *hillbilly.* The meaning of *hoosier*, according to McDavid, "is fairly consistent: basically, an uncitified—and by implication, uncivilized—dweller in out-of-the-way communities . . ."[68] *Hoosier,* as a derogatory name, is still current in West Virginia, the Upper Piedmont of Virginia, the Carolinas, and Georgia; however, it appears to be rare as a derogatory term west of the Appalachians, where it simply means a native of Indiana. According to McDavid,

> As a social designation, *hoosier* is found along the Atlantic Seaboard, from West Virginia to Georgia . . . it may well have occurred—it may even still occur—in Alabama, Tennessee, and Mississippi, but so far we have little field work from those states. It is basically an upland term, characteristic of the foothill and mountain sections, but it occurs occasionally in the coastal plain and even in the North Carolina tidewater. It is heard more frequently from rural informants than from urban, from older speakers than from younger, from uneducated than from educated. It is often commented on as old, rarely as an innovation.[69]

McDavid suggests that the term *Hoosier* probably was applied first to early settlers in southern Indiana, themselves from southern states, who were considered uncouth rustics by their relatives back home in more established states. Ultimately, he says, the term probably comes from an English dialect. He notes:

> Unfortunately there is little solid evidence on *hoosier* before it was transplanted to North America. The pattern of its American distribution, however, suggests an origin in the north of England, Lowland Scotland, or Ulster—the areas from which came the pioneer stock of western Pennsylvania and the Southern uplands. From Cumberland, the northwesternmost shire in England, Wright (1898-1905), regrettably incomplete, records *hoozer* 'something big, monstrous.' Possibly this indicates an association with huge; certainly it would suggest a relationship to *cracker*— which in early records seems to have been synonymous with *boaster* or *braggart*—and possibly with (*mountain*) *boomer*. It was a term suggestive of the raw strength of the frontier, of the yeoman farmers in contrast with the alleged refinements of plantation and mercantile society. And it was this group—epitomized by Daniel Boone—that thrust across the Appalachians into the Ohio Valley. One can reasonably suppose that the Southern *hoosiers* made up the bulk of the original population of Kentucky as well as in Indiana . . .[70]

Most scholars now agree with Dunn and McDavid that *Hoosier* comes from a southern dialect word meaning "a rough or uncouth person." Warren Roberts, for one, says this explanation "is the one that makes most sense to me"[71] and argues that the family name Hoosier offers proof of the age of the word. According to Roberts, "At first glance, then, the family name Hoosier would seem to indicate that the word 'hoosier,' meaning a wild, uncouth person, has been used in Great Britain for a long time. It was brought to this country and flourished in the mid-South where it retained its meaning. It was eventually applied to the residents of Indiana and has been retained until today because its original meaning has been forgotten."[72] There are, in fact, several legends that hold that *Hoosier* comes from a family name. In one of these, a Louisville contractor named Hoosier preferred hiring Indiana men, and his employees were known as "Hoosier men" or "Hoosiers." The notion that "Hoosier" may have come from a family name has some supporters, though Dunn, after examining a number of city directories in which Hoosier did not appear as a family name, discounts this explanation. According to Dunn, "it is hardly possible for a family name to disappear completely."[73] But Roberts found the family name *Hoosier* in the telephone directories of Indianapolis, Saint Louis, and Cincinnati.[74]

The Floridian who wrote to the *Wall Street Journal* editor argued that "the important point is not the derivation but the meaning of the word. To be a Hoosier," he said, "means to be at a distance from both New

York and California. As Kurt Vonnegut observed, 'Hoosiers are everywhere.'" Today—bolstered by the contributions of Hoosier authors such as Vonnegut to American letters and the success of the Indiana University Hoosiers on the basketball court, with NCAA championships in 1940, 1953, 1976, 1981, and 1987—people living in Indiana no longer agree with Meredith Nicholson that "Hoosier" was unfortunately applied to Indianians. In fact, as the Hoosier letter writer to the *Journal* pointed out, they much prefer *Hoosier* to *Indianian*. Thus, *Hoosier,* as applied to one who lives in Indiana, according to McDavid, "seems to be accepted almost everywhere in the state, without resentment, as a neutral designation if not a compliment."[75]

As even the nineteenth-century writers of subliterature recognized, Hoosiers have a sense of humor. Hoosiers know that Kentucky was the home state of many people who settled parts of Indiana, and in jokes about themselves, Hoosiers define a Hoosier as a Kentuckian who ran out of money on the way to Michigan. Hoosiers know that they have a penchant for basketball, automobile racing, and mushrooms, and they define *Hoosier* as "a person dribbling a basketball around the Indianapolis 500 race track looking for mushrooms." Hoosiers know that easterners think people from Indiana are uncouth, and they tell jokes about a Hoosier on the Harvard campus asking a Harvard person "where the library's at." When the Harvard person informed the Hoosier that "at Harvard we don't end our sentences with prepositions," the Hoosier replied, "Oh, can you tell me where the library's at, asshole?"[76]

Among those Americans who aren't interested in basketball or knowledgeable about literature, *Hoosier* may remain a pejorative term, but as John Finley wrote in 1833 in "The Hoosier's Nest," a poem that helped make the word *Hoosier* both popular and respectable:

> With feelings proud we contemplate
> The rising glory of our State;
> Nor take offense by application
> Of its good-natured appellation.[77]

County Names in Indiana

Since 1790, when the first Hoosier county, Knox, was organized under the famous Ordinance of 1787 that created the Northwest Territory, ninety-two counties have been established in Indiana. Most of the names of Indiana's counties came from personal names, especially from the names of military heroes. Of the seventy-nine counties that bear personal names, fifty-four were named for heroes of the Revolution, the War of 1812, or the Indian wars. Of the latter wars, the Battle of Tippecanoe (1811) especially made a deep impression on the Hoosier mind, for ten counties were named for heroes of that famous battle in what is now northern Indiana. Of course, many of these war heroes won distinction in civil life, too; thus, men like William Henry Harrison—who was governor of the Indiana Territory and president of the United States, as well as a successful military commander—fall into more than one class of place names. Nevertheless, the names of Hoosier counties suggest strong feelings of patriotism in those who named the counties. Besides wars, virtually every epoch of U.S. history, from the Native American occupation of the land through the early nineteenth century, is reflected in the names of Indiana's counties.

The Native American occupation of what is now Indiana, though, is scarcely remembered in the names of Hoosier counties. Counties, arbitrary territorial divisions, usually were created after the Native Americans were forced off the land; consequently, the Native American influence on the naming of counties would be negligible, for Native Americans would not have had names for these nonexistent legal entities. Moreover, sometimes there were strong feelings against Native American names. For instance, one Hoosier county, Howard, first was named Richardsville, honoring the famous Miami chief, when the county was organized in 1844, but there was enough resentment against the name that two years later the name was changed to Howard, for the Hoosier statesman Tilghman A. Howard.

Still, as a map prepared by Daniel Hough for a state geological report of 1882 shows, before the conquest of George Rogers Clark, tribes of the great Algonkin family occupied much of the territory that is now Indiana.[78] Foremost among them were the Miami tribes, which gave their name to Miami County. After the Delawares were forced from their homes in the eastern United States, they moved west and settled in the territory claimed by the Miamis. This event is recalled in one county name, Delaware, although the name itself is actually European in origin and not Native American. Another county name, Tippecanoe, is ultimately Native American, but the county name was borrowed from the Tippecanoe River. For Hoosiers, however, the name *Tippecanoe* really does not commemorate the Native American occupation of the land. On the contrary, the name generally recalls the Battle of Tippecanoe which was fought and won against Native Americans by William Henry Harrison and his troops. Besides Tippecanoe, other Native American names of rivers applied to Indiana counties are Ohio and Wabash.

Two other county names, Vermillion and Elkhart, are literal translations of Native American names of nearby streams. Vermillion County was named for the Vermilion River, a tributary of the Wabash. An Algonkin name of the Vermilion River was Osanamon, a compound of *osawa* ("yellow") and *unimun* (a plant from which Native Americans made red dye). The stream was so named because the Native Americans found red earth there with which they painted themselves. The French name of the stream was Vermillon Jaune ("Red-Yellow"), a direct translation of the Native American name. Similarly, Elkhart County was named for the Elkhart River. Earlier the name of the stream was written Elk Heart or Elksheart in English and Coeur de Cerf in French, both literal translations of the Potawatomi name of the stream, Me-sheh-weh-ou-deh-ik. Apparently the name comes from a heart-shaped island at the mouth of the river.

The early French exploration and settlement of what is now Indiana is reflected in at least one county name, La Porte. The name was applied first to a settlement within the present county and then became the name of the county as well as its seat. La Porte, "the door," is a descriptive name, since, in a sense, it served as the door to the north. Trade between southern Indiana and the north passed through a natural opening in the forest there. Other French names of Indiana counties are Fayette, named for the Marquis de Lafayette, and Lagrange, named for Lafayette's country home near Paris, but these two names honor a famous soldier and really do not reflect the early French occupancy of the state. Since the French were explorers and adventurers much more than they were colony builders, they gave names to the rivers on which they traveled, and since many of them were Catholics spreading the gospel to Native Americans, frequently they applied the names of saints to rivers in the New World. Such is the case with the Saint Joseph River, for which Saint Joseph County was named.

Seven Hoosier counties were named for signers of the Declaration of Independence. Carroll County was named in honor of Charles Carroll, who was the sole survivor of the fifty-six signers when the county was organized in 1828. Other signers of the Declaration of Independence remembered in county names are Benjamin Franklin, Alexander

Hamilton, John Hancock, Samuel Huntington, Thomas Jefferson, and Dr. Benjamin F. Rush. Most of these men won distinction in other pursuits, too—one, Jefferson, as president of the United States. Six more county names honor U.S. presidents. Harrison County honors William Henry Harrison; Madison County was named after James Madison; and Monroe County was named for James Monroe. Washington County, of course, is one of several Indiana place names honoring the first president of the United States, George Washington. Jackson County was named for Andrew Jackson, who became the seventh president, though the county was organized before Jackson became president. Consequently, the name remembers Jackson as a famous general in the Battle of New Orleans.

Governors of either the Indiana Territory or the State of Indiana are honored in the names of six counties. The versatile William Henry Harrison, for whom Harrison County was named, was the first governor of the Indiana Territory as well as U.S. president. Gibson County was named for General John Gibson, who served as acting governor of the Indiana Territory for about a year. Another general, Thomas Posey, was governor of the Indiana Territory from 1813 to 1816, and Posey County, organized in 1814, was named for him. Jennings County was named for the first governor of the State of Indiana, Jonathan Jennings. Hendricks County was named for William Hendricks, who was governor when the county was organized. When Noble County was organized in 1836, Noah Noble was governor, and it seems likely that the county was named for him, though some sources maintain that Noble County was named for James Noble, the first U.S. senator from Indiana.

Governors, statesmen, and famous citizens from other states also are honored in the names of Hoosier counties. Scott County was named for General Charles Scott, who after serving in the Revolution became governor of Kentucky. Isaac Shelby, for whom Shelby County was named, served in the Revolution as well as in the War of 1812 and became governor of Kentucky, too. Clinton County was named for a famous governor of New York, De Witt Clinton. Benton County honors a U.S. senator from Missouri, Thomas Hart Benton. Two Indiana counties are named for famous orators—Henry County for the orator of the American Revolution, Patrick Henry, and Clay County for the orator and statesman from Kentucky, Henry Clay. Another famous civilian, Robert Fulton, the inventor of the steamboat, is remembered in one county name, Fulton.

Hoosier esteem for the law is shown in the names of jurists applied to six counties. Federal jurists are commemorated in the names of two counties. Jay County was named in honor of John Jay, who served as chief justice of the United States, and Marshall County was named for another chief justice, John Marshall. Territorial judges are remembered in the names of two other counties. Vanderburgh County was named for Henry Vanderburgh, judge of the first court in the Indiana Territory, and Parke County was named for another territorial judge, Benjamin Parke. Judges on the Indiana Supreme Court are honored in the names of Blackford County, for Isaac Blackford, and Johnson County, for John Johnson.

Ten, or possibly eleven, county names were derived from names of previously existing places. Of the loan names, two are foreign. Switzerland County honors Swiss settlers who came to the area in 1802. Lagrange County, as noted, was named for the Marquis de Lafayette's home near Paris. One county name, Orange, was borrowed from a county name in another state, as early settlers came from Orange County, North Carolina, and brought the name with them. Possibly another Hoosier county, Randolph, was named for a county of the same name in North Carolina from which early settlers came, too, although some sources suggest the county was named for Thomas Randolph, who was killed in the Battle of Tippecanoe, or for Thomas Mann Randolph, the Virginia statesman. Most of the borrowed names, however, are local transfers, coming from names of natural features. Elkhart, Ohio, Saint Joseph, Tippecanoe, Vermillion, and Wabash counties got their names from nearby streams, while Lake County got its name from Lake Michigan, which borders the county on the north.

In most place-name surveys, subjective names are relatively rare; therefore, it comes as no surprise that only one of Indiana's counties, Union, has an inspirational name. Sources disagree on the origin of the name, though. Bitter battles for county seats were fought between rival towns in some Hoosier counties, and some people say that when Union County was organized in 1821, it was named Union to discourage such fights. Probably, however, the name reflects a more general feeling of patriotism, as do most county names in Indiana.

Settlement Names in Indiana

Names borrowed from personal names, especially surnames of national or state heroes and local settlers, founders, and families are among the most common kinds of American settlement names. It follows that the largest group of Hoosier settlement names comes from personal names. Unlike Hoosier counties, however, most settlement names derive from local rather than nonlocal people.

Indiana settlement names for a nonlocal person include Bainbridge, Colfax, Decatur, Ekin, Fillmore, Grant City, Huntington, Jeffersonville, Knox, Lafayette, Madison, Napoleon, Owensville, Pierceton, Reno, Sheridan, Tennyson, Vilas, Wallace, and Yenne. Hoosier settlement names honoring a local person or family include Ade, Banta, Crumstown, Doolittle Mills, Eckerty, Fickle, Grammer, Hamlet, Ijamsville, Judyville, Klemmes Corner, Leisure, Moonville, New Carlisle, Ogden, Peppertown, Poland, Redkey, Speed, Tower, Upton, Veedersburg, Walesboro, Yeoman, and Zipp. While most place names honoring local people are borrowed surnames, some settlement names come from first names, middle names, or nicknames. Examples are Bud, Dale, Edna Mills, Frankton, Granville, Hobart, Idaville, Jasonville, Kenneth, Leota, Marysville, Otterbein, Pleasantville, Saint Wendel, Tab, Virgie, Williamsport, and Zelma.

Names borrowed from other places constitute the second largest group of settlement names. Local transfers are the most popular of these borrowed names, and names borrowed from other states are more popular than names borrowed from other countries. Beanblossom, which was named for nearby Beanblossom Creek, is an example of a local transfer. Most printed accounts, as mentioned, say the stream received its name from a man named Bean Blossom who drowned or nearly drowned in the stream. Usually Bean Blossom is identified as either a soldier in Tipton's army or an Indian horse thief pursued by Tipton's army. Some local informants, however, think the town and stream were named for a wild bean plant that grew along the stream,[79] and these oral sources might be closer to the truth than some printed sources. Since a Miami name for the stream, Ko-chio-ah-se-pe, translates "Bean River," the stream name seems to be a translation of a Native American descriptive name.[80] Other Hoosier settlements named for a nearby place include Beaver City, Dune Acres, Elkhart, French Lick, Merom Station, Nineveh, Orangeville, Patoka, Raccoon, Sullivan, Universal, and Wabash.

Names borrowed from other states include Atlanta, Boston, Cincinnati, Dayton, Florida, Greencastle, Hartford, Huron, Ligonier, Manhattan, Nevada, New Harmony, Ontario, Philadelphia, Raleigh, Sitka, Toledo, Utica, Vermont, Worthington, and Zanesville. Examples of Indiana settlement names from other countries are Aberdeen, Brazil,

China, Denmark, Elberfeld, Fulda, Holland, Ireland, Jalapa, Lapland, Moscow, New Alsace, Norway, Paris, Runnymede, Scotland, Syria, Tangier, Vienna, Warsaw, and Yeddo.

Descriptive names constitute the third largest group of Hoosier settlement names, though they rank far behind settlement names borrowed from personal names and from other places. Descriptive names may be either objective or subjective. Objectively descriptive settlement names identify places by noting some characteristic of the feature or locale. Some objectively descriptive names—such as Bluecast, Lapel, Long Beech, and probably some of the several Pinhooks—are descriptive of shape, size, or color, while others are for local flora or fauna. Local flora has been much more influential than fauna on settlement names, though, as a number of Hoosier settlements bear names such as Ash Grove, Beechwood, Cloverdale, Maple Valley, Oaklandon, Pine, Plum Tree, and Sycamore. Some of these names seem commendatory as well as descriptive. Names descriptive of fauna include Badger Grove and Oriole.

Some Hoosier settlement names, such as Cannelburg, Carbon, Gas City, Limedale, Petroleum, and Saline City, are descriptive of mineral and soil. The most popular objectively descriptive settlement names are those inspired by landscape, situation, or association. This group features names such as Alta, Bridgeton, Canal, Cementville, Edgewood, Five Points, Hillsdale, Milford, Prairieton, Quakertown, River, Shoals, and Tunnelton. Locational names—for instance, East Columbus, East Union, North Anderson, North Madison, South Elwood, South Richmond, West Clinton, and West Terre Haute—indicate direction or position and may be treated as a subtype of objectively descriptive names. Settlement names of this sort also are local transfers, since they bear directional prefixes applied to nearby place names.

Personal judgment or taste enters in subjectively descriptive settlement names. While objectively descriptive names are very popular, subjectively descriptive settlement names—such as Aroma, Grandview, Mount Healthy, and Pleasant Ridge—account for a relatively small percentage of Indiana settlement names. Other kinds of subjective place names also are rare in Indiana, as apparently they are in other states. Idealistic Hoosier settlement names include Granger, Harmony, Patriot, and Union City. Among the classical settlement names in Indiana are Argos, Delphi, Hymera, Mount Olympus, and Rome. Literary names such as Waverly, New Waverly, and Rob Roy suggest that Sir Walter Scott's novels were once among the most popular pieces of literature in

Indiana. Other Hoosier settlement names inspired by literature include Banquo, Lochiel, Medora, Romona, and Tell City. Biblical or religious names, including Bethany, Canaan, Carmel, Lebanon, Merom, and Mount Sinai, are only slightly more popular than literary names, with Palestine being one of the most common biblical names applied to Indiana settlements. Often biblical names are local transfers that have been borrowed from nearby churches. Most inspirational settlement names are commendatory names, a label used by George R. Stewart to identify names that have pleasant connotations.[81] Sometimes these names were applied to attract settlers. Commendatory settlement names include Acme, Bloomingdale, Emporia, Fairfield, Friendship, Garden City, Home Place, Magnet, Mechanicsburg, Onward, Progress, Prosperity, Retreat, and Solitude.

Humorous settlement names are not common in Indiana, although amusing anecdotes explain a number of names such as Gnaw Bone, Pinhook, and Popcorn. Needmore and Pumpkin Center, both applied to more than one Hoosier community, may be humorous derogatories, but their origin, explained only by legends, is uncertain. Santa Claus, too, may be a humorous name, although for some people the name no doubt has commendatory value. Lacking contextual information, we can't be certain, however, that these and other names were humorously applied, and we can't be sure that the stories about the origin of these names are believed by the people who pass them along. Though not commonly collected and studied, there are humorous narratives of place naming. Unlike place-name legends, place-name jokes aren't taken seriously by people who pass them along. A joke about the naming of Indianapolis, for example, goes like this: "Do you know how Indianapolis got its name? Well, there was an Indian who put some apples in his teepee for safekeeping. One day he went hunting buffalo, and while he was gone another Indian came by and stole the apples from the tepee. The Indian who did this left the first Indian appleless."[82] Jokes such as this one sometimes have been reported as legends by place-name collectors who have been interested only in texts and not in the informant's attitude toward the material. In other words, when asked the origin of a place name, a local trickster sometimes tells the collector a joke, and the greenhorn collector, who does not determine whether the informant or anyone else in the community believes the tale, reports the joke either as a legend or as a fact.

The Native American occupation of what we now call Indiana is hardly remembered in the names of Hoosier settlements, for only a few Hoosier settlement names are Native American or pseudo–Native American—that is, Native American names applied or reshaped by people other than Native Americans. Some settlement names, such as Ockley and Toto, are thought to be of Native American origin, but have uncertain origins. Other names, such as Mongo, have been reshaped considerably from their Native American forms. Of the Native American names of settlements, the most popular ones are for personal names, with about half of these remaining close to Native American languages (for example, Coesse, Kewanna, Kokomo, Majenica, Metea, Monoquet, Osceola, Winamac) and the other half (for example, Anderson, Blackhawk, LaFontaine, Lagro, Logansport, Red Cloud, Strawtown) being either translated Native American names or European-language names of Native Americans. Native American tribes—including Erie, Miami, Mohawk, Muncie, and Wyandotte—influenced the naming of several Hoosier settlements.

A few settlements bear incident names, those that generally arise from local happenings. Cyclone, for example, was named for a cyclone there in 1880. Two incident names were inspired by the Battle of Tippecanoe. Armiesburg was so named because William Henry Harrison's army camped there on the way to that battle, and Battle Ground received its name because the battle was fought there. The explanation of one supposedly incident name, Rome City, actually appears to be legendary.

Folk etymology occurs when an unfamiliar name is reshaped to make it more familiar. Since most Hoosier place names are of English-language origin, folk etymology is not common in Indiana settlement names, although it has occurred with a few names. Koleen apparently was reshaped from kaolin, a type of clay used in making pottery, and Gnaw Bone may be a reshaping of Narbonne, a French city, though this explanation is merely an educated guess. Russiaville appears to have been named for the country, but actually the name is a form of Richardsville, the French name of a Miami chief.

Place names coined from reversed letters, from other names, or from initials provide some of the most interesting names in place naming, though coined names are rare in Indiana. Some examples of coined names include boundary names such as Kyana and Michiana Shores. Kyana was coined from the abbreviation for Kentucky and the last three letters of Indiana, while Michiana Shores was coined from the first four letters of Michigan and the last four letters of Indiana. Bromer and Elwren are acronyms formed from the names of founders or settlers, and Gimco is another acronym formed from the name of a local company. Some Hoosier place names were formed from parts of two personal names. Broad Park, for instance, comes from the names of two landowners, Broadstreet and Parker. Carwood also comes from two surnames, Carr and Wood. Hanfield was coined from the names of two statesmen, Hancock and Garfield. Loogootee apparently also comes from two personal names, Lowe and Gootee, as does Wilfred, which honors two local mine operators, Wilford and Fredmon. Both Holton and Woodbury supposedly were coined from the names of their founders, Holman and Ellingwood. Perhaps the most celebrated coined name in the state is Trevlac, which is the name of one of the founders, Calvert, spelled backwards. According to one source, the locale now called Trevlac was first a railroad stop, and since there already was a station called Calvert on the line, the name was spelled backwards to avoid confusion.[83]

A few Hoosier settlement names are mistake names that generally have their origin in errors made by the U.S. Post Office Department or local postal clerks. For instance, one community applied for a post office as Comet, but misunderstandings changed the name to Correct. Another town was called Moores Mill until a mistake was made when it applied for a post office, and it became Moores Hill. Siberia originally was named Sabaria; the Post Office Department tried to correct what it thought was an error but made one itself when it changed the name to the more familiar Siberia. Perkinsville was supposed to honor early settler William Parkins, but an error was made when the plat was recorded. A clerical error also changed Laswell, a personal name, to Taswell.

Place names from European languages other than English are rare in Indiana. Of the settlement names, Terre Haute preserves a French influence, as do Vincennes and Saint Croix, although the latter apparently was applied for devotional reasons. Another French name, Amity, probably is commendatory, as is the Latin Amo. The influence of other European languages on Indiana place names is minimal and largely indirect. Haubstadt, named for local storekeeper Henry Haub, uses a German generic, -stadt, which is rare in Indiana. Greek names such as Eureka and Philomath are incident or commendatory names and not direct applications. The Spanish Plano probably is a transfer name from a western state. Thus, the names of Indiana's populated places reflect a settlement history of mainly English-speaking immigrants. Although during the late nineteenth and early twentieth centuries there was considerable foreign immigration from other European countries, later settlers had scant influence on Hoosier place naming, as English remained the basic language in the state and most names had been fixed by then.

Method of Presentation

This study of Indiana place names includes only names of settlements (villages, towns, cities) and counties listed in *The National Gazetteer of the United States of America—Indiana, 1988*.[84] The emphasis has been on primary names listed in this gazetteer; however, within the entries, variant names and spellings frequently are given and cross referenced.

The primary entries in this book are arranged alphabetically, generally according to the present currently approved spelling as it appears in *The National Gazetteer*, though in a few cases, such as Wolf Lake, the preferred local spelling is used. Some of the cross-referenced names (those followed merely by "See . . ."), especially post office names, do not appear in *The National Gazetteer*, so the spelling is that appearing in other sources, generally in county histories and Marie Kaminsky and J. David Baker's useful list of post offices.[85] Some older post office names were spelled with genitive apostrophes; but here, in accordance with the guidelines of the U.S. Board on Geographic Names, apostrophes indicating possession or association have not been used within the body of place names.

Following the spelling is the locally accepted pronunciation, or pronunciations, in brackets. Then, in parenthesis, is the county in which the settlement is located. Ideally, geographical coordinates are used in place-name studies if the place is emphasized rather than the name; however, since locating by latitude and longitude is impossible for readers who do not have access to adequate maps, location is provided in this book merely by county. Readers who want a more precise location should consult *The National Gazetteer* for geographical coordinates and the title of the U.S. Geological Survey topographic map on which the populated place appears.

Entries include the date of settlement and/or establishment of the place, if this information is available. In many cases, though, the name is older than the official establishment or platting of a settlement. Post office information is provided if a post office was located in or near a settlement or if a post office name is associated somehow with an earlier name or with the present name of a settlement. Post office locations obviously present a problem, for the location of a post office often changed when a postmaster changed, since the post office usually was located in the postmaster's store, mill, or home. Moreover, a post office name sometimes changed when a post office was discontinued and reestablished at a nearby site. What place-name scholar Robert M. Rennick found in Kentucky is equally true of Indiana: "Over the years community boundaries shifted and even streams sometimes altered their courses. Post office sites moved with nearly every change in postmaster, for these were usually in that official's home or store. In the course of history of some of these offices, the shifts covered several square miles. Few post offices, when they closed, were at the sites they were established on."[86] Consequently, although a current settlement may bear a post office name and although a post office may have had another name or other names, the location of a post office generally should be interpreted as being only somewhere in the general vicinity of the current location of a settlement.

Generally only the dates of establishment and closing of a post office are given. An asterisk (*) following the post office dates indicates that the post office was discontinued and reestablished or that there are dates of other kinds of changes, so the reader wanting more complete post office records should consult Kaminsky and Baker's list of Indiana post offices. What's more, there are many Hoosier post offices in that source that do not appear in this book because they are not identified as populated places in *The National Gazetteer*.

The kind of populated place—for example, city, town, village—and cross references generally are provided within the entry. Besides community, settlement, and populated place, other feature labels used are state, county (given as part of the name), county seat (given with location), city, town, village, and post office. Populated places are classified according to population, following roughly the categories established under the general laws of Indiana. Cities are populated places of more that 1,500 population. Towns are incorporated settlements with fewer than 1,500 people, though some populated places have a population of over 1,500 but still are classified as towns because they have not held elections to become cities. Very small and unincorporated populated places have been classified here as villages, though unlike the usual concept of village, some of these communities were established as railroad stops, post offices, or resort communities. Some have a scattered population, and some may have been incorporated. Variant spellings and alternate names are given within the primary entry and are cross referenced if the variation is major. To conserve space, minor variations in names and spellings, such as settlement names ending with generic *-burg* or *-burgh,* are not cross referenced, since these names can easily be located with a single entry under the currently approved spelling. Some of the variant names from *The National Gazetteer* are those of small settlements or other features once located near the present populated place. As stated in the gazetteer, because it "is designed to be a reference tool, it does not always reflect the true relationship between the current and the historical name of a place. Historical places, such as forts, Indian villages, and small settlements, that once existed close to or within the current boundaries of a present-day populated place often are listed as separate places but are also listed as appropriate variants."[87]

The history of the present name—that is, the name given in *The National Gazetteer*—has been emphasized rather than etymology. Possible origins are suggested for some names, but since it's risky to guess about place-name origins, such guesses are clearly qualified and should not be considered factual. The namers may be noted when known; however, most namers of Indiana settlements remain anonymous.

A book on state place names must be a compromise. To represent speech sounds, scholars prefer the precise International Phonetic Alphabet, but general readers like a more familiar pronunciation key, such as the one used by the Indiana Broadcasters Association[88] and adapted for its readability in this book. Scholars also like documentation, while many general readers prefer legends and anecdotes. Folk legends and anecdotes are included here for their cultural value and popular appeal, but in all cases, legendary accounts are clearly identified. To conserve space and to improve readability, most documentation within entries has been suppressed, though two unpublished manuscript collections, the WPA files and the Indiana State University Folklore Archives, have been cited as WPA and ISUFA in parentheses. Printed sources are listed in the bibliography, and all post office information comes from Kaminsky and Baker's list of post offices.

Acknowledgments

This book owes a great deal to a number of place-name scholars, including Frederic G. Cassidy, Robert M. Rennick, W. F. H. Nicolaisen, Donald J. Orth, Allen Walker Read, and W. Edson Richmond. I also thank David E. Vancil and Robert L. Carter of the Rare Books and Special Collections Department of the Cunningham Memorial Library at Indiana State University for their cooperation and assistance in making the excellent Indiana collection and WPA manuscript materials available. Local librarians and county historians throughout the state generously provided many of the pronunciations. Graduate student Monty Records spent two years and graduate students Cheryl Horst, Janis Bond, and Floyd Reed spent summer terms as research assistants on the Indiana Place-Name Survey. Another graduate assistant, Kristi Boardman, was especially helpful in verifying local pronunciations. I also am grateful to Mona Dean, Mary Ann Duncan, and Nelta Pippins, secretaries in the Department of English at Indiana State University, who helped with the preparation of the manuscript.

NOTES

1. Richard M. Dorson, *American Folklore and the Historian* (Chicago, 1971), p. ix.

2. Richard M. Dorson, "Interpretation of Research," in *Handbook of American Folklore,* ed. Richard M. Dorson (Bloomington, 1983), p. 325.

3. Richard M. Dorson, "Oral Tradition and Written History: The Case for the United States," *Journal of the Folklore Institute,* 1 (1964), 220.

4. Lawrence W. Levine, "How to Interpret American Folklore Historically," in *Handbook of American Folklore,* ed. Richard M. Dorson (Bloomington, 1983), p. 338.

5. *Webster's Ninth New Collegiate Dictionary* (Springfield, Mass., 1983).

6. Henry Glassie, "Folklore and History," *Minnesota History,* 50 (1987), 188.

7. Alexander H. Krappe, *The Science of Folklore* ([1930] New York, 1964), p. 203.

8. Glassie, p. 190.

9. George Laurence Gomme, *Folk-Lore as an Historical Science* (London, 1908).

10. Jan Vansina, *Oral Tradition: A Study in Historical Methodology* (Chicago, 1961).

11. Wm. Hugh Jansen, "Reality the Non-Story and Realism the Story," *Midwestern Journal of Language and Folklore,* 1 (1975), 54.

12. Jansen, p. 57.

13. Jansen, p. 59.

14. D. K. Wilgus and Lynwood Montell, "Beanie Short: A Civil War Chronicle in Legend and Song," in *The American Folk Legend,* ed. Wayland D. Hand (Berkeley, 1971), p. 133.

15. Gordon Gerould, *The Ballad of Tradition* ([1932] Oxford, England, 1957), p. 131.

16. Gerould, p. 134.

17. Francis James Child, *The English and Scottish Popular Ballads,* 5 vols. ([1888] New York, 1965).

18. Gerould, p. 134.

19. Child, III, 42.

20. J. C. Holt, *Robin Hood* (London, 1982), p. 40.

21. Holt, p. 7.

22. Robert S. Rudolph, *Wood County Place Names* (Madison, Wisc., 1970), p. viii.

23. Linda Dégh, "Importance of Collecting Place-Name Legends in Indiana," in *The Study of Place Names,* ed. Ronald L. Baker (Terre Haute, 1970), p. 86.

24. For instance, see Edward Clodd, *Tom Tit Tot, an Essay on Savage Philosophy in Folk-Tale* (London, 1897).

25. W. F. H. Nicolaisen, *Scottish Place-Names: Their Study and Significance* (London, 1976), p. 4.

26. Kenneth Burke, "Literature as Equipment for Living," in *The Philosophy of Literary Form* ([1941] New York: 1961), pp. 253–262.

27. See Ronald L. Baker, "The Role of Folk Legends in Place-Name Research," *Journal of American Folklore,* 85 (1972), 367–373.

28. Robert M. Rennick, "The Role of Oral History in Place-Name Research," in *The Study of Place Names,* ed. Ronald L. Baker (Terre Haute, 1970), p. 71.

29. H. L. Mencken, *The American Language* (New York, 1962), p. 527.

30. Ronald L. Baker, *Hoosier Folk Legends* (Bloomington, 1982), p. 192.

31. Glassie, p. 190.

32. Glassie, p. 191.

33. Scott Russell Sanders, *Staying Put* (Boston, 1993), pp. 149–150.

34. Arthur W. Shumaker, *A History of Indiana Literature* (Indianapolis, 1962), p. 325.

35. Meredith Nicholson, *The Hoosiers* ([1900] New York, 1915), p. 2.

36. William Blane, *An Excursion through the United States and Canada during the Years 1822–1823* (London, 1824), p. 140.

37. Quoted in Jacob Piatt Dunn, *The Word Hoosier.* Indiana Historical Society Publications, vol. 7, no. 2 (Indianapolis, 1907), p. 9.

38. Richard M. Dorson, *Davy Crockett: American Comic Legend* (New York, 1977), pp. 123–124.

39. Richard Lyle Power, "The Hoosier as an American Folk-Type," *Indiana Magazine of History,* 38 (1942), 108–109.

40. Power, p. 109.

41. Power, p. 109.

42. Power, p. 109.

43. Power, p. 110.

44. Power, pp. 112–113.

45. *Wall Street Journal,* January 27, 1987, p. 1; February 9, 1987, p. 19; February 24, 1987, p. 33; March 18, 1987, p. 31; March 26, 1987, p. 37.

46. *Webster's New World Dictionary of the American Language* (Cleveland and New York, 1964).

47. *Wall Street Journal,* March 18, 1987, p. 25.

48. Baker, *Hoosier Folk Legends,* p. 174.

49. Dunn, *The Word Hoosier,* pp. 14–15.

50. Baker, *Hoosier Folk Legends,* p. 174.

51. Baker, *Hoosier Folk Legends,* pp. 171–172.

52. *Wall Street Journal,* March 26, 1987, p. 35.

53. See H. L. Mencken, *The American Language: Supplement II* (New York, 1962), pp. 617–618.

54. Dunn, *The Word Hoosier,* p. 12.

55. Indiana State University Folklore Archives (ISUFA), Terre Haute.

56. R. Carlyle Buley, *The Old Northwest: Pioneer Period, 1815–1840* (Bloomington, 1950), p. 617.

57. Mencken, *The American Language: Supplement II,* p. 617.

58. Dunn, *The Word Hoosier,* p. 13.

59. Quoted in Dunn, *The Word Hoosier,* pp. 13–14.

60. ISUFA, Terre Haute.

61. ISUFA, Terre Haute.

62. ISUFA, Terre Haute.

63. Dunn, *The Word Hoosier,* p. 18.

64. Dunn, *The Word Hoosier,* p. 26.

65. Baker, *Hoosier Folk Legends,* pp. 174–175.

66. Dunn, *The Word Hoosier,* pp. 28–29. See Joseph Wright, *The English Dialect Dictionary,* 6 vols. (London, 1898–1905).

67. Dunn, *The Word Hoosier,* p. 19.

68. Raven McDavid, "Word Magic, or Would You Want Your Daughter to Marry a Hoosier?" in *Dialects in Culture: Essays in General Dialectology by Raven I. McDavid, Jr.,* ed. William A. Kretzschmar, Jr. (University, Ala., 1979), p. 256.

69. McDavid, p. 56.

70. McDavid, pp. 256–257.

71. Warren E. Roberts, *Viewpoints on Folklife: Looking at the Overlooked* (Ann Arbor, 1988), p. 50.

72. Roberts, p. 51.

73. Dunn, *The Word Hoosier,* p. 17.

74. Roberts, p. 48.

75. McDavid, p. 255.

76. Ronald L. Baker, *Jokelore: Humorous Folktales from Indiana* (Bloomington, 1986), pp. xxxvii–xxxix.

77. Reprinted in Dunn, *The Word Hoosier,* pp. 5–8.

78. Hough's map has been reprinted in several books, including Logan Esarey, *A History of Indiana from Its Exploration to 1850* (Indianapolis, 1970), p. 241.

79. Frank A. Hoffman, "Place Names in Brown County," *Midwest Folklore,* 11 (1974), 60.

80. Card file in the Indiana Historical Society Library, Indianapolis.

81. George S. Stewart, *American Place Names* (New York, 1970), p. xxx.

82. ISUFA, Terre Haute.

83. Hoffman, p. 61.

84. *The National Gazetteer of the United States of America—Indiana, 1988,* U.S. Geological Survey Professional Paper 1200-IN (Reston, Va., 1988).

85. J. David Baker, *The Postal History of Indiana,* 2 vols. (Louisville, 1976).

86. Robert M. Rennick, "Research in Placenames, a Cautionary Note," *Names,* 40 (1992), 230–231.

87. *The National Gazetteer,* p. xi.

88. *A Guide to the Pronunciation of Indiana Cities and Towns* (West Lafayette, n.d.), p. 2.

Pronunciation Guide

[a]	as in h*a*t		[g]	as in *g*un
[ay]	as in f*a*te		[kw]	as in *qu*ick
[ah]	as in *a*rm		[ch]	as in *ch*urch
[e]	as in m*e*t		[sh]	as in ca*sh*
[ee]	as in tr*ee*		[zh]	as in a*z*ure
[i]	as in s*i*t		[s]	as in *s*oft
[eye]	as in *i*ce		[z]	as in bu*zz*
[o]	as in s*o*		[ng]	as in si*ng*
[oo]	as in sh*oo*t		[th]	as in *th*rough
[u]	as in f*oo*t		[*th*]	as in *th*en
[uh]	as in c*u*p		[ks]	as in ta*x*
[yoo]	as in *u*se			
[er]	as in farm*er*			
[ehr]	as in *ai*r			
[ahr]	as in *a*re			
[awr]	as in *o*r			
[ow]	as in c*ow*			
[aw]	as in s*aw*			
[oy]	as in b*oy*			
[k]	as in *c*at			
[j]	as in e*dg*e			

CAPITALS indicate accented syllables.

☞ Alphabetical List of Hoosier Place Names

 **A**

Aaron [EHR-uhn] (Switzerland). A post office was established here on June 26, 1871; closed on April 15, 1907. Aaron, usually from a personal name, is not a common place name in the United States, though it also is found in Kentucky, where it was applied to a post office in 1908.

Abbey Dell (Orange). See Abydel.

Aberdeen [AB-er-deen] (Ohio). This village was settled around 1814 and named about five years later for Aberdeen, Scotland, by Dr. Robert Gillespie, a Scottish settler. The name literally means "mouth of the Don"—a Celtic river name. A post office was established on July 20, 1852; closed on August 23, 1880. A variant name is Bascom, as another post office was established on December 22, 1880, with Robert B. Bascom as postmaster, and closed on September 30, 1924.

Abington [AB-ing-tuhn] (Wayne). This village was platted on December 5, 1817, by John and Joseph Cox. John Cox purchased land here in 1806. A post office was established on March 17, 1824; closed on December 31, 1903. This English, Irish, and Scottish place name also is found in Connecticut, Massachusetts, and Pennsylvania; consequently, the name of the Indiana community probably was borrowed from one of these places or from the personal name, which generally comes from the English place name.

Aboite [uh-BOYT] (Allen). A post office was established on July 30, 1833; closed on March 31, 1921.* According to local tradition, this village was named for an Indian chief or derived from the French *abattoir*, "slaughterhouse," because of a French defeat by Indians here in 1780; however, the town name is a local transfer from Aboite Creek. Aboite Creek, sometimes Aboite River, comes from the French name for the stream, Rivière à Boitte, or à Bouette—supposedly referring to minnows used as bait. Variant names are Aboit and Aboit Station.

Abydel [AB-ee-del] (Orange). A post office was moved from Lick Creek (cf. Prospect) to Abydel on January 14, 1889; closed on February 28, 1907. The origin of this unique place name is unknown; however, most American place names with the similar Abby or Abbie as the specific name are from women's names. A variant spelling is Abbey Dell.

Academie [uh-KAD-uh-mee] (Allen). This village was platted in 1874 by Samuel Evans and named for the nearby Academy of the Sacred Heart. A post office was established as Academie on May 29, 1878; changed to Academy on August 9, 1880; closed on October 7, 1893.* A variant name is Academie Station, and a variant spelling is Academy.

Acme [AK-mee] (Jackson). A post office was established here on January 22, 1884, but closed on March 21, 1891, when a post office was established at nearby Surprise. Acme, suggesting "best," is a common commendatory place name found in at least nine other states.

Acton [AK-tuhn] (Marion). This village was platted on October 22, 1852. It first was named Farmersville, but since there already was a Farmersville in Posey County, the name was changed to Acton, for a local resident, General Acton. A post office was established on March 6, 1854; closed on June 21, 1963.

Adams [AD-uhmz] (Decatur). A post office was established on February 29, 1828; closed on February 16, 1963.* The village was laid out on January 1, 1855, by Aaron H. Womack. The name comes from Adams Township, in which it is located. The township was named for President John Quincy Adams.

Adamsboro [AD-uhmz-ber-o; AD-uhmz-ber-uh] (Cass). This village was platted in the fall of 1872 by George E. Adams and named for him. A post office was established as Adamsborough on December 19, 1872; closed on April 29, 1905.

Adams County [AD-uhmz]. This county, one of Indiana's leading producers of grain and livestock, was formed from Allen County in 1835, organized in 1836, and named for the sixth president of the United States, John Quincy Adams. Located here is Limberlost State Historic Site, the home of Hoosier novelist and naturalist Gene Stratton Porter. Seat: Decatur.

Adams Mill [AD-uhmz MIL] (Carroll). Located about a mile east of Cutler, this community also was called Adams Mills. Adams is a local family name. The post office here, called Wild Cat or Wildcat,

was established on December 17, 1832; closed on September 26, 1894.* Cf. Burlington.

Adayeville (Perry). See Adyeville.

Ade [ayd] (Newton). A post office was established on December 10, 1904; closed on October 15, 1912. The village was laid out in March 1906 and named for John Ade, first recorder of Newton County.

Adel [ay-DEL] (Owen). Originally called Pleasant Valley, this village was laid out on April 28, 1859, by Levi Carpenter, proprietor. A post office was established on January 16, 1889; closed on September 29, 1906. Normally deriving from a woman's name, Adel also is found as a place name in Georgia, Iowa, and Oregon. The first postmaster was Sylvester E. Adkins, and the name may have been coined from his name. The village was nicknamed Dog Walk.

Adriance (Newton). See Kentland.

Advance [AD-vants] (Boone). This town was laid out in 1820 and first named Osceola, for the Seminole chief, but since there was another town and post office in Saint Joseph County named Osceola, in 1872 the name was changed to Advance, supposedly a commendatory name "in anticipation of the advancement which the coming of the Midland railway would bring to the community." A post office was established on September 24, 1873.

Adyeville [AY-dee-vil] (Perry). A post office was established on January 28, 1862; closed on September 23, 1966. The village was platted in 1873. The name honors a local family. The first postmaster was Andrew J. Adye. Adayeville and Adyville are variant spellings.

Aetna [ET-nuh] (Lake). A post office was established here on March 8, 1894; closed on July 15, 1919.

Ainsworth [AYNZ-werth] (Lake). This village was founded around 1880 and supposedly was named for a railroad official (WPA). A post office was established on January 10, 1882; closed on February 15, 1934. Variant spellings have been Ainesworth and Answorth.

Aix [ayks] (Jasper). A post office was established on September 2, 1892; closed on October 30, 1909. The village apparently was named for the French city Aix, or Aix-en-Provence.

Akron [AK-ruhn] (Fulton). This town was settled in 1836, laid out in 1838, and called Newark by settlers from Ohio. A post office was established as Wesley on August 9, 1837, but changed to Akron, for the city in Ohio, on January 6, 1853. In 1855 the name of the town also was changed to Akron. One account says that Newark was chosen as the first name because the settlers were from Newark, Ohio. Another account says that when the settlers arrived here, the leader said, "This is the New Ark, consummating the covenant seeking homes in a new land."

Alamo [AL-uh-mo] (Montgomery). This town was laid out in 1837, and a post office was established on July 11, 1844. The name comes from the fort in San Antonio, Texas. "The Bard of Alamo," Hoosier poet James B. Elmore (1857–1942), lived on a farm near here.

Alaska [uh-LAS-kuh] (Owen). This village is located on the Owen-Morgan county line. A post office was established as West Salem in Morgan County on March 24, 1849. The post office was changed to Graysville, for a local family, on April 24, 1855. David W. Gray settled in the township in 1836; Benjamin Gray built the first mill in the township also in 1836; and Francis M. Gray was appointed postmaster on April 24, 1855. The post office was changed to Sheasville on July 28, 1855; changed to Alaska on May 4, 1868; changed to Owen County on December 1, 1875; changed back to Morgan County on April 24, 1897; and closed on June 15, 1904. Russian America, renamed Alaska, from an Aleutian word meaning "mainland," was purchased by the United States in 1867, so it was in the news when the post office was named Alaska.

Albany [AWL-buh-nee] (Delaware). The town was laid out on December 11, 1833, by William Venard, and a post office was established on January 27, 1851. Apparently the name was borrowed from Albany, New York.

Albion [AL-bee-uhn] (county seat, Noble). Formerly called The Center before becoming the county seat, this town was laid out in November 1846 by Samuel Hanna, William F. Engle, John White, Warren Chaffee, and James L. Worden. A post office was established on August 19, 1847. The present name is from the ancient name of Britain, via Albion, New York, home of a county commissioner.

Albion [AL-bee-uhn] (Scott). This village was platted on December 12, 1837, by Henry Cochran. Ultimately this place name is from the ancient name of Britain.

Alcinda (Putnam). See Indian Village.

Aldine [AWL-deen] (Starke). This village was established as a railroad station in 1882. A post office was established on December 11, 1883; closed on August 30, 1919.

Alert [uh-LERT] (Decatur). A post office was established on March 21, 1866; closed on January 31, 1951.* Although the name appears to be commendatory and unique to Indiana, supposedly an early settler, Ben Peterson, named the post office for his hometown in Ohio. The village was laid out on August 30, 1886, by James Bannister.

Alexander (Adams). See Geneva (Adams).

Alexander (Clay). See Cardonia.

Alexandria [el-ig-ZAN-dree-uh; al-ig-ZAN-dree-uh; al-iks-AN-dree-uh] (Madison). This city was laid out on June 3, 1836, by William Conner and John D. Stephenson. A post office was established on April 1, 1837. Possibly the name is for Alexandria, Virginia, though some say it's for the ancient Egyptian city of Alexandria, some say it's for the wife of a founder, and others say that like the Egyptian Alexandria, it's for Alexander the Great.

Alfont [AL-fahnt] (Madison). A local post office established on February 27, 1851, was moved to nearby Ingalls, June 30, 1893. The village, platted around 1850, was named for William Alfont, who built a sawmill here in 1835.

Alford [AWL-ferd; AL-ferd] (Pike). Formerly called Alfords, this village was laid out on November 8, 1856, by Elijah, Nathaniel, and Samuel Alford (sometimes given as Alfords) and named for them.

Alfordsville [AL-ferdz-vil; AWL-ferdz-vil] (Daviess). This town was laid out on June 3, 1845, by Isaac Harris and named for James Alford, an early settler. A post office was established on April 1, 1856; closed on December 31, 1968.*

Algiers [al-JEERZ] (Pike). A nearby post office was established as Delectable Hill on February 1, 1838; changed to Algiers on December 16, 1885; and closed on March 15, 1955.* The village, formerly called Cross Roads, was platted first on October 21, 1836. The present name, apparently for the city in North Africa, was suggested by one of the early settlers, Wesley Coleman.

Aliceville (Knox). See Ragsdale.

Alida [uh-LEYE-duh] (La Porte). This village, formerly called Alida Station, was established as a railroad junction. A post office established as Burton on July 31, 1876, was changed to Alida on August 23, 1876, and closed on February 15, 1932.* This unusual place name also is found in Saskatchewan.

Allen [AL-uhn] (Allen). Apparently this settlement was named for the county in which it is located.

Allen (Miami). See Macy.

Allen County [AL-uhn]. This county was organized in 1823 and named for Colonel John Allen, Kentucky lawyer and Indian fighter, who aided in the liberation of Fort Wayne in 1812 and was killed at the Battle of the River Raisin. The county's many attractions include Historic Fort Wayne, a replica of the military post constructed here in 1815–1816. Seat: Fort Wayne.

Allens Ferry (Dearborn). See West Harrison.

Allensville [AL-uhnz-vil] (Switzerland). This village was laid out in 1816 and named for the local Allen family. A post office was established on June 3, 1823; closed on September 30, 1908.* Allensville is sometimes given as a variant name of nearby East Enterprise, q.v., because for a time the post office moved back and forth between these two villages.

Alliance [uh-LEYE-uhnts] (Madison). Formerly this village was called Alliance Station, as it developed as a railroad station. According to oral tradition, the name is descriptive: "Alliance Station is a small town in Adams Township, Madison County, Indiana. That's where two or three railroads junction, and that's why they call it Alliance Station" (ISUFA).

Allisonville [AL-uh-suhn-vil] (Marion). A post office was established here on September 23, 1832, and named for John Allison, first postmaster, who also laid out the village on February 8, 1833. The post office was moved to Castleton, q.v., on December 7, 1853.* A variant name is Allison.

Alma Lake [AL-muh LAYK] (Parke). This village was named for the lake of the same name, which was named for Alma Creek.

Alpine [AL-peyen] (Fayette). According to the WPA files, this village was founded about 1832 and named Ashland, for ash trees in the vicinity, but Allen Crisler built a sawmill here around 1814. A post office called Alpine was established on February 24, 1868; closed on May 20, 1966. Supposedly the name *Alpine* was selected for its similarity to Ashland when it was discovered that there already was a post office named Ashland in Henry County. Cf. Nulltown for a post office in this county named Ashland.

Alquina [al-KWEYE-nuh] (Fayette). A post office was established on December 15, 1832; closed on July 14, 1903.* The settlement dates from 1813, with Joseph VanMeter as the original proprietor. Joseph D. Ross and Isaac Darter laid out the south addition on November 2, 1838, and Jacob Reed laid out the north addition on December 27, 1841. Allegedly the village was named around 1830 by a local merchant, Green Larimore. Though the origin of the name is not known, it may have been borrowed from Alquines, France.

Alta [AL-tuh] (Vermillion). This village was platted in 1871. The name, meaning "elevation," may be descriptive and may have been influenced by Hillsdale, which is located a mile north across Little Raccoon Creek. Hillsdale and Alta generally are regarded as a single village.

Altamont Switch [AWL-tuh-mahnt SWICH] (Tippecanoe). Also called Alamont, this village was established as a railroad switching station.

Alto [AL-to] (Howard). This village was laid out in 1848 and named for the Battle of Palo Alto in the Mexican War. A post office was established on August 16, 1848; closed on June 16, 1907.

Alton [AWL-tuhn] (Crawford). The town was platted on July 5, 1838. A post office established as Nebraska on March 8, 1847, was changed to Alton on July 2, 1860, and was closed on February 26, 1965. Alton is a fairly popular place name that is found in Great Britain, Canada, Australia, and New Zealand as well as in at least eleven states. Ultimately, the name comes from the English town, but in the United States generally it is a borrowing from New England or from a personal name derived from the English town. According to a legend, "They've called upper Alton 'Pie Town' for years and years. Some old-timers don't call it by any other name. There was a federal penitentiary in town during the Civil War. Soldiers used to bring prisoners in and march them right through the town. Then sometimes just the soldiers would come through on their way to and from the wars. . . . Those soldiers would march through town, to and from the war, and the women would know that they were coming. They'd all bake a lot of pies, as many as they could afford, and when the soldiers marched through, they'd run out along the streets and give the pies to the soldiers. You know, they didn't get much to eat, sometimes nothing at all. The soldiers spread the word around and upper Alton began to be called 'Pie Town.' For years and years the paper was called the *Pie Town Journal*" (ISUFA).

Altona [al-TO-nuh] (DeKalb). A post office was established on October 29, 1874, with Henry Gettel as the first and only postmaster; closed on September 15, 1913. The name may have been borrowed from the city of the same name in Germany, or it may have been borrowed from Pennsylvania, since apparently an earlier spelling was Altoona.

Altoner (Cass). See Lucerne.

Alvarado [al-vuh-RAY-do] (Steuben). A post office was established here on June 21, 1855; closed on October 15, 1904. Originally the village was called Richland Center. The present name may come from the Mexican city.

American City (Dubois). See Ireland.

Ambia [AM-bee-uh] (Benton). The name of this settlement was changed from Weaver City, for the nearby post office in Illinois, to Ambia on May 5, 1873, when a post office was established. The town was laid out by Mr. and Mrs. Ezekiel M. Talbot on February 22, 1875. Possibly the name was borrowed from Ambialet, France, though supposedly the town was named for the Talbots' daughter (ISUFA).

Amboy [AM-boy] (Miami). This town was platted on October 9, 1867, by Bennet Fellows, John A. Lamb, John P. Tomey, and Abijah Ridgeway as a station on the Pan Handle Railroad, completed in Miami County in the same year, and named for Perth Amboy, New Jersey, home of the surveyor, A. M. Goodrich, who was born in Scotland. A post office was established on January 21, 1868. According to a local legend, the town was named when someone saw a visitor wearing kilts and said, "He am girl." Overhearing this, the visitor replied, "No, am boy."

America [uh-MEHR-uh-kuh] (Wabash). A post office with this patriotic name was established here on February 18, 1837; closed on February 16, 1881.* The village was platted on October 16, 1837, by Jesse D. Scott and Elihu Garrison. Until the railroad was completed through La Fontaine, America was the local trade center.

Americus [uh-MEHR-ee-kuhs] (Tippecanoe). This village was laid out in 1832 by William Digby, who also founded Lafayette. A post office was established on December 30, 1833; closed on October 15, 1902.* The name, a masculine form of America, is patriotic.

Amity [AM-uh-tee] (Johnson). A post office was established on February 22, 1849; closed on April 30, 1906.* The village was platted on June 15, 1855, by John Adams. The name comes from the French word *amitié*, "friendship." This commendatory name sometimes is applied to churches, as in Hancock and Morgan counties, both with an Amity Church.

Amo [AY-mo] (Hendricks). The town was laid out in 1850 by Joseph Morris and first called Morrisville for him. A post office was established as Morrisville, with Joseph Morris as postmaster, on June 1, 1852, but the name was changed to Amo "by some classical-minded citizens" on August 13, 1855. The present name often is said to be a Potawatomi word, *a-mo*, "honeybee," but probably it is from the Latin *amo*, "I love."

Amsterdam (Harrison). See New Amsterdam.

Anderson [AN-der-suhn] (county seat, Madison). A post office was established as Andersontown, sometimes spelled Andersonton, in 1823; changed to Anderson on June 9, 1849. The city was named for Captain William Anderson, a Delaware chief whose Indian name was Kok-to-wha-nund, sometimes spelled Kikthawenund, "Making a Cracking Noise." The Delaware name of an Indian village here was Wa-pimins-kink, "Chestnut Tree Place."

Andersonville [AN-der-suhn-vil] (Franklin). A post office called Andersonville, for the local Anderson family, was established on March 25, 1828, with Joseph Anderson as the first postmaster; closed on April 2, 1906. The village was laid out first in November 1837 by Fletcher Tevis and called Ceylon. On May 24, 1849, Thomas Anderson made an addition to the village.

Andrews [AN-drooz] (Huntington). This town was surveyed on December 12, 1853, and named Antioch by the proprietor, Andrew Leedy. A post office called Antioch was established on February 21, 1856. Apparently with some local opposition, the post office name was changed to Andrews on April 14, 1882. The present name supposedly comes from the name of the railroad yards, Andrewsia, located here in 1881 and named for an official of the Wabash Railroad.

Angola [an-GO-luh] (county seat, Steuben). A post office was established on January 3, 1838. The city was surveyed on April 5, 1838, and incorporated in October 1866. The name is a transfer from Angola, New York, home of some early settlers.

Annapolis [an-AP-uh-luhs; an-AP-luhs] (Parke). This village was laid out in 1837, though settled around 1825. A post office was established on July 24, 1837; closed on June 30, 1905. Probably the name was borrowed from Annapolis, Maryland.

Anoka [uh-NO-kuh] (Cass). A post office named Anoka was established on February 1, 1856; closed on September 14, 1903.* A village was laid out here on September 29, 1876, by F. Herman Smith and named Herman City for him. Anoka, according to some sources, is an invented name, but according to Jacob P. Dunn, the name probably comes from a Sioux adverb meaning "on both sides." This place name also is found in Minnesota and Nebraska.

Answorth (Lake). See Ainsworth.

Anthony [AN-thuh-nee] (Delaware). A post office was established on July 8, 1850; closed on October 14, 1901.* The town probably was named for the Anthony family, including Thomas, Samuel, and Penelope, who registered land in this county in the 1830s.

Anthonys Location (Pulaski). See Radioville.

Antioch [AN-tee-ahk] (Clinton). This village was first settled in 1828 (WPA). The name is from the biblical city, probably via a local church, since this is a very common name for churches throughout the United States. The name has been popular as a place name in Indiana, too, for in addition to the settlements named Antioch that follow, a post office named Antioch was established in Jefferson County on December 22, 1884, though it closed on August 26, 1885.

Antioch (Huntington). See Andrews.

Antioch [AN-tee-ahk] (Jay). This village was laid out in 1853 and named by C. H. Clark, one of three founders, for Antioch College in Ohio. The post office established on August 10, 1870, was called Hawkins for a local family. John Hawkins built the first cabin in the township in 1829. The post office was closed on June 9, 1881.*

Antioch [AN-tee-ahk] (Switzerland). A post office was established here on June 18, 1894; closed on May 14, 1904. Cf. Antioch (Clinton).

Antioch Junction [AN-tee-ahk JUHNK-shuhn] (Greene). This village, also called Antioch, was settled in 1829 and named for a church that was built here shortly after settlement.

Antiville [AN-tuh-vil] (Jay). A post office was established on September 11, 1889, but closed on October 31, 1900. According to a local legend, "In about 1865 a group of people lived in the vicinity of Antiville which were very much opposed to all secret organizations, such as Masons, KKK, Knights of the Golden Circle, etc. Because of this strenuous stand against the secret orders they were given the name of Anti-Masons, Anti-Circles, etc., by surrounding communities. This was changed to Antiville when the blacksmith and sawmill appeared" (WPA). Other accounts agree that the people living here when the settlement was established were opposed to Masons, or opposed to slavery, or opposed to most subjects and institutions.

Apalona [ap-uh-LO-nuh] (Perry). A post office was established as Lushers on June 7, 1858; changed to Apalona June 2, 1864; closed on August 31, 1955.*

Arabia [uh-RAY-bee-uh] (Parke). According to local tradition, this village was named by Isaac Silliman in the 1820s because local hog thieves were called Arabs, a colloquial term for vagrants and petty thieves.

Arba [AHR-buh; AHR-bee] (Randolph). This village was settled as early as 1815, when a Friends' meetinghouse was established here, although it was not platted until October 30, 1855. A post office was established on September 24, 1849; closed on January 31, 1911. Possibly the name was borrowed either from a personal name or from the river in Spain.

Arcadia [ahr-KAY-dee-uh] (Hamilton). The town was laid out in 1849 by John Shafer and Daniel Waltz, and a post office was established on October 19, 1852. Apparently the name comes from the ancient Greek district noted for its pastoral simplicity and beauty. Arcadia glass, now a collector's item, was made here.

Arcadia (Pike). See Coe.

Arcana [ahr-KAN-uh] (Grant). This village was laid out in 1852. A post office was established on June 7, 1858; closed on December 14, 1900.* The name is probably plural of *arcanum*, "hidden," suggesting "secluded," hence commendatory.

Arcola [ahr-KO-luh] (Allen). A post office called Taw Taw, established on July 14, 1849, was changed to Arcola on April 17, 1858. The town was platted on April 25, 1864. Arcola, as a place name, is found in several other states and comes from Arcole or Arcola, a town in Italy where Napoleon won a victory over the Austrians in 1796.

Arcola (Owen). See Vilas.

Arcole (Lawrence). See Spring Mill Village.

Arctic (DeKalb). See Artic.

Arda [AHR-duh] (Pike). The name of this village may come from the Arda River in Bulgaria or Italy.

Ardmore [AHRD-mawr] (Saint Joseph). This village, laid out on the farm of Congressman Abraham Brick, may have been named for the town in Ireland, perhaps via Pennsylvania.

Argos [AHR-guhs] (Marshall). This town was platted on January 8, 1851, and called Sidney, for Sidney Williams, an early settler and circuit judge. A post office was established as Argos, for the

Greek city, on August 3, 1857. The post office name was applied to the town in 1859.

Ari [EHR-ee] (Allen). This village is located on the Allen-Noble county line. A post office called Ari was established in Noble County on January 29, 1872; changed to Allen County on October 15, 1887; closed on June 30, 1914. The railroad station here was called Potters Station for a local family. Galutia Potter was the first postmaster, and James Potter was the second postmaster.

Arlington [AHR-ling-tuhn] (Monroe). This village was platted on February 25, 1893.

Arlington [AHR-ling-tuhn] (Rush). This village was laid out on April 12, 1832, and called Burlington, but since there was another town and post office of the same name in Carroll County, the post office, established on July 11, 1833, was called Beech Grove. On December 23, 1875, the post office name was changed to Arlington, for Arlington, Virginia, site of the national cemetery, and since then the community has been called Arlington.

Armery (Warrick). See Stevenson.

Armiesburg [AHR-meez-berg] (Parke). This village was laid out in 1833. A post office established as Armiesburgh on January 2, 1844, was closed on May 31, 1902.* The village was so named because General William Henry Harrison's army camped here on the way to what became the Battle of Tippecanoe. According to a local legend, "Armiesburg was first called Stringtown because the village ran from Christman Dazney's tepee, which was right out there about where Luther Myers' barn is, to about where the houses are now. The cabins were all in a row, all strung out, so they called it Stringtown. Then after Harrison's armies camped there, somebody decided to call it Armiesburgh" (ISUFA). It also has been reported that General Hopkins as well as General Harrison camped here and that the earlier name was Stringtown because a row of log houses here was connected by logs. The village also has been called Armiesburg Mills.

Armour (Lake). See Cedar Lake.

Armstrong [AHRM-strawng] (Vanderburgh). A nearby post office called Cross Roads was established on July 8, 1850; closed on October 6, 1851. Another post office called Armstrong was established on August 5, 1856; closed on May 31, 1957.* The village also was called Armstrong Crossroads, and the railroad station was called Armstrong. The name is for Armstrong Township, in which the village is located. The township was named for John Armstrong, Sr., an early settler.

Arney [AHR-nee] (Owen). The village was laid out in 1852, though the settlement dates from about 1830, and originally was called Middletown. A post office was established as Arney on September 11, 1856; closed on March 31, 1912.*

Aroma [uh-RO-muh] (Hamilton). The village was founded around 1836. A post office was established on September 28, 1870; closed on October 15, 1902. Allegedly the village was named for pleasant odors from flowering trees, from new-mown hay, or from something else when a name was being selected.

Art [ahrt] (Clay). A post office was established on June 2, 1873; closed on February 28, 1903. It was named by W. W. Carter, a lawyer engaged to correspond with the postal department when the post office was established. Supposedly Carter chose Art for the name because it was short and easier to spell and write than Science or Philosophy.

Artesian City (Morgan). See Martinsville.

Arthur [AHR-ther] (Pike). A post office was established on October 18, 1873; closed on August 31, 1903.* Perhaps the name honors Arthur Thompson, postmaster from 1876 until the closing of the post office in 1903, though he was not the first postmaster.

Artic [AHR-dik] (DeKalb). A post office was established on September 5, 1848; closed on September 15, 1903.* A former spelling was Arctic, so apparently it was named for the arctic region.

Ascension (Sullivan). See Farmersburg.

Ashboro [ASH-ber-o] (Clay). A post office was established as Ashborough on June 23, 1858; closed on February 28, 1918. The spelling was changed to Ashboro on November 15, 1886. The name was borrowed from Asheboro, North Carolina. Located on the old Bloomington Trail, Ashboro was once called Barrows Inn. It was laid out by Charles W. Moss, the second postmaster, in July 1860. Moss operated a large sawmill and hoped to relocate the county seat here from Bowling Green. Later, two additions were made by Mrs. Norton Dilsaver and F. P. Barrows.

Asherville [ASH-er-vil] (Clay). This village was laid out on September 13, 1873, by John Asher and named for him. Asher built the first building, which was used as a store operated by John Vonewitz. The village became a shipping point for two coal mines: the Globe and the Aetna. A post office was established on December 19, 1873; closed on February 29, 1912.

Ash Grove [ash GROV] (Tippecanoe). A post office was established on June 14, 1864; closed on October 31, 1910. The name is said to be descriptive of ash trees in a wooded area here (WPA).

Ashland (Fayette). See Alpine and Nulltown.

Ashland [ASH-luhnd] (Henry). A post office was established on April 11, 1848; closed on July 15, 1910. The village, formerly called Mullens Station for a local pioneer family, was never laid out. The name is for Ashland, Ohio, home of some settlers.

Ashland (Wabash). See La Fontaine.

Ashley [ASH-lee] (Steuben). The DeKalb-Steuben county line divides this town. A post office was established on August 15, 1892, the same year the town was laid out. Ashley is a popular English place name and family name, so this name may be a transfer name, perhaps from Pennsylvania; however, according to the WPA files, the name honors the Ashley family, owners of the town site. A variant name is Ashley-Hudson.

Ashton (Henry). See Ashland.

Asphaltum [ASH-fuhl-tuhm; ASH-fawl-tuhm] (Jasper). About 1900 there was an oil boom in this area, and this village grew up around a refinery that produced heavy oil used for lubrication and paving, hence the name. A post office was established on August 23, 1901; closed on September 15, 1904.

Athens [ATH-uhnz] (Fulton). A post office established as Grant, on December 20, 1875, was changed to Athens, May 28, 1896. Originally the village was called Hoover Station, for the Hoover family who lived near here. The present name is for Athens, Greece.

Atherton (Parke). See West Atherton.

Atherton [ATH-er-tuhn] (Vigo). This village was platted on October 7, 1871. A post office was established on June 21, 1881; closed on January 31, 1934. The line of the north part of the plat divides Vigo and Parke counties. An earlier name was Athertons Island, as the surveyor, a geologist named Atherton, for whom it was named, said the site once had been an island.

Atkinson [AT-kuhn-suhn; AT-kuh-suhn] (Benton). A post office was established on March 5, 1873; closed on April 14, 1923. The name honors W. J. Atkinson, a prominent cattleman in this area.

Atkinsonville [AT-kin-suhn-vil] (Owen). This village was laid out in 1850 and named for the proprietor, Stephen Atkinson. A post office was established on May 10, 1854; closed on August 15, 1907.*

Atlanta [at-LAN-tuh] (Hamilton). A post office was established on November 28, 1845, as Shielville, sometimes spelled Shielsville, for landowner James Shiel, but the town was called Buena Vista as early as 1854. On January 18, 1886, the post office, and subsequently the town, became Atlanta, apparently for the city in Georgia.

Attica [AD-uh-kuh] (Fountain). This city was platted on March 19, 1825, and a post office was established on July 20, 1826. The name is classical, coming from the district in ancient Greece, perhaps via New York.

Atwood [AT-wud] (Kosciusko). The village was laid out on September 29, 1857, by Agnes Teegarden and Harvey Hunt. A post office was established as Atwood, allegedly for early settler John Wood, on November 23, 1864. The village first was called Mount Ruska, but by petition renamed Atwood in 1865. Wood is a variant name.

Auburn [AW-bern] (county seat, DeKalb). This city was laid out in 1835, and a post office was established on March 5, 1839. The name comes from the English village via New York. According to local legend, Auburn is an incident name. Several Indians were sitting around a fire, and one Indian stuck his finger in the fire and said, "Ah, burn!" (WPA).

Auburn Junction [aw-bern JUHNK-shuhn] (DeKalb). A post office was established on December 22, 1884; closed on May 15, 1931. The village developed as a railroad junction near Auburn, for which it was named.

Augusta (Bartholomew). See Waynesville.

Augusta [uh-GUHS-tuh] (Marion). The village was laid out in 1832. A post office was established on February 3, 1835; closed on February 28, 1859. The name may be a transfer from Virginia or Georgia.

Augusta [uh-GUHS-tuh; aw-GUHS-tuh] (Pike). This village was founded by Charles Beech, who came here in the early 1860s. A post office was established on July 27, 1874; closed on November 15, 1920.* Possibly the name was borrowed from either Georgia or Virginia.

Augusta Station (Marion). See New Augusta.

Au Poste (Knox). See Vincennes.

Aurora [uh-RAWR-uh] (Dearborn). A post office was established on December 30, 1819. The city, laid out the same year, was named for the Roman goddess of dawn by Judge Jesse Lynch Holman, who, among other things, served on the Indiana Supreme Court, wrote fiction and poetry, and helped organize the Indiana Historical Society.

Austin [AWS-tuhn] (Scott). The town was laid out on May 3, 1853, and a post office was established on January 10, 1854. The town was named for Austin, Texas, by veterans who were stationed there during the Mexican War. According to a local legend, Austin had a couple of nicknames: "Ivan Morgan, I guess, came from Kentucky. I don't really know. But he was one of the original people who came to Austin and started the food canning factory, which was the town's livelihood. The main reason they built Austin there was because the railroad was coming through there. At that time, North Vernon was probably the largest town in the area, but as the canning factory grew, called Morgan Packing Company, the town grew also. Either everyone in Austin originated in East Kentucky, or their ancestors came from there. One of Austin's nicknames is 'Little Kentucky' or 'Pistol City.' Now a reason they call it Pistol City is that in eastern Kentucky you just don't mess with mountain men, and by the same token, you don't mess with mountain folks from Austin, and that's really true. Mountain folks are just real easy going. They work hard for a living, and they are generally very close to their families. And if you mess with one person, you've got the whole family to deal with. They really stick together" (ISUFA).

Avery [AY-vuh-ree; AY-vree] (Clinton). A post office was established on May 9, 1879; closed on June 30, 1903. The name is for a local family. Jacob Avery, a farmer, settled here around 1857.

Avilla [uh-VEL-uh; uh-VIL-uh] (Noble). A post office was established on January 20, 1846, with Noah J. Hill as postmaster. Hill built the first house here and opened a tavern, which apparently attracted most of the early settlers. The town, dating from around 1835, was incorporated in 1876. Possibly the name was borrowed from Avila, the Spanish city.

Avoca [uh-VO-kuh] (Lawrence). This village was laid out around 1819. A post office was established on February 20, 1856; closed on April 15, 1859; and re-established March 2, 1870. Avoca, ultimately from Vale of Avoca (Wicklow, Ireland), is a fairly common place name, as it is found in nine states as well as in Australia, Canada, New Zealand, South Africa, and Tasmania. The Hoosier community supposedly was named by Dr. Winthrop Foote for the Irish place name in the fourth stanza of Thomas Moore's poem "The Meeting of Waters." Foote said the cold springs here reminded him of the poem:

Sweet vale of Avoca! how calm could I rest
In thy bosom of shade, with the friends I love best,

Where the storms that we feel in this cold world should cease,
And our hearts, like thy waters, be mingled in peace.

Avon [AY-vahn] (Hendricks). This community was settled about 1830. A post office was established as Smootsdell, for John Smoot, on April 17, 1868. The post office was changed to Avon on November 28, 1870, for a railroad station; closed on October 31, 1902. Avon Station is a variant name. Found in seventeen states, Avon is a very popular place name in the United States. Avon also is found throughout the United States in conjunction with a number of place-name generics, such as Avonburg, which follows. Virtually all of these names come from the English river made famous by its association with Shakespeare. Former names of post offices near Avon were Hampton, q.v., and White Lick, q.v.

Avonburg [AY-vahn-berg] (Switzerland). Soapville was an earlier name of this village. Apparently the current name is for the English river associated with Shakespeare. Cf. Avon.

Aylesworth [AYLZ-werth] (Fountain). A post office was established on June 2, 1884; closed on January 2, 1907.* The village was named for its founder (WPA).

Aylesworth [AYLZ-werth] (Porter). This village was named for Giles Aylesworth, local schoolteacher.

Ayrshire [ASH-er] (Pike). A post office was established on September 22, 1886; closed on July 14, 1917. Probably the name comes from the county in Scotland.

Azalia [uh-ZAYL-yuh] (Bartholomew). The village was platted first on April 1,

1831. A post office was established on July 11, 1833; closed on September 15, 1934. The name is for the flower, though apparently it is commendatory rather than descriptive. According to local history, the namers hoped the community would be pure, undefiled, and worthy of its namesake.

 **B**

Babcock [BAB-kahk] (Porter). A post office was established on January 7, 1889; closed on November 14, 1904. The name honors the local Babcock family, early settlers (WPA).

Bacon [BAY-kuhn] (Orange). A post office was established on July 27, 1904; closed on January 31, 1935.*

Badger Grove [baj-er GROV] (White). A post office was established as Badger on September 19, 1881; closed on November 10, 1900.* Allegedly this village was so named because there were a lot of badgers in a grove located about fifty yards northwest of the present site of the village (WPA).

Bainbridge [BAYN-brij] (Putnam). This town was laid out on March 5, 1831, by Levi A. Pearcy and named for naval hero William Bainbridge by Colonel John Osborne. A post office was established on February 13, 1835.

Bainter Town [BAYN-ter town] (Elkhart). This village has had several names, all associated with mills here: Wylands Mills, simply The Mills, and Bainter Town. In 1831 a man named Ingle built a sawmill near the Benton and Jackson township line, and soon after, Jonathan Wyland built another sawmill around which this village developed. Wyland sold his mill to a man named Bainter. Other owners of the mills included William Reddin, and the mills were called the New Paris Mills (cf. New Paris) when he owned them.

Baker [BAY-ker] (Sullivan). This village was established as a mining community around 1920 and named for the nearby Baker coal mine (WPA).

Bakers Corner [bay-kerz KAWR-ner] (Hamilton). This village was laid out in 1831. A post office was established on February 7, 1873; closed on December 31, 1900.* Apparently the name was borrowed from a local family name, as the second postmaster was William H. Baker, and the fourth postmaster was Anthony Baker. A variant spelling is Bakers Corners.

Bakers Corners (Tippecanoe). See Stockwell.

Balaka (Randolph). See South Salem.

Balbec [BAL-bek] (Jay). A post office was established on October 27, 1865; closed on January 13, 1919. Supposedly the name, sometimes rendered as Balbee, is a misspelling of Baalbec, or Baalbek, the ancient Syrian city, once a Roman colony and famous for its ruins.

Baldridge [BAWLD-rij] (Sullivan). According to an oral account, this village was named for a local coal mine (ISUFA).

Baldwin [BAWLD-win; BAWLD-wuhn] (Allen). A post office was established on February 15, 1890; closed on November 15, 1917. The village was platted by Timothy Baldwin in 1890 and named for him.

Baldwin Heights [bawld-wuhn HE-YETS] (Gibson). This village was platted by Edwin J. Baldwin and named for him.

Ballengers (Tipton). See Sharpsville.

Ballstown [BAWLZ-town] (Ripley). A post office was established on February 14, 1844; closed on March 31, 1904. The post office was named for Samuel Ball, the first postmaster, who platted the village on May 15, 1848.

Baltimore (Porter). See Boone Grove.

Bancrofts Mill (Saint Joseph). See Osceola.

Bandon [BAN-duhn] (Perry). A post office was established on August 22, 1905; closed on March 31, 1955. This place name is found in Australia and Oregon as well as Indiana. The name comes from the county in Ireland. A local folk poem about Bandon, Indiana, goes:

> The Bandon town,
> The Boudart Street,
> The Massey Hotel,
> And nothing to eat. [ISUFA]

Banner Mills [ban-er MILZ] (Parke). A post office was established on November 23, 1855; closed on March 20, 1863.

Bannersville (Bartholomew). See Waynesville.

Banquo [BAN-kwo] (Huntington). Originally this community was called Priceville, for a post office that was established on April 19, 1871, and named for the local Price family. This post office was closed on January 30, 1874. Another post office was established as Banquo on July 13, 1882; closed on November 14, 1903. The village was platted in 1906. Supposedly a local supernatural legend inspired the naming of the village Banquo for the ghost in Shakespeare's *Macbeth*. The name *Banquo* also is found in a number of old genealogies of Scottish kings.

Banta [BAN-tuh; BAN-tee] (Morgan). A post office was established on November 22, 1883; closed on March 31, 1904. This village probably was named for the local Banta family.

Barbee [BAHR-bee] (Kosciusko). Big Barbee Lake and Little Barbee Lake, which appear as Barbers Lake on the 1876 Baskin, Forster map, are nearby and were named for a local family. Willard Barbee laid out nearby Oswego, q.v. A post office was established on March 30, 1898; closed on July 15, 1898.

Barbers Mills (Wells). See Rockford (Wells).

Barbersville [BAHR-berz-vil] (Jefferson). A post office, with Timothy Barber as the first postmaster and named for the local Barber family, was established on December 7, 1826; moved to nearby Canaan, q.v., on November 29, 1838. Another post office in Ripley County was established as Buchanans Station on February 12, 1840; moved to Jefferson County and Barbersville on June 27, 1848; and closed on May 31, 1906. The town was laid out on December 18, 1848, by Enoch Bray and Thomas H. Bray. A variant spelling is Barboursville.

Barce [bahrs] (Benton). A post office was established on June 12, 1897; closed on July 15, 1907. The village was founded around 1890 and named for Lyman Barce.

Bargersville [BAHR-gerz-vil] (Johnson). This village, first called New Bargersville, was named for Old Bargersville, q.v., formerly called Bargersville, too. It was founded in 1906 when a railroad came through here. A post office was established on January 22, 1908.

Bark Works (Switzerland). See Quercus Grove.

Barnard [BAHR-nerd] (Putnam). This village was laid out in 1876 by William DeMoss, the first postmaster. A post office was established as Fort Red on March 1, 1876; changed to Barnard on March 29, 1880; closed on June 30, 1912. Fort Red received its name for a red schoolhouse here. When a railroad depot was established, it was called Barnard for Calvin Barnard, on whose farm it was established.

Barren (Harrison). See Ramsey.

Barrett [BEHR-uht] (Posey). A variant name is Kilroy for a post office established on October 26, 1895; closed on July 14, 1906.

Barrows Inn (Clay). See Ashboro.

Bartholomew County [bahr-THAHL-uh-myoo]. This county was organized in 1821 and named for General Joseph Bartholomew, who was wounded at the Battle of Tippecanoe and was cosponsor of the county when it was established. John Tipton also was instrumental in establishing the county. Seat: Columbus.

Bartle [BAHR-tuhl] (Washington). A post office was established on December 20, 1880; closed on June 30, 1906.

Bartlettsville [BAHRT-luhts-vil] (Lawrence). The village, which also has been called Bartlett, was named for Samuel J. Bartlett, who platted it on January 19, 1860. A post office was established on August 17, 1886; closed on October 31, 1905. Steven A. Bartlett became postmaster in 1889.

Bartonia [bahr-TO-nee-uh; bahr-TON-yuh] (Randolph). This village was platted on October 1, 1849, and named for the proprietor, Edward Barton. A post office was established on September 14, 1852; closed on May 15, 1903. Variant names are Barton and Jacksonboro.

Bartons Location [bahr-tuhnz lo-KAY-shuhn] (Pike). This village probably was named for the local Barton family, who owned property in this county and in the adjoining county, Gibson.

Bartsville (Ripley). See Batesville.

Bascom (Ohio). See Aberdeen.

Bascom Corner [bas-kuhm KAWR-ner] (Ohio). This village was named for a local family.

Bass Lake [bas LAYK] (Starke). A post office named Bass Lake, for an adjoining lake of the same name, was established in September 1892; changed to Bass on August 28, 1894; and closed on August 31, 1948. The adjoining 1,345-acre lake, third-largest natural lake in Indiana, was named for the large number of black bass in it. Cedar Lake is a variant name of the lake.

Bass Station [bas STAY-shuhn] (Starke). This village was established as a railroad station about a mile south of the village of Bass Lake, for which it was named. A variant name is Bass Lake Station.

Batesville [BAYTS-vil] (Ripley). This city was platted on November 3, 1852, by the Callahan Trust Company and named for the surveyor, Joshua Bates, Callahan's chief engineer. A post office was established on December 2, 1853. Variant spellings have been Bartsville and Bates Ville. Middleton, a variant name, is for a town laid out here on June 5, 1866, and now part of Batesville.

Bath (Franklin). See New Bath and Old Bath.

Battle Ground [BAT-uhl grownd] (Tippecanoe). A post office was established here on July 8, 1835, when it was moved from nearby Harrisonville. The town was laid out in March 1858. The name comes from the Battle of Tippecanoe, which was fought here. A variant spelling is Battleground, and a variant name is

Prophets Town, also spelled Prophets-town. Prophets Town was established in 1808 by Tecumseh and his half brother, Tenskwatawa, "The Prophet," and burned after the Battle of Tippecanoe.

Bay (Fulton). See Lake Bruce.

Beal [beel] (Knox). A post office was established here on September 19, 1891; closed on September 30, 1901. A variant spelling is Beall.

Beanblossom [BEEN-blaw-suhm] (Brown). This village was platted in 1833 and first named Georgetown for the first settler and founder, George Grove. A post office named Bean Blossom, for the nearby stream of the same name, was established on July 8, 1842; closed on Au-gust 15, 1911. The Miami name for Beanblossom Creek was Ko-chio-ah-se-pe, which also was the Miami name for the Saint Joseph River and means "Bean River"; consequently, the name seems to be a translation of the Indian name. One traditional account of the naming, though, says in 1812 a man by the name of Bean Blossom nearly drowned trying to swim the creek, and General Tipton named the stream for him. Another traditional tale holds that Captain Beanblossom was an officer in Harrison's army and nearly drowned in the stream in 1811. According to other traditional accounts, the name comes from wild bean plants that grew along the stream or for beans that early settlers raised as their main crop.

Bear Branch [BEHR branch] (Ohio). This village, settled as early as 1815, was laid out in 1845 by Jonathan Cole, who named it Coles Corner, sometimes spelled Coles Corners. The village also has been called Freedom, apparently a commendatory name. A post office named Bear Branch, for nearby Bear Creek, was established on August 28, 1849; closed on February 27, 1937.

Bear Creek (Brown). See Trevlac.

Bear Creek (Jay). See Bloomfield and West Liberty (Jay).

Beard [beerd] (Clinton). This village was established around 1839 and named for the local Beard family. In 1834 John Beard entered 160 acres of government land here. A post office was established on July 7, 1888; closed on June 30, 1905.

Beardstown [BEERDZ-town] (Pulaski). This village was laid out in 1901 and named for Beardstown, Illinois. A post office named Beardstown was established on August 5, 1903; closed on October 31, 1905. A variant name, Voltz, for the man on whose farm the town was built, was applied to another post office established on October 2, 1915.

Beattys Corner [bay-deez KAWR-ner] (La Porte). This village, also called Beattys Corners, was laid out in 1842 by James Whittem and named for a local family. Only one lot was sold, so George Selkirk bought the whole town and added it to his farm. Around 1833 John Beatty, one of the earliest settlers, with Purdy Smith established a sawmill in the southwest corner of Coolspring Township.

Beaver City [bee-ver SIT-ee; bee-ver SID-ee] (Newton). A post office, named for its location on Beaver Prairie, was established on February 19, 1866; closed on December 31, 1913. The village was platted on March 23, 1893. According to the WPA files, "The first settlers were

hunters and trappers who caught many beavers along the streams and in the marshes of Beaver Prairie."

Beaver Dam [bee-ver DAM] (Kosciusko). Julia Burns named this village for the dam here of the same name. According to the WPA files, the village is located "on the dam of the same name. The dam was built on the site of a large beaver dam, on a creek of the same name." A post office was located here on January 30, 1844, at the house of Samuel Rickel, first postmaster. The spelling of the post office name was changed to Beaverdam on October 10, 1894, and the post office was closed on June 29, 1901.

Becks Grove [beks GROV] (Brown). A post office established as Becks Grove on August 7, 1868, was changed to Beck on June 8, 1895; closed on October 31, 1905.* The name comes from the local Beck family. According to an oral account, the place was named for David Beck, early settler, who came to Brown County from Lawrence County in 1850 (WPA). John Beck was the first postmaster, and later John B. Beck and James Beck served as postmasters.

Becks Mill [beks MIL] (Washington). This village, founded around 1808, was named for the Beck family, who for several generations operated a mill here. A variant spelling is Becks Mills. A post office established on August 3, 1858, with David Beck as postmaster, closed on June 15, 1900.

Beckville [BEK-vil] (Montgomery). In 1928 Solomon Beck and others took out patents for land, and Beckville, named for him, was established later on land owned by Beck. A post office named Beckville was established on June 14, 1860; closed on August 17, 1865.

Bedford [BED-ferd] (county seat, Lawrence). This city was platted on March 30, 1825, and named by Joseph Rawlins for Bedford County, Tennessee. A post office was established in April 1825.

Beech Grove [beech GROV] (Marion). A post office established as Ingallston, for a railroad official, on November 11, 1879, was moved to Beech Grove on March 22, 1883. The city was incorporated in 1906. The name was borrowed from Beech Grove Farm, which was named for a wooded area here.

Beech Grove (Rush). See Arlington.

Beechwood [BEECH-wud] (Crawford). A post office, named for a large beech grove here (WPA), was established on June 22, 1875; closed on May 10, 1963.*

Bee Creek (Wells). See Ossian.

Beehunter [BEE-huhnt-er] (Greene). This village was named for a local stream, Beehunter Creek, allegedly so named because along its banks was a good place to find honey. There was a marsh here called Beehunter, too. According to an oral account, "It's called Beehunter because all that marshland was just covered with flowers in the summertime, and all the bee hunters would go there to see which way the bees went when they went back to their trees. They would see which way the bees went and then they would locate the right trees and get the honey. Do you know how they usually did it? Well, we'd get a jar of syrup and pour it out and draw the bees to it. Then we'd watch them to see which way they went. Sometimes you had to follow them for miles, and sometimes we'd have to use another jar of syrup before

we found the trees. I suppose that the marsh was a sort of starting point" (ISUFA). It is also said that the stream was named for a Piankishaw chief named Beehunter.

Beelers Station (Marion). See Maywood.

Bee Ridge [bee RIJ] (Clay). This community, dating from about 1828, was one of the earliest settlements in Clay County. It was named by early settlers for the many bee trees found along the ridge on the south side of Otter Creek, where the community is located.

Beesons [BEE-suhnz] (Wayne). This village, earlier called Beesontown and sometimes called Beeson, sprang up around several businesses owned by the local Beeson family. Three brothers—Silas H., Benjamin Franklin, and Ithamar Beeson—operated a gristmill, tannery, and other businesses here. A post office called Beeson was located here on August 25, 1865; closed on November 22, 1890.* The second postmaster was Florence Beeson.

Behlmer Corner [bel-mer KAWR-ner] (Ripley). This village was laid out on September 2, 1844, as Lynnville by James H. Oliver.

Belknap [BEL-nap] (Vanderburgh). Possibly this village was named for the American general and politician William Worth Belknap (1829–90). A variant name is Belknap Station.

Belle Union [bel YOON-yuhn] (Putnam). A post office was established on April 6, 1870; closed on May 14, 1906. The village was platted on March 6, 1873. The name appears to be commendatory, though it is thought to have come from the local Bell family and the church they attended, Union Valley Baptist Church, founded in 1869.

Belleview [BEL-vyoo] (Jefferson). A post office called Mud Lick was established on March 2, 1855, but the name was changed to the more commendatory Belleview on March 15, 1890. The post office was closed on May 31, 1906. Allegedly, a saloon fight made the participants muddy, so the village was called Mud Lick (WPA). According to the WPA files, "Some of the old citizens got together and decided to name their village Belleview, meaning 'beautiful to look upon.'"

Belleville [BEL-vil] (Hendricks). The village was laid out in 1829 by William H. Hinton, Lazarus B. Wilson, and Obediah Harris. A post office was established on December 29, 1831; closed on October 31, 1902. Belville was an earlier spelling.

Bellfountain [bel-FOWN-tuhn] (Jay). This village was platted on October 29, 1851. An earlier spelling of the name was Bellefontaine, so perhaps the name is a transfer from Belgium via Ohio, though the name also has commendatory value. Another plausible explanation is that the name is descriptive of ebullitions on nearby Limberlost Creek. The post office, called Hector, was established on May 28, 1851; closed on May 31, 1904.*

Bellmore [BEL-mawr] (Parke). A post office named Bellmore was established on January 21, 1852. According to tradition, the village earlier was known as Northampton, sometimes spelled North Hampton, for the city in Massachusetts, but the name was changed in 1852, allegedly for Thomas Moore's beautiful daughters; a visitor, General George K.

Steele, is said to have admired them and suggested the town be named Belle Moore in their honor. According to one version of the local legend, "The small town of Bellmore was originally platted as Northampton by a homesick settler who had come from Connecticut. Then he discovered that Indiana had another Northampton. It was called Northampton for a while anyway until General George Steele happened to be out there visiting in the home of a man named Moore. Mr. Moore had some daughters who were unusually beautiful and charming, so General Steele remarked to Mr. Moore that 'This town should be named Belle Moore in honor of your daughters'" (ISUFA). It's possible, though, that this place name is a combination of the specific "Bell," for the personal name, and the Gaelic generic "more," as in Inishmore.

Belmont [BEL-mahnt] (Brown). A post office was established on July 7, 1884; closed on December 31, 1916. This is a common place name in the United States and abroad and may be a transfer.

Belmont [BEL-mahnt] (Marion). This community also was called West Indianapolis. Cf. Belmont (Brown).

Belshaw [BEL-shaw] (Lake). Once called Belshaw Station, the village was named for the Belshaw family who owned land here. William Belshaw, a native of England, settled near here in 1836 and developed a large farm, and George Belshaw settled here in 1842.

Ben Davis [ben DAY-vuhs] (Marion). This village, previously called Ben Davis Station, was named for Benjamin Davis, a railroad superintendent who supervised the building of the railroad station here in 1877. A post office was established on May 8, 1877; closed on January 31, 1906.

Benefiel Corner [BEN-uh-feel KAWR-ner] (Sullivan). This village was named for the local Benefiel family. William Benefiel, a veteran who died in 1863, and other members of his family are buried in nearby Benefiel Cemetery.

Bengal [BENG-guhl; BENG-gol] (Shelby). Never platted, this village probably was named for the state in India. A post office was established on June 1, 1881; closed on December 6, 1902.

Benham [BEN-uhm] (Ripley). This village was founded around 1857 and formerly called Benhams Station and Benhams Store, for the Benham family here. A post office called Benham Store, with John Benham, Jr., as postmaster, was established on March 27, 1866; changed to Benham on April 10, 1888; and closed on February 28, 1934. Lincolnville, for Abraham Lincoln, is another variant name.

Bennetts Switch [ben-uhts SWICH] (Miami). Founded around 1854 (WPA), this village was established as a station on the Lake Erie and Western Railroad, on a tract of land belonging to Baldwin N. Bennett and named for him. A post office, with Baldwin N. Bennett as postmaster, was established on May 19, 1862; closed on July 15, 1935. Variant names and spellings have been Bennets, Bennett, and Bennetts.

Bennettsville [BEN-uhts-vil] (Clark). The village, first called New Town, was laid out in September 1838, and a post office was established on February 23, 1847. Supposedly the name was formed from the Christian name of the first merchant, Benedict Nugent.

Bennington [BEN-ing-tuhn] (Switzerland). This village was laid out in 1847. A post office called Slawson, for a local family, was established on March 7, 1838. On July 11, 1848, the post office was changed to Bennington, possibly a transfer from Vermont.

Benton [BENT-uhn] (Elkhart). Matthew Boyd settled here in 1828 and opened an inn in 1830. The village was laid out in 1832 by Captain Henry Beane and named for Thomas Hart Benton, senator from Missouri. A post office was established on October 28, 1835.

Benton (Steuben). See Hudson.

Benton County [BENT-uhn]. This county was organized in 1840 and named for Thomas Hart Benton, senator from Missouri. This county is famous for its rich farmland and as the birthplace of the famous standardbred trotter Dan Patch (1896–1916), who achieved legendary status because he never lost a race. Seat: Fowler.

Bentonville [BENT-uhn-vil] (Fayette). Around 1819–1822 several families from New England settled in this area, and the community was known locally as Yankeetown. A post office, established as Plum Orchard on November 28, 1827, was changed to Bentonsville on February 13, 1838. The village was platted on August 7, 1838, by Joseph Dale. The name honors Senator Thomas Hart Benton of Missouri.

Benwood [BEN-wud] (Clay). This village was laid out in 1869 and supposedly named for Ben Davis, an official with the Vandalia Railroad. A post office was established on June 17, 1881; closed on January 6, 1882.

Berlien [ber-LEEN] (Steuben). This village was founded around 1908 and named for the local Berlein family (WPA). A variant spelling is Berlein.

Berne [bern] (Adams). This city was laid out in 1871 and named by Joe Crawford, a county commissioner, for Bern, Switzerland, in honor of Swiss Mennonites who settled here in 1852. A post office was established on November 27, 1872. Bern is a variant spelling.

Berryville (Knox). See Wheatland.

Bethany (Bartholomew). See South Bethany.

Bethany [BETH-uh-nee] (Morgan). Members of the Disciples of Christ Church established Bethany Park here in 1884 to hold camp meetings before they built a large tabernacle, hotel, and restaurant. Later the community became a resort area. The village of Bethany, established in 1955, was named for the park.

Bethany [BETH-uh-nee] (Parke). A post office named for the biblical village, possibly via a local church, was established on May 11, 1852; closed on February 13, 1873.

Bethel [BETH-uhl] (Delaware). A variant name of this village is Stout, for Isaac Stout, who was a merchant here for many years.

Bethel (Washington). See Livonia.

Bethel [BETH-uhl] (Wayne). This village was settled in 1817 by the Harlan family from Kentucky. A post office, named for a local Christian church organized in 1821, was established on January 7, 1850; closed on May 15, 1915.

Bethleham (Union). See Philomath.

Bethlehem [BETH-lee-hem; BETH-luh-ham] (Clark). This village was platted in 1812 and, according to the WPA files, probably named for Bethlehem, Pennsylvania. An Indiana Territory post office was established here on March 6, 1816.

Bethlehem (Hamilton). See Carmel.

Bethlehem (Knox). See Freelandville.

Beverly Shores [BEV-er-lee SHAWRZ] (Porter). This town was developed as a residential and resort village on Lake Michigan in 1934. A post office was established on May 16, 1935. According to the WPA files, Frederick Bartlett established the community around 1928 and named it for his daughter, Beverly.

Bibler (Lake). See Winfield (Lake).

Bicknell [BIK-nuhl] (Knox). A post office was established on November 30, 1868, and named for local merchant John Bicknell, who laid out the town on October 1, 1869. Another local merchant, George W. Fuller, owned land here before the town was laid out. From the 1870s through the 1940s the town served as a coal mining center.

Bigrest (Decatur). See Harper.

Big Saint Joseph Station (Saint Joseph). See South Bend.

Big Springs [big springz] (Boone). A post office was established as Big Springs on December 4, 1883; changed to Bigsprings on November 22, 1894; closed on November 15, 1900.*

Big Springs (Crawford). See Marengo.

Billie Creek Village [bil-ee kreek VIL-ij] (Parke). This reconstructed historical village covering seventy-five acres was named for a local stream, Billy Creek, a variant of Williams Creek.

Billingsville [BIL-ingz-vil] (Union). A post office, named for the local Billings family, was established on May 8, 1833; closed on October 14, 1903. The village also has been called Billings.

Billtown [BIL-town] (Clay). Settled around 1826, this village, formerly called Williamstown, sometimes spelled Williamtown, developed after the National Road, now S.R. 340, was completed west of Brazil. The Van Buren post office also was established just west of Brazil on May 30, 1835, in a private residence. After a few months, the post office was moved to Williamstown, now Billtown, but the post office, which was closed on August 17, 1865, always was called Van Buren.

Bingen (Adams). See Williams.

Bippus [BIP-uhs; BIF-uhs] (Huntington). A post office named Bippus was established on August 23, 1883. The village was platted on July 25, 1885. The name honors George J. Bippus, who secured the right-of-way for the railroad here. Earlier the railroad station was called West Point. Allegedly West Point was named by William Stults, who taught singing schools in the county, including one at a schoolhouse where Bippus now stands. This was his "most western" singing school, so Stults referred to it as West Point. When the post office was established, the name was changed to Bippus because there already was a post office named West Point in Tippecanoe County.

Birchim [BER-chuhm] (La Porte). This village was established as a resort community and named for the local Birchem family, "presumably for Abraham Birchem, a settler there, or his son, John A. Birchem" (WPA).

Birdseye [BERDZ-eye] (Dubois). A post office named Birdseye was established on June 24, 1856. The town was platted on January 24, 1880. According to a local legend reported in the WPA files, several names were suggested but rejected by the Post Office Department. Finally Bird, for Reverend Bird Johnson, postmaster at Worth (now Schnellville), was suggested, and he was invited to help select the post office site. When he decided on the location, he said, "This spot suits Bird's eye to a T-y-tee." Neither Worth nor Schnellville had a postmaster named Bird Johnson, though, so apparently this account is apocryphal. According to another account, the town was "named for Rev. Benjamin T. (Bird) Goodman, who was my great uncle" (ISUFA). It seems likely that the town was named for Reverend Benjamin Talbott "Bird" Johnson, who served as state legislator. Variant names and spelling have been Bird, Birdsey, and Birds Eye.

Birmingham [BERM-ing-ham] (Miami). A post office named Birmingham was established on June 15, 1869, with Isaac Caulk as postmaster; closed on June 15, 1901. The village was laid out by Isaac Caulk and Solomon Jones on November 20, 1868. A small railroad station, with Caulk also as the railroad agent, was located here, but the railroad closed the station because Caulk refused to advertise and sell tickets for Sunday excursions. The name probably comes from the city in England.

Blackford County [BLAK-ferd]. This county, Indiana's fourth smallest, was formed from part of Jay County in 1838, organized in 1839, and named for Isaac Blackford, speaker of the first state legislature and pioneer justice of the Indiana Supreme Court. Seat: Hartford City.

Blackhawk (Shelby). See Mount Auburn (Shelby).

Blackhawk [BLAK-hawk] (Vigo). A post office was established on February 19, 1901, and named for the famous Sauk chief, Ma-ka-ta-mi-ci-kiak-kiak, "Black Sparrow Hawk"; closed on July 30, 1927.* According to the WPA files, however, a church here was called the Blackhawk because of dissension within it over the slavery issue during the Civil War. A variant spelling is Black Hawk.

Blackhawk Beach [blak-hawk BEECH] (Porter). This community, named for the Sauk chief Blackhawk, was laid out in 1928.

Black Oak [blak ok] (Daviess). This village was settled around 1819 and named for the black oak timber on the site (WPA).

Black Oak [blak ok] (Lake). A post office was established as Blackoak on August 29, 1899; closed on August 14, 1905.

Blacks (Parke). See Rosedale.

Blaine [blayn] (Jay). A flag station on the Lake Erie and Western Railroad, this village was platted on ten acres by R. T. Hammons on January 1, 1883, and named for James G. Blaine, presidential candidate in 1884. The post office was established on July 14, 1882; closed on April 30, 1914. Blane is a variant spelling.

Blair (DeKalb). See Saint Joe.

Blairsville [BLEHRZ-vil] (Posey). This village was laid out on July 4, 1837, by Ebenezer Phillips and Stephen Blair, for whom it was named. A post office, with Stephen Blair as postmaster, was established on May 26, 1838; closed on March 5, 1894.

Blakesburg [BLAYKS-berg] (Putnam). A post office named Blakesburgh was established on May 26, 1828; closed on October 19, 1839. According to an oral account, "Blakesburg was named for a man named Blake. It should have been 'Fosher-something' because John Fosher [an ancestor of the informant] built the first cabin there" (ISUFA).

Blanford [BLAN-ferd] (Vermillion). This village was platted on October 26, 1912, and named for L. S. Blanford, a local landowner. A post office was established on June 16, 1915.

Blocher [BLACH-er] (Scott). The village was laid out in 1860 and named for Daniel Blocher, founder. A post office named Holman Station, locally called Holman, was established on May 13, 1870; the name was changed to Blocher on March 23, 1888; and the post office became a rural station of Scottsburg on September 10, 1965. Jefferson H. Blocher was postmaster from 1871 to 1874.

Bloomer [BLOOM-er] (Madison). Earlier called Bloomer Station, this community was named for the local Bloomer family.

Bloomfield [BLOOM-feeld] (county seat, Greene). The town was laid out on May 11, 1824, and named by Dr. Hallet B. Dean for his birthplace, Bloomfield, New Jersey. A local legend reported in the WPA files says early settlers named the town Bloomfield because they saw blooming fields here. A post office called Bloomfield was established on May 28, 1825. A variant name is Bloomington.

Bloomfield [BLOOM-feeld] (Jay). This village was founded before 1840 (WPA). A post office called Bear Creek (cf. West Liberty [Jay]), for the township in which it was located, was established on February 7, 1840; closed on April 5, 1875.

Bloomfield (Parke). See Bloomingdale.

Bloomfield [BLOOM-feeld] (Spencer). The village was laid out in August 1853 by James McCoy. A post office called Grass was established on January 21, 1878; closed on December 31, 1904.* Yearbyville is a variant name.

Bloomingdale [BLOOM-ing-dayl] (Parke). This town was settled around 1823 by Quakers and named Elevatis (sometimes spelled Elevalis, Elevatus, and Ellevalas) for the elevation where their meetinghouse was built. In 1827 the name was changed to Bloomfield, supposedly because a Quaker leader wanted a name with more "bloom" in it. According to another account, "After different names had been suggested and none chosen, one man said it should be *Bloom* something. After much serious thought, *field* was added to it. The name was soon changed to Bloomingdale" (WPA). When a post office was established on March 28, 1860, the name was changed to Bloomingdale to avoid confusion with another post office named Bloomfield in Greene County. Java is another variant name.

Blooming Grove [bloom-ing GROV] (Franklin). This village was laid out on July 23, 1816, and originally called Greensboro for a town in Maryland by the founders, who were from Maryland. When a post office was established on May 18, 1832, the village was renamed for Blooming Grove Township because there already was a post office named Greensboro in Henry County. The post office was closed on April 2, 1906.

Bloomingport [BLOOM-ing-pawrt] (Randolph). This village was platted on September 30, 1829, and formerly called Bloomingsport.

Bloomingsburgh (Fulton). See Talma.

Bloomington (Greene). See Bloomfield.

Bloomington [BLOOM-ing-tuhn] (county seat, Monroe). This city was settled around 1815 and platted on April 10, 1818. A post office was established on February 15, 1825. According to local legend, the name was "suggested when a group of early settlers, gazing from an elevation commanding a view of the site, was impressed by the flowers and foliage" (WPA). Another oral tradition says the name honors an early settler, William Bloom (ISUFA).

Blountsville [BLUHNTS-vil] (Henry). This town was platted in July 1832 and named for the proprietor, Andrew D. Blount. A post office was established on January 22, 1835; closed on May 8, 1964.

Blue [bloo] (Ohio). A post office was established here on March 15, 1890; closed on October 15, 1907.

Bluecast [BLOO-kast] (Allen). Supposedly the name of this village is descriptive of a nearby spring. Traditional accounts say that a Mr. Gouge name the village.

Blue Creek (Franklin). See Klemmes Corner.

Bluegrass [BLOO-gras] (Fulton). A post office was established as Blue Grass on March 10, 1851; changed to Bluegrass on October 26, 1893; and closed on April 30, 1906. Marshtown, for a local family, is a variant name of the village.

Blue Lick [bloo lik] (Clark). A post office, named for nearby Blue Lick Creek, was established on February 11, 1837; closed on May 31, 1905. The creek was named for the blue slate forming its bed.

Blue Ridge [BLOO rij] (Shelby). This village was platted on August 18, 1835, by Andrew Snyder and Isaac Springer and named Cynthiana, sometimes spelled Cynthiann, for the town in Kentucky. A post office established on January 4, 1847, was named Blue Ridge by James Marshall for his home in Kentucky because there was another Cynthiana in Posey County. The post office was closed on June 15, 1907.*

Blue River [BLOO riv-er] (Washington). A post office named Blue River, for the nearby stream of the same name, was established on July 2, 1893; closed on April 30, 1904. Blue is a descriptive name applied to a number of streams and lakes in Indiana.

Bluff Creek [bluhf KREEK] (Johnson). A post office named Bluff Creek, for a nearby stream of the same name, was established on June 24, 1856; changed to Bluffcreek on July 12, 1895; and closed on January 14, 1904. The village, which was never platted, was first called Brownstown, for the local Brown family, early settlers (WPA). According to the WPA files, "From the best authority obtained, the place [Bluff Creek] got its name from the fact that the creek runs by a bluff, which is one-half mile to the south."

Bluff Point [bluhf POYNT] (Jay). Supposedly this community first was called Iowa because a number of settlers in the area came from that state. A post office called Van was established on December 17, 1840; closed on April 14, 1849. Another post office called Bluff Point, apparently named for its location on a small hill (WPA), was established on September 19, 1853; closed on May 31, 1904.* The village was laid out in 1854.

Bluffs [bluhfs] (Johnson). This village first was laid out in September 1821 and was named for the Bluffs, a nearby cliff. Thomas Lee was the proprietor. Before the War of 1812, the French from Vincennes established temporary trading posts here with the Delawares. Christopher Ladd, who wanted to establish the state capital at the Bluffs, settled here around 1819 and kept a tavern before the county was organized. The village also was called Port Royal, for Port Royale, the French name of the trading area, and a post office by that name, with Christopher Ladd as postmaster, was established on July 3, 1824; closed on January 29, 1834. Far West is another variant name, as a village of that name was laid out here in 1833. A post office was established as Far West on May 25, 1835; moved to Waverly, q.v., on September 14, 1855.

Bluffton [BLUHF-tuhn] (county seat, Wells). This city was laid out in March 1838 and named for its location on the bluffs of the south bank of the Wabash River. A post office was established on August 6, 1839.

Bobo (Adams). See Rivare.

Bobtown [BAHB-town] (Jackson). This community must have been established after 1900, because it does not appear on maps of 1878 or 1900.

Boggstown [BAWGZ-town] (Shelby). This village was first platted on June 16, 1838, and called Houghburg for a local family. In 1867 the name was changed to Boggstown, for a pioneer settler, Joseph Boggs, and his family. A post office called Boggstown was established on May 16, 1867; closed on December 31, 1908.

Bogle Corner [bo-guhl KAWR-ner] (Clay). This community was named for the local Bogle family.

Bolivar [BUL-uh-vahr] (Wabash). A post office was established on November 16, 1886; closed on September 7, 1898.* The unplatted village was established as a railroad junction and apparently named for Simon Bolivar, the South American revolutionary hero.

Bonds [bawndz] (Orange). A post office was established on January 8, 1894; closed on May 14, 1906.

Bonnell [BAHN-el] (Dearborn). A post office called Kennedy, for a railroad official (WPA), was established on November 5, 1885; closed on May 31, 1929. According to the WPA files, the present name also is for a railroad official.

Bono [BO-no] (Lawrence). This village, the oldest in the county, was laid out on April 4, 1816, and, according to local legend, was named for a French settler who was driven out of town a few years after settlement (WPA), but local history says the village was named for the Bono brothers, early settlers. The township, also called Bono, in which the village is located, is said to have been named for Nicholas and Charles Bono, "patriots" (WPA). This name also is found in other states, where it is an adaptation of the Latin word for "good." A post office was established on October 15, 1818; closed on February 13, 1904.*

Bono [BO-no] (Vermillion). The village was established in 1848 by Tilly Jenks and others, though it was never platted. The name, found in Lawrence County and in other states, may be commendatory, meaning "good." The nearby post office was called Toronto, q.v.

Boone County [boon]. Organized in 1830, this county was named for the famous frontiersman Daniel Boone. There is a legend that this county is swampy and that people living here have webbed feet: "Boone County had the reputation of being one of the swampiest counties in the state of Indiana. Every night from early spring clear through the summer you could hear the frogs in every creek and field pond in the county. It was like a constant dull roar so that pretty soon you just got used to it and didn't hear it anymore. The story started going around in the surrounding counties that people who lived in Boone County had webbed feet, and if a Boonite visited another county, he was always asked to show everybody his feet. When the first test gas well was being drilled in the county, the story got started that a wagon tire and a rubber boot had been found at a depth of 100 feet" (ISUFA). Seat: Lebanon.

Boone Grove [boon GROV] (Porter). This village, named for a local family, was founded about 1857 when a store was established here by Joseph Janes. For a time the community was known as Baltimore. A post office established in this county as Jumbo on June 14, 1883, was changed to Boone Grove on July 20, 1883.

Boonville [BOON-vil] (county seat, Warrick). This city was laid out in Boon Township on May 15, 1818. Both the city and township were named for the Boon family. Ratliff Boon, early settler and prominent politician, was instrumental in locating the county seat here. According to an oral tradition, "Boonville gets its name from the Boon family. Ratliff Boon, the first representative to the legislature from Boonville, established the first township. The town of Boonville was supposedly named after Jesse Boon, Ratliff's father, because of his contributions to finding the site of the town. Jesse owned the land and gave it to the commissioners to start the city of Boonville. Most people of Boonville believe the town to be named after Ratliff. There are also rumors of the town being named after Daniel Boone. Most of these thoughts have been brought in from others just talking and trying to establish a reason for it being called Boonville" (ISUFA). It is also said that Ratliff was Daniel Boone's cousin (WPA). A post office was established on January 8, 1820. Variant spellings have been Booneville and Boonsville.

Borden [BAWR-duhn] (Clark). A town called New Providence, for Providence, Rhode Island, was laid out in 1817 by Stephen, John, and Asa Borden, and a post office named New Providence was established on May 11, 1826. On January 7, 1891, the post office was changed to Borden, for the local Borden family, who came here from Rhode Island. On February 19, 1891, the post office was changed back to New Providence. On April 19, 1892, the post office was changed again to Borden.

Boston (Harrison). See New Boston.

Boston (Washington). See South Boston.

Boston [BAW-stuhn] (Wayne). This town was platted in 1832 and apparently named for Boston, Massachusetts (WPA). A post office was established on March 21, 1837.

Boston Station (Crawford). See Eckerty.

Boston Store (Montgomery). See Elmdale.

Boswell [BAHZ-wel] (Benton). A post office was established on November 3, 1870, and named for a local family in the cattle business. A pioneer settler was Charles P. Boswell. Among other early landowners were Parnham Boswell and John F. Boswell. The town was laid out on October 27, 1871, by Charles Moore, who sold it to Elizabeth H. Scott, who platted it on July 18, 1872. One informant said that Boswell "is called the hub of the universe" (ISUFA).

Boundary City [BOWN-duh-ree SIT-ee; bown-dree SID-ee] (Jay). A post office, with Daniel Heister as postmaster, was established as Boundary, sometimes spelled Boundry, for its location on an Indian treaty line, on May 11, 1852; closed on July 30, 1904. The village was laid out January 4, 1854.

Bourbon [BER-buhn] (Marshall). A post office was established on September 29, 1843, and named for its location in Bourbon Township, which was named for Bourbon County, Kentucky, former home of the Parks family, who came here in 1836. The village was laid out on April 23, 1853. John F. Parks was the first postmaster.

Bovine (Gibson). See Wheeling.

Bowers [BOW-erz] (Montgomery). A post office called Clousers Mills was established here on August 27, 1861, and named for a local family. Daniel Clouser was the second postmaster. On April 5, 1876, the name was changed to Bowers, for the local Bowers family. Abner Bowers settled near here in 1844 and donated the land for a station, called Bowers Station. The post office was closed on May 31, 1924.

Bowling Green [BO-ling green] (Clay). Bowling Green is the oldest settlement in Clay County, as David Thomas settled here in 1812. A post office was established on September 15, 1825, and the village was laid out in 1827. It is commonly thought that the name was borrowed from Bowling Green, Kentucky, since one of the early settlers, Benjamin Parks, came here from Shelby County, Kentucky, but more likely the village was named for Bowling Green, Virginia, where Parks was born. According to oral tradition, Bowling Green was founded in an unusual way: "How was Bowling Green founded? Well, it's been said that, you know, Spencer was founded first. It's been said that these three boys decided to play leapfrog, you know, from Spencer, and after they went so far, they got tired and quit right here in the heart of Bowling Green. Right then and there they decided to start a town, and it's grown ever since" (ISUFA).

Bowman [BO-muhn] (Pike). This village was named for Jonathan Bowman, who settled in this area in 1838 and owned the property on which the village was established. A post office was established on June 22, 1888; closed on January 31, 1901.

Bowrie (Noble). See Brimfield.

Boxley [BAHKS-lee] (Hamilton). This village was laid out in 1836 and named Boxleytown for the local Boxley family. George Boxley, father of the founders, Addison and Thomas P. Boxley, was an early settler. A post office called Boxley, with Thomas P. Boxley as postmaster, was established on April 13, 1837; closed on April 30, 1907.*

Boydstons Mills (Kosciusko). See North Webster.

Boyleston [BOYLZ-tuhn] (Clinton). The village was named for Louis N. Boyle of Indianapolis who platted the town in 1875. A post office was established on February 27, 1877; closed on January 31, 1951. A variant spelling is Boylestown.

Bracken [BRAK-uhn] (Huntington). This village was platted in 1853 as Claysville, but since there already was a post office named Claysville in Washington County, the name was changed to Bracken, for the Kentucky county, home of the founders. A post office named Bracken was established on July 23, 1868; closed on February 28, 1905.

Brackenridge (Harrison). See Brecken-ridge.

Bradford [BRAD-ferd] (Harrison). This village was laid out on July 20, 1838, by Ulrick H. How, who became the first postmaster when a post office was established on February 13, 1844.

Bramble [BRAM-buhl] (Martin). The village was founded about 1875 and named for local landowners (WPA). "Some fellow named Bramble had a farm up there. He was popular because he played the fiddle" (ISUFA). A post office was established on April 7, 1879; closed on March 15, 1906.

Branchville [BRANCH-vil] (Perry). This village was laid out in 1874. A post office named Oil Creek, for a nearby stream of the same name, was established on June 15, 1864. On May 22, 1878, the post office name was changed to Branchville. The present name comes from the location of the village near the branches of Oil Creek.

Braysville [BRAYZ-vil] (Owen). A post office named Braysville, for the proprietor, Hiram Bray, was established on August 18, 1853; closed on July 20, 1861. Bray had the village surveyed in January 1860.

Braytown [BRAY-town] (Switzerland). A variant name of this community is Craig for the post office established here on September 18, 1849; closed on April 15, 1907. The post office was named for Craig Township, in which it was located, and the township was named for George Craig, early settler.

Brazil [ber-ZIL; bruh-ZIL; BRAY-zil] (county seat, Clay). This city was settled before 1834, laid out on July 4, 1844, by Owen Thorpe, and named for Brazil, South America, which was in the news at the time. A post office, with Owen Thorpe as postmaster, was established on January 25, 1844. Locally, several legends and a place-name joke explain the name:

1. "One of the teachers asked me how Brazil got its name. Well, it got its name when they were laying out the town. A man named Owen Thorpe laid it out, and I guess they were talking about calling it Thorpeville or different things. Well, there was an old newspaper, and Brazil, South America, was having a revolution. So they named it Brazil" (ISUFA).

2. "As I recall, as it was told to me, when Clay County was getting its start, about 120 years ago, the town which was later to be called Brazil was just getting its start. A coal town, I guess you could call it a boom town, and it had about 20,000 to 25,000 people in it. All of these people kept pouring into this town, and it didn't have a name, and they didn't know what to call it, and, of course, it didn't have a mayor, city council, or anything like that. The town existed for a couple of years, and the town just didn't have a name. People just went there. And, as the story goes, a bunch of local men were sitting in a tavern, getting drunk, and they were discussing this problem, and they didn't know what to call the town. So, as it goes, a fellow picked up a local paper, and it said that there was a revolution going on in the country of Brazil in South America. So while they were still drunk, they decided to call the town Brazil" (ISUFA).

3. "There's lots of stories about how Brazil got its name. One story goes like this: When Brazil was first founded, it was by a family called Taylor. And, at first, they had thought about calling the town Taylor; however, they did not re-

ceive the right to do so by the government. So they set out to find a better name. They held a contest. People submitted names, and the best was to be chosen. However, it was at this time that South America was having some turmoil in their country, and a country called Brazil in South America was making the news almost every day. In these days, the oldest family of the community, which was also the family with the most money, literally ran the town and made all of the important decisions. This family particularly liked the name Brazil. So it was agreed that the community would, from then on, be called Brazil" (ISUFA).

4. "In the early days, a man named Bray worked in the train station here. Once when a train came in, the conductor asked for Mr. Bray and was told, 'Bray's ill.' That's how Brazil got its name" (ISUFA).

Breckenridge [BREK-uhn-rij] (Harrison). A post office named Breckenridge was established on May 6, 1858; closed on January 14, 1905.* A variant spelling is Brackenridge.

Bremen [BREE-muhn] (Marshall). A post office called Brothersville, for David Brothers, first postmaster, was established on December 16, 1847, and changed to Bremen on July 28, 1848. The town, formerly called New Bremen, for the city in Germany, by German settlers who settled here around 1836, was platted on October 21, 1851.

Brems [brimz] (Starke). This village was platted in 1881 and named for Louis Brems, a local landowner. A post office established on May 17, 1883, as Nickel Plate, for the railroad, was changed to Brems on May 12, 1911; closed on May 15, 1924.

Brendonwood [BREN-duhn-wud] (Marion). This community was established as a private residential area in 1917 (WPA).

Bretzville [BRETS-vil] (Dubois). This village was laid out in 1866 by William Bretz and named for the Bretz family. A post office called Bretzville was established on August 22, 1866; closed on June 30, 1915.* William Bretz also was the second postmaster, appointed on October 17, 1867. Variant names are Newton and Newtown.

Brewersville [BROO-erz-vil] (Jennings). This village was named for Jacob Brewer, who laid it out on September 1, 1837. A post office was established on January 22, 1844; closed on August 31, 1931.*

Briant (Jay). See Bryant.

Brice [breyes] (Jay). A post office named Brice was established on April 24, 1883; closed on January 15, 1901. The village was platted on November 3, 1886.

Brick Chapel [brik CHAP-uhl] (Putnam). A post office called Brick Chapel was established on April 28, 1873; closed on February 28, 1905.* The village was established around a church built here in the early 1830s and named for it.

Bridgeport [BRIJ-pawrt] (Harrison). This village was laid out in September 1849 by Thomas Joyes and David M. Farnsley, who donated land for the village. A post office named Rock Lick was established in this county on May 1, 1873; changed to Locust Point on December 13, 1875; closed on March 31, 1934.* Bridgeport may be a descriptive name, as this was a shipping port.

Bridgeport [BRIJ-pawrt] (Marion). Probably named for Bridgeport, Connecticut, home of early settlers (WPA), this village was platted on May 17, 1831. A post office was established on June 8, 1832; closed on June 1, 1958.

Bridgeport (Washington). See Fredericksburg.

Bridgeton [BRIJ-tuhn] (Parke). Lockwood and Silliman built the first mill here about 1823. Originally called Lockwood Mills, for the mill owner, the village was platted in 1857. A post office named Bridgeton, was established on October 24, 1849. The present name comes from a timber bridge here over Big Raccoon Creek. Locally the community also was called Sodom, a name suggested by a distillery operating here in the 1820s.

Bright [breyet] (Dearborn). A post office called Bright was established on June 2, 1847; closed on May 14, 1904. A variant name is Bunkuin.

Brighton [BREYET-uhn] (Lagrange). The village was laid out in July 1836 by John Kromer, surveyor, for Abraham K. Brower and Joseph Skerritt and originally called Lexington. The post office, established on November 21, 1837, was named Brighton because there already was a post office named Lexington in Jefferson County. The post office closed on June 15, 1911.*

Brimfield [BRIM-feeld] (Noble). This village was platted in March 1861 by William Bliss, proprietor, and perhaps named for the English village via New England. A post office named Bowrie, established on March 17, 1858, was changed to Brimfield on May 17, 1867.

Brinckley [BRINK-lee] (Randolph). A post office was established on July 13, 1881, with Alonzo Brinckley as postmaster and named for him; closed on July 31, 1901. Shedville is a variant name.

Bringhams Groves (Tippecanoe). See Montmorenci.

Bringhurst [BRING-herst] (Carroll). A post office was established on September 26, 1872. Known earlier as U Know and as Plank, for a local family, the village, platted in 1872, received its present name for Colonel Bringhurst of Logansport. Moses Plank was the first postmaster.

Brintonville (Owen). See Romona.

Bristol [BRIS-tuhl] (Elkhart). This town was founded in 1830; platted around 1835 by Samuel P. Judson, Lewis M. Alverson, and Hiram Doolittle; and, according to the WPA files, named for Bristol, England, by New England settlers. A post office was established on November 2, 1835.

Bristow [BRIS-to] (Perry). The village, established as a mill site, was laid out in 1875 and named for a local family. A post office was established on September 19, 1879.

Broad Park [brawd PAHRK] (Putnam). A post office called Broadpark was established on March 26, 1892; closed on December 31, 1903. The village was surveyed in 1893. The name was coined from the names of two local landowners, J. C. Broadstreet and Hugh Parker.

Broad Ripple [BRAWD rip-uhl] (Marion). This locale, incorporated into Indianapolis in 1922, developed as two adjacent communities, Broad Ripple and

Wellington, which merged into one, Broad Ripple. Broad Ripple was laid out on April 20, 1837, and named for the nearby ripple on White River, at that time the widest in the county. Wellington was laid out on May 17, 1837, and named for the Duke of Wellington. A post office named Broad Ripple was established on February 20, 1846; changed to Ripple on November 24, 1894; changed back to Broad Ripple on February 16, 1900; and closed on April 15, 1913.*

Brockville (Steuben). See Fremont.

Bromer [BRO-mer] (Orange). A post office was established on June 16, 1884; closed on April 14, 1904.* Supposedly the name is an acronym formed from the first letters of the names of six early settlers: Boyd, Roll, Oldham, McCoy, Ellis, and Reid.

Bronson (Randolph). See Losantville.

Brook (Bartholomew). See Corn Brook.

Brook [bruk] (Newton). This town was settled around 1832. A post office called Brook was established in Jasper County on August 23, 1837; changed to Newton County in 1860. Supposedly the name comes from a small stream running through town.

Brookfield [BRUK-feeld] (Shelby). This village, which began as a trading post in the 1850s, was first called Brookville. A post office was established as Brookfield on July 23, 1859; closed on June 15, 1904.

Brooklyn [BRUK-lun; BRUK-luhn] (Morgan). This town, probably named for the borough in New York City, was settled as early as 1819, when Benjamin Cuthbert built a mill here. About 1853

Frank Landers opened a store, and soon after that he laid out the town. A post office was established on April 2, 1856.

Brooklyn (Ripley). See Milan.

Brooksburg [BRUKS-berg] (Jefferson). This town was laid out by Fletcher Tevis on November 21, 1843, though it was named about 1839 for cofounder Noah Brooks. A post office named Brooksburgh was established on October 19, 1880. The spelling was changed to Brooksburg on March 31, 1893.

Brookston [BRUKS-tuhn] (White). This town was laid out on April 26, 1853, by Benjamin Gonzales, Isaac Reynolds, and Joel B. McFarland and named for James Brooks, president of the Louisville, New Albany, and Chicago Railroad. A post office established as Prairie Ridge on September 19, 1851, was changed to Brookston on October 16, 1853. A variant spelling is Brookstown.

Brookville [BRUK-vil] (county seat, Franklin). This town was planned by Amos Butler and Jesse Brooks Thomas, laid out by Thomas on August 8, 1808, and named Brooksville for Thomas's mother, whose maiden name was Brooks. The sale of lots, however, was postponed because Butler produced papers showing that Thomas had not paid his share, and 87.5 acres were deeded to Butler and the remainder to the law firm settling the case. In 1812 the town was surveyed again. An Indiana Territory post office was established here on February 1, 1813. The name has been spelled Brookville since 1811.

Brookville (Shelby). See Brookfield.

Broom Hill [broom HIL] (Clark). This village was established in 1851 by

Thomas Littell, who made brooms, thus giving the village its name. A post office was established on May 17, 1855; closed on November 24, 1857.

Brothersville (Marshall). See Bremen.

Brown County [brown]. This county was organized in 1836 and named for Major General Jacob J. Brown, hero of the War of 1812. Brown County State Park, the largest in the state, is located in this scenic county. Seat: Nashville.

Brownsburg [BROWNZ-berg] (Hendricks). This town was laid out in 1835 by William Harris, who called it Harrisburg, also spelled Harrisburgh. The name was changed to Brownsburgh when the post office was established on March 17, 1836. The spelling was changed to Brownsburg on April 25, 1893. The present name is for James Brown, who settled in this area in 1824.

Browns Corner [brownz KAWR-ner] (Huntington). A post office was established as Browns Corners on April 14, 1870; changed to Toledo, for the Toledo Railroad, which was supposed to come through here, on October 3, 1893. The village, platted on April 10, 1875, developed as a local trading point.

Browns Crossing [brownz KRAWS-ing] (Morgan). According to the WPA files, it is believed that a man named Brown owned a store at a crossroads here.

Brownstown [BROWNZ-town] (Crawford). This village was named for the local Brown family. A variant name is Mount Prospect for the post office established here on February 23, 1835; closed on May 15, 1918.*

Brownstown [BROWNZ-town] (county seat, Jackson). This town was platted in 1816 and named for Major General Jacob J. Brown, hero of the War of 1812. An Indiana Territory post office was established on October 4, 1816. Cf. Ewing.

Brownstown (Johnson). See Bluff Creek.

Browns Valley [BROWNZ VAL-ee] (Montgomery). The village was laid out by Matthias M. Van Cleave in 1836 as Brownsville for its location in Brown Township. A post office was established as Browns Valley on October 4, 1850; closed on February 15, 1945.*

Brownsville (Montgomery). See Browns Valley.

Brownsville [BROWNZ-vil] (Union). Aaron Ashbrook and Charles McGathlin purchased land here from the government in 1811. The village was laid out on October 27, 1815, in Wayne County and named for the Brown family, early settlers. A post office named Brownsville was established in Union County on March 13, 1819.

Brubakers Mill (Marion). See Millersville.

Bruce Lake [BROOS layk] (Fulton). A post office called Bruces Lake, for the nearby lake of the same name, was established on June 7, 1855; changed to Bruce Lake on June 27, 1895; closed on December 10, 1942. The lake, formerly called Keewaunay, was named for the Bruce family, local landowners. Bruce Lake Station is a variant name.

Bruceville [BROOS-vil] (Knox). This town was named for the first settler, Major William Bruce, who came here in

1805 and laid out the town on December 10, 1829. A palisaded fort called Fort Bruce was built on the Bruce farm near the present town site in 1812. A post office was established on February 9, 1818, with William Bruce as postmaster.

Bruins Crossroads (Parke). See Guion.

Brunerstown [BROO-nerz-town] (Putnam). This town was named for Joseph Bruner, who laid it out in 1837. A post office named Brunertown was established on November 29, 1839; closed on August 8, 1859. A variant name is Clinton Falls.

Brunswick [BRUHNZ-wik] (Clay). Established about 1831, this village was once the site of two boatyards, at which flatboats for shipping goods to New Orleans were built. According to the WPA files, "Mr. Ferguson, who had been a native of [New] Brunswick, N.J.," named the village.

Brunswick [BRUHNZ-wik] (Lake). A post office established on December 9, 1857, as Hanover, for the township in which it was located, was changed to Brunswick on February 16, 1860, when the name of the South Hanover post office in Jefferson County was changed to Hanover. The post office here was closed on August 14, 1905. The present name, for the state and city in Germany, supposedly was selected by the Post Office Department.

Brushy Prairie [bruhsh-ee PREHR-ee] (Lagrange). A post office was established here on June 12, 1834; closed on June 29, 1907.*

Bryant [BREYE-uhnt] (Jay). This town was laid out on December 8, 1871, by William McClellen, William R. Gillum, William K. Sanders, and William Carson. It was originally named Bryan, for a railroad construction boss who helped establish a railroad station here, but the railroad called the station Briant. The plat was filed on January 5, 1872. Locally the town has been called Billtown, since all four of the founders were named William. The post office established here on August 23, 1872, was called Bryant. North Briant was laid out October 6, 1873, by Ezekiel Rowlett, and the two plats now constitute one village.

Bryantsburg [BREYE-uhnts-berg] (Jefferson). This village was laid out in 1834 by Jacob Bryant and named for him. A post office was established as Bryantsburgh on January 18, 1872; closed on July 29, 1907.*

Bryants Corner (Monroe). See Hindustan.

Bryantsville [BREYE-uhnts-vil] (Lawrence). This village, first called Paris, was platted on May 28, 1835, and named for Robert Bryant, local pioneer farmer. A post office was established on March 9, 1846; closed on August 31, 1905.*

Brynville (Harrison). See Byrneville.

Buchanan (Parke). See Judson.

Buchanans Springs (Parke). See Judson.

Buchanans Station (Ripley). See Barbersville.

Buck Creek [BUHK kreek] (Tippecanoe). This village was platted in 1856 by Samuel Miller and originally called Transitville, and a post office called Transitville was established on January 8, 1858. On January 20, 1885, the post office name was changed to Buck Creek, for the nearby stream of the same name.

Buckeye [BUHK-eye] (Huntington). A post office was established on April 8, 1879; closed on June 30, 1920. The village was laid out in the spring of 1879.

Buckskin [BUHK-skin] (Gibson). A post office was established on August 19, 1847. This name, said to be descriptive of local deerskin operations, has inspired several legends, including the following:

1. "The town of Buckskin got its name from the deerskins that hung on the trading post walls. In the early 1800s there was a small trading post at what now is Buckskin. The owners of the post used to hang deerskins on the side of the building to dry. When people had skins or furs to sell they would go to the Buckskin trading post. When it became a town the name of Buckskin was used as the name" (ISUFA).

2. "You know, I don't know what the guys' names were, but there were two guys, and they were hunting. And they ran into this buck, and they shot him, and they skinned him, and they hung it up on the fence, and they said, 'This is Buckskin.'" (ISUFA).

3. "Buckskin was named after an experience of an early mail carrier who traveled on horseback from Princeton to the site of the town. About 1829, Mr. McCormick and Mr. Polk killed a deer on the route. One took the hide and the other the deer meat. . . . The carrier hung the hide on a tree and said, 'When I return, I'll get my buckskin.' Thus the settlement was named" (WPA).

Bud [buhd] (Johnson). The first store was built here around 1832, and the village was named for Bud Vandivier, son of the first merchant, Madison Vandivier (WPA). A post office was established on December 6, 1889; closed on November 29, 1902.

Buddha [BOO-duh; BOO-dee] (Lawrence). A post office was established on May 7, 1895; closed on February 13, 1904.* According to local tradition, the name was suggested by a traveling salesman who stopped at a store here: "It is said the name Buddha was first suggested by a traveling salesman who stopped at John Beasley's store there during the early 90s. No one seems to know why the suggestion was made" (WPA). Another legend, though, says the traveler was a tramp named Buddha: "Buddha was named for a tramp. Back in [the] 1800s, according to legend, a tramp named Budha [sic] used to pass through the town, and it was later named after him. He's now buried in an old cemetery west of here" (ISUFA). Buda, for one of the two cities now Budapest, Hungary, was applied to post offices in Illinois and Iowa in the nineteenth century and likely is the source of this name, too. A former name was Flynns Cross Roads.

Buell (Sullivan). See Cass.

Buena Vista (Adams). See Linn Grove.

Buena Vista [byoo-nuh VIS-tuh; bo-nuh VIS-tuh] (Franklin). This village was platted on July 18, 1848, by William Pruet and named for the Battle of Buena Vista in the Mexican War. The post office established on December 15, 1832, and closed on August 14, 1909,* was called Stipps Hill, for Isaac Stips, who came here in 1814.

Buena Vista (Gibson). See Giro.

Buena Vista (Hamilton). See Atlanta.

Buena Vista [boo-nuh VIS-tuh; byoo-nuh VIS-tuh] (Harrison). This village was laid out in 1850 on land donated by William Wallace. This popular name commemorates the Battle of Buena Vista. The post office established on April 28, 1878, and closed on April 30, 1904, was called Convenience, supposedly because getting the mail here was more convenient than getting it farther away at Elizabeth.

Buenavista [byoo-nuh VIS-tuh] (Monroe). This village was laid out in March 1849 by Henry Farmer on land owned by Jesse W. East, who named the village Buena Vista, "a name then peculiarly fresh and distinct in the minds of all Hoosiers," for the battle in the Mexican War. A post office was established on July 25, 1873; closed on December 15, 1925.

Buena Vista (Pulaski). See Monterey.

Buena Vista [byoo-nuh VIS-tuh] (Randolph). This village was platted on July 1, 1851. A post office called Cerro Gordo, probably for the American victory in Mexico in 1847, was established on October 7, 1852; closed on March 31, 1902. Apparently the present name commemorates another battle in the Mexican War.

Buffalo (Adams). See Geneva.

Buffalo [BUHF-uh-lo] (Brown). This village, dating from around 1854, grew up around George Harland's store.

Buffalo (Ohio). See French.

Buffalo (Spencer). See Buffaloville.

Buffalo [BUHF-uh-lo] (White). A post office was established here on January 16, 1851, and named for Buffalo, New

York, former home of the first postmaster. The village was platted in 1886 by John C. Karr.

Buffaloville [BUHF-uh-lo-vil] (Spencer). This village was laid out on January 26, 1860. A post office called Buffalo was established on June 20, 1860. On July 10, 1860, the name was changed to Buffaloville. According to tradition, the name comes from Buffalo Grounds, the name early settlers gave to Clay and Jackson townships (WPA).

Buffington [BUHF-ing-tuhn] (Lake). A post office was established on July 10, 1908; closed on September 30, 1912. Buffington is a familiar name in this county, which also has a Buffington Harbor and Buffington Park.

Bufkin [BUHF-kin] (Posey). A post office was established here on April 3, 1890; closed on July 14, 1902.

Bugtown (Posey). See Rapture.

Bullocktown [BUL-uhk-town; BUL-ik-town] (Warrick). A post office named Bullock, for a local pioneer family, was established on March 10, 1892; closed on December 31, 1903.* John A. Bullock was the first postmaster.

Bull Town (Shelby). See Saint Paul.

Buncombe (Parke). See Parkeville.

Bunker Hill [buhnk-er HIL] (Miami). This town was platted on August 8, 1851, by Alexander Galbraith, James Myers, and John Duckwall. Myers built the first house here in 1851. A post office established as Leonda on February 25, 1852, was changed to Bunker Hill, sometimes spelled Bunkerhill, on October 6, 1860. According to local tradition, a group of young men, led by James A.

Meek, went to Leonda one night, stole the post office equipment and supplies, took them to Bunker Hill in a saddlebag, and established the post office here. The town was incorporated on November 6, 1882. According to the WPA files, the town was named for the Battle of Bunker Hill, though a local legend says that it was so named because it was located on the highest point along the railroad between Indianapolis and Michigan City, and trains stopped here to have their bunkers filled in order to climb the hill (ISUFA).

Bunker Hill [buhnk-er HIL] (Washington). Apparently this village was named for the famous battle.

Bunkuin (Dearborn). See Bright.

Burdick [BER-dik] (Porter). A post office was established on July 18, 1871; closed on May 15, 1933. The village was laid out on October 22, 1875. The name is for A. C. Burdick, a lumber dealer from Coldwater, Michigan, who owned a sawmill here.

Burkehart Station (Vanderburgh). See Smythe.

Burket [BER-kuht; ber-KET] (Kosciusko). This town was platted in the spring of 1882 by Elias Burkett and named for him. A variant spelling is Burkett, the name of the post office established here on September 25, 1882.

Burkhart Station (Vanderburgh). See Smythe.

Burlington [BER-ling-tuhn] (Carroll). This town was laid out in 1828 and, according to a tradition printed in *Indiana: A Guide to the Hoosier State* (p. 446), named for a Wyandotte, Chief Burling-

ton, "who lived in this vicinity for many years." A post office established on December 17, 1832, as Wildcat was moved to Burlington on May 21, 1833; moved back to Wildcat on December 19, 1850; and closed on September 26, 1894. The Wildcat post office was located east of Burlington at Adams Mills, q.v., which was near Cutler, in Democrat Township. Burlington is located in Burlington Township, which was established in 1832.

Burlington (Rush). See Arlington.

Burnett [ber-NET] (Vigo). A post office called Burnett, for a local family who owned a local tanyard, was established on May 19, 1870; closed on January 31, 1934. The village, first called Otterville for nearby Otter Creek, was subdivided on March 17, 1873, by William Campbell. Grant Station is a variant name.

Burnettsville [BER-nuhts-vil] (White). A post office called Burnetts Creek, for a nearby stream named for Abraham Burnett, local landowner and fur trader, was established here on May 27, 1837. The post office name was changed to Burnettsville on June 26, 1922. The town was laid out in March 1854 by Franklin J. Herman. The community was called Farmington before the post office was established. The Farmington Male and Female Seminary, the first normal school in Indiana, was located here, 1852–1863.

Burney [BER-nee] (Decatur). This village was laid out on May 2, 1882, by James C. Pulse and named for the Burney family, early settlers. A post office was established on August 26, 1884. According to oral tradition, Burney once was called Mudsock: "I do know the old-timers around here called Burney

'Mudsock' because the sidewalks around here were so damn muddy that they had to pull socks on over their shoes when they got all dressed up to go to church or something" (ISUFA).

Burns City [BERNZ SID-ee] (Martin). A post office called Kecks Church, for the local Keck family, was established on July 14, 1849; changed to Burns City on September 15, 1890; and closed on November 15, 1957. Christian Keck, the first postmaster, purchased land here in 1845 and built a nondenominational church. Lee Keck was the second postmaster. The village was first platted as Kecksville on May 29, 1852. According to the WPA files, the current name was applied by a railroad engineer whose wife's maiden name was Burns.

Burns Harbor [bernz HAHR-ber] (Porter). This community was named for Burns Waterway, a drainage channel completed in 1926. Burns International Harbor, an artificial port, was built between 1965 and 1969.

Burnsville [BERNZ-vil] (Bartholomew). This village was platted in 1845 by Brice Burns and named for him. A post office was established on October 27, 1852; closed on March 14, 1903.*

Burr Oak [ber ok] (Marshall). This village was platted on December 16, 1882. A post office called Oakington was established on January 19, 1882; changed to Burr Oak on July 10, 1883.

Burr Oak [ber ok] (Noble). A post office named Burr Oak was established on October 25, 1848; closed on June 25, 1850. Another post office called Strouse, with Martin V. Strouse as postmaster, was established on January 21, 1899; closed on December 31, 1902. The variant name, Strouse, honors the local Strouse family, early settlers. The community may have derived its name from the Burr Oak school, built of round logs near here in 1840.

Burrows [BER-uhz; BER-oz] (Carroll). A post office called Cornucopia was established here on December 2, 1853; changed to Burrows, for a local family, on September 14, 1864. The village was laid out in 1856.

Burton (Parke). See Howard.

Bushrod [BUSH-rahd] (Greene). This village was laid out around 1889 and, according to the WPA files, named for Bushrod Taylor, who laid out the switches here for the Penn Central Railroad. It's also said that Bushrod was the first name of a railroad official's son (ISUFA).

Busseron [BUHS-er-uhn] (Knox). This village was laid out on May 30, 1854, and named for Busseron Township, in which it is located. The township was named for Busseron Creek, which was named for Francis Busseron, a judge of the Northwest Territory. A post office was established on June 9, 1855; closed on July 15, 1872.*

Butler [BUHT-ler] (DeKalb). A post office called Oak Hill was established near here on June 13, 1851; changed to Norristown, for Charles Norris, real estate promoter, on June 11, 1853; changed to Jarvis on August 20, 1859; changed to Butler on July 6, 1868. According to a local tradition reported in the WPA files, the name probably honors David Butler, an early settler in this county, though apparently he settled closer to Butler Center, q.v., in the southern part of the county. Some local history buffs claim the name honors a railroad executive.

Butler Center [buht-ler SEN-ter] (De-Kalb). A post office called Butler was established on February 7, 1840; moved to New Era, q.v., on January 14, 1868. The name is descriptive of its location near the center of Butler Township, apparently named for a local family, perhaps for pioneer David Butler, who settled in this county around 1833. Cf. Butler.

Butler Switch (Jennings). See Grayford.

Butlerville [BUHT-ler-vil] (Jennings). A post office was established near here on November 17, 1851, and the first postmaster, John Morris, named the post office for his hometown in Ohio. The village, named for the post office, was platted on July 27, 1853.

Buzzards Glory (Whitley). See Lorane.

Buzzards Roost (Jay). See Redkey.

Buzzards Roost (Putnam). See Hoosier Highlands.

Byrneville [BERN-vil] (Harrison). The spelling of the name of this village and post office has varied. The spelling is Byrnville in a county history, but supposedly the community first was named Brynville for Temple C. Bryn, who came here from North Carolina in 1809 and laid out the town in October 1838. A post office called Byrenville was established on March 6, 1851; closed on July 31, 1906.

Byron [BEYE-ruhn; BEYE-ern] (La Porte). William Hunt built a cabin here in the summer of 1835, and the village was platted on May 22, 1837. A post office called Kankakee, for the township in which it is located, was established on June 7, 1832; changed to Byron on September 8, 1841; and moved to Rolling Prairie, q.v., on April 23, 1857.

Byron [BEYE-ruhn; BEYE-ern] (Parke). A post office, supposedly named for Lord Byron, the British poet, was established on November 14, 1884; closed on June 15, 1905.* According to a traditional account, "Byron got its name from some people here by the name of Banta. This name was sent to Washington, D.C., and since there was already a town so named this town became known as Byron. *The Corner* was the first name given, but this was changed when a post office was made" (WPA).

 **C**

Cabel (Pike). See Hartwell.

Caborn [KAY-bawrn] (Posey). A post office called Hickory Branch, established on April 11, 1860, was changed to Caborns on August 29, 1876; closed on March 31, 1911. The village was laid out by Cornelius Caborn in 1871 and named for him. Variant names have been Caborns, Caborn Station, Caborn Summit, and Caborn Summit Station.

Cabot (Gibson). See Crawleyville.

Cadiz [KA-dis; KA-diz; kuh-DIZ] (Henry). This town was laid out on September 11, 1836, by David Pickering and named for Cadiz, Ohio, county seat of Harrison County, which was the former home of a number of settlers here. A post office was established on December 18, 1837; closed on May 15, 1923. Ultimately the name comes from the Spanish city. According to an oral account, "Cadiz is a small town in Henry County, Indiana. Cadiz was named after Cadiz, Spain." (ISUFA). Another oral tradition refers to an earlier name of the community: "Uncle Otts Town, this was the name used by the people surrounding Cadiz, Indiana, for many years, until the town was formally named Cadiz. Ott Holloway lived in the town called Cadiz now and owned a furniture store. He was a friend to all and well known and loved by a lot of the people in that area. People developed 'Uncle Otts Town' to give a reference to the place where the familiar Ott Holloway lived" (ISUFA).

Cagle Mill (Putnam). See Hoosier Highlands.

Cairo [KEYE-ro] (Tippecanoe). This village apparently was named for the city in Egypt.

Calcutta [kal-KUH-duh] (Clay). This community, which developed as a result of coal mining interests in the county, was surveyed in August 1870 by M. B. Crist for John M. and Sarah Brown, proprietors. A post office was established on May 11, 1870; closed on June 25, 1879.

Cale [kayl] (Martin). A post office was established on March 17, 1884; closed on November 28, 1887. The village was platted in 1889 as Cale City. Apparently the name comes from nearby Kale School, supposedly named for a resident.

Caledonia [kal-uh-DO-nee-uh; kal-uh-DON-yuh] (Sullivan). A post office was established on March 18, 1902; closed on December 31, 1909. Scottish coal miners named this mining village for the poetic name of Scotland.

Calumet (Porter). See Chesterton.

Calvertville [KAL-vert-vil] (Greene). The village, named for the local Calvert family, was founded around 1885. A post office was established on March 24, 1888, with John O. Calvert as postmaster; closed on February 28, 1910. According to local oral tradition, Calvertsville "was called so because the settlement was made mostly of people named Calvert" (ISUFA).

Cambria [KAM-bree-uh] (Clinton). A post office was established here on September 10, 1883; closed on June 15, 1915. The name comes from the Latin name of Wales, perhaps via New York or Pennsylvania.

Cambridge City [kaym-brij SIT-ee; kaym-brij SID-ee] (Wayne). According to the WPA files, this town was platted as Vandalia on June 1, 1824, but other sources say the town was laid out in 1836. A post office called Vandalia was established in this county on January 25, 1828; closed on June 27, 1833. A post office named Cambridge was established on March 11, 1835. On June 30, 1864, the post office name was changed to Cambridge City. This former depot on the Whitewater Canal was named for the English county or town, perhaps via New England.

Camby [KAM-bee] (Marion). The village was platted in 1890 by Don Carlos Morgan and formerly called West Union Station. A post office was established here on April 16, 1890. According to the WPA files, the first postmaster, Don Carlos Morgan, gave the town its present name "because it was short and different from any post office in the state and was the name of a river in South America."

Camden [KAM-duhn] (Carroll). A post office was established on February 20, 1833, around the same time that the town was platted. The name apparently is a transfer from an eastern state.

Camden (Jay). See Pennville.

Cameron Springs (Warren). See Kramer.

Cammack [kuh-MAK; KAM-uhk] (Delaware). This village was laid out on April 15, 1882, by David Cammack, for whom it was named. A post office was established on November 10, 1882; closed on January 15, 1907.

Campbell Corner [kam-buhl KAWR-ner] (Sullivan). This village was named for a local family (ISUFA).

Campbell Siding [kam-buhl SEYE-ding] (Morgan). According to the WPA files, this community was named for a local family. Variant names are Campbells and Hastings Station.

Campbellsburg [KAM-buhlz-berg] (Washington). This town was laid out by Robert Campbell in December 1851 and named for him. A post office named Campbellsburgh was established on April 3, 1852. The spelling was changed to Campbellsburg on June 9, 1893.

Campbelltown [KAM-buhl-tuhn] (Pike). This village was named for Samuel Campbell, who owned the first general store here. A variant spelling is Campbell Town.

Camp Creek (Kosciusko). See Etna Green.

Camp Flat Rock [kamp FLAT rahk] (Shelby). This village, first called Mount Pleasant, was established on June 2, 1831.

Canaan [KAY-nuhn] (Jefferson). This village was platted on August 1, 1836, and named for the promised land in the Bible, although the name of the founder, John Cane, may have suggested the name. A post office moved here from nearby Barbersville, q.v., on November 29, 1838; closed on January 15, 1911.

Canal (Warrick). See Millersburg (Warrick).

Cannelburg [KAN-uhl-berg] (Daviess). Originally called Clarks Station, for A. Clark, the first settler, the town was laid out on September 26, 1872, and named for the cannel coal mined here by the Buckeye Cannel Coal Company. A post office was moved from Black Oak Ridge, located west of here, to Cannelburgh on April 10, 1873. The spelling was changed to Cannelburg on April 14, 1893.

Cannelton [KAN-uhl-tuhn] (Perry). First called Coal Haven, this city was founded by the American Cannel Coal Company in 1837 and laid out by that company in 1841 as Cannelsburg, for the cannel coal mined here. The present name was adopted when a post office was established here on April 29, 1844. According to local oral tradition, "It was named after the Cannel Coal Company that had all of the land around there" (ISUFA). Another variant name is Cannelton Heights, though this name actually refers to an area overlooking the city.

Canton (Tipton). See Tipton.

Canton [KAN-tuhn] (Washington). Formerly called Greensburg, for the local Green family, and Eggharbor, for the large quantity of eggs sold here, the village was laid out in 1838 by Eli Overman. The present name, probably borrowed from an eastern state, was suggested when the post office was established on March 11, 1835. The post office was closed on November 30, 1905.

Cape Sandy [KAYP SAN-dee] (Crawford). A post office was established here on October 26, 1877; closed on February 26, 1965.*

Carbon [KAHR-buhn] (Clay). This town was laid out on June 7, 1870, by the Carbon Coal Company, which was so named for the coal here. A post office was established on September 13, 1870.

Carbondale [KAHR-buhn-dayl] (Warren). A post office was established here on January 17, 1855, and named Clarks Cross Roads, for the local Clark family. This post office was closed on June 30, 1858. On October 9, 1873, another post office called Carbondale, for local coal deposits, was established. It was closed on July 30, 1904.

Cardonia [kahr-DON-yuh; kahr-DO-nee-uh] (Clay). This village was laid out

on July 17, 1871, by the Clay Coal Company and named for John F. Card, then president of the company. A post office named Alexander was established here on February 23, 1872; changed to Cardonia on March 18, 1879; and closed on November 15, 1909. The Alexander post office was named for John Alexander, who platted a village here called Alexander on May 20, 1872.

Carlisle [kahr-LEYEL; KAHR-leyel] (Sullivan). Apparently named for Carlisle, Pennsylvania, former home of some settlers, this town, the earliest settlement in the county, was settled in 1803 and platted in 1815. An Indiana Territory post office was established here in 1812.

Carlos [KAHR-luhs] (Randolph). A post office was established as Carlos City on December 13, 1882. The post office name was changed to Carlos on March 14, 1895.

Carlton (Hancock). See Carrollton (Hancock).

Carmel [KAHR-muhl] (Hamilton). Originally called Bethlehem, sometimes spelled Bethleham, this town was platted on April 13, 1837. A post office named Carmel was established here on January 20, 1846, and the name of the town was changed to Carmel, too, when the town was incorporated on March 21, 1871. The name was suggested by Levi Haines, Sr., probably for the biblical mountain. According to an oral account, "Carmel was first named Bethlehem, and in later years the name was changed to Carmel. My grandmothers could not remember the reason for this" (ISUFA).

Carmel (Saint Joseph). See Tamarack Grange.

Carp [kahrp] (Owen). A post office was established on October 21, 1885; closed on March 31, 1904.

Carpenters Creek (Jasper). See Remington.

Carpenters Station (Jasper). See Remington.

Carpentersville [KAHR-puhn-terz-vil] (Putnam). This village was laid out in 1840 and named for Philip Carpenter, who came here about 1831, established a tannery and harness factory, and later became postmaster. The post office was established on May 23, 1850; closed on October 15, 1910. Carpenterville Town is a variant name.

Carroll (Carroll). See Wheeling (Carroll).

Carroll County [KEHR-uhl]. This county, mostly agricultural, was organized in 1828 and named for Charles Carroll, a signer of the Declaration of Independence. Lake Freeman, a popular recreational area, is located in this county. Seat: Delphi.

Carrollton [KEHR-uhl-tuhn] (Carroll). This village was platted in 1835 and named for its location in Carrollton Township. A post office was established on February 1, 1838; closed on April 4, 1839. Darwin is a variant name for a post office established on May 15, 1871; closed on December 15, 1905. Delphi, q.v., also was once called Carrollton.

Carrollton [KEHR-uhl-tuhn] (Hancock). This village has had more names than any other settlement in the county. A post office called Kinder was established here on April 28, 1847. On January 26, 1869, the post office name was changed to Carrollton, probably for Charles Carroll, and this remained the name until September 30, 1905, when the post office was closed. The railroad called its station here Reedville or Reedville Station. In 1913 the post office was reestablished as Finly, sometimes spelled Finley, for Congressman Finly Gray. A local name, Tailholt, was immortalized by James Whitcomb Riley. Hiram Comstock laid out the village in February 1854. Variant spellings have been Carlton and Carrolton.

Carrollton Location (Carroll). See Wheeling (Carroll).

Cartersburg [KAHR-terz-berg] (Hendricks). This village, named for the local Carter family, was laid out in 1850 by John Carter. David Carter built the first house here. A post office was established as Cartersburgh on October 7, 1852. The spelling was changed to Cartersburg on July 7, 1893.

Carthage (Putnam). See Mount Meridian.

Carthage [KAHRTH-ij; KAHRTH-eej] (Rush). This town was laid out on August 18, 1834, and named for Carthage, North Carolina, home of Quaker settlers. The post office here was established on February 27, 1835.

Carwood [KAHR-wud] (Clark). A post office was established on May 5, 1858, as Muddy Fork, for Muddy Fork of Silver Creek, on which it was located. On February 26, 1902, the name was changed to Carwood, supposedly a coined name honoring General John Carr, an early settler and prominent citizen, and General Wood, but its location in Carr Township, named for General John Carr, may have influenced the name. The post office was closed on October 31, 1933.

Caseyville (Parke). See Diamond.

Cass [kas] (Sullivan). A post office was established here on July 12, 1877, and named for Cass Township, in which it is located. The village was laid out in the summer of 1880. Formerly the community was called Lyontown and Buell, for Lieutenant Colonel Pratt Buell, a railroad official.

Cass County [kas]. This county, predominantly farmland, was formed in 1828, organized in 1829, and named for General Lewis Cass, who was in the War of 1812, governor of the Michigan Territory (1813–31), and Democratic candidate for president in 1848. Seat: Logansport.

Cassville [KAS-vil] (Howard). Surveying of the I.P.&C. Railway led to the origin of this village, which was laid out in September 1848 by William and Nathan Stanley and named for Lewis Cass, general, senator, and presidential candidate. The Cassville post office was established on July 21, 1854; closed on August 15, 1906.*

Cassville (Lake). See Leroy.

Castleton [KAS-uhl-tuhn] (Marion). This town was platted on February 25, 1852, by Thomas P. Gentry, who named it for his former home, Castleton, North Carolina. The post office was moved from Allisonville, q.v., to Castleton on December 7, 1853; closed on April 30, 1960.

Cataract [KAT-er-ak] (Owen). A post office established on March 31, 1846, was named for the cataract (waterfall)

here on Mill Creek. The post office was closed on April 15, 1936. Laid out in December 1851, the village grew up around a flour mill and sawmill owned by T. C. Jennings, who made additions in March 1860 and September 1863.

Cates [kayts] (Fountain). A post office established on April 2, 1883, was named for the local Cates family. David Cates settled here around 1844, and William Cates was the first postmaster. The village was platted on May 23, 1903.

Catlin [KAT-luhn] (Parke). This village was named for Thomas Catlin, who built a warehouse here in 1861 and became the first postmaster when the post office was established on June 19, 1861. The post office was closed on December 30, 1965.

Cato [KAY-to] (Pike). A post office called Cato was established here on April 21, 1894; closed on August 31, 1903. This classical name possibly is a transfer name from New York.

Cavender (Marshall). See Rutland.

Cayuga [keye-YOO-guh; kay-YOO-guh; kuh-YOO-guh] (Vermillion). First called Osonimon, for an Indian chief, and formerly called Eugene Station, for the township in which it is located, the town was platted in 1827. The post office was established on February 12, 1886. The present name is for the New York lake and city. The name derives from the Iroquois name Gwa-u-geh, "the place of taking out," referring to the beginning of a portage. A local legend explaining the name goes: "When the Model T Ford first was made, the people would drive through Cayuga and blow their horns. The sound of the horn seemed to say CAYUGA. And that is how Cayuga, Indiana, received its name" (ISUFA).

Cedar [SEE-der] (DeKalb). Settled in 1868, the village was laid out in 1872. A post office named Cedar Creek was established on December 2, 1872, and the name was changed to Cedar on June 20, 1894. The post office was closed on March 15, 1914. The community also was called Cedar Creek Station. The name comes from the stream Cedar Creek, which is a literal translation of the Potawatomi name Mes-kwah-wah-se-pe.

Cedar Beach (Kosciusko). See Wawasee.

Cedar Grove [see-der GROV] (Franklin). A post office called Cedar Grove was established on January 30, 1833. Apparently the post office originated from local canal activity. The town was platted in September 1837 by John Ward and originally called Rochester.

Cedar Lake [see-der LAYK] (Lake). The first post office named Cedar Lake, for the nearby lake of the same name, was established in 1839 (cf. Creston). The second post office named Cedar Lake was established on May 6, 1886, but was changed to Armour on July 28, 1899. The Armour post office, named for the Armour brothers, meatpackers from Chicago who had an ice-cutting business here, was closed on August 14, 1905. The Paisley post office, established April 25, 1890, was changed to Cedar Lake on August 29, 1899. Armour, or Armour Town, a residential area, was established in 1870 and thrived until about 1920. The community of Cedar Lake, established as a resort town, was not incorporated until 1969. Formerly called The Lake of the Red Cedars, the lake

was named for the red cedars along its shores.

Cedarville [SEE-der-vil] (Allen). This village, once the site of a Potawatomi settlement, was platted in 1838 and named for Cedar Creek. A post office was established on March 23, 1844; closed on November 15, 1905.*

Celestine [SEL-uhs-teen; SEL-uhs-teyen] (Dubois). This village was platted on November 16, 1843, by Father Joseph Kundek and named in honor of the Right Reverend Celestine René Lawrence de la Hailandière, bishop of Vincennes. A post office was established here on April 16, 1851.

Celina [suh-LEYE-nuh] (Perry). A post office named Celina was located here on March 24, 1870; closed on January 31, 1940. The name possibly was borrowed from Celina, Ohio.

Cementville [see-MENT-vil] (Clark). A post office was established here on January 4, 1869; closed on May 14, 1904.* The name comes from the local cement industry.

Centenary [SENT-uhn-ehr-ee] (Vermillion). This village was platted on October 19, 1910, and perhaps named for a local church.

Center [SEN-ter] (Howard). This village, first called Tampico, was laid out in 1852 and named Center because a Pennsylvania Railroad survey showed its location as midway between Cincinnati and Chicago (WPA). A post office was established as Centre on August 26, 1854. The spelling was changed to Center on July 31, 1893, and the post office was closed on September 15, 1972.

Center [SEN-ter] (Jay). This village received its name because of its location near the center of Greene Township (WPA).

Center Point [SEN-ter poynt] (Clay). A post office called Centre Point was established here on April 19, 1855. The spelling was changed to Center Point on June 15, 1893. The town was platted on September 18, 1856. The post office received its name because it was located near the center of the county. An oral tradition apparently based on a printed account in a county history goes: "Center Point . . . was laid out for the apparent purpose of securing the county seat, to which it seemed entitled on account of its close proximity to the geographical center of the county on Upper Bloomington Road, ten miles south of Brazil. It was from this geographical location that it received its name, Center Point. Martin H. Kennedy, who was its founder, was a descendant of a long line of early pioneers" (ISUFA). Another variant spelling has been Centerpoint.

Center Square [sen-ter SKWEHR] (Switzerland). This town received its name from the fact that it was laid out in 1835 in the form of a square near the center of the county. A post office was moved here from Jacksonville, q.v., and named Centre Square on January 30, 1867. The spelling was changed to Center Square on April 25, 1892.

Centerton [SENT-er-tuhn] (Morgan). This village was laid out in March 1854 and apparently named by Hiram T. Craig, the surveyor, for its location near the center of the county. A post office was established on August 15, 1854, with William H. Spencer, who opened the first store here, as the first postmaster; closed on September 14, 1869.

Center Valley [sen-ter VAL-ee] (Hendricks). This village is located near the Hendricks-Morgan county line. A post office called Centre Valley (see Center Valley [Morgan]) was changed from Morgan County to Hendricks County on March 25, 1872; closed on October 31, 1902.

Center Valley [sen-ter VAL-ee] (Morgan). A post office called Centre Valley was established here on April 30, 1856, but moved to Hendricks County (see Center Valley [Hendricks]) on March 25, 1872.

Centerville (Lake). See Merrillville.

Centerville [SEN-ter-vil] (Spencer). This village was laid out in the early 1840s. Centreville is an earlier spelling. Oakland is a variant name for a post office established on May 24, 1847; closed on October 29, 1895.*

Centerville (Vigo). See Lewis.

Centerville [SEN-ter-vil] (Wayne). This town was platted on October 20, 1814, and named for its location near the center of the county. A post office called Centreville was established here on June 3, 1818. The spelling was changed to Centerville on July 10, 1893.

Central [SEN-truhl] (Harrison). A post office was established on October 2, 1879, and so named because of its location as a central point of mail delivery (WPA). The village was laid out on May 31, 1890, by William Smith.

Central Barren [sen-truhl BEHR-uhn] (Harrison). A post office was established here on June 7, 1890; closed on May 15, 1905. The Buffalo Trace passed through this village.

Centre (Grant). See Jonesboro (Grant).

Cerro Gordo (Randolph). See Buena Vista (Randolph).

Ceylon [suh-LAHN; see-LAHN] (Adams). This village was platted in 1873 by Dr. B. B. Snow and named Florence for Snow's deceased daughter. The name was changed to Ceylon, apparently for the island in the Indian Ocean, by Dr. Snow when it was discovered there was another community in Indiana named Florence. A post office called Ceylon was established on January 25, 1884; closed on October 19, 1895.

Ceylon (Franklin). See Andersonville.

Chain-O-Lakes [chayn-uh-LAYKS] (Saint Joseph). This community was named for the nearby Chain O'Lakes (Bass Lake and Chain Lake).

Chalmers [CHAL-merz] (White). A post office called Mudge Station was established here on April 21, 1854. The post office name was changed to Chalmers on May 25, 1860. The original name, Mudge Station, or sometimes Mudges Station, was for a local storekeeper, Gardner Mudge, who built a house here in 1853 and became the first postmaster. The town was laid out on July 24, 1873, by Mr. and Mrs. Jacob Raub. Allegedly the present name is for Alexander Chalmers, Scottish biographer and editor.

Chambersburg [CHAYM-berz-berg] (Orange). This village was laid out in September 1840 by Samuel Chambers, who purchased land here from the government on September 13, 1821, and named the village for himself. A post office was established as Chambersburgh on May 10, 1849. On September 14, 1894, the spelling was changed to Chambersburg. The post office was closed on October 15, 1912.

Chandler [CHAND-ler; CHAN-ler] (Warrick). A post office established as Lee on June 28, 1847, was changed to Chandler on December 10, 1874.

Chapel Hill [chap-uhl HIL] (Monroe). This village was platted on October 11, 1856, by David Miller and John Smith and named for the local Chapel Hill Methodist Church, organized in the early 1850s. Miller was a member of the church. A post office called Chapelhill was established here on September 13, 1897; closed on December 15, 1925.

Chapmanville (Tippecanoe). See Colburn.

Charlestown [CHAHR-uhlz-town] (Clark). This city, fifth oldest in the state, was laid out in 1808 and named for Charles Biggs, who, with John Hay, surveyed the town. An Indiana Territory post office named Charleston was established on October 31, 1812. The post office name was changed to Charlestown in 1831.

Charlottesville [SHAHR-luhts-vil] (Hancock). This village was platted June 1, 1830, by David Templeton and probably named for Charlottesville, Virginia, though it is also said that it was named for the daughter of the founder (WPA). A post office was established on May 9, 1831.

Charlottesville [SHAHR-luhts-vil] (Union). According to the WPA files, this village was named for a local person.

Chase [chays] (Benton). A post office was established on February 12, 1873;

closed on April 15, 1918. The village was named for a local landowner, Simon P. Chase.

Chatterton [CHAT-er-tuhn] (Warren). This village was founded in 1896, and a post office was established on January 27, 1900; closed on January 15, 1906. Allegedly the Post Office Department selected the name from several suggested names (WPA).

Chauncey (Tippecanoe). See West Lafayette.

Chelsea [CHEL-see] (Jefferson). A post office was established on June 1, 1883. The name apparently comes from the district in London, perhaps via Maine.

Cherry Grove [chehr-ee GROV] (Montgomery). A railroad switching station was established around 1851. Supposedly the name is descriptive of wild cherry trees here.

Cherryvale [CHEHR-ee-vayl] (Vigo). Also called Cherryville, this village, located on the Clay-Vigo county line, was never laid out. A post office was established on March 30, 1899; closed on October 15, 1904. Francis M. Hamilton, local storekeeper and postmaster, named the village for wild cherry trees growing in a narrow valley here.

Chester [CHES-ter] (Wayne). This village was settled about 1820 and platted in September 1866. A post office was established on December 13, 1848; closed on September 30, 1901.

Chesterfield [CHES-ter-feeld] (Madison). This town was platted on April 19, 1830, and first called West Union for its location in Union Township. The name was changed to Chesterfield in 1834.

The name is for an early settler and Indian trader named McChester, according to a local legend repeated in printed sources. A post office, with Amasa Makepeace as postmaster, established as Mill Creek on March 15, 1827, was changed to Chesterfield on February 9, 1848, and closed on December 31, 1954. Possibly the name was borrowed from Chesterfield, New Hampshire, home of the Makepeace family, local merchants.

Chesterton [CHES-ter-tuhn] (Porter). A post office established in La Porte County on January 29, 1835, as Coffee Creek, for a nearby stream, was changed to Porter County on April 7, 1840; changed to Calumet, for another stream, on December 31, 1849; and changed to Chesterton on January 24, 1870.* The town was platted as Calumet in 1852 and became Chesterton in 1869. The present name comes from Westchester Township, in which the town is located.

Chesterville [CHES-ter-vil] (Dearborn). A post office was established here on January 11, 1884; closed on April 30, 1907.

Chestnut City (Perry). See Oriole.

Chestnut Hill [ches-nuht HIL] (Washington). A post office was established as Chestnut Hill on March 8, 1837; changed to Sturdevants Store on December 13, 1837; changed back to Chestnut Hill on January 31, 1840; closed on December 31, 1901.

Chestnut Ridge [ches-nuht RIJ] (Jackson). This village was a trading center in the early 1830s and later became a railroad station. A post office named Chestnut Ridge was established here on April 22, 1878; changed to Chestnut on October 11, 1894; closed on October 31, 1902.

Chetwynd [CHET-wind] (Morgan). A post office was established here on June 21, 1887; closed on October 15, 1900. This place name also is found in Australia.

Chili [CHEYE-leye] (Miami). This village was laid out on the north bank of Eel River on October 16, 1839, and called New Market. Before that, the settlement was called Liberty and North Liberty in the 1830s. Another early settlement, established in 1829, though on the south bank of Eel River, was called Springs, for local natural springs. Chili is an older spelling of Chile, and the presence of populated places named Mexico and Peru in this county probably influenced the renaming of this town for the country in South America. The spelling and pronunciation, though, are found in a New York place name, so there is a possibility of borrowing from New York. A post office named Chili was established on February 13, 1843; closed on May 26, 1961. Chile is a variant spelling.

China [CHEYE-nuh] (Jefferson). This village first was called Indiana Kentucky, but the name was changed by the Post Office Department to China, apparently for the country, on January 30, 1833, when a post office was established. The final closing of the post office, after two earlier interruptions in service, was on February 28, 1902.

Choppeen (Wells). See Zanesville.

Chrisney [KRIS-nee] (Spencer). This town first was called Spring Station, or sometimes Springs Station, for a spring here beside the railroad. A post office named Spring Station was established on January 5, 1874. On September 3, 1883, the post office name was changed to Chrisney for John B. Chrisney, who first owned the site and arranged for the local post office and railroad station. Chrisney established a distillery here around 1866. An oral account provides the following additional information: "The town of Chrisney was first called Spring because of a spring of water which ran in the vicinity and had a pump. Later, when the railroad was built and stopped at Spring, it had a post office, and the name was changed to Spring Station. One of the residents of Spring Station was John B. Chrisney, who had immigrated there from France and bought some farmland. He built a store and the post office there. He was also instrumental in the construction of roads and other enterprises in the settlement. In 1882, Spring Station was changed to Chrisney in honor of this man" (ISUFA).

Christiansburg [KRIS-chuhnz-berg] (Brown). This village was founded about 1850 by Thomas Carmichael, and a post office named Christiansburg was established on December 6, 1850. The post office was changed to Valley Hill on February 29, 1860; changed back to Christiansburg on August 29, 1879; and closed on September 30, 1902.* The name is found in other states, where it sometimes honors Colonel William Christian, who was killed by Indians in Kentucky in 1786.

Churubusco [chehr-uh-BUHS-ko; chehr-yu-BUHS-ko] (Whitley). Two towns were platted here: Franklin on August 17, 1845, and Union on April 25, 1855. On December 28, 1848, a post office was established and named for Churubusco, the town where in 1847 American troops had won a battle in the

Mexican War. In 1870, Franklin and Union merged and assumed the post office name. According to a local tradition, an old fiddler always played a dance tune that he called "Churubusco," and Thomas Cunningham, with whom the fiddler lived, selected the title of the tune for the post office name. A variant spelling is Cherubusco.

Cicero [SIS-uh-ro; SIS-er-o] (Hamilton). This town was laid out in 1835 and named for nearby Cicero Creek. According to local tradition, the stream was named for an early settler's son, Cicero, who fell into the stream while fishing or for a surveyor's son who fell into the stream when attempting to drink from it. According to another account, Cicero was "an old Indian chief of this vicinity" (WPA). A variant name of the creek is Cezaro Creek. A post office was established on March 5, 1839.

Cincinnati [sints-uh-NAD-ee] (Greene). Founded about 1840, this village was named for Cincinnati, Ohio. A post office was established on January 13, 1874; closed on December 31, 1934. According to a legend, "It sprang up around an inn located along an old cattle trail in 1840. The inn was a favorite stopping and carousing place for the rough cattle drivers of that era and was often visited by cattle buyers from various parts of the middle west. One night, during the first year of its existence, a drunken cattle buyer at the inn jokingly remarked that the place reminded him of his hometown, Cincinnati, Ohio, on account of its high hills and abundance of good whiskey. The suggestion seemed to take well with the owner of the inn and the cattle drivers who were present, so the name was adopted and has remained ever since" (WPA).

Circleville (Porter). See Scircleville.

City West (Porter). See Wheeler (Porter).

Clanricarde [klan-ri-KAHRD] (Porter). This village was established as a railroad siding in 1865 and named for Clanricarde, Wales, hometown of the wife of Jim Burke, co-owner of a cattle ranch here.

Clapboard Corner (Switzerland). See East Enterprise.

Clare [klehr] (Hamilton). This village was settled around 1830 and allegedly named by William W. Conner, one of the founders, for a son of an early settler. A post office was established on February 25, 1878; closed on January 31, 1902.*

Clark County [klahrk]. This county was established by William Henry Harrison in 1801 and named for General George Rogers Clark, hero of the Revolution. Seat: Jeffersonville.

Clarke (Randolph). See Stone.

Clarke Junction [klahrk JUHNK-shuhn] (Lake). A post office was established in this county as Clarke Station on July 17, 1860; closed on June 15, 1918.* Another variant name of this village is Clarke. The name is for a local landowner named Clarke, who came here from England (WPA).

Clarksburg (Daviess). See Odon.

Clarksburg [KLAHRKS-berg] (Decatur). This village was laid out by Woodson Clark on April 9, 1832, and named for him. Clark built the first house here, and the settlement was called Clarksburg before the village was laid out. According to local legend, the community received its name from "Dr. Clark. He was the veterinarian around here and founded the town" (ISUFA). A post office named Clarksburgh was established on March 16, 1835. The spelling was changed to Clarksburg on April 19, 1893.

Clarksburg (Johnson). See Rocklane.

Clarks Cross Roads (Warren). See Carbondale.

Clarks Hill [klahrks HIL] (Tippecanoe). This town was named for Daniel D. Clark, who platted the town in 1850 and became the third postmaster in 1858. A post office was established here on July 26, 1853. Variant names are Clarkhill, Clarkshill, and Clarksville.

Clarks Prairie (Daviess). See Odon.

Clarks Station (Daviess). See Cannelburg.

Clarks Station (Madison). See Florida.

Clarkstown (Boone). See Hamilton (Boone).

Clarksville [KLAHRKS-vil] (Clark). After the Revolution, Virginia rewarded George Rogers Clark with 150,000 acres in what is now Clark, Scott, and Floyd counties, and Clark founded this city in 1783. Named for Clark, Clarksville is the oldest American city in the Old Northwest Territory. Clarkville is a variant spelling.

Clarksville [KLAHRKS-vil] (Hamilton). This village supposedly was named for General George Rogers Clark. A post office named Poinsett was established in this county on June 1, 1840; on Oc-

tober 4, 1850, the post office was changed to Nicklesonville, with Abraham Nickleson as postmaster; and on December 12, 1850, the post office was changed to Clarksville. The post office was closed on October 15, 1902.* Nickleson (also spelled Nicholson) is credited with founding the village in 1849.

Clay City [KLAY SID-ee] (Clay). This town was laid out by Barbara Storm on June 16, 1873, and called Markland, for Colonel Markland, Hoosier soldier and statesman. Since another Indiana town and post office in Switzerland County had the same name, a local committee changed the name to Clay City, for the county in which it is located. A post office established on November 8, 1875, as Huntersville, with Elizabeth Hunter as postmaster, was changed to Clay City on December 17, 1875.

Clay County [klay]. This county, once known for its coal mines and clay plants, was organized in 1825 and named for Henry Clay, Kentucky orator and statesman. Seat: Brazil.

Claypool [KLAY-pool] (Kosciusko). A post office named Claypool was established on October 26, 1841; closed on June 19, 1868; reestablished April 14, 1873. The town was platted on May 10, 1873, by John and Nelson Beigh and named for the post office. Reuben Beigh was appointed postmaster on March 27, 1874.

Claysville (Hendricks). See Clayton.

Claysville (Huntington). See Bracken.

Claysville [KLAYZ-vil] (Washington). This village was laid out on October 24, 1828, and first called Middletown. A post office called Claysville was established August 19, 1825; closed on September 15, 1906.

Clayton [KLAY-tuhn] (Hendricks). This town was platted in 1851 by George W. Willis and originally called Claysville, for Henry Clay, Kentucky statesman. A post office was established June 21, 1852, and named Clayton because there already was a post office called Claysville in Washington County.

Clear Creek [KLEER kreek] (Monroe). This village was founded around 1854 and named for a nearby stream of the same name. A post office was established on March 2, 1870.

Clear Lake [KLEER layk] (Steuben). A post office named Clear Lake, for a nearby lake of the same name, was established on May 23, 1870, but the postal service was moved to Ray, q.v., on July 12, 1872. Another post office named Clear Lake was established on April 12, 1890, but on October 31, 1903, it was closed, too, when the mail again was sent to Ray. The present town of Clear Lake was incorporated in 1933.

Clear Spring [KLEER spring] (Jackson). This village was laid out on March 2, 1839, and named for a spring in the village. A post office called Mooney, for a local shop owner, was established here on May 4, 1848; closed on July 31, 1930.

Cleona (Monroe). See Gatesville.

Clermont [KLEHR-mahnt] (Marion). A post office was established as Clermont on May 31, 1831. The town was laid out by Perry Hosbrook on April 6, 1849, as Mechanicsburg, but it was renamed for the post office about six years later because there were several other Indiana communities and a post office in Henry County named Mechanicsburg. Clermont is a common place name in France and Belgium and is also found in Canada and Australia as well as throughout the United States. Ultimately a transfer name from France, the name sometimes is selected for its commendatory quality.

Cleveland [KLEEV-luhnd] (Hancock). This village was laid out on July 8, 1834, and called Portland until about 1855. A post office called Cleveland was established on August 31, 1852; closed on January 15, 1903. The origin of the present name is unknown but perhaps is for the city in Ohio.

Clifford [KLIF-erd] (Bartholomew). This town was laid out on September 2, 1853, and a post office was established on October 1, 1853; closed on October 31, 1941.

Clifton [KLIF-tuhn] (Union). A post office was established here on March 24, 1852; closed on October 14, 1903.*

Clifty (Decatur). See Milford.

Clinton [KLINT-uhn] (Ripley). This village was laid out on March 30, 1833, by John and Samuel Boldrey and Minor Canfield.

Clinton [KLINT-uhn] (Vermillion). A post office was established on November 11, 1823. This city was laid out first in 1824 by William Harris, a government surveyor from Martin County. The name is for De Witt Clinton, governor of New York.

Clinton County [KLINT-uhn]. This county was organized in 1830 and named for De Witt Clinton, governor of New York, who unsuccessfully ran against James Madison for president. Seat: Frankfort.

Clinton Falls [klint-uhn FAWLZ] (Putnam). This village was called Quincy before a post office was established here on August 31, 1874. The present name is for the township in which the village is located and for nearby falls. The post office was closed on August 31, 1901.

Clinton Falls (Putman). See Brunerstown.

Clinton Locks (Parke). See Lyford.

Clousers Mills (Montgomery). See Bowers.

Cloverdale [KLO-ver-dayl] (Putnam). A post office established here on February 11, 1836, was named Clover Dale, supposedly "for the many large fields of clover, and the lovely shady dales." The town, located in Cloverdale Township, was laid out in 1839 by Andrew T. McCoy and Moses Nelson.

Cloverland [KLO-ver-land] (Clay). This village was founded in 1834 by Charles Modesitt, though perhaps not laid out until 1848, and supposedly named for a growth of native clover on the site. The earliest clay plant, probably pottery, and the second steam gristmill in the county were located here. A post office was established on February 5, 1850; closed on June 30, 1920.

Clunette [kloo-NET] (Kosciusko). This village was laid out in 1846 by Felix Miller and apparently first called Galveston and then North Galveston. The post office, established on April 13, 1883, and closed on January 31, 1901, was called Clunette.

Clymers [KLEYE-merz] (Cass). Founded by George Clymer around 1856 and named for his family, this village was laid out in 1869 by David Clymer. A post office was established on August 7, 1890; closed on December 15, 1919.

Coal Bluff [KOL bluhf] (Vigo). Local coal mining operations contributed significantly to the origin and development of this village, which was named for the Coal Bluff Mining Company, purchaser of Webster's Coal Mine, one of the first in the county, as Daniel Webster first operated his mine here about 1871. A post office was established on May 15, 1876; closed on February 28, 1969.

Coal City [kol SID-ee] (Owen). When work began here on the Cincinnati and Terre Haute Railroad, Charles D. Wilber and Asa Turner, who were associated with the Indiana Block Coal Company, laid out a town and called it Frazier, for the president of the railroad; however, when they could not pay for the land, the plat was not recorded, and the land reverted to the original owners. The village then was laid out in 1875 by Henry and Charity Grim and named for the local coal mines. Additions were made in 1877, 1880, and 1881. A post office was moved from nearby Stockton, q.v., to Coal City on November 22, 1877.

Coal Creek [KOL kreek] (Fountain). A post office was established on January 23, 1840, as Headleys Mills. On February 24, 1864, when Samuel J. Snoddy was postmaster, the name was changed to Snoddys Mills; and on July 11, 1888, it was changed to Coal Creek for a nearby stream of the same name. The post office was closed on May 16, 1899. The stream received its name from a rich coal bank discovered near its mouth.

Coal Haven (Perry). See Cannelton.

Coalmont [KOL-mahnt] (Clay). The village was founded in 1900 and named for the coal here and allegedly the elevation of the site. A post office was established on March 1, 1901.

Coatesville [KOTS-vil] (Hendricks). The original plat and records for this town have been lost, but a church was established in the 1830s, and a post office called Coatsville was established on July 28, 1851. Allegedly the name honors a man named Coates who owned a lot of land along the railroad here.

Coats Spring [kots SPRING] (Pike). This village first was called West Saratoga Springs for the New York resort. Andrew Johnson discovered the springs here in 1850, and James Coates opened a resort in 1867. The present name, also spelled Coates Spring, is for him.

Coburg [KO-berg] (Porter). This village was named by Jacob T. Forbes, who settled here in 1854, for his former home, Cobourg, Ontario. Forbes owned the land on which the town was laid out. A post office was established on May 8, 1876; closed on January 15, 1906.

Cochran [KAHK-ruhn] (Dearborn). A post office was established on May 4, 1858; closed on April 30, 1917.* The community, which adjoins Aurora, was laid out on August 25, 1860, by George Cochran, for whose family it was named.

Coe [ko] (Pike). This village was laid out in 1869 by Simeon LeMasters and called Arcadia.

Coesse [ko-ES-ee] (Whitley). A post office established on March 15, 1843, was converted to a branch of Columbia City on March 24, 1967. The village was laid out in 1854 or 1855. The name is a derivation of a Potawatomi nickname of a Miami chief, Ku-wa-zi, "Old Man." The Miami pronunciation was Ko-wa-zi.

Coesse Corners [ko-ES-ee KAWR-nerz] (Whitley). This village is located just north of Coesse, q.v.

Coffee Creek (Porter). See Chesterton.

Coffins Station (Henry). See Dunreith.

Coke Oven Hollow [kok uh-vuhn HAH-lo] (Parke). Foundry is a variant name of this village on Sugar Creek where flatboats once were built.

Colburn [KOL-bern] (Tippecanoe). This village first was laid out in 1858 by Jacob Chapman and called Chapmanville for him. A post office was established as Colburn on September 12, 1863, with Nathan Chapman as the first postmaster.

Cold Springs [KOLD springz] (Dearborn). This station on the O. & M. Railroad originally was called Jones Station, and a post office by that name was established here on January 21, 1857. The name was changed to Cold Springs on March 5, 1874. The post office was closed on March 10, 1874. A variant spelling is Cold Spring, and a variant name is Cold Spring Station.

Cold Springs (Whitley). See Ormas.

Cole [kol] (Grant). A post office called Coleboro was established on September, 14, 1900; closed on September 15, 1902.

Coles Corners (Ohio). See Bear Branch.

Colfax [KOL-faks] (Clinton). A post office called Colfax was established on September 6, 1853. The town was laid out in 1849 by Montgomery Stroud and originally named Medway (Midway, according to the WPA files). In 1857 the town name was changed to Colfax for the post office. The name honors Schuyler Colfax (1823–1885), prominent Hoosier who became vice president of the United States (1869–1873).

Collamer [KAHL-mer; KAHL-uh-mer] (Whitley). This village was platted in 1846 and formerly called Slabtown or Slab, for slabs used for siding the local sawmill workers' cabins, and Millersburg, for Elias Miller, who had a gristmill here. The village was renamed for the local post office, which was established as Collamer on September 18, 1849; closed on February 28, 1922. The name honors Jacob Collamer, postmaster-general, 1849–1850.

College Corner [KAHL-ij KAWR-ner] (Jay). This village was laid out by Dr. Joseph Watson in 1850. Subsequently, in opposition to a college at nearby Liber that enrolled an African American student, Farmers Academy was established here with the understanding that the college would never educate black students. A local post office was established on May 30, 1862, but it was moved to Liber on January 10, 1872.

College Corner [KAHL-ij KAWR-ner] (Wabash). In 1859 the Disciples of Christ congregation built a frame church here. The name is of uncertain origin.

College Corner Station (Union). See West College Corner.

Collegeville [KAHL-ij-vil] (Jasper). This village was founded in 1889 and named for Saint Josephs College, which was incorporated here the same year. A post office was established on May 9, 1893; closed on March 31, 1958.

Collett [KAHL-uht] (Jay). This village was platted on February 13, 1872, by John Collett, for whom it was named. A post office was established on April 23, 1872, with Collett as the first postmaster; closed on December 15, 1922. According to a local legend, the village was nicknamed Poodle because an Irish construction boss had a poodle that was killed and buried without his knowledge, and the whole town helped him search for it (WPA).

Collins [KAHL-uhnz] (Whitley). This village was platted in 1872 and named for James Collins, president of the Detroit, Eel River, and Illinois Railroad. A post office was established on February 13, 1872; closed on September 5, 1913.*

Coloma [kuh-LO-muh; ko-LO-muh] (Parke). This village was settled in 1830 and first called Rocky Run for a nearby stream. It was renamed Coloma in 1868, probably for Coloma, California, famous in the Gold Rush of 1849. The village was laid out in 1876. A post office was established March 16, 1868; closed on May 31, 1905.*

Columbia [kuh-LUHM-bee-uh] (Fayette). This village was platted on June 15, 1832, and named for the township in which it is located. A post office was established on February 16, 1833; closed on July 14, 1903.*

Columbia (Tippecanoe). See Corwin.

Columbia City [kuh-LUHM-bee-uh SID-ee] (county seat, Whitley). This city was platted on November 26, 1839, and first called Columbia. The name, a Latinized form of Columbus, is a very popular place name in the United States and was chosen here for its inspirational quality or as "personification of the U.S.," according to the WPA files. A post office was estab- lished as Columbia City on January 16, 1854. *City* was added to the name to distinguish it from the post office and village called Columbia in Fayette County.

Columbus [kuh-LUHM-buhs; kuh-LUHM-bus] (county seat, Bartholomew). This city was settled by General John Tipton, John Lindsay, and Luke Bonesteel in 1820 and called Tiptonia for General Tipton, who in 1821 offered thirty acres for the county seat if it were named for him. The county commissioners readily accepted the land but renamed the seat Columbus on March 20, 1821. According to an oral narrative, "This was once a village called Tiptonia in honor of Colonel Tipton of the War of 1812. He led an army through Madison and was searching for a road. But he settled and was granted land. He built a mansion on the highest point of the river, and a village grew up around that. The river was the east fork of the White River. Later, in 1821, they had a celebration after the corporation of the village and . . . named it after Christopher Columbus" (ISUFA). A post office was established on August 22, 1821.

Comet (Ripley). See Correct.

Commiskey [kuh-MIS-kee] (Jennings). This village was platted on February 10, 1870, and a post office was established on July 7 of the same year.

Como [KO-mo] (Jay). This village was founded in 1879 and perhaps named for the Italian city and lake. A post office was established on December 7, 1882; closed on December 30, 1904.

Concord [KAHN-kawrd] (DeKalb). Apparently this village, platted in 1832, was named for Concord Township, in which it is located. A post office was established on January 19, 1876; closed on March 30, 1929.*

Concord [KAHN-kawrd] (Tippecanoe). This village was platted in the summer of 1832 by James B. Johnson, who built a mill here. A post office was established on May 5, 1837; closed on June 24, 1868.* Probably the name is a transfer name from an eastern state.

Connersville [KAHN-erz-vil] (county seat, Fayette). This city was named for John Conner, founder, who established a fur-trading post here in 1808 and platted the city in 1813. A post office was established on January 24, 1818.

Conns Creek (Shelby). See Waldron.

Conologue [KAHN-uh-lawg] (Jackson). A post office was established on April 6, 1866; closed on July 5, 1876. Conlogue is a variant spelling.

Conrad [KAHN-ruhd; KAHN-rad] (Newton). This village was named for Jennie M. Conrad, who laid it out in December 1908. A post office was established on October 25, 1906; closed on June 14, 1924.

Contreras [kuhn-TREHR-uhs] (Union). Apparently the village was named for the Mexican town of the same name, site of the American victory over the Mexicans in August 1847.

Convenience (Harrison). See Buena Vista (Harrison).

Converse [KAHN-vers] (Blackford). A flag station was established here around 1860 and named for Dr. Converse, president of the Pan Handle Railroad.

Converse [KAHN-vers] (Miami). This town was laid out on April 7, 1849, by Willis Elliott, and the first plat was recorded on October 31, 1849 by Willis Elliott and Oliver H. P. Macy. The town first was named Xenia, for Xenia, Ohio, and a post office called Xenia was established on July 5, 1854, with Macy as the first postmaster. Additions were platted in 1856, 1867, and 1869, the latter by J. W. Edward and J. N. Converse. The town was renamed for the local Converse fam-ily. William Converse was an early land-owner. In 1873 the county auditor directed that all irregular lots in the town be surveyed for tax purposes, and that 1873 plat is considered the official plat of Converse. The post office was changed from Xenia to Converse on June 25, 1892.

Conwells Mills (Franklin). See Laurel.

Cook [kuk] (Lake). This village was established in Hanover Township around 1855 and named Hanover Center by German immigrants. It developed after 1906 as a railroad station that was named Cook for a railroad worker, D. A. Cook. By 1920 the village, too, was called Cook.

Cooks Station (Elkhart). See Millersburg.

Cope [kop] (Morgan). A post office was established on December 9, 1870; closed on July 14, 1904.* Before the post office was established, James Crocker and Henson Martin opened the first store here in a log house.

Copeland (Parke). See Rockport.

Cork (Dearborn). See Weisburg.

Corn Brook [KAWRN bruk] (Bartholomew). A variant name of this community is Brook.

Cornelius [kawr-NEEL-yuhs] (Brown). This village once was known locally as Cottonwood, supposedly for a tree near a present cemetery (WPA). The official name, Cornelius, honoring an early settler, was applied to the local post office established on June 19, 1893; closed on June 15, 1907.

Cornettsville [KAWR-nuhts-vil] (Daviess). This village was laid out on May 22, 1875, and named for Samuel Cornett, who, with John F. and David Myers, laid out the town. A post office was established on April 9, 1878; closed on November 29, 1902.

Corning [KAWR-ning] (Daviess). The village was settled around 1828 and allegedly named by a priest for the corn growing here (WPA). The name is both a personal and place name in the United States, though, so the name perhaps comes from a person or another place. A post office was established on May 27, 1893; closed on November 29, 1902.

Cornucopia (Carroll). See Burrows.

Correct [kuh-REKT] (Ripley). A post office was established as Jimacoy, apparently coined from James W. McCoy, the name of the first postmaster, on August 19, 1881; changed to Correct on September 27, 1881; closed on September 14, 1905. According to an oral account,

William Will, postmaster at Versailles, was asked to suggest a name when a post office was established here in 1881. Since it was at the time of Halley's Comet, he wrote "Comet" on the form and sent it to the Post Office Department. The department found his handwriting difficult to read so re- turned a card with "Comet" on it and asked Will to verify the name. He wrote "correct," and that became the name of the town (ISUFA).

Cortland [KAWRT-luhnd] (Jackson). This village was founded in 1847 by Cyrus L. Dunham, who named it for his birthplace, Cortland, New York. A post office was established on May 4, 1850.

Corunna [kuh-RO-nuh] (DeKalb). This town was settled around 1855 and perhaps named for Corunna, Michigan, platted in 1837, although ultimately the name comes from a Spanish city. A post office was established on March 4, 1858.

Corwin [KAWR-wuhn] (Henry). This community developed as a railroad station. The place name also is found in Ohio and Kansas as well as in Tippecanoe County. It may be a variant of Corwen, a Welsh place name, though probably it came from a personal name.

Corwin [KAWR-wuhn] (Tippecanoe). This village was platted on August 29, 1832, by John Peterson and first called Columbia. A post office named Corwin was established on October 6, 1854; closed on November 30, 1854. Located on the Louisville, New Albany, and Chicago Railroad, it was earlier called Corwin Station. Cf. Corwin (Henry).

Cory [KAWR-ee] (Clay). This village was platted on April 5, 1872, and named for Simeon Cory, pioneer hardware merchant of Terre Haute. A post of- fice was

established on October 4, 1872. A local legend reflects the fact that Cory was famous for its apple orchards: "Cory, Indiana, got its name from its reputation as a great apple growing region. Cory is associated with the apple core" (ISUFA). Cory High School's teams were called the Apple Boys. Cory no longer has the big orchards developed after 1916 by E. A. Doud, who died in 1965, but holds an annual Apple Festival in the fall.

Corydon [KAWR-uh-duhn] (county seat, Harrison). This town was laid out in 1808 by Harvey Heth on land purchased from William Henry Harrison, and a post office was established on January 10, 1811. General Harrison, who purchased land here in 1804, named the place Corydon when he was governor of the Indiana Territory for the shepherd in his favorite song, "The Pastoral Elegy," which was in the popular songbook *Missouri Harmony*. Corydon was the seat of the Indiana Territory (1813–1816) and the first state capital (1816–1825).

Corydon Junction [KAWR-uh-duhn JUHNK-shuhn] (Harrison). This village was platted north of Corydon, for which it was named, by Joseph DeWeese on May 13, 1833, on the Corydon, New Albany, and Louisville Railroad.

Coryville (Wells). See Curryville.

Cosperville [KAHS-per-vil] (Noble). Formerly called Springfield, this village was laid out in 1844. A post office called Cosperville was established on January 28, 1891; closed on January 31, 1903. The name is for local farmer George Cosper, who apparently donated land for the village.

Cottage Grove [kahd-ij GROV] (Union). A post office was established on

March 24, 1848; closed on August 31, 1951. According to the WPA files, an old resident reported that this village was so named because all the original houses were of the "cottage type."

Cottonwood (Brown). See Cornelius.

Coulters Corner (Franklin). See Old Bath.

Courter [KAWR-ter] (Miami). This village was platted on March 8, 1871, by R. F. Donaldson on the Indianapolis, Peru, and Chicago Railroad. A post office named Courter, for a local family, already had been established here on July 26, 1869; closed on October 19, 1895.

Coveyville [KO-vee-vil; KUHV-ee-vil] (Lawrence). This village formerly was called Goat Run.

Covington [KUHV-ing-tuhn] (county seat, Fountain). A post office was established on May 28, 1827. The city was platted on December 24, 1828, by Isaac Coleman, a Virginian who settled here in 1826, so possibly the city was named for Covington, Virginia.

Cowan [KOW-uhn; KOW-wuhn] (Delaware). This village was laid out on November 5, 1869, by several men, including Charles McCowen, for whom it was named. A post office was established December 13, 1869; closed on June 15, 1923. Cowen is a variant spelling.

Coxborough (Wayne). See Richmond.

Coxton [KAHKS-tuhn] (Lawrence). This village was established as a railroad station. A post office was established on November 22, 1890; closed on January 31, 1903.

Coxville [KAHKS-vil] (Parke). A post office was established in 1823 and named Roseville, for Chauncey Rose, early settler and prominent citizen, who came here in 1819. The post office name was changed to Coxville on January 27, 1890, for William Cox, local miller; closed on November 30, 1906.

Crackaway (Boone). See Dover.

Crackaway (Decatur). See New Point.

Cradick Corner [krad-ik KAWR-ner] (Putnam). A variant spelling of the name of this village is Cradnick Corner.

Craig [kreg] (Switzerland). This village was established as a post office on September 18, 1849, and named for Craig Township, in which it is located. The township was named for George Craig, early settler. The post office was closed on April 15, 1907.

Craigville [KREG-vil] (Wells). This village was laid out on April 21, 1879, and named for William J. Craig, county clerk at that time. A post office was established on April 29, 1879.

Cranberry (Delaware). See Wheeling (Delaware).

Crandall [KRAN-duhl] (Harrison). This town was laid out on June 11, 1872, by Cornelius F. Crandall, for whom it was named. A post office was established on December 8, 1873, with Crandall as the first postmaster. Crandall Station is a variant name.

Crane [krayn] (Martin). In 1940 this area first was called the Burns City Ammunition Depot for nearby Burns City. When a housing unit was completed in 1943, it was renamed Crane, for Commodore William Montgomery Crane, first chief of the Navy Bureau of Ordinance and Hydrography in 1842. A post office was established at the Crane Naval Ammunition Depot on June 9, 1943.

Cranes Mills (Jackson). See New Elizabethtown.

Crawford County [KRAW-ferd]. This county, home of Marengo Cave and Wyandotte Cave, was organized in 1818 and probably named for Colonel William Crawford, Indian fighter and land agent for George Washington. Seat: English.

Crawfordsville [KRAW-ferdz-vil] (county seat, Montgomery). This city was platted in March 1823 by Major Ambrose Whitlock, who named it for Colonel William H. Crawford, a famous Indian fighter from Virginia, who was secretary of war, 1815–1816, secretary of the treasury, 1816–1825, and candidate for the presidency, 1824. A post office was established on May 30, 1820.

Crawleyville [KRAW-lee-vil] (Gibson). Formerly called Cabot, this village was settled in 1811 and named for a prominent local family whose name was spelled Crowley (WPA). Variant names are Crowley and Crowleyville.

Cresco [KRES-ko] (Whitley). A post office was established on May 10, 1888; closed on February 29, 1904. Supposedly the name, Latin for "I grow," is for Cresco Miller, a boy who lived nearby when the post office was established (WPA).

Creston [KRES-tuhn] (Lake). This village was settled around 1845. The Cedar Lake post office, named for a nearby lake, was established about a half mile from the present site of Creston around

1842 and relocated here in 1875. The post office name was changed to Creston on May 12, 1882; closed on September 15, 1935.

Creswell (Jefferson). See Smyrna.

Crete [kreet] (Randolph). A post office was established on December 13, 1882; closed on November 15, 1918. Allegedly the name is for a local resident's sweetheart whose name was Lucretia or Cretia. Perhaps the present spelling was influenced by the Mediterranean island, although not necessarily, since Crete, North Dakota, also was named for the nickname of a girl named Lucretia.

Crisman [KRIS-muhn] (Porter). This village was named for the local Crisman family, as B. G. Crisman was the founder, and Isaac Crisman was the first postmaster when a post office was established on May 15, 1871. The post office closed on August 31, 1933.

Crocker [KRAHK-er] (Porter). This village was laid out in 1875 by Fred LaHayn and called LaHayn for him. The present name, originally spelled Croker, allegedly was for the engineer of the first train to pass through here or for the surveyor who laid out the village (WPA). A post office named Croker was established on June 24, 1893; changed to Crocker December 13, 1894; closed on June 15, 1905.

Cromwell [KRAHM-wel] (Noble). This town was laid out in June 1853 by Harrison Wood, who allegedly said, "[Oliver] Cromwell was a good republican and I'll name the town in his honor." A post office was established on July 22, 1851.

Crossed Roads (Lawrence). See Fayetteville (Lawrence).

Crossing (La Porte). See Otis.

Cross Plains [kraws PLAYNZ] (Ripley). This village was laid out on February 2, 1826, and so named for its location on a crossroads on level ground. A post office was established on September 4, 1826.

Cross Roads [KRAWS rodz] (Delaware). John C. Gustin opened a small, short-lived store here at the crossing of the Muncie Road and Yorktown Road around 1832, and about 1838 William and Erasmus Moffett opened another store on the same corner. A post office called Cross Roads was established on June 16, 1879; changed to Crossroads on October 4, 1895; closed on October 14, 1901. The name is descriptive of the settlement's location at the crossing of two roads.

Cross Roads (Parke). See Guion.

Cross Roads (Pike). See Algiers.

Cross Roads (Posey). See Wadesville.

Cross Roads [KRAWS rodz] (Ripley). According to the WPA files, this village first was called Hackmans Cross Roads "because a man named Hackman had a store here and it was located where two roads crossed. . . . When Hackman died nobody carried on with the store so the people dropped the name of Hackman." Another variant name is Spanglerville.

Cross Roads [KRAWS rodz] (Vanderburgh). A post office was established here on July 8, 1850; closed on October 6, 1851. Cf. Armstrong.

Crothersville [KRUH-therz-vil] (Jackson). This town was founded in 1835 and originally called Haysville, allegedly because the land was suited for growing hay. Shortly after, the name was changed to Crothersville, supposedly for Dr. Crothers, a railroad superintendent who promised to build a depot here. A post office was established as Crothersville on December 17, 1857.

Crowleyville (Gibson). See Crawleyville.

Crown Center [krown SEN-ter] (Morgan). Originally this community was called Mount Tabor, but apparently because there was another Hoosier town of that name, the Post Office Department applied the present name on March 27, 1891. The post office was closed on May 15, 1905.

Crown Point [krown POYNT] (county seat, Lake). This city was founded about 1834 and first known as Robinsons Prairie, for Solon and Milo Robinson. Allegedly, when Solon Robinson saved his neighbors' lands from speculators, he was nicknamed "King of the Squatters," and the settlement was renamed Crown Point: "Crown" for the "king" and "Point" for the elevation on which the courthouse and Robinson's cabin stood. The town was laid out in 1840 as a new county seat, and according to one source, "The name Crown Point was applied under the following circumstances: 'I have a name to propose,' said George Earle, Agent. 'So have I,' replied Solon Robinson. 'What is your name?' 'Crown Point.' 'And that is also mine.'" Possibly the name was suggested by that of a nearby settlement, West Point, and borrowed from New York for its commendatory value. The post office was established on June 26, 1845.

Crows Nest [KROZ nest] (Marion). This community was laid out and incorporated on May 8, 1927, and so named, according to the WPA files, because crows nested in a tree here.

Crums Point (Saint Joseph). See Crumstown.

Crumstown [KRUHMZ-town] (Saint Joseph). This village, platted on April 21, 1875, formerly was called Crums Point, for the family of Nathaniel H. Crum, early settler and prominent citizen. A post office was established as Crums Point on May 6, 1875; changed to Crumtown on February 3, 1888; closed on December 31, 1918.

Crystal [KRIS-tuhl] (Dubois). This village, founded around 1880, was never platted, but a post office was established here on September 11, 1889; closed on February 28, 1919.

Cuba [KYOO-buh] (Allen). This village was laid out in 1855 and apparently named for the island.

Cuba [KYOO-buh] (Owen). This village was laid out in 1851 for William L. Hart, proprietor, and called Santa Fe. The post office, established June 18, 1851, was called Cuba, apparently for the island; closed on December 31, 1909.

Culver [KUHL-ver] (Marshall). This town was laid out on June 8, 1844, and called Union Town. The present name is for the founder of Culver Military Academy, Henry Harrison Culver. Other former names were Marmont, for the French general, and Culver City. A post office established in this county as Yellow River on December 26, 1850, was changed to Marmont on April 3, 1860, and to Culver on January 12, 1897.

Culvertown (Starke). See San Pierre.

Cumback [KUHM-bak] (Daviess). This village was settled in 1883 and named for Hoosier politician William Cumback. A post office was established on August 3, 1881; closed on November 15, 1905.

Cumberland [KUHM-ber-luhnd] (Marion). This town was platted in the summer of 1831 and named for the Cumberland Road, on which it was located. A post office was established on January 10, 1834; closed on June 1, 1958.

Cunningham (Clark). See Hamburg (Clark).

Cunot [KYOO-naht] (Owen). A post office was established on October 31, 1894; closed on February 28, 1905. According to an oral account, the name may be descriptive of a winding road with a Q-shaped turn through here. The variant name, Needmore, comes from an alleged statement—either "We need more stables," according to an oral account (ISUFA), or the place would "need more houses in order to make a town," according to a printed account.

Curby [KER-bee] (Crawford). A post office was established on February 3, 1904; closed on June 15, 1915.

Curryville [KER-ee-vil] (Sullivan). A post office called Currysville was established on April 24, 1840; closed on October 9, 1861.* The name probably comes from Curry Township, in which the village, laid out in 1885, is located. The township was named for William Curry, who came here from Kentucky in 1817.

Curryville [KER-ee-vil] (Wells). Located on the Adams-Wells county line, this village was platted on March 25, 1859, and called Coryville, for Peter Corey, on whose land it was located. A post office called Curryville was established on May 15, 1879; closed on April 16, 1880; reestablished April 27, 1880; closed on June 29, 1907.

Curtisville [KER-tuhs-vil] (Tipton). About 1859 L. B. Colvin built a sawmill here along the railroad and sold lots in order to establish a railroad station. A post office was established July 13, 1858; closed on June 30, 1951.

Cutler [KUHT-ler] (Carroll). This village was settled in 1828 and named for a railroad official named Cutler (WPA). A post office was established on January 21, 1873.

Cuzco [KUHZ-ko] (Dubois). A post office was established on June 20, 1902; closed on March 31, 1955. This village was platted on September 27, 1905, and originally named Union Valley because residents were opposed to slavery. The present name comes from the city in Peru, South America.

Cyclone [SEYE-klon] (Clinton). A post office was established on June 29, 1883; closed on October 14, 1933. The village was named for a cyclone of June 14, 1880.

Cynthiana [sin-thee-AN-uh] (Posey). This town was laid out on March 6, 1817, and named by William Davis for Cynthiana, Kentucky, home of Davis and other settlers. The Kentucky community was named for Cynthia and Anna Harrison, daughters of the donor of the land on which the town was built, and a local tradition is that this Hoosier town, too, was named for two daughters of the founder. A post office was established on May 30, 1820.

Cynthiana (Shelby). See Blue Ridge.

Cypress [SEYE-pruhs] (Vanderburgh). A post office called Cypress was established on April 21, 1882; closed on September 30, 1933. An oral account explains the variant name, Dogtown: "When they were building the railroad south of town along the river, all the railroad men camped at this one place. And when they threw the food out, a bunch of dogs gathered around, so they called the place Dogtown" (ISUFA). According to the WPA files, the village is "better known as Dogtown" and "received the name Dogtown from the large number of dogs owned by the inhabitants of the village, which barked fiercely at people passing through the village."

 **D**

Dabney [DAB-nee] (Ripley). A post office was moved here from Otter Village, q.v., on December 2, 1856, and called Poston. The post office name was changed to Dabney on September 14, 1897, and the post office was closed on February 15, 1934. The village was laid out on May 16, 1855, and named

Poston, but allegedly because it sounded so much like Holton, people often got off the train at the wrong station. According to a local legend, a train dispatcher got the communities mixed up and almost caused a wreck, so the railroad company called the community Dabney for the postmaster, whose name was Dabney (WPA). There is no record of a postmaster named Dabney, however.

Daggett [DAG-it; DAG-uht] (Owen). This village was laid out in March 1880 and named for Charles Daggett, co-owner of a large sawmill and planing mill here. A post office was established on November 22, 1880, with William A. H. Coday as postmaster; closed August 28, 1896.*

Dale [dayl] (Spencer). This town was laid out on April 26, 1843, and named Elizabeth, supposedly for Elizabeth Jones, the first nonnative child born in Center Township (ISUFA), but since there already were two other communities named Elizabeth in the state, it was renamed Dale, for Robert Dale Owen of New Harmony, who was a congressman when the name was changed. A post office named Dale was established on August 15, 1844.

Daleville [DAYL-vil] (Delaware). This village was platted on November 10, 1838, by Campbell Dale and originally called Dalesville for him. A post office was established on September 1, 1857.

Dalton [DAWL-tuhn] (Wayne). According to the WPA files, this village was platted in January 1828. Probably it was named for the township in which it is located. A post office called Palmyra was established on March 25, 1835; changed to Dalton on February 13, 1838; closed on October 31, 1901.

Dana [DAY-nuh] (Vermillion). A post office established on April 5, 1838, at nearby Toronto was moved here on January 22, 1874. The town was platted on August 18, 1874. The name honors Charles Dana, a stockholder in the Indianapolis, Decatur, and Western Railroad, which came through here in 1874.

Dante (Marshall). See Hibbard.

Danville [DAN-vil] (Clay). This community was platted by Daniel Shidler, for whom it was named, in 1874.

Danville (Fayette). See Orange (Fayette)

Danville [DAN-vil] (county seat, Hendricks). This town was laid out in 1824 by Thomas Hinton on land donated by Daniel Beals, George Mattock, Robert Wilson, and James Downard, each of whom donated twenty acres. Supposedly it was named by William Watson Wick, judge of the fifth circuit, for his brother Daniel. A post office was established on April 1, 1825.

Danville (Lawrence). See Fayetteville.

Dan Webster (Henry). See Hillsboro (Henry).

Darby (Adams). See Pleasant Mills.

Dark Hollow [dahrk HAH-lo] (Lawrence). This village, named for a quarry of the same name, was founded about 1875. According to the WPA files, the quarry was named Dark Hollow "because it is located between two large hills and in a natural hollow." A post office was established on July 7, 1893; closed on January 15, 1901.*

Darlington [DAHR-ling-tuhn] (Montgomery). According to the WPA files, this town was first settled in 1823. It was platted in February 1836 by Enoch Cox. Supposedly it was named for the English community of the same name by Quaker settlers. According to an oral account, Darlington was "once named Darling Town, although it was nicknamed the Sweet Town because it's at the point where Sugar Creek meets Honey Creek" (ISUFA). A post office was established on October 9, 1837.

Darmstadt [DAHRM-stat] (Vanderburgh). This village was established about 1860 by Germans who named it for Darmstadt, Germany. A variant spelling is Darnstadt.

Darsyville (Parke). See Rosedale.

Darter (Putnam). See Russellville.

Daughertys Shoals (Martin). See Shoals.

Daviess County [DAY-vuhs]. This county was organized in 1817 and named for Colonel Joseph Hamilton Daviess, who was killed in the Battle of Tippecanoe. Jacob Piatt Dunn says the "Colonel's name was Daveiss and he always wrote it that way."

Darwin (Carroll). See Carrollton.

Davidsburg (Owen). See Stockton.

Davidson [DAY-vuhd-suhn] (Harrison). A post office was established here on June 18, 1838, with David Aistin as postmaster and presumably named for him. The post office was closed on April 30, 1924.*

Davis [DAY-vuhs] (La Porte). Also called Davis Station, this community supposedly was named for "Mr. Davis,"

who "built a shanty and fished and trapped here for over fifty years" (WPA).

Daylight [DAY-leyet] (Vanderburgh). A post office was established on April 4, 1900. Allegedly this community was named for a remark of a railroad engineer. Each evening when he dropped off a construction crew here, he said, "I'll pick you men up at daylight"; eventually Daylight became the name of the village.

Dayton [DAYT-uhn] (Tippecanoe). This village was laid out in 1827 by William Bush on his land and named Fairfield. About the same time, Timothy Horram divided eighty acres into town lots and named his division Marquis. In 1830 David Gregory platted a north division to the village and, at his suggestion, the village was renamed Dayton for the city in Ohio. A post office named Dayton was established on April 19, 1831.

Dayville [DAY-vil] (Warrick). According to the WPA files, this village was named for the Day family, descendants of Thomas Day, who settled in the county in 1850. A post office was established here on January 12, 1900, with George O. Day as the postmaster; closed on November 30, 1901.

Deacon [DEE-kuhn] (Cass). Never platted, this village was named for William C. Deacon, merchant and first postmaster, when a post office was established on June 6, 1884. The post office was closed on July 31, 1903.

Dearborn County [DEER-bern]. This county was organized in 1803 and named for Major General Henry Dearborn, who served in the Revolution and was secretary of war, 1801–1809.

Decatur [dee-KAY-ter; di-KAY-ter] (county seat, Adams). This city was platted in 1836 by Thomas Johnson and Samuel Rugg and named for naval hero Stephen Decatur. A post office was established on April 1, 1837.

Decatur County [di-KAY-ter]. This county was organized in 1821 and named for Commodore Stephen Decatur, naval hero of the War of 1812. Seat: Greensburg.

Decker [DEK-er] (Knox). A post office was established as Deckers Station on May 21, 1858, with Isaac Decker as the first postmaster; changed to Decker on November 28, 1882. Formerly called Deckertown, also spelled Decker Town, and Deckers, the town was laid out in June 1869 by Isaac Decker. The township also is named Decker for the Decker family, early settlers.

Decker Chapel [dek-er CHAP-uhl] (Knox). This village is located in Decker Township, and a Methodist church was located here. Cf. Decker.

Deeds Creek (Kosciusko). See Pierceton.

Deedsville [DEEDZ-vil] (Miami). After the Cincinnati, Chicago, and Louisville Railroad was completed through here in 1869, William Deeds built a warehouse on his farm to handle grain and produce, and the village, platted in July 1870 by Deeds, was named for him. The post office was established on February 18, 1870.

Deep River [deep RIV-er] (Lake). According to the WPA files, this village was first settled in 1836 and named for the nearby stream of the same name. A post office named Deep River was established

on June 23, 1838; changed to Deepriver on September 10, 1895; closed on February 28, 1910.

Deer Creek [DEER kreek] (Carroll). A post office called Deer Creek, for the nearby stream of the same name, was established on December 17, 1832; closed on July 25, 1911.* The stream name comes from the Miami name, Passeanong, "The Place of the Fawn." A variant name is West Sonora.

Deer Creek [DEER kreek] (Lake). This village was named for the nearby stream of the same name.

Deerfield [DEER-feeld] (Randolph). This village was laid out on September 28, 1833. A post office named Mississinewa, for the nearby river, was established on June 22, 1833, and changed to Deerfield on May 5, 1837. This post office was moved to nearby Randolph, q.v., on October 8, 1869, and was closed on August 15, 1900. On December 22, 1869, another post office was established here as Deerfield, and this post office was closed on January 15, 1915.

Deer Mill [DEER mil] (Montgomery). This community was named for Joel G. Deer, who built a gristmill here on his land.

De Gonia Springs [duh GON-yuh SPRINGZ; dee GO-nee-uh SPRINGZ] (Warrick). A post office was established on August 14, 1879; closed on December 15, 1926. According to an informant from this area, "It is said that in the 1920s, it was a prosperous summer resort area. There were cabins to be rented for lodging and plenty of things to do for entertainment. It is said that the biggest reason that people went there for was the water—mineral water. . . . It was supposedly magical and worked wonders for your health. It was a very smart move and a very popular place to go for vacations or to get the water" (ISUFA). Degonia Springs is a variant spelling.

Dekalb (DeKalb). See Saint Johns.

DeKalb County [di-KALB; dee-KALB]. This county was organized in 1837 and named for Baron Johann de Kalb, Revolutionary War general. Baron de Kalb, a Bavarian who entered the French service in 1743 and the American service in 1777, was killed at Camden in 1780. Seat: Auburn.

Delaware [DEL-uh-wehr] (Ripley). This village was platted on May 16, 1870. A post office was established as Delaware Station on January 10, 1860; changed to Rei on August 7, 1861; changed to Delaware on January 21, 1889; and closed on October 31, 1933. There was another post office called Delaware, which was located north of here in the same township at Melissaville, q.v. Both post office names were for Delaware Township, in which they were located.

Delaware County [DEL-uh-wehr]. This county, home of Ball State University, was organized in 1827 and named for the Delaware Indians, who had villages in the area from 1770 to 1818. Seat: Muncie.

Delectable Hill (Pike). See Algiers.

Delong [dee-LAWNG; duh-LAWNG] (Fulton). According to the WPA files this village was founded in 1871 and named for early settlers, though it developed around 1883 as a railroad station and may have been named for the railroad station agent. A post office was estab-lished as De Long on September 26, 1884; changed to Delong on February 20, 1894; and closed on April 30, 1955.

Delphi [DEL-feye] (county seat, Carroll). This city was laid out as the county seat in May 1828 and first called Carrollton, for the county, but nine days later the name was changed to Delphi, for the Greek city and shrine, at the suggestion of General Samuel Milroy, a leader in the organization of the county. A post office was established on July 2, 1828.

Delta (Parke). See West Union.

Deming [DEM-ing; DEM-eeng] (Hamilton). This village, first called Farmington, was laid out on August 10, 1837, by Elihu Pickett, Solomon Pheanis, and Lewis Jessup. According to the WPA files, the current name is for an abolition candidate for president. A post office established as Penfield on April 7, 1846, was changed to Deming on January 14, 1854, and closed on October 15, 1902.

DeMotte [dee-MAHT; duh-MAHT] (Jasper). A post office was established as De Motte on June 5, 1882, and the spelling was changed to Demotte on May 25, 1893. The town (written De-Motte) was laid out on August 23, 1884. The name honors Congressman Mark L. DeMotte of Valparaiso. DeMotte served as a colonel during the Civil War and founded Valparaiso University's law school.

Denham [DEN-uhm] (Pulaski). A store was opened here in 1868. A post office established as Gundrum on March 17, 1870, was changed to Denham on July 17, 1888. The original name was for the first merchant, Paul Gundrum. Supposedly the name was changed by railroad officials.

Denmark [DEN-mahrk] (Owen). A post office was established at this unplatted village on September 16, 1874; closed on September 30, 1905.* In the early days, the center of activity in this community was a store operated by William Herstine, who became the first postmaster. Apparently the name is for the country.

Denver [DEN-ver] (Miami). Earlier called Urbana, the town was laid out as Denver by Harrison Grimes in August 1872, about the time that the Eel River Railroad was being built through the county. The present name, for Denver, Colorado, was applied to the local post office, established on June 29, 1869. There was another settlement called Urbanna, sometimes spelled Urbana, established by Andrew Wolpert on April 21, 1854, in the southern part of Miami County near McGrawsville.

Depauw [dee-PAW] (Harrison). This village was platted on April 8, 1884. The name probably is from the personal name, perhaps for industrialist Washington C. DePauw of nearby New Albany, for whom DePauw University was named the same year. A post office named De Pauw was established on May 7, 1884, and the spelling was changed to Depauw on January 19, 1894. A variant spelling has been Depaw.

Depot (Knox). See Oaktown.

Deputy [DEP-yu-dee] (Jefferson). A post office was established on May 5, 1870, and the village was laid out by Foster C. Wilson on March 29, 1871. The name honors the local Deputy family. James Deputy was an early settler.

Derby [DER-bee] (Perry). This village was laid out in 1835 and named by Samuel Frisbie for Derby, Ireland, the home of his ancestors. A post office was established on October 19, 1852.

Desoto [dee-SO-to; di-SO-to; duh-SO-to] (Delaware). This village was platted on January 8, 1881, and originally called Woodlawn. Because of confusion with a community of the same name in Allen County, the name was changed to Desoto, for the Spanish explorer. A post office called De Soto was established on August 1, 1881; changed to Desoto on February 6, 1895; and closed on May 31, 1956.

Deuchars [DOO-shahr] (Crawford). A post office was established on July 13, 1925; closed on January 31, 1960. Variant spellings have been Deuchara and Deuchers.

Devore [duh-VAWR; dee-VAWR; di-VAWR] (Owen). Originally this community was called Mill Grove, for a mill here. The village was surveyed in March 1835 for John Hallenback, proprietor, and named for the Devore family, early settlers. Nicholas Devore, a pioneer preacher, settled in the county around 1822, and Henry Devore entered the county around 1828. A post office was established on November 1, 1893; closed on March 31, 1904. Hugh B. Devore was the second postmaster.

Dewberry [DOO-behr-ee] (Ripley). A post office was established here on May 17, 1882; closed on February 3, 1887.

Dexter [DEKS-ter] (Perry). A post office was established on June 15, 1870; closed on December 31, 1948.*

Diamond [DEYE-muhnd; DEYE-muhn] (Parke). Originally called Caseyville, for a local storekeeper, this village was renamed Diamond for the coal, "black diamond," here when a post office was established on October 19, 1891. The post office was closed on September 15, 1934.

Dickeyville [DIK-ee-vil] (Warrick). A post office was established on June 17, 1884; closed on October 31, 1903. The name honors a local family.

Dicksons Mills (Parke). See Mansfield.

Dillman [DIL-muhn] (Wells). According to the WPA files, this village was named for Andrew Dillman, who came here in 1854 from Ohio. A post office was established on May 31, 1880; closed on June 29, 1907.

Dillsboro [DILZ-ber-o] (Dearborn). This town was laid out on March 16, 1830, by Mathias Whetstone and originally called Dillsborough. A post office was established as Dillsborough on February 4, 1837. The spelling of the name was changed to Dillsboro on August 2, 1893. Probably the name is for General James Dill, prominent in the history of the county.

Dillsboro Station [DILZ-ber-o STAY-shuhn] (Dearborn). The name of this village, also spelled Dillsborough Station, is for Dillsboro, q.v. According to a local legend, "Dillsboro Station is located in a hollow that is called Station Hollow. The station was an old station that the railroad used to make stops there for the farmers to take their produce to the city of Cincinnati. There is a legend concerning the hollow that tells of a couple that got killed crossing the railroad tracks on their way to a dance. The name of the crossing isn't on the map, but the local people call it Blinking Light Crossing, and it has been said that the lights on the railroad sign blink even when there isn't a train coming" (ISUFA).

Dinwiddie [DIN-wid-ee] (Lake). This village was named for the local Dinwiddie family. Oscar Dinwiddie, oldest son of pioneer J. W. Dinwiddie, was a farmer and officer in the state and national granges. William Dinwiddie was the first physician in the township.

Disko [DIS-ko] (Wabash). This village was platted by George Gearhart on July 1, 1856, and originally called New Harrisburg, probably for Harrisburg, Pennsylvania. A post office established as New Harrisburg on January 4, 1871, was changed to Disko on August 28, 1883. According to the WPA files, the present name is for the railroad station here. A variant spelling is Disco, and the name may come from Disco, a bay and island west of Greenland, but the name is found in Michigan, too, where it comes from a nineteenth-century school named for the Latin "I learn."

Dixie [DIK-see] (Harrison). A post office was established on June 28, 1892; closed on November 15, 1905.*

Dixon [DIK-suhn] (Greene). Daniel Dixon, the proprietor, laid out this village, named for him, in November 1872. A post office was established on April 14, 1873; closed on October 31, 1904.

Dixons Mills (Parke). See Mansfield.

Doans [donz] (Greene). According to the WPA files, this town originally was called Snake Hollow for a rattlesnake found here. According to Baber's county history, Snake Hollow was "named by old Jimmy, the well-digger. Mr. Webb, the old Englishman who came over the ocean to look for Katydids, found a rattlesnake in that hollow, after it had bitten his finger." It was renamed Doans, for nearby Doans Creek, when a post office was established on October 7, 1899. The small stream was named for an early settler, Isaac Doan.

Doblestown (Shelby). See Pleasant View.

Dodd [dahd] (Perry). A post office was established on March 19, 1898; closed on November 30, 1935.* The name is for a local family. According to the WPA files, George Dodd was an early settler. Betty Dodd was the fourth postmaster.

Dodsons Landing (Perry). See Magnet.

Dogtown (Vanderburgh). See Cypress.

Dog Walk (Owen). See Adel.

Dogwood [DAWG-wud] (Harrison). A post office was established here on April 10, 1890; closed on November 30, 1922. Apparently the name is for the tree.

Dolan [DO-luhn] (Monroe). This village was laid out in April 1851 and named for a pioneer miller, John Dolan. A post office was established on August 2, 1888; closed on December 31, 1904.

Domestic [duh-MES-tik] (Wells). This village formerly was called Ringville. A post office called Domestic, apparently a commendatory name, though the origin is unknown, was established on March 17, 1884; closed on February 15, 1905.

Donaldson [DAHN-uhld-suhn; DAHN-uhl-suhn] (Marshall). This village was platted on October 25, 1871, and a post office was established on February 7, 1871. An earlier spelling was Donelson.

Donaldsonville [DAHN-uhld-suhn-vil] (Clay). This village was laid out by Mrs.

E. D. Rardan on September 9, 1867, and named for her maiden name, Donaldson.

Dongola [dawng-GO-luh] (Gibson). This village was laid out in March 1851 by William Carpenter and Isaac Street. A post office was established on September 9, 1851; closed on March 24, 1862. This Sudanese place name also is found in Kentucky and Illinois.

Doolittle Mills [DOO-lut-uhl MILZ] (Perry). A post office called Doolittles Mills was established on July 18, 1870, and named for the Doolittle family, who operated a mill here. Henry B. Doolittle was the second postmaster, and Isaac C. Doolittle was the sixth postmaster. The post office name was changed to Doolittle Mills on March 26, 1892, and the post office was closed on March 10, 1967.

Door Village [dawr VIL-ij] (La Porte). This village was settled about 1830 and surveyed in 1836 on Door Prairie. The name of the town and prairie are translations of the name of the county, La Porte. French traders and explorers found a natural opening in the forest in this area and called it La Porte, "the door." A post office was established on January 6, 1834; closed on September 15, 1900.*

Dotyville (Parke). See Rosedale.

Douglas [DUHG-luhs] (Gibson). This village was platted in 1851 and originally called Maxam, sometimes spelled Maxams, for Napoleon Maxam, early settler. A post office was established as Maxams on January 20, 1890; closed on August 13, 1904. The present name comes from the local Douglass family. Jasper N. Douglass was the first postmaster.

Dover [DO-ver] (Boone). First known as Crackaway, the village was laid out by Aris Pauly in 1850. On February 27, 1860, a post office was established here and called Dover, perhaps a transfer from an eastern state. The Dover post office was closed on August 20, 1872. A nearby post office, established on March 21, 1873, and closed on January 31, 1901, was called Cason, for Thomas J. Cason of Lebanon.

Dover [DO-ver] (Dearborn). John Kelso, a native of Ireland, settled in the county in 1813, and a township and this town were named for him. A post office called Kelso was established on December 1, 1830; closed on November 30, 1936.* McKenzie Cross Roads, for Henry McKenzie, who became the second postmaster, was another former name.

Dover (Saint Joseph). See North Liberty.

Dover (Wayne). See Webster.

Dover Hill [do-ver HIL] (Martin). This village, said to be the highest locale in the county, was laid out on September 12, 1845, and called Hillsborough. A few years later the name was changed to Dover Hill, supposedly because the high cliffs here reminded English settlers of the cliffs of Dover, England. A post office called Dover Hill was established on July 24, 1846; changed to Doverhill on July 28, 1894; closed on April 14, 1906.

Downeyville [DOW-nee-vil] (Decatur). Never platted, the village was named for early settler J. F. Downey, who with his sons had a general store here. When a post office was established on June 13, 1876, Amos F. Downey became the first postmaster. The post office was closed on March 31, 1903.

Down Hill (Crawford). See Eckerty.

Doyle [doyl] (Miami). This unplatted village was established as a siding on the Lake Erie and Western Railroad for the convenience of nearby farmers and was named for a local family.

Dresser (Vigo). See Taylorville.

Drewersburg [DROO-erz-berg] (Franklin). Originally called Edinburg, this village was platted in November 1833 and named for a resident, William S. Drewer, who lived here when the town was laid out. A post office was established on March 21, 1837; closed on September 15, 1903.* Drewersburgh has been a variant spelling.

Drexel Gardens [dreks-uhl GAHR-duhnz] (Marion). This community perhaps was named for nearby Drexel Run.

Drusilla [droo-SIL-uh] (Jackson). A post office was established on December 20, 1831; closed on April 16, 1838. The village was laid out by John J. Judy on September 27, 1833. Drucilla is a variant spelling.

Dublin (Parke). See Mansfield.

Dublin [DUHB-luhn] (Wayne). This town was settled around 1821 and laid out in 1830 by Harmon Davis. A post office was established on January 8, 1833. Probably the name is for the Irish city, but according to local anecdote, "Dublin, in the early days, was a famous mud hole just west of Cambridge City. Wagons and stagecoaches when passing this spot had to double team to get through. This condition continued until the National Road was built. When the town was platted, it was decided to call it Dublin, because of always having to double team at that place. There is a marker to designate the place" (WPA). According to another legend, "Dublin, Indiana, got its name from the old home place, [the] Huddleston House. The home place used to be called Double Inn because it had double doors" (ISUFA).

Dubois [DOO-boyz] (Dubois). A post office established on December 8, 1879, and named Polsonton, for the local Polson family, was changed to Dubois, for the county in which it is located, on August 2, 1880. The village, platted on November 5, 1885, was settled in 1826 by Andrew Kelso and called Kelsos Mill. It also has been called Polsons Mill and Knoxville.

Dubois County [DOO-boyz]. This county was organized in 1817 and named for Toussaint Dubois, a French merchant and soldier from Vincennes who fought with General William Henry Harrison at Tippecanoe. Dubois recorded land in this area in 1807.

Dubois Crossroads [DOO-boyz KRAWS-rodz] (Dubois). This community, named for the county, dates from 1928, when a gas station was established here.

Duck Creek (Madison). See Elwood.

Dudleytown [DUHD-lee-town] (Jackson). This village was laid out on April 12, 1837, by James Dudley, for whom it was named. A post office was established on September 13, 1847; closed on December 31, 1904.

Duff [duhf] (Dubois). According to the WPA files, this village was founded in 1833 and named for Colonel B. B. "Duff" Edmonstan. A post office was established

on March 10, 1868; closed on March 31, 1955.*

Duff (Dubois). See Millersport.

Dugger [DUHG-er] (Sullivan). This town was laid out in 1879 by Francis M. Dugger and Henry T. Neal and named for Dugger. An oral account says that "it was established as a coal town and there was a coal operator named Dugger" (ISUFA), which is true. First the town was called Fairchild, for John Fairchild, a superintendent for the Dugger Coal Company, but in a short time the name was changed to Dugger for the coal company and the town's founder. When a post office was established as Dugger on March 22, 1881, Edgar A. Fairchild was the postmaster. The community's history of coal mining is reflected in the local Coal Museum.

Duncan [DUHNK-uhn] (Floyd). A post office was established here on January 16, 1899; closed on September 30, 1915. The name honors the local Duncan family. Spergheum Duncan owned land here.

Dundee (Blackford). See Roll.

Dundee [duhn-DEE] (Madison). Originally called Mudsock, for the marshy quality of the soil, this town was platted on December 6, 1883, by Riley Etchison. A post office named Dundee was established on December 26, 1876; closed on August 15, 1902. Probably the name is for the city in Scotland.

Dune Acres [doon AY-kerz] (Porter). This town was laid out in 1923, incorporated in 1925, and named for the Indiana Dunes, some of the highest of which are here. According to the WPA files, the name was "suggested by the large number of acres of the estate located on the Dunes."

Dune Acres Station [doon ay-kerz STAY-shuhn] (Porter). This railroad station was named for nearby Dune Acres, q.v.

Duneland Beach [doon-luhnd BEECH] (La Porte). This community was named for the Indiana Dunes.

Dunfee [DUHN-fee; DUHM-fee] (Whitley). A post office called Dunfee was established here on April 6, 1883; closed on April 30, 1917. The name probably is for a local family, as Jonathan S. Dunfee settled in Jefferson Township in 1850. According to the WPA files, though, the name is for a railroad official.

Dunhams Station (Jackson). See Shields.

Dunkirk [DUHNG-kerk] (Jay). This city was platted first on December 10, 1853, by Isaiah Sutton and originally called Quincy. The name was changed because there was another community named Quincy in the state. The present name might be for Dunkirk, New York, home of glass blowers who came here to work in a glass manufacturing plant. It also has been suggested that the name comes from the local Dunkirk Masonic Lodge, which supposedly bore the name before the city. A post office named Dunkirk was established on February 28, 1856.

Dunlap [DUHN-lap] (Elkhart). Unplatted, this village was named for a railroad official. When a post office was established on December 2, 1886, the name was spelled Dunlaps. The post office was closed on December 15, 1902.

Dunlapsville [DUHN-laps-vil] (Union). This village was platted in September 1817 and named for John Dunlap, early settler, mill owner, proprietor, and first postmaster. The post office was established on January 22, 1818; closed on October 14, 1903.*

Dunn [duhn] (Benton). A post office was established here on October 26, 1907, and named for Captain James Dunn, who founded nearby Dunnington. The post office was closed on May 31, 1913.

Dunnington [DUHN-ing-tuhn] (Benton). This village was named for its founder, Captain James Dunn. Manvella Dunn was the first postmaster when a post office was established on October 6, 1888. The post office was closed on September 30, 1903.

Dunns Bridge [duhnz brij] (Jasper). This unincorporated village was named for the local Dunn family. Cf. Tefft, a nearby village earlier called Dunnville.

Dunns Settlement (Jefferson). See Hanover (Jefferson).

Dunnville (Jasper). See Tefft.

Dunreith [DUHN-reeth] (Henry). This town, laid out on July 22, 1865, earlier was called Coffins Station, for Emery Dunreith Coffin, and the post office was established as Coffins Station on July 2, 1861. The post office name was changed to Dunreith, for Coffin's middle name, on October 7, 1867.

Dupont [DOO-pahnt] (Jefferson). This town was laid out on January 2, 1849, by James Tilton of Wilmington, Delaware, who earlier had named the town for the Du Pont family, Delaware manufacturers of gunpowder. A post office established as Lancaster on March 16, 1830, was changed to Dupont on August 30, 1839.

Durbin [DER-buhn] (Hamilton). A post office was established on February 6, 1890; closed on January 31, 1905.

Durham [DER-uhm] (La Porte). This village sprang up around 1837, was laid out in 1847, and was named for New Durham Township, which was named for Durham, Greene County, New York. A post office was established on September 14, 1880; closed on February 5, 1884.

Durkees Ferry (Vigo). See Tecumseh (Vigo).

Dye [deye] (Martin). A post office was established here on September 1, 1858; closed on October 20, 1874.

Dyer [DEYE-er] (Lake). A post office named Dyer was established on February 11, 1857. According to official records, the town, which developed around a railroad station, was platted on June 1, 1855, but a note in the plat book states that the plat actually was recorded on March 28, 1858.

Dyes Grove (Hancock). See Spring Lake.

 **E**

Eagletown [EE-guhl-town] (Hamilton). This village, laid out on March 21, 1848, by Jesse Waller and Ephraim Stout, was established as a railroad station and named after Little Eagle Creek. A post office was established on December 20, 1849; closed on April 11, 1925.

Eagle Village [ee-guhl VIL-ij; ee-guhl VIL-eej] (Boone). This village, which also has been called Eagle, was laid out in 1829 in Eagle Township, for which it was named. A post office was established on December 15, 1832; closed on January 29, 1858.

Eagleville (Steuben). See Jamestown (Steuben).

Eames [eemz] (Warrick). A post office was established on January 31, 1882; closed on July 25, 1894.*

Earle [erl] (Vanderburgh). This village was named for John Earle, an English settler who came here in 1828. A post office was established on February 27, 1871; closed on June 15, 1901. A variant spelling is Earl.

Earl Park [erl PAHRK] (Benton). A post office was established on June 26, 1872, and the town was laid out on July 31, 1872, by Mr. and Mrs. Adams Earl and A. D. Raub and named for the Earls. There is a large park here, too. Earl and Raub also built a general store here in 1872.

East Chicago [eest shi-KAH-go; eest shi-KAW-go] (Lake). A post office was established here on January 14, 1889, the same year the city was incorporated. The name is locational, as the city is located east of Chicago, which means "place of wild onions."

East Columbus [eest kuh-LUHM-buhs; eest kuh-LUHM-bus] (Bartholomew). This village was platted on February 20, 1873. The name is locational, since the village is situated east of Columbus, q.v.

East Enterprise [eest EN-ter-preyez] (Switzerland). This village formerly was called Clapboard Corner for a local clapboard mill. A post office was moved here from nearby Allensville, q.v., on February 6, 1864. Because the post office moved back and forth between these two villages until March 1, 1865, when a post office remained here, Allensville sometimes is given as a variant name of East Enterprise.

East Gary (Lake). See Lake Station.

Eastgate [EEST-gayt] (Hancock). East Gate is a variant spelling of this village.

East Germantown [eest JER-muhn-town] (Wayne). This town was platted on August 1, 1827, and named Georgetown for the proprietor, George Shortridge. In 1832 it was renamed Germantown for German settlers from Pennsylvania, although the post office, established on March 31, 1846, was called East Germantown to distinguish it from another Hoosier post office called Germantown. On August 4, 1917, the post office name was changed to Pershing, for General J. J. Pershing, since there was so much bitterness against Germany during World War I.

East Glenn [eest GLEN] (Vigo). This community was named for nearby Glen Ayr, q.v., although East Glenn actually is north of Glen Ayr. East Glen is a variant spelling.

East Liberty [eest LIB-er-dee] (Allen). This village was laid out in 1848 by John Burger. A post office was established on July 24, 1850; closed on October 30, 1866.* Apparently the name is commendatory.

East Mount Carmel [eest mownt KAHR-muhl] (Gibson). This village was established about 1885 by Jess Wiseman. The name is locational, as Mount Carmel, Illinois, is located just across the Wabash River. A variant name is Fetters.

Easton (Marion). See West Newton.

East Oolitic [eest o-LIT-ic] (Lawrence). This village was platted on September 1, 1900, by James D. Farmer. The name is locational, as the town is east of Oolitic, q.v. Formerly the village was called Spien Kopj for the South African battle in the Boer War in 1900.

East Shelburn [eest SHEL-bern] (Sullivan). This village has a locational name, as it is located east of Shelburn, q.v.

East Union [EEST YOON-yuhn] (Tipton). Apparently this name is commendatory.

Easytown [EE-zee-town] (Vermillion). According to an oral account, "very easygoing people" lived here, "most of whom didn't have a job" (ISUFA).

Eaton [EE-tuhn] (Delaware). This town was laid out in 1854, and a post office was established on May 20, 1856.

Eby [EE-bee] (Warrick). A post office was established on March 24, 1870; closed on December 31, 1903.* This unique place name, probably for the personal name, is found only in Indiana.

Eckerty [EK-er-dee] (Crawford). This village was named for Christopher Eckerty, who laid out the town in 1873. A post office was established on January 23, 1861, as Down Hill. On November 13, 1882, the post office was changed to Boston Station, and on August 21, 1886, the post office was changed to Eckerty.

Economy [ee-KAHN-uh-mee] (Wayne). This town was named by Charles Osborn in 1825 when, according to one tradition, he was short of funds and laid out his land in lots and sold them, as "this was the most economical way of proceeding" (WPA). According to another local tradition, the town formerly was called Ninevah, but the town site was moved from an unhealthy spot along a creek to a higher location and renamed Economy because it was considered more prudent to move. Economy, however, is a common commendatory name, meaning "thrift," in the United States. A post office was established on January 17, 1827.

Eddy [ED-ee] (Lagrange). A post office was established here on May 3, 1893; closed on May 14, 1904.

Eden [EE-duhn] (Hancock). A post office called Eden was established on March 15, 1834; closed on August 31, 1905. The village, laid out on August 21, 1835, formerly was called Lewisburg. The origin of the present name is unknown, but possibly, influenced by the biblical garden, it is commendatory.

Eden Mills (Lagrange). See Emma.

Edgerton [EJ-er-tuhn] (Allen). This village was platted in 1889. A post office was established on February 5, 1890; closed on August 14, 1954.

Edgewood [EJ-wud] (Madison). This town was laid out by General Motors Corporation as a residential area west of Anderson in 1916 and supposedly so named because a forest bordered it on the east (WPA).

Edgewood [EJ-wud] (Marion). This village was platted on August 4, 1907, and allegedly so named because it was located "at the edge of a large wood" (WPA).

Edgewood Lake [ej-wud LAYK] (Putnam). This community was named for the nearby reservoir of the same name.

Edinburg (Franklin). See Drewersburg.

Edinburgh [ED-uhn-berg] (Johnson). This town was founded by 1822 and named for Edinburgh, Scotland, possibly by Alexander Thompson, a Scotsman and a cofounder of the town. The Scottish city received its name from the ancient fortress Eidyn. According to a local tradition, the Hoosier town was named Eddiesburg for Eddie Adams, brother-in-law of Louis Bishop, one of the town's founders; Adams had a reputation for hitting the bottle and demanded that the town be named in his honor. A post office called Edinburgh was established on December 4, 1823. In 1899 the spelling of the post office name was changed to Edinburg, which remained the spelling until 1977.

Edna Mills [ed-nuh MILZ] (Clinton). This village was never formally laid out. A post office was established on July 26,

1861; closed on August 14, 1905. The first mill in Ross Township was located here. The name is for Edna Kellenberger, wife of a local mill owner. Daniel Kellenberger was the first postmaster. According to the WPA files, a former name was Blackberry because a local blacksmith named Michaels liked blackberry brandy.

Edwardsport   [ED-werdz-pawrt] (Knox). A post office was established on January 30, 1833, and the town was laid out on August 25, 1839. The name honors Edward Wilkes, first postmaster, who was instrumental in laying out the town. This village once was a prominent flatboat landing place, thus the generic *port.*

Edwardsville [ED-werdz-vil] (Floyd). This village was laid out in 1853 by Henry Edwards, for whom it was named. A post office was established on January 23, 1859; closed on August 14, 1905.

Eel River [eel RIV-er] (Clay). This village was named for the nearby stream of the same name. The stream name is a translation of the Delaware name, Schack-a-mak, "slippery fish," i.e., "eel."

Effner [EF-ner] (Newton). According to the WPA files, this village was established about 1860. A post office was established on April 11, 1899; closed on May 31, 1901. An earlier name was State Line or State Line Junction for the village's location on the Indiana-Illinois state line

Eggharbor (Washington). See Canton.

Ehrmandale [ER-muhn-dayl] (Vigo). A post office was established as Elsie on April 13, 1896, but the name was changed to Ehrmandale on February 3, 1898, for the Ehrman family, local

landowners. The post office was closed on September 22, 1905.

Ekin [EE-kin] (Tipton). A post office was established on February 1, 1875, and, according to the WPA files, named for General Ekin, supervisor of a government depot in Jeffersonville. The post office was closed on August 30, 1902.*

Elberfeld [EL-ber-feeld] (Warrick). A post office was established on June 29, 1868, and the town was platted in 1885. The name is for Elberfeld, Germany, as many settlers were Germans.

Elevatis (Parke). See Bloomingdale.

Elizabeth [uh-LIZ-uh-buhth; uh-LIZ-buhth] (Harrison). This town was platted on April 17, 1812; incorporated on March 8, 1819; and named for Elizabeth Veach, wife of the man who donated land to the town. A post office was established on May 15, 1821.

Elizabeth (Spencer). See Dale.

Elizabeth City (Henry). See Maple Valley.

Elizabethtown   [uh-LIZ-uh-buhth-town; LIZ-buhth-town] (Bartholomew). A post office was established on May 17, 1844, with George W. Branham as postmaster, and the town was platted on June 11, 1845, by Branham. The name honors Branham's wife, Elizabeth.

Elizabethtown (Jackson). See New Elizabethtown.

Elizabethtown (Wayne). See Hagerstown.

Elizaville [uh-LEYE-zuh-vil] (Boone). This village was settled around 1834 and laid out in 1851 or 1852 on the farm of Hiram Brinton. A post office was established on February 5, 1855; closed on June 15, 1907.

Elkhart [EL-kahrt] (Elkhart). George Crawford and a man named Huntsman built the first gristmill here in 1829. A post office, with Crawford as postmaster, was established on the north side of the Elkhart River and called Pulaski on June 6, 1829. The post office name was changed to Elkhart and the location was changed to the south side of the river on March 14, 1839. Dr. Havilah Beardsley built another gristmill in 1831 and a sawmill in 1832, and he platted the city, named for the Elkhart River, on April 30, 1832. Local legend offers another derivation of the name: "There's this story about the naming of two cities in the northern Indiana area. A long, long time ago, when savage Indians lived in this part of Indiana, there was a famous Indian chief who was a hero-like image to his people. He always wanted to be remembered even after he died. The same Indian chief had a beautiful daughter, and he wanted his princess daughter to be remembered too. Well, anyway, the Indian chief's name was eventually given to his main camp on the river here. His daughter, the beautiful princess, had her name used in naming a smaller camp a couple miles away on the same river. The Indian chief's name was Chief Elkhart, for whom Elkhart was named. Today, there is a city near there often called the 'Princess City' after Chief Elkhart's daughter. Her name was Princess Mishawaka. This is the name for the city called Mishawaka, Indiana" (ISUFA). Cf. Elkhart County.

Elkhart County [EL-kahrt]. This county was organized in 1830 and named for the Elkhart River. On early maps the name of the river was written Elkheart or Elksheart in English and Coeur de Cerf in French, which are literal translations of the Potawatomi name of the stream, Me-sheh-weh-ou-deh-ik. The stream derives its name from an island at its mouth, which Native Americans thought resembled an elk's heart. Seat: Goshen.

Elkinsville [EL-kinz-vil; EL-kuhnz-vil] (Brown). This village was named for William Elkins, first settler and founder, who arrived here, according to traditional accounts, around 1816. A post office was established on September 29, 1860; closed on September 15, 1941. Members of the Elkins family who served as postmaster were Lewis and Granderson.

Ellettsville [EL-uhts-vil] (Monroe). This town was laid out in February 1837 and named Richland for the township in which it is located. When a post office was established on September 25, 1837, the name was changed to Ellettsville, for Edward Ellett, Jr., since there was another post office called Richland in Rush County. Ellett had a tavern here for several years before the town was platted, and he also established a sawmill and blacksmith shop. Variant names have been Ellettville and Elliotville.

Elliotville (Grant). See Radley.

Elliotville (Monroe). See Ellettsville.

Ellis [EL-uhs] (Clinton). According to the WPA files, Ellis is a former name of Kilmore, q.v., but Ellis is located about two miles north of Kilmore.

Ellis [EL-uhs] (Greene). This village was founded about 1873 and named for William Ellis, who donated land for a school here.

Ellis [EL-uhs] (Steuben). A post office was established here on March 22, 1888; closed on October 31, 1903.

Elliston [EL-uhs-tuhn] (Greene). This village was platted in 1885 and named for an early settler named Ellis. A post office was established on November 20, 1885; closed on July 15, 1910. A variant name was West Bloomfield for its location.

Ellsworth [ELZ-werth] (Dubois). A post office was established on November 8, 1878; closed on July 31, 1916. According to the WPA files, the name honors the Ellsworth family, early settlers; however, the first three postmasters were members of the Ellis family, so conceivably the name was coined from this local family name or borrowed from a given name. Ellsworth E. Ellis was postmaster at Elon in an adjacent county, Orange.

Elmdale [ELM-dayl] (Montgomery). A post office called Boston Store was established on February 1, 1866; changed to Elmdale on October 24, 1882; and closed on April 15, 1905. The present name probably is descriptive for the tree, although Elm, especially with the generic *dale*, has commendatory quality. Local legend explains the name this way: "Back in the 1800s, it was a town with one grocery store and a church and was filled with many trees. I think at that time it was called by the name of some man. Then about twenty years after, the people—as they started moving into the area and maps were beginning to come into existence—they used to have a blue book, and as the blue book told it, it gave directions, like go to the Y in the road, and turn right, and go straight until you hit a big tree, and curve to your right, and go to the Williams' farm, and

veer to your left, and go straight for several miles, and go past a road which is located at the Moore's place. When you go past this, there is a clump of trees, and that is Elmdale. The man who first settled there was called Dale, and they eventually changed it to Elmdale because of all of the elm trees" (ISUFA).

Elmira [el-MEYE-ruh] (Lagrange). Apparently this village was named for Elmira, New York.

Elnora [el-NAWR-uh] (Daviess). This town, earlier called Owl Town, was laid out on September 25, 1885, by local merchant William C. Griffith and A. R. Stalcup and named for Griffith's wife, Elnora. A post office established as Owl Prairie on December 20, 1831, was changed to Elnora on December 11, 1885. It's said that Owl Prairie and Owl Town were named for the variety and large number of owls here in early times, but according to local legend, the names honor an Indian chief: "A great many years ago, the red men roamed over the trackless forests and the open prairies, seeking knowledge from the great school of nature. The great chief, Owl, encouraged the braves to gather learning from all sources. When the white men came, they set up schools and built a town upon the site of Chief Owl's favorite camp. This town was called Owl Town. Later the name was changed to Elnora" (ISUFA).

Elon [EE-lahn; EE-luhn] (Orange). A post office named Elon was established on December 16, 1892, with Ellsworth E. Ellis as postmaster; closed on December 31, 1915. Earlier, 1863–1864, there was another post office with this name in Pulaski County. There also was a Kentucky post office called Elon that was established in 1888 and a North

Carolina college named Elon that was established in 1889.

Elrod [EL-rahd] (Ripley). A post office, named for the local Elrod family, was established on February 22, 1849; closed on December 31, 1903. An early settler and the first postmaster was George W. Elrod. James Elrod also served as postmaster from 1880 to 1885.

Elsie (Vigo). See Ehrmandale.

Elston [ELS-tuhn] (Tippecanoe). According to the WPA files, the name of this village honors Isaac Compton Elston. In 1850 Major Elston, a resident of Crawfordsville, developed the Crawfordsville and Wabash Railroad, of which this village was the northern terminus. A post office was established on June 29, 1883; closed on April 25, 1892.

Elsworth Station (Vigo). See North Terre Haute.

Elwood [EL-wud] (Madison). This city was laid out on March 1, 1853, and called Quincy, but since there was another settlement of that name in Indiana, the name was changed to Elwood in 1869. A post office called Duck Creek, established on February 5, 1855, was changed to Elwood on July 21, 1869. Explanations of the origin of the present name vary. One account says the name was arbitrarily selected from a directory, and a more likely one says the name honors Homer Elwood Frazier, seven-year-old son of one of the founders.

Elwren [EL-ruhn] (Monroe). A railroad station was established here in 1906. A post office was established on April 6, 1910; closed on January 15, 1934. Supposedly the name is an acronym coined to satisfy four local families who wanted the local railroad station named for them: *El*ler, *Wh*aley, Bak*er*, and Breed*en*.

Eminence [EM-uhn-uhnts] (Morgan). This village was laid out in July 1855 by William Wigal. The name possibly is commendatory; but according to some accounts, it is descriptive, as the village site allegedly was the highest point between Indianapolis and Vincennes when State Road 67 was surveyed. A post office was established on July 20, 1857.

Emison [EM-uh-suhn; IM-uh-suhn] (Knox). This village was laid out in May 1867 and named for the proprietor, Samuel A. Emison. A post office established as Emersons Station on October 11, 1866, was changed to Emison Station on January 15, 1869, and to Emison on November 28, 1882. Another nearby post office in this county was established as Emisons Mills, with Thomas Emison as postmaster, on January 7, 1828, and changed to West Union on August 14, 1836. At the latter site, now a county park called Emison's Mill Park, Emison built a mill around 1808, and the mill, first powered by water, then steam, was operational until about 1891.

Emma [EM-uh] (Lagrange). This village first was called Eden Mills, apparently for the Garden of Eden and a sawmill owned by the Schrock family. A post office called Eden Mills was established on August 23, 1868; closed on September 7, 1875. Another post office called Emma was established on September 21, 1880; closed on May 15, 1903. Jacob and Andrew Hostetler owned a store here and became the first and second postmasters of Emma.

Emporia [im-PAWR-ee-uh; em-PAWR-ee-uh] (Madison). This village was founded in 1891 as a railroad station, and a post office was established on January 25, 1892; closed on March 30, 1907. Emporium means "a commercial center" or "place of trade," so the name may be commendatory; however, since the name was applied to two ancient cities and several American settlements, the name may have been borrowed. Local legend, though, offers the following explanation: "Emporia is a small town in Adams Township, Madison County, Indiana. Emporia, that's where Elmer Pasco's grain elevator was. Well, an emporium is a super cool store, and it has lots of stuff in it. The elevator had goods in it and was the only one around for miles" (ISUFA).

English [AYNG-glish; ING-glish] (county seat, Crawford). This town was laid out as Hartford in 1839. A post office named English was established on April 1, 1856. The present name honors William Hayden English, Hoosier congressman who helped get the post office here.

English Lake [ing-glish LAYK] (Starke). A post office was established on October 23, 1860, and named for an adjoining lake, now drained; closed on September 20, 1960.*

Ennes (Gibson). See Mount Olympus.

Enochsburg [EE-niks-berg] (Franklin). This village was laid out on March 12, 1836, by Woodson Clark and Enoch Abrahams, for whom it was named. A post office was established on July 21, 1837; closed on April 2, 1906.* Cf. New Point.

Enos [EE-nuhs] (Newton). This village was laid out by R. and L. Bartlett in June 1907.

Enos Corner [ee-nuhs KAWR-ner] (Pike). A variant name of this village is Enosville.

Enterprise [EN-ter-preyez] (Spencer). A post office with this commendatory name was established on March 24, 1852; closed on July 15, 1915. This village was laid out on August 12, 1862.

Enterprise (Steuben). See Hamilton.

Epsom [EP-suhm] (Daviess). This village was settled in 1815 or 1816 by Peter Yount and allegedly named for a local well that tasted like Epsom salts, but the name also is found in England and New Hampshire and may be a transfer. A post office was established on July 25, 1856; closed on July 14, 1905. Tophet was a nickname.

Erie [EER-ee] (Lawrence). A post office named Erie was established on March 29, 1864; closed on April 14, 1900. The village was laid out in 1867. The name ultimately comes from the Indian tribe, perhaps via Lake Erie or one of the other populated places in the United States called Erie.

Erie [EER-ee] (Miami). This unplatted village, established as a trading center, was named for Erie Township, in which it is located. The township was named for the Wabash-Erie Canal, which once crossed it.

Erin (Switzerland). See Lamb.

Ethel [ETH-uhl] (Orange). A post office was established here on March 13, 1891; closed on April 29, 1939.

Etna [ET-nuh] (Whitley). This village was laid out on September 11, 1849, and named for the township in which it is located. A post office established as Popano on April 11, 1848, was changed to Etna on June 30, 1851. On October 7, 1851, the Etna post office was moved to nearby Noble County, and on May 22, 1852, it was renamed Hecla, perhaps for the Ohio town. On October 7, 1861, the Hecla post office was returned to Whitley County, and on February 29, 1904, the post office was closed.

Etna Green [et-nuh GREEN] (Kosciusko). The post office established here on June 14, 1849, first was called Camp Creek, and the name was changed to Etna Green on September 19, 1854, when Leve Kehler became postmaster. The town was laid out in 1853 by Kehler and David Carr, who followed Kehler as postmaster. The town is located in Etna Township, for which it was named. The entire name perhaps is a variant of Gretna Green, a Scottish town.

Eugene [YOO-jeen] (Vermillion). A post office was established here in Eugene Township on March 9, 1826; closed on March 15, 1954. The village was laid out in 1827 by S. S. Collett around the Big Vermillion Mill of James Groenendyke. The actual origin of the name is unknown, but according to local legend, an habitual drunk frequently searched for his wife, calling "Oh, Jane!" "But his condition rendered his speech ineffective, and his call would sound more like, 'Eu, Jene!' Finally his popular call became the name of the town" (WPA).

Eugene Station (Vermillion). See Cayuga.

Eureka [yu-REE-kuh] (Lawrence). This village, also known as Geiberson, sprang up in the early 1800s near the Geiberson stone quarry. The Shiloh Church was built here before 1840.

Eureka [yu-REE-kuh] (Spencer). A nearby village was laid out in March 1858 by John Atkinson and named French Island City for the nearby island on the Ohio River. A post office called French Island already had been established here on September 13, 1847. Atkinson's store was the only business in the village, and in May 1858 Atkinson was persuaded by three other merchants to lay out another village around their businesses, which were north of French Island at the present site of Eureka. The post office remained at French Island, though, until August 9, 1869. On October 24, 1872, another post office called Eureka, for the latter settlement, was established, and this post office was closed on December 15, 1921. According to a local legend reported in the WPA files, early settlers were looking for a tract of land opposite French Island. A watchman sighted the island at dawn and shouted "Eureka," which became the name of the settlement.

Evans Landing [ev-uhnz LAN-ding] (Harrison). A post office, named for the local Evans family, was established on February 9, 1870; closed on November 30, 1947. William M. Evans was the first postmaster. According to the WPA files, this settlement dates back to the late 1700s; first called Boones Ford because Daniel and Squire Boone forded the river here, it later was called New Boston. Another variant name is Flannagans Landing.

Evanston [EV-uhnz-tuhn] (Spencer). A post office was established here on March 27, 1891.

Evansville [EV-uhnz-vil] (county seat, Vanderburgh). Colonel Hugh McGary bought land and built a cabin here in 1812. In 1817 he sold a large section of land to General Robert Evans and James Jones; the city was replatted, becoming the seat of newly created Vanderburgh County, and named for General Evans. A post office was established on February 20, 1818.

Everroad Park [EV-er-rod PAHRK] (Bartholomew). This community perhaps was named for Everroad Lake, a nearby reservoir. A variant name is Everroad Park West.

Everton [EV-er-tuhn] (Fayette). A post office was established as Everton on October 10, 1827; closed on January 15, 1937. The village, founded around 1840, originally was called Lawstown or Laws-burg, then West Union. It was renamed for the post office.

Ewing [YOO-ing] (Jackson). This village, named for the local Ewing family, was laid out about a mile west of Brownstown, q.v., on May 14, 1857, by William Ewing. A post office, with Ewing as postmaster, was established on December 31, 1857. The post office remained open until May 5, 1967,* though the community merged with Brownstown before the turn of the century.

Ewington [YOO-ing-tuhn] (Decatur). A post office was established here on May 31, 1871; closed on March 31, 1900.

Exchange [EKS-chaynj] (Morgan). A post office was established on June 7, 1880; closed on May 28, 1904.*

Fairbanks [FEHR-banks] (Sullivan). This village, laid out in 1840 by Benjamin Ernest, Samuel Myers, and James Pogue, was named for the township in which it is located. The township was named for Lieutenant Fairbanks, who, along with most of his small command, was killed here by Indians in 1812 while carrying supplies to Fort Harrison. A post office was established on July 5, 1842. Fairbank is a variant spelling.

Fairchild (Sullivan). See Dugger.

Fairdale [FEHR-dayl] (Harrison). This village was platted on October 15, 1867, by John McPheeters.

Fairfax [FEHR-faks] (Monroe). N. Whisenand and R. Wilson opened a tavern in this village around 1835. A post office was established on August 9, 1837; closed on December 31, 1904.* A recreation area on Lake Monroe now encompasses the site of this village.

Fairfax (Wayne). See Webster.

Fairfield (Franklin). See New Fairfield.

Fairfield (Howard). See Oakford.

Fairfield (Tippecanoe). See Dayton.

Fairfield Center [fehr-feeld SEN-ter] (DeKalb). A post office was established as Fairfield Centre on June 25, 1852. On October 5, 1893, the spelling was changed to Fairfield Center, and on April 14, 1906, the post office was closed. The name comes from the village's location near the center of Fairfield Township.

Fair Fight (Spencer). See Hatfield.

Fairland [FEHR-land] (Shelby). This village was platted on October 21, 1852, by Henry Jenkins and Isaac Odell. A post office was established on January 10, 1854, with Odell as postmaster. Odell came here when the railroad was being constructed and sold supplies and other merchandise to the railroad workers and farmers. Later he established a bank. According to the WPA files, the name is descriptive of the area's "beautiful land."

Fairmount [FEHR-mownt] (Grant). This town, settled mainly by Quakers and earlier called Pucker, was laid out in 1850 and named by J. Baldwin for the Fairmount waterworks of Philadelphia "because of its resemblance in cleanliness and beauty." A post office established as Grant, for the county, on November 19, 1849, was changed to Fairmount on May 20, 1864. Actor James Dean grew up near here.

Fair Oaks [fehr OKS] (Jasper). A post office was established here on February 11, 1884.

Fair Play [fehr PLAY] (Vanderburgh). A post office was established on May 12, 1871; closed on September 10, 1883.* Earlier (1833–1856) there was another post office named Fair Play in Greene County. The Greene County village was laid out in 1819 and supposedly named for the motto of Solomon Dixon, who donated land for the village.

Fairview [FEHR-vyoo] (Fayette). William Powers built a log house here around 1828. A post office was established on February 17, 1835; closed on August 3, 1836.

Fairview [FEHR-vyoo] (Randolph). This village was laid out in 1838. A post office was established on August 19, 1843; closed on July 31, 1901.*

Fairview [FEHR-vyoo] (Rush). This village was platted around 1828. A post office was established on July 29, 1830; closed on February 17, 1835. Fairview Academy was located here. A variant name is Grove.

Fairview [FEHR-vyoo] (Switzerland). This village is unplatted. The post office, established on September 27, 1835, was called Sugar Branch. The post office name was changed to Fairview on September 16, 1911, and the post office was closed on October 31, 1935.

Fairview Park [fehr-vyoo PAHRK] (Vermillion). This town was platted in 1902. Fairview, generally a subjectively descriptive name, is the name of five other communities in Indiana. Fairview Park is especially commendatory.

Faithsville (Montgomery). See Parkersburgh.

Fall Creek (Marion). See Germantown.

Fall Creek Highland [fawl kreek HEYE-luhnd] (Marion). A variant spelling of the name of this community, named for Fall Creek, is Fall Creek Highlands. For the origin of the stream name, see Germantown (Marion).

Falmouth [FAL-muhth] (Fayette). Originally called Old Baker Settlement for the local Baker family, this village was laid out in 1832 and renamed for the English town Falmouth, supposedly the ancestral home of the Baker family, who came here from Kentucky around 1825. A post office called Falmouth was established on September 7, 1847, in Fayette County. It was moved to Rush County on February 18, 1873, but back to Fayette County on June 1, 1915.

Farabee [FEHR-uh-bee] (Washington). A post office established as Foresters Station, with Alfred Farabee as postmaster, on August 19, 1856, was changed to Farabees Station on December 28, 1859, to Farabee on November 28, 1882, and closed on July 14, 1934. Apparently Alfred Farabee, for whom the village was named, was the first agent at the railroad station here, too. A variant spelling is Farrabee.

Fargo [FAHR-go] (Orange). A post office called Fargo was established on February 29, 1888; closed on May 31, 1928. The village was called Pittsburg, supposedly for a local family named Pitman. Short-Peg was a nickname of the village, and according to a county history, "Whence this unenviable appellation came is past finding out, even by the inquisitive historian."

Farlen [FAHR-luhn] (Daviess). Originally this village was called McFarlen for the McFarlen family, who had a general store here. A post office was established on April 21, 1884; closed on November 29, 1902.* Wyatt M. McFarlen became postmaster in 1884.

Farmers [FAHRM-erz] (Owen). A post office named Farmers Station was established here on November 24, 1869. On November 28, 1882, the name was changed to Farmer, and on December 15, 1931, the post office was closed. The name honors a local storekeeper named Farmer.

Farmersburg [FAHRM-erz-berg] (Sullivan). This town was settled by Seventh-Day Adventists and platted in 1853 along the Evansville and Terre Haute Railroad. In 1865, W. T. Crawford established Ascension Seminary here, and the town was called Ascension as well as Farmersburg. In 1872 the seminary was moved to Sullivan, and in 1875 the townsfolk settled on Farmersburg as the name of the town. The name reflects the fact that the town is located in a rural area and served farmers. A post office called Ascension was established on March 30, 1855; changed to Farmersburgh on June 12, 1882; closed on June 15, 1893.

Farmers Retreat [fahrm-erz ri-TREET] (Dearborn). A post office established here on October 7, 1852, was closed on April 30, 1925, and the village was named for it. Apparently this name is subjectively descriptive. A variant name of the community was Opptown.

Farmersville (Marion). See Acton.

Farmersville [FAHRM-erz-vil] (Posey). Settled about 1812, this village formerly was called Yankee Settlement and Yankeetown, as the settlers were from New England. It also has been called The Corners, for its location at the corner of four farms, and apparently the present name is for these surrounding farms. A post office called Farmersville was established on May 30, 1850; closed on January 31, 1902.*

Farmington [FAHRM-ing-tuhn] (Rush). This village was platted as Marcellus on September 27, 1836. A post office called Farmington was established on February 14, 1846; closed on April 9, 1858.

Farmington (White). See Burnettsville.

Farmland [FAHRM-land] (Randolph). This town was platted on July 28, 1852, and presumably named for the rich farmland surrounding it. A post office was established on November 16, 1853.

Farnsworth [FAHRNZ-werth] (Sullivan). A post office was established on December 4, 1886; closed on June 14, 1913.* The village, also founded in 1886, was named for the Farnsworth Coal Company (WPA).

Farrville [FAHR-vil] (Grant). A post office was located here on March 12, 1887; closed on August 14, 1902. The name is for a local family. Samuel Farr (1774–1832) of Virginia and Mahala Wallace Farr (1782–1860) of Georgia were the founders, and Alfred C. Farr was the first postmaster.

Far West (Johnson). See Bluffs.

Fawcetts (Greene). See Furnace.

Fayette [fay-ET] (Boone). There was a settlement here in the 1830s, but the village was laid out after that on land owned by Edmond Shurly. Apparently the name is for the Marquis de Lafayette.

Fayette County [fay-ET]. This county was organized in 1819 and named for the Marquis de Lafayette, the French general who fought in the American Revolution. Seat: Connersville.

Fayetteville (Fayette). See Orange.

Fayetteville [FAY-uht-vil] (Lawrence). This village, settled around 1818 and earlier called Crossed Roads, was platted on February 6, 1838, by Ezra Kern. Ambrose Kern was the first postmaster. According to the WPA files, it was named for John Fayette, early settler. A post office called Fayetteville was established here on December 28, 1846; closed on April 30, 1907.

Featherhuffs Mills (Carroll). See Pyrmont.

Fellows Mill (Greene). See Mineral City.

Fenns [fenz] (Shelby). This village, located in Shelby Township, should not be confused with a Shelby County post office, also called Fenns, that was established in Sugar Creek Township near Boggstown on July 6, 1870; closed on December 31, 1904.

Ferdinand [FERD-nand; FERD-uh-nand] (Dubois). This town was platted on January 8, 1840, by Reverend Joseph Kundeck, who named it for the Austrian emperor Ferdinand I. According to local legend, Kundeck named this place Ferdinand to get a donation from the emperor and was successful. A post office was established on January 9, 1850; closed on August 3, 1865; reestablished on August 26, 1865.

Ferdinand Station (Dubois). See Johnsburg.

Ferguson Hill [FER-guh-suhn HIL] (Vigo). This village was named for a farmer named Ferguson who owned much of the land here (WPA).

Ferndale [FERN-dayl] (Parke). According to the WPA files, this village was settled in 1839 and named for the abundance of ferns growing here. A post office was established on January 29, 1884; closed on December 31, 1904.

Fetters (Gibson). See East Mount Carmel.

Fez (Jasper). See Rensselaer.

Fiat [FEYE-uht] (Jay). A post office was established on March 10, 1881; closed on January 30, 1926.* Fiat money is that which is not convertible into coin, and, according to local tradition, this village received its name from greenbackers who advocated paper money backed only by the U.S. government. A variant spelling is Fiatt, and variant names are Winona and Woinona.

Fickle [FIK-uhl] (Clinton). This village was named for the Fickle family, who bought land here in the early 1830s. William Fickle settled here in the spring of 1834 on 320 acres. A post office was established on March 24, 1888; closed on October 15, 1928. Apparently the family name also was spelled Fickel, for the fourth postmaster was Joseph Fickel.

Fidelity (Pike). See White Sulphur Springs.

Fido (Fountain). See Roberts.

Fields Station [feeldz STAY-shuhn] (Gibson). A post office, named for the local Field family, was established on February 20, 1856; closed on October 6, 1857. Reuben Field was the first and only postmaster.

Fillmore (Porter). See Wheeler (Porter).

Fillmore [FIL-mawr] (Putnam). According to one account, this village was laid out in 1837 and named Nicholsonville, sometimes spelled Nicholsville, for one of the founders, Carter F. Nicholson. According to other accounts, the village was laid out in 1851 or 1852 by Benjamin Nicholson, Hardin Wilcox, and Moses T. Bridges, though this may have been an addition to the original village. A post office named Eberle was estab-lished on August 10, 1848; changed to Nicholsonville on November 19, 1849; and changed to Fillmore on December 5, 1861. The present name is for President Millard Fillmore.

Fincastle [FIN-kas-uhl] (Putnam). This village was laid out in 1838 by John Obenchain. Apparently the name is for Fincastle, Virginia, or for the old county of Fincastle in Virginia. Kentucky was part of Fincastle County, Virginia, until it was made a separate county in 1776. A post office was established on October 21, 1847; closed on January 14, 1905.*

Findley Mill (Jackson). See Maumee.

Finley (Hancock). See Carrollton (Hancock).

Finleys Cross Roads (Scott). See Leota.

Finly (Hancock). See Carollton (Hancock).

Fischlies Mills (Jackson). See Rockford.

Fishers [FISH-erz] (Hamilton). This town was named for Salathel Fisher, who laid it out on June 11, 1872. A post office was established as Fishers Switch on September 20, 1872; changed to Fishers on September 15, 1908. The town also was called Fishers Station.

Fishersburg [FISH-erz-berg] (Madison). This village was laid out on May 10, 1837, by Reverend Fletcher Tivis and named for the local Fisher family. Charles Fisher, who became the second postmaster, operated a general store here, and his father, John Fisher, was an early settler. According to the WPA files, the name is for Ben Fisher, "who was killed and scalped by Indians near Strawtown." A post office was established on June 19, 1837; closed on July 30, 1904.*

Fish Lake [fish LAYK] (La Porte). The name of this village is a local transfer from the lake of the same name.

Fishtown [FISH-town] (Harrison). A post office was established here on March 18, 1904; closed on April 30, 1907.

Five Points [FEYEV poynts] (Marion). This village was so named "from the fact that five roads converge at this point" (WPA). This is a common descriptive place name in Indiana, as it is also found in Allen, Jefferson, Morgan, Knox, Switzerland, Union, Warren, Wells, and Whitley counties.

Five Points [FEYEV poynts] (Morgan). This village was named for five converging roads here.

Five Points Corner [feyev poynts KAWR-ner] (Porter). The name of this community is descriptive of five roads once converging here.

Flackville [FLAK-vil] (Marion). This village was founded in 1884 on land owned by Joseph F. Flack, for whom it was named (WPA). A post office was established on February 25, 1888; closed on February 14, 1902.

Flannagans Landing (Harrison). See Evans Landing.

Flat Rock [FLAT rahk] (Shelby). A post office was established on January 9, 1828. A railroad station on the Jeffersonville, Madison, and Indianapolis Railroad, the village was laid out on January 4, 1855, by Thomas Woolley, who served as postmaster in 1860. The name is for nearby Flatrock River. The name of the stream comes from the Delaware name, Puck-op-ka. *Puck* means "rock," though *op-ka* does not mean "flat," as the translation implies. It may mean "bed of a stream."

Flat Rock Park [flat rahk PAHRK] (Bartholomew). This village was named for Flat Rock Creek, now Flatrock River. A variant name is Flat Rock Park North. Cf. Flat Rock.

Fleener [FLEE-ner] (Monroe). A post office, named for the local Fleener family, with Isaac N. Fleener as postmaster, was established on November 18, 1886; closed on June 30, 1912. A variant name is Fleenersburgh.

Fleming [FLEM-ing] (Jackson). This community developed as a railroad station. A post office was established on August 18, 1892; closed on December 31, 1904.

Fletcher [FLECH-er] (Fulton). A post office was established on June 2, 1888; closed on July 15, 1904. Fletcher Lake is a variant name.

Flint [flint] (Steuben). Never platted, this village formerly was called Thompsons Mills. A post office established as Jackson Prairie, for the local Jackson family, on May 15, 1839, was changed to Flint on January 14, 1850. Robert C. Jackson was the second postmaster, and Samuel B. Jackson was the third postmaster of the Jackson Prairie post office. The post office was closed on July 31, 1907.

Flora [FLAWR-uh] (Carroll). This town was laid out in 1872 by John Flora and named for him. A post office was established on August 25, 1873.

Flora [FLAWR-uh] (Miami). Sometimes called Floras Subdivision, this community was established on July 12, 1955, and named for the developers, Norman D. and Clara E. Flora.

Florence (Adams). See Ceylon.

Florence [FLAWR-uhnts] (Switzerland). This village was laid out by Benjamin Drake in 1817 and called New York. The post office, also called New York, was established on July 20, 1827. On April 28, 1847, the post office name was changed to Florence.

Florida [FLAWR-uh-duh] (Madison). This village was laid out in 1856 and named Clarks Station, for T. G. Clark, resident. The present name comes from the railroad station here, Florida Station, apparently named for the state. A post office called Florida was established on March 15, 1864; closed on July 31, 1903.

Floyd County [floyd]. This county was organized in 1819 and is commonly thought to have been named for Colonel John Floyd, who was killed by Indians on the Kentucky side of the Ohio River; however, Colonel Davis Floyd (1772–1834), an associate of Aaron Burr and member of the Indiana General Assembly, was an important figure in the history of the county, and it is more likely that the county was named for him. A village in the county, Floyds Knobs, also honors Davis Floyd. Seat: New Albany.

Floyds Knobs [floyd NAHBZ; floydz nahbz] (Floyd). A gristmill was built here in 1815, and the present name was adopted in 1843 in honor of Colonel Davis Floyd of Jeffersonville. Earlier

called Mooresville, for founder James Moore, the town is located in a valley surrounded by hills, locally called "knobs." A post office was established on September 27, 1852.

Flynns Cross Roads (Lawrence). See Buddha.

Folsomville [FOL-suhm-vil] (Warrick). This village formerly was called Lickskillet. The present name is for Benjamin Folsom, proprietor, who laid out the village on January 27, 1859, and became the second postmaster. The post office was established as Folsomville on September 5, 1863.

Foltz (Jefferson). See Middlefork.

Fontanet [fown-tuhn-ET; fahn-tuhn-ET] (Vigo). This village formerly was called Fountain Station, sometimes Fountain, allegedly because "the village sprang up overnight" (WPA), though it may have been named for a local spring. On December 7, 1870, a post office called Fountain Station was established; closed on November 12, 1877. On November 26, 1877, another post office called Hunter was established, and on September 27, 1881, the post office name was changed to Fontanet, apparently formed from Fountain Station.

Foraker [FAWR-ay-ker; FAWR-uh-ker] (Elkhart). A post office was established here on June 25, 1891; closed on September 23, 1966. The village, promoted by two men named Blosser and Bechtel, was platted in 1892. The name honors Senator Joseph B. Foraker of Ohio.

Foresman [FAWRZ-muhn] (Benton). This village developed as a railroad station between Templeton and Otterbein in the southeastern corner of the county.

Foresman [FAWRZ-muhn] (Newton). This village was laid out in 1882 by J. B. Foresman and named for him. A post office called Foreman was established in this county on February 15, 1883; closed on April 30, 1934.

Forest [FAWR-uhst] (Clinton). This village was laid out on September 1, 1874, by H. Y. Morrison and supposedly named for the dense forest here when the village was established. A variant spelling in the WPA files and on the 1876 Baskin, Forster map is Forrest, suggesting the influence of a personal name. A post office called Forest was established on August 4, 1875.

Forest (Whitley). See Laud.

Forest City [fawr-uhst SIT-ee; fawr-uhst SID-ee] (Jasper). According to the WPA files, this village was so named "because of the abundance of wild, uncultivated land and forest surrounding the community."

Foresters Station (Washington). See Farabee.

Forest Hill [fawr-uhst HIL] (Decatur). This village was laid out on March 17, 1852, by Newberry Wheeldon and called Newburg, also spelled Newburgh. According to oral tradition, the present name is descriptive, as the village site "was heavily wooded and stood on a hill" (ISUFA). A post office was established as Forest Hill on October 1, 1849; closed on July 4, 1904.*

Forest Hills (Miami). See Wells.

Fort Branch [fawrt BRANCH] (Gibson). First called LaGrange, for Aaron La-Grange (WPA), this town was laid out in 1852 and named for a pioneer outpost, Fort Branch, built in 1811 near the present town. A post office established as York on September 18, 1849, was changed to Fort Branch on March 11, 1856.

Fort Harrison [fawrt HEHR-uh-suhn] (Vigo). Now the property of the Elks Country Club, this locale along the Wabash River in northwestern Terre Haute is the site of Fort Harrison, built in 1811, for which it was named.

Fort Miami (Allen). See Fort Wayne.

Fort Red (Putnam). See Barnard.

Fort Ritner [fawrt RIT-ner] (Lawrence). This village was named for Michael Ritner, foreman of a construction crew building the railroad tunnel near here, who platted the town on May 29, 1857. A post office, with Ritner as postmaster, was established on September 4, 1856; closed on November 30, 1933.* There are several local legends concerning the naming of the town, including the following: (1) "Fort Ritner, as legend has it, was an old Indian fort and went by the name of Fort Ritnar with an 'a' rather than an 'e'" (ISUFA). (2) "Fort Ritner was named for Michael Ritner. He was a construction worker and built a few houses on the site, and it was then called Ritners Fort" (ISUFA).

Fortville [FAWRT-vil] (Hancock). This town was laid out on February 12, 1849, by landowner Cephas Fort and was named for the Fort family. Before the town was platted, a local name was Phoebe Forts Corner. A post office established on October 22, 1851, with Cephas Fort as postmaster, was called Walpole, for Thomas D. Walpole, a prominent attorney. When the town was incorporated in 1865, the official name became

Fortville, and the post office name was changed to Fortville on February 5, 1866.

Fort Wayne [fawrt WAYN] (county seat, Allen). Called Kekionga by the Miamis, this city was platted in 1824 and named for General Anthony Wayne, who built a stockade here after defeating Little Turtle in 1794. A post office was established on February 4, 1820. Other variant names have been Fort Miami, Frenchtown, Kisakon, Miami Town, Omee Town, Post Miami, and Twightwee Village.

Foster (Porter). See Kouts.

Foster [FAWS-ter] (Warren). A post office was established on June 25, 1883; closed on January 15, 1905. The village was platted on March 25, 1893. The name honors the local Foster family. Joseph Foster was an early settler here.

Fosters Ridge [faws-terz RIJ] (Perry). A post office, named for the local Foster family, established on June 7, 1858, was moved to nearby Uniontown on May 28, 1890. Alexander Foster was the first postmaster, and Hiram Foster was the second postmaster.

Foundry (Parke). See Coke Oven Hollow.

Fountain [FOWN-tuhn] (Fountain). This village was platted on April 26, 1828, by Major Whitlock, William Miller, and Barnard Preble and called Portland, since it was an important trading port at that time. A post office established as Portland on June 26, 1828, was changed to Fountain on January 10, 1868, and closed on December 29, 1904. The present name comes from the county in which it is located. Cf. Fountain County.

Fountain (Vigo). See Fontanet.

Fountain City (Fountain). See Riverside.

Fountain City [fown-tuhn SIT-ee; fown-tuhn SID-ee] (Wayne). A Quaker settlement, this town was laid out in 1818 as New Garden. When it was incorporated in 1834, it was renamed Newport. A post office called New Garden was established on August 23, 1824. The name of the post office was changed to Fountain City on June 10, 1878, and the name of the town was changed the same year, for the local sulphur fountains, or natural springs. A legend about a traveler through here is reported in a local history: "It was before the railroad was built and traveling was done in covered wagons. The traveler had reached the tavern late in the evening; after supper they fell to talking about the town and then the fountains. Somehow, the poor stranger conceived the idea that it was hollow underneath and probably the town would sink before morning. Immediately he had his horses and wagon brought and started on for a safer resting place."

Fountain County [FOWN-tuhn]. This county was established in 1825 and named for Major James Fountain of Kentucky, who was killed near Fort Wayne in the Battle of Maumee in 1790. Seat: Covington.

Fountain Station (Vigo). See Fontanet.

Fountaintown [FOWN-tuhn-town] (Shelby). This village was platted on December 23, 1854, by Matthew Fountain and named for him. A post office established on September 19, 1853, and called Davisville was changed to Fountaintown on March 24, 1869.

Fountainville (Fountain). See Kingman.

Four Corners (Allen). See Zulu.

Four Corners (Wabash). See Lincolnville (Wabash).

Four Presidents Corners [fawr PREZ-uh-duhnts KAWR-nerz] (Allen). Dating from September 22, 1917, this village was named for its location at the intersection of four townships bearing the names of four presidents: Jefferson, Jackson, Madison, and Monroe.

Fowler [FOW-ler] (county seat, Benton). A post office was established on August 26, 1872, and the town was first platted on October 26, 1872, by Moses Fowler, a Lafayette businessman, for whom it was named.

Fowlerton [FOW-ler-tuhn] (Grant). This town originally was called Leach for a local family. The present name also comes from a local family. Albert and Jeff Fowler built a mill here in 1895. A post office, with Albert Fowler as postmaster, was established as Leach on September 6, 1895; changed to Fowlerton on March 21, 1902.

Fox [fahks] (Grant). This village, apparently never platted, formerly was called Fox Station for resident Edward Fox. A post office called Fox was established on February 7, 1884; closed on May 31, 1906.

Frances [FRAN-suhs] (Johnson). According to the WPA files, this village was named for the wife of a railroad official or a local man who helped establish a railroad station here and assisted in laying out the town.

Francesville [FRAN-suhs-vil] (Pulaski). This town was laid out in 1852 by James Brooks, a railroad president from New Albany, and supposedly named for his daughter, Frances. A post office was established on December 20, 1853. Variant spellings are Francisville and Franesille.

Francisco [fran-SIS-ko] (Gibson). This town was platted in January 1851 by John Perkins. According to legend, it was named for a Spanish laborer working on the Wabash and Erie Canal. He was fired, built a shack here, and became the first settler (WPA). A post office was established on August 19, 1854.

Frankfort [FRANK-fert] (county seat, Clinton). This city was laid out on May 9, 1830, and probably named for Frankfurt am Main, Germany, home of the grandfather of the Pence brothers, who owned the land on which the city is located; however, some say the name is for Frankfort, Kentucky. A post office was established on August 30, 1830.

Frankfort (Scott). See New Frankfort.

Franklin [FRANK-luhn; FRANK-lun] (county seat, Johnson). This city was laid out in 1823 and named for Benjamin Franklin (WPA). George King built a log house here in 1823 and became the first postmaster, and Samuel Herriott, who admired Franklin, suggested the name. A post office was established on March 15, 1824.

Franklin [FRANK-luhn] (Wayne). This village was platted on January 7, 1832. The post office established on February 3, 1829, was called Nettle Creek for the nearby stream; closed on November 14, 1890.

Franklin (Whitley). See Churubusco.

Franklin County [FRANK-luhn]. This county was organized in 1811 and named for the famous statesman, Benjamin Franklin. Seat: Brookville.

Frankton [FRANK-tuhn] (Madison). This town was laid out on March 3, 1853, by Alfred Makepeace and Francis Sigler and possibly named for Sigler's nickname, Frank. A post office established as Pipe Creek on July 12, 1838, was changed to Frankton on April 13, 1854. Sigler was postmaster of the Pipe Creek post office from 1851 to 1854, when the name was changed to Frankton.

Frazier (Owen). See Coal City.

Fredericksburg (Marshall). See Walnut.

Fredericksburg [FRED-riks-berg] (Washington). This town was settled in 1805 and called Bridgeport, apparently for a toll bridge here. It was laid out in 1815 by Frederick Royse and named for him. A post office name Fredericksburg was established on January 25, 1819. Fredericksburgh is a variant spelling.

Frederickville (Montgomery). See Mace.

Fredonia [free-DON-yuh; free-DO-nee-uh] (Crawford). This village was platted on June 22, 1818, by Allan D. Thom, who built a two-story brick courthouse and was instrumental in getting the county seat moved here from Mount Sterling in 1822. In 1843 the county seat was moved to Leavenworth, where it remained until 1894. The name was coined around 1800 by giving a Latin ending to freedom, and by 1876 it had been applied to at least twelve post offices in the United States. Since the name means "place of freedom," the name is commendatory. A post office, with Thom as postmaster, was established on February 15, 1819; closed on February 26, 1965.

Freedom (Ohio). See Bear Branch.

Freedom [FREE-duhm] (Owen). This village was laid out on November 18, 1834. The name was formed from the name of the proprietor, Joseph Freeland, a Quaker who came here from Maryland in 1818 and settled near the present village for about ten years before returning to Maryland. Later he returned to Freedom, where he remained until his death in 1838. A post office was established on January 30, 1834.

Freeland Park [free-luhnd PAHRK] (Benton). This village was platted in 1898 and named for Antone Freeland, who owned the land. A post office was established on December 21, 1901.

Freelandville [FREE-luhnd-vil] (Knox). Settled in the 1830s by German immigrants and first called Bethlehem and Kreuzweg, "Crossroads," this village was laid out on July 31, 1866, and renamed Freelandville for Dr. John T. Freeland, local physician. A post office established as Maria Creek on January 27, 1834, was changed to Freelandville on December 31, 1860. An earlier spelling was Freelandsville.

Freeman [FREE-muhn] (Owen). A post office named Freeman was established on November 24, 1886; closed on January 31, 1915.* According to the WPA files, the name is for a local family.

Freeport [FREE-pawrt] (Shelby). This village was platted by Ira Bailey, Alexander Rittenhouse, and John McCormick on March 17, 1836. Bailey operated a gristmill here, and the mill served as a trading post. According to the WPA files, the village was so named because the trading post was "a free place to load cargo." A post office was established on August 9, 1837; closed on August 30, 1902.* Both Rittenhouse and Bailey served as postmaster.

Freetown [FREE-town] (Jackson). This village was laid out on March 15, 1850. It first was called Freeport, apparently a commendatory name, but the name was changed to Freetown because another village in Shelby County was called Freeport. A post office was established as Freetown on May 4, 1850.

Fremont [FREE-mahnt] (Steuben). Originally called Willow Prairie, for willow trees growing here, this town was platted in 1837 and renamed Brockville, for a local family. At the time there was another settlement in Indiana named Brockville, according to the WPA files, so the town was renamed Fremont, for the famous explorer, John C. Fremont. A post office was established as Brockville on April 24, 1837; changed to Fremont on September 11, 1848. Fremount is a variant spelling.

French [french] (Ohio). A post office called French was established here on June 22, 1897; closed on September 30, 1905. A variant name is Buffalo.

French Island (Spencer). See Eureka (Spencer).

French Lick [french LIK] (Orange). A post office was established on November 26, 1847, and the town, though settled earlier, was laid out on May 2, 1857, by postmaster William Bowles in French Lick Township, for which it was named. The township was called Southwest Township until 1847, when it was renamed for the famous springs and stream within its boundaries. According to tradition, salt deposits in this area attracted French settlers from Vincennes in the late eighteenth century, but Indians chased them away. Salty water, commonly called a lick, also attracted deer and other animals. Thus French settlers and a salt lick allegedly combined to give a name to a stream, a township, and a town in Orange County. Once a famous resort, French Lick is the home of Hoosier folk hero Larry Bird, basketball star of the Indiana State University Sycamores and the Boston Celtics. A common place-name joke about French Lick goes: "The state of Indiana didn't name its cities properly because North Vernon isn't in the part of the state you think it is in, South Bend isn't in the part of the state you think it is, and French Lick isn't what you think it is" (ISUFA). A variant name is French Lick Springs.

Frenchtown (Allen). See Fort Wayne.

Frenchtown [FRENCH-town] (Harrison). This village was settled in 1840 by about fifty families from France and first called Saint Bernard for a local church. When a post office was established on August 19, 1873, the name was changed to Frenchtown, for French settlers. The post office was closed on January 31, 1905.

Friendship [FREN-ship; FREND-ship] (Ripley). A post office called Harts Mills, sometimes spelled Hart Mills, with Hiram A. Hart as postmaster and named for the Hart family, was established on February 3, 1837. On January 14, 1868, the post office name was changed to Friendship. According to the WPA files, the postmaster changed the name to Friendship "because most of the people were friendly." Others say that a local committee changed the name because the settlement was built on friendship. The village first was laid out on July 5, 1849, by William Hart and called Harts Mills (WPA).

Friendswood [FRENZ-wud] (Hendricks). This village was settled in 1820 and developed as a railroad station. A post office called Friendswood, a commendatory name perhaps suggesting a Quaker influence, was established on February 27, 1868; closed on October 30, 1909.

Frishies Mills (Warrick). See Yankeetown.

Fritchton [FRICH-tuhn] (Knox). This village was laid out on March 31, 1839, as Richland, for the quality of the soil here. On July 20, 1893, a post office named Frichton, sometimes spelled Frishton, for the Fritch family, was established. Emil H. Fritch was the first postmaster. The post office was closed on February 20, 1915.

Fruitdale [FROOT-dayl] (Brown). A post office was located here on May 1, 1909; closed on January 31, 1937.* The name is of unknown origin, although it is generally believed that it comes from the location of the village, in the fruit belt (WPA).

Fulda [FUL-duh] (Spencer). This village was laid out in 1845 by German surveyors for Milton Jackson, who settled here in 1829. The surveyors suggested naming the village for their hometown, the German city of the same name. A post office was established on January 22, 1850. A variant spelling is Fuldah.

Fullerton (Parke). See Lodi.

Fulton [FUL-tuhn] (Fulton). This town was named for Fulton County, in which it is located. A post office was established on September 8, 1843; closed on January 24, 1845; and reestablished on November 1, 1850.

Fulton County [FUL-tuhn]. This county was formed in 1835, organized in 1836, and named for the inventor of the steamboat, Robert Fulton. Seat: Rochester.

Funks Station (Madison). See Linwood.

Fuquay (Warrick). See Stevenson.

Furnace [FER-nuhs] (Greene). According to the WPA files, this village was founded before 1897 and named Fawcetts for the Fawcett family, local landowners. On maps as early as 1876, it is called Richland Furnace, for an iron furnace that was located near Richland Creek in Richland Township. According to local legend, Richland Creek "was named this because all of the land around those parts was found to be fertile and rich, and the water of the creek was rich with the soil from the land" (ISUFA). On recent maps the name is Fawcetts.

Furnessville [FER-nuhs-vil] (Porter). This village earlier was called Murrays Side Track and Morgans Side Track.

Gilbert Morgan built the first frame building here in 1853; Edwin L. Furness built the second one in 1855 and opened a store in his basement in 1856.

A post office called Furnessville, with Furness as postmaster, was established on July 9, 1861; closed on November 29, 1919.

 **G**

Gadsden [GADZ-duhn] (Boone). A post office was established on August 25, 1887; closed on August 14, 1909. A variant spelling has been Glasden.

Gale [gayl] (Hendricks). A post office was established on January 20, 1882; closed on May 14, 1906.

Galena [guh-LEE-nuh] (Floyd). This village was platted in 1837 and first called Germantown for German settlers. When a post office was established on May 23, 1843, it was named Galena, a name descriptive of the principal ore of lead, but the name may be a transfer from another state. The post office was closed on November 30, 1933.

Galveston [gal-VES-tuhn] (Cass). This town was laid out by James Carter in May 1852. A post office was established as Chancery in Howard County on October 14, 1847, was moved to Cass County on February 10, 1853, and was changed to Galveston on June 21, 1853. The name is explained by an amusing anecdote: "Mr. Carter was puzzled as to what name to give it, and on looking out the window noticed a girl passing by with a vest on. The name of Galveston sprang up in his mind" (WPA). More likely the name was borrowed from Texas.

Gar Creek [gahr KREEK; gahr KRIK] (Allen). A post office was established here on May 5, 1873, and named for Gar Creek, a nearby stream, now dredged; closed on April 15, 1926.

Garden City [gahr-duhn SIT-ee; gahr-duhn SID-ee] (Bartholomew). This village, which also has been called simply Garden, was established in 1886 and allegedly so named because "most everyone living there has a large vegetable garden" (WPA).

Garfield [GAHR-feeld] (Montgomery). A post office was established here on July 2, 1880, and probably named for James A. Garfield, who was elected president of the United States that year. The post office was closed on January 31, 1907.

Garrett [GEHR-uht] (DeKalb). Though surveyed earlier in 1853 and 1871, this city was platted in 1875 by Beverly L. Randolph, son of James L. Randolph, chief engineer for the B. and O. Railroad, and named for John W. Garrett, president of the B. and O. Railroad. A post office was established on April 21, 1875.

Garretts (Gibson). See Johnson.

Gary [GEHR-ee] (Lake). This city was founded in 1906 and named for Judge Elbert H. Gary, chairman of the board of directors of U.S. Steel. A post office was established on June 9, 1906.

Garyton [GEHR-ee-tuhn] (Porter). This village was laid out around 1912–1914 by a Gary real estate firm and named for Gary, Indiana (WPA).

Gasburg [GAS-berg] (Morgan). A post office named Gasburgh was established on January 13, 1874. The spelling was changed to Gasburg on October 12, 1892, and the post office was closed on May 31, 1904. According to local legend, "Gideon Johnson, an early settler of Monroe Township, Morgan County, was regarded in his day as the 'windiest' man in that part of Morgan County. In fact, a little village in Monroe Township, which he is accredited as having founded, soon became named or nicknamed Gas Burg on account of his 'gas' and 'tall' stories" (WPA).

Gas City [gas SIT-ee; gas SID-ee] (Grant). This city was named for the natural gas discovered here in 1887. The town was laid out in 1867 and formerly called Harrisburg, for John S. Harris, a local lawyer, who laid it out. Burr M. Harris was the first postmaster. A post office was established as Gas City on April 16, 1892.

Gaston [GAS-tuhn] (Delaware). A post office was established as New Corner on July 6, 1852; changed to Gaston on November 11, 1892. The town was platted on February 27, 1855, also as New Corner. The current name is for the gas boom here in the 1880s.

Gatchell [GACH-ul] (Perry). According to a local legend, this village was "named after Roy Gatchell who ran the post office in his house" (ISUFA), but post office records do not list any postmaster with that name. A post office was established here on August 1, 1895; closed on January 31, 1944. A variant spelling is Gatchel.

Gates Corner [GAYTS KAWR-ner] (Delaware). This village was named for the local Gates family. Albert L. Gates settled in Perry Township in 1838 and divided his 250 acres among his children. A post office called Gates was established in this county on January 22, 1898; closed on October 14, 1901.

Gates Corner [GAYTS KAWR-ner] (Porter). This village was named for L. L. Gates, who owned a hotel here (WPA).

Gatesville [GAYTS-vil] (Monroe). A variant name of this village is Cleona, as a post office named Cleona was established on May 17, 1855; closed on March 31, 1903.

Gaynorsville [GAY-nerz-vil] (Decatur). A post office was established here on February 14, 1871; closed on July 14, 1904. The village was never platted.

Geetingsville [GEE-deengz-vil] (Clinton). According to the WPA files, this village was founded about 1830. A post office was established on March 14, 1856; closed on February 28, 1905. The name honors the local Geeting family.

Henry W. Geeting was the first postmaster. According to local tradition, a variant name was Shave Town because a farmer who wanted to trade his lazy horse shaved it where the harness would have worn the hair off to make it look like a hard worker (WPA). Another variant name has been Greetingsville.

Gem [jem] (Hancock). A post office named Gem, for Gem Station, a railroad station already here, was established on August 29, 1877; closed on January 2, 1907. The village has not been platted.

Geneva [juh-NEE-vuh; ji-NEE-vuh] (Adams). According to the WPA files, a town named Alexander was platted by Charley Lindley here in 1838 and named for the first settler, Alexander Hill. Another town called Buffalo was platted in 1853 by David Studebaker. In 1871 Alexander and Buffalo were consolidated to form Geneva, named for the Swiss city or lake "because of the predominance of Swiss people" or perhaps for the daughter of the station agent (WPA). The post office established on May 8, 1841, was called Limber Lost, sometimes spelled Limberlost, for Limberlost Creek, which was named for a swamp formerly called Loblolly. According to local legend, the name of the swamp was changed in the early days to Limber Lost when an athletic young man, "Limber Jim" McDowell, went bear hunting in the swamp and was lost for three days (WPA). The legendary quality of this widely accepted explanation is obvious, though, as variant stories have arisen, such as the following one from a county history: "A man named James Miller, while hunting along its banks, became lost. After various fruitless efforts to find his way home, in which he would always come around to the place of starting, he determined he

would go on a straight course, and so, every few rods would blaze a tree. While doing this he was found by his friends who were hunting him. Being an agile man, he was known as 'limber Jim,' and after this, the stream was called 'Limberlost.'" On January 11, 1872, the post office name was changed to Geneva.

Geneva (Jennings). See Scipio (Jennings).

Geneva [ji-NEE-vuh; juh-NEE-vuh] (Shelby). This village was platted by Louis Kline, sometimes spelled Cline, on October 28, 1853, and named for the Swiss city. The post office here was established as Sulphur Hill, sometimes spelled Sulpher Hill, on March 29, 1836; closed on December 15, 1904.*

Gentryville [JEN-tree-vil] (Spencer). This town was platted in 1854 and named for James Gentry, one of the town's first merchants, who came to this county from North Carolina in 1818 and first operated a store on his farm. A post office called Gentrys Store was established on June 15, 1826; changed to Gentryville on December 10, 1835; changed to Jonesboro, for William Jones, who operated a nearby trading post, on May 1, 1837; changed back to Gentryville on March 14, 1844. Gentrysville is a variant spelling.

Georgetown (Boone). See Northfield.

Georgetown (Brown). See Beanblossom.

Georgetown [JAWRJ-town] (Cass). This village was platted in July 1835 by Major Daniel Bell and named for George Cicott, a Native American whose reservation was partly in the town's plat.

Georgetown [JAWRJ-town] (Floyd). This town was laid out around 1833 by George Waltz, for whom it was named. A post office was established on February 8, 1837.

George Town [JAWRJ town] (Randolph). This village was platted in 1850, although settled as early as 1830. A variant spelling is Georgetown.

Georgetown (Wayne). See East Germantown.

Georgia [JAWR-juh] (Lawrence). This village, a station on the B. and O. Railroad, was platted on February 14, 1853, by John and Alexander Case. A post office was established on February 12, 1857; closed on September 29, 1917.

Gerald [JEHR-uhld; jer-AHLD] (Perry). A post office called Gerald was established on November 3, 1905; closed on August 31, 1955.

Germantown [JER-muhn-town] (Decatur). This fairly common name usually indicates a German settlement and here honors the large number of Germans who settled in the county.

Germantown (Floyd). See Galena.

Germantown [JER-muhn-town] (Marion). This village was laid out as Germantown on March 1, 1834. A post office called Germantown was established on April 24, 1837. The variant name, Fall Creek, is for the stream of the same name. The stream name is a translation of the Delaware word for a waterfall, *sokpehellak* or *sookpehelluk*, which refers to the falls near Pendleton. The Miami name of the stream was Chank-tun-oon-gi, "Makes a Noise Place," which also refers to the falls.

Germantown (Wayne). See East Germantown.

Germany [JER-muh-nee] (Clark). This village was laid out in 1829 and named for German settlers.

Gessie [GES-ee] (Vermillion). This village was platted on April 6, 1872, and named for Robert J. Gessie, owner of the townsite. A post office was established on August 20, 1872; closed on October 20, 1967.

Gibson (Clark). See Prather.

Gibson [GIB-suhn] (Lake). This village, formerly called West Point, was established as a railroad station and probably was so named because it was the western terminal of the Michigan Central Railroad (ISUFA). A post office established as Gibsons Station on August 5, 1857, was changed to Gibson on November 28, 1882; closed on March 31, 1912.

Gibson County [GIB-suhn]. This county, famous for its melons, was organized in 1813 and named for General John Gibson, secretary of the Indiana Territory, 1800–1816, and acting governor for about a year after William Henry Harrison's resignation. Seat: Princeton.

Gibson Station (Clark). See Prather.

Gifford [GIF-erd] (Jasper). This village was founded in February 1899 by Benjamin J. Gifford and named for him. A post office was established on August 29, 1899; closed on July 31, 1920.

Gilderoy (Parke). See Lodi (Parke).

Gilead [GIL-ee-ud] (Miami). This village was platted on March 23, 1844, by

Adam E. Rhodes and apparently named for the biblical district and mountain. Rhodes settled on the village site in 1835 and by 1840 had established a community here. A post office was established on March 7, 1846; closed on April 30, 1917.

Gilman [GIL-muhn] (Madison). This village may have been laid out as early as 1880 by Jacob Miller (WPA), though apparently it was laid out again on June 15 1893, by the Gas Center Land Company. The name is for an early resident. A post office established as Purdue on August 25, 1876, was changed to Gilman on June 10, 1878; closed on June 30, 1908.

Gilmer Park (Saint Joseph).

Gilmour [GIL-mawr] (Sullivan). Located on the Sullivan-Greene county line, this village was established in 1900 and named for the local Gilmour family. According to the WPA files, Jackson Gilmour operated a local coal mine, which closed in 1921. A post office, with John P. Gilmour as postmaster, was established as Embury on March 6, 1902; changed to Gilmour, with John P. Gilmour remaining as postmaster, on October 7, 1903; closed on March 15, 1919.

Gimco City [gim-ko SIT-ee; gim-ko SID-ee] (Madison). This community was established in 1929 near a factory of the General Insulating and Manufacturing Company and named for the company's initials. Alexandria annexed Gimco City in 1973.

Gings [gingz; geengz] (Rush). A post office called Star, with William Ging as postmaster, was established on February 19, 1853; changed to Gings on February 6, 1890, and to Ging, with Lewis E. Ging as postmaster, on January 26, 1894;

closed on April 29, 1905.* Storekeeper Michael Ging, the original proprietor of the village, also was postmaster of the Star post office from 1870 to 1878. The village, formerly Gings Station, for the Ging family, was platted on September 26, 1870.

Giro [GEYE-ro] (Gibson). This village was laid out in 1848 and named Buena Vista for the Mexican War battle of February 22 and 23, 1847. A post office called West Buena Vista was established on March 25, 1854; closed on February 5, 1877. Another post office called Giro was established on February 9, 1887; closed on July 14, 1902.* Giro also is found in Australia and Africa as a place name.

Glasden (Boone). See Gadsden.

Glen Ayr [glen EHR] (Vigo). This village originally was a mining community owned by the Glen Ayr Coal Company and named for the coal company. Glenn Post Office was established on March 9, 1887; closed on October 31, 1902. Variant spellings are Glen Ayre and Glenn Ayr, and a variant name is Glenn.

Glendale [GLIN-dayl] (Daviess). This village was laid out on February 7, 1866, and named for Glendale, Ohio. A post office was established on April 19, 1866; closed on February 28, 1907.

Glendenning Corners (Adams). See Perryville.

Glendora [glin-DAWR-uh] (Sullivan). Founded around 1893, this village was named for the local Glendora coal mine (WPA).

Glenhall [GLEN-hawl] (Tippecanoe). According to the WPA files, this village was platted in 1831 by Joseph Hall, who named it Glen Hall for himself. A post office was established as Glen Hall on May 22, 1866; changed to Glenhall on July 21, 1894; closed on October 31, 1904.

Glenn (Vigo). See Glen Ayr.

Glenns Valley [glenz VAL-ee] (Marion). This village was founded in 1831 and named for the local Glenn family. A post office was established on May 11, 1838; closed on November 30, 1903.* Located close to the Marion-Johnson county line, the post office moved back and forth across the county line, and Archibald Glenn served as postmaster in both locations. Variant spellings are Glen Valley and Glens Valley.

Glen Park [glen PAHRK] (Lake). This village developed as a Nickel Plate station just south of the crossing of the Joliet Cut Off and Nickle Plate Railroad. One source indicates that the name suggests a Chicago origin because "Lake County people are not inclined to the name of Park." The alternate name, Kelley or Kelly, was a post office name, as a post office named Kelly was established on March 4, 1898; closed on January 14, 1902.* Glenpark is a variant spelling.

Glenwood [GLEN-wud] (Elkhart). This fairly common commendatory American place name may be a transfer from an eastern state.

Glenwood [GLEN-wud] (Rush). A post office called Steeles, for postmaster David Steele, was established on January 19, 1833; changed to Glenwood on December 14, 1874. The town, earlier called Vienna, was laid out on January 23, 1882. Gleenwood is a variant spelling.

Glezen [GLEE-suhn; GLEE-zuhn] (Pike). This village was laid out on January 23, 1854, by Stephen R. Hosmer and named Hosmer Town, later Hosmer, for him. A post office called Hosmer was established on October 19, 1870; closed on January 9, 1873. Another post office called Glezen, sometimes spelled Glezon, was established on August 10, 1883; closed on April 23, 1965. Glezon is the name of a family in the county, as Joseph C. Glezon was a member of the first board of trustees of Petersburg. According to local history, Mary Glezen of Petersburg drove to Hosmer every Sunday to teach Sunday school, and she was so well liked by the citizens of Hosmer that in 1939 they changed the name of the village to honor her.

Glidas [GLID-uhs] (Harrison). A post office was established on June 14, 1899; closed on July 13, 1905.

Glory (Whitley). See Lorane.

Gnaw Bone [NAW bon] (Brown). Several legends try to explain this colorful name. One story says the Hawkins family built a store and sawmill here, and when one man asked another if he had seen Hawkins, the latter replied, "I seed him settin' on a log above the sawmill gnawin' a bone" (WPA). Another legend tells of a drunk who got lost on the way home, and one of his friends who found him said, "Thar he sets on that er' log gnawin' his bones" (WPA). Other stories tell about early settlers who were snowed in, and when help arrived the settlers were found gnawing on old bones. An educated guess, or legend of the educated, is that French settlers named the town Narbonne, for the French city, and through folk etymology the town became Gnaw Bone. Another educated guess that has not reached legendary status is that the Gaelic word for bone, *gnamh*, is pronounced like *gnaw*, so in oral English Bone may follow Gnamh in the place name as a literal translation of the Gaelic word.

Goat Run (Lawrence). See Coveyville.

Goblesville [GO-buhlz-vil] (Huntington). This village was named for the local Goble family. Peter R. Goble settled here around 1855, and John Goble had a sawmill here. The village, which grew up around the sawmill, was never platted. A post office was established on May 14, 1883; closed on February 28, 1905.

Goddard (Rush). See Homer.

Goldsmith [GOLD-smith] (Tipton). This village was laid out in 1876 for the proprietors—John Wolford, J. A. Teter, McDonald Teter, and Hiram Fulkerson—and named for a railroad official. A post office was established on July 31, 1876.

Goodland [GUD-luhnd; GUD-luhn] (Newton). A post office was established on May 28, 1861, and the town was laid out the same year by Timothy Foster. Apparently the fertile prairie here suggested the name. The local flag station was called Tivoli.

Goodwins Corner [gud-wuhnz KAWR-ner] (Union). A post office was established on December 8, 1871; closed on October 14, 1903. The post office and village were named for the local Goodwin family. Bonaparte L. Goodwin had a store here and became the second postmaster.

Goshen (Bartholomew). See Hope.

Goshen [GO-shuhn] (county seat, Elkhart). On May 2, 1831, Oliver Crane

was appointed agent for the county seat, and on June 21, 1831, he was directed to lay off lots here for the establishment of the county seat. According to one local tradition, Crane donated the land that includes the courthouse square, and he suggested that the proposed county seat be named for his hometown, Goshen, in Orange County, New York. Another local tradition says the land was rich and productive, like the biblical Goshen, and thus the city was named for the biblical land (WPA). A post office was established on January 12, 1832.

Goshen [GO-shuhn] (Scott). According to the WPA files, this village was never laid out and was named "for the Goshen of the Scriptures."

Gospel Grove [gahs-pul GROV] (Vigo). Two oral accounts explain the name of this community: (1) "Gospel Grove . . . was named by Gertrude Myers. Mrs. Myers and her husband, ministers, bought the area and allowed only members of their particular church to buy the land from them. The area was a religious community" (ISUFA). (2) "Approximately one half mile of the first stoplight in Seelyville is a residential area set in an isolated surrounding. The first occupants of this area were all of the same religious sect and allowed no others to move in. This area soon became known as Gospel Grove and still is today" (ISUFA).

Gosport [GAHS-pawrt] (Owen). This town was laid out in June 1829 and named for Ephraim Goss, a native of North Carolina, who came to Washington County, Indiana, in 1810, bought land here in 1817, settled here in 1819, and died in 1833. Wiley A. Goss became postmaster in 1892. As the place name suggests, the town developed as a shipping port for flatboats on White River. A post office was established on November 21, 1831.

Gowdy [GOW-dee] (Rush). According to the WPA files, this village was founded as a church community as early as 1830. A post office was established on April 29, 1890; closed on July 14, 1903. The post office name honors the Gowdy family. John K. Gowdy (1843–1918) of Rushville was a prominent Republican politician who was appointed consul general to Paris in 1897.

Grab All (Jay). See Redkey.

Grabill [GRAY-buhl; GRAY-bil] (Allen). This town was named for Joseph A. Grabill, the first postmaster, who laid it out in 1901. The post office was established on August 2, 1902.

Grafton [GRAF-tuhn] (Posey). This village was laid out on June 6, 1852, by George W. Thomas, who owned a local flour mill, and was named for Grafton, Illinois. A post office, with Noah McFadden as postmaster, was established as McFadden on October 7, 1858; changed to Grafton on July 23, 1861; closed on January 31, 1902.*

Graham [gram; GRAY-uhm] (Daviess). According to the WPA files, this village was founded about 1900 and named for nearby Graham Farms.

Graham [gram; GRAY-uhm] (Fountain). This village and the nearby creek of the same name were named for the Graham family, who settled here about 1823.

Graham [gram; GRAY-uhm] (Jefferson). A post office named Graham, for the township in which it was located, was established on January 8, 1844; closed on July 30, 1904.

Grammer [GRAM-er] (Bartholomew). This village was platted in 1896. A railroad was built through here in 1891, and allegedly the name comes from the surname of a railroad conductor. According to oral history, "Grammer was a railroad town. Back in the 1890s or around that time the railroad was built through this part of the country. The railroad was supposed to go from Terre Haute to Cincinnati, but it went bankrupt and ended at Westport. Anyway, the people built a livestock holding pen close to Ross Williams' old house and where Danny Arnholt lives now. The Springers and the Wynns were prominent families back then. The Wynns wanted to start a town about where Jim Williams lives and call it Wynette. The Springers wanted to start a town about the same place as the livestock holding pens and call it Springer. The railroad company had to build a depot station at this time, so to stay out of the argument between the Wynns and the Springers, they went on down the tracks and built the depot where Grammer is now. Anyway, nobody knew what the name of the town was going to be. When they were going to break ground for the depot, the officials of the railroad company came down to break ground. Well, everybody in the community wanted to know what the name of the town was going to be, so everybody was there when the officials from Chicago came in. The train came in, and everybody clapped when it stopped. Then this official came out and made the announcement that the town would be called Grammer. They named it Grammer after some railroad executive named Grammer. This is a firsthand story I got from Dorie Hubbard who was there because he worked for the railroad, and that's the story they used to tell at the store" (ISUFA). Other oral accounts say that Grammer earlier was called Springs Crossing and Cushman (WPA, ISUFA). A post office was established as Springer on January 23, 1891; changed to Cushman on February 28, 1891; and changed back to Springer on May 25, 1891. The Springer post office was changed to Grammer on July 12, 1893; closed on January 31, 1972.* Cyrus N. Clapp was postmaster at all three of these post offices.

Grand Rapids Crossing (Noble). See Laotto.

Grandview [GRAND-vyoo; GRAN-vyoo] (Spencer). This town was laid out in the fall of 1851, and according to one source, it was so named because of its location on a bluff that offers a view of the Ohio River in each direction. According to an oral account, "The residents of this community chose this name because of its location on the Ohio River and therefore its 'grand view'" (ISUFA). Another account says the "grand view" was from the portico of Alfred Lamar's home (WPA). A post office was established on May 12, 1854.

Grange Corner [graynj KAWR-ner] (Parke). This village first was named Grangeburg about 1871 for John Lundgren's Grange Store and the local Jefferson chapter of the National Grange. It received its current name around 1879.

Granger [GRAYN-jer] (Saint Joseph). This village was founded on April 3, 1883, by Thomas J. Foster, who named it in commemoration of the Grange, a farmers' organization.

Grant (Fulton). See Athens.

Grant City [grant SIT-ee; grant SID-ee] (Henry). This village was laid out on October 31, 1868, by Jacob and Margaret Green, who named it for General U. S. Grant, under whom Jacob Green served in the Civil War. The local post office—

established on January 7, 1888; closed on June 29, 1901—was called Snyder, for the local Snyder family.

Grant County [grant]. This county, home of Indiana Wesleyan University and Taylor University, was organized in 1831 and named for Samuel and Moses Grant, Kentuckians who were killed by Indians in 1789 in Switzerland County. Seat: Marion.

Grantsburg [GRANTS-berg] (Crawford). A post office was established on May 23, 1848, and called Sterling. On April 19, 1854, the name was changed to Grantsburgh, supposedly for General U. S. Grant (WPA), but more likely for the local Grant family, since Grant was not nationally known until the Civil War. John V. Grant was the third postmaster. The spelling of the post office name was changed to Grantsburg on July 25, 1894.

Grants Creek (Ohio). See Norths Landing.

Grant Settlement (Wabash). See La Fontaine.

Grants Land (Wabash). See La Fontaine.

Grants Station (Vigo). See Burnett.

Granville [GRAN-vil; GRAN-vuhl] (Delaware). This village was laid out on May 9, 1836, and named for Granville Hastings, who established two mills and a store here. A post office was established on May 8, 1840; closed on October 14, 1901.*

Grass (Spencer). See Bloomfield.

Grass Creek [GRAS kreek] (Fulton). This village was established in 1882 and named for a nearby stream of the same name. A post office called Grasscreek Village was established on January 25, 1884; closed on December 30, 1964.* Grasscreek is a variant spelling.

Gravel Hill [grav-uhl HIL] (Benton). Formerly this village was called The Summit, for a hill here composed largely of gravel; thus, the present name is descriptive.

Gravelton [GRAV-uhl-tuhn] (Kosciusko). This village, located on the Elkhart-Kosciusko county line, was laid out on the Baltimore and Ohio Railroad in 1876 by David Brumbaugh, who twice served as postmaster, and apparently was named for a gravel pit once here (WPA). A post office was established on January 19, 1876; closed on June 15, 1906.

Grayford [GRAY-ferd] (Jennings). A post office was established as Butlers Switch, sometimes spelled Butler Switch, on May 18, 1875; changed to Grayford on May 23, 1889; closed on March 15, 1922.*

Graysville (Owen). See Alaska.

Graysville [GRAYZ-vil] (Sullivan). A post office was established on July 14, 1849, and named for Joseph Gray, owner of a store and woolen mill in this village.

Greeley (Gibson). See Warrenton.

Greenbrier [GREEN-breye-er] (Orange). A post office called Green Brier was established on June 28, 1861; closed on May 15, 1938.*

Greencastle [GREEN-kas-uhl] (county seat, Putnam). This city was named for Greencastle, Pennsylvania, hometown of the earliest settler, Ephraim Dukes, who came here in 1821 and donated land for the county seat in 1823. A post office called Green Castle was established on March 15, 1824. One local legend that attempts to explain the name goes: "The first man that settled in this area built a home and built it on—I don't know whether it was on posts or he had it laying down for a footing—but they started, after the house was built, they started to sprout, you know, and grow, so he called it his green castle" (ISUFA). Variant spellings have been Greencastel and Green Castle.

Greencastle Junction (Putnam). See Limedale.

Green Center [green SEN-ter] (Noble). This village was settled about 1836 and so named because it is near the center of Green Township. A post office called Green Centre was established on January 7, 1870; closed on January 31, 1903.

Greendale [GREEN-dayl] (Dearborn). This town was laid out in 1883 by Stephen Ludlow. A post office established on March 13, 1882, was closed on March 6, 1883. Apparently the town was named for the local Greendale Cemetery, dedicated on September 21, 1867.

Greene [green] (Jay). A post office was established here on May 22, 1862, and named for the township in which it is located. The township was named for Greene County, Ohio, home of settlers. The post office was closed on September 29, 1900. A variant spelling is Green.

Greene County [green]. This county was organized in 1821 and named for Nathaniel Greene, Revolutionary War general. According to a local oral account, though, "Greene County is called so because of all the fertile soil and green hilltops. It's so pretty and green" (ISUFA). Seat: Bloomfield.

Greenfield [GREEN-feeld] (county seat, Hancock). On April 11, 1828, a committee chose this city as the seat of Hancock County and ordered that it "shall be known and designated by the name and title of Greenfield," for reasons unknown. An early settler in the county was John Green, for whom Green Township was named, so the name may have come from a local family name. The city was laid out in June 1828. A post office established as Brandywine in May 1820 was changed to Hancock on May 15, 1829, and to Greenfield on April 15, 1833.

Greenfield (Johnson). See Greenwood.

Green Hill [green HIL] (Warren). This village was platted on March 5, 1832, by William B. Bailey, who named it Milford, for the Delaware town. In 1869 the name was changed to Green Hill when the Green Hill Seminary was established here by the United Brethren. A post office established as Poolsville on December 2, 1837, was changed to Green Hill on October 18, 1877; closed on August 13, 1904. According to the WPA files, "The United Brethren Church gave Green Hill its name because of the natural scenery thereabouts."

Green Oak [green OK] (Fulton). A post office was established on September 19, 1853; closed on October 31, 1901. Allegedly this commendatory name is for a large oak tree on the land where a general store was built (WPA). Greenoak is a variant spelling.

Greensboro (Franklin). See Blooming Grove.

Greensboro [GREENZ-ber-uh; GREENZ-ber-o] (Henry). This town was first platted on February 27, 1830, and named for Greensboro, North Carolina, by settlers from there. A post office was established on April 18, 1831. A variant spelling is Greensborough.

Greensburg [GREENZ-berg] (county seat, Decatur). This city was laid out on August 26, 1822, by John B. Potter on ground donated by Thomas Hendricks and John Walker. Hendricks is credited with founding the city in 1820 and his wife with naming it for Greensburg, Pennsylvania, her hometown. Allegedly, since Mrs. Hendricks had "four interesting daughters," her choice for the name of the town was supported by seventeen young men. A post office was established on October 24, 1823.

Greensburg (Washington). See Canton.

Greens Fork [GREENZ fawrk] (Wayne). This town was platted on September 28, 1818, and originally called Washington, but since there already was a town of that name in the state, it was renamed for a nearby stream, Greens Fork. Supposedly the stream was named for John Green, a Native American. A post office was established on August 22, 1828. Greensfork is a variant spelling.

Greens Station (Washington). See New Pekin.

Greentown [GREEN-town] (Howard). This town was platted in April 1848 on the site of a Miami town called Greens Village, which was named for Chief Green. One account says the name is for a green meadow here, but the name probably is a form of Greens Village. A post office established on January 20, 1848, at nearby Jerome was moved to

Greentown on September 21, 1848, back to Jerome on April 3, 1849, and back to Greentown on February 8, 1850.

Greenville [GREEN-vil] (Floyd). This town was settled in 1807 and platted in 1818 near the center of Greenville Township. An Indiana Territory post office called Greenville was established on October 12, 1816.

Greenville (Lawrence). See Williams (Lawrence).

Greenville [GREEN-vil] (Sullivan). Established about 1901, this village was named by an early resident, Mrs. Eva Sharp (WPA).

Greenwood [GREEN-wud] (Johnson). This city was founded in 1823 by the Smock brothers of Mercer County, Kentucky, and first called Smocktown. James Smock was the first postmaster when the post office was established on March 31, 1828, as Greenfield, probably to avoid confusion with a post office in Jefferson County called Smockville. Supposedly the post office was named Greenfield for a local church, but it's also said that the name is for surrounding evergreen trees (WPA). Since there already was a town called Greenfield east of Indianapolis, the post office name was changed to Greenwood on March 6, 1833. According to local tradition, the name honors "a man well liked in the Greenwood area, Jo Jo Greenwood" (ISUFA). The city was platted in 1864.

Greenwood [GREEN-wud] (Wells). This village was platted on October 3, 1872, by Samuel Greenwood and named for him.

Greetingsville (Clinton). See Geetingsville.

Griffin [GRIF-uhn] (Posey). This town, first called Prices Station, was laid out on August 11, 1881, by William Price and named for him. A post office named Griffin, for Samuel Griffin, first postmaster, was established on May 9, 1881.

Griffith [GRIF-ith; GRIF-uhth] (Lake). This town dates from around 1854 when the Michigan Central Railroad was constructed through here and railroad workers settled in the area. It was named for Benjamin Griffith, civil engineer for a railroad. Later the town was developed by Jay Dwiggins and Company, then of Chicago, as "the grandest railroad crossing in Lake County," as four (later five) railroad lines converged here. A post office was established on November 27, 1891.

Griswold Station [griz-wawld STAY-shuhn] (Knox). A post office called Griswold was established on September 3, 1862; closed on January 9, 1877.*

Groomsville [GROOMZ-vil] (Tipton). This village was established in 1860 when Enoch Smith drew up a petition for a post office, which he named for Dr. Groom of Tipton. The post office was established on February 16, 1860; closed on October 15, 1900.* A variant spelling is Groomville.

Grove (Rush). See Fairview.

Groveland [GROV-luhnd] (Putnam). A post office was established on July 19, 1852; closed on March 31, 1905. The village was laid out on March 18, 1854, by Benjamin F. and Daniel Summers. The name may be for the forest here, but Groveland was a popular commendatory name applied to nine post offices in the United States by 1875.

Grovertown [GRO-ver-town] (Starke). According to the WPA files, this village was laid out in 1858 and named for Stephen Grover, engineer on the Pennsylvania Railroad. A post office called Grover Town was established on January 20, 1859, and the spelling was changed to Grovertown on April 22, 1893. A variant spelling is Grovestown.

Gudgel [GUHJ-uhl] (Gibson). According to the WPA files, Andrew Gudgel settled here around 1835, and the village was named for him.

Guernsey [GERN-zee] (White). A post office was established on July 28, 1882; closed on July 31, 1907. In 1883 a railroad station was established here, but the village was never platted.

Guilford [GIL-ferd] (Dearborn). This village was laid out on May 29, 1850, and possibly was named for the English town via an eastern state. A post office established as Miller on June 5, 1837, was changed to Tanners Creek on July 30, 1841, and to Guilford on December 19, 1850.

Guion [GEYE-uhn] (Parke). This village was settled in 1821 and called Bruins Crossroads, for a local family. A post office established as Bruins Crossroads on December 3, 1839, was moved to nearby Judson, q.v., on July 5, 1872. Another post office called Guion was established on November 11, 1878; closed on August 31, 1943. Robert F. Bruin was the third postmaster. The present name is for William H. Guion, a New York stockholder in the railroad that was constructed through here in 1872. The village was platted on January 7, 1882, by Robert Bruin. Variant names have been Bruens Crossroads, Bruins, and Cross Roads.

Guionsville [GEYE-uhnz-vil] (Dearborn). This village was named for the local Guion family. A post office, with Thomas Guion as postmaster, was established here on February 3, 1837, but the post office and the name were moved to Ohio County. Cf. Milton.

Guionsville (Ohio). See Milton.

Gundrum (Pulaski). See Denham.

Gundys Deadening (Allen). See New Haven.

Guthrie [GUHTH-ree] (Lawrence). This village first was called Slick Rock Ford "from the slick rock bottoms of Salt Creek where early settlers forded" (WPA). A post office called Guthrie was established on August 1, 1855; closed on December 31, 1907.* The name may be for Daniel Guthrie, one of the first settlers in the county, or his family. The village was laid out on December 10, 1865. Guthrie is a familiar name in Lawrence County, as a township and a stream also bear this name. Alfred H. Guthrie (1828–1913) of Tunnelton was at one time the county's largest landowner and served on the state legislature in 1877.

Guy [geye] (Howard). A post office was established here on February 6, 1890; closed on August 30, 1902.

Gwynneville [GWIN-vil] (Shelby). This village was laid out by Alexander D. Pollitt on January 25, 1881, and named for O'Brien Gwynne, merchant from Carthage, Indiana, who owned land here. A post office was established on February 14, 1881.

 **H**

Hackleman [HAK-uhl-muhn] (Grant). A post office was established on July 20, 1871; closed on August 14, 1902. The name is for Brigadier General Pleasant Adams Hackleman, the only Hoosier general killed in the Civil War.

Hadley [HAD-lee] (Hendricks). This village, which developed as a railroad station, was platted on March 28, 1872, and named for the local Hadley family. A post office established as Mimosa on May 1, 1871, was changed to Hadley on March 23, 1874, and closed on November 20, 1936. Members of the Hadley family who served as postmaster were Luther and William Hadley.

Hageman (Porter). See Porter.

Hagerstown [HAY-gerz-town; HAG-erz-town] (Wayne). This town was settled around 1815, laid out in 1830, and first called Elizabethtown. In 1832 it was replatted as Hagerstown, for Hagerstown, Maryland, allegedly the former home of some settlers. On June 20, 1836, a post office was moved here from nearby Nettle Creek, and the post office name was changed to Hagerstown.

Halberts Bluff (Martin). See Shoals.

Haleysburg [HAY-leez-berg] (Washington). A post office, named for the local Haley family, was established on March 1, 1883; closed on January 26, 1885. All three of the postmasters were members of the Haley family: Benjamin D., James E., and Elias R. Haley.

Half Way (Jay). See Redkey.

Hall [hawl] (Morgan). This village was laid out in the fall of 1861, though it had its beginning with the establishment of a store here around 1851 or 1852 and may have been settled as early as 1830. A post office was established on September 9, 1854; closed on April 22, 1966.

Halls Corners [hawlz KAWR-nerz] (Allen). A post office, named for the local Hall family, was established here on March 10, 1851; closed on January 14, 1905. Isaac Hall was the first postmaster. A variant spelling is Halls Corner.

Hamburg [HAM-berg] (Clark). This village was platted on April 27, 1837, by Abram Littell and Thomas Cunningham and named for the German city. A post office called Cunningham, for the Cunningham family, was established on March 8, 1836; changed to Hamburgh, a variant spelling, on December 29, 1836; closed on February 16, 1857.

Hamburg [HAM-berg] (Franklin). This village was platted on April 27, 1864, by Wesley Martin and named for the city in Germany. The Martins were early settlers. A post office called Hamburgh was established on September 11, 1867. On April 12, 1893, the spelling was changed to Hamburg, and on January 15, 1929, the post office was closed.

Hamilton (Allen). See Leo.

Hamilton [HAM-uhl-tuhn] (Boone). This village was laid out around 1833 on land owned by Jacob Hoover and first called Clarkstown, for Walter Clark, who came here from Ohio. In 1838 or 1839 the name was changed to Hamilton.

Hamilton [HAM-uhl-tuhn] (Clinton). This village was platted on April 19, 1839, and named for Alexander Hamilton.

Hamilton [HAM-uhl-tuhn] (Madison). This village was laid out in 1836 by Henry Devlin, agent of William Conner and John D. Stephenson of Noblesville, who were active in establishing settlements and stores along the Indiana Central Canal when it was under construction. Supposedly the name is for Robert Hamilton, local educator. A post office called Hamilton was established here on March 31, 1838; closed on December 10, 1841. A post office called Zinsburgh was established on September 11, 1857; closed on July 24, 1878.* Another post office named Halford, for Indianapolis journalist Elijah Halford, was established on August 17, 1889; closed on July 31, 1902.

Hamilton (Rush). See Sexton.

Hamilton [HAM-uhl-tuhn] (Saint Joseph). This village, earlier called Terre Coupee, "plowed land," the French name for the prairie here, was platted on April 12, 1837. A post office called Terrecoupe was established on January 10, 1831; closed on April 24, 1893. The present name is for Hamilton's Tavern, once here.

Hamilton [HAM-uhl-tuhn] (Steuben). This town was platted as Enterprise in 1836 by Samuel Tuttle and F. W. Bingham. Since the town did not prosper, Tuttle sold it to a group of New York merchants, who, it's said, changed the name to Hamilton, supposedly for one of the new proprietors. According to other accounts, though, the town was named for Alexander Hamilton. A post office established on May 15, 1837, as Enterprise, with Samuel Tuttle as postmaster, was changed to Hamilton on August 15, 1844.

Hamilton County [HAM-uhl-tuhn]. This county, still mainly agricultural but fast becoming a residential area for people working in Indianapolis, was organized in 1823 and named for Alexander Hamilton, the American statesman. Seat: Noblesville.

Hamlet [HAM-luht] (Starke). This town was named for John Hamlet, who platted it in 1863. A post office was established on October 20, 1864.

Hammond [HAM-uhnd; HAM-muhnd] (Lake). This city was settled in 1851 and platted on April 12, 1875, by M. M. Towle. Towle and his five brothers operated a hotel, meat market, packing house, and publishing house here. A post office called Hammond was established on April 11, 1873. Formerly the settlement was called Hohman, for Ernest Hohman, an early settler, and then State Line for its location on the Indiana-Illinois line. It was renamed Hammond for George H. Hammond, a Detroit butcher who founded the local slaughterhouse and adapted the refrigeration boxcar for shipping dressed beef. Hoosier author Jean Shepherd uses the former name of this city, Hohman, as the setting of his humorous novel, *In God We Trust, All Others Pay Cash* (1964), and other stories.

Hampton [HAMP-tuhn] (Hendricks). A post office was established here on December 4, 1833; closed on December 9, 1852.* Cf. Avon.

Hamricks Station [ham-riks STAY-shuhn] (Putnam). This village developed as a railroad station between Lime-dale and Reelsville. A post office called Hamricks Station, for the local Hamrick family, was established on October 11, 1866. The post office name was changed to Hamrick on November 28, 1882, and the post office closed on October 31, 1902. Ambrose D. Hamrick served several terms as postmaster here.

Hancock Chapel [han-kahk CHAP-uhl] (Harrison). This village, sometimes called Hancock, was named for a local family, probably via a former post office. A nearby post office named Hancock, but shown on the 1876 Baskin, Forster map as Hancocks Post Office, was established on July 19, 1852; closed on May 31, 1907. William Hancock was postmaster in 1852 when the post office was changed from Davidson, q.v.

Hancock County [HAN-kahk]. This county, mainly agricultural, was organized in 1827 and named for John Hancock, first signer of the Declaration of Independence. Seat: Greenfield.

Handy [HAN-dee] (Benton). According to the WPA files, this village was named for a man who operated a local grain business.

Handy [HAN-dee] (Monroe). The name probably honors Joseph D. Handy, a native of Franklin County, Virginia, who came to Monroe County in February 1833. Handy taught in various Monroe County schools for about fourteen years before settling in Perry Township in

1864. He served as township trustee and county commissioner.

Haney Corner [hay-nee KAWR-ner] (Ripley). This village is located near, and probably was named for, the former Haneys Corner post office, which was established on December 5, 1871. On May 21, 1892, the name was changed to Haneys Corner, and on July 15, 1905, the post office was closed.

Hanfield [HAN-feeld] (Grant). A post office was established on March 22, 1881; closed on February 28, 1928. According to the WPA files, the name was coined as a compromise between advocates of the names Garfield and Hancock.

Hanging Rock (Spencer). See Rockport.

Hangman Crossing [hang-man KRAWS-ing] (Jackson). This locale west of Seymour at the B. and O. Railroad Crossing, also called Hangmans Crossing, was so named because on two separate occasions in 1868, vigilantes hanged three members of the Reno gang from a beech tree that was once here. According to an oral account, "Did you ever hear about Hangman's Crossing? Well, you know that crossing down by my house where the road crosses the railroad track and goes over the highway? Well, back in the time when the Reno Brothers were robbin' trains, they had the first train robbery in the history of the world in Seymour; the Reno brothers robbed a train. That's another story. Well, they . . . a bunch of 'em robbed a train down near Hangman's Crossing, and it wasn't called Hangman's Crossing then. They just robbed this train, and the posse caught up with 'em. And they caught 'em. They took 'em off the train down there. None of the Reno brothers were on the train. They were waitin' somewhere else, I guess. And instead of takin' 'em down for trial, they just decided to hang 'em right there. An' there's this big ol' tree; it's not there anymore, but it used to be down the road from the crossing. And they strung a bunch of 'em up on this tree. I guess about three or four of 'em. One of 'em had never been in a robbery before. His father was part of the posse. So his own father has to string up his son. And that's why Hangman's Crossing is called Hangman's Crossing 'cause they hung those guys there" (ISUFA).

Hanna [HAN-uh] (La Porte). This village was laid out in 1858 and named for Judge Hanna of Fort Wayne, who was involved with building a railroad here. A post office called Hanna Station was established on January 18, 1860; changed to Hanna on November 28, 1882. According to a local legend, a trainman called for his wife, Hannah, as he passed through here, and that's how the village got its name (WPA).

Hanna (White). See Idaville.

Hanover [HAN-o-ver] (Jefferson). Williamson Dunn moved here with his family from Kentucky in 1809, and the community was called Dunns Settlement. The town was platted in 1832 and named for Hanover Church, which was named as a compliment to the wife of Reverend Thomas Searle, who before her marriage lived in Hanover, New Hampshire. A post office established as South Hanover on December 13, 1830, was changed to Hanover on February 16, 1860.

Hanover (Lake). See Brunswick (Lake).

Hanover (Shelby). See Morristown.

Hanover Center (Lake). See Cook.

Hansells Station [han-suhlz STAY-shuhn] (Dearborn). A post office called Hansells was established at this railroad station on March 29, 1870; closed on October 20, 1871.

Hardenburgh (Jennings). See Hayden.

Hardingrove [HAHRD-ing-grov] (Perry). A post office, named for the local Hardin family, was established here on November 1, 1893; closed on July 31, 1937. Louise Hardin was the first postmaster.

Hardinsburg [HAHRD-uhnz-berg] (Dearborn). Settled in 1796 by Henry Hardin and his family, for whom it was named, this town was laid out on Hardin's land in May 1815. A post office was established on November 7, 1820; closed on March 1, 1836. Variant names are Hardentown, Hardinsburgh, and Hardintown.

Hardinsburg [HAHRD-uhnz-berg] (Washington). This town was laid out by Aaron Hardin in 1838 and named for him. A post office called Hardinsburgh was established on April 30, 1838. On December 2, 1891, the spelling was changed to Hardinsburg.

Hardscrabble (Cass). See Mount Pleasant (Cass).

Harlan [HAHR-luhn] (Allen). A post office called Harlan was established on March 10, 1851, and the village was laid out in 1853 by Mr. and Mrs. Lewis Reichelderfer, who named the settlement Harlan. In 1859 an adjoining village, Maysville, was laid out by Ezra May and named for him. Although Harlan remained the post office name, for a time residents called both villages Maysville.

Harley [HAHR-lee] (Carroll). This village, not the same settlement as Harley Siding, q.v., was named for the local Harley family.

Harley Siding [hahr-lee SEYE-ding] (Carroll). A railroad switch was built here on land owned by the local Harley family. The village also is called Harley. Cf. Harley.

Harmonie (Posey). See New Harmony.

Harmony [HAHR-muh-nee] (Clay). This village originally was laid out by John Graves in 1839, but since his estate was insolvent, the land was sold and the plat vacated. After the Vandalia Railroad was completed through here, the village was platted again on November 30, 1864, by Isaac Marks. According to local history, the name is inspirational: "There is no reason to be assigned for the naming of this and the post office, also, other than that of euphony and suggestiveness." The post office established here on August 9, 1837, was called McKinleys Store, for the McKinley family, with G. McKinley as postmaster. The post office name was changed to Harmony on January 13, 1846.

Harmony (Posey). See New Harmony.

Harper [HAHR-per] (Decatur). A post office established as Bigrest on August 3, 1881, was changed to Harper on January 20, 1882; closed on July 31, 1907.

Harris [HEHR-uhs] (Marshall). A post office named Linkville, q.v., was established near here on August 8, 1884. On December 17, 1888, the post office was moved along the railroad and called Harris Station. On November 18, 1889, the post office was moved back to Linkville, and on November 30, 1903 the post office was closed.

Harrisburg [HEHR-uhs-berg] (Fayette). A post office called Harrisburgh was established here on March 17, 1828; closed on November 14, 1902.

Harrisburg (Grant). See Gas City.

Harrisburg (Hendricks). See Brownsburg.

Harris City [hehr-uhs SID-ee] (Decatur). A post office called Harris City was established on January 23, 1874. On April 18, 1895, the post office name was changed to Harris, and the post office was closed on August 18, 1898. The name of the village is for B. B. Harris, who rode through here with General John Hunt Morgan in 1863 and returned in 1869 to open a quarry.

Harrison (Dearborn). See West Harrison.

Harrison [HEHR-uh-suhn] (Vigo). This village was platted by Ann Potts on August 4, 1837, on the west side of the Wabash River from Fort Harrison, q.v., for which it was named.

Harrison County [HEHR-uh-suhn]. This predominantly rural county was organized in 1808 and named for William Henry Harrison, first governor of the Indiana Territory, commander at the Battle of Tippecanoe, and ninth president of the United States. Seat: Corydon.

Harrisonville (Martin). See Trinity Springs.

Harristown [HEHR-uhs-town] (Washington). This village was laid out on July 18, 1850, by Thomas Harris, for whom it was named. A post office named Harristown, with Harris as postmaster, was established on March 10, 1851; closed on December 15, 1914. According to the WPA files, the railroad station here was called Norris, for the first station agent, Thomas B. Norris, to avoid confusion with Harrisburg. Norris was appointed postmaster on September 13, 1883.

Harrisville [HEHR-uhs-vil] (Randolph). This village was platted on January 17, 1854, by John Harris and named for the Harris family. A post office was established on January 16, 1854; closed on April 30, 1920.

Harrodsburg [HEHR-uhdz-berg] (Monroe). Formerly called Newgene, this village was platted on December 16, 1836, by Alexander Buchanan. When an addition was laid out in 1837, the name was changed to Harrodsburg "for some reason unknown," but perhaps for the Kentucky city. The Marysville post office in Lawrence County was moved here and called Harrodsburgh on February 7, 1840; moved back to Marysville in Lawrence County on June 24, 1841; and changed back again to Harrodsburgh in Monroe County on June 3, 1845. On April 13, 1893, the spelling of the post office name was changed to Harrodsburg.*

Hartford (Benton). See Oxford.

Hartford (Crawford). See English.

Hartford [HAHRT-ferd] (Ohio). This village apparently was laid out in 1817, but there is no record. An Indiana Territory post office called Hartford was established on April 1, 1816, and moved from Dearborn County to Ohio County on January 4, 1844. On November 25, 1891, the post office was changed to

Laughery, for Laughery Creek, on which it is located. The stream was named for Colonel Archibald Laughery, who was killed by Indians in 1781 near its mouth. The Laughery post office was closed on April 15, 1907. Hartford may be for the English town, perhaps via an eastern state.

Hartford (Vigo). See Pimento.

Hartford City [hahrt-ferd SIT-ee; hahrt-ferd SID-ee] (county seat, Blackford). A post office called Blackford, for the county, was established on August 13, 1840. On March 20, 1854, the post office name was changed to Hartford City. In 1839, when the city was platted, the county commissioners named the city Hartford, but since there already was a village named Hartford in Ohio County, S. R. Shelton, who became postmaster in 1864, suggested adding "City" to the name. The name may come from Hartford, Connecticut, former home of early settlers, although according to a local legend reported in the WPA files, the name honors the local Hart family, who forded Lick Creek on their farm.

Hartleyville [HAHRT-lee-vil] (Lawrence). Charles Hartley named this village for himself.

Hart Mills (Ripley). See Friendship.

Hartsdale [HAHRTS-dayl] (Lake). This village was established around 1832 and named for the Hart estate, on which it was built (WPA). The Harts were a pioneer family.

Harts Mills (Ripley). See Friendship.

Hartsville [HAHRTS-vil] (Bartholomew). This town was laid out in 1832

and probably named for local pioneer Gideon B. Hart or his family; however, according to the WPA files, the name may come from John Everhart, early landowner and merchant, though this explanation is not generally accepted. A post office was established on July 6, 1838. Hartsville College, which moved to Huntington in 1897 and eventually became Huntington College, was established here in 1850.

Hartwell [HAHRT-wel] (Pike). A post office named Cable, sometimes spelled Cabel, was established on April 30, 1898; closed on August 31, 1903. Another variant name of this coal mining community is Hartwell Junction.

Harveysburg [HAHR-veez-berg] (Fountain). This village was first laid out in 1856 by L. B. Lindley and named for his wife's father, Harlan Harvey, who lived here and suggested that the village be named for him. A post office was established on July 20, 1857; closed on November 15, 1900.* Variant spellings have been Harveys Burg and Harveysburgh.

Haskell [HAS-kuhl] (La Porte). This village, sometimes called Haskells, formerly was called Haskell Station, as the junction of the Monon and Grand Trunk railroads was here. A store was opened in 1855 by Samuel Brush, and a post office, with Brush as postmaster, was established on August 20, 1857; closed on May 15, 1937.* The name is for a local family. James Haskell, one of the early settlers, came to this township from Massachusetts in 1834.

Hastings [HAY-stingz] (Kosciusko). Settled around 1837, this village probably was named for a local family (WPA).

A post office was established on May 2, 1891; closed on November 30, 1903.

Hastings Station (Morgan). See Campbell Siding.

Hatfield [HAT-feeld] (Spencer). Originally called Fair Fight, this village was founded in 1883 by storekeeper James Hatfield, who became the first postmaster when a post office was established on December 4, 1886, and named for him.

Hathaway (Steuben). See York.

Haubstadt [HAHBZ-staht] (Gibson). This town was laid out in 1855 by James Oliver and originally called Haubs Station for Henry Haub, who had a general store and stage station here. A post office, with Haub as postmaster, was established on January 8, 1856. Haub had been postmaster of nearby Warrenton, q.v., from May 21, 1852, until the post office was moved to Haubstadt. The German generic -*stadt*, "town," is rare in Indiana place names.

Hausertown (Owen). See Marion Mills.

Hawkins (Jay). See Antioch (Jay).

Hayden [HAYD-uhn] (Jennings). This village was platted in 1854. A post office established on March 8, 1837, as Six Mile, for the nearby creek of the same name, was changed to Hayden on March 15, 1890. Hardenburgh, for the railroad superintendent who was in charge of building the section of track through here, was an earlier name of the village, and according to local tradition, the present name comes from railroaders who call Hardenburgh the "hay den" of Indiana.

Hayden (Porter). See Malden.

Haymond (Franklin). See St. Marys (Franklin).

Haysville [HAYZ-vil] (Dubois). This village was platted in 1835 and named for Judge Willis Hays, who bought acreage here in 1818 and donated land to the village. A post office was established on January 20, 1846; closed on July 15, 1914.*

Haysville (Jackson). See Crothersville.

Haw Patch (Lagrange). See Topeka.

Hazel (Delaware). See Mount Pleasant (Delaware).

Hazelrigg [HAY-zuhl-rig] (Boone). This village was laid out on land owned by H. G. Hazelrigg and named for him. A post office was established on September 10, 1873; closed on June 29, 1935.*

Hazelwood [HAY-zuhl-wud] (Hendricks). This village was named for Daniel Hazelwood, who settled here in 1832. A post office was established on January 25, 1884; closed on March 15, 1934.

Hazleton [HAY-zuhl-tuhn] (Gibson). This town was laid out in 1856 and named for a local family, who were early settlers in this county. A post office established as Robbs Mills on December 17, 1853, was changed to Hazelton, a variant spelling, on December 22, 1856. An earlier Indiana Territory post office (established in 1814 and closed in 1822) in this county, with Gervase Heazleton (sometimes spelled Gervas Hazleton) as postmaster, was Heazletons Ferry or, interchangeably, Heazletons Furnace, also spelled Hazeltons Ferry and Hazeltons Furnace.

Headlee [HED-lee; HAD-lee] (White). A post office was established on January 15, 1877; closed on August 31, 1907.* The name is for a local family. Harvey Headlee was appointed the third postmaster on November 25, 1878, and, with others, platted the village in 1888.

Headleys Mills (Fountain). See Coal Creek.

Heath [heeth] (Tippecanoe). A post office was established here on February 29, 1888; closed on October 15, 1902.

Heaton (Greene). See Ridgeport.

Hebron [HEE-bruhn] (Porter). Originally called The Corners, this town first was laid out in 1844 and named for the biblical city by Reverend Hannan. A post office was established on December 30, 1843.

Hecla (Whitley). See Etna.

Hector (Jay). See Bellfountain.

Hedrick [HED-rik] (Warren). This village was platted on July 31, 1881, by P. G. Smith and G. W. Compton and named for an early resident. A post office was established on January 14, 1880; closed on January 31, 1959.

Heffren (Washington). See Smedley.

Heilman [HEYEL-muhn] (Warrick). A post office was established on August 1, 1881; closed on December 31, 1903. The name is for the Heilman family, early settlers.

Helltown (Marshall). See Hibbard.

Helmer [HEL-mer] (Steuben). This village was platted in May 1892 by Cyrus

Helmer, for whom it was named. A post office was moved here from DeKalb County on November 12, 1892.

Helmsburg [HELMZ-berg] (Brown). This village was named for John Helms, an early settler. A post office established as Helms on July 23, 1904, was changed to Helmsburg on May 16, 1905.

Heltonville [HELT-uhn-vil] (Lawrence). This village was platted on September 8, 1845, by local merchant Andrew Helton and his wife and named for them. A post office, with Andrew Helton as postmaster, was established on April 11, 1846. Heltonsville is a variant spelling.

Helvetia (Perry). See Tell City.

Hemenway [HEM-uhn-way] (Warrick). A post office was established here on January 15, 1900; closed on December 31, 1903.

Hemlock [HIM-lahk; HEM-lahk] (Howard). Originally called Terre Hall, this village was surveyed in 1852 by John Newlin for Asa Parker, proprietor. When a post office was established on May 2, 1881, it was named Hemlock, apparently for the tree.

Henderson [HEN-der-suhn] (Rush). This village was named for Ida M. Henderson, who laid it out on August 1, 1890. A post office was established on August 16, 1890; closed on May 15, 1903.*

Hendricks County [HEN-driks]. This largely agricultural county was organized in 1823 and named for William Hendricks, governor of Indiana when the county was established. Seat: Danville.

Hendricksville [HEN-driks-vil] (Greene). A post office was established on September 21, 1888; closed on March 15, 1921. The name is for the local Hendricks family. Philip Hendricks was an early settler.

Hen Peck (Adams). See Honduras.

Hen Peck (Cass). See Twelve Mile.

Henry County [HEN-ree]. This county was organized in 1821 and named for Patrick Henry, famous orator of the Revolution, perhaps via Henry County, Kentucky. Seat: New Castle.

Henryville [HEN-ree-vil] (Clark). This village was laid out in 1850 and first called Morristown. In 1853 the name was changed to Henryville for Colonel Henry Ferguson. A post office established on February 25, 1837, as Pine Lick, for a nearby stream, was changed to Hubbard on January 20, 1853, and to Henryville on April 22, 1865.

Hensley (Johnson). See Trafalgar.

Hepburn [HEP-bern] (Posey). A post office was established here on July 21, 1898; closed on December 15, 1905.

Herbamount [HERB-uh-mownt] (Morgan). A post office called Herbemont was established on July 16, 1873; closed on May 15, 1905. Another spelling is Herbamont.

Herbst [herbzd; herpst] (Grant). A post office, named for August H. Herbst, the first storekeeper and postmaster, was established on October 19, 1880; closed on November 30, 1962.

Herculaneum (Clark). See Owen.

Herman City (Cass). See Anoka.

Hermann (Ripley). See Penntown.

Herod (Bartholomew). See Taylorsville (Bartholomew).

Hessen Cassel [has-uhn KAS-uhl; hes-uhn KAS-uhl] (Allen). This village was platted in 1863 and named by early settlers from Hesse, Germany, for Hessen-Kassel, a former landgraviate. Variant spellings have been Hessan Cassel, Hessan Castle, Hesse Cassel, Hessen Kassel.

Hesston [HES-tuhn] (La Porte). This village formerly was called Mayes Corners, for Matthew Mayes, who settled here in 1834 and operated a blacksmith shop for many years. Mayes visited the area a year earlier and helped John Tolbert set up a sawmill on Galena Creek. The mill, completed in 1834, changed hands several times and once was operated by the Hess family, for which this village was named. A post office was established on September 11, 1877, with storekeeper Peter M. Hess as postmaster; closed on September 15, 1900.

Hessville [HES-vil] (Lake). This village was named for the proprietor, Joseph Hess, an Alsatian cattleman who settled here around 1850. A post office was established on August 4, 1886; closed on July 31, 1927.* Several members of the Hess family, including Joseph, served as postmaster. The village was annexed to Hammond in 1923.

Heusler [HOOS-ler] (Posey). A post office, named for the local Heusler family, was established on August 7, 1893; closed on February 28, 1903. Ernest H. C. Heusler was the first and only postmaster.

Hibbard [HIB-erd] (Marshall). This village was platted on November 1, 1883.

Formerly it was known officially as Dante and informally as Helltown, apparently for the Italian poet Dante Alighieri and Part I, Inferno (Hell), of his *Divine Comedy*. Hibbard, perhaps for a personal name, was applied to the railroad station and post office here. The post office was established on April 29, 1887; closed on January 10, 1958.

Hibernia [heye-BER-nee-uh] (Clark). This village was never platted, but a post office named Hibernia, the literary name of Ireland, was established on January 12, 1835; closed on October 12, 1868. A variant name is Solon.

Hibernia [heye-BER-nee-uh] (Montgomery). This village, which bears the poetic name of Ireland, also has been called Hibernia Mills.

Hickory Grove (Dubois). See Thales.

Hicksite (Wabash). See Lincolnville (Wabash).

Highbank Town [HEYE-bank town] (Pike). This village, settled as early as 1813 and first laid out on November 19, 1819, was one of the earliest settlements in the county. A post office called High Banks, descriptive of the village's location on the high banks of the East Fork of White River, was established on October 25, 1819; closed on July 2, 1859.*

Highland (Clay). See Staunton.

Highland [HEYE-luhnd] (Lake). This village owes its existence to the establishment of a railroad station in 1882, though there were a few residences here before then. A post office established on August 13, 1883, was named Clough. On January 21, 1888, the name was changed to Highland for its location on land higher than the surrounding area. The post office was closed on February 29, 1944. According to a local tradition, "I was over in the [Calumet] region the other day visiting John and Dave. I asked them if they knew any legends, and they were duds. The only one that they could come up with is this one about the railroad. After the Great Lakes receded, they left the area rather low. Many years ago, a railroad company wanted to build a track from Chicago to the east. Most of the land was low and swampy, but they reached one area that was raised above the surrounding area. This they called 'Highlands.' Big deal!" (ISUFA).

Highland [HEYE-luhnd] (Vanderburgh). This place name, popular in the United States, often is commendatory, though sometimes descriptive.

Highland [HEYE-luhnd] (Vermillion). Located on the route between Terre Haute and Lafayette, this village, one of the oldest trading points in the county, developed as a stage station. A post office was established on January 6, 1838; closed on June 12, 1868.* Supposedly it was so named "because it is the highest spot in that area" (ISUFA).

Highwoods [HEYE-wudz] (Marion). This community was laid out and incorporated in 1927. A variant spelling is Highwood.

Hillcrest [HIL-krest] (Porter). This village was laid out around 1914 and named "from its location" (WPA). The name also has commendatory value and was applied to communities in Allen, Harrison, and Madison counties. In Warrick County there is a community called Hillcrest Terrace, an especially commendatory name.

Hill Grove (Wabash). See Somerset (Wabash).

Hillham [HIL-ham; HIL-uhm] (Dubois). This village was never platted, but a post office was established here on February 3, 1864; closed on July 31, 1937.

Hillisburg [HIL-uhs-berg] (Clinton). This village, established around 1850, was named for John E. Hillis, who platted it in 1874. A post office called Hillisburgh was established on August 17, 1876. The spelling was changed to Hillisburg on May 7, 1893.

Hillsboro [HILZ-ber-o] (Fountain). This town was platted on July 21, 1826, by Jesse Kester and, according to the WPA files, named for its location. A post office called Hillsborough was established on February 4, 1829. On March 31, 1893, the spelling was changed to Hillsboro.

Hillsboro [HILZ-ber-uh; HILZ-ber-o] (Henry). This village was platted on July 26, 1831, and named for its elevation. According to one local history, "The name undoubtedly comes from the fact that one can hardly reach the place from any direction without climbing a hill." Since there was a post office named Hillsboro in Fountain County, the post office established here on March 10, 1851, and closed on June 26, 1867,* was called Dan Webster.

Hillsborough (Wayne). See Whitewater.

Hillsdale [HILZ-dayl] (Vermillion). On February 14, 1872, a post office was established, and in 1873 the village was laid out by Everlin Montgomery, then postmaster. The name is descriptive of the village's location on high ground.

Hillsdale Junction [hilz-dayl JUHNK-shuhn] (Vermillion). Established at the junction of two railroads near Hillsdale, this locale has a descriptive name.

Hindostan Falls [hin-DAWS-tuhn FAWLZ] (Martin). A post office named Hindostan was established here on July 22, 1819; closed on December 29, 1830. The village was named Hindostan by Captain Caleb Fellows, the oldest lot owner here, who had served in India for many years.

Hindustan [hin-DUHS-tuhn; hin-DUHS-tan] (Monroe). This village was laid out in June 1853 by Charles G. Corr, proprietor. A variant spelling has been Hindostan. Apparently it was named for India, or a region of it. A variant name is Bryants Corners.

Hitchcock [HICH-kahk] (Washington). A post office called Hitchcock Station, sometimes spelled Hitchcocks Station, for the local Hitchcock family, with storekeeper William Hitchcock as postmaster, was established here September 27, 1858; closed on February 6, 1860. Another post office established on January 23, 1861, at nearby Heffren (see Smedley), was relocated here and called Hitchcocks Station on April 1, 1865; it was renamed Hitchcock on November 28, 1882. On April 19, 1900, the post office name was changed to Oxonia by O. K. Hobbs, apparently for Oxford University graduates or residents of Oxford, England.

Hoagland [HOG-luhnd; HOG-land] (Allen). This village was platted in 1872 and named for the Honorable Pliny Hoagland. A post office was established on March 7, 1872.

Hoards Station (Lawrence). See Huron.

Hobart [HO-bert] (Lake). A post office was moved here from nearby Liverpool on May 26, 1847, and named Hobart. The city was platted on May 8, 1849, and named for Hobart Earle—brother of George Earle, who was the third postmaster of Liverpool, first postmaster of Hobart, and founder of the city. A local legend explains the name: "The people of the town were standing in front of the old country store when a man came through with his horse and buggy and said, 'Whoa, Bart!' to his horse. So the name just stuck" (ISUFA). A longer version goes: "One of the stories of how Hobart, Indiana, got its name is common knowledge in Hobart, and it goes something like this. There was a wagon train of settlers coming west back in the early days. The first wagon was driven by an old man, and his team of horses was headed by a horse named Bart. When they got into this area, the old man decided he liked it here and they should settle here. So he yelled, 'Whoa, Bart!' to stop his horse, and they just decided to call their settlement Hobart because that's what it sounded like when the old man yelled to stop his horse" (ISUFA).

Hobbieville [HAH-bee-vil] (Greene). Settled in 1816 and laid out on September 29, 1837, this village first was called Jonesboro. A post office called Hobbieville was established on January 6, 1840; closed on May 15, 1935. Allegedly the village informally was called Screamersville because residents voiced their opinions loudly on election day.

Hobbs [hahbz] (Tipton). A post office, named for the local Hobbs family, was established on September 28, 1876. Zachariah T. Hobbs became the second postmaster in 1878, and Martin M. Hobbs became the third postmaster in 1881. A small railroad station was established here about 1878 by Henderson Hobbs on his farm.

Hoffman Crossing [hahf-muhn KRAWS-ing] (Clay). This community, located where Indiana Highway 46 crosses the Monon Railroad, was named for the local Hoffman family, instrumental in building a loading station for grain here.

Hoggatts (Vigo). See Prairieton.

Hohman (Lake). See Hammond.

Hole-in-the-Wall (Daviess). See Lettsville.

Holland [HAHL-uhnd] (Dubois). A post office was established on July 11, 1856. The town was laid out on May 20, 1859, by the first postmaster, Henry Kunz, who named the settlement for his native country.

Hollandsburg [HAHL-uhnz-berg] (Parke). A post office was established on February 10, 1853, with Abraham Collings, Jr., as postmaster. Members of the Collings family named the village, established the same year, for a Kentucky Baptist minister. The post office was closed on May 31, 1902.

Holloway Town (Wabash). See Lincolnville (Wabash).

Holman Station (Scott). See Blocher.

Holmesville [HOLMZ-vil] (La Porte). Jacob Bryant built the first house and a sawmill here in 1833. A post office was established on April 21, 1854; closed on June 17, 1895.* The village was platted on October 5, 1855. The name is for Hiram Holmes, who owned the land on which the village was located.

Holsbrook (Marion). See New Augusta.

Holton [HOLT-uhn] (Ripley). This village was laid out on June 29, 1854, on land owned by Jesse Holman. According to local tradition, some people wanted to name the town Holman, but Holman did not agree, so they settled on Holton. A post office was established on September 19, 1854.

Home Place [hom plays] (Hamilton). This village was laid out in 1814. The name was selected from several suggested names by vote of the residents, probably for its commendatory quality.

Homer [HO-mer] (Rush). Established along the J. M. and I. Railroad and originally called Slabtown for a sawmill built here around 1850 by Nathan Murphy and Samuel Craig, this village was laid out in 1876. The name was changed to Homer because it was felt that the original name was derogatory and might hurt business. A post office called Goddard, with Joseph Goddard as postmaster, was established on June 3, 1840; changed to Swinehart on December 2, 1852; and changed to Homer on May 10, 1854.

Homestead [HOM-sted] (Dearborn). A post office was established here on April 19, 1895; closed on November 15, 1910.

Honduras [hahn-DER-us; hahn-DER-uhs] (Adams). A WPA informant born in 1867 recalled that this village, apparently named for the Central American republic, was here in the 1870s. A post office was established on June 23, 1890; closed on December 31, 1904. According to local tradition, an earlier name of the village was Hen Peck, supposedly because in the early days the women here quarreled a lot (WPA).

Honey Creek [HUH-nee kreek] (Henry). This village, originally called Warnock Station for a pioneer landowner, was founded in 1858. The present name is for a nearby stream. A post office called Honey Creek was established on June 18, 1861; closed on July 14, 1864.

Honey Creek (Vigo). See Prairieton.

Honeyville [HUH-nee-vil] (Lagrange). A variant name of this village is Schrock, sometimes spelled Shrock.

Hoosier [HOO-zher] (state nickname). A number of legends have arisen to explain Hoosier, the state nickname. According to the most widely held account, pioneers in Indiana greeted visitors at the doors of their log cabins by calling out, 'Who's 'ere?'—as in the following versions:

1. "How the word Hoosier got started? Back in pioneer days the Indians in Indiana would go by the house of the pioneers and knock, and when they did, the pioneer, who was friendly and lazy, would say, 'Who's there?' And the Indians thought they were saying 'Hoosiers,' so they started calling Indiana settlers 'Hoosiers'" (ISUFA).

2. "I can't remember where I first heard this story, but the story answers a question often asked about how we Hoosiers got our nickname. Long ago when Indiana was first being settled, it was not uncommon for the new settlers to stop by the cabins as they went on their journey. As the new settlers stopped before the cabins, they would shout to the occupants, and in typical, friendly Indiana fashion, the people would shout out, 'Who's there?' Of course, heard through the heavy wooden doors, the question was somewhat distorted and came out sounding more like 'Hoosier?'" (ISUFA).

3. "It's funny how we got our name, Hoosier. When this state was first here, there was this guy from Kentucky came up, and he was sort of drunk, and he knocked on this guy's door. Well, the guy inside the house was kind of drunk, too, so he says, 'Who's der?' The Kentuckian walked off and said, 'Those damn Hoosiers'" (ISUFA).

4. "Now, I'm not sure about this, but this is the way I had it explained to me. I think one of my grade school teachers told us. It is kind of dumb, but here it is anyway. Well, anyway, it seems that the first people to settle in Indiana came up from the south. They couldn't speak too clearly, had an accent or something, so everything they said came out with a drawl. Well, I guess that when someone would come to their cabin door and should knock on it, the owner of the cabin would holler out 'Who's there?' but with that southern twang, it would come out something like 'hoosier'" (ISUFA).

5. "Shortly after Indiana was admitted to the Union as a state in 1816, the language of the people living there was considered to be somewhat different from the rest of the country. Many natives of Indiana commonly said 'hows come you do this or that,' and this was considered to be rather strange language by some of the people from other areas of the country. Along with this saying and others, the people of Indiana had another very distinct saying. When someone came to visit at a person's home, after knocking on the door, they were greeted with a 'Who's 'ere?' Evolving from this, the saying gradually became 'Hoosier,' and the people of Indiana became known as the Hoosiers" (ISUFA).

According to a related legend, people living in Indiana called "Who's here?" rather than "Who's there?":

6. "Another man told me that the nickname Hoosier came from the question 'Who's here?' that people would yell whenever they came into a tavern" (ISUFA).

Other oral accounts suggest that people living in Indiana asked "Who's your . . . ?"

7. "The name Hoosier originated according to the name of 'Who's your ma' or 'Who's your pa.' The story was told to me by an old man down in Kentucky about 70 years ago. It was the first and last time that I had ever heard this version. I noticed that if you went somewhere the first thing people would ask is where you were from and if they were familiar with this area, so they would ask 'Who's your ma?' and 'Who's your pa?'" (ISUFA).

8. "Do you know how Indiana got the nickname Hoosier? When it was first settled everyone ran around saying 'Who's your daddy? Who's your daddy?'" (ISUFA).

9. "The name for Indiana people is Hoosier. The word used to be associated with a phrase that people used when crossing over the state. They would have to stay in different people's homes along the way, and they would ask 'Who's your neighbor?' Then when the visitors would leave, they would carry the news to the next door neighbors. Later on, the phrased question became a description of Indiana people by running the phrase together and coming up with a word that makes Hoosier" (ISUFA).

10. "Back in the old days, a lot of things were moved by flatboat; the men who ran them were rough characters. The Indiana boys were especially rough. When an unfamiliar boat came by, the Indiana boys would call out 'Who's your

state?' If they weren't from Indiana, they got the hell beat out of them. The term Hoosier was then attached to Indiana from the 'Who's your' part of the statement" (ISUFA).

11. "I do know how we people from Indiana came to be called Hoosiers. We were talking about the early days in history here, of how we prospered because of commercial interest that began to develop after the [Civil] war was finally ended. And this young captain had acquired his grant from the U.S. Army, or government, and in due time he began to prosper by the fact that he had built the grain mill, pork processing plant. They had a tannery, and they did some weaving, did some weaving. They had all of these things, and their business was so good that they had to look for different outlets. So at this time they began to search for places to sell. And, of course, the natural was in the South because the South didn't have a lot of the things that we had at this time. So here came an era of the flatboat. They'd build a flatboat and send tons of material south. And these flatboats were generally built of the tulip tree, a large tree growing in our area. And they were not only used for the boat, but upon arrival there, they would sell the cargo and, along with that, the boat. And, of course, they would have to tread their way back north. Many people, of course, were lost on the way down because of severe weather and so forth. The story that we hear around here was that these traders that would go south were friendly, sociable people, but they were not always welcomed with open arms in being transit, of course. But once they were there and established in the community in the South, why, they were welcome. And they were accepted and taken into the homes and given a night's lodging or a week, if necessary. If they had a friend along, they had to account

for him and identify him. And maybe at a late hour they'd say, 'Well, there are two of us here.' They'd say, well, 'Who's your friend?' And here is where we have heard that the word Hoosier originally started" (ISUFA).

Another anecdote holds that a Louisville contractor named Samuel Hoosier preferred hiring Indiana men, and his employees were known as "Hoosier men" or "Hoosiers." Other sources maintain that there was a lot of fighting in early Indiana taverns, and the frontiersmen scratched, gouged, and bit—often biting off noses and ears. Frequently following a fight a settler found an ear on the sawdust floor of a tavern and asked, "Whose ear?":

12. "Okay, this is a story I heard about how Hoosiers got their name. Apparently a man got his ear cut off in a town somewhere. People found the ear, somebody found the ear and took it around town asking 'Who's ear? Who's ear?' And whose ear, Hoosier, is how Hoosiers got their name" (ISUFA).

13. "Taverns at that time had sawdust on the floors, and it wasn't uncommon for two men to get to fighting. They'd kick and scratch and bite and maybe bite somebody's ear off. The next day some guy would come in, kicking through the sawdust, and kick up an ear. He'd say, 'Whose ear?' And that's where the word 'Hoosier' comes from" (ISUFA).

14. "When my dad was running for office, this man was telling me how the name Hoosier came about. He said that when the state capital was in Corydon, there was a tavern that most of the people went to, and there was a jar on the bar that had an ear in it, and when strangers came in, they would ask, 'Whose ear?' In time, this phrase became popular and was eventually shortened to Hoosier for a nickname for people that came from around there" (ISUFA).

Other accounts generally agree that early settlers or Ohio River boatmen were vicious fighters and were called "hussars" because they fought like those European soldiers or "hushers" because they could hush any opponent:

15. "Early in 1819 many squatters, principally from Kentucky, had built cabins and had made some improvements on a part of the public domain. Some of these squatters hastened back to Kentucky to tell their friends that the country was now opened for settlement and to insist on coming to the 'New Purchase.' They gave such glowing accounts of the soil, fine timber, abundance of wild game, and the level country that they were deemed by some who heard them as extremely visionary. Many of their listeners were the Pennsylvania Dutch, who had always lived in a mountainous region. They were especially incredulous. After listening to what they regarded as exaggerations, they would turn away and say to others, 'Well, he is a hoosher'— meaning a husher, a silencer. This epithet became proverbial until all who returned from Indiana were facetiously called 'hooshers.' This, my Kentucky parents told me, was the origin of the name 'Hoosier,' as it was pronounced later" (WPA).

16. "The way I heard it was that the people that first came to Indiana Territory were pretty rough. They settled down on the Ohio River and worked flatboats and stuff. They were really big and tough. I guess that the south, near the river, was a rough place to live and there used to be lots of fights, guys getting killed and things. Well, from what I hear, those guys that worked on the river loved to get in and mix it up. They were so big and strong that any fight they got into they usually won. I guess the word they used to describe them

was 'husher' 'cause they quieted things down so well. I guess that it somehow got changed to 'Hoosier,' but it means the same thing" (ISUFA).

17. "Throughout the Midwest, men were extremely proud of their physical strength and displayed it at log rollings or house raisings. They were called 'hushers' by fellow citizens because of their ability to silence an opponent. The boatmen of Indiana were a primitive set and delighted in showing their strength upon the levee at New Orleans. One day a man who was not a native of the western world was showing his strength, and in all the excitement, he yelled in a foreign accent, 'I'm a hoosier. I'm a hoosier.' Some of the New Orleans papers reported this, and the name 'Hoosier' was applied to all" (ISUFA).

18. "This is another tale that I have known for many years. I don't remember where I first heard it. This legend also answers the question 'Where did the Hoosiers get their nickname?' Back when flatboat travel was one of the few ways to get to St. Louis and New Orleans, many Indiana men hired out as boat hands. The men were quite muscular from the farm work that they had done as children and again from the hard work that they did on the flatboats. These men were big enough to hush any man who said anything that did not agree with their opinion; consequently, they acquired the name 'Husher,' which later developed into our present-day Hoosier" (ISUFA).

Other accounts hold that Hoosier comes from a non-English language— for example, from the French *houssières*, "bushy places," or from an English dialectical word, "hoose," for roundworms. Apparently this disease of cattle caused the animals' hair to turn back and gave their eyes a wild look, as Indiana frontiersmen in their coonskin caps appeared to others. Still other explanations are that the nickname comes from *hoosa*, an alleged Native American word for maize. One legend suggesting a Native American origin of Hoosier goes:

19. "Sure, I know why we are called 'Hoosiers.' I thought everybody knew that. My mother told me that it is an old Indian word. See, the first people to come to Indiana were terrible liars and braggers. The one thing they had going for them was they could raise corn. I guess they talked a lot about what great farmers they were, especially about the corn. Anyway, lots of people got tired of hearing them brag, so they hung this Indian word, hoosier, on them. I guess it means one who brags a lot" (ISUFA).

Other folk explanations say that Hoosier comes from "huzza," an exclamation of early settlers, or from a southern dialectical word meaning hick or hayseed:

20. "Hoosier was at one time a slang word in the South referring to a 'jay' or 'hayseed.' The term originated from England, where 'hoose' was a common name for a disease of calves. This disease causes the calves' hair to turn back, and it gives them a wild, staring look. The coonskin caps which the pioneer men and boys wore made their hair lay funny, and the homemade whiskey produced the wild-eyed look. Thus, the word 'hoosier' was used to describe these early pioneers, and then it was later applied to all Indiana folk" (ISUFA).

There may be some truth in the latter legend, for field records for the Linguistic Atlas of the Middle and South Atlantic States reveal that in the southern states *hoosier* is a derogatory epithet connoting uncouthness and is synonymous with *hick, hayseed,* and *hillbilly.* Probably the term first was applied to settlers in southern Indiana, themselves from southern states, who were considered rustics by their relatives back home in more established states. *Hoosier,* as a derogatory term, is still current in West Virginia, the Upper Piedmont of Virginia, the Carolinas, and Georgia; however, it is rare as a derogatory term west of the Appalachians, where it simply means a native of Indiana.

Hoosier [HOO-zher] (Greene). This village was named for the nearby Hoosier coal mine (WPA).

Hoosier Highlands [hoo-zher HEYE-luhnz] (Putnam). This village, established as a recreational area, was platted in 1924. The name was suggested by the Hoosier poet William Herschel, from the state nickname and the hills here. A variant name, Cagle Mill, is for an early mill that was located nearby. Another variant name is Buzzards Roost.

Hoosierville [HOO-zher-vil] (Clay). This village was laid out in 1871 and so named for its location in the Hoosier state. A post office was established on June 24, 1874; closed on January 31, 1902. Variant names are Wittigton and Wittington.

Hoover [HOO-verz; HOO-ver] (Cass). A post office was established on September 10, 1873; closed on December 31, 1928. The settlement, sometimes called Hoovers, was named for Riley Hoover, who platted the village in April 1874.

Hoover Station (Fulton). See Athens.

Hope [hop] (Bartholomew). This town was settled in 1830 by a Moravian congregation from North Carolina and called Goshen, a biblical name, until a post office was established on February 8, 1834, when the name was changed to Hope, for an earlier Moravian settlement in North Carolina. The town was platted on November 17, 1836.

Hopewell [HOP-wel] (Johnson). This village was settled in 1831 by French Huguenots and supposedly named Hopewell for a spring they found here. Nearly twenty post offices in the United States bore this name by 1876, however, so possibly the name was borrowed for its commendatory quality. Ultimately the name comes from Hopewell, England.

Horace [HAWR-uhs] (Decatur). This village was laid out on February 23, 1881, by James Wyncoop and first called Wyncoop for his family. Horace was the name of the post office, which was established on June 15, 1881; closed on March 31, 1929.*

Hord (Lawrence). See Huron.

Hortonville [HAWRT-uhn-vil] (Hamilton). A post office established on January 31, 1883, was named for the first postmaster, John B. Horton. The post office closed on September 30, 1933. A variant name is Horton.

Hosbrook (Marion). See New Augusta.

Hosmer (Pike). See Glezen.

Houghburg (Shelby). See Boggstown.

Houston [HOWS-tuhn] (Jackson). A post office was established on January 24, 1850; closed on November 30, 1911.* The village was laid out in 1853. The name honors an early settler, Leonard Houston (WPA).

Hovey [HUH-vee] (Posey). A post office was established on July 20, 1881; closed on July 14, 1902.* The name is for a local family. Union officer and

Hoosier governor (1888–1891) Alvin P. Hovey is buried nearby in Bellefontaine Cemetery.

Howard [HOW-erd] (Parke). A post office called Burton, with Josephus Burton as postmaster, was established on March 3, 1840; changed to Howard on January 15, 1850. The village was platted in 1848 and named for Tilghman A. Howard, soldier and politician, who lived here. Westport, a variant name, was an area of the community that was located on the Wabash and Erie Canal.

Howard County [HOW-erd]. This county was organized in 1844 as Richardville, named for the famous Miami chief Jean Baptiste Richardville, who was the son of a Miami woman and a French trader. In 1846 the name was changed to Howard, for Tilghman A. Howard, Hoosier soldier and statesman. Seat: Kokomo.

Howe [how] (Lagrange). A post office called Lima was established on August 26, 1833; changed to Howe on June 23, 1909. The village, also first called Lima, was laid out on October 22, 1834, on the site of a Potawatomi village called Mongoquinong, "Big Squaw." In 1884 the village was renamed for lawyer John B. Howe, who bequeathed Howe School here the same year. Established as a grammar school affiliated with the Episcopal church, Howe School became a military academy, Howe Military School, in 1895.

Howesville [HOWZ-vil] (Clay). This village was named for Robert C. Howe, who founded it in 1856, though it was not formally platted until 1867. When a post office was established on January 14, 1858, Howe was the first postmaster. The post office was closed on December 31, 1909.

Hubbard (Clark). See Henryville.

Hubbell [HUHB-uhl] (Owen). A post office, named for the local Hubbell family, with Mary E. Hubbell as postmaster, was established on August 30, 1881; closed on April 10, 1883. A variant name is Hubbells Station.

Hubbells Corner [huhb-uhlz KAWR-ner] (Dearborn). Formerly called Hubbells Cross Roads, also spelled Hubbells Crossroads, this village was named for local storekeeper Merritt Hubbell, who settled here around 1832.

Hudnut (Parke). See Lyford.

Hudson [HUHD-suhn] (Steuben). A post office called North Benton, apparently to distinguish it from an existing post office named Benton in Elkhart County, was established on December 10, 1868; closed on November 22, 1869. The town, platted in August 1869, also was named North Benton, though sometimes called Benton. On January 15, 1875, a post office called Hudson was established.

Hudson Lake [huhd-suhn LAYK] (La Porte). This village was settled between 1829 and 1833 and first called Lakeport for its location on the east shore of Hudson Lake. The village also has been called Hudson, for the township in which it is located. The present name is the same as that of the adjoining lake.

Hudsonville [HUHD-suhn-vil] (Daviess). This village was laid out in 1856 by Nelson and Daniel Jackson and named for the Hudson family, who were among the early settlers. A post office was established on February 24, 1858; closed on December 31, 1904.*

Huff (Spencer). See New Boston (Spencer).

Huffman [HUHF-muhn] (Spencer). A post office was established on April 19, 1882; closed on March 30, 1935. The village originally was called Huffmans Mills, as the Huffman family built a mill around 1815 and eventually owned a gristmill, sawmill, and store here. John H. Huffman was the second postmaster.

Hunter (Vigo). See Fontanet.

Hunters Ford (Fulton). See Leiters Ford.

Huntersville (Clay). See Clay City.

Huntersville [HUHNT-erz-vil] (Franklin). This village was laid out on February 25, 1841, by the trustees of the local German Lutheran Church and supposedly was named for a man named Hunter who was instrumental in founding the village.

Huntersville (Tippecanoe). See Monroe (Tippecanoe).

Huntertown [HUHNT-er-town] (Allen). A post office called Perry, established on May 5, 1837, was changed to Huntertown on January 12, 1870.* The town also was platted in 1870, although settled in the 1830s. The name is for a local family. William T. Hunter purchased a tract of land here on the old Lima Plank Road and became the second postmaster of the Perry post office. John C. Hunter was appointed postmaster in 1875.

Huntingburg [HUHNT-ing-berg; HUHN-ing-berg] (Dubois). This city was founded in 1839 by Joseph Geiger, who named it Huntingdon, supposedly be-

cause he came to this area from Kentucky to hunt even before he purchased 1,920 acres of land here in 1837. Since the name was confused with Huntington, it was changed to Huntingburg. A post office called Huntingburgh was established on September 23, 1842. On June 13, 1893, the spelling was changed to Huntingburg.

Huntington [HUHNT-ing-tuhn; HUHN-ing-tuhn] (county seat, Huntington). This city was settled in 1831 on the site of a Miami village, Wepecheange, "place of flints." In 1833 General John Tipton had the city laid out, and it became the county seat in 1834. It was named for Samuel Huntington, member of the Continental Congress and signer of the Declaration of Independence. A post office was established on March 6, 1834.

Huntington County [HUHNT-ing-tuhn; HUHN-ing-tuhn]. This county was formed in 1832, organized in 1834, and named for Samuel Huntington (1731–1796) of Connecticut, member and president (1779–1781) of the Continental Congress and signer of the Declaration of Independence. Seat: Huntington.

Huntsville [HUHNTS-vil] (Madison). This village was laid out on May 24, 1830, by Enos Adamson and Eleazer Hunt and named for the Hunt family, who were among the earliest settlers. A post office was established on February 15, 1847; closed on July 15, 1878.

Huntsville [HUHNTS-vil] (Randolph). This village was named for the proprietors, William and Miles Hunt, who platted it on March 6, 1834. A post office established on January 2, 1822, as Smiths, with William Smith as postmaster, was changed to Vulcan on June 8, 1829, and to Hunts Cross Roads, with

William Hunt as postmaster, on June 8, 1832. On February 15, 1849, the post office was changed to Trenton, and it was closed on July 31, 1902.

Huntsville (Whitley). See Larwill.

Hurlburt [HERL-buht] (Porter). A post office was established on June 20, 1883; closed on March 30, 1918. According to the WPA files, the village was founded in 1833 and named for an early settler. David Hurlburt settled in the township around that time.

Huron [HYUR-uhn] (Lawrence). Originally this settlement was called Hoards Station, for William Hoard, pioneer landowner, but it was renamed for Huron, Ohio, by settlers who came from there about 1855. A post office established as Hord, a variant spelling of Hoard, on August 5, 1857, was changed to Huron on July 15, 1858. The village was platted early in 1859.

Hursh [hersh] (Allen). A post office, named for the local Hursh family, was established on February 23, 1882; closed on December 14, 1903. Arrison Hursh was the second postmaster, and Isaac Hursh was the third postmaster.

Hutton [HUHT-uhn] (Vigo). This village was settled in 1833 (WPA) and named for a local family. A post office, with Charles N. Hutton as the first postmaster, was established on October 19, 1889; closed on August 15, 1906.

Hymera [heye-MEHR-uh] (Sullivan). A post office called Hymera was established on August 1, 1855.* The town was platted in 1870 and called Pittsburg, also spelled Pittsburgh, for William Pitt, who owned land here, and, according to some accounts, "because, like Pittsburgh, Pennsylvania, it was a coal town." According to one legend, the town was named Hymera by John Badders, the postmaster, for his unusually tall adopted daughter, whose nickname was "High Mary": "I'm not exactly sure just what class it was. I think, oh, yes, it was . . . my high school literature teacher who told us one time how Hymera got its name. He said that the postmaster in the town had a very tall daughter, and when the people saw her taking his lunch to him they would say, 'There goes High Mary.' You know, like high, meaning tall. They kept this up, and pretty soon the town itself got the name of Hymera" (ISUFA). Another legend says: "Hymera, Indiana, did not always have that name. It used to be called Philadelphia, Indiana. When it was a town of about 200 people, it had a makeshift post office. The woman that worked in the post office was named Mary, and everyone that passed by would wave and call, 'Hi, Mary.' It soon became so widely known that the town officially changed its name to Hymera" (ISUFA). According to another tale, High Mary was a high-priced prostitute (ISUFA). It seems more likely, however, that the name is classical, for the ancient city, Himera, founded 648 B.C. on the northern coast of Sicily. The town's name was changed to Hymera, already the post office name, in 1890.

Hyndsdale [HEYENZ-dayl] (Morgan). This village, named for a local family, was founded soon after the railroad became operational through here. John Hynds settled in this area around 1825. A post office, with William Hynds as postmaster, was established on June 15, 1869; closed on September 30, 1904. A variant name is Hynds Station.

Iba (DeKalb). See Sedan.

Idaville [EYE-duh-vil] (White). This village was laid out on March 20, 1860, by Andrew and Margaret Hannah, John B. and Rebecca E. Townsley, and John and Murha S. McCully and called Hannah for Andrew Hannah. The post office established on April 13, 1860, however, was named Idaville, apparently because there already was a post office called Hanna Station in La Porte County. According to the WPA files the present name is for Ida M. Baxter, a woman "who was a local favorite with the early settlers."

Ijamsville [EYE-juhmz-vil] (Wabash). This village was platted on September 9, 1872, by Daniel Van Buskirk, proprietor, and originally called South Laketon, for its location south of Laketon. A post office called Ijamsville—for the Ijam brothers, Philip and John, who operated a sawmill here—was established on October 29, 1874; closed on July 31, 1923.

Ilene [eye-LEEN] (Greene). This village was named for the daughter of John Lyman Morgan, local landowner (WPA, ISUFA).

Illion (Marshall). See Tippecanoe.

Illinoi [il-uh-NOY] (Lake). A post office established here on February 2, 1900, was named for the State of Illinois; it was moved to that state on April 21, 1902.

Independence (Madison). See Rigdon.

Independence [in-duh-PEN-duhnts; in-di-PEN-duhnts] (Warren). A trading post was located here as early as 1811. The village was laid out on October 5, 1832, by Zachariah Cicott—a French-Indian trader and scout for General William Henry Harrison—on Cicott's Reserve, ground given him by the government for his services. A post office was established on March 24, 1834; closed on January 31, 1950.

Independence Hill [in-duh-PEN-duhnts HIL] (Lake). This village was platted in 1926. A post office branch was established on November 1, 1958. "As it was laid out by a real estate company, it was no doubt named with the idea that it would afford an opportunity for the city dweller to get out into the open country and own a home—in other words, to be independent" (WPA).

Indiana [in-dee-AN-uh; in-di-AN-uh] (state). Indiana, the nineteenth state, was admitted to the Union on December 11, 1816, and named for the Indiana Territory, established in 1800. The first use of the name *Indiana* was for a tract of land in Pennsylvania ceded by Native Americans in 1768.

Indiana Harbor [in-dee-AN-uh HAHR-ber] (Lake). A post office was established on January 17, 1902; closed on September 30, 1918.

Indiana Kentucky (Jefferson). See China.

Indiana Mineral Springs (Warren). See Kramer.

Indianapolis [in-dee-uh-NAP-uh-luhs; in-dee-NAP-luhs] (state capital, county seat, Marion). Settled in February 1820, this city, Indiana's largest, first was called the Fall Creek Settlement by fur traders. On June 7, 1820, the site was selected for a new state capital because of its geographic location near the center of the state. It was platted in April 1821 and named Indianapolis, coined by adding the Greek -polis, "city," to the state name. The name was suggested by Judge Jeremiah Sullivan when legislators found another name, Tecumseh, unacceptable. A post office was established on March 8, 1822.

Indian Creek Estates [IN-dee-uhn kreek uh-STAYTS] (Marion). This community was named for a nearby stream of the same name. Indian Creek is one of the most popular stream names in Indiana, with around twenty-five streams bearing this name. Most of these streams were so named because allegedly Native Americans either lived or camped nearby.

Indian Creek Settlement [IN-dee-uhn kreek SET-uhl-muhnt; IN-dee-uhn krik SET-uhl-muhnt] (Knox). This village was named for a nearby stream of the same name.

Indian Lake [IN-dee-uhn LAYK] (Marion). This community was named for the lake of the same name.

Indian Prairie (Tipton). See Tetersburg.

Indian Springs [in-din SPRINGZ; IN-dee-uhn SPRINGZ] (Martin). A post office was established on November 20, 1885.* The village was laid out on October 23, 1889. The name is for local mineral springs, Sulphur Springs, also called Indian Springs.

Indian Village (Kosciusko). See Alcinda.

Ingalls [ING-guhlz] (Madison). This town was platted by the Ingalls Land Company on June 5, 1893, and named for M. E. Ingalls, then president of the Big Four Railroad. A post office established at nearby Alfont on February 27, 1851, was moved to Ingalls on June 30, 1893.

Ingallston [ING-guhlz-tuhn] (Marion). A post office was established at this railroad station on November 17, 1879; moved to Beech Grove on March 22, 1883.

Inglefield [ING-guhl-feeld] (Vanderburgh). A post office established as Saundersville, perhaps for local resident Saunders Hornbrook, with John Ingle as postmaster, was established on November 27, 1823. Ingle settled here in 1818. On November 17, 1869, the post office was changed to Inglefield. The village, laid out by Ingle in 1819, first was called Saundersville, too. Ingle, also an alternate name of the community, was the name of the local railroad station.

Ingleside (Franklin). See Peoria (Franklin).

Inwood [IN-wud] (Marshall). A post office established as Lycurgus on September 22, 1851, was changed to Inwood on September 10, 1860. The village was platted on December 29, 1854, by Ezra G. Pearson, local sawyer, who also served as postmaster, 1856–1858, and it was named Pearsonville for him. In 1856 railroad officials, wanting a shorter name for the local station, changed the name to Inwood, allegedly descriptive of thick woods here.

Iona [eye-O-nuh] (Knox). A post office was established on July 13, 1888; closed on October 31, 1903.

Iowa (Jay). See Bluff Point.

Ireland [EYE-er-luhnd] (Dubois). This village first was called American City. A post office called Ireland was established on July 26, 1853, and the village was platted on May 20, 1865. According to the WPA files, the settlement was so named because most of the early settlers were Irish.

Ironton [EYE-ern-tuhn] (Martin). This village was laid out in 1873 by the Southern Indiana Coal and Iron Company and formerly called Irondon for the iron industry here.

Irvington [ERV-ing-tuhn] (Marion). This community was laid out on November 7, 1870, and named for author Washington Irving. A post office was established on January 5, 1874; closed on November 2, 1899. It was annexed to Indianapolis in February 1902.

Iva [EYE-vuh] (Pike). A post office was established here on June 6, 1893; closed on October 31, 1901.

Ivanhoe [EYE-vuhn-ho] (Lake). A post office was established on November 10, 1891; closed on March 14, 1895. This village also has been called West Gary. The name is said to be for the character Ivanhoe in Sir Walter Scott's novel of the same name.

 **J**

Jackson (Elkhart). See New Paris.

Jacksonboro (Randolph). See Bartonia.

Jacksonburgh (Brown). See Nashville.

Jacksonburg [JAK-suhn-berg] (Wayne). This village was platted in 1814 and named for Jackson Township, as it was then the voting precinct of that township. A post office was established as Jacksonburgh on May 18, 1822. On September 15, 1892, the spelling was changed to Jacksonburg, and on June 30, 1903, the post office was closed.

Jackson County [JAK-suhn]. This county was organized in 1816 and named for Andrew Jackson, general in the Battle of New Orleans in 1815 and later president of the United States. Seat: Brownstown.

Jackson Hill [jak-suhn HIL] (Sullivan). This village was named for the local Jackson Hill Coal Company.

Jackson Prairie (Steuben). See Flint.

Jacksons [JAK-suhnz] (Tipton). Newton Jackson founded a settlement named Jackson, for himself, around 1846. About 1851 Jackson, with George Kane, built a steam sawmill here. On June 29, 1863, a post office named Jackson Station was established about two miles south of the sawmill. On November 28, 1882, the post office name was changed to Jackson. The post office was closed on December 31, 1905. Parrottsville, a variant name, was established as a railroad station in 1853 and served as a shipping point for the sawmill.

Jacksonville (Fountain). See Wallace.

Jacksonville [JAK-suhn-vil] (Switzerland). This village was laid out in 1815 by Peter Harris and named for the local Jackson family. A post office, moved here from Mount Sterling, q.v., on July 29, 1841, was moved again to Center Square, q.v., on January 30, 1867.

Jadden [JAD-uhn] (Grant). A post office was established on December 26, 1850; closed on December 12, 1900. The name honors a local family. William Jadden was the first postmaster.

Jalapa [juh-LAP-uh] (Grant). This village was laid out in 1849 and named for the Mexican city occupied by Americans during the Mexican War. A post office established as Dallas on June 15, 1848, was changed to Jalapa on November 13, 1849; closed on September 29, 1900.

James Mills (Ohio). See Milton (Ohio).

James Switch (Marion). See Mallot Park.

Jamestown [JAYMZ-town] (Boone). This town, formerly the county seat, was platted in 1832 and named for James Mattlock (or Mattock), one of the founders. A post office was established on September 5, 1831.

Jamestown [JAYMZ-town] (Elkhart). This village, formerly called Jimtown, was laid out by James Davis, for whom it was named, in 1835.

Jamestown (Henry). See New Lisbon (Henry).

Jamestown (Ohio). See Milton (Ohio).

Jamestown [JAYMZ-town] (Steuben). This village was settled about 1835 and apparently first laid out around 1836. It was platted by Simeon Gilbert and Joseph Hutchinson on April 21, 1853. An earlier name of this village was Eagleville, supposedly for two eagles that each year built a nest on the shore of a nearby lake. The post office established on May 5, 1837, and closed on October 31, 1903, was called Crooked Creek, for a nearby stream of the same name.

Jarvis (DeKalb). See Butler.

Jasonville [JAY-suhn-vil] (Greene). This city was named for local storekeeper Jason Rogers, who purchased the original plat from Philbert Wright in 1853. Rogers and William B. Squires laid out the city on January 23, 1859 (WPA). A post office was established on June 23, 1858.* According to a version of a local legend, about 1855 Billy Buckalew came to Rogers's store to exchange butter and eggs for groceries. While loafing outside the store, Buckalew dipped a paddle in a tar bucket hanging on his wagon and scrawled "Jasonville" on the side of the store, and this prank gave the city its name.

Jasper [JAS-per] (county seat, Dubois). This city was founded about 1818 and platted in September 1830. When it was suggested that the city be named for her, Eleanor Enlow, wife of one of the founders, substituted the name Jasper from the biblical description of Jerusalem: "And her light was like unto a stone most precious, even like a jasper stone, clear as crystal" (Rev. 21:11). A post office was established on January 11, 1832. Oral traditions explaining the name include:

1. "As the first family in the new settlement, they were reading about the gates of heaven. The first stone mentioned in the Bible was that of jasper, so the lady of the family named the settlement Jasper" (ISUFA).

2. "Jasper was named when some ol' lady opened the Bible and put her finger on the word Jasper. She was the oldest in the community, so she got the honor of naming the town" (ISUFA).

3. "Yeah, the people around Jasper have always been religious people. Back in the beginning when they were going to name the city, they had a hard time deciding what to call it. They had a bunch of commissioners, and they voted on it and decided to name it after one of the founder's wives. Her first name was Eleanor, and that's what they were going to call the town. However, this woman, being very religious, wanted to name it after something in the Bible. She found this passage in the Book of Revelations which said that the city was built on precious stones and that jasper was the foundation stone. I guess she wanted this town to stay for a long time" (ISUFA).

Jasper County [JAS-per]. This county was formed in 1835, organized in 1838, and named for Sergeant William Jasper of Fort Moultrie, South Carolina, who was killed in the Revolution. Most of the county is farmland. Seat: Rensselaer.

Java (Parke). See Bloomingdale.

Jay City [jay SIT-ee; jay SID-ee] (Jay). This village was laid out on June 7, 1840, by Samuel Hall and David Hite and named for Jay County, q.v.

Jay County [jay]. This county was organized in 1836 and named for John Jay, American statesman who served as the first chief justice of the Supreme Court and governor of New York. Seat: Portland.

Jeff [jef] (Wells). A post office was established on September 5, 1891; closed on February 28, 1903. Allegedly the name is for Jeff Jones, son of the owner of the land on which the town was located. Supposedly, Mr. Jones said, "Jeff is a good boy, so Jeff ought to be a good town" (WPA). John T. Jones was the first postmaster.

Jefferson [JEF-er-suhn] (Clinton). This village was laid out by David Kilgore, John Ross, and Samuel Olinger in 1829 and, according to the WPA files, named for President Thomas Jefferson. A post office was established on March 16, 1830; closed on October 31, 1905.

Jefferson County [JEF-er-suhn]. This county was organized in 1811 and named for President Thomas Jefferson. Hanover College is located in this scenic county. Seat: Madison.

Jeffersonville [JEF-er-suhn-vil] (county seat, Clark). A settlement was made here at Fort Steuben in 1786. In 1802 the city was laid out according to a grid plan suggested by Thomas Jefferson and named in honor of him by William Henry Harrison. An Indiana Territory post office was established on September 13, 1803.

Jennings County [JEN-ingz]. This county was formed in 1816, organized in 1817, and named for Jonathan Jennings, first governor of the State of Indiana (1816–1822). Seat: Vernon.

Jericho [JEHR-uh-ko] (Sullivan). This place name, from the biblical city, may have been influenced by other biblical place names in this county (Merom, New Lebanon).

Jerome [juh-ROM] (Howard). This village was laid out in 1847 by Hampton Brown, who named it for his son, Jerome. A post office was established on January 20, 1848; closed on September 13, 1902.* Cf. Greentown.

Jessup [JES-uhp] (Parke). A post office was established on December 4, 1867, and called Jessups Station, for local landowner C. Jessup. According to local history, Jessup, "an old resident of the neighborhood," moved near the Pumpkin Vine Railroad after it was completed, and Pleasant Hawkins and Monroe Barns contributed to the naming of the village when they marked "Jessup" on a barrel of salt shipped here from Terre Haute. The post office name was changed to Jessup on November 28, 1882, and it was closed on April 30, 1948.

Jewell Village [jool VIL-ij] (Bartholomew). According to a traditional account, this village was named for two local families named Jewell (ISUFA).

Jimtown (Crawford). See Marengo.

Jimtown (Elkhart). See Jamestown (Elkhart).

Jimtown (Henry). See New Lisbon (Henry).

Jockey [JAHK-ee] (Warrick). This name is of uncertain origin; however, one explanation is that residents had a reputation for shrewd dealings, so the community was named Jockey. According to another local tradition, the village was so named because a man traded horses at a small racetrack here.

Johnsburg [JAHNZ-berg] (Dubois). A post office called Johnsburgh was established on August 6, 1879; closed on February 15, 1930. A nearby railroad station was called Ferdinand Station, apparently for the township or town, both called Ferdinand and located east of this village.

Johnson [JAHN-suhn] (Gibson). This village was settled in 1911 along the Penn Central Railroad and named for a railroad construction superintendent. According to the WPA files, former names were Garretts and Nip and Tuck. A post office was established on May 22, 1914; closed on June 30, 1930.

Johnson County [JAHN-suhn]. This county was established in 1822 and named for John Johnson, judge of the Indiana Supreme Court. The first Indiana college to admit women (1841), Franklin College, a Baptist-supported school, is located in this county. Seat: Franklin.

Johnsonville [JAHN-suhn-vil] (Warren). This village was laid out on July 8, 1874, and named for the local Johnson family. A post office was established on December 2, 1875, with George W.

Johnson as postmaster; closed on August 31, 1907.*

Johnstown [JAHNZ-tuhn] (Greene). A post office was established here on May 15, 1872; closed on December 15, 1886.*

Jolietville [jahl-ee-ET-vil] (Hamilton). A post office named Jollietville was established on March 11, 1875. On August 17, 1883, the spelling was changed to Jolietville. The village was established by John Corbin, who came here from Kentucky, and apparently was named for the French explorer Louis Jolliet.

Jonesboro [JONZ-ber-o] (Grant). This town was platted in 1837 by Obediah Jones, for whom it was named. A post office, with Jones as postmaster, was established as Centre, for the township in which it was located, on October 2, 1840, and changed to Jonesboro on July 19, 1848.* Jonesborough is a variant name.

Jonesboro (Greene). See Hobbieville.

Jonesboro (Huntington). See Warren.

Jonesboro (Spencer). See Gentryville.

Jones Station (Dearborn). See Cold Springs.

Jonestown [JONZ-town] (Vermillion). This village was platted in 1862 by Phillip Jones and named for him. A post office called Jones was established on April 26, 1862; moved to nearby Saint Bernice, q.v., on March 26, 1867.

Jonesville [JONZ-vil] (Bartholomew). This town, named for a local family, was laid out on March 10, 1851, by Benjamin Jones. A post office was established on June 28, 1852, with Smith Jones as

postmaster. According to an oral account, "A fellow by the name of Jones used to have a flour mill and lived down around there" (ISUFA).

Joppa [JAW-puh] (Hendricks). This village was named for the biblical seaport. The name also was applied to a post office in Hancock County (1880–1903).*

Jordan (Jay). See Salem (Jay).

Jordan [JAWR-duhn; JER-duhn] (Owen). A post office called Jordan Village was established on August 8, 1854; closed on April 29, 1922. Apparently the name is for the local Jordan family (WPA).

Jordon [JAWR-duhn] (Daviess). This village was named for the Jordan family, early settlers (WPA).

Judah [JOO-duh; JOO-dee] (Lawrence). Around 1882 Judah School was built here on land owned by John W. Judah, for whom it was named, and the village took its name from the school. A variant name is Judy.

Judson [JUHD-suhn] (Howard). A Baptist Church called Judson was established about two miles east of the Ervin post office.

Judson [JUHD-suhn] (Parke). Originally called Buchanans Springs, or sometimes simply Buchanan, for a local family, this town was platted in 1872 by Alexander Buchanan, who named it for Adoniram Judson, a Kentucky minister and missionary who died in 1850. The Bruins Crossroads post office (cf. Guion) was moved here on July 5, 1872.

Judyville [JOO-dee-vil] (Warren). This village, named for the local Judy family, was platted by John Judy on February 9, 1903. The post office, with Ole R. Judy as postmaster, was established on October 1, 1903; closed on January 6, 1961.

Julian [JOO-lee-in; JOO-lee-uhn] (Newton). This village was platted in October 1882 by Martha and J. B. Julian, for whom it was named.

Juliett (Lawrence). See Tarry Park.

Julietta [joo-lee-ET-uh] (Marion). A post office was established at this railroad community on July 19, 1869; closed on May 31, 1917. The village was platted on February 5, 1870.

Junction (Hancock). See Maxwell (Hancock).

 K

Kale School (Martin). See Cale.

Kankakee [kang-kuh-KEE] (La Porte). This community was named for the nearby stream of the same name. The river's name is a form of the Potawatomi name, Tian-kakeek, meaning "low land" or "swampy country." Another form of the name, Kiakiki, appeared in French as Qui-que-que and Quin-qui-qui, the latter pronounced about the same as Kankakee. Cf. Byron for a post office called Kankakee in this county.

Kansas [KANZ-uhs] (Bartholomew). This village was laid out on February 15, 1855, by William A. Ergenbright. A post office was established on May 21, 1856; closed on May 9, 1863. In 1942 Camp Atterbury opened in this area on 40,351 acres, including this village, which became a target range.

Kappa Corner [kap-uh KAWR-ner] (Howard). A post office called Kappa was established on June 9, 1886; closed on July 14, 1917. Although the name appears to be the tenth letter of the Greek alphabet, it perhaps comes from the Indian tribal name Kappa, sometimes spelled Quapaw.

Kasson [KAS-uhn] (Vanderburgh). A post office was established here on June 28, 1861; closed on October 15, 1902.

Kautz (Porter). See Kouts.

Kecks Church (Martin). See Burns City.

Kecksville (Martin). See Burns City.

Kekionga (Allen). See Fort Wayne.

Keller [KEL-er] (Vigo). A post office was established as Ferrell on January 9, 1903. On February 24, 1903, the name was changed to Keller, probably for the personal name, by the Southern Indiana Railroad. The post office was closed on November 15, 1913.

Kellers Settlement (Wabash). See Richvalley.

Kellers Station (Wabash). See Richvalley.

Kellerville [KEL-er-vil] (Dubois). This village, which has not been platted, was established around 1867 and named for local merchant John C. Keller. A post office was established on January 5, 1870; closed on May 29, 1931.*

Kelley (Lake). See Glen Park.

Kelso (Dearborn). See Dover (Dearborn).

Kelso (Huntington). See Majenica.

Kelsos Mill (Dubois). See Dubois.

Kempton [KEMP-tuhn; KEM-tuhn] (Tipton). This town, an outgrowth of the Lake Erie and Western Railroad, was established in 1874 on land owned by David Kemp and named for him. A post office was established on May 29, 1876.

Kendall (Allen). See New Haven.

Kendallville [KEN-duhl-vil] (Noble). This city was settled around 1832, and a post office was established on December 7, 1836, but it was relocated to nearby Lisbon on May 29, 1849. The city was platted in 1849, and on July 11, 1849, another post office was established. The name honors Postmaster General Amos Kendall, who served under President Jackson.

Kennard [KEN-erd] (Henry). This town was platted on September 6, 1882, and named for Jenkins Kennard, a local farmer who was an early resident. A post office was established on September 12, 1882.

Kennedy (Dearborn). See Bonnell.

Kennedy [KEN-uh-dee] (Spencer). This village, named for a local family, earlier was called Madrid and Kennedy Station. A post office named Madrid was established on March 13, 1888; closed on April 30, 1915. David F. Kennedy was the second postmaster.

Kenneth [KEN-uhth] (Cass). A post office was located here on December 17, 1892; closed on March 3, 1929.* According to the WPA files, the community was named by railroad officials.

Kenny (Newton). See Thayer.

Kent [kent] (Jefferson). A post office called Ramseys Mills, established on December 19, 1832, was changed to Kent, for James Kent, chief justice of New York, on January 14, 1848. The village was platted by James Blankinship on April 9, 1853.

Kentland [KENT-luhnd] (county seat, Newton). This town was platted in February 1860 by Alexander J. Kent and named Kent for him. A post office was established as Kent on August 20, 1860; changed to Kent Station on October 25, 1860; changed to Adriance on February 9, 1864; and changed to Kentland on July 20, 1868. The name Kentland supposedly was suggested by Schuyler Colfax (1823–1885), South Bend native who served as vice president of the United States (1869–73) under Grant. The name was changed to avoid confusion with another town and post office called Kent in Jefferson County.

Kercheval [KER-chuh-vul] (Spencer). A post office was established on February 23, 1882; closed on April 14, 1904.* Located near the Lincoln family homestead, this village was named for the Kercheval family, prominent in the early history of the county. Samuel Edward Kercheval published the *Rockport Journal* and served as a state legislator among other activities.

Kersey [KER-zee] (Jasper). A post office, named for a local family, was established on May 25, 1900; closed on February 28, 1955.

Kewanna [kee-WAH-nuh; kuh-WAH-nuh] (Fulton). This town was laid out in 1845 as Pleasant Grove, but the post office established on February 18, 1847, was called Kewanna, probably because there already was a post office called Pleasant Grove in Jasper County. The present name is for a Potawatomi chief, Ki-wa-na, "Prairie Chicken."

Keys Ferry (Boone). See Stringtown (Boone).

Keystone [KEE-ston] (Wells). A post office was established on January 20, 1871, and the village was platted on April 19, 1872, by Luther Twibell, and named for the Keystone State—Pennsylvania. According to the WPA files, Mrs. Twibell chose the name.

Kilmore [KIL-mawr] (Clinton). A post office called Kilmore was established in this county on October 22, 1851; closed on October 11, 1854. Another post office called Killmoreville was established on January 12, 1871; changed to Killmore on March 27, 1872; closed on July 31, 1903. The community first was called Penceville, for Abner Pence, who laid out the village on March 27, 1854. The present name is for a nearby stream, Kilmore (formerly spelled Killmore) Creek, named for early resident John Killmore. A local legend suggests that the village was named Killmore because a number of railroaders were killed here.

Kilroy (Posey). See Barrett.

Kimberlin (Boone). See Terhune.

Kimmell [KIM-uhl] (Noble). This village was settled in 1831 and named for the local Kimmell family. Orlando Kimmell was a prominent farmer and member of the state legislature. A post office was established on January 7, 1888.

Kinder (Hancock). See Carrollton (Hancock).

Kinder [KIN-der] (Johnson). A post office was established here on August 17, 1886; closed on November 29, 1902. The name probably is for a local family. William Kinder was an early settler (WPA). It's also said, though, that the name was adapted from Kinderhook, New York (WPA).

King [king] (Gibson). A post office called Kings Station was established on November 30, 1868; closed on November 28, 1882. The village was named for John King, who settled here around 1818 (WPA). Kings is a variant spelling.

Kingman [KING-muhn] (Fountain). This town was platted in January 1886 by David Ratcliff, proprietor. A post office was established on December 16, 1886. Another village called Fountainville was platted across the road from Kingman on October 30, 1886, by John Russell. In June 1900 the two villages were incorporated as Kingman.

Kingsbury [KINGZ-behr-ee] (La Porte). One of the oldest settlements in the county, this town was laid out in 1835, and the plat was recorded on February 6, 1836. A post office was established on August 30, 1839. According to the WPA files and a county history, the town was named for an early settler named Kingsbury who came here in 1834; however, the name may honor the local King family, as Polaski King, one of the town's founders, was an early local merchant. It's also said that the name was borrowed from Kingsbury, New York, former home of settlers.

Kingsford Heights [kingz-ferd HEYETS] (La Porte). This community developed during World War II as a residential area for workers at the nearby Kingsford Ordnance Plant, constructed in 1941 and at one time employing over 20,000 workers. A post office was established on April 14, 1943.

Kingsland [KINGZ-luhnd] (Wells). This village was laid out on June 11, 1883, and originally called Parkinson, for Ebenezer Parkinson, first postmaster. The post office, established as Parkinson on January 9, 1882, was changed to Kingsland on April 21, 1884. The town was renamed by Isaac Hatfield.

Kings Station (Gibson). See King.

Kingston [KINGZ-tuhn] (Decatur). A post office, named for the local King family, was established on February 15, 1849; closed on May 15, 1905. The village was laid out on June 12, 1851, by John King and others.

Kingston (Tippecanoe). See West Lafayette.

Kingston (Tipton). See Tipton.

Kinsey [KIN-zee] (Kosciusko). A post office called Kinzie was established in this county on January 24, 1882; closed on August 31, 1907.

Kirby [KER-bee] (Monroe). This village was named for the local Kirby family (WPA).

Kirklin [KERK-luhn] (Clinton). A post office called Kirks Cross Roads was established on December 17, 1832; changed to Kirklin on July 2, 1879. The name honors Nathan Kirk, who bought land here in 1828, built a tavern, became the first postmaster, and laid out the town in 1837.

Kirkpatrick [kerk-PAT-rik] (Montgomery). This village was platted in 1882 and named for James Wesley Kirkpatrick, a farmer from Ohio who settled here in December 1872 and owned the land on which the town was laid out. A post office, with Kirkpatrick as postmaster, was established on December 13, 1881; closed on June 15, 1931.

Kirksville (Gibson). See Wheeling (Gibson).

Kirksville [KERKS-vil] (Monroe). A post office was established on March 3, 1879; closed on January 14, 1905. The village, sometimes called Kirkville, was named for the Kirk family, early settlers who bought and operated the local Lane and Carmichael store here. George W. Kirk became the third postmaster.

Kiskakon (Allen). See Fort Wayne.

Kitchel [KICH-uhl] (Union). A post office was located here on September 25, 1901; closed on September 15, 1951. The village was named for the local Kitchel family, who owned land on which the village was established. A variant spelling is Kitchell.

Klaasville [KLAHS-vil] (Lake). This village was named for the local Klaas family. An early German settler was H. Klaas, who came here in 1850, and a local storekeeper, considered the founder, was August Klaas. The post office, established on March 8, 1882, was called Klassville, but apparently that was a mistake, for the name was changed to Klaasville about two weeks later on March 21, 1882. The post office was closed on November 29, 1902.

Klemmes Corner [klem-eez KAWR-ner] (Franklin). A post office called Blue Creek, for the nearby stream of the same name, was established on December 4, 1849; closed on March 31, 1904. The name of the village, Klemmes Corner, honors a local family. Albert Klemme operated a general store here, and Joseph F. Klemme was appointed postmaster in 1882.

Klondike [KLAHN-deyek] (Tippecanoe). A post office, apparently named for the region or river in Canada famous for gold discoveries, was established on December 14, 1897; closed on December 31, 1900. Klondyke is a variant spelling.

Klondyke [KLAHN-deyek] (Parke). This village was platted in 1907 and supposedly named for the Canadian Klondike, noted for the Gold Rush of 1898, the same year the Marion Brickworks opened nearby and the village sprang up. A variant name is Smoky Row.

Klondyke [KLAHN-deyek] (Vermillion). This village was named for the Klondyke mines, which were active in this area during the first of this century. Earlier the community was called Tar Town for the tarpaper houses here (ISUFA).

Knight Ridge [neyet rij] (Monroe). This village was named for the local Knight family. John Knight was an early settler (WPA).

Knightstown [NEYETS-town] (Henry). This town was laid out by Waitsel M. Cary in 1827 and named for Jonathan Knight, an engineer on the construction of the National Road through here. A post office was established on January 30, 1833. Variant names are La Fayette and West Liberty.

Knightsville [NEYETS-vil] (Clay). This town was laid out on July 13, 1867, by Dr. A. W. Knight of nearby Brazil on land owned by him, and it was named for Knight. A post office was established on February 1, 1870.

Kniman [NEYE-muhn] (Jasper). This village was laid out on January 20, 1887, by H. Kniman, for whom the village was named.

Knob Creek (Harrison). See Salina.

Knox [nahks] (county seat, Starke). A post office was established here on October 30, 1850, and the city was laid out in 1851. The name honors Major General Henry Knox, officer in the Revolution and member of Washington's cabinet.

Knox County [nahks]. This county, the first in the state, was organized in 1790 and named for Major General Henry Knox, artillery officer during the Revolution and secretary of war, 1785–1794. Vincennes University, the oldest comprehensive junior college in the United

States, is located in this county. Seat: Vincennes.

Knoxville (Dubois). See Dubois.

Kokomo [KOK-uh-mo] (county seat, Howard). David Foster, an Indian trader from Carroll County, came here in the spring of 1842 and in 1844 purchased the northeast corner of an Indian reservation. On December 5, 1844, he deeded forty acres to the county commissioners to establish a county seat here. A post office was established on November 19, 1845. The city is named for a Thorntown Miami Indian, Ko-ka-ma, sometimes spelled Kokomoko, "The Diver." In an oral text, a native of Kokomo explains the city's two nicknames: "Kokomo actually has two nicknames. One given to it by those who have to drive around it is 'Stoplight City' because they have managed to put up ten stoplights on the bypass. The formal nickname given to it years ago by our forefathers is 'The City of Firsts.' What firsts, you say? Well, one of the local McDonalds has commemorative plaques on its wall displaying our achievements, such as the first canned tomato juice made in Kokomo, Indiana, the first push button car radio, the first automatic corn picker, the first pneumatic rubber tire, Elwood Haynes' first car, the world's largest steer, and the world's largest sycamore stump" (ISUFA).

Koleen [ko-LEEN] (Greene). This village was platted in 1853 by Elijah Mitchell and apparently named by railroad officials because kaolin clay, used in making pottery, was mined here. A local legend offers another explanation of the name: "The name Cullen, maiden name of the wife of a merchant there, was sent to Washington as a name for the village when the post office was established, but the officials made a mistake, and the name established was 'Koleen'" (WPA). A post office was established on October 29, 1877. A variant name is Robison.

Koontz Lake [koonts LAYK] (Starke). This village was named for nearby Koontz Lake, which was named for Samuel Koontz, who operated a nearby mill.

Kosciusko County [kahs-kee-UHS-ko; kahs-ee-AWS-ko]. This county was formed in 1835, organized in 1836, and named for Brigadier General Thaddeus Kosciusko, a famous Polish soldier who served with Washington in the Revolution. One of the many lakes in this county is Wawasee, the largest natural lake in the state. Seat: Warsaw.

Kossuth [kah-SOOTH; kuh-SOOTH] (Washington). A post office was established on February 18, 1850; closed on December 31, 1901. Probably the name is for the Hungarian orator and patriot Lajos Kossuth (1802–1894).

Kouts [kowts] (Porter). This town, earlier called Kouts Station for a local family, was laid out on November 3, 1864, by Barnhardt (also given as Bernard) Kouts. According to most accounts, the name of the town dates from around 1865, when railroad surveyors boarded at the home of Kouts, first spelled Kautz, and named the place Kouts Station. A post office established as Foster on July 24, 1866, was changed to Kouts Station on May 14, 1867, to Kout on November 28, 1882, and to Kouts on December 10, 1890.

Kramer [KRAY-mer] (Warren). A post office called Cameron Springs, for William Cameron, first postmaster, was established on November 5, 1885. On

June 12, 1889, the name was changed to Indiana Mineral Springs; and on March 23, 1901, it was changed to Kramer for Harry L. Kramer, who built a resort hotel here to take advantage of the springs, which were thought to have therapeutic properties.

Kreitzburg [KREETS-berg] (Lake). A former spelling of the name of this village is Kreutzburg.

Kriete Corner [kree-dee KAWR-ner] (Jackson). This village was named for the Kriete family, who owned a grocery store here. A variant spelling is Kriete Corners.

Kreuzweg (Greene). See Freelandville.

Kurtz [kerts] (Jackson). This village was formed in 1890 and named for an engi-neer named Kurtz who assisted in build-ing the railroad through here (WPA). A post office was established on October 7, 1890.

Kyana [keye-AN-uh] (Dubois). This village was platted on August 11, 1882, by John L. Wheat, president of the Louisville Mining and Manufacturing Company. The name, coined by the com-pany, consists of the abbreviation for Kentucky and the last three letters of In-diana. A post office was established on September 4, 1882.

Kyle [keyel] (Dearborn). A post office called Kyle was established on April 2, 1883; closed on February 29, 1904. Earlier the village was called Manches-ter, for the township in which it is located.

 **L**

Laconia [luh-KON-yuh; luh-KO-nee-uh] (Harrison). This town was platted on March 9, 1816, and said to be named by settlers from New England for La-conia, New Hampshire, but ultimately the name comes from the name of a dis-trict in ancient Greece. A post office was established on April 12, 1823.

LaCroix (La Porte). See Otis.

La Crosse [luh-KRAWS] (La Porte). A post office was established on April 16, 1866.* Supposedly the name is French and means "The Crossing," de-scriptive of the location of the town at the junction of four railroads. But "crossing" in French is *croisement* and a railroad crossing is *passage à niveau*. *Crosse* means "crosier" or "hooked stick," and *lacrosse* is the name of an Indian game played with a crosierlike stick. Thus, either Native Americans played lacrosse here, the name was borrowed from one of the other American settle-ments called La Crosse, or the name was misapplied. LaCrosse is a variant spelling.

Lacy [LAY-see] (Martin). A post office was established on May 8, 1901; closed on June 15, 1904. Probably the name honors a local family, but according to a local anecdote, "some of the villagers claim the town is so named because of the small lace caps which the women of a peculiar religious sect near the village always wear to church" (WPA).

Ladoga [luh-DO-guh] (Montgomery). This town was laid out by John Myers on March 26, 1836, and named for the largest lake in Europe, Lake Ladoga in Russia. Supposedly a resident saw the name on a map and suggested the name. A post office was established on August 9, 1837.

La Fayette (Henry). See Knightstown.

Lafayette [lahf-ee-ET; laf-ee-ET; layf-ee-ET] (county seat, Tippecanoe). This city was laid out on May 24, 1825, and named by its founder, William Digby, for the Marquis de Lafayette, who was then touring the United States. It was selected as the county seat in 1826, and a post office was established on April 24, 1826. A variant spelling is La Fayette.

La Fontaine [luh-FOWN-tuhn] (Wabash). This town was settled around 1833 by William Grant and called Grants Land or Grant Settlement for him. On January 14, 1845, Daniel Grant platted the town and called it Ashland for Henry Clay's home in Kentucky. The post office, established on May 31, 1848, was called La Fontaine because there was another post office in Henry County called Ashland. The name honors Chief François la Fontaine, who was elected leader of the Miami nation in 1841. La-Fontaine is a variant spelling.

Lagrange (Gibson). See Fort Branch.

Lagrange [luh-GRAYNJ] (county seat, Lagrange). This town was platted on June 18, 1836, by Reuben J. Dawson, William F. Beavers, George F. Whittaker, and James McConnell and named for Lagrange County. A post office was established on March 30, 1844. A variant spelling is La Grange.

Lagrange County [luh-GRAYNJ]. This county, still mostly farmland, was organized in 1832 and named for the Marquis de Lafayette's country home near Paris. Seat: Lagrange.

Lagro [LAY-gro] (Wabash). This Wabash River town, once a French and Indian trading post between Quebec and Vincennes, was settled around 1829 and named for Le Gros ("The Big" or "The Fat"), the French nickname of a Miami chief who lived here. Originally the town was laid out in Grant County in the spring of 1834 by General John Tipton. It was platted in Wabash County on March 6, 1838. A post office spelled La Gro was established on May 17, 1834; spelling changed to Le Gros, sometimes spelled LeGros, on October 25, 1869; spelling changed back to La Gro on December 9, 1869; spelling changed to Lagro on April 5, 1893.

LaHayn (Porter). See Crocker.

Lake (Spencer). See Richland City.

Lake Bruce [layk BROOS] (Fulton). This village is located on Lake Bruce, also called Bruce Lake, for which it was named. The post office, called Bay, was established on October 1, 1902; closed on September 11, 1905.

Lake Cicott [layk SEYE-kaht; layk SEE-kuht] (Cass). This village was laid out on July 9, 1868, and named for the lake of the same name, which was named for George Cicott, a fur trader whose reserve was here. A post office was established on March 3, 1873.

Lake County [layk]. This county was formed in 1836, organized in 1837, and named for Lake Michigan, which borders the county on the north. Seat: Crown Point.

Lake James [layk JAYMZ] (Steuben). A post office was established on September 9, 1851; closed on October 6, 1851. The name is for the nearby lake of the same name.

Lakeland [LAYK-luhnd] (Parke). A post office was established here on May 23, 1894; closed on October 28, 1899.

Lakeport (La Porte). See Hudson Lake.

Lakeside [LAYK-seyed] (Pulaski). A post office was established on August 26, 1885; closed on June 15, 1906. Other communities named Lakeside are located in Hendricks and Lagrange counties.

Lake Station [LAYK stay-shuhn] (Lake). This city, laid out on March 9, 1852, was established as a station on the Michigan Central Railroad and was an important shipping point in the county until other railroads were built. A post office was established as Lake Station on October 21, 1852, but the name was changed to East Gary on December 7, 1908. On December 16, 1976, the Common Council of the city passed an ordinance changing the name back to Lake Station.

Laketon [LAYK-tuhn] (Wabash). This village was laid out on September 8, 1836, by Hugh Hanna, Isaac Thomas,

and Jacob D. Cassatt and named for its location between Long and Round lakes. A post office was established on August 7, 1839.*

Lake View [LAYK vyoo] (Porter). Earlier called Lake View Park, this village, established as a summer resort, was laid out on April 6, 1917. Supposedly it was so named "because one has a good view of Long Lake from there" (WPA). Another community called Lake View is located in Franklin County, and a community called Lakeview is located in Lagrange County. A community called Lakeview Spring is located in Kosciusko County.

Lake Village [LAYK VIL-ij; LAYK VIL-eej] (Newton). This village was laid out in January 1876, and a post office was established on September 13, 1876. Though the village likely was named for Lake Township, in which it is located, the WPA files state that this area was "once covered with water and from which fact it derives its name."

Lakeville [LAYK-vil] (Saint Joseph). Settled in 1833, this village was platted first on August 18, 1857. A post office was established on November 11, 1850. The name is for a chain of small lakes nearby.

Lamar [luh-MAHR] (Spencer). A post office was located here on April 28, 1888.

Lamb [lam] (Switzerland). This village was laid out in 1815 and called Erin. The present name is for the local Lamb family who established the post office here on May 3, 1882. William Lamb was the first postmaster. The post office closed on August 31, 1907.

Lamong [luh-MAHNG] (Hamilton) A post office was established on February 2, 1874; closed on October 15, 1902.

Lancaster [LANG-kuhs-ter] (Huntington). This village, laid out in May 1836, earlier was called New Lancaster, probably for its location in Lancaster Township. The post office, however, was established on September 21, 1875, as River, for its location on the Salamonie River. The River post office was closed on February 28, 1905. The present name ultimately comes from the English town and county.

Lancaster (Jay). See Salamonia.

Lancaster [LANG-kuhs-ter] (Jefferson). A post office was established on March 16, 1830; closed on May 15, 1907.* The village was named for Lancaster Township, in which it is located.

Lancaster (Orange). See Leipsic.

Lancaster (Owen). See Patricksburg.

Landersdale [LAN-derz-dayl] (Morgan). This village was named for the local Landers family. William Landers, a Virginian, arrived in Morgan County from Kentucky in 1819 and purchased a large tract of land from the government. Landers was an associate judge, county commissioner, and justice of the peace. A post office was established on June 13, 1870; closed on November 15, 1906.

Landess [LAN-duhs] (Grant). Formerly called Landesville, the town was laid out in 1882 by local storekeeper William Landess, for whom it was named. A post office, with Landess as postmaster, was established on February 19, 1884.

Lanesville [LAYNZ-vil] (Harrison). The Pennington family settled here in 1792, and Edward Pennington platted the town on December 11, 1817. The town was named for the government surveyor, whose last name was Lane. A post office was established on March 1, 1832.*

Langdon [LANG-duhn] (Jackson). This village was founded by and named for a man named Langdon who operated a mill here around 1820, but the business was abandoned by 1886. A post office called Langdons Station was established on October 9, 1877; changed to Langdon on November 28, 1882; closed on October 1, 1897.

Laotto [lay-AH-to] (Noble). The first post office in this vicinity, called Simons Corners for a local family, was established on August 19, 1856, and closed on September 18, 1861. David Simon built a steam sawmill here in the winter of 1871–1872, and Martin Belger opened a blacksmith shop in 1872. In October 1871 David Vorhees, Martin Belger, David Simon, Solomon Simon, and Jonathan Simon laid out a village, which they called Simonville, at a railroad junction. The railroad, however, named the junction Grand Rapids Crossing. The post office was established as Grand Rapids Crossing on September 19, 1872. The post office name was changed to La Otto on July 20, 1875, and the spelling was changed to Laotto on May 25, 1893. Supposedly the name La Otto was suggested by Reverend Benjamin F. Stultz.

La Paz [luh PAZ] (Marshall). This town was laid out on August 5, 1873, and apparently named for the capital of Bolivia or the city in western Mexico. According to "an old informant," however, the town "is called La Paz because of the rail junction, the path" (WPA). A nearby post office established as Walnut Hill on

May 20, 1864, was moved to La Paz on November 17, 1873. On August 1, 1893, the spelling of the post office was changed to Lapaz.

La Paz Junction [luh paz JUHNK-shuhn] (Marshall). This community was established about 1876 nearly a mile east of La Paz at a railroad junction, hence the name. Lapaz Junction is a variant spelling.

Lapel [luh-PEL] (Madison). This town was laid out on April 27, 1876, by David Conrad and Samuel E. Busby and so named by Busby because when the railroad was built through here a strip of land was left between it and the Pendleton Turnpike in the shape of a lapel. A post office was established on March 17, 1882. A variant spelling is Lapell.

Lapland [LAP-land] (Montgomery). A post office, apparently named for the northern European region, was established here on February 24, 1885; closed on August 7, 1899.

La Porte [luh PAWRT] (county seat, La Porte). Because of its location on the Sauk Trail, this city was chosen as the county seat in 1832 when La Porte County, q.v., was organized and named for the county. Walter Wilson first bought land here on October 19, 1831, and along with Hiram Todd, John Walker, James Andrew, and A. P. Andrew, founded the city, which was platted in 1833. An oral account includes a nickname: "Toni told me that La Porte was named by a Frenchman, and it means 'the door.' Because of the roads leading from it to the west, it was considered the door to the new west. It also has the nickname of Maple City because of the maple trees growing there" (ISUFA). A post office was established

on July 3, 1832. Variant spellings are La-Porte and Laporte.

La Porte County [luh PAWRT]. This county was organized in 1832 and called La Porte, "the door." The French had used the name because a natural opening through the forest in this area served as a gateway to the north. Seat: La Porte.

Larimer Hill [LEHR-uh-mer HIL] (Vigo). This village was named for a local family, whose name sometimes is spelled Larimar. W. H. Larimar came to nearby Terre Haute in 1880.

Larwill [LAHR-wil] (Whitley). This town was laid out on November 13, 1854, and formerly called Huntsville, for local taverner Truman Hunt, owner of some of the land on which the town was located. The present name honors two engineers, William and Joseph Larwill, who supervised the building of a railroad here. A post office established as Summit on December 21, 1846, was changed to Larwill on March 28, 1866.

Laswell (Crawford). See Taswell.

Latta Yard [lad-uh YAHRD] (Greene). Railroad yards were established here in 1901 and named for the local Latta family, who owned the land on which the yards were located (WPA). Also called Latta, the village served coal mining operations in this area.

Laud [lawd] (Whitley). This community, earlier called Sodom and Lickskillet, dates from 1854, when a sawmill was built here. A post office called Laud was established on June 27, 1855; closed on February 28, 1903. The village, laid out around 1866, was named Forest, supposedly for dense forests, according to the WPA files.

Lauer [lahr; lowr] (Perry). A post office was established on June 19, 1930; closed on December 15, 1945. The name honors a local family. Mittie A. Lauer was the first and only postmaster.

Laughery (Ohio). See Hartford.

Laugheryville [LAHK-ray-vil] (Ripley). A post office named Laughery was established on November 28, 1827; closed on September 19, 1845. The name is for Laughery Creek via Laughery Township, in which it is located. The stream was named for Colonel Archibald Laughery (sometimes spelled Lochry), who was killed in 1781 near its mouth. The village was platted by Jonathan Merrick on May 5, 1847. A variant name is Laughery Switch.

Laura [LAWR-uh] (Jasper). This village was founded about 1897 and named by B. J. Gifford. A post office was established on May 3, 1902; closed on September 15, 1913.

Laurel [LAHR-uhl] (Franklin). This village was platted on November 30, 1836, by James Conwell, who named it for his hometown—either Laurel, Maryland, or Laurel, Delaware, depending on the source. Formerly it was called Somerset and Conwells Mills. A post office established on May 31, 1832, as Conwells Mills, with James Conwell as postmaster, was changed to Laurel on July 26, 1837. An oral account of a nearby mound goes: "This mound is about 150 feet above the valley of Laurel and is said to be a genuine prehistoric mound, the northern most of several mounds that dot the Whitewater Valley. It overlooks a landscape that Meredith Nicholson, a famous Indiana writer, had once said was 'one of the loveliest in Indiana.' The mound was

once the site of an Indian village. An eminent archaeologist termed it the finest Algonquin village location that he had ever seen" (ISUFA). A variant name is Laurel City.

Lawrence (DeKalb). See Sedan.

Lawrence [LAHR-uhnts; LAWR-uhnts] (Marion). This city was platted on February 27, 1849, and formerly called Lanesville; however, since there was another town in Indiana with that name, the name was changed to Lawrence, for the local post office, which was established on November 13, 1846, and closed on July 31, 1950. The post office was named for its location in Lawrence Township.

Lawrenceburg [LAHR-uhnts-berg] (county seat, Dearborn). This city was laid out in April 1802 and named by one of the proprietors, Captain Samuel C. Vance, for his wife, Mary Morris Lawrence. An Indiana Territory post office called Laurenceburgh was established on November 26, 1806. On June 6, 1829, the spelling was changed to Lawrenceburgh, and on August 3, 1894, the spelling was changed to Lawrenceburg. Another variant name is New Lawrenceburgh.

Lawrenceburg Junction [LAHR-uhnts-berg JUHNK-shuhn] (Dearborn). This village was named for nearby Lawrenceburg, q.v.

Lawrence County [LAHR-uhnts; LAWR-uhnts]. This scenic county was organized in 1818 and named for Captain James Lawrence, of the United States frigate *Chesapeake*. Seat: Bedford.

Lawrenceport [LAHR-uhnts-pawrt] (Lawrence). This village, overlooking

White River, was platted on May 17, 1837, and named for early landowner Josiah Lawrence. A post office was established on January 16, 1851; closed on April 16, 1859. Cf. Rivervale.

Lawrenceville [LAHR-uhnts-vil] (Dearborn). This village, named for the local Lawrence family, was laid out in 1836 by John Lawrence. James and Philip Lawrence owned the first store here. An adjoining village called Morgantown, apparently for R. L. Morgan, who managed the store owned by the Lawrence family, also was laid out in 1836 and was absorbed by Lawrenceville. A post office called Lawrenceville was established on June 12, 1846; closed on December 31, 1904.

Lawsburg (Fayette). See Everton.

Lawstown (Fayette). See Everton.

Lawton [LAWT-uhn] (Pulaski). A post office was established on August 14, 1902; closed on June 15, 1906. According to the WPA files, Jesse Lowther, on whose farm the village was founded, chose the name.

Layton [LAYT-uhn] (Fountain). A post office was located here on August 26, 1891; closed on November 15, 1900.

Layton Mills (Decatur). See Slabtown.

Leach (Grant). See Fowlerton.

Leases Corner [lees-uhz KAWR-ner] (Cass). This village was named for George Lease, a local storekeeper.

Leatherwood [LETH-er-wud] (Parke). A post office was established on September 10, 1880; closed on May 17, 1894.

The village was named for Leatherwood Branch.

Leavenworth [LEV-uhn-werth] (Crawford). This town was platted on July 14, 1819. A post office, with Zebulon Leavenworth as postmaster, was established on November 8, 1819. The town was virtually destroyed by a flood in 1937, relocated on a bluff behind the old site, and rebuilt in 1938. It was named for the proprietors, Seth and Zebulon Leavenworth, who were cousins. The Leavenworth cousins were active in state as well as in local affairs, for both served in the state legislature.

Leavenworths Mill (Crawford). See Milltown.

Lebanon [LEB-uh-nuhn] (county seat, Boone). This city was platted in 1832 and named for the biblical mountains noted for their cedars. Tall hickory trees apparently suggested the name to the county commissioners. According to a local anecdote, A. M. French, the youngest of the commissioners, gazed at the tall trees around him, thought of the cedars of Lebanon, and shouted "Lebanon" at a meeting on May 1, 1831, when the commissioners were deciding on a name for the county seat. It's also said that French named the city for his hometown in Ohio. A post office was established on December 15, 1832.

Lebanon (Warren). See West Lebanon.

Lee [lee] (White). A post office was established on October 25, 1880; closed on June 30, 1933. The village was named for John Lee, president of the Indianapolis, Delphi, and Chicago Railroad, who developed a grain market here.

Leesburg [LEEZ-berg] (Kosciusko). This town, the oldest in the county, was named for Levi Lee, who laid it out in 1835. A post office established as Turkey Creek on September 5, 1836, was changed to Leesburgh on September 20, 1839.

Leesville [LEEZ-vil] (Lawrence). This village was laid out in June 1818 and named by its founders for their former home, Lee County, Virginia. Apparently it was platted again on February 27, 1840, by William Flinn, Sr., and William Flinn, Jr. A local tradition says that Daniel Guthrie was the founder, and the place originally was called Leahsville, for Guthrie's wife, Leah (WPA). A family legend collected from another informant suggests a similar origin of the name: "According to records in my family (for whose accuracy I cannot vouch and pass along the statement for what it is worth either as history or as folklore), Leesville was named for . . . my great-great-great grandmother, Leah Spear Flinn, and it seems to be indeed folklore, for the historical marker says that it was named for Lee County, Virginia" (ISUFA). A post office was established on August 28, 1824; closed on September 15, 1906.

LeGros (Wabash). See Lagro.

Leipsic [LEEP-sik] (Orange). This village was laid out in October 1851 by David S. Lewis and Isaac Edwards and called Lancaster. Leipsic, apparently for the German city, was the name applied to the post office established on December 10, 1852.

Leisure [LAY-zher; LEE-zher] (Madison). A post office, named for a local family, was established here on February 6, 1888; closed on February 14, 1903.

Leiters Ford [leyet-erz FAWRD] (Fulton). Settled around 1836, this village originally was called Hunters Ford, for the local Hunter family. William Hunter settled here in 1840 and sold his property to John Leiter in 1845. When a post office was established on May 21, 1872, it was named Leiters Ford, for the Leiter family.

Lena [LEE-nuh] (Parke). This village was laid out in 1870 by Robert King, and a post office was established on June 20, 1871, in Clay County; consequently, Marysville, q.v., a Clay County community adjoining Lena on the south, also popularly was known as Lena. On March 29, 1880, the post office moved across the county line to Parke County, and on March 31, 1936, the post office was closed. The name is of uncertain origin, although local legends say Lena was named for an Indian maiden or for a white girl captured by Indians. Since the community was established along a railroad during coal mining days, railroad officials perhaps named the place.

Leo [LEE-o] (Allen). A post office called Leo was established on September 22, 1846.* The name comes from St. Leo's Church, which was named for Pope Leo XII. The village was platted in 1849 and first called Hamilton, for one of the platters, James Hamilton.

Leopold [LEE-uh-pold] (Perry). This village was founded in November 1842 and named by Father Augustaus Bessonies for King Leopold I of Belgium. A post office was established on February 18, 1846. According to an oral account, "Leopold was named after France's

Ferdinand II. I know that for a fact" (ISUFA).

Leota [lee-O-duh] (Scott). A post was established on August 8, 1884; closed on September 30, 1901. Never officially laid out, the village was named for a local woman whose Christian name was Leota (WPA). A variant name is Finleys Cross Roads.

Leroy [LEE-roy] (Lake). A railroad station called LeRoy was established about 1865. The village was platted on December 11, 1875, and originally called Cassville, for Dr. Levi Cass, who owned land near here. The post office, established on July 15, 1869, was called LeRoy. On April 7, 1893, the spelling was changed to Leroy.

Letts [lets] (Decatur). This village was laid out on September 30, 1882, and named for the local Lett family. A post office called Letts Corner, q.v., with Allen W. Lett as postmaster, was established near here on February 8, 1871. On February 10, 1896, the post office apparently was moved here, and the name was changed to Letts. On January 31, 1954, the post office was closed.

Letts Corner [lets KAWR-ner] (Decatur). This community, named for the local Lett family, was a railroad station and post office located about a half mile west of Letts, q.v.

Lettsville [LETS-vil] (Daviess). This village, laid out by Warden C. Lett on May 10, 1871, was named for the local Lett family. A post office, with Warden C. Lett as postmaster, was established on July 15, 1869, and closed on January 26, 1887. According to local tradition, a nickname was Hole-in-the-Wall for a makeshift door knocked through a brick wall of a basement saloon.

Lewis [LOO-us] (Vigo). This village first was called Centerville, but when a post office was established on April 17, 1840,* the name was changed to Lewis, supposedly by the Post Office Department because there already was a post office called Centerville in Wayne County.

Lewisburg [LOO-us-berg] (Cass). This village was laid out in September 1835 by Lewis Boyer, for whom it was named. A post office was established on November 9, 1835; closed on May 18, 1868. Boyer served as postmaster from 1843 to 1845.

Lewisburg (Hancock). See Eden.

Lewis Creek [loo-us KREEK] (Shelby). This village was founded around 1856 and named for the nearby stream of the same name. A post office was established on February 6, 1861; closed on October 31, 1931.

Lewiston [LOO-us-tuhn] (Jasper). This village was platted on September 9, 1901, by Benjamin J. Gifford, who also named it.

Lewisville [LOO-us-vil] (Henry). This town was laid out on December 25, 1829, and named for cofounder Lewis C. Freeman, who also was the first postmaster when a post office was established on May 27, 1831.

Lewisville [LOO-us-vil] (Morgan). This village was established as a small collection of houses about a half mile east of Alaska on the Morgan-Owen county line and was named for a local pioneer family.

Lexington [LEKS-ing-tuhn] (Carroll). This village, sometimes locally called Lex, was established around 1835. It is thought that the name is for the Battle of Lexington (WPA).

Lexington (Lagrange). See Brighton.

Lexington [LEKS-ing-tuhn] (Scott). This village was founded between 1810 and 1813 and named for Lexington, Massachusetts, apparently because of the famous battle there. An Indiana Territory post office was established on July 14, 1814.* A variant name is New Lexington.

Liber [LEYE-ber] (Jay). This village was platted on April 30, 1853, and named for Liber College, which was located here in the same year. A post office established on January 10, 1872, was closed on April 10, 1902.* Cf. College Corner (Jay).

Liberal [LIB-er-uhl; LIB-er-ul] (Spencer). A post office was established here on August 19, 1887; closed on April 30, 1907.

Liberty (Johnson). See Trafalgar.

Liberty (Miami). See Chili.

Liberty [LIB-er-dee] (county seat, Union). This town was laid out on April 9, 1822, by Thomas Brown on land purchased from the government on December 18, 1813, by Wright Cook and probably was named for Liberty, Virginia, home of some early settlers. A post office was established on June 23, 1824.

Liberty Center [LIB-er-tee SEN-ter] (Wells). A post office, named for its location near the center of Liberty Township, was established as Liberty Centre on November 18, 1857, and the spelling was changed to Liberty Center on July 27, 1893.* The village was laid out in November 1878.

Liberty Mills [LIB-er-dee MILZ] (Wabash). This village was platted on June 24, 1837, by John Comstock—first post-

master, judge, state representative, and cattleman. The first part of the name is patriotic, and the second part is descriptive of the early saw, grist, woolen, and carding mills around which the village was built on Eel River. The post office was established on July 27, 1837.

Libertyview [LIB-er-dee-vyoo] (Porter). This village was laid out in 1909. A post office called Liberty View was established on February 5, 1910; closed on December 31, 1913. The name is commendatory.

Libertyville [LIB-er-dee-vil] (Vermillion). This village is located on the Vigo-Vermillion county line. A post office named Libertyville was established as a Vigo County post office on November 24, 1871; closed on March 31, 1904.

Lick Creek (Orange). See Prospect.

Lickskillet (Daviess). See South Washington.

Lick Skillet (Jay). See Redkey.

Lick Skillet (Jennings). See North Vernon.

Lick Skillet (Miami). See McGrawsville.

Lickskillet (Morgan). See Wilbur.

Lickskillet (Warrick). See Folsomville.

Liggett [LIG-it; LIG-uht] (Vigo). This village probably was named for early settlers named Liggett (WPA).

Ligonier [lig-uhn-EER; lig-uh-NEER] (Noble). This city was platted in May 1835 by Isaac Cavin and named for his hometown, Ligonier, Pennsylvania. A local tradition held that the name was of Native American origin and meant "place where bones and other refuse was piled" (WPA). Another humorous story says that someone going through here in the 1880s got his leg and ear cut off, and the name comes from that misfortune. A post office established as Good Hope on August 28, 1832, in Lagrange County was moved to Noble County on August 26, 1841, and changed to Ligonier on June 15, 1848.

Lilly Dale [LIL-ee dayl] (Perry). A post office called Lilly Dale was established here on August 8, 1855; closed on February 15, 1918.* Lillydale is a variant spelling.

Lima (Lagrange). See Howe.

Limberlost (Adams). See Geneva.

Limedale [LEYEM-dayl] (Putnam). Hellens, Butcher, and Steeg opened a lime and stone quarry here in 1856. The village was laid out in 1864 and called Greencastle Junction. On December 16, 1873, when a post office was established, it was renamed Limedale for the limestone quarries and lime kiln here. The post office was closed on October 30, 1909.

Limestone (Lawrence). See Oolitic.

Lincoln [LINK-uhn] (Cass). This village was laid out in May 1852 and named for Theodore Lincoln, who surveyed part of the town. A post office was established on November 9, 1855; closed on October 31, 1953.

Lincoln (Miami). See Macy.

Lincoln City [link-uhn SIT-ee; link-uhn SID-ee] (Spencer). This village was laid out in 1872 on land that once belonged to Abraham Lincoln's father, Thomas

Lincoln, and named for the Lincoln family. A post office was established on March 25, 1892; closed on August 14, 1901.

Lincoln Pioneer Village [LINK-uhn PEYE-uh-neer VIL-ij] (Spencer). Located near the city park in Rockport, this reconstructed village with about twenty buildings dates from 1934–1935. The village illustrates what life was like when Lincoln lived in the county.

Lincolnville (Ripley). See Benham.

Lincolnville [LINK-uhn-vil] (Wabash). A post office, named for Abraham Lincoln, was established on July 11, 1870; closed on June 15, 1907. The village was platted by J. V. Straugh on June 24, 1876. Variant names before the post office was established were Hicksite, for a branch of Quakers here, and Holloway Town, for the Holloway families, local farmers and merchants. The community also was called Four Corners.

Linden [LIN-duhn] (Montgomery). A post office, apparently named for the tree, was established on June 30, 1851, and the town was platted in 1852 by Hiram Hughes, Joel Lee, and Nathan Harwood.

Lindley (Saint Joseph). See Lydick.

Linkville [LINK-vil] (Marshall). This village, earlier called Linksville, was laid out on June 9, 1866, and named for M. J. Link, one of the founders. A post office called Linkville was established on August 8, 1884, closed on November 30, 1903.* Cf. Harris.

Linn Grove [lin grov] (Adams). A post office called Linn was established on September 5, 1848; changed to Linn

Grove on November 19, 1849; changed to Linngrove on April 15, 1895; and closed on December 31, 1904. On May 1, 1964, the post office was reestablished as Linn Grove. The village was laid out around 1856 by Robert Simison and originally called Buena Vista, a popular name in Indiana commemorating an American victory in the Mexican War.

Linnsburg [LINZ-berg] (Montgomery). This village was laid out in April 1870 and named for the local Linn family. Asbury Linn was a local merchant, farmer, and third postmaster. A post office was established on February 10, 1887; closed on January 31, 1934. Mace is a variant name.

Linton [LINT-uhn] (Greene). This community was settled around 1816 and first called New Jerusalem. A post office established on January 2, 1833, as New Jerusalem was changed to Linton on November 19, 1835. The city was laid out in 1850, according to most sources. The name honors Colonel William C. Linton, congressional candidate from Terre Haute who made a speech here. Linton once was called the Pittsburgh of the West because of the many coal fields in the area.

Linwood [LIN-wud] (Madison). This village earlier was called Funks Station for the local Funk family, instrumental in establishing a local railroad station. A post office called Funks was established on January 2, 1878; changed to Linwood, apparently for the tree, on March 25, 1887; and closed on June 14, 1929.*

Lippe [LIP-ee] (Posey). A post office was established on September 25, 1890; closed on July 14, 1902. German settlers named this village for Lippe, Germany.

Lisbon [LIZ-buhn] (Noble). Asa Brown built a house and sawmill here about 1837 and platted the city in October 1847. A post office was established on May 29, 1849; closed on August 30, 1919.* Brown also served as the second postmaster (1850–1853). The name probably comes from the city in Portugal.

Little Flat Rock (Rush). See Milroy (Rush).

Little Marion (Shelby). See Marion (Shelby).

Little Point [LID-uhl poynt] (Morgan). According to the WPA files, this village was founded in 1829, though a post office was not established as Little Point until June 16, 1876. On June 4, 1894, the spelling of the post office name was changed to Littlepoint, and on December 18, 1908, the post office was closed.

Little Rock [lid-uhl RAHK] (Knox). A post office was established as Littlerock on March 1, 1901; closed on July 31, 1903.

Littles [LIT-uhlz] (Pike). A post office was established on January 8, 1890; closed on August 31, 1929. From around 1900 to 1920 this village was a thriving coal mining community. The name is for an Evansville man named Little who owned a deep shaft coal mine here.

Littleton (Saint Joseph). See Wyatt.

Little Walnut (Putnam). See Morton.

Little York [lid-uhl YAWRK] (Washington). This town was laid out by George Davis on August 3, 1831, and so named because the settlers were from New

York. A post office was established on February 18, 1837.*

Liverpool (Daviess). See Washington (Daviess).

Liverpool [LIV-er-pool] (Lake). This village, the first seat of Lake County, was laid out in 1835. A post office established on January 28, 1837, was moved to Hobart, q.v., on May 26, 1847.

Livonia [leye-VON-yuh] (Washington). This town was laid out in 1819 and first called Bethel for a local church. A post office called Livonia was established on May 9, 1818; closed on January 15, 1925.* The present name probably is for the Baltic province.

Lizton [LIZ-tuhn] (Hendricks). This town was laid out in 1851 by Jesse Veiley and named New Elizabeth for his wife, Elizabeth. A post office was established as New Elizabeth on July 29, 1854; changed to Lizton on May 1, 1873. According to the WPA files, the railroad shortened the name to Lizton.

Lochiel [lo-KEEL] (Benton). A post office established as Kaarland, for the local Kaar family, on November 17, 1882, was changed to Lochiel on May 25, 1883, and closed on July 15, 1907. The present name honors "the head of the clan Cameron" (WPA). "Lochiel," the title of the chief of the Camerons, is perhaps most familiar in Thomas Campbell's poem "Lochiel's Warning," of which Donald Cameron of Lochiel is the subject.

Locke [lahk] (Elkhart). A post office, named for its location in Locke Township, was established on October 14, 1847; closed on December 9, 1893.* According to the WPA files, the township was named for the first settler, Samuel Lockwood. The village was laid out by George Eby, M. H. Morlan, and L. B. Winder in 1867.

Lockport [LAHK-pawrt] (Carroll). This village was laid out in 1836 on the Wabash and Erie Canal and named for the locks here. A post office established as Burnettsville on January 23, 1835, was changed to Lockport on March 3, 1838; closed on October 15, 1904.*

Lockport (Vigo). See Riley.

Lockridge (Putnam). See Raccoon.

Lockwood Mills (Parke). See Bridgeton.

Locust Point (Harrison). See Bridgeport.

Lodi (Fountain). See Silverwood.

Lodi [LO-deye] (Parke). Around 1832–1833 this village was called Gilderoy, but was platted in 1836 as Fullerton. In 1837 the name was changed to Lodi for nearby artesian springs. In 1857 the name was changed again to Waterman, for Dr. Richard Waterman who settled here in that year and improved commercial interests. Lodi is an Italian town, site of Napoleon's victory in 1796. A post office called Lodiville was established on December 28, 1844; changed to Waterman on January 19, 1860.* Cf. Silverwood for a nearby post office called Lodi.

Logan [LO-guhn] (Dearborn). This village formerly was called Logan Cross Roads (also spelled Logan Crossroads) and Logan Cross. A post office called Logan, for the township in which it was located, was established on January 29, 1836; closed on August 15, 1927. Logan Township, organized in November 1826, was named for Logan Creek, which was named for early settler James

Logan, who dug two salt wells on the creek.

Logan [LO-guhn] (Lawrence). This village was established as a switching station on the Monon Railroad.

Logansport [LO-guhnz-pawrt] (county seat, Cass). This city was laid out on April 10, 1828, and named for Captain James John Logan, a Shawnee chief, whose Indian name was Spemica Lawba, "High Horn." Logan was killed near Fort Wayne in 1812 while serving with the United States Army. A post office established as Eel River on January 1, 1827, was changed to Logansport on August 25, 1828. According to an oral account, "Back when the Miami Indians were living in Cass County, Indiana, they frequently made trips up and down the Eel River. All along the river were small villages and settlements of various peoples. Most of these small settlements had some kind of name already attached to them. However, there was one fairly large community, which, for some unknown reason, had no permanent name yet. At this time, the Miami Indians were in the process of changing chiefs. They could think of no more fitting gesture than to name a settlement after their new chief. The Miami Indians, being the peace-loving Indians that they were, went to this new settlement and counseled with the people. They agreed to name their community after the new Indian chief. From that day on, this small settlement was named Logansport, after Chief Logansport. . . ." (ISUFA). According to local tradition, citizens participated in a shooting match to determine who would get to name the city (WPA). Some sources say that Colonel John B. Duret won the shooting match and therefore the honor of naming the city. Loganport has been a variant spelling.

Lomax [LO-maks] (Starke). This village was established around 1882 and named for a local landowner (WPA).

London [LUHN-duhn] (Shelby). This village was laid out on July 21, 1852—at the time when the Indianapolis, Cincinnati, and Lafayette Railroad was being surveyed—by Aaron House and named for London, England. A post office was established on January 10, 1854; closed on February 28, 1959.

Lone Tree [lon tree] (Greene). This village has had two different sites, which were over two miles from each other. A post office called Lone Tree was established on September 11, 1857; closed on November 7, 1862. Another post office, apparently at a different site, called Lonetree was established on August 2, 1897; closed on July 14, 1906. According to a local tradition, the village was named for a single oak tree that stood in the yard of a store at the original site. The name may have been applied first to Lone Tree Prairie, also said to have been named for a single oak tree that stood on the prairie.

Long Beach [LAWNG beech] (La Porte). The name of this town, located on Lake Michigan, is descriptive of "the long stretch of beautiful sandy beach along which the town was originally started and upon which it now fronts" (WPA). Frank Lloyd Wright's son, John Lloyd Wright, designed several public buildings, including the elementary school and the town center, as well as several houses here between 1923 and 1946, when he moved to California.

Long Lake Island [lawng layk EYE-luhnd] (Porter). This community was named for Long Lake, which was named for its long, cigarlike shape.

Long Run [LAWNG ruhn] (Switzerland). A post office was established on March 13, 1874; closed on April 15, 1907. The name is for a nearby stream of the same name. A variant name is Long Branch.

Long Siding (Parke). See Tangier.

Longwood Crossing [lawng-wud KRAWS-ing] (Fayette). A post office established as Philpotts Mills, with William Philpotts as postmaster, on December 15, 1832, was changed to Longwood on April 24, 1837, and closed on March 15, 1901.*

Loogootee [lo-GO-dee; luh-GO-dee] (Martin). This city was platted in 1853 by Thomas N. Gootee, who homesteaded here in 1818. A post office was established on July 6, 1857; closed on December 28, 1957. The name apparently was coined from Gootee's name and another name. Some say the first part of the place name comes from Lowe, the engineer of the first train through here, and some say it's for Lucinda, Gootee's wife. Other legends of the city's naming include:

1. "Ever since I was old enough to go to school, I've been hearing about how Loogootee got its name. It was at the time they were building the B & O Railroad through the midwest to St. Louis. At the time, they had already built it to Shoals, but they didn't know whether to go on to Mount Pleasant or to make a straighter route through what's now called Loogootee. This guy named Gootee who owned this land offered his land to the railroad for a very good price. The engineer, who knew how she felt about his son, said, as a joke, that he'd let his daughter marry Gootee's son if he would name the town after him. Of course, Gootee agreed, and the Lowe girl married the Gootee boy. It didn't take long for the name Lowe-Gootee to catch on then" (ISUFA).

2. "There are so many, many people named Godie in Loogootee, and people would go along and say, 'Hello, Godie.' Finally, it was shortened to 'Lo, Godie'" (ISUFA).

3. "People, when they built the town, couldn't decide on a name, so they opened an atlas and put their finger down, and it was on Loogootee, which is in Russia, and that is what they named the city" (ISUFA).

4. "Some people say that the town was named for the wife of Thomas Gootee, the man who founded the town. Her name, I think, was Mary Lou Gootee or something like Lou Gootee" (WPA).

Lookout [LUK-owt] (Ripley). A post office was established here on February 28, 1889; closed on August 31, 1906.

Lorane [lo-RAYN; luh-RAYN] (Whitley). A post office called Loran was established in this county on July 28, 1851; closed on March 24, 1855. Another post office called Lorane was established on May 21, 1872; closed on February 29, 1904. According to the WPA files, the village earlier was called Steam Corners, for local steam-powered sawmills, and Buzzards Glory, for an incident. A traveler crossed a stream near here and stopped all night with the Lord family. "The next morning, he said he crossed the river Jordan, went through Glory, and stayed all night with the Lord, and from that time on the little place was called Glory. Someone added the name Buzzard. Why, no one knows." The present name seems to be a phonetic spelling of Lorraine, the French province. Lorain is a variant spelling.

Loree [luh-RAY; LAWR-ee] (Miami). The Pan Handle Railroad established a siding here in 1888 and named this unplatted village for a railroad official. Soon after, E. B. Bottorff opened a general store, and a post office was established on March 13, 1888; closed July 14, 1926.

Losantville [luh-SANT-vil] (Randolph). This town was platted on February 22, 1851, and originally called Hunts Cross Roads, for landowner Howard Hunt, who platted the town. Losantville, established as a post office on June 29, 1854, is a form of Losantiville, the original coined name of Cincinnati. "L" stands for Licking Creek, "os" is Latin for mouth, and "anti" is Greek for opposite. These were combined with the generic *ville* to identify "the town opposite the mouth of Licking Creek." Kentucky historian John Filson is sometimes credited with coining the name Losantiville for what later became Cincinnati. An alternate name, Bronson, apparently comes from the name of a railroad official, as a railroad station called Bronson was established about three-quarters of a mile south of the original site of Losantville.

Lost River [LAWST RIV-er] (Orange). A post office was established on August 15, 1837; closed on January 28, 1878.* The name comes from a local stream of the same name, which was so named because it sinks and runs underground for several miles before it rises again. Several legends attempt to explain the stream name:

1. "In Orange County at Spring Mill State Park, there is a river that has no beginning known as the Lost River. Scientists have been searching for the answer to the mystery, but no one can find the river's beginning. They can trace it to a certain point where it seems to fall into the ground. It seems that it would flow underground, but no such underground route can be located. The river just disappears" (ISUFA).

2. "Lost River is located east of Orleans, Indiana. The river received the name because it disappears for about ten miles. It is believed that it goes under into limestone caves. People have put such things as ducks and other material objects in the river at its origin and never see them again. At the place where it comes up, there's a high rock, and the water goes up rolling. At the place where it comes up, it is like a big hole" (ISUFA).

3. "Well, you know how Lost River got its name, don't you? I've never seen the place myself, but everybody around here almost has been up where the river just goes right into a hill. It's up there north of Boggs Creek somewhere. There's like a big hole in the side of a hill, and the river flows right into it. There's supposed to be an awful suction where the river goes into the hill, and one time when they still drove horses and wagons, a man drove too close to the side of the road and fell in the river. He was pretty close to that hole anyway, and the river was up, so the current just carried his horses, wagon, and all right to where the suction was. The suction pulled them all in under the hill, and they've never been able to recover them since" (ISUFA).

4. "Have you ever heard of this opening in the river at Orangeville? There have been divers that have put green food coloring in it to see if it comes up anywhere else because they don't think it is a part of Lost River, which supposedly doesn't have a bottom. About two years ago, whenever it was that they used horses and carriages, somehow or something, he drove his horses and everything out into the river there. Everybody went out to see what had happened, and so when they got out there, they could see the bubbles and everything and knew he had drowned. Now they say that every so often you can hear him screaming and his horses

hollering and stuff. But the real thing that gets me is, you know, they thought the carriage and pieces of it would float back up, but they never did. So not too long ago they sent more divers down to look for traces of it, you know. But they can't find anything because they can't find a bottom. Now isn't that mysterious?" (ISUFA).

Lottaville [LAHT-uh-vil] (Lake). A railroad station was established here in 1879 and called Redsdale, although the post office was named Lottaville when it was established on May 26, 1881. The post office was closed on June 15, 1905.

Lotus [LO-duhs] (Union). A post office was established here on February 6, 1865; closed on October 14, 1903.

Lovely Dale (Knox). See Monroe City.

Lovett [LUHV-uht] (Jennings). This village was platted in 1855 and named for a railroad official. A post office was established on April 11, 1870; closed on August 5, 1934.*

Lowell [LO-uhl; lol] (Lake). This town was laid out in 1853 by Samuel Halstead, who registered a claim for land in 1835 and built a mill here. According to the WPA files, the name was borrowed from Lowell, Massachusetts. A post office established as Outlet on December 30, 1843, was changed to Lowell on June 15, 1864.

Lowry Station (Madison). See Orestes.

Lucerne [lu-SERN; loo-SERN] (Cass). This village was laid out on September 29, 1883, and first called Altoner, allegedly for Mr. or Mrs. Al Toner, instrumental in building the railroad through here. The post office, established on January 16, 1884, was called Nebo. On

April 23, 1891, the post office and village names were changed to Lucerne, apparently for the lake or city in Switzerland.

Luray [lu-RAY; loo-RAY] (Henry). A settlement here first was called Virginia, former home of settlers (WPA). The village was laid out by Lot Hazelton on January 19, 1836, and called Luray, for Luray, Virginia. A post office was established on May 15, 1838; closed on June 15, 1901.

Lushers (Perry). See Apalona.

Lusks Mills [luhsks MILZ] (Parke). A post office called Lusks Mills was established on December 13, 1837; closed on March 17, 1845. The name honors the local Lusk family. Salmon Lusk was the first and only postmaster. Lusk, a Vermonter, built a gristmill on Sugar Creek in 1826, but the mill was destroyed by a flood in 1847. The house Lusk built in 1841 is now a museum. Another post office called Lusks Springs, for a local spring, also named for the Lusk family, was established on December 27, 1867; closed on May 31, 1902.*

Luther [LOO-ther] (Whitley). A post office, named for Myron Luther Pray, local storekeeper and first postmaster, was established on January 2, 1894; closed on February 15, 1905. The village also was called Sawdust Mill, descriptive of the piles of sawdust accumulated at four local sawmills (WPA).

Lycurgus (Marshall). See Inwood.

Lydick [LEYE-dik] (Saint Joseph). A post office established on August 12, 1839, as Warren Center, for its location in Warren Township, was changed to Sweet Home on July 9, 1885; to Lindley, for a local family, on March 21, 1902; to Lydick on July 27, 1909; and closed in 1913. The village, established about 1851 as a shipping point, first was called Warren Center, but it was platted as Lindley on September 6, 1901, by Ashbury and Mina Lindley. The present name apparently is for a member of the local Milliken family (WPA).

Lyford [LEYE-ferd] (Parke). This village was platted in 1892 and named for W. H. Lyford, vice president of the railroad built through here. The village first was called Clinton Locks, for nearby Clinton and the Wabash and Erie Canal locks located here. Hudnut and Company from Terre Haute bought a warehouse nearby, and the name of a community just north of this site was called Hudnut. A post office named Hudnut, established on March 16, 1887, was changed to Lyford on May 24, 1892, and closed on September 30, 1912.* Another variant name was Williamson.

Lyles [leyelz] (Gibson). This village was known as the Cherry Grove Vicinity before the Civil War. After the war, Joshua Lyles, an African American, bought land here, other blacks settled, and the name was changed to Lyles Station for Lyles. A post office called Lyles was established on August 21, 1886; closed on January 31, 1921. Variant names are Lyle and Lyle Station.

Lynhurst [LIN-herst] (Marion). This community was laid out and incorporated in 1928.

Lynn [lin] (Randolph). A post office was established on November 29, 1838,* and the town first was laid out in 1847. It was platted by Philip Brown on October 4, 1850.

Lynnville (Ripley). See Behlmer Corner.

Lynnville [LIN-vil] (Warrick). This town was named for John Lynn, who platted it in 1839 and opened a saddle and harness shop the same year. A post office, with Lynn as postmaster, was established on July 19, 1839.

Lyons [LEYE-uhnz] (Greene). This town was platted in 1869 and named for Squire Joe Lyon, Bloomfield resident who held several county offices, including treasurer and auditor. A post office was established on April 26, 1870.

Lyonsville [LEYE-uhnz-vil] (Fayette). A post office called Lyons Station was established on January 2, 1863; closed on July 15, 1916. The name is for a local family. Abraham Lyons settled here around 1808.

Lyontown (Sullivan). See Cass.

 **M**

McCallens Cross Roads (Harrison). See Palmyra (Harrison).

McCanns (Rush). See Raleigh.

McCool [muh-KOOL] (Porter). This village was established in 1872 and named for a local family. Walter McCool was an early settler (WPA). A post office called

McCool was established on April 24, 1884; closed on April 27, 1962.

McCordsville [muh-KAWRDZ-vil] (Hancock). A post office called McCordsville was established on April 19, 1855, and named for the local McCord family, who had a store here. An early settler was Elias McCord. The village was laid out by James Negley on September 11, 1865.

McCoy [muh-KOY] (Decatur). This village, named for a local family, was platted on August 11, 1871, by J. C. Adams. A post office called McCoys Station, with William A. McCoy as postmaster, was established on May 27, 1856; changed to McCoy on November 28, 1882; closed on November 15, 1899. Charles D. and James T. McCoy also served as postmasters.

McCoysburg [muh-KOYZ-berg] (Jasper). This village was established in 1877 and named for a local family. Alfred McCoy owned land here. A post office established as Zard on February 9, 1882, was changed to McCoysburg on December 4, 1895.

McCutchanville [muh-KUHCH-uhn-vil] (Vanderburgh). This village was established about 1845 and named for the local McCutchan family. A post office, with Samuel McCutchan as postmaster, was established on April 26, 1850; closed on March 15, 1906.* Variant names are McCutchan, McCutchan Station, McCutchanville Station.

Mace [mays] (Montgomery). This village first was called Frederickville, for Frederick Long, who laid out the village in 1839 or 1840. A post office called Mace was established on February 10, 1853; closed on November 30, 1912.

McFarlen (Daviess). See Farlen.

McGary [muh-GEHR-ee] (Gibson). A post office called Marsh, with Sarah C. McGary as postmaster, was established on January 9, 1880. On December 13, 1882, the post office name was changed to McGary, for the local McGary family. The post office was closed on December 14, 1901. Hugh D. McGary, who became postmaster in 1889, opened a general store here in 1880. A variant name is McGarys Station.

McGrawsville [muh-GRAWZ-vil] (Miami). A post office was established on June 4, 1867, with John M. McGraw as postmaster; closed on December 15, 1942. The village was established as a Pan Handle Railroad station, which was named for the McGraw family. Nelson McGraw built a small store about two years before the railroad was completed to this point. The village earlier was called Lick Skillet, according to the WPA files, because "railroad workers who ate at McGraw's store complained of the scanty lunches, saying they had to lick the skillet."

McGregor (Miami). See Peru.

McGregors Hill [muh-GREG-erz HIL] (Pike). This village was named for the McGregor family, early settlers. McGregor Hill is a variant spelling.

McFaddens Bluff (Posey). See Mount Vernon (Posey).

McKenzie Cross Roads (Dearborn). See Dover.

McHaleysville (Greene). See McVille.

Mackey [MAK-ee] (Gibson). This town was established around 1882 and, according to the WPA files, named for O. J. Mackey, local railroad owner. A post office was established on January 7, 1885, with Mackel Market as postmaster.

McKinley [muh-KIN-lee] (Washington). A post office was established on October 2, 1891, and allegedly named for William McKinley, who became president of the United States in 1897.

McKinleys Store (Clay). See Harmony (Clay).

Macksville (Vigo). See West Terre Haute.

Macksville (Randolph). See Maxville.

McVille [muhk-VIL] (Greene). This village was laid out in 1836 by John McHaley, who first called it McHaleysville but then shortened it to McVille.

Macy [MAY-see] (Miami). This town was laid out on June 14, 1860, by two brothers, George and Anderson Wilkinson, and called Lincoln, probably for Abraham Lincoln. In 1869, when the post office was moved from Five Corners to Lincoln, it was discovered that there already was a post office called Lincoln in Cass County; therefore the post office name was changed to Allen, apparently for the township in which the post office is located. Having towns called Lincoln in both Cass County and Miami County still caused confusion; consequently, in 1875 the townsfolk petitioned the county commissioners to change the name to Macy, for David Macy, president of the Indianapolis, Peru, and Chicago Railroad. The post office was changed from Allen to Macy on May 6, 1880.

Madalline [mad-uhl-EEN] (Parke). A post office called Medelline, a variant spelling, was established on February 9, 1852; closed on June 5, 1862.

Madison [MAD-uh-suhn] (county seat, Jefferson). One of the oldest settlements in the state, this city was settled in 1805. The site was purchased in 1808 by John Paul, a Revolutionary War soldier, Jonathan Lyons, and Lewis Davis. According to the WPA files, Paul named the city for President James Madison, though an 1873 newspaper account says the name honors an African American named Madison who first lived here. An Indiana Territory post office was established in 1812.

Madison (Madison). See Pendleton.

Madison County [MAD-uh-suhn]. This county, noted for its auto parts industries as well as for its agriculture, was organized in 1823 and named for James Madison, fourth president of the United States. Seat: Anderson.

Magee [muh-GEE] (La Porte). The name of this community may have been borrowed from a personal name or another place name, as it is found in Northern Ireland, New York, Mississippi, and Idaho.

Magley [MAG-lee] (Adams). This village began as a station on the Erie Railroad in 1882 and was named for Jacob J. Magley, the first station agent who operated a general store here. A post office, with Magley as postmaster, was established on June 29, 1883; closed on November 15, 1927.

Magnet [MAG-nuht] (Perry). This village, located on the Ohio River, first was called Dodsons Landing for a pioneer family, but the post office established on July 29, 1857, was named

Rono, allegedly for a local dog owned by Jesse Martin, who operated a wood-yard here (ISUFA). On February 24, 1899, the name was changed to Magnet, apparently by the Post Office Department. The current name, Magnet, might be commendatory, suggesting the settlement is attractive.

Magnolia [mag-NOL-yuh] (Crawford). A post office was established on March 16, 1848; closed on June 15, 1937.* The village was platted on July 4, 1838. This place name, usually for the tree, is common in the United States, but as applied here may be a transfer name from a southern state.

Mahalasville [muh-HAHL-uhs-vil] (Morgan). A post office, named for Mahala VanSickle, was established on July 17, 1854, with Jacob VanSickle as postmaster; closed on November 30, 1928.* Mahala Vansickle became the second postmaster.

Mahon [MAY-hahn] (Huntington). This village, an outgrowth of the Wabash and Erie Canal, was platted on June 20, 1853, by Archibald Mahon and named for his family. William Mahon was a local landowner, and Samuel Mahon supervised a construction crew building the railroad that passed through here. A post office was established on August 18, 1853; closed on May 16, 1867.

Maidstone (Parke). See Mecca.

Majenica [muh-JEN-uh-kuh] (Huntington). Formerly called Kelso, this village was laid out on November 8, 1856, by J. Crosby. Kelso is a Scottish place name that has been popular in Australia, Canada, New Zealand, and South Africa as well as in the United States. Since there already was a post office

named Kelso in Dearborn County, the post office established on July 13, 1858, was called Majenica, for the Miami chief Man-ji-ni-kia, "Big Frame." The post office was closed on February 27, 1909.*

Makin [MAY-kuhn] (Huntington). A post office was established here on May 8, 1882; closed on December 31, 1902. The name honors a local family. Abraham S. Makin was the first postmaster.

Malden [MAWL-duhn] (Porter). This village was founded around 1902 and called Hayden for an early settler, but since there was already a Hoosier town of that name, it was renamed Malden for the city in Massachusetts.

Malott Park [mal-uht PAHRK] (Marion). A post office established as James Switch, for a local family, on July 16, 1862, was changed to Malott Park, for the Malott family, on May 21, 1877.* The village was laid out on May 4, 1872. Mallott Park is a variant spelling.

Manchester [MAN-ches-ter] (Dearborn). This village was settled in 1818 and named for the township in which it is located. Ultimately the township name comes from Manchester, England, but Manchester has been a popular place name in the United States, as it is found in about half of the states, and here may be a transfer name from another state. Since Kyle, q.v., a nearby village, also was called Manchester, this village earlier was called Upper Manchester. A nickname of the village was Muletown, supposedly because Daniel Northrop owned a breachy mule that usually did what it pleased (WPA). A post office was established on May 7, 1822; closed on July 31, 1914.

Manchester (Wabash). See North Manchester.

Manhattan [man-HAT-uhn] (Putnam). This village was laid out in 1829 by John M. Coleman and Thomas H. Clark and named for Manhattan Island, New York. A post office, with Clark as postmaster, was established on March 13, 1830; closed on October 31, 1905. Coleman became the second postmaster.

Manilla [muh-NEL-uh] (Rush). This village was settled in 1824, laid out on January 4, 1836, and originally called Wilmington, for the city in North Carolina, former home of settlers. A post office established as Walker on June 22, 1833, was changed to Manilla on March 14, 1840. Apparently the present name is for the Philippine city.

Mansfield [MANZ-feeld] (Parke). This village first was called New Dublin, then Dicksons Mills, for Francis Dickson, co-owner of a mill built here in 1821, and then Strains Mills before the name was changed to Mansfield, probably for Mansfield, Ohio. The village was platted in 1852. The post office established as Dicksons Mills on February 26, 1824, with Dickson as postmaster, was changed to Mansfield on September 13, 1852. Other variant names have been Dixons Mills and Dublin.

Manson [MAN-suhn] (Clinton). A post office was established on January 9, 1873; closed on February 28, 1917. The village was platted on June 30, 1874, by Lucinda, David, and Rebecca Clark. The name honors General Mahlon D. Manson, who commanded the Tenth Indiana Regiment during the Civil War.

Manville [MAN-vil] (Jefferson). A post office called Buena Vista established on August 19, 1847, was changed to Manville on December 22, 1858, and closed on April 30, 1907. The present name is for a local family. Nicholas Manville was postmaster when the name was changed to Manville. Robert, Josephus, and Abyssinia Manville also were postmasters.

Maples [MAY-puhlz] (Allen). This village was laid out by O. Bird on November 17, 1853, and named for the local Maples family. A post office was established on September 12, 1854; closed on May 11, 1921. Lewis S. Maples, part owner of a stave factory here, served as postmaster for a brief time in 1867.

Mapleton [MAY-puhl-tuhn] (Marion). This village was platted on September 18, 1871. A post office was established on December 15, 1881; closed on August 22, 1898.

Maple Valley [may-puhl VAL-ee] (Henry). This village, laid out by Robert Overman on September 17, 1838, first was called Elizabeth City, for Overman's former home, Elizabeth City, North Carolina, but the post office established on February 12, 1878, was called Maple Valley. The post office closed on April 30, 1903.*

Maplewood [MAY-puhl-wud] (Hendricks). A post office called Progress established on May 6, 1880, was changed to Maplewood on March 11, 1881. According to the WPA files, the present name is descriptive of a dense maple forest on the site of the settlement, though the name has commendatory value.

Marble Hill [mahr-buhl HIL] (Jefferson). A post office was established on May 27, 1889; closed on November 15,

1921. The name of this village is for a nearby hill of the same name. According to the WPA files, the name is from "a stone quarry on this hill. For a time this stone was rated as pure marble."

Marcellus (Rush). See Farmington.

Marco [MAHR-ko] (Greene). This village was settled around 1816 and laid out in 1868. A post office named Marco was established on August 2, 1853; closed on September 8, 1967. According to local tradition, the name was coined from the names of two early residents, March and Coker (ISUFA), though some say the name is for Marco Polo, and others say that the Post Office Department chose the name.

Marcy (Lagrange). See Woodruff.

Mardenis [mahr-DEE-nuhs] (Huntington). This village, established as a small station on the Wabash Railroad, first was called Miners Switch and then Union Station. The name was changed to Mardenis for storekeeper William R. Mardenis, who settled here in 1870 and became the local railroad agent and first postmaster when a post office was established on August 11, 1884. The post office closed on February 29, 1904.

Marengo [muh-RAYNG-go; muh-RENG-go] (Crawford). Earlier called Big Springs, for two local springs, as well as Spring Town and Jim Town (WPA), this town was platted on April 15, 1839, by David Stewart, a minister who bought property here from the government in 1833. A post office established as Tuckersville on February 11, 1824, and changed to Proctorsville on January 12, 1835, was relocated and renamed Marengo on July 13, 1852. Proctor and Tucker are local family names. The first

store was opened in 1838 by William Proctor, who also served as postmaster of both Tuckersville and Proctorsville. David Tucker opened a saloon in 1848. According to the WPA files, Joseph Thornton of Leavenworth named the town "Marengo after one of Napoleon's great victories" over the Austrians in 1800 at Marengo, Italy, but according to county history, Dr. Mattingly, who served on a committee charged with moving the post office from Proctorsville to this location, suggested the name.

Maria Creek (Knox). See Freelandville.

Mariah Hill [muh-REE-uh HIL; muh-REYE-uh HIL] (Spencer). This village was platted on April 21, 1860, for the trustees of the local parish Catholic church of Maria Hilf aus Kristiens (Mary, Help of Christians) and named Maria Hilf. Apparently the Post Office Department changed the name to Mariah Hill when a post office was established on June 19, 1862.

Marietta (Crawford). See West Fork.

Marietta [mehr-ee-ET-uh] (Shelby). This village was laid out on August 31, 1835, by John Heistand, David Engles, John French, S. Robertson, and Redding Money. A post office was established on May 23, 1848; closed on February 29, 1904.

Marion [MEHR-ee-uhn] (county seat, Grant). This city was settled by Martin Boots, John Ballinger, and David Branson in 1826. When Grant County was formed in 1831, Boots and Branson donated land for the county seat, and when the city was laid out on September 30, 1831, it was called Marion, for General Francis Marion, cavalry officer in the

Revolutionary War. A post office established as Grant Court House on January 18, 1832, was changed to Marion on September 5, 1836.

Marion (Ripley). See New Marion.

Marion [MEHR-ee-uhn] (Shelby). This village was laid out by John Sleeth for James Wilson on December 27, 1820, and named for General Francis Marion, hero of the Revolutionary War. Wilson and his family settled here in 1819. A post office established as Marion on January 20, 1823, was changed to Noah on September 5, 1836, and closed on February 28, 1902.* A variant name is Little Marion.

Marion County [MEHR-ee-uhn]. This county was organized in 1882 and named for General Francis Marion, officer in the American Revolution. The state's capital, Indianapolis, encompasses the whole county, for in the late 1960s a consolidated city-county government for Indianapolis and Marion County was established. Seat: Indianapolis.

Marion Heights [MEHR-ee-uhn HEYETS] (Vigo). This community was named for Marion McQuilton, local landowner (WPA).

Marion Mills [MEHR-ee-uhn MILZ] (Owen). This community was named for Marion Township, organized in 1839, in which it is located, and for local mills. A post office called Hausertown, with George Hauser as postmaster, was established on April 25, 1848; closed on May 31, 1907.

Markland (Clay). See Clay City.

Markland [MAHRK-luhnd] (Switzerland). A post office was established on November 24, 1873; closed on December 15, 1944. The village was platted on March 18, 1874. The name honors local merchant Charles Markland, who laid out the village.

Markle [MAHRK-uhl] (Wells). Located in both Huntington and Wells counties, this town was platted on June 25, 1836, and originally called Tracy for a local storekeeper. A post office established as Tracy on May 10, 1849, was changed to Markle, for a local family, on June 28, 1852.

Markles [MAHRK-uhlz] (Vigo). This community was established as a flag station on the Indianapolis and St. Louis Railroad and formerly called Markle Station or Markles Station. It was named for the Markle family, who operated a mill near the station. Abraham Markle, one of the founders of Terre Haute, settled here around 1816 and built a house and the mill. Nearby, Markle's son, Frederick, built a large Greek Revival house in 1848. A post office established as Markles Mills on October 5, 1821, with Henry Markle as postmaster, was relocated and renamed Otter Creek on January 26, 1826.

Markleville [MAHRK-uhl-vil] (Madison). This town was laid out in 1852 by John D. Markle, for whom it was named. A post office, with John Markle as postmaster, was established on May 31, 1860.

Marmont (Marshall). See Culver.

Marrs Center [mahrz SEN-ter] (Posey). This village was named for Marrs Township, which was named for Samuel R. Marrs, one of the first county commissioners.

Marshall [MAHR-shuhl] (Parke). This town was platted in 1878 and named for Mahlon W. Marshall, who donated land for a railroad station here. A post office was established on November 25, 1878.

Marshall County [MAHR-shuhl]. This county, noted for its lakes and orchards, was formed in 1835, organized in 1836, and named for John Marshall, chief justice of the United States Supreme Court, 1801–1835. Seat: Plymouth.

Marshfield [MAHRSH-feeld] (Scott). This community developed as a railroad station. Here, on the night of May 22, 1868, the Reno gang pulled off what is considered to be the nation's second train robbery, netting $96,000.

Marshfield [MAHRSH-feeld] (Warren). A post office was established on April 6, 1857, and the village was platted on May 22, 1857. The name is for Marshfield, Massachusetts, home of Daniel Webster, or, according to the WPA files, for swampy land nearby.

Marshtown (Fulton). See Bluegrass.

Martin [MAHRT-uhn] (Vanderburgh). This village was named for a local family. Among the earliest settlers were James Martin and his two sons, Thomas and Charles, who came here from North Carolina.

Martin County [MAHRT-uhn]. This county, one of the most scenic in the state, was organized on January 7, 1820. Although the origin of the name is uncertain, most sources say it was named for Major John P. Martin of Newport, Kentucky, though one source says for Kentucky frontiersman and Indian fighter John T. Martin and another source says for either Major John P.

Martin or Major Thomas Martin of Kentucky. Seat: Shoals.

Martinsburg [MAHRT-uhnz-berg] (Washington). This village was laid out on September 18, 1818, by Dr. Abner Martin, for whom it was named. A post office was established on May 18, 1830; closed on October 31, 1919. A variant spelling is Martinsburgh.

Martinsville [MAHRT-uhnz-vil] (county seat, Morgan). This city was laid out as the county seat in May 1822 on an old Delaware trail and named for John Martin of Washington County, senior member of the board of commissioners, who located the county seat here. A post office was established on February 11, 1823. Mineral springs accidentally discovered here in 1884 gave the city its nickname, Artesian City.

Martz (Clay). See Middlebury.

Marysville [MEHR-eez-vil] (Clark). This village was laid out in 1871, and a post office was established on April 6, 1871. The name is for Mary Kimberlain, who lived in this county.

Marysville [MEHR-eez-vil] (Clay). This village was laid out adjacent to Lena, q.v., on January 17, 1870, by Mary Wyatt and named for her.

Matamoras [mat-uh-MAWR-uhs] (Blackford). Organized in 1875, this village probably was named for the Mexican city captured by American troops in the Mexican War.

Matthews [MATH-yooz] (Grant). A post office established as New Cumberland on April 1, 1865, was changed to Matthews on June 25, 1895. The town was named for Claude Matthews, Indiana governor (1893–1897) and major stockholder in the Matthews Land Company, which founded the town during a natural gas boom. The town of Matthews absorbed New Cumberland, about a mile away, which had been founded in 1833.

Mattix Corner [mat-iks KAWR-ner] (Clinton). This village, which dates from 1839, was named for the local Matix family (WPA).

Mauckport [MAHK-pawrt] (Harrison). This town, first called New Market, was platted on May 7, 1827, and renamed for the founder, Frederick Mauck, who came to Harrison County between 1808 and 1811 and established a ferry. Mauck owned the land on which the town was laid out. The post office was established on December 24, 1827. A variant spelling is Maucksport.

Maumee [MAW-mee] (Jackson). A post office was established on December 20, 1880; closed on August 31, 1928. *Maumee* is a form of the Native American word *Me-ah-me*, of which *Miami* is another form (cf. Miami County). Variant names are Findley Mill and Finleys Mill, for the local Finley family, who owned a mill here.

Mauzy [MAW-zee] (Rush). This village originally was called Griffin Station for the local Griffin family. A post office named Mauzy, also for a local family, was established on March 10, 1884, with Marion Griffin as postmaster; closed on August 15, 1905. William Mauzy was an early settler in the county.

Max [maks] (Boone). A post office was established here on November 13, 1886; closed on June 15, 1907.*

Maxams (Gibson). See Douglas.

Maxinkuckee [MAKS-uhn-kuh-kee] (Marshall). A post office, named for nearby Lake Maxinkuckee, was established on March 20, 1857; closed on January 31, 1902. *Maxinkuckee* is a form of the Potawatomi name of the lake, Mog-sin-kee-ki, "Big Stone Country." Apparently the lake was named for its extensive rock bars.

Maxville [MAKS-vil] (Randolph). This village was laid out about 1832 by Robert McIntyre and apparently named for him. An earlier spelling was Macksville.

Maxville [MAKS-vil] (Spencer). This village was laid out on April 12, 1841, and probably named for James McDaniel, proprietor.

Maxwell [MAKS-wel] (Hancock). Laid out in 1881, this village first was called Junction, but when a post office was established on June 12, 1882, the name was changed to Maxwell in honor of a man involved in building the railroad through here.

Mayes Corners (La Porte). See Hesston.

Mayfield [MAY-feeld] (Scott). A post office, named for a local family, was established on January 21, 1857; closed on January 4, 1860. James Mayfield was was the first postmaster.

Maynard [MAY-nerd] (Lake). Established on part of the Hart estate, this community was named for Maynard Hart, "son of the elder Hart" (WPA).

Mays [mayz] (Rush). A post office called Mays was established on October 9, 1883. The village, first called Mays Station, for a local family, was laid out on June 25, 1884.

Maysville (Allen). See Harlan.

Maysville [MAYZ-vil] (Daviess). Eli Hawkins of South Carolina settled near here in 1806. The village, which developed during canal days, was laid out first in 1834 by John McDonald. A post office established as Zanesville on June 25, 1852, was changed to Maysville on March 2, 1855.

Maysville Crossing [mayz-vil KRAWS-ing] (Fountain). A post office called Maysville was established on March 21, 1840; closed on May 28, 1842. A village called Maysville, which became a station on the Wabash and Erie Canal, was laid out in 1882 by Z. Wade.

Maywood [MAY-wud] (Marion). Originally called Beelers Station for a local miller, Fielding Beeler, this town was laid out on June 4, 1873, by John and Clay Campbell, who apparently named the town for Maywood, Illinois. A post office called Maywood was established on September 5, 1873; closed on July 31, 1955.

Meadowbrook [MED-o-bruk] (Madison). This community was established as a residential area of Anderson by General Motors Corporation in 1925. The name, also found in Allen and Porter counties, generally is commendatory.

Mecca [MEK-uh] (Parke). A post office established as Maidstone on August 11, 1887, was changed to Mecca Mills on April 12, 1888, and to Mecca on May 2, 1894. The village was platted in 1890. According to the WPA files, a church near here was nicknamed the Arabian Church for its location on a dry, sandy hill. Each spring when the roads became passable, the residents near the church came to the store of Alexander McCune, who remarked that the Arabians were coming on their annual visit to Mecca, hence the name for the Arabian city. Another local legend offers this explanation of the name: "Mecca is a town, and it was first settled about the early 1840s. In 1898 they built a tile plant, and so they needed workers, and they needed cheap workers, so they sent over to the Near East and got these Moslems, in that general area. They lived there outside town, and when they got paid, they'd come to town and say it was almost like coming to Mecca, and so they called the town Mecca" (ISUFA). It's also said that in the 1880s Arabs were brought here to train Arabian horses.

Mechanicsburg [muh-KAN-iks-berg] (Boone). This village was laid out in 1835 by James Snow. Mechanicsburg is a common commendatory name. Here it supposedly remembers the manual skills of many early settlers, who included carpenters, wagon makers, and a blacksmith. Mechanicsburgh is a variant spelling.

Mechanicsburg [muh-KAN-iks-berg] (Clay). This village was laid out on March 8, 1871, by Elisha Adamson, who named it Mechanicsburg because he envisioned a model community composed of mechanics, miners, and laborers.

Mechanicsburg [muh-KAN-iks-berg] (Decatur). This village was laid out by Robert Garrison and others on October 10, 1846. Mechanicsburg is a common commendatory name.

Mechanicsburg [muh-KAN-iks-berg] (Henry). A post office called Mechanicsburgh was established on July 14, 1849; the spelling was changed to Mechanicsburg on April 18, 1894, and it was closed on January 15, 1907. The village was laid out on September 22, 1858. The name, probably commendatory as well as descriptive, supposedly honors the many mechanics who settled here.

Mechanicsburg (Marion). See Clermont.

Mechanicsville (Vanderburgh). See Zipp.

Medaryville [muh-DEHR-ee-vil] (Pulaski). This town was platted on February 25, 1853, by William Clark and Josiah Walden. Carter Hathaway, the surveyor, named the town for Joseph Medary, Ohio governor. A post office established as White Post on May 2, 1838, was changed to Medaryville on December 22, 1853.

Medelline (Parke). See Madalline.

Medford [MED-ferd] (Delaware). This village, platted on September 18, 1901, by Clarissa Phillips, originally was called Phillips for the founder. The present name might be for the town in Maine.

Medora [muh-DAWR-uh] (Jackson). This town was laid out on May 23, 1853. Commonly it is believed that the town was named by the founder, music teacher West Lee Wright, for the first three notes of the scale—do, re, mi—with the order changed, but possibly the name comes from the name of pirate chief Conrad's true love, Medora, in Lord Byron's narrative poem "The Corsair" (1814).

Medway (Clinton). See Colfax.

Melissaville [muh-LIS-uh-vil] (Ripley). A post office called Delaware, for Delaware Township, in which it was located, was established on January 3, 1838;

closed on January 12, 1889. When another village also named Delaware, q.v., was established about a mile south of here, this village was referred to locally as Old Delaware, though it was officially platted as Melissaville.

Mellott [MEL-uht; muh-LAHT] (Fountain). This town was platted on October 7, 1882, by John B. and Syrena C. Mellott, for whom it was named. A post office called Melott, with John B. Mellott as postmaster, was established on November 23, 1882. The spelling of the post office name was changed to Mellott on February 18, 1884.

Melners Corners (Hancock). See Milners Corners.

Meltonville (Vigo). See Sandcut.

Meltzer [MELT-ser; MELT-zer] (Shelby). This village, named for the local Meltzer family, grew up in the 1870s around a country store owned by John Meltzer. A post office was established on January 21, 1880; closed on May 15, 1905.

Memphis [MEM-fus] (Clark). This village was platted in 1852 and probably named for Memphis, Tennessee, since early settlers came from that area. A post office was established on February 22, 1854.

Memphis (Martin). See Shoals.

Mentone [MEN-ton; men-TON] (Kosciusko). This town was laid out by Albert Tucker in May 1882, and a post office was established as Mentone on December 6, 1882. The name comes from Menton, a city on the Mediterranean in France, although the WPA files say it is for Mennonites who settled here in 1885, three years after the name was officially applied to this community.

Mentor [MENT-er] (Dubois). This village was platted on September 29, 1881.

Meridian Hills [muh-RID-ee-uhn HILZ] (Marion). This community, named for Meridian Street, on which it was developed, was laid out and incorporated in 1937.

Merediths Mills (Fulton). See Yellowbanks.

Merom [MEER-uhm] (Sullivan). This town was laid out in 1817 and actually named for the biblical lake, although local legend says that the town received its name from Native Americans who, coming here for liquor, said, "Me rum!" A post office was established on January 22, 1818. A variant name is Miriam.

Merom Station [meer-uhm STAY-shuhn] (Sullivan). This village was named for the nearby town of Merom, q.v., as around 1854 the railroad passed through here instead of through Merom (WPA).

Merriam [MEHR-ee-uhm] (Noble). A post office was established on September 19, 1853; closed on March 30, 1907. The name probably is for a local family, as Mason M. Merriam was a storekeeper in this area in 1844.

Merrillville [MEHR-uh-vil; MEHR-uhl-vil] (Lake). A post office named Merrillville, for a local family, was established on December 9, 1847. Storekeeper Dudley Merrill became postmaster in 1861, and John Merrill succeeded him in 1875. Before the post office was established, the settlement locally was called Centerville, possibly for its location mid-way between Michigan City and Joliet (WPA), by a few families who settled near an old Indian village called Mc-Gwinnis. Merrillville was not incorporated until 1970.

Messick [MES-ik] (Henry). This village, never platted, was established around 1882 and named for the local Messick family, who kept a store here. A post office was established on March 28, 1884; closed on May 15, 1926.

Metamora [met-uh-MAWR-uh] (Franklin). This village was laid out on March 20, 1838, by David Mount and William Holland. A post office established in April 1826 as Duck Creek Crossing was changed to Metamora, with William Holland as postmaster, on June 11, 1838. Mrs. John A. Matson named the village for the heroine in J. A. Stone's popular romantic tragedy, *Metamora, or the Last of the Wampanoags,* produced in 1829 and revised in 1836.

Metea [MEE-dee-uh] (Cass). A post office was established on April 25, 1834; closed on October 14, 1903.* The village, formerly called New Hamilton, was laid out in 1853 by local storekeeper George Allen. The present name honors the Potawatomi chief Mi-ti-a, "Kiss Me," who was poisoned, supposedly by disgruntled followers, in 1827.

Metz [mets] (Steuben). A post office was established on May 10, 1849.* The village was surveyed by Erastus Farnham on August 22, 1854, for Justus Barrow and Jared Graves. According to the WPA files, the name is for Metz, France, home of early settlers.

Mexico [MEK-see-ko] (Miami). This village was laid out in August 1834 by John B. and Simeon Wilkinson and developed around a trading post that was established soon after the village was founded. It was named for the country, apparently because of sympathy for the Mexican struggle for independence. According to legend, though, the village was so named because "many Mexicans made it their trading point when the town was just a trading post" (WPA). A post office established on July 8, 1842, as Coles Mill, with Charles Cole as postmaster, was changed to Mexico on January 30, 1844.

Miami [meye-AM-ee] (Miami). This village was platted on August 16, 1849, by Isaac Herrell and named for the county in which it is located. Soon after the village was platted, Alexander Blake, the first merchant, built the first house. A post office was established on November 19, 1849. Cf. Miami County.

Miami County [meye-AM-ee]. This county was formed on February 2, 1832, and organized in 1834, though the early boundaries were altered and the county did not assume its present shape until January 15, 1838. The name is for the Big Miami Reserve, on which the county was established, and for the Miami nation, whose people once inhabited the area. Early French chroniclers wrote the name Oumiamiouek and Oumiamiak, apparently a form of Wemiamik, literally "all beavers," but figuratively "all friends," the Delaware name for the Miamis. The river name Maumee is a form of Miami close to the native pronunciation, Me-ah-me. Seat: Peru.

Miamisport (Miami). See Peru.

Miami Town (Allen). See Fort Wayne.

Michaelsville [MEYE-kuhlz-vil] (Grant). A post office called Michael, for a local family, was established on April 1, 1892; closed on October 15, 1902. William Michael was the first and only postmaster.

Michiana Shores [mish-i-AN-uh SHAWRZ] (La Porte). The name of this community, which is located on Lake Michigan, was coined from the first four letters of Michigan and the last four letters of Indiana. Northern Indiana and southern Michigan, with common social and economic ties, constitute a region commonly called Michiana.

Michigan City [mish-i-guhn SID-ee] (La Porte). This city was laid out by Major Isaac C. Elston in October 1832 on Lake Michigan in Michigan Township as the terminus of the Michigan Road, so the name is a local transfer. "Although an impression has prevailed that Michigan City took its name from the Michigan (state) territory in which it was once located, it is generally accepted that the city took its name form the fact that it was the northern terminus of the Michigan Road and that it lies on Lake Michigan" (WPA). The plat was recorded on September 17, 1832. A post office was established on August 26, 1833.

Michigantown [MISH-ee-guhn-town] (Clinton). This town was laid out in Michigan Township in September 1830 by Joseph Hill and Robert Edwards and named for the Michigan Road, which passes through here and for a time was the most important north-south highway in Indiana. The post office was established on December 17, 1832. The northern part of the town sometimes was called Lowdenville for William Lowden, owner of a local brickyard and grain elevator, who made two additions to the town in 1874 and 1876.

Middleboro [MID-uhl-ber-o] (Wayne). Formerly this village was called Coxs Mills, for Jeremiah Cox, who had a gristmill here, and Limetown, for several local lime kilns. A variant spelling is Middleborough.

Middlebury [MID-uhl-behr-ee] (Clay). John Cooprider founded Middlebury in 1836. Allegedly his son, Elias, selected the name from a list of geographical names in a spelling book. Since there already was a post office named Middlebury in Elkhart County, when a post office was established here on April 18, 1854, it was called Martz, apparently for Arthur Martz, who, according to local history, earlier laid out a town here in 1827. The post office closed on April 30, 1907.*

Middlebury [MID-uhl-behr-ee] (Elkhart). This town was platted in 1835 or 1836 by three men named Winslow, Warren, and Brown and named for Middlebury Township, which, according to the WPA files, was named for Middlebury, Vermont, home of the first settler. A post office was established on April 27, 1836.

Middlebury Station (Elkhart). See Vistula.

Middlefork [MID-uhl-fawrk] (Clinton). On August 9, 1836, a post office called Middle Fork, for the nearby stream of the same name, was established here. The spelling was changed to Middlefork on May 3, 1893, and on September 30, 1907, the post office was closed.

Middlefork [MID-uhl-fawrk] (Jefferson). This village was named for Middle Fork Creek. A variant name is Foltz, as a post office named Foltz, for the local Foltz family, was established on December 26, 1883; closed on August 15, 1927. Nicholas Foltz was the first postmaster.

Middleton (Ripley). See Batesville.

Middleton (Tippecanoe). See Westpoint.

Middletons Station (Howard). See West Middleton.

Middletown [MID-uhl-town] (Allen). This village was laid out by Louis Lopshire in 1851. Apparently the name is locational for its position between Fort Wayne and Decatur.

Middletown (Daviess). See Odon.

Middletown (Harrison). See New Middletown.

Middletown [MID-uhl-town] (Henry). This town was laid out by Jacob Koontz (also spelled Coontz) on October 9, 1829, and so named because of its location between New Castle and Anderson. A post office, with Koontz as postmaster, was established on September 10, 1830. Middleton is a variant spelling.

Middletown (Montgomery). See Waynetown.

Middletown (Owen). See Arney.

Middletown [MID-uhl-town] (Shelby). This village was platted on June 19, 1829, by William Hammond and Daniel French.

Middletown (Tippecanoe). See Westpoint.

Middletown (Vigo). See Prairie Creek.

Middletown (Washington). See Claysville.

Midland [MID-luhnd] (Greene). A post office was established on February 20, 1884,* and the village was platted in 1901 by the Midland Coal Company. It is generally thought that the name comes from the village's location midway between Sullivan and Worthington on an old mail route, though the name may come from the coal company. A variant name is Wright, for the nearby Wright post office, established on March 10, 1848, and named for the township in which it is located. The Wright post office was closed on June 11, 1897.

Midland Junction [mid-luhnd JUHNK-shuhn] (Greene). This railroad station was named for nearby Midland, q.v.

Midway (Clinton). See Colfax.

Midway [MID-way] (Spencer). A post office was established on January 6, 1831; closed on August 31, 1905. This popular place name, found in five other Indiana counties (Clinton, Elkhart, Franklin, Jefferson, and Parke), is locational, although accounts vary as to what this Spencer County village is midway between. One account says the village is so named because of its location between Boonville and Rockport. Another account says it is the halfway point between Evansville and Troy (WPA).

Mier [mier] (Grant). This village was laid out on September 11, 1848, and named for Mier, Mexico, which was on General Scott's route to Mexico City during the Mexican War (WPA). A post office was established on January 15, 1849; closed on December 31, 1928.

Mifflin [MIF-luhn] (Crawford). A post office was established on March 16, 1848; closed on April 21, 1967.* The name ultimately comes from the personal name, especially from General Thomas Mifflin of the Revolution, who was governor of Pennsylvania, 1790–1799. Several eastern towns bear this name, so it may be a transfer.

Milan [MEYE-luhn] (Ripley). This town was laid out by David Brooks in 1854 just across the railroad from South Milan, also laid out in 1854, and named Brooklyn, sometimes spelled Brooklin, for Brooks. These two villages merged into one, now called Milan. The original village named Milan, now Old Milan, q.v., was located a mile north of here, but with the coming of the railroad through here in 1854, the population and name shifted to this location. A post office, with Stephen Harding as postmaster, established as Hardings Store on February 3, 1837, was changed to Milan on March 1, 1842.

Milan Center [meye-luhn SEN-ter] (Allen). This village was named for Milan Township, which was established in 1838 and named by Stephen Heath for his home township in Huron County, Ohio.

Milersburg (Whitley). See Collamer.

Milford [MIL-ferd] (Decatur). John Brinson moved here and opened a saloon in 1824, and William Crawford may have made a plat of the town in the same year. The town, first called Needmore, was platted again on August 25, 1835, by James Edwards. According to local history, the present name is for a mill built at a ford here. The first millers in the area were the Critsers, who operated several mills on Clifty Creek. The post office, named Clifty for the creek, was established on March 3, 1838; closed on September 31, 1951.

Milford [MIL-ferd] (Kosciusko). This town was platted on April 10, 1836, by Judge Aaron M. Perine, who opened a hotel here. According to a local tradition reported in the WPA files, the name is for a ford at a mill here on Turkey Creek. A post office was established on March 21, 1837.

Milford (Warren). See Green Hill.

Milford Junction [mil-ferd JUHNK-shuhn] (Kosciusko). This railroad junction, established about 1874, is located just north of Milford, for which it was named. An earlier name of the community was Shakespeare.

Millageville (Boone). See Milledgeville.

Millboro (Union). See Quakertown.

Mill Creek [mil KRIK; mil KREEK] (La Porte). This village was platted in 1834 and named for a nearby stream of the same name. Water mills for sawing wood and grinding flour were essential and numerous in Indiana during the nineteenth century, and this is reflected in the names of several streams named Mill Creek in the state. Invariably these streams are so named for one or more mills on them. In this case, a sawmill was built on a stream called Spring Run, and the name was changed to Mill Creek. A post office was established on May 5, 1875, near the stream and a railroad crossing.

Milledgeville [MIL-uhj-vil] (Boone). A post office called Millageville was established on September 4, 1874; changed

to Milledgeville on December 1, 1875; closed on June 15, 1899.* Millidgeville is another variant spelling.

Miller [MIL-er] (Lake). A post office called Millers Station was established on February 7, 1865; changed to Vanderbilt on September 8, 1874; changed back to Millers Station on June 13, 1879; changed to Miller on November 28, 1882; and closed on February 15, 1927. Established as a railroad junction, the community, annexed to Gary in 1918, was settled mainly by Swedish Lutherans and named for a local tavern owner named Miller.

Millerburg (Whitley). See Collamer.

Millersburg [MIL-erz-berg] (Elkhart). This town was laid out in 1855 by Solomon Miller on his land and named for him. Miller, who was born in Tennessee in 1803, was a captain in the Black Hawk War. He purchased land here in 1834 and returned in 1842. A post office established as Cooks Station on August 20, 1857, was changed to Millersburgh on March 27, 1861. On September 2, 1893, the spelling was changed to Millersburg.

Millersburg [MIL-erz-berg] (Hamilton). This village was laid out in 1860 and named for early settler and cofounder Peter Miller.

Millersburg [MIL-erz-berg] (Orange). This village was named for Greenup Miller, who opened the first store here in 1833. A post office called Stampers Creek was established on February 27, 1855; closed on May 15, 1905. Stampers Creek, also the name of the township in which the post office was located, was named for a man named Stamper who lived near the springs that are the source of the stream.

Millersburg [MIL-erz-berg] (Warrick). This village was platted in 1852 and named for the local Miller family, descendants of Phillip Miller, early settler who built a mill here in 1824. Since there are other towns of the same name in Indiana, the post office—established on June 21, 1851; closed on December 31, 1903—was called Canal for its location on the Wabash and Erie Canal. Millersburgh is a variant spelling.

Millersburg (Whitley). See Collamer.

Millersport [MIL-erz-pawrt] (Dubois). This village was founded in 1833 by Robert Small and named Duff for Colonel B. B. Edmonston's nickname (WPA). Stapleton is another variant name.

Millersville [MIL-erz-vil] (Marion). This village, founded in 1838, formerly was called Brubakers Mill for a local family who operated a mill. The present name may come from the milling industry once here; may honor a local family, as W. H. H. Miller owned ninety-one acres here; or may be for Millersville, Pennsylvania, former home of early settlers (WPA). A post office, with Jacob Brubaker as postmaster, was established as Millersville on June 18, 1840; closed on November 17, 1843; reestablished on March 20, 1850; moved to James Switch on July 16, 1862; reestablished as Millersville on January 7, 1878; closed on December 2, 1884.

Millgrove [mil-GROV] (Blackford). A sawmill was built here in 1866, and the village was laid out in 1867 on land owned by Robert Sawyer and named by John C. Robbins. According to the WPA files, it was so named because the mill built here in 1866 was located in a shady grove. A post office, with John C. Robbins as postmaster, was established on February 25, 1868; closed on June 30, 1934. Variant spellings are Milgrove and Mill Grove.

Mill Grove (Owen). See Devore.

Millhousen [MIL-howz-uhn] (Decatur). This town was settled in 1838 by Maximilian Schneider and other German Catholics and named for Schneider's home in Germany. On June 29, 1840, Schneider donated forty acres to establish a Catholic church and a town. The church was built in 1840, but the town was not officially platted until April 10, 1858. A post office was established on May 23, 1844.* Schneider kept the first store here and became the first postmaster. Bernard Harderbeck, who succeeded Schneider as both storekeeper and postmaster, built the first mill here.

Millidgeville (Boone). See Milledgeville.

Milligan [MIL-uh-guhn; MIL-ee-guhn] (Parke). This village first was called South Waveland for its location south of Waveland, q.v. The present name is for local merchant Joseph Milligan. A railroad station was established here in 1878, and a post office was established on December 18, 1882. The post office was closed on July 12, 1957.

Millport [MIL-pawrt] (Washington). A post office established as Druscilla in Jackson County on December 20, 1831, was changed to Millport on April 16, 1838, and closed on December 31, 1901.*

Mills Corner (Jay). See West Liberty.

Milltown [MIL-town] (Crawford). A post office, named for local mills, was established on January 6, 1831, and the town was laid out in 1839. According to some sources, the Leavenworth cousins, Seth and Zebulon, who founded Leavenworth on the Ohio River in this county in 1818, also built a sawmill and gristmill here in 1818, and the settlement first was called Leavenworths Mill. Later the Hostetter brothers operated a local mill.

Millville [MIL-vil] (Henry). This village was laid out on December 4, 1854, and named for a nearby mill. A post office was established on June 7, 1855; closed on April 30, 1928.

Millville (Steuben). See Nevada Mills.

Millwood (Hamilton). See Sheridan.

Milners Corner [mil-nerz KAWR-ner] (Hancock). This unplatted village commenced as a center of business about 1850 when James Milner, for whose family it was named, settled here. Another early merchant was Henry Milner. A post office was established on December 4, 1868; closed on April 30, 1903. A variant spelling is Melners Corners.

Milo [MEYE-lo] (Huntington). A post office named for Milo M. Sharp, first postmaster, was established on March 14, 1881; closed on April 14, 1923.

Milroy (Benton). See Oxford.

Milroy [MIL-roy] (Rush). This village was laid out on November 3, 1830, and probably named for Samuel Milroy, speaker of the Indiana House, who signed the act creating Rush County.

There's also a tradition, though, that the name was coined from that of a local distiller, Roy Miller. A post office established as Little Flat Rock on January 16, 1828, was changed to Milroy on August 31, 1832.

Milton [MILT-uhn] (Ohio). This village was laid out in 1825 by Pinkney James and named Jamestown for the James family. James built a mill here the same year, and the place also was known as James Mills. In fact, several mills were established here to support boat building. The alternate name, Guionsville, for a local family, first was applied to a small settlement on the opposite side of Laughery Creek. On February 3, 1837, a post office was established in Dearborn County and named Guionsville. Thomas Guion was the first postmaster. The post office name was changed to Milton Mills, sometimes called Milton, on February 18, 1847. On March 19, 1850, the post office was moved back to Dearborn County and called Guionsville. On September 1, 1899, the Guionsville post office again was moved back to Ohio County, and on November 15, 1905, the post office was closed.

Milton [MILT-uhn] (Wayne). This town was platted on July 5, 1824, and allegedly was so named because there were several mills here. According to the WPA files, there were eleven mills operating locally at the same time. Possibly, though, the name was influenced by Milford Meeting, a society of Friends established here in 1819. A post office was established on March 19, 1825.

Mineral City [MIN-er-uhl SID-ee] (Greene). This village earlier was called Fellows Mill, but the post office established on September 17, 1877, was called Mineral City, a descriptive name applied by the railroad for coal or mineral springs here. The post office name was changed to Mineral on March 7, 1895, and the post office was closed on November 30, 1950.

Miner City [meye-ner SIT-ee; meye-ner SID-ee] (Sullivan). According to an oral account, "Farmersburg's original name was Miner City due to the great population of miners and mines in the Farmersburg region. After the coal mines had died out, farmers of many countries moved in and settled the region and built farms, and so the name Miner City was changed to Farmersburg" (ISUFA). Actually, Miner City is located just east of Farmersburg, q.v., but it was a mining community named for the coal mines and miners in this area.

Minshall [MIN-shuhl] (Parke). A variant name of this village is Odd, and a variant spelling is Minchell. A post office called Odd was established on February 20, 1884; closed on February 28, 1901. According to the WPA files, the present name is for a "class of coal found here."

Miriam (Sullivan). See Merom.

Mishawaka [mish-uh-WAW-kuh] (Saint Joseph). This city was laid out in 1833, and according to local legend it was named for an Indian princess who died in 1818. Actually the name is a form of the Potawatomi *m'seh-wah-kee-ki*, "country of dead trees," referring to a deadening, generally where trees are girdled with axes as a first step toward clearing a forest. Apparently there was a tract of dead timber here. A post office called Mishawaka was established on December 11, 1833. Variant spellings are Mishawauka and Mishewaka.

Mishwah (Miami). See Wawpecong.

Missisinewa [mi-si-SIN-uh-wah; mi-SIN-uh-wah] (Miami). The name of this historical settlement, comes from the stream of the same name. The stream name is a form of the Miami name, Na-mah-chis-sin-wi, which literally means "an ascent" but as applied to the river means "much fall in the river." Formerly the Miami name was written Mas-sis-sin-e-way.

Mississinewa (Randolph). See Deerfield.

Mitchell [MICH-uhl] (Lawrence). Although land near here was settled as early as 1813, this city was not platted until September 29, 1853, by George W. Cochran and John Sheeks. The community first was called The Crossing, descriptive of a railroad crossing. A post office established as Woodland on December 10, 1852, was changed to Mitchell on June 15, 1854. The name honors Major General Ormsby McKnight Mitchell, chief engineer and surveyor for the Ohio and Mississippi Railroad, which was built through here.

Mixersville [MIKS-erz-vil] (Franklin). This village was named for William Mixer, who filed the first plat on March 1, 1846, and the second plat in 1849. Mixer also was the first postmaster when the Mixersville post office was established on March 8, 1851; closed on June 30, 1903. Mixerville is a variant spelling.

Moberly [MO-ber-lee] (Harrison). A post office was established here on April 24, 1884; closed on January 31, 1907.

Modesto [muh-DES-to] (Monroe). A post office was established on April 6, 1892; closed on October 31, 1903. This Spanish name meaning "modest" is found in California dating from 1870 and most likely is a transfer.

Modoc [MO-dahk] (Randolph). This town was platted around 1882 and named for the Indian tribe. Supposedly the name is the Shasteeca word for "enemy." Local legend says the name was suggested by a picture of a Modoc chief on a cigar box. A post office, with Ira Swain as postmaster, was established as Swains Hill on April 23, 1879, and changed to Modoc on December 11, 1883.

Moffitt [MAHF-uht] (Jasper). This village probably was named from the personal name. Moffett is a variant spelling.

Mohawk [MO-hawk] (Hancock). A post office was established on November 23, 1882; closed on December 31, 1955. The village was platted on January 25, 1883. The name is for the Mohawk tribe. *Mohawk* is probably a form of *maugwawogs*, "maneaters." According to local legend, once there was a flight of hawks overhead, and some residents ran out and called, "More hawks, more hawks!" (WPA).

Mollicay (Adams). See Pleasant Mills.

Mongo [MAHNG-go] (Lagrange). A post office was established as Mongoquinong on June 25, 1832, at the site of a French fur trading post. On February 25, 1874, the post office name was changed to Mongo.* The village was laid out as Mongoquinong in March 1840 by Drusus Nichols. Mon-go-quin-ong, "Big Squaw," was the Potawatomi name for the Elkhart River.

Monitor [MAHN-uh-ter] (Tippecanoe). A settlement was located here about 1823. On February 3, 1864, a post office was established and allegedly named for the Union ironclad *Monitor*, which fought the Confederate *Merrimack* on March 9, 1862 (WPA). The post office was closed on October 15, 1902.

Monmouth [MAHN-muhth] (Adams). This village was platted in 1836 and named for Monmouth, New Jersey, by Quaker settlers from the east. A post office was established on February 13, 1839; closed on November 15, 1904.

Monon [MO-nahn] (White). A post office was established on May 9, 1849, and named Monon for the township in which it was located. When the town was platted on March 18, 1853, by James Brooks, it was called New Bradford, or sometimes Bradford, but in 1879 when the town was incorporated, it assumed the name of the post office. The present name ultimately comes from a Potawatomi word equivalent in usage to the southern "tote," but probably was influenced by the Monon Railroad, which passed through here and connected the Ohio River with Lake Michigan.

Monoquet [muh-NUH-kwet] (Kosciusko). This village was laid out in 1834 and named for a Potawatomi chief. A post office was established on January 29, 1844; closed on April 17, 1851.

Monroe [muhn-RO] (Adams). This town was platted in 1847 by John Everhart, proprietor, and named for the fifth president of the United States, James Monroe. A post office was established on March 7, 1872.

Monroe [muhn-RO] (Tippecanoe). This village was laid out in December 1832 by William Major and probably named for President James Monroe. A post office established as Huntersville on September 22, 1836, was changed to Monroe on May 7, 1840.*

Monroe City [muhn-ro SID-ee] (Knox). A post office established as Lovely Dale on May 12, 1854, was changed to Monroe City on February 27, 1883. The town, earlier called Nashville and the City of Three Names, was laid out on August 29, 1856, by W. C. Davenport. The current name is for Monroe Alton, proprietor.

Monroe County [muhn-RO]. This county, home of Indiana University, was formed on January 14, 1818, and named for James Monroe, fifth president of the United States. Seat: Bloomington.

Monroeville [muhn-RO-vil] (Allen). This town was settled in 1841 by Peter Barnhart, according to the WPA files, and founded in 1851 by John Barnhart, according to a local history. When a post office was established on June 12, 1856, John Barnhart was the first postmaster. Incorporated in 1865, the town was named for Monroe Township, in which it is located.

Monrovia [muhn-RO-vee-uh] (Morgan). This village was laid out in June 1834 by Gideon Johnson and George Hubbard. The name is a Latinized form of Monroe Township, in which the village is located. A post office was established on May 15, 1834.

Montclair [mahnt-KLEHR] (Hendricks). A post office was established on June 21, 1880; closed on February 15, 1929. The name probably was borrowed from an eastern city for its commendatory value. Montclaire is a variant spelling.

Monterey [mahnt-uh-RAY] (Pulaski). This town was laid out in 1849 by Eli and Peter W. DeMoss, proprietors, and named Buena Vista for the site of a battle in the Mexican War. When a post office was established on March 10, 1851, with Peter W. DeMoss as postmaster, the name was changed to Monterey, also a site of a battle in the Mexican War, because there was already a post office called Buena Vista in Jefferson County.

Montezuma [mahnt-uh-ZOO-muh] (Parke). This town was settled in 1821 and named by early settlers for the last Aztec emperor of Mexico. It was laid out first in 1823 or 1824 and platted again on July 20, 1849, by Ambrose Whitlock. A post office was established on September 15, 1825. Montezuma was an important canal town, for in a basin here canal boats were stored and turned around. Montazuma has been a variant spelling.

Montgomery [mahnt-GUHM-ree] (Daviess). A post office called Montgomerys Station, for the local Montgomery family, was established on February 16, 1859. On February 12, 1880, the name was changed to Montgomery. James C. Montgomery was the first postmaster. The village was laid out on November 23, 1865.

Montgomery County [mahnt-GUM-ree; mahnt-GUHM-uh-ree]. This county was formed in 1822, organized in 1823, and named for General Richard Montgomery, Revolutionary War officer who was killed in the Battle of Quebec in 1775. Wabash College, the General Lew Wallace Study and Museum, and the Lane Place, a memorial to Indiana and Civil War history, are located in this county. Seat: Crawfordsville.

Monticello [mahnt-uh-SEL-o] (county seat, White). A post office was established on January 8, 1834, and the city was laid out as the county seat on November 3, 1834, under the supervision of county agent John Barr. County commissioners—John Killgore, John B. King, and James H. Steward—named the post office and city for Thomas Jefferson's home in Virginia.

Montmorenci [mahnt-muh-RENTS-ee] (Tippecanoe). This village was laid out in 1838 by Sampson Hinkle, one of the first merchants in the township, who established a store here in 1830. The post office, established on June 25, 1846, was called Bringhams Groves, for the local Bringham family. John Bringham was the first postmaster, and Allen Bringham was the second postmaster. On July 26, 1853, the post office was changed to Montmorency, supposedly for the Duke de Montmorency-Laval, a French general in the Revolutionary War. On June 29, 1881, the spelling of the post office name was changed to Montmorenci. The name ultimately comes from the commune in France. The first bishop of Quebec, Monsignor François Xavier Montmorenci-Laval, perhaps influenced the naming of this settlement as well as the river in Quebec and the town in South Carolina.

Montpelier [mahnt-PEEL-yer] (Blackford). This city was laid out on September 5, 1837, by Abel Baldwin, who, with other early settlers, came from Montpelier, Vermont, and named the town for the Vermont city. A post office was established on February 12, 1840.

Moody [MOO-dee] (Jasper). This village was named for Granville Moody, who founded it in 1893. A nearby post office established as Pleasant Grove on November 11, 1842, was changed to Moody on July 23, 1914. The post office was closed on July 14, 1923.*

Mooney (Jackson). See Clear Spring.

Moonville [MOON-vil] (Madison). This village was founded around 1835 by local landowner Zimri Moon and named for him. Moonsville is a variant spelling.

Moore [mawr] (DeKalb). A post office established as Moores Station, for a local family, on May 17, 1875, was changed to Moore on November 28, 1882; closed on April 30, 1909. G. S. Moore was an early settler, and Aaron D. Moore served as the third postmaster.

Moorefield (Miami). See North Grove.

Moorefield [MAWR-feeld] (Switzerland). A post office, named for the local Moore family, was established on July 5, 1817; closed on June 30, 1916.* A variant spelling of the post office name in 1817 was Moorfield. The village was laid out in 1834.

Mooreland [MAWR-luhnd] (Henry). This town was laid out August 9, 1882, and named for the local Moore family. Miles M. Moore was the proprietor, and his brother, Henry H. Moore, was the first postmaster when the post office was established on August 21, 1882.

Moores Hill [mawrz HIL] (Dearborn). A post office, with Adam Moore as postmaster, was established on April 9, 1823,* and the town was laid out on March 10, 1838 (WPA), by Moore and Andrew N. Stevens. Moore, for whom the town was named, was a Methodist preacher who owned a local mill and founded Moores Hill College. The community first was called Moores Mill, but through a mistake when the town applied for a post office, the name became Moores Hill.

Mooresville (Floyd). See Floyds Knobs.

Mooresville [MAWRZ-vil] (Morgan). This town was laid out in the fall of 1824 by Samuel Moore and named for him. In 1823 Moore came to Morgan County from Salem, Indiana, and established a dry goods store in a vacant blacksmith shop about a quarter of a mile from what is now Mooresville. Later he opened the first store in Mooresville and was a storekeeper here for forty-four years. A post office was established on August 30, 1826.

Moores Vineyard (Bartholomew). See North Ogilville and Ogilville.

Moran [muh-RAN] (Clinton). A post office was established on May 23, 1872; closed on March 31, 1955. The village was laid out in 1873 by Noah L. Burnell (WPA). The name is for a railroad official.

Morgan County [MAWR-guhn]. This county was formed in 1821, organized in 1822, and named for Brigadier General Daniel Morgan, who served under Benedict Arnold in Canada in 1775 and with around a thousand men defeated a British force led by Colonel Balastre Tarleton at Cowpens in 1781. Seat: Martinsville.

Morgans Side Track (Porter). See Furnessville.

Morgantown (Dearborn). See Lawrenceville.

Morgantown [MAWR-guhn-town] (Morgan). This town was laid out first in

March 1831 by Robert Bowles and Samuel Teeters, proprietors. Teeters, who came here in 1828, probably was the first resident. A post office was established on January 10, 1833. According to the WPA files, the town was named for a pioneer family named Morgan, but possibly it was named for the county in which it is located.

Morocco [muh-RAH-ko] (Newton). This town was laid out on January 18, 1851, and apparently named for the country in North Africa, although according to local legend the town was named for a stranger's boots, which were topped with red morocco leather. A post office called Morocco established in Jasper County on June 24, 1854, was moved to Newton County on August 3, 1860.*

Morris [MAWR-uhs] (Ripley). German Catholic families settled here around 1840. Earlier called Springdale, for "three springs located in a little dale," the town was laid out on March 31, 1858, and named Morris for a resident. A post office called Morris was established on April 14, 1858.

Morristown (Clark). See Henryville.

Morristown [MAWR-uhs-town; MAHR-uhs-town] (Shelby). This town was laid out on May 3, 1828, by Rezin Davis and Samuel Morrison and named by Nancy Davis for Morrison. A post office established as Hanover on October 23, 1820, was changed to Morristown on January 23, 1834.

Morrisville (Hendricks). See Amo.

Morton [MAWRT-uhn] (Putnam). A post office established as Little Walnut, for the stream of the same name, on

October 9, 1855, was changed to Morton on July 17, 1857, and was closed on January 14, 1905. The village supposedly was named for Oliver Perry Morton, governor of Indiana, 1861–1867, though a former name, Mortons Corners, suggests a more immediate influence.

Morven [MAWR-vuhn] (Shelby). A post office was established on April 20, 1826; closed on September 19, 1842.* The second store in the county, owned by Alfred Major, the first postmaster, and operated by William Reid, was located here. This Scottish place name also is found in Australia and New Zealand as well as in Georgia and North Carolina.

Morvins Landing [mawr-vuhnz LAN-ding] (Harrison). Harvey Heth platted Morvin, a variant name, just east of Mauckport on September 7, 1816. According to local tradition, this was the first station on the Underground Railroad in Indiana. David Bell was accused of helping slaves escape from Kentucky and was imprisoned before the Civil War. It is also said that on July 8, 1863, General Morgan and his raiders invaded the village and shot a cannon through a house before crossing the Ohio River. Variant spellings are Morvan and Morvan Landing.

Moscow [MAHS-ko] (Rush). John Woods, the proprietor, and David Querry built a mill here in 1822. A post office, probably named for the Russian city, was established on December 22, 1827; closed on January 2, 1907. The village was laid out in 1832. According to the WPA files, the origin of the name is unknown: "Its meaning is hidden in obscurity of time and history. There is a view that being a place off the railroad, a derisive name for its numerous hills, banks, woods, and streams would apply best.

This opinion is not regarded as fact, for the reason that for half a century, Moscow was the milling center of three counties. . . ."

Mott Station [maht STAY-shuhn] (Harrison). A post office called Mott was established on May 29, 1888; closed on November 9, 1897.* Motts Station is a variant spelling. The village was platted on May 12, 1883, by Charles A. Crosby.

Mount Auburn [mownt AW-bern] (Franklin). This village was platted on February 25, 1850.

Mount Auburn [mownt AW-bern] (Shelby). This village was platted on January 18, 1837, by John Warner, Christopher M. Allen, Daniel A. Allen, and William P. Records, and originally called Black Hawk, sometimes spelled Blackhawk, for the Sauk chief. A post office was established as Black Hawk on November 23, 1838. On March 13, 1844, the name was changed to Mount Auburn, apparently to avoid confusion with the other town called Blackhawk in Vigo County.

Mount Auburn [mownt AW-bern] (Wayne). This town was platted on April 18, 1864, by Rudolph Burkets.

Mount Ayr [mownt EHR] (Newton). This town was laid out on an elevated tract in October 1882 by Louis Marion, who named it for his home, Mount Airy, North Carolina. Previous spellings have been Mount Airy and Mount Ayer. A post office established as Pilot Grove on September 12, 1854, was changed to Mount Ayr on July 22, 1886.*

Mount Carmel [mownt KAHR-muhl] (Franklin). This town was first laid out in February 1832 by two local merchants, J. and S. S. Faucett, who were brothers, and named for the local Mount Carmel Presbyterian Church, which was organized by Reverend John Thompson in 1824, making it the oldest local church. A post office established as Sentinel on January 12, 1832, was changed to Mount Carmel on February 14, 1840; closed on March 31, 1906.

Mount Carmel [mownt KAHR-muhl] (Washington). This village was laid out on December 20, 1837, by John and William Brown. The name comes from the biblical mountain, perhaps via a local church. Mount Carmel Ridge also is in this county.

Mount Comfort [mownt KUHM-fert] (Hancock). A post office was established on September 22, 1851; closed on February 24, 1956. The village was platted on October 25, 1885. Although the name is commendatory, its origin is unknown.

Mount Corbin (Ripley). See Otter Village.

Mount Etna [mownt ET-nuh] (Huntington). This town was founded in November 1839 and named for the Sicilian volcano. A post office was established on March 16, 1848; closed on May 15, 1920.

Mount Healthy [mownt HEL-thee] (Bartholomew). This village was laid out in 1851 by William Howbert and supposedly so named because it is located on high ground "free of miasmatic vapors" (WPA). A post office established on June 13, 1850, as White Creek, with Howbert as postmaster, was changed to Mount Healthy on January 6, 1851; closed on November 23, 1888.*

Mount Jackson [mownt JAK-suhn] (Marion). A post office was established on July 9, 1832; closed on January 6, 1898.* The village was laid out around 1838 (WPA).

Mount Liberty [mownt LIB-er-dee] (Brown). A post office was established here on June 17, 1856; closed on October 15, 1932.*

Mount Meridian [mownt muh-RID-ee-in] (Putnam). This village was laid out in 1833 by William Heavin and Bryce W. Miller and called Carthage. When a post office was established on July 24, 1835, the Post Office Department named it Mount Meridian because there already was another post office named Carthage in Rush County, and the village was renamed for the post office, which was closed on February 28, 1905.

Mount Olive [mownt AHL-iv; mownt AHL-uhv] (Martin). A post office was established on August 19, 1887; closed on February 15, 1916. Mount Olive, from the biblical Mount of Olives, is a common name for churches, which frequently influence the naming of settlements, such as this one.

Mount Olympus [mownt uh-LIM-puhs] (Gibson). Originally this village was called Ennes, for a pioneer blacksmith, William Ennes. Samuel Kelly, a schoolteacher, gave the village its present name, the home of the Greek gods, because it reminded him of the Greek mountain.

Mount Pisgah [mownt PIS-gee; mownt PIZ-guh] (Lagrange). A post office was established on January 14, 1848; closed on April 30, 1907.* This name comes from the biblical mountain, but often it is applied first to a local church, from which the community takes its name.

Mount Pleasant [mownt PLEZ-uhnt] (Cass). This village, also called Hardscrabble, was laid out in June 1836. Mount Pleasant, a common commendatory name in Indiana that is sometimes suggested by a local church, is found in eight other counties (Delaware, Jay, Johnson, Martin, Perry, Randolph, Shelby, and Warrick).

Mount Pleasant [mownt PLEZ-uhnt] (Delaware). This village was laid out in September 1837 and probably named for the nearby Mount Pleasant United Brethren Church. Mount Pleasant is a common name for churches in Indiana, and sometimes a settlement takes its name from the name of a local church. A variant name is Hazel.

Mount Pleasant (Jay). See New Mount Pleasant.

Mount Pleasant [mownt PLEZ-uhnt] (Martin). A post office was established on February 27, 1824; closed on December 20, 1862. The village was laid out in 1826. Apparently, the name is commendatory. According to tradition, "The people who settled Mount Pleasant came there from a place called Hindostan Falls whence they had been forced to leave on account of a plague which infested that vicinity. The settlement of Mount Pleasant is located on a hill and the surroundings were a very agreeable change to the first settlers over the plague-ridden Hindostan they had left. Hence the name" (WPA).

Mount Pleasant [mownt PLEZ-uhnt] (Perry). A post office was established on August 19, 1869; closed on February 27, 1943. According to an oral account, the village is located "on a high plateau, which accounts for its name" (ISUFA).

Mount Pleasant (Randolph). See Snow Hill.

Mount Pleasant (Shelby). See Camp Flat Rock.

Mount Pleasant (Warrick). See Newburgh.

Mount Prospect (Crawford). See Brownstown.

Mount Prospect (Warrick). See Newburgh.

Mount Ruska (Kosciusko). See Atwood.

Mounts [mownts] (Gibson). This village was established around 1880 as a flag station. A post office was established on May 3, 1886; closed on November 15, 1919. The name is for a local family. Mathias and Smith Mounts settled in this area around 1806. Smith Mounts fought with General Wayne at Tippecanoe, and many of his relatives lived in this vicinity.

Mount Sinai [MOWNT SEYE-neye] (Dearborn). This village was named for the Mount Sinai Methodist Episcopal Church, which was built here prior to 1836.

Mount Sterling [mownt STER-ling] (Switzerland). This village was laid out in 1816 by Philo Averil, allegedly on a hill and named for the Sterling family. A post office was established on April 6, 1819; closed on April 15, 1907.*

Mount Summit [mownt SUHM-uht] (Henry). This town was platted on July 11, 1854. A post office was established on July 15, 1869. Surrounded by hilly farmland, the town supposedly is situated on one of the higher elevations in the county, from which it received its name.

Mount Tabor [mownt TAY-ber] (Monroe). John Burton bought land here in 1819, was operating a sawmill by 1820, and bought additional land in 1824. The village was platted on April 21, 1828, and a post office was established on October 20, 1831, though it closed on January 23, 1860. Ultimately this name is for the biblical mountain, but frequently it is applied first to a local church and from the church the community takes its name. According to the WPA files, there was a hill here named Tabor Hill, so the name may have been influenced by a local family.

Mount Tabor (Morgan). See Crown Center.

Mount Vernon (Jay). See Redkey.

Mount Vernon [mownt VER-nuhn] (county seat, Posey). This city, formerly known as McFaddens Bluff and McFaddens Landing, was settled by Andrew McFadden about 1805 and first platted by John Wagoner on March 11, 1816. A post office called Mount Vernon was established on March 9, 1818. The present name is for Washington's home. Supposedly the name was suggested by Samuel Rowe at a meeting held to select a name (WPA).

Mount Vernon [mownt VER-nuhn] (Wabash). This village was platted on October 15, 1847, by William Dayton and named for George Washington's home. Locally it is sometimes called Vernon.

Mount Walleston (White). See Norway.

Mount Zion [mownt ZEYE-uhn] (Wells). A post office was established on May 26, 1873; closed on April 30, 1917.* The village was platted on August 27, 1895. The name is for a church around which the village was built.

Muddy Fork (Clark). See Carwood.

Mudge Station (White). See Chalmers.

Mudlavia Springs [mud-LAV-ee-uh SPRINGZ] (Warren). This village once was considered part of Kramer, q.v. After a fire in 1920 destroyed the Mudlavia Springs Hotel, Kramer developed on a hill overlooking Big Pine Creek, and the area of the fire at the foot of the hill was called Mudlavia or Mudlavia Springs.

Mud Lick (Jefferson). See Belleview.

Mudsock (Decatur). See Burney.

Mudsock (Madison). See Dundee.

Mulberry [MUHL-behr-ee; MAWL-behr-ee] (Clinton). This town was platted in 1858 by William Perrin and allegedly named for a tall mulberry tree here (WPA). A post office established as Winships Mill, with Edwin Winship as postmaster, on October 1, 1853, was changed to Mulberry on March 5, 1860.*

Muletown (Dearborn). See Manchester (Dearborn).

Mull [muhl] (Randolph). A post office was established here on September 15, 1897; closed on July 31, 1901.

Mullens Station (Henry). See Ashland (Henry).

Muncie [MUHN-see; MUHNTS-ee] (county seat, Delaware). This city was settled as early as 1818 and platted in 1827. A post office called Muncietown was established on April 10, 1828; closed on December 6, 1855; reestablished as Muncie on December 29, 1857. Formerly the settlement, too, was called Munseetown, Muncey Town, or Muncietown because so many Delawares of the Munsee band lived here. The name of the band, Min-si or Min-thi-u (sometimes spelled Monsy and Monthee), means "people of the stony country." Munsey is another variant spelling.

Mundy Station [muhn-dee STAY-shuhn] (Owen). A post office was established as Mundy on February 6, 1883; closed on March 29, 1886, when the Romona, q.v., post office was established. Murdy Station is a variant spelling.

Munster [MUHNS-ter] (Lake). This town was settled in 1855, and a post office was established on February 5, 1892,* with storekeeper Jacob Munster as postmaster. The name honors the pioneer Munster family. Early settler Eldert Munster was a native of Holland.

Murdock [MER-dahk] (Lawrence). This village was established as a switching station on the Monon Railroad.

Murray [MER-ee] (Wells). This village, first called New Lancaster, was settled in 1829 and laid out on October 17, 1839. A post office was established on September 16, 1837; closed on July 15, 1902. Supposedly the Post Office Department changed the name to Murray.

Murrys Side Track (Porter). See Furnessville.

Musselman (Johnson). See Samaria.

 N

Nabb [nab] (Clark). This village was platted in 1855 and named for a railroad superintendent, General Nabb. Since this village is located on the Clark-Scott county line, the post office has moved back and forth across the county line. A post office established as Nabb on October 2, 1878, in Scott County was changed to Clark County on February 25, 1881, and was changed back to Scott County on May 20, 1907.

Napoleon [nuh-POL-yuhn] (Ripley). This town was platted on February 9, 1820, by William Wilson and named for Napoleon Bonaparte. A post office was established on January 19, 1821.

Nappanee [nap-uh-NEE] (Elkhart). This city was laid out in 1874 by Daniel Metzler, John Culp, Jr., and Henry Stahly, Sr. A post office was established on March 15, 1875. Ultimately the name comes from the Missisauga *na-pa-ni,* "flour." The Hoosier town gets its name from a Canadian town, Napanee, which received its name from a gristmill there. A local legend offers another explanation: "Nappanee was founded in about 1870. It supposedly got its name from an Indian maiden found there knee deep in mud. Supposedly, Nappanee is the Indian name for mud" (ISUFA).

Nash Depot (Vanderburgh). See Stacer.

Nashville [NASH-vil] (county seat, Brown). Banner Brummet, county agent, built a log building here in 1835 and laid out the town in August 1836. Brummet called the town Jacksonburg for the township in which it was then located. The old township was named for Andrew Jackson. The post office, with Brummet as postmaster, was established as Nashville, for Nashville, Tennessee, on February 25, 1837.

Nashville [NASH-vil] (Hancock). This village was laid out on December 30, 1834, by John Kennedy and Daniel Blakeley.

Natchez [NACH-ee; NACH-uhz] (Martin). This village, once a stagecoach stop, was platted in 1839 by John P. Davis. A post office was established on April 17, 1844; closed on July 14, 1905.* Apparently the name was borrowed from the city of the same name in Mississippi, which was named for the Native American tribe. Natches is a variant spelling.

Nauvoo (La Porte). See Rolling Prairie.

Navilleton [nuh-VIL-tuhn] (Floyd). This village was founded around 1845. A post office was established on May 18, 1894; closed on May 19, 1902.

Nead [needz; need] (Miami). A post office was established on March 15, 1894; closed on August 31, 1901. Ac-
cording to the WPA files, this unplatted village was named for Samuel Nead, an early settler. Locally, the name is pronounced as if it were spelled Neads.

Nebo (Cass). See Lucerne.

Nebraska (Crawford). See Alton.

Nebraska [nuh-BRAS-kuh] (Jennings). This village was platted in November 1856 and apparently named for the territory of Nebraska, established in 1854 and named for the Native American name of the Platte River. A post office established as Otter Creek on November 26, 1858, was changed to Nebraska on February 27, 1861.

Needham [NEED-uhm] (Johnson). This village was platted in April 1866 and named for a local family. The proprietor was Noah Needham, and the first postmaster was William H. Needham. The post office, first called Needhams Station, was established on December 20, 1866; on November 28, 1882, the post office name was changed to Needham.

Needmore [NEED-mawr] (Brown). A post office was established on October 16, 1872; closed on January 31, 1919. According to a local legend, a storekeeper or a threshing crew boss said that he had never seen a community that needed more, so the village was called Needmore (WPA).

Needmore [NEED-mawr] (Lawrence). This village was settled in 1873. According to a local legend, it was named by Lou Goodman "during the Cleveland administration, who said the people were always needing more bread and meat than they had" (WPA).

Needmore (Owen). See Cunot.

Needmore (Sullivan). See Pleasantville (Sullivan).

Needmore [NEED-mawr] (Vermillion). This village was platted in 1904. Needmore is a widespread name, with at least five Hoosier settlements and a Hendricks County post office (established on April 21, 1868; closed on May 25, 1871) as well as eight Kentucky communities bearing the name. Stewart calls the name a "humorous derogatory" suggesting that "the place needs more of everything."

Negangards Corner [NEG-an-gahrdz KAWR-ner] (Ripley). This village developed around a general store located at a junction of two roads. A post office called North Hogan was established on January 11, 1844; closed on August 14, 1877.

Nettle Creek (Wayne). See Franklin.

Nevada [nuh-VAD-uh] (Tipton). This village was platted on October 28, 1852, by Samuel Denny and William Marshall. The county recorder, Sylvester Turpen, offered not to charge them for recording the plat if they would let him name the village. Denny and Marshall agreed, and Turpen named it Nevada, supposedly "after a town in Mexico." Perhaps he named the village for the mountain range, for which the territory ceded by Mexico in 1848 was named. A post office was established on September 19, 1857; closed on March 14, 1908.

Nevada Mills [nuh-VAD-uh MILZ] (Steuben). Originally this village was called Millville for sawmills here. A local landowner named Dean, who had lived in Nevada County, California, during the Gold Rush, suggested the name Nevada. When a post office was estab-lished on July 23, 1867, Mills was added to the name to distinguish it from another post office named Nevada in Tipton County. The post office was closed on August 15, 1905.*

New Albany [noo AWL-buh-nee] (county seat, Floyd). This city was platted in 1813 by Joel, Abner, and Nathaniel Scribner, who named it for the capital of their home state, New York. An Indiana Territory post office, with Joel Scribner as postmaster, also was established in 1813.

New Alsace [noo AL-suhs] (Dearborn). This village was laid out in 1837 and apparently named for the region and former province in France. An early settler, Anthony Walliezer, who came here in 1833, was a native of the province of Alsace in eastern France. A post office established as Alton on December 10, 1834, was changed to New Alsace on December 9, 1845, and closed on May 14, 1904.

New Amsterdam [noo AM-ster-dam] (Harrison). This town was platted on September 19, 1815, by Jacob Funk and Samuel McAdams and apparently named for the Dutch city, though perhaps influenced by the former name of New York. A post office was established on March 17, 1838; closed on April 30, 1950. Amsterdam is a variant name.

Newark (Fulton). See Akron.

Newark [NOO-erk] (Greene). This village was founded around 1860 and named for Newark, Ohio, home of early settlers. A post office was established on May 8, 1866; closed on May 15, 1910.

New Augusta [noo uh-GUHS-tuh] (Marion). This village, first called Hosbrook, or Holsbrook (WPA), was platted in 1852. Hosbrook is a family name in this county, as Perry Hosbrook laid out Clermont, q.v. The railroad depot here was named Augusta Station for a nearby town, Augusta. A post office established as Augusta Station on January 31, 1854, was changed to New Augusta on August 24, 1876. The post office was closed on January 20, 1961.*

New Baltimore [noo BAWL-tuh-mawr] (Posey). This village was settled in 1819 by James Allen. Located at the mouth of Black River, where it empties into the Wabash, the village once was an important river landing.

New Barbersville (Jefferson). See Barbersville.

New Bargersville (Johnson). See Bargersville.

New Bath [NOO bath] (Franklin). This village developed as a station on the Chesapeake and Ohio Railroad and was named for the Bath post office, which was named for its location in Bath Township. Cf. Old Bath, where the Bath post office was located.

New Bellsville [noo BELZ-vil] (Brown). This village was settled in the 1830s and supposedly named by settlers from Bellville, Ohio (WPA). Joseph Campbell was the founder. A post office was established on July 11, 1856; closed on December 31, 1909.

Newbern [NOO-bern] (Bartholomew). This village was laid out on July 14, 1832, by Aaron Davis and Aaron P. Taylor and named for New Bern, North Carolina, Davis's home. A post office was established on January 2, 1833; closed on October 14, 1901.

Newberry [NOO-behr-ee] (Greene). A post office called Slinkards Mills, with Frederick Slinkard as postmaster, was established on July 12, 1823. On August 15, 1849, the post office name was changed to Newberry. According to the WPA files, the town first was laid out in 1822, though surveyed and platted again on May 6, 1830, and named for Newberry, South Carolina; however, a local history says the town was laid out in 1842 by M. Newberry and named for him.

New Bethel (Marion). See Wanamaker.

New Boston [noo BAW-stuhn] (Harrison). Apparently this village was named for the English town via Massachusetts. A variant name is Boston.

New Boston [noo BAW-stuhn] (Spencer). This village, laid out in August 1851, probably was named for Boston, Massachusetts. The post office, established on July 8, 1852, was called New Boston until it closed on December 29, 1868. Another post office located here from December 30, 1881, to July 15, 1918, was called Huff, for the township in which it was established.

New Bremen (Marshall). See Bremen.

New Britton [noo BRIT-uhn] (Hamilton). This village was laid out by William Brandon on March 8, 1851. A post office was established on January 8, 1856; closed on January 2, 1907. The name is spelled New Britain in one county history, so possibly the village was named for the commonwealth.

New Brunswick [noo BRUHNZ-wik] (Boone). This village was platted in 1850. A post office was established on July 3, 1858; closed on March 15, 1901.*

The name may have been borrowed from an eastern state.

New Brunswick [noo BRUHNZ-wik] (Clay). This village was laid out in February 1831 by A. R. Ferguson and William Maxwell, the county surveyor. Located on Eel River, the principal businesses were in staves, hogs, poultry, and grain. Most of these things were shipped to New Orleans on flatboats that were built and launched here.

Newburg (Clay). See Turner.

Newburg (Decatur). See Forest Hill.

Newburg (Johnson). See Samaria.

Newburg (Randolph). See Spartanburg.

Newburgh [NOO-berg] (Warrick). This town was settled as early as 1803 by John Sprinkle and named Sprinklesburg for him, although the settlement also was known locally as Mount Prospect, according to the WPA files, or Mount Pleasant, according to other sources, supposedly for the high bluff on which it was located on a steep hill northeast of the settlement and for the rich soil west of the settlement (WPA). Sprinklesburg was laid out by Chester Elliott for John Sprinkle in 1818. An adjoining town called Newburgh was laid out by Abner Luce on October 23, 1829. In 1837 the two towns were consolidated and called Newburgh. A post office called Newburgh, with Abner Luce as postmaster, was established on November 30, 1829.*

New Burlington [noo BER-ling-tuhn] (Delaware). This village was platted on August 22, 1837, on the Burlington Pike and probably named for it. A post office was established on March 9, 1838; closed on October 14, 1901.

New Carlisle [noo kahr-LEYEL] (Saint Joseph). This town was platted on August 15, 1835, by Richard R. Carlisle, traveler and adventurer, for whom it was named. A post office was established on February 25, 1837.

New Carrollton [noo KEHR-uhl-tuhn] (Ripley). A post office was established here on December 11, 1837; closed on March 26, 1839.

New Castle [NOO kas-uhl] (county seat, Henry). This city first was platted on April 8, 1823, and named by Ezekiel Leavell, an early settler, for his home, New Castle, Kentucky. A post office was established as New Castle on April 12, 1823; changed to Newcastle on February 5, 1894; and changed back to New Castle on August 1, 1938. According to an oral account, "New Castle is called [nicknamed] the Rose City in honor of the Heller brothers. The Heller brothers, through crossbreeding, developed the now famous long-stemmed [American] Beauty Rose" (ISUFA). Place-name legends give other origins of the name: (1) "New Castle was just named after New Castle, Spain. That was a Spanish settlement around there" (ISUFA). (2) "New Castle, Indiana, was named after a New Castle in England by the settlers of that area. . . . The town of New Castle in its early stages in 1821 consisted of 20 families, 150 people, two stores, two bars, and a post office. Later, settlers moved from New Castle, Indiana, and established a New Castle in Kentucky" (ISUFA). New Castle, of course, is not a Spanish name, and the Kentucky city, founded in 1798, is older than the Hoosier city.

New Chicago [noo shu-KAH-go; noo shu-KAW-go] (Lake). This village was platted in 1893 and named for the nearby city in Illinois. A post office was established on October 19, 1907; closed on August 15, 1917. Cf. East Chicago.

New Columbus [noo kuh-LUHM-buhs] (Madison). This village was laid out in 1834 by Abraham Adams, who was from Ohio, and called New Columbus, a name it still shares with Ovid, the name of the post office established here on March 25, 1837.* Apparently the post office was called Ovid to avoid confusion with Columbus in Bartholomew County. New Columbus possibly is for Columbus, Ohio, and Ovid probably is for the classical poet, perhaps via New York.

New Corner (Delaware). See Gaston.

New Corydon [noo KAWR-uh-duhn] (Jay). This village was platted in the spring of 1844 and named for Corydon, Indiana. A post office was established on September 7, 1844; closed on January 31, 1960. Cf. Corydon.

New Discovery [noo duh-SKUHV-ree; noo duh-SKUHV-er-ee] (Parke). Supposedly this village was named by early settlers who discovered unclaimed land here after they were led to believe that all of the desirable land in the county had been claimed.

New Dublin (Parke). See Mansfield.

New Durham (La Porte). See Pinhook (La Porte).

New Elizabeth (Hendricks). See Lizton.

New Elizabethtown [noo uh-LIZ-uh-buhth-town] (Jackson). This village, earlier called Elizabethtown, was laid out by Asa Crane on November 12, 1836. The post office, established as Cranes Mills,

for the local Crane family, on February 8, 1858, was moved to Shields, q.v., on January 10, 1866.*

New Era [NOO EHR-uh] (DeKalb). A post office was established here on January 14, 1868; closed on May 14, 1906.*

New Fairfield [noo FEHR-feeld] (Franklin). A village named Fairfield was platted in October 1815 by Hugh Abernathy, George Johnston, Thomas Osborn, and James Wilson, whose adjoining lands met in the center of the village. Supposedly the name, also applied to the township, was suggested by the "general beauty" of its setting. It is also said that the village site was a neutral meeting ground where various Indian tribes met and camped. A post office named Fairfield was established on January 19, 1818; closed on April 2, 1906. When Brookville Reservoir was constructed during the late 1960s and early 1970s, the village of Fairfield was razed, and this relocated village was called New Fairfield for the old village.

New Farmington [noo FAHRM-ing-tuhn] (Jackson). This village was laid out on July 30, 1852. The name may be a transfer from an eastern state. A post office was established on December 10, 1852; closed on June 22, 1868.

New Frankfort [noo FRANK-fert] (Scott). This village was platted on February 10, 1838, and named by settlers from Kentucky for the capital of their native state. A post office established as New Frankfort on September 11, 1838, was moved to nearby Woostertown on October 17, 1861; back to New Frankfort on March 17, 1865; back to Woostertown on April 25, 1865; back to New Frankfort on September 13, 1875;

closed on May 31, 1901. Frankfort is a variant name.

New Garden (Wayne). See Fountain City.

Newgene (Monroe). See Harrodsburg.

New Germantown (Boone). See Whitestown.

New Goshen [noo GO-shuhn] (Vigo). A post office was established here on March 14, 1851.* The village was laid out on May 17, 1853, by Hamilton Smith, William Ferguson, George Smith, and John Hay. The name Goshen is fairly popular in the United States and comes from the biblical land. The adjective *New* distinguishes this village from the city in Elkhart County.

New Harmony [noo HAHR-muh-nee] (Posey). This town was settled in 1814 by George Rapp and associates and named for Harmonie, Pennsylvania, site of their first settlement. On December 25, 1825, it was sold to Robert Owen, who renamed it New Harmony. An Indiana Territory post office established as Harmony on August 17, 1816, was changed to New Harmony on February 21, 1825.

New Harrisburg (Wabash). See Disko.

New Haven [NOO HAY-vuhn] (Allen). A settlement here was called Gundys Deadening, as an early settler named Gundy deadened timber prior to clearing his land. Gundy sold his land to Samuel Hanna, who sold it to Egen Burgess, who sold it to his son, Henry, who platted the city in June 1839 and named it for New Haven, Connecticut. A post office established as Kendall on June 13, 1839, was changed to New Haven on June 17, 1842.

New Hope [noo hop] (Owen). This village dates from about 1870 and was named for a church of the same name that was here when the village was founded.

New Jerusalem (Greene). See Linton

New Lancaster (Huntington). See Lancaster.

New Lancaster [noo LANG-kuhs-ter] (Tipton). Settled around 1845, this village, apparently unplatted, was established as a trading point. A post office was established on April 5, 1847; closed on July 14, 1903. The original site of this village was owned by Carter Jackson, who from time to time sold parts of his farm to other settlers. The name comes from the English county and town, probably via an eastern state.

New Lancaster (Wells). See Murray.

Newland [NOO-luhnd] (Jasper). A post office was established on February 25, 1901; closed on May 15, 1925. The village was laid out on February 28, 1906, on reclaimed marshlands, hence the name (WPA).

New Lawrenceburgh (Dearborn). See Lawrenceburg.

New Lebanon [noo LEB-uh-nuhn] (Sullivan). This village was settled around 1827 by Methodists and named for the biblical mountains. Since there was another town named Lebanon in Indiana, *New* was added. A post office was established on March 31, 1840; closed on February 11, 1966. According to another account, "This town was settled by Methodists and, according to local history, was probably named after the Methodist town of Lebanon in northern Indiana" (ISUFA).

New Lexington (Clark). See Lexington.

New Liberty [noo LIB-er-dee] (Washington). Liberty, a common place name in the United States, generally is borrowed for its commendatory value.

New Lisbon [noo LIZ-buhn] (Henry). This village was platted first on July 19, 1833, and named for Lisbon, Ohio. Originally the settlement was called Jamestown, locally Jimtown, for one of the original proprietors, James Donaldson. A post office established as Jamestown on September 5, 1836, was changed to New Lisbon on November 28, 1836.

New Lisbon (Jay). See Pennville.

New Lisbon [noo LIZ-buhn] (Randolph). This village was platted in 1848. The name comes from the city in Portugal, perhaps via an eastern state.

New London [noo LUHN-duhn] (Howard). This village was laid out in 1845 by John Lamb and Reuben Edgerton and probably was named for the city in Connecticut, perhaps via Ohio. A post office was established on February 23, 1847; closed on August 15, 1918.

New London [noo LUHN-duhn] (Jefferson). A post office was established here on May 13, 1818; closed on February 14, 1840.

New Madison (Wabash). See Servia.

New Marion [noo MEHR-ee-uhn] (Ripley). This village, probably named for Francis Marion, first was called Marion, but because there already was a town of that name in Indiana, the name was changed to New Marion on July 12, 1832, the year the town was laid out. A

post office was established on January 8, 1833; closed on December 31, 1949.

New Market [NOO mahr-kuht] (Clark). Formerly called Oregon, this village was laid out in 1839. Allegedly it was named New Market because market wagons assembled here.

New Market (Miami). See Chili.

New Market [NOO mahr-kuht] (Montgomery). This town was platted on July 1, 1872, and a post office was established on December 17, 1872. Allegedly, when a local gristmill burned, another mill was rebuilt south of the first one, other businesses followed, and the new site was called New Market (WPA). Another account says that the town was so named because it served as a convenient trading center (ISUFA).

New Market (Vigo). See Sandford.

New Maysville [noo MAYZ-vil] (Putnam). This village was laid out in 1832 by R. Biddle on land owned by John Johnson, William Welch, and Aquila Talbott and named by Biddle for Maysville, Kentucky. A post office was established on June 14, 1834; closed on August 30, 1919.

New Middletown [noo MID-uhl-town] (Harrison). Formerly called Middletown, this town was laid out on October 16, 1860, by Henry Sechrist, who donated land for the town. A post office established as Spring Dale on May 1, 1852, was changed to New Middletown on September 13, 1865.*

New Mount Pleasant [noo mownt PLEZ-uhnt] (Jay). This village was platted in March 1838 by J. H. Sanders, who named it Mount Pleasant for a Quaker meeting house in Ohio. A post office was established on October 4, 1839; closed on August 31, 1907.

New Otto (Clark). See Otto.

New Palestine [noo PAL-uhs-teen; noo PAL-uhs-teyen] (Hancock). The post office established here on August 20, 1834, was called Sugar Creek, the railroad station Palestine, and the town, laid out on October 1, 1838, New Palestine. Since three different names caused confusion and since there already was a Palestine in Kosciusko County, the post office was renamed New Palestine on January 16, 1889, and the railroad station was renamed New Palestine the same year.

New Paris [noo PEHR-uhs] (Elkhart). This village was laid out by Isaac Abshire and Enoch Wright in 1838 and named for the French city, probably via New Paris, Ohio, home of the founders. Early settlers, however, were from Alsace-Lorraine, according to the WPA files. A post office established as Jackson on April 22, 1840, was changed to New Paris on September 16, 1852; closed on December 30, 1938.

New Pekin [NOO PEE-kuhn] (Washington). This town, earlier called Greens Station and Pekin Station, developed as a railroad station near Pekin, q.v., for which it was named. The Pekin post office, now located here, was established on March 14, 1840.* Charles D. Green, who became postmaster in 1851, built a brick house along the railroad, and his house served as a depot and general store as well as the post office.

New Pennington [noo PIN-ing-tuhn] (Decatur). This village, named for the local Pennington family, was laid out on

July 28, 1851, by Eli Pennington. A post office, with Eli Pennington as postmaster, was established on February 9, 1852; closed on July 13, 1886.*

New Philadelphia [noo fil-uh-DEL-fee-uh] (Washington). A post office was established on January 8, 1833; closed on December 31, 1938. The village was laid out as Philadelphia, for the city in Pennsylvania, on November 30, 1837, by John I. Morrison for William Hamilton, proprietor.

New Pittsburg [noo PITS-berg] (Randolph). This village was platted on July 3, 1859, and named for Pittsburgh, Pennsylvania. A post office was established on April 24, 1858; closed on March 30, 1907.

New Point [NOO poynt] (Decatur). A post office established on July 21, 1837, at Enochsburgh, q.v., was relocated here and called Rossburgh (cf. Rossburg) on February 20, 1838. On April 5, 1870, the Rossburgh post office was changed to New Point. The town was laid out on September 8, 1854, shortly after the Indianapolis and Cincinnati Railroad was built. New Point was a trading point for lumber and staves. According to the WPA files, the town formerly was called Crackaway. Newpoint is a variant spelling.

Newport (Porter). See Porter.

Newport [NOO-pawrt] (county seat, Vermillion). A post office was established on December 16, 1820.* The town, selected for the county seat in 1824 and first platted on July 28, 1828, may have been named for Newport, Delaware, though this popular English place name is found in a number of states.

Newport (Wayne). See Fountain City.

New Prospect (Orange). See Prospect.

New Providence (Clark). See Borden.

New Richmond [noo RICH-muhnd; noo RICH-muhn] (Montgomery). Samuel Kincaid laid out this town in 1830 and named it for his hometown, New Richmond, Ohio (WPA). A post office was established on February 8, 1850.

New Ross [NOO raws] (Montgomery). A post office called New Ross first was established on August 9, 1837, about a mile from this site, then called Valley City, which was founded around 1841. In 1868 the post office was moved to this locale, which then assumed the post office name, as there already was a post office named Valley City in Harrison County. New Ross was named by local innkeeper George Dorsey for the English town, Ross, scene of an English battle.

Newry [NOO-ree] (Jackson). This village was never platted, but it was one of the earliest settlements in Vernon Township. A post office was established on April 15, 1846; closed on April 13, 1860.*

New Salem (La Porte). See Otis.

New Salem [noo SAY-luhm] (Rush). This village was laid out in February 1831 by Moses Thompson. A post office was established on October 20, 1831; closed on April 15, 1943.* Salem is a very popular name in the United States and generally is borrowed for its commendatory value.

New Salisbury [NOO SAHLZ-behr-ee] (Harrison). This village was platted on August 28, 1830, by John Kepley and named for his former home, Salisbury, North Carolina. A post office was established on May 27, 1837.

New Santa Fe [NOO san-tuh FAY] (Miami). This village was platted on July 25, 1902, by Alpheus and Sally Haynes and named for another town, Santa Fe, q.v., located one and one-half miles south of here in the same county.

New Switzerland (Switzerland). See Vevay.

Newton (Dubois). See Bretzville.

Newton (Jasper). See Rensselaer.

Newton (Marion). See West Newton.

Newton [NOOT-uhn] (Newton). This English place name has been extremely popular in the English-speaking world, where it generally is a transfer name. In the case of this community, established as a small railroad station, it comes from the county in which it is located.

Newton [NOOT-uhn] (Wabash). Never platted, this village, also called Newton Crossing, was established about 1883 at a railroad crossing with a water tower, signal tower, round house, and hotel.

Newton County [NOOT-uhn]. This county, mainly agricultural, was organized in 1859 and named for Sergeant John Newton, who served under Francis Marion in the Revolutionary War. This was the last county organized in the state. Seat: Kentland.

Newton Station (Crawford). See Riceville.

Newton Stewart [NOOT-uhn STOO-ert] (Orange). This village was laid out on April 17, 1839, by mill owners

William and Henry Stewart, who named it Newton Stewart. According to a local history, to their name they added the name of their birthplace in Ireland; however, Stewart is one of the most common Scottish surnames, and Newton is one of the most common English place names. Newton also has been a popular place name in Scotland, though not in Ireland, and Newton Stewart is a Scottish place name. A post office was established on October 4, 1850.*

Newtonville [NOOT-uhn-vil] (Spencer). A post office was established on July 6, 1860, and the village was laid out in March 1865. The name honors the local Newton family, early merchants. One of the founders was Bezaleel Newton. According to an oral account, "Newtonville is located about nine miles east of Chrisney on State Road 70. Newtonville was named after a family called the Newtons. Calvin Newton had sold drugs and other goods in the community, and his brother Bezaleel sold whiskey" (ISUFA).

New Town (Clark). See Bennettsville.

Newtown (Dubois). See Bretzville.

Newtown [NOO-town] (Fountain). Aaron Hetfield of southern New York settled here in 1824 and platted the town on June 30, 1829. A post office was established on May 12, 1831.

Newtown (Randolph). See Ridgeville (Randolph).

New Trenton [NOO TRENT-uhn] (Franklin). This village was laid out on December 31, 1816, by Solomon Manwarring, surveyor for Samuel Rockafeller and Ralph Wildridge, proprietors. A post office, with Rockafeller as postmaster, was established on April 5, 1817. Rockafeller came here from New Jersey and named the village for Trenton, New Jersey.

New Unionville [NOO YOON-yuhn-vil] (Monroe). This village was established around 1906 and named for nearby Unionville, q.v.

Newville [NOO-vil] (DeKalb). This village was surveyed in March 1837 by George W. Weeks for Washington Robinson, early settler and proprietor. Formerly the village was called Vienna, though the post office—established on July 5, 1839; closed on March 30, 1907—was called Newville for its location in Newville Township.

New Washington [NOO WAW-shing-tuhn] (Clark). This village was laid out in 1815 by David Copple, Bala Johnson, and Adam Keller, and a post office was established on April 6, 1819.

New Watson [NOO WAHT-suhn] (Clark). This village was established about a mile southeast of Watson, q.v., and named for it.

New Waverly [NOO WAY-ver-lee] (Cass). This village was laid out in December 1855 by John Forgy, and a post office was established on September 16, 1857. Probably the name is for Sir Walter Scott's popular *Waverley* novels, with *New* added to distinguish it from the town in Morgan County.

New Winchester [NOO WIN-ches-ter] (Hendricks). This village was laid out in 1832 by Wesley Morgan and James Bronaugh. A post office was established on February 15, 1837; closed on December 31, 1904.* The name probably is for the English town via an eastern state.

New York (Switzerland). See Florence.

Nicholsonville (Putnam). See Fillmore.

Nickle Plate (Starke). See Brems.

Nine Mile [neyen meyel] (Allen). A post office was established on November 9, 1855; closed on December 31, 1904.* The name is locational, for the village is located about nine miles southwest of Fort Wayne. A variant name is Nine Mile Place.

Nineveh [NIN-uh-vuh] (Johnson). This village was settled in 1821 by Amos Durlin, John S. Miller, and Robert Worl and named for nearby Nineveh Creek. The township in which it is located also is called Nineveh. A post office established as Woodruffs, with J. Woodruff as postmaster, on November 26, 1832, was changed to Ninevah on February 22, 1839. The village was platted on May 24, 1834, as Williamsburg. Although the stream name appears biblical, according to a local tradition repeated in a county history, the stream first was named Nineveh's Defeat, for Nineveh Berry, who fell into the stream and nearly drowned while carrying a deer's carcass across the stream. A number of Hoosier streams, according to legends, were named for men who fell in them and nearly drowned.

Nip and Tuck (Gibson). See Johnson.

Nixville (Huntington). See Pleasant Plain.

Noah (Shelby). See Marion (Shelby).

Noble [NO-buhl] (Jay). This village was named for Noble Township, which was named for Noah Noble, Indiana governor.

Noble County [NO-buhl]. This county, located in the state's lake country, was organized in 1836 and named for one or both of the Noble brothers from Dearborn County—James Noble (1785–1831), the first United States senator from Indiana (1816–1831), and Noah Noble (1794–1844), who was governor of Indiana (1831–1837) when the county was organized. Seat: Albion.

Noblesville [NO-buhlz-vil] (county seat, Hamilton). This city was laid out in 1823 and probably named for James Noble, first United States senator from Indiana. Local legend, however, says the town was named by one of the founders for his fiancee, Lavinia or Kathleen Noble. A typical oral account is: "John Conner and James Polk founded the town of Noblesville in 1823. At that time Polk was engaged to marry a woman from Indianapolis by the name of Kathleen Noble. Polk built a new home for his bride in the center of his newly discovered town. He planted a garden of vegetables in an outline which spelled out her name. He thought that this would symbolize his great love for Miss Noble. However, Miss Noble was not pleased. Instead, she was greatly enraged and insulted by the vegetable garden. Thus she broke her engagement to Polk. Sometime later a couple passing through the territory came to the Polk cottage, which was deserted, and saw the garden which he had planted. The man turned to the woman and asked, 'What is the name of this town?' His wife replied that this must be Noblesville because the garden said so" (ISUFA). According to the WPA files, "Perhaps both [accounts of naming] are right, for although Polk may have named it for his sweetheart, people in general considered Senator Noble a more fitting person to honor." A post office was established on March 10, 1824.

Nora [NAWR-uh] (Marion). When the post office was established here on December 11, 1871, Peter Lawson, first postmaster, named the post office Nora for the town in southern Sweden. Lawson was born in Sweden (WPA). The post office was closed on December 6, 1924. A local tradition offers another explanation of the naming of this village: "This community received its name from the wife of the first storekeeper in the town. He was Swedish" (ISUFA).

Normal [NAWR-muhl] (Grant). This village was never laid out. A post office established as Slash on September 27, 1852, was changed to Normal on July 8, 1880; closed on August 30, 1902.

Norman [NAWR-muhn] (Jackson). This village was founded in 1889 by John A. Norman, for whom it was named. A post office established as Norman Station on March 3, 1890, was changed to Norman on February 1, 1935.

Normanda [nawr-MAN-duh] (Tipton). This village was laid out in 1849 by M. P. Evans, Edward Jackson, and Matthew Jones, proprietors, and a post office was established on February 9, 1852; closed on February 28, 1921.

Norris (Washington). See Harristown.

Norristown (DeKalb). See Butler.

Norristown [NAWR-uhs-town] (Shelby). This village was platted on November 22, 1851, by David Winterowd, William Winterowd, and Henry Deiwert and named for Dr. James M. Norris,

local physician. Deiwert, who settled here as early as 1845, was the first merchant.

North (Ohio). See Norths Landing.

Northampton (Parke). See Bellmore.

North Anderson [nawrth AN-der-suhn] (Madison). This community, now the site of Shadyside Park, was named for its location north of Anderson, which annexed North Anderson in 1932.

North Belleville [NAWRTH BEL-vil] (Hendricks). The name is locational, as the village was established on the railroad north of Belleville.

North Benton (Steuben). See Hudson.

Northfield [NAWRTH-feeld] (Boone). A post office established as Georgetown—for the first postmaster, George Shirts—on December 19, 1832, was changed to Northfield on June 4, 1834; closed on August 2, 1897. The village was laid out in 1834.

North Galveston (Kosciusko). See Clunette.

North Grove [nawrth grov] (Miami). Originally this town was platted early in 1854 by John Parks and called Moorefield. On March 16, 1854, William North made an addition to the original plat and called the combined town North Grove for his family. A post office was established as North Grove on April 16, 1868; changed to Northgrove on March 5, 1894; and closed on June 30, 1934.

North Hampton (Parke). See Bellmore.

North Hogan (Ripley). See Negangards Corner.

North Indianapolis [nawrth in-dee-uh-NAP-uh-luhs] (Marion). A post office was established here on September 1, 1875; closed on January 6, 1898. The name is locational.

North Judson [NAWRTH JUHD-suhn] (Starke). A post office was established on September 24, 1860,* and the town was laid out first in 1861, though apparently the plat was not recorded. It was laid out again in 1866. Probably the name is a transfer from one of the communities named Judson south of here.

North Landing (Ohio). See Norths Landing.

North Liberty (Miami). See Chili.

North Liberty [NAWRTH LIB-er-dee] (Saint Joseph). This town was laid out on January 12, 1836 (or in 1837, according to the WPA files and other sources). A post office established as Dover on January 22, 1845, was changed to North Liberty on December 16, 1847. The name is locational, for the town is located in northern Liberty Township.

North Madison [NAWRTH MAD-uh-suhn] (Jefferson). This village was platted on October 27, 1846, by Robert J. Elvin, William H. Branham, and David Branham and named for nearby Madison, q.v. A post office was established on January 13, 1848; closed on August 31, 1957.

North Manchester [NAWRTH MAN-ches-ter] (Wabash). This town was platted on February 13, 1837, by Peter Ogan, who settled here in 1834 and surveyed the town site in 1836. Originally the town was called Manchester, presumably for the city in England, perhaps via New England. When a post office was established on October 6, 1838, it was called North Manchester, since there already was a post office called Manchester in Dearborn County. Located here is Manchester College, established by the United Brethren Church in 1860 as Roanoke Classical Seminary in Roanoke, Indiana.

North Ogilville [NAWRTH O-guhl-vil] (Bartholomew). The name of this village is locational (cf. Ogilville). A variant name is Moores Vineyard.

Northport [NAWRTH-pawrt] (Noble). This village was laid out in 1838 by Francis Comparet. A post office was established on January 14, 1846; moved to nearby Rome City, q.v., on January 21, 1868.

North Salem [NAWRTH SAY-luhm] (Hendricks). This town was laid out in 1835 by John Claypool, Davis Claypool, and John S. Woodward, and a post office was established on July 5, 1839. Probably the name is a transfer from southern Indiana or a southern state.

Norths Landing [NAWRTH LAN-ding; NAWRTHS LAN-ding] (Ohio). This village, also called North Landing, was founded in 1831 by Royal F. North. Originally it was called Grants Creek for a nearby stream. A post office, with Royal F. North as postmaster, was established as Grants Creek on June 17, 1831; changed to Norths Landing on March 27, 1866; changed to North on June 2, 1894; closed on November 29, 1919. Other members of the North family, for whom the village was named, also served as postmaster.

North Terre Haute [NAWRTH TEHR-uh HOT; nawrth tehr hot] (Vigo). According to the WPA files, this community first was called Stringtown because all the houses were on one side of the road, and later it was called Edwards and Elsworth for local families. Elsworth Station was near here. A post office called North Terre Haute was established on March 18, 1912; closed on January 31, 1957. The name is locational. Cf. Terre Haute.

North Union [NAWRTH YOON-yuhn] (Montgomery). A post office was established here on December 19, 1871; closed on October 11, 1899.*

North Vernon [NAWRTH VER-nuhn] (Jennings). This city was platted on June 24, 1854, north of the older town of Vernon; thus the present name is locational. Earlier names were Lick Skillet and Tripton. Tripton, the name of the post office established in 1842, is for Hagerman Tripp, who platted the town and changed the name from Lick Skillet to Tripton. The post office name was changed to North Vernon on March 12, 1867. Only legends explain the variant name Lick Skillet:
  1. "Lick Skillet is the former name for North Vernon. The train used to go through there and stop, and every time it stopped, the conductor could see the dogs and cats licking the skillet. The housewives would set out the pans and skillets for the animals to clean, so it was named Lick Skillet. Later it was named North Vernon because it was three miles up the pike from Vernon" (ISUFA).
  2. "Vernon, Indiana, used to be Lick Skillet. When they first settled, they

were building houses, and this guy was working so hard he was getting hungry. He came back to camp where his wife was and told her that he was so hungry that he could lick the skillet. So they called it Lick Skillet. Then eventually the people all died out, and people by the name of Vernon moved in and changed the name" (ISUFA).

North Webster [NAWRTH WEBZ-ter; NAWRTH WEB-ster] (Kosciusko). This town was platted on May 2, 1837. The original proprietor was John Ridinger. According to the WPA files, the town was named for Malcolm Webster, local landowner, but according to a local history, the town was "named in honor of Daniel Webster by Mr. Shoemaker." A post office established as Boydstons Mills, with Thomas G. Boydston as postmaster, was established on June 14, 1848, and changed to North Webster on August 19, 1879. It's said that when the post office was at Boydstons Mills, the patrons didn't have to pay any box rent because all of the mail was kept in an empty flour barrel.

Northwood Park [nawrth-wud PAHRK] (Porter). Formerly called North Woods, this village was laid out in 1923 as a summer resort on Long Lake and was so named "because of a wood at the north end of the lake" (WPA).

Norton [NAWRT-uhn] (Dubois). A post office established as Dillon on February 9, 1907, was changed to Norton on March 21, 1908, and closed on December 31, 1938.

Nortonburg [NAWRT-uhn-berg] (Bartholomew). Never platted, this town was named for the local Norton family. William Norton operated a general store here. On June 15, 1886, a post office was established with Ephraim B. Norton as first postmaster. The post office closed on September 30, 1912. A variant spelling is Nortonsburg.

Norway [NAWR-way] (White). The name of this village comes from the Scandinavian country, home of the founder, Hans Erasmus Hjort, and several other settlers. It was laid out in March 1845 and originally called Mount Walleston, for the ship that brought Hjort to the United States from Norway. In his will, probated in 1845, Hjort instructed his executors to "lay out a village on my place to be called Mount Wolleston in honor of the first ship that landed me in America." A post office named Norway was established on January 14, 1898; closed on December 30, 1899.

Nottingham [NAHD-ing-ham] (Wells). A post office was established on July 13, 1848; closed on February 28, 1905. The village was platted in 1895. The name is for the township in which the village is located.

Nowlington (Parke). See Nyesville.

Nulltown [NUHL-town] (Fayette). This village was founded in 1847 and named for the Null brothers, Israel and Michael, who established a sawmill and gristmill here in the 1830s. The post office was established as Ashland on February 26, 1847; changed to Nulls Mills on April 6, 1848; changed to Nulltown on December 14, 1895; closed on May 14, 1906.* Null Town is a variant spelling.

Numa [NOO-muh] (Parke). This village was settled first by John Wilson, who laid out the village on part of his farm in 1837 and served as the first postmaster when a post office was established on May 1, 1844; closed on June 14, 1899.* The village was initially a stagecoach stop and then a canal stop. The origin of the name is uncertain, although some residents believe the name is Native American. The name may be classical, though, for the traditional second king of Rome. Variant names are Walkers Bluff and Walkertown.

Nutwood [NUHT-wud] (Saint Joseph). This village was established along the Vandalia Railroad. A post office was established on October 11, 1886; closed on January 31, 1901.

Nyesville [NEYEZ-vil] (Parke). This village was platted in 1871 by the Sand Creek Coal Company and named for its president, William H. Nye. A post office was established on October 4, 1872; closed on May 31, 1902. According to local legend, "Nyseville was started in the late 1800s by a coal miner. When he first arrived, there was nothing but wilderness. He opened a coal mine and a general store to get things started. Well, after the news of a mine opening, meaning jobs, many people moved into the area. It is said that at one time Nyseville had 21 taverns. Nyseville flourished for a while, but died out when the mine closed. Nyseville is now just a small community with a few houses and a church" (iSUFA). The outstanding baseball pitcher Mordecai "Three Finger" Brown was born here on October 19, 1876, and died in Terre Haute on February 14, 1948. A variant name, Nowlington, is for a local family. Martin Nowling served as the first postmaster of Nyesville.

 **O**

Oak (Pulaski). See Thornhope.

Oakford [OK-ferd] (Howard). This village, a product of the growth of the I. P. and C. Railroad, was laid out by John Stephens in 1849 as Fairfield. Since there already was a town of that name in Indiana, the post office, established on August 23, 1854, was called Oakford. Apparently both names are commendatory.

Oak Forest [OK FAWR-uhst] (Franklin). A post office named Oak Forest was established on April 6, 1848. On September 17, 1894, the spelling of the post office name was changed to Oakforest, and on November 15, 1907, the post office was closed. Apparently the name is commendatory as well as descriptive.

Oakington (Marshall). See Burr Oak.

Oakland (Spencer). See Centerville.

Oakland City [OK-luhnd SID-ee; OK-luhn SID-ee] (Gibson). This city was platted on January 15, 1856, by James W. Cockrum and Warrick Hargrove and originally called Oakland, supposedly for oak groves on the town site. A post office was established as Oakland City on March 15, 1860.

Oaklandon [ok-LAN-duhn] (Marion). This village was platted on June 18, 1849, and originally called Oakland for the numerous oak trees here. The name was changed to distinguish it from another town named Oakland. A post office established as Germantown on April 24, 1837, was changed to Oaklandon on January 24, 1870; closed on May 31, 1960.*

Oak Ridge (Greene). See Owensburg.

Oaktown [OK-town] (Knox). A post office established as Oak Station on July 28, 1855, was changed to Oaktown on September 14, 1866. The town was laid out on May 20, 1867, by Samuel E. Smith for George Bond, who built the first gristmill here. A variant name is Depot.

Oakville [OK-vil] (Delaware). This village was laid out on December 30, 1873, and called Pleasant Hill. The post office established on February 15, 1876, was called Oakville, supposedly because the Post Office Department would not accept Pleasant Hill as the post office name.

Oakwood [OK-wud] (La Porte). A post office was established here on December 7, 1875; closed on May 31, 1914.

Oatsville [OTS-vil] (Pike). A post office was established on June 28, 1876; closed on August 31, 1903. Oatville is a variant spelling.

Ober [O-ber] (Starke). A post office was established here on April 5, 1883, and the village was platted on June 1, 1889. The name honors Ober Heath, early settler.

Occident [AHK-si-dent; AHK-suh-dent] (Rush). Originally called Tail Holt, this village was renamed Occident when a post office was established on June 8, 1882; closed on May 31, 1900.

Oceola (Saint Joseph). See Osceola.

Ockley [AHK-lee] (Carroll). This village was laid out in 1884. A post office was established on April 7, 1884. Locally the name is thought to be Native American of unknown meaning (WPA), though the name also is found in England.

Octagon [AHK-tuh-guhn] (Tippecanoe). A post office was established here on July 17, 1866; closed on December 31, 1900.*

Odd (Parke). See Minshall.

Odell [o-DEL; O-del] (Tippecanoe). This village was named for Major John W. O'Dell, of the War of 1812 and the Black Hawk War. Soon after he arrived here in 1831, a settlement, O'Dells Corners, sprang up. A post office named Odell was established on January 12, 1872; closed on September 6, 1900.

Odon [O-duhn] (Daviess). This town was laid out as Clarksburg in December 1846 by John Hastings. A post office established as Perkins Store, with William A. Perkins as postmaster, was established on July 25, 1856; changed to Walnut Hill on July 29, 1857; changed to Clarks Prairie on May 13, 1848; and changed to Odon on April 4, 1881. An earlier name of the settlement was Clarks Spring, as well as Clarksburg and Clarks Prairie—all for George Rogers Clark. The present name supposedly was inspired by the name of a Norse god, Odin; however, according to a letter, "the town was named Clarksburg, [but] the post office was Clark's Prairie. That name began to sound too rural to the young people and progressive citizens who expected the place to become a second Terre Haute. There was a lot of argument around the store hot stoves during the winter of 1881 as to what the name should be. Lon Caughy wanted the name to be Garfield for the newly elected president. Joe Dun Laughlin and Caleb O'Dell had been two of the principal agitators for a new name. It was finally decided to name the town for them, 'O' for O'Dell and 'don' for Joe Dun. The syllables put together spelled Odon. Nobody had the old Norse god, Woden, in mind. Nobody there but Joe Dun and Wesley Neal had ever heard of him. There already was an Odin in Illinois and the knowledge of that place helped to blend 'O' and 'Dun' into Odon" (ISUFA).

Ogden [AHG-duhn] (Henry). This village was platted on December 18, 1829, by Hiram Crum. First it was named Middletown for its location between Richmond and Indianapolis; however, it was discovered that another town in Henry County had been platted and named Middletown two months earlier, so this village was renamed Odgen for an engineer who worked on the construction of the National Road. A post office was established on July 15, 1840; closed on April 30, 1906.

Ogden Dunes [AHG-duhn DOONZ] (Porter). This town was laid out in 1925 and named for Francis A. Ogden, who once owned land, including a dunes tract, here.

Ogilville [O-guhl-vil] (Bartholomew). A nearby post office, with Burris Moore as postmaster, was established as Moores

Vineyard, for the local Moore family, on December 12, 1850; changed to Taylor Mills, for the local Taylor family, on January 18, 1893; and changed to Ogilville on June 5, 1893. One informant suggests the present name comes from a local family name: "A lot of Ogilvies lived around there, but I don't know. That's the way a lot of them places got named" (ISUFA). Cf. North Ogilville.

Ohio County [o-HEYE-uh; o-HEYE-o]. Organized in 1844, this county, the smallest in both size and population in the state, is bordered on the east by the Ohio River, for which it was named. *Ohio* comes from an Iroquois word meaning "beautiful." In 1680, LaSalle wrote of the river: "the Iroquois call it Ohio, and the Ottawas Oligh-in-cipau." Seat: Rising Sun.

Oil Creek (Perry). See Branchville.

Old Baker Settlement (Rush). See Falmouth.

Old Bargersville [OLD BAHR-gerz-vil] (Johnson). This village was laid out in February 1850 by local merchant Jefferson Barger (or Joshua Bargers, according to some sources), and first called Bargersville for him. A post office called Bargersville was established on July 28, 1851; closed on November 29, 1902.* The village now is called Old Bargersville to distinguish it from a nearby community also called Bargersville, q.v.

Old Bath [old BATH] (Franklin). This village first was called Coulters Corner, but it was renamed Bath, for the township in which it is located, when the Springfield post office was moved here and renamed Bath on December 14, 1838. The post office was closed on March 8, 1851.* The township was named for nearby medicinal springs. The present name, Old Bath, distinguishes it from New Bath, q.v.

Oldenburg [OLD-uhn-berg] (Franklin). This town was settled by Irish in 1817 but founded by German immigrants, including Father Franz Joseph Rudolf from Alsace. Named for Oldenburg, Germany, it was laid out on July 10, 1837, by John H. Runnebaum and John Henry Raspohl. A post office called Oldenburgh was established on December 9, 1845. On June 24, 1893, the spelling was changed to Oldenburg.

Old Milan [OLD MEYE-luhn] (Ripley). Formerly called Milan, this village was laid out on November 9, 1836, and apparently named for the Italian city. With the coming of the railroad in 1854, the population moved a mile south to the present town called Milan, q.v.

Old Otto (Clark). See Otto.

Old Pekin (Washington). See Pekin.

Old Porter (Porter). See Porter.

Old Saint Louis [old saynt LOO-us] (Bartholomew). This village was laid out on July 13, 1836, by Lewis Reed and Abraham Zeigler and formerly called Saint Louis, presumably suggested by Reed's first name, though some say the village was named for Saint Louis, Missouri. Old was added to distinguish it from nearby Saint Louis Crossing, q.v. Edward Eggleston's portrayal of Lewisburg, the fictional village in *The Hoosier Schoolmaster*, was influenced by this village.

Old Santa Fe (Miami). See Santa Fe.

Old Tip Town [OLD TIP town; OL TIP town] (Marshall). This village was platted on December 12, 1850, as Tippecanoe Town, for the river on which it is located. When it was bypassed by the railroad (cf. Tippecanoe), it was referred to as Old Tippecanoe Town, of which the present name is a variant form.

Old Tulip (Greene). See Tulip.

Old Watson [OLD WAHT-suhn] (Clark). This village was laid out in 1876 and called Watson. The present name distinguishes it from nearby New Watson, q.v.

Olean [o-lee-AN] (Ripley). A post office was established on February 14, 1844; closed on August 31, 1905.* The village was laid out on January 15, 1858. The name is for Olean, New York, former home of settlers.

Olive [AHL-iv; AHL-uhv] (Saint Joseph). A post office was established on July 14, 1836; closed on June 27, 1837. The village was named for Olive Township, which was named for Olive Stanton Vail, wife of Charles Vail, who settled in the township around 1830.

Oliver [AHL-iv-er; AHL-uhv-er] (Posey). A post office was established on January 29, 1883; closed on October 31, 1934. The name is for a local family. Thompson Oliver was the first postmaster, and Kisiah Oliver was the second postmaster.

Omee Town (Allen). See Fort Wayne.

Omega [o-MEG-uh] (Hamilton). A post office was established on July 27, 1870; closed on October 15, 1902. The name is for the last letter in the Greek alphabet. According to a local anecdote, the name was selected when a post office was es-

tablished because the former name, Dogtown, was not acceptable; therefore, "it was the last of 'Dogtown.'" The village was called Dogtown "because Finly Smock, a rural mail carrier, said he had never seen so many dogs in one town" (WPA).

Ontario [ahn-TEHR-ee-o] (Lagrange). This village was laid out by Nathan Jenks, proprietor, in March 1837 and named for Lake Ontario. Jenks built a mill here in 1843. Earlier, around 1836, he founded the LaGrange Collegiate Institute, modeled after Oberlin College in Ohio. A post office was established on September 12, 1846; closed on March 31, 1943.

Onward [AWN-werd] (Cass). A post office was established on August 12, 1852.* The town was laid out on May 24, 1869. The name appears to be commendatory, but local legend says it comes from a remark local citizens made after loafing at the local store: "I must now plug onward."

Oolitic [o-LID-ik; oo-LID-ik] (Lawrence). According to the WPA files, this town was platted first in June 1888 and called Limestone, for limestone quarried here. Apparently the town was platted again on March 23, 1896, by the Bedford Quarries Company and named for the oolitic texture of local limestone. A post office was established on March 23, 1892.

Opptown (Dearborn). See Farmers Retreat.

Ora [AWR-uh] (Starke). A post office was established on April 21, 1882, and named for Ora Keller, son of Ezekiel Keller, who platted the village in 1882 and served as first postmaster.

Orange [AWR-inj; AWR-uhnj] (Fayette). Earlier called Danville and Fayetteville, this village was laid out on October 12, 1824. A post office called Orange, for the township in which it was located, was established on September 7, 1826; closed on February 29, 1908.* The township was named for Orange, New Jersey, by settlers from there.

Orange County [AWR-inj; AWR-uhnj]. This county—noted for limestone, underground streams, and scenic hills—was organized in 1816 and named for Orange County, North Carolina, former home of early settlers. Seat: Paoli.

Orangeville [AWR-uhnj-vil] (DeKalb). When this village was platted in November 1836 it was named Orange, a name it still bears on some maps.

Orangeville [AWR-uhnj-vil] (Orange). This village was laid out on June 14, 1849, by Samuel Hicks, Harvey Denny, and Nathaniel B. Wilson and named for the county in which it is located. The township in which the village is located also is called Orangeville. The post office was established as Orange Valley on January 13, 1849; changed to Orangeville on June 2, 1849; closed on March 30, 1907.

Orchard Grove [awr-cherd GROV] (Lake). A post office was established here on July 21, 1854; closed on May 31, 1904.

Oregon (Clark). See New Market (Clark).

Orestes [aw-RES-tuhs] (Madison). First called Lowry Station for nearby landowner Nathan Lowry, this town was founded around 1876 and is said to have been named for Orestes McMahon, son of the first postmaster (WPA), though Frank McClead was the first postmaster when a post office was established on June 3, 1880. It's also said that the name honors Orestes McMahan, a local farmer. According to a county history, though, Nathan Lowry named the town for Orestes, son of Agamemnon, in Aeschylus's *Oresteia*.

Organ Springs [awr-guhn SPRINGZ] (Washington). A post office called Organ Spring was established on July 20, 1858. On May 9, 1894, the spelling of the post office name was changed to Organspring, and on May 31, 1901, the post office closed.

Oriole [AWR-ee-ol] (Perry). This village earlier was called Chestnut City for chestnut trees once here, but apparently many of the trees became diseased and died (ISUFA). The name was changed to Oriole, for the bird, supposedly by the Post Office Department, when a post office was established on June 14, 1890. The post office closed on February 10, 1967.

Orland [AWR-luhnd] (Steuben). This town, probably the oldest in the county, was settled in 1834 by Vermonters and first called The Vermont Settlement. A post office called Orland was established on March 9, 1837, and the town was platted on March 19, 1838, by Samuel Barry, Cyrus Choate, Alexander Chapin, and Chester Stocker. Chapin, the first postmaster, allegedly opened a hymnbook and named the post office and town for the title of the first hymn he saw (WPA), although another account says the hymnbook was opened to the phrase "O'er land and sea" (ISUFA). Still another account says that church fathers randomly opened a hymnbook to select the name. This English place name may be a transfer, though, as it is found in Maine and California as well as in England.

Orleans [awr-LEENZ] (Orange). This town, the oldest in the county, was platted on March 11, 1815, by William McFarland and Samuel Lewis two months after Andrew Jackson's victory at New Orleans, for which it was named. A post office was established on February 1, 1823.

Ormas [AWR-muhs] (Noble). This village was laid out on May 9, 1856, and named for Ormas Jones, a resident (WPA). A post office was established on July 16, 1880; closed on February 29, 1904. A variant name was Cold Springs, descriptive of a number of local springs containing very cold water (WPA).

Orrville [AWR-vil] (Knox). A post office was established on July 11, 1891; closed on June 30, 1904.* The name honors a local family. McAdam Orr was the third postmaster, and Edgar J. Orr was the fourth and final postmaster.

Osceola (Boone). See Advance.

Osceola [o-see-O-luh] (Saint Joseph). This town, earlier called Bancrofts Mills for a mill owned by a local family, was laid out on November 17, 1837. The name is for the famous Seminole chief, whose name comes from *os-y-o-hul-la*, a ceremonial drink. Chief Osceola was taken prisoner in October 1837, a few weeks before the town was platted. A post office established as Oceola on February 27, 1854, was changed to Osceola on November 17, 1881.

Osgood [AHZ-gud] (Ripley). A post office established as Ripley, for the county, on April 18, 1854, was changed to Osgood on March 27, 1855. The town was platted in March 1857. The name honors A. L. Osgood, chief engineer of the O. and M. Railroad. Osgood was in charge of the surveying crew when the railroad was constructed through here.

Ossian [AW-see-uhn] (Wells). This town was laid out on March 14, 1850, and named for Ossian Hall, County Old, Scotland, former home of some of the early settlers. A post office established as Bee Creek on September 28, 1846, was changed to Ossian on May 11, 1850.

Oswego [ahs-WEE-go] (Kosciusko). This village was laid out on the site of a former Indian reservation in 1837 and named for the town in New York. The Iroquoian name, meaning "flowing out," is appropriate, for the Hoosier village is located at the outlet of Tippecanoe Lake. A post office was established on September 24, 1840; closed on August 31, 1935.

Otis [O-dis; O-dus] (La Porte). A railroad station was established here in 1852. The village first was called New Salem or Salem Crossing by the Michigan Southern Railroad in 1852, then LaCroix by the Louisville, New Albany, and Chicago Railroad. Solomon Tucker, who platted the village in 1870, first accepted LaCroix as the name of the village, but it was renamed Packard, for Congressman Jasper Packard. Packard himself suggested the present name. A post office established as Crossing on December 14, 1855, was changed to Packard on June 10, 1872; to Otis on September 12, 1872; and closed on October 25, 1963.

Otisco [o-TIS-ko] (Clark). This village was founded in 1854 and perhaps named for Otisco Lake in New York. Apparently *Otisco* is Iroquoian for "water-dried." A post office was established on April 21, 1870.

Otterbein [AH-der-beyen; AH-der-buhn] (Benton). Located on the Benton-Tippecanoe county line, this town was laid out by Mr. and Mrs. John Levering on October, 25, 1872. A post office named Pond Grove, with schoolteacher William Otterbein Brown as postmaster, was established on May 25, 1863; changed to Otterbein on August 23, 1872. Some sources say the name honors Otterbein Brown, an early settler, and other sources say the name is for William Otterbein Brown, the first postmaster. Possibly they are the same person or from the same family.

Otter Creek (Vigo). See Markles.

Otter Creek Junction [ah-der kreek JUHNK-shuhn] (Vigo). This flag station established at a railroad crossing was named for the nearby stream of the same name.

Otter Village [ah-der VIL-ij] (Ripley). This village, named for nearby Otter Creek, was platted on January 3, 1837. A post office established as Mount Corbin, with John Corbin as postmaster, was established on October 5, 1837; changed to Otter Village on November 14, 1838; moved to Poston (cf. Dabney) on December 2, 1856.

Otterville (Vigo). See Burnett.

Otto [AH-to] (Clark). A post office called Otto, for Judge Otto, was established in this county on March 12, 1864; closed on August 15, 1950. This village is called Old Otto to distinguish it from New Otto, which is located about a half mile from here.

Otwell [AHT-wel] (Pike). This village was laid out on January 15, 1855, and until 1864 was called Pierceville for President Franklin Pierce (1853–1857). A post office established as White Oak Grove on July 11, 1844, was changed to Otwell on March 23, 1864.* The present name is for Robert Otwell Brown, son of Dr. Perry Brown, who laid out the village. A variant spelling is Ottwell.

Outlet (Lake). See Lowell (Lake).

Ovid (Madison). See New Columbus.

Owasco [o-WAHS-ko] (Carroll). A post office was established on November 5, 1883, and the village was laid out in 1884. The name, borrowed from the lake in New York, is Iroquois and means "floating bridge."

Owen [O-uhn] (Clark). A post office called Owen was established on April 25, 1878; closed on October 13, 1933.* The name is for Owen Township, which was named for John Owen, a county commissioner. The village was laid out in 1830 as Herculaneum, apparently for the ancient city in southern Italy.

Owen County [O-uhn]. This county, nicknamed "Sweet Owen," was established in 1818 and named for Abraham Owen, an officer from Kentucky who was killed in the Battle of Tippecanoe. Seat: Spencer.

Owensburg [O-uhnz-berg] (Greene). This village was platted on March 10, 1848 (WPA), and named for the local Owens family. Silbern Owens opened a blacksmith shop here in 1842. A post office established as Oak Ridge on May 15, 1844, was changed to Owensburgh on May 1, 1851.

Owensville [O-uhnz-vil] (Gibson). This town was laid out on February 18, 1817, by Philip Briscoe, a Kentuckian, and named for Thomas Owen, famous Kentuckian. A post office, with Briscoe as postmaster, was established on April 25, 1818.

Owl Prairie (Daviess). See Elnora.

Owl Town (Daviess). See Elnora.

Oxford [AHKS-ferd] (Benton). This town was laid out in 1843 as the county seat. A post office was established on December 6, 1844. The settlement originally was called Milroy, for a local commissioner, then Hartford, for the city in Connecticut. Since there already was a Hartford as well as a Milroy in Indi-ana, Judge David J. McConnell, who settled here in 1834 and became the first postmaster, suggested the name Oxford, hoping that it might become an educational center. One local folk explanation says that Pine Creek was crossed at a ford here by wagons drawn by oxen. Another story says that Judge McConnell drained bogs here with a team of oxen. In one spot he put straw in the bog for better footing for the oxen, and the place became known as Oxford. Oxford is a popular American place name coming from the English town and university, and the original Oxford apparently was named for a ford used by oxen. Some locate the original English ford near Folly Bridge.

Oxonia (Washington). See Hitchcock.

 **P**

Packard (La Porte). See Otis.

Packerton [PAK-er-tuhn] (Kosciusko). A post office was established on December 31, 1881; closed on March 30, 1926. The village was laid about 1882 by John C. Packer and named for him. Packertown is a variant spelling.

Page [payj] (Steuben). A post office was established here on August 21, 1897; closed on October 31, 1903.

Paisley (Lake). See Cedar Lake.

Palestine [PAL-uhs-teyen] (Franklin). This village was laid out by Paul Holliday in October 1847 and called Palestine for the biblical region. The post office—established on February 21, 1848; closed on April 2, 1906*—was called Wynn, for John Wynn, local surveyor and justice of the peace.

Palestine (Hancock). See New Palestine.

Palestine [PAL-uhs-teyen] (Kosciusko). A nearby post office called Tipicanunk, a form of Tippecanoe, established on January 6, 1838, in the house of postmaster James Wooden, was moved to Palestine on March 14, 1839, with Isham Summey as postmaster. Summey platted the lakeside village in 1837. The name is for the biblical region.

Palestine (Posey). See Poseyville.

Palmer [PAH-mer; PAHL-mer] (Lake). This village, formerly called Palmer Station, established as a railroad station in 1881 and platted in 1882, was named for local farmer and founder Dennis Palmer, who entered the township in 1854 and purchased land at this site in 1866. A post office was established on May 22, 1882; closed on March 30, 1935.*

Palmyra [pal-MEYE-ruh] (Harrison). This town was founded in 1810 by Hayes McCallen and called McCallens Cross Roads for his family. In 1836 the town was laid out and called Carthage. In 1839 lots were added, and the name was changed to Palmyra. A post office called McCallens Cross Roads, with Hayes McCallen as postmaster, was established on October 27, 1823; changed to Palmyra on June 23, 1838.* The present name probably is for the ancient city allegedly built by Solomon.

Palmyra (Wayne). See Dalton.

Paoli [pay-O-luh; pay-O-lee] (county seat, Orange). This town was platted in 1816 and named for either Pasquale Paoli (1725–1807), a Corsican patriot and general, perhaps via Paoli, Pennsylvania, or Pasquale Paoli Ashe, son of Samuel Ashe, governor of North Carolina and friend of Pasquale Paoli. According to one local legend, the name comes from a Swede named Oley who operated a toll road. People traveling along the road had to "pay Oley." A post office was established on September 15, 1822.

Paradise [PEHR-uh-deyes] (Warrick). According to the WPA files, this settlement was called Paradise because it was thought to be a good location for a mining town. A post office was established on March 2, 1891; closed on July 31, 1902.

Paragon [PEHR-uh-gahn] (Morgan). This town was platted on April 18, 1851, around the time J. D. Newton opened a store here. The name, suggesting a model of perfection, probably is commendatory. According to a local tradition, an early settler viewing the town site from a hill declared that the small settlement already established in a valley was a paragon. A post office was established on February 10, 1868.*

Paris [PEHR-uhs] (Jennings). This village, near the Jennings-Jefferson county line, was laid out in 1829, though it was settled around 1810. A post office called Paris was established in Jefferson County on January 22, 1820; changed to Jennings County on July 7, 1841; closed on June 30, 1908. Apparently the name was chosen by French Huguenot settlers for the French city.

Paris (Lawrence). See Bryantsville.

Paris (Posey). See Stewartsville.

Paris Crossing [PEHR-uhs KRAWS-ing] (Jennings). This village was established in the 1850s along the railroad about a mile northwest of Paris, for which it was named. A post office was established on January 17, 1876.

Parisville (Pulaski). See Thornhope.

Park [pahrk] (Greene). Originally this village was called Parker, for the local Parker family, early settlers here. A post office called Park was established on May 16, 1866; closed on March 15, 1908.

Park (Parke). See Rockville.

Parke County [pahrk]. This county, famous for its covered bridges and festivals, was organized in 1821 and named for Benjamin Parke, territorial congressman and judge, who served as the first president of the Indiana Historical Society. Seat: Rockville.

Parker City [PAHRK-er SID-ee] (Randolph). This town was platted on November 15, 1851, and formerly called Morristown, probably for a local family (WPA). An early settler was Thomas W. Parker, and the present name perhaps honors him or his family. A post office called Parker was established on September 19, 1853.

Parkersburg [PAHRK-erz-berg] (Montgomery). This village, located near the Montgomery-Putnam county line, was laid out first in 1829 by Jacob and Christoper Shuck and called Somerset. A post office established in Putnam County as Swanksville on June 8, 1829, with Nathaniel Parker as postmaster, was changed to Parkersburgh, for the local Parker family, and to Montgomery County on February 27, 1835. The post office was changed to Faithsville, for a local family, on January 28, 1837; back to Parkersburgh on July 21, 1837; and closed on July 31, 1903.*

Parkers Settlement [pahrk-erz SET-uhl-muhnt] (Posey). A post office was established here on November 17, 1851; closed on July 14, 1902. A variant name is Poskers Settlement.

Parkeville [PAHRK-vil] (Parke). This village, named for the county, was laid out on October 4, 1837, by Presley Doggett. A post office called Parkville was established on December 10, 1852; closed on May 31, 1902.* Other variant names and spellings of this village have

been Buncombe, Park Ville, Park Village, Payton Place, and Pin Hook.

Parkinson (Wells). See Kingsland.

Park View Heights [pahrk vyoo HEYETS] (Miami). This subdivision was established on August 1, 1955, on the Jean B. Richardville Reserve No. 5 by Clyde E. Williams Associates. The name is commendatory, though probably influenced by its location east of Maconaquah Park.

Parr [pahr] (Jasper). A post office was established on November 14, 1893; closed on December 27, 1968. The village was platted on April 19, 1895. The name is for Judge Simon Parr Thompson or, according to the WPA files, Judge Simon Parr Kenton, who donated land for a railroad depot and switch here.

Parrottsville (Tipton). See Jacksons.

Patoka [puh-TO-kuh] (Gibson). This town, the oldest in the county, was settled in 1789 by John Severns and platted in October 1813. A post office was established on April 4, 1833. The name is for the Patoka River. *Patoka* is a word used by the Miami people to refer to the Comanche people, who often were held as slaves by the Illinois and Miamis. In French chronicles the Comanches are called Padocquia or Padouca. According to local legend, *Patoka* means "log on the bottom" and was applied to the stream because there were a lot of logs stuck in the mud on the river's bottom. Former names of the town were, depending on the source, Smithville or Smithfield, for John Smith, an early settler, and Columbia, for Christopher Columbus.

Patricksburg [PAT-riks-berg] (Owen). This village—first called Lancaster for

Lancaster, Pennsylvania, former home of the wife of the cofounder, Dr. R. B. McAlister—was laid out in 1851 by Patrick Sullivan and McAlister. A post office was established as Patricksburgh, for Patrick Sullivan, on May 6, 1854. On August 18, 1893, the spelling was changed to Patricksburg.

Patriot [PAY-tree-uht] (Switzerland). This town was laid out in 1820 and named Troy, for Troy, New York. A post office named Patriot was established on March 15, 1827. Supposedly, the present inspirational name is for the patriotism of the people living here. One local legend says the name comes from "the Patriots," veterans of the Revolution who settled here, while another account says that when the name was changed from Troy, town leaders wanted to rename the town Washington for the greatest patriot, but since there already were several towns with that name in Indiana, they settled for Patriot.

Patronville [PAY-truhn-vil] (Spencer). A post office was established here on July 21, 1875; closed on December 31, 1904.

Patton [PAT-uhn] (Carroll). A post office was established on May 7, 1880; closed on November 15, 1913. The village was laid out on October 23, 1883, by H. Patton, for whom the village was named.

Pattonville [PAT-uhn-vil] (Lawrence). This village, named for the local Patton family, was platted on March 10, 1891, by Enoch Patton. A variant name is Patton Hill.

Paul Town (Shelby). See Saint Paul.

Paxton [PAKS-tuhn] (Sullivan). A post office was established here on May 26, 1864, and the village was platted in 1868 by W. P. Walter. The name, first applied to a nearby railroad station, honors Dr. James H. Paxton, an early merchant and physician of Carlisle.

Paynesville [PAYNZ-vil] (Jefferson). This village was named for Miller Payne, an early settler.

Payton Place (Parke). See Parkeville.

Peabody [PEE-bah-dee] (Whitley). A post office, named for local businessman James Peabody, was established on January 16, 1883; closed on December 15, 1923.

Pearsonville (Marshall). See Inwood.

Pecksburg [PEKS-berg] (Hendricks). A post office was established on October 7, 1852; closed on November 15, 1913.* The village was platted in 1853. The name is for the first president of the Vandalia Railroad.

Peerless [PEER-lus] (Lawrence). This village was platted on November 13, 1891, by John Williams and named for the local Peerless quarry. A post office was established on June 8, 1894; closed on May 31, 1932.

Pekin [PEE-kin] (Washington). The original village of Pekin, apparently named for the city in China romanized as Peking, was laid out on Mutton Fork of Blue River on November 15, 1831. When the railroad was completed across the river, a station was built there, and Pekin lost population. This village is sometimes called Old Pekin to distinguish it from New Pekin, q.v., where the Pekin post office is located.

Pekin Station (Washington). See New Pekin.

Pelzer [PEL-zer] (Warrick). A post office was located here on March 31, 1898; closed on December 15, 1900. The village was named for the local Pelzer family.

Pembroke [PEM-brok] (Newton). This village may have been named for the Welsh county or town via an eastern state.

Pence [pents] (Warren). This village was founded around 1902 by Frank R. Pence and named for the Pence family. A post office was established on October 12, 1903; closed on April 5, 1957.

Penceville (Clinton). See Kilmore.

Pendleton [PEN-duhl-tuhn; PEN-uhl-tuhn] (Madison). A post office established as Madison, for the county, in 1802 was changed to Pendleton on October 31, 1826. The name is for the local Pendleton family. Thomas Pendleton settled here in 1823 and platted the town in January 1830.

Penntown [PEN-town] (Ripley). This village was laid out on August 16, 1837, and originally called Pennsylvaniaburg, as most of the settlers were from Pennsylvania. The present name is an abbreviated form of the earlier name. A post office established at nearby Sunman on September 27, 1833, was moved here and called Hermann on April 27, 1849. The Hermann post office was closed on January 19, 1883.

Pennville [PEN-vil] (Jay). This town was laid out on August 27, 1836, by Samuel Grisell. Originally it was called New Lisbon, but in August 1837, Grisell changed the name to Camden. Since there already was a post office called Camden in Carroll County, the name was changed to Penn, for Penn Township, which was named by Samuel Grisell for William Penn and in honor of Quakers who settled here. A post office called Penn was established on January 19, 1839. Since Penn often was confused with Peru, the name, supposedly at the suggestion of the Post Office Department, was changed to Pennville on March 10, 1848.

Pennville [PEN-vil] (Wayne). This village may have been named for the Penn Central Railroad near here.

Pennyville [PEN-ee-vil] (Daviess). According to the WPA files, this village was named "by a Bierhaus salesman. They called him 'the penny drummer,' so he said he would name the town after himself and gave it the name of Pennyville."

Peoga [pee-O-guh] (Brown). A post office established on June 21, 1898, closed on March 31, 1903.* The origin of the name is uncertain, but some villagers have claimed that Peoga is a Native American word for "village" (WPA). According to a local legend, the name comes from a holler, "Pe-o-ga," that a Brown County farmer used every morning to call his hogs (WPA).

Peoria [pee-AWR-ee-uh] (Franklin). A post office was established on December 6, 1850; closed on January 2, 1907.* An alternate name of this village has been Ingleside, for Ingleside Institute, an academy once located here. Peoria is from the name of a subtribe of the Illinois tribe, first applied to the city in Illinois.

Peoria [pee-AWR-ee-uh] (Miami). This village was platted on October 16, 1849, by Isaac Litzenbarger. According to local legend, settlers passed through here on the way to Peoria, Illinois, and were so pleased with the locale that they stayed and named the place for their destination (WPA). The post office was called the Reserve Post Office, for Ozahshinquah's reservation, which was located just north of the village. The post office was established on December 7, 1843; closed on January 15, 1910.*

Peppertown [PEP-er-town] (Franklin). A post office, with August Pepper as postmaster, was established on May 14, 1857; closed on August 15, 1910. The village was laid out by Fielding Berry in August 1859 for the proprietor, John Koerner. August Pepper, for whom the village was named, came here from Germany around 1851. Pepertown is a variant spelling.

Perkins Store (Daviess). See Odon.

Perkinsville [PER-kuhnz-vil] (Madison). This village was laid out on August 1, 1837, and named for William Parkins, who settled here in 1825; however, when the plat was recorded an error was made, and the name became Perkinsville. A post office was established on March 9, 1844; closed on August 31, 1912.*

Perry (Allen). See Huntertown.

Perry County [PEHR-ee]. This county, with 56,000 acres of the Hoosier National Forest within its boundaries, was organized in 1814 and named for Commodore Oliver Hazard Perry, who defeated the British in the Battle of Lake Erie in 1813. Seat: Tell City.

Perrysburg [PEHR-eez-berg] (Miami). This village was platted on June 13, 1837, by Matthew Fenimore and John R. Wilkinson and, according to the WPA files, presumably named for a resident or friend of the founders, though possibly the name is for Perrysburg, Ohio. A post office was established on January 26, 1838; closed on February 15, 1907.

Perrysville [PEHR-eez-vil] (Vermillion). This town was laid out by James Blair in 1826 and named for Commodore O. H. Perry by Blair, who served under Perry in the War of 1812. Major Blair, allegedly a sharpshooter on Lake Erie during the War of 1812, settled here in 1818 or 1819. A post office, with Blair as postmaster, was established on October 3, 1827.

Perryville [PEHR-ee-vil] (Adams). This crossroads settlement first was called Glendenning Corners for the Glendenning family, who came here and started a store in the 1840s. The current name comes from Perry Glendenning, the owner of the store.

Pershing [PER-shing] (Fulton). A village named Germany sprang up after the railroad passed through here in 1882. During World War I, the name was changed to Pershing for General J. J. Pershing. A variant patriotic name is Loyal.

Pershing (Wayne). See East Germantown.

Perth [perth] (Clay). This village was laid out on November 1, 1870, by Michael McMillan and named for Perth, Scotland, birthplace of his ancestors. The village, initially inhabited mainly by miners working in the Iron Mountain mine, was built along the railroad as a shipping point for coal. A post office was established on March 24, 1880; closed on January 31, 1929.

Peru [PEE-roo; pu-ROO] (county seat, Miami). A post office named McGregor, with John McGregor as postmaster, was established on January 29, 1829; changed to Miamisport on March 31, 1829; changed to Peru on March 6, 1835. A trading post named Miamisport, for the Miami Reserve and nation, was laid out on the north bank of the Wabash River by Joseph Holman on March 12, 1829, though the plat was not recorded until July 15, 1830. Peru was laid out as the county seat in 1834 by Jesse L. Williams, Richard L. Britton, and William H. Hood on land adjacent to Miamisport that Hood had purchased from Holman. The name probably is for the country in South America, via Peru, New York, home of early settlers, though it is also said to be a Miami word meaning "a straight place in the river." Miamisport has been a part of Peru since June 9, 1841. Once famous as the winter home of several circuses, Peru is nicknamed Circus City. Songwriter Cole Porter (1891–1964) was born here.

Petersburg (Clark). See Speed.

Petersburg [PEE-terz-burg] (county seat, Pike). Settled in 1813, this city was laid out on April 3, 1817, and named for Peter Brenton, an early settler, carding mill owner, and principal donor of land. A post office was established on April 21, 1823.*

Peterson [PEE-der-suhn] (Adams). This village was founded in the 1870s and named for Smith Peterson, a lawyer from nearby Decatur, who obtained the right-of-way through the county for the Cloverleaf Lines Railroad Company in 1878. A post office was established on February 2, 1848; closed on January 31, 1940.

Peters Switch [pee-terz SWICH] (Jackson). This community, established near the Pennsylvania Railroad, was named for the Peters family, who owned land here.

Petersville [PEE-terz-vil] (Bartholomew). This village, according to the WPA

files, was named for Peter S. Blessing, who laid out the town in 1874, although an oral account says the name honors Peter B. Glick (ISUFA). Both Blessing and Glick are local family names, and Peter S. Blessing was the second postmaster. A post office was established on June 2, 1873; closed on December 15, 1900.

Petroleum [puh-TROL-yuhm] (Wells). This village was laid out in June 1894 in the midst of an oil field, for which it was named. A post office was established on January 22, 1894.

Pettit [PET-uht] (Tippecanoe). A post office was established on February 18, 1854; closed on July 15, 1902.* The name honors the local Pettit family, early settlers. Judge John Pettit was a Lafayette lawyer and congressional representative from this area.

Pettysville [PET-eez-vil] (Miami). This village, named for the local Petty family, was platted in 1872 by Daniel Petty, who opened a store when the railroad was completed through here. A post office, with Daniel Petty as postmaster, was established on January 13, 1875; closed on August 31, 1917. Other members of the Petty family also served as postmaster.

Phelps (Allen). See Woodburn.

Phenix [FEE-niks] (Wells). A post office was established on May 16, 1889; closed on July 15, 1904. Phenix, a variant spelling of Phoenix, is for the mythological bird. The name has been fairly popular in the United States, so possibly it was borrowed from another state.

Philadelphia [fil-uh-DEL-fee-uh] (Hancock). This village was laid out on April 11, 1838, by Charles Atherton and named for Philadelphia, Pennsylvania. A post office was established on June 1, 1838; closed on January 2, 1907.

Philadelphia (Washington). See New Philadelphia.

Philanthropy (Franklin). See Scipio (Franklin).

Phillips (Delaware). See Medford.

Philomath [feye-LO-muhth] (Union). On September 29, 1832, Jonathan Kidwell and Joseph Adams announced in a Cincinnati newspaper that they had purchased this site, then called Bethleham, and had renamed it Philomath, Greek for "lover of learning." They platted the village on June 29, 1833. The name reflects the founders' aspirations, as Western Union Seminary was established here in 1833. Kidwell and S. Tizzard published a Universalist paper, the *Sentinel and Star in the West*, which became the *Star and Covenant*; and Kidwell edited the *Philomath Encyclopedia*. A post office, with Jonathan Kidwell as postmaster, was established on May 27, 1837; closed on January 2, 1907.*

Philpotts Mills (Fayette). See Longwood Crossing.

Phlox [flahks] (Howard). This village, apparently named for the flower, was established by Quakers around 1847. A post office was established on July 24, 1890; closed on August 30, 1902.*

Phoebe Forts Corner (Hancock). See Fortville.

Piattsville [PEYE-uhts-vil] (Parke). This village was known for a short time as Van Ness Town, for a local family. Piatt also was a local family name. A post office called Piattsville was estab-lished on February 29, 1856; closed on August 8, 1862.

Pickard [PIK-erd] (Clinton). This village, formerly called Pickards Mills, was laid out by James Ward in 1844 and named for the local Pickard family. Jacob Pickard came here in 1839, built a sawmill and gristmill, and later opened a general store. A post office called Pickards Mills was established on December 7, 1860, in Tipton County; changed to Clinton County on April 3, 1873; changed to Pickard on July 24, 1895; closed on May 31, 1906. According to an oral account, "There's a little town of Pickard just about 35 miles straight north of Indianapolis whose nickname is Tailholt, and I've been told through the years the way that the town of Tailholt got its name was back in years past it was prairie land and very marshy. And when they used to drive the hogs to Indianapolis, the farmers always rode their horses, and when they got to Tailholt, because of the marshy conditions, it was easier to grab the pigs by the tail and drag them through than try to drive through because they just wanted to stop and wallow in the mud. So that's how the name of Pickard became Tailholt, known by this name to this day. We realize that James Whitcomb Riley immortalized the little town of Tailholt in a poem many years ago. According to the founder of the town, he spent several days in their home just prior to composing the poem of 'The Little Town of Tailholt'" (ISUFA).

Pierceton [PEERS-tuhn] (Kosciusko). This town was laid out on December 6, 1852, by Lewis Keith and John B. Chapman and named for President Franklin Pierce. A post office office established on July 19, 1850, as Deeds Creek was changed to Princeton on November 11, 1853, and to Pierceton on November 17,

1853. Pierceton Junction is a variant name.

Pierceville (Pike). See Otwell.

Pierceville [PEERS-vil] (Ripley). A post office named for the local Pierce family was established on April 14, 1854; closed on January 31, 1936. The village was laid out on May 11, 1860, by J. C. Kennedy.

Pierre (Starke). See San Pierre.

Pie Town (Crawford). See Alton.

Pigeon [PIJ-uhn] (Spencer). A post office named for Little Pigeon Creek was established on February 13, 1883; closed on May 15, 1920. According to a local tradition, "Pigeon Creek [the stream] got its name because it has so many branches that it resembles a pigeon foot" (ISUFA).

Pigeon Roost Station [PIJ-uhn roost STAY-shuhn] (Scott). A post office called Pigeon Roost was established on March 20, 1857; closed on July 12, 1862. The community supposedly was so named because for many years wild pigeons roosted on nearby Pigeon Roost Creek. It seems likely that the village was named for the stream and the stream named "from the abundance of wild pigeons which came here to roost especially in the fall and winter season. . . ." The village "was called Pigeon because the railroad built a sidetrack at that place [near Pigeon Roost Creek] to load the lumber from the sawmills along the creek. The track was called Pigeon Switch by the employees of the railroad" (WPA).

Pike [peyek] (Boone). A post office established as Pikes Crossing on September 18, 1885, was changed to Pike on

March 13, 1895; closed on December 14, 1900.*

Pike County [peyek]. This county was formed on December 21, 1816, officially organized on February 1, 1817, and named for General Zebulon Montgomery Pike, who was killed in 1813 while commanding the attack on York, Canada. This was the first county organized after Indiana became a state. Seat: Petersburg.

Pikes Peak [peyeks peek] (Brown). A post office was established on August 18, 1868; closed on June 29, 1907.* According to local legend, an early settler, James Ward, founder of the village, hearing of the California gold rush, set out in a prairie schooner that carried the sign "Pikes Peak or Bust." When he arrived at Madison, however, he became homesick, so he purchased enough supplies to open a store and returned to Brown County. When his customers visited his store, they would say, "Guess I'll go over to Pikes Peak for supplies," and the settlement became known as Pikes Peak (WPA).

Pikeville [PEYEK-vil] (Pike). This village was laid out on September 18, 1859, and named for Pike County. A post office was established on September 13, 1867; closed on December 31, 1938.

Pilot Knob [PEYE-luht NAHB] (Crawford). A post office was established on September 9, 1850; closed on March 31, 1955.* The name comes from a nearby summit also called Pilot Knob, which supposedly was an island in a Paleozoic sea.

Pimento [peye-MENT-o] (Vigo). This village was laid out in 1852 by Israel French on land owned by him. A post office was established on March 30, 1855, with Thomas French, who established the first store here, as postmaster. The village formerly was called Hartford, but it was renamed by the Post Office Department because there already was a post office called Hartford in Ohio County. Apparently the name comes from the sweet pepper, usually spelled "pimiento." According to an oral account, "Pimento, Indiana, was founded in the early part of the 19th century. It was called Hartford until about 1872. The post office changed the name to Pimento because it kept mixing up the Hartford mail with the Hartford City mail" (ISUFA).

Pinch [pinch] (Randolph). This village was so named "because everybody was short of spondulix [cash]" (WPA).

Pine [peyen] (Lake). Now located within the Gary city limits, this community was named for pine trees on the original site (WPA).

Pine Lick (Clark). See Henryville.

Pine Station [PEYEN STAY-shuhn] (Saint Joseph). This village supposedly was named for the tree. Pine is a variant name.

Pine Village [PEYEN VIL-ij] (Warren). This town was platted in 1851 by Isaac and John R. Metsker, proprietors, and a post office was established on February 18, 1854. According to the WPA files, a local trading post first was called Pine Village, allegedly for a lone pine tree that stood on a creek bluff. The town is located on Big Pine Creek, though, and it is possible the name comes from the stream name.

Pinhook [PIN-huk] (La Porte). This village, first called New Durham for the township in which it is located, was settled around 1830 and platted on April 15, 1847. A post office called New Durham was established on May 10, 1842.* New Durham Township was named for Durham, Greene County, New York. The village was nicknamed Pinhook, probably for a jog in the main road here, which became the official name. According to the WPA files, "The old settlers' story of the origin of this nickname [Pinhook] is that a woman entered a store in the town and left with a package of pins, having failed to pay for them." Another account says citizens of a nearby rival town, Floods Grove, gave New Durham its nickname, and the citizens of New Durham retaliated by referring to Floods Grove as Squatham. Pinhook, sometimes spelled Pin Hook, has been a fairly popular place name in Indiana, as it also is found in Decatur, Franklin, Lawrence, Parke, and Wayne counties.

Pinhook [PIN-huk] (Lawrence). This village was settled first about 1818. A post office called Pin Hook was established on August 12, 1852; closed on January 14, 1904.* According to a local legend collected in the 1930s, the town "received its name through the sale of pins in an illegal manner. No person in the community had a permit to sell whiskey by the drink. But in order to evade the law, one of the early merchants of the little community is said to have hit upon the idea of selling a customer a bent pin to use for a fishhook and giving him a drink of whiskey as a premium. Hence the name Pinhook" (WPA). Two other oral accounts collected more recently also suggest that the name comes from the illegal sale of liquor:

1. "My roommate's grandparents live in Pinhook, Indiana. Her grandparents told me this story. During the 1800s in Lawrence County near Bedford, Indiana, there was an owner of a general store who did not have a liquor license. So what he would do is pour the customer a glass of liquor and take a woman's long old-fashioned hat pin, bend it, and hook it over the shot glass. The customer was not buying the drink but the pin that was hooked over the glass, so he could not be arrested for selling liquor because he was selling the pin and giving the drink away. So whenever anyone said 'Let's go to Pinhook,' one knew they were going to get some booze. Eventually the area around the general store came to be known as Pinhook, and it is on the map today" (ISUFA).

2. "Pinhook was thought to be named because people not wanting to be charged with illegal sale of liquor purchased a quantity of pins. A customer would purchase a pin for an exaggerated price, and the seller would throw in a bottle of moonshine for good measure" (ISUFA).

Another anecdote says, "Pinhook's name is related to the making of fish hooks from pins in earlier days" (ISUFA), and a final oral account perhaps explains the name: "Pinhook, it was thought, was named from a peculiar twist in the road at the little village" (ISUFA).

Pin Hook (Parke). See Parkeville.

Pinola [pin-O-luh] (La Porte). This village supposedly was named for pine trees on the site of the settlement (WPA).

Pioneer [peye-uh-NEER] (Wabash). A post office called Pioneer was established on November 13, 1897; closed on January 11, 1905. The postmaster was Isaac Conrad, and he and his wife named the post office in commemoration of the pioneers. From April 7, 1879, to August 14, 1897,* the Pucker Brush post office was located on the site of the present village of Pioneer.

Pipe Creek (Madison). See Frankton.

Pittsboro [PITS-ber-o] (Hendricks). This town was settled around 1830 and laid out in 1834 by Simon T. Hadley and William L. Matlock. Hadley originally called the town Pittsburg, but the post office established on February 9, 1849, was called Pittsborough, apparently because there already was a post office called Pittsburg in Carroll County. The spelling of the post office name was changed to Pittsboro on June 2, 1893.

Pittsburg [PITS-berg] (Carroll). This village was laid out in 1836 by Merkle, Kendall, and Company and probably named for Pittsburgh, Pennsylvania. A post office was established on February 1, 1838; closed on May 15, 1915.* A variant spelling is Pittsburgh.

Pittsburg (Sullivan). See Hymera.

Pittsburgh (Orange). See Fargo.

Plainfield [PLAYN-feeld] (Hendricks). A post office was established on September 5, 1835, and the town was laid out by Elias Hadley and Levi Jessup in 1839. The settlement was named by Quakers, "the plain people," so apparently the name is commendatory.

Plainfield [PLAYN-feeld] (Saint Joseph). This village was laid out on December 23, 1833. The name may have been selected for its commendatory value.

Plainville [PLAYN-vil] (Daviess). Formerly called Stump Town because the timber had been cut and only stumps remained here (WPA), this town was laid out in December 1855. Allegedly it received its present name for the level terrain of the site (WPA). A post office was established on August 11, 1860.*

Plank (Carroll). See Bringhurst.

Plano [PLAY-no] (Morgan). A post office was established on June 21, 1889; closed on September 15, 1904.* The name is Spanish for "plain" or "level" and presumably is a transfer from a western state.

Plato [PLAY-to] (Lagrange). A post office, apparently named for the ancient Greek philosopher, was established on January 18, 1890; closed on October 15, 1901.*

Plattsburg [PLATS-berg] (Washington). This village was platted by Perry Baley on September 19, 1837. A post office established on September 10, 1834, as Walnut Ridge, for a ridge of the same name on which black walnut trees grew, was changed to Plattsburgh on December 30, 1844, back to Walnut Ridge on February 7, 1845, and closed on February 7, 1857. The name may be a transfer from New York or Ohio.

Pleasant [PLEZ-uhnt] (Switzerland). This village, named for the township in which it is located, was settled in 1817, but it was never platted. A post office was established on February 27, 1829; closed on December 15, 1917.

Pleasant Gardens [PLEZ-uhnt GAHR-duhnz] (Putnam). This village was laid on the National Road in 1830 by John Matkins. Pleasant Garden is a variant spelling.

Pleasant Grove (Fulton). See Kewanna.

Pleasant Grove (Jasper). See Moody.

Pleasant Hill (Delaware). See Oakville.

Pleasant Hill (Montgomery). See Wingate.

Pleasant Lake [plez-uhnt LAYK] (Steuben). A post office was established on June 2, 1851.* The village was first laid out in February 1846 and was platted again by William Thompson and Sheldon Ball in November 1870. The name is for a nearby lake of the same name. The subjectively descriptive name of the lake supposedly comes from a Native American name, Nipcondish, "Pleasant Waters" (WPA).

Pleasant Mills [plez-uhnt MILZ] (Adams). This village was platted in 1846 by E. A. Goddard and George Heath, proprietors. Although the first settlers called the settlement Mollicay, the official name became Pleasant Mills because the only gristmill in the area was located here. Pleasant is subjectively descriptive of the "pleasant surroundings near the mill" (WPA). A post office established as Darby on October 7, 1847, was changed to Pleasant Mills on January 14, 1850.

Pleasant Plain [plez-uhnt PLAYN] (Huntington). This village was laid out in 1875 as Nixville by Levin Wright, Mark R. Wright, Eli J. Scott, Samuel Satterthwaite, and others; however, the post office established on April 16, 1875, was named Pleasant Plain, which soon became the name of the village. The post office closed on February 28, 1905. The name is subjectively descriptive: "Old settlers say that the name was adopted because of the beautiful location of the place" (WPA).

Pleasant Ridge [plez-uhnt RIJ] (Greene). A post office was established on August 19, 1843; closed on August 31, 1877.*

Pleasant Ridge [plez-uhnt RIJ] (Jasper). A post office was established on April 1, 1878; closed on August 15, 1923. The settlement, dating from around 1870, supposedly was named for the pleasant view and ridges here (WPA).

Pleasant Ridge [plez-uhnt RIJ] (Jay). According to the WPA files, this village was named for the pleasant view and its location on a watershed divide.

Pleasant Valley [plez-uhnt VAL-ee] (Martin). This village was platted in 1850, and a post office was established on January 8, 1850; closed on January 29, 1859.* The name is subjectively descriptive.

Pleasant Valley (Owen). See Adel.

Pleasant View [plez-uhnt VYOO] (Shelby). This village began as a trading post in 1835, when Frederick Thatcher moved here and established a small store. It was platted by Alexander Means on July 6, 1836. A post office called Wrights, with Jordan Wright as postmaster, was established on April 8, 1828; changed to Doblestown, with William A. Doble as postmaster, on October 3, 1837; changed to Pleasant View on August 23, 1841; closed on July 12, 1859.

Pleasantville (Howard). See Plevna.

Pleasantville (Pike). See Spurgeon.

Pleasantville [PLEZ-uhnt-vil] (Sullivan). Earlier called Needmore (WPA), this village was platted in 1864 by Pleasant O'Haver and named for him. A post office was established on June 19, 1865; closed on December 4, 1964. Pleasant O'Haver became the second postmaster on June 4, 1867, and served until June 5, 1871.

Plevna [PLEV-nuh] (Howard). Originally this village was called Pleasantville, then Pomeroy, for a local politician. The post office established on April 7, 1879, was called Plevna, probably for the Bulgarian city of the same name. The post office closed on December 31, 1902.

Plummer [PLUHM-er] (Greene). A post office was established on January 10, 1889; closed on February 28, 1921. The name is for the local Plummer family. Thomas Plummer was an early resident of this county and a member of the first board of county commissioners. A small stream, Plummers Creek, and a township in this county were named for Thomas Plummer.

Plum Orchard (Fayette). See Bentonville.

Plum Tree [PLUHM tree] (Huntington). This unplatted village once was called Yankee Town. A post office called Plum Tree was established on August 2, 1876; changed to Plumtree on October 30, 1893; closed on August 31, 1904. The name supposedly comes from a large wild plum tree on the site of the settlement (WPA).

Plymouth [PLIM-uhth] (county seat, Marshall). This city was platted on October 20, 1834, and apparently named for Plymouth, Massachusetts. A post office was established on October 17, 1836.*

Poe [po] (Allen). A post office called Po, perhaps simply the abbreviation for post office, was established on December 20, 1856, with William Essig as postmaster. Essig platted the village in 1874 (or in 1848, according to the WPA files) and named it Williamsport for himself. On June 6, 1881, the post office name was changed to Poe, and on October 31, 1916, the post office was closed.

Point Commerce [poynt KAH-mers] (Greene). This village was laid out by the Allison brothers of Spencer in April 1836. They named it Point Commerce because two proposed canals, one on the Wabash and one on White River, were supposed to join here, and they thought this village would develop into a commercial center. A post office was established on April 1, 1837; closed on October 15, 1869.*

Point Isabel [POYNT IZ-uh-bel] (Grant). This village was never laid out. According to the WPA files, it was named for an Ohio town; however, the name appears to be uniquely Hoosier. A post office was established on February 11, 1859; closed on March 31, 1911.

Poke Patch (Warrick). See Selvin.

Poland [PO-luhnd] (Clay). This village was founded in 1841 as a trading point and named for James Alexander Poland, the settlement's first blacksmith. A post office was established on January 20, 1846. John B. Nees, William Crafton, Isaac Anderson, and Tillman Chance owned land on which the village was established.

Poling [PO-ling] (Jay). Formerly called Polingtown, this village was named for a local family. A post office called Poling was established on October 24, 1887; closed on June 15, 1907.* On December 22, 1888, William Poling was appointed postmaster.

Pollytown (Randolph). See South Salem.

Polk Patch (Warrick). See Selvin.

Polsonton (Dubois). See Dubois.

Pomeroy (Howard). See Plevna.

Pond Creek Mills [pawnd kreek MILZ] (Knox). A post office named Pond Creek Mills, for Pond Creek, was established on June 21, 1851; changed to Pondcreek on March 28, 1894.*

Pond Grove (Tippecanoe). See Otterbein.

Poneto [puh-NET-o] (Wells). This town was platted on September 4, 1871, and formerly called Worthington for a railroad superintendent. Since there was another Hoosier town of that name, confusion resulted, and allegedly residents coined Poneto because it did not resemble the name of any other town in the United States, and apparently this is the only settlement in the United States with this name. A post office established as Worthington Crossing on October 19, 1870, was changed to Poneto on April 21, 1881.

Pontiac [PAHN-tee-ak] (Clay). This village, named for the Ottawa chief Pontiac (1720?–1769), located about a mile south of Carbon, was laid out in October 1871 as a speculative venture by Aaron Lovell, who thought it would become a railroad station.

Pony [PO-nee] (Jay). A post office named Pony, perhaps for Pony Run, was established here on June 26, 1886; closed on November 30, 1900.

Popcorn [PAHP-kawrn] (Lawrence). This village was settled before 1875 and named for a nearby stream, Popcorn Creek. A post office named Popcorn was established on February 11, 1891; closed on July 31, 1905. Only local legends explain this colorful name. One goes: "A family came to visit from Vincennes to a family in Perry Township. The two families were always arguing about who raised the best corn. The man from Vincennes said, 'Your corn is popcorn compared to what we grow.' That's how Popcorn got its name" (ISUFA).

Poplar Grove [PAHP-ler GROV] (Howard). This village was settled around 1847, and a post office was established on August 8, 1855; closed on July 29, 1896. The name is for a large grove of poplars on the site of the settlement (WPA).

Poplar Grove [PAHP-ler GROV] (Marion). A post office was established here on July 28, 1854; closed on March 26, 1855.

Portage [PAWRT-ij] (Porter). This city was named for Portage Township, which was named for Portage County, Ohio. A post office station was established on June 17, 1961.

Porter [PAWR-ter] (Porter). A town called Porter Station, for the county, was laid out on September 11, 1855. Henry Hageman founded another town a mile from Porter Station in 1872 and named it Hageman. After the railroad station was moved from Porter Station to Hageman in 1872, locally Porter Station was called Old Porter, and Hageman was called New Porter. A post office established as Porter Station on September 7, 1865, was changed to Porter on November 28, 1882, and closed on June 6, 1892. Another post office founded as Hageman on June 19, 1874, was changed to Porter on June 25, 1892, and closed on November 19, 1965.

Porter County [PAWR-ter]. This county was formed in 1835, organized in 1836, and named for Commodore David Porter, commander of the *Essex* in the War of 1812. Valparaiso University is located in this county. Seat: Valparaiso.

Porter Crossroads [pawr-ter KRAWS-rodz] (Porter). A post office called Porters Cross Roads was established on May 1, 1844; closed on August 19, 1873.*

Portersville [PAWR-terz-vil] (Dubois). This village was founded around 1818 as the first county seat and supposedly was named for a relative of one of the town proprietors, Arthur Harbison. A post office was established on November 9, 1821; closed on December 31, 1909.*

Portersville (Porter). See Valparaiso.

Portland (Fountain). See Fountain.

Portland (Hancock). See Cleveland.

Portland [PAWRT-luhnd] (county seat, Jay). This city was laid out on June 5, 1837, by Daniel W. McNeal and named for his hometown, Portland, Maine. A post office established as Jay on February 13, 1838, was changed to Portland on January 10, 1868.*

Portland (La Porte). See Rolling Prairie.

Portland Mills [PAWRT-luhn MILZ; PAWRT-luhnd MILZ] (Putnam). This village, located on the Parke-Putnam county line, was founded around 1821 and earlier was called Upper Raccoon, for Big Raccoon Creek, and Portland. Mills, apparently for a gristmill built here in 1825, was added to Portland to distinguish it from another post office named Portland in Fountain County. A post office called Portland Mills was established in Parke County on May 25, 1835; changed to Putnam County on September 11, 1837; changed back to Parke County on September 15, 1851; changed back to Putnam County on November 6, 1854; changed back to Parke County on January 25, 1875; changed back to Putnam County on December 7, 1888; closed on December 31, 1904.

Port Mitchell [pawrt MICH-uhl] (Noble). This village was laid out in May 1838 by Samuel Hanna and William F. Engle, proprietors. According to one source, it was named for a local miller or one of his family; however, according to another source, it was named for a "good looking canal engineer." Port Mich is a variant name.

Port Royal (Morgan). See Bluffs.

Posey County [PO-zee]. This county was organized in 1814 and named for General Thomas Posey, officer in the Revolution and governor of the Indiana Territory, 1813–1816. The state's southernmost point is in this county. Seat: Mount Vernon.

Poseyville [PO-zee-vil] (Posey). This town, formerly called Palestine, was laid out by Talbott Sharp and Elison Cole on February 18, 1840. A post office called Poseyville was established on February 10, 1843. The name is for Posey County.

Poskers Settlement (Posey). See Parkers Settlement.

Poste Ouabache (Knox). See Vincennes.

Post Miami (Allen). See Fort Wayne.

Poston (Ripley). See Dabney.

Post Saint Ange (Knox). See Vincennes.

Post Saint Vincent (Knox). See Vincennes.

Post Vincennes (Knox). See Vincennes.

Potters Station (Allen). See Ari.

Pottersville [PAHT-erz-vil] (Owen). This village was laid out in 1858 by William M. Kinnaman, Owen County surveyor.

Powers [POW-erz] (Jay). This village was platted on June 17, 1868, and named for Andrew Powers, Jr., who laid out the town. A post office was established on November 19, 1867; closed on October 10, 1935.*

Prairie City [PREHR-ee SID-ee] (Clay). This village was laid out in 1869 by Absalom B. Wheeler and so named because it borders on what was already known as Wheelers Prairie or Clay Prairie. A post office established as Prairie City on June 28, 1888, was changed to Prairie on June 10, 1895, and closed on January 31, 1902.

Prairie Creek [PREHR-ee kreek] (Vigo). A post office called Prairie Creek was established in Prairie Creek Township on September 7, 1822. The village was laid out on August 24, 1831, as Middletown. The present name ultimately is for Prairie Creek, a nearby stream. Although *prairie* frequently is a place-name generic, it has become a rather common place-name specific for streams in Indiana, for there are fifteen streams in Indiana called Prairie Creek and two streams called Prairie Run. As a stream name, *Prairie* generally is descriptive of the landscape through which the stream flows.

Prairie Ridge (White). See Brookston.

Prairieton [PREHR-ee-tuhn] (Vigo). This village was laid out on July 22, 1836, by Robert Hoggatt and formerly was called Hoggatts Store, as Moses Hoggatt and his son, Robert, owned a store here. The post office, established as Hoggatts on May 11, 1818, was changed to Prairieton on November 4, 1840. The present name is for the village's location on the Honey Creek prairie. According to an oral account, "Prairieton means Prairie Town. It was named this because of the rolling prairie on which the settlers built" (ISUFA).

Prairie West (Lake). See Saint John.

Prather [PRAY-ther] (Clark). A post office, named for the Prather family who owned a store here, was established on March 4, 1878; closed on October 14, 1933. David L. Prather was the fourth postmaster. Variant names are Gibson and Gibson Station.

Prattsburg [PRATS-berg] (Ripley). A post office, named for the local Pratt family, was established on August 16, 1849; closed on October 24, 1857. The Pratt family owned a sawmill, store, and saloon here. D. Pratt served as the second postmaster.

Preble [PREB-uhl] (Adams). A post office was established on June 4, 1883, and the village was platted in 1884 by Daniel Hoffman and David Werling, proprietors. The name is for Preble Township, which was organized in 1838.

Prescott [PRES-kaht; PRES-kuht] (Shelby). A post office called Prescott was established on March 8, 1860; closed on May 15, 1905. The town, a way station on the Jeffersonville, Madison, and Indianapolis Railroad, was laid out by S. L. Dorsey on June 29, 1867.

Priam (Blackford). See Trenton.

Prices Station (Posey). See Griffin.

Priceville (Huntington). See Banquo.

Princes Lakes [prints-uhz LAYKS] (Johnson). This community was named for four nearby reservoirs: Princes East Lake, Princes Northeast Lake, Princes North Lake, and Princes White Lake. Princes Lake is a variant spelling.

Princeton [PRINTS-tuhn] (county seat, Gibson). This city was platted first on March 28, 1814, and named for Captain William Prince, local attorney and judge, who became a representative in Congress. An Indiana Territory post office was established on March 3, 1816. According to one informant, a local schoolteacher, "Gibson County had become a separate unit of the Indiana Territory on 1813. Prior to 1813, it had been part of Knox County. On February 14, 1814, the Gib-son county Court of Common Pleas met, which resulted in locating the proposed county seat where the city of Princeton stands today. The court convened again on February 16, 1814, at the home of Henry Hopkins, which was located at what is now 608 South Main Street in Princeton. To select a name for the new town, the names of the county commissioners were placed in a hat. These names were William Prince, Robert Elliot, Abel Westfall, and William Polk. The name drawn out of the hat was that of Captain William Prince; therefore, the new town and county seat was called

'Prince Town,' which has evolved into Princeton" (ISUFA). The local tradition that Captain Prince's name was drawn out of a hat is a strong one, as the following text corroborates: "Steve just told me about how Princeton got its name. In class we were talking about how Edwin Arlington Robinson's parents drew his name from a hat at her weekly club meeting. He said that that's how Princeton got its name. They couldn't decide, so they just drew that out of a hat" (ISUFA).

Prince William [prints WIL-yuhm] (Carroll). A post office established as Xenia on July 20, 1835, was changed to Prince Williams on June 22, 1840; closed on June 9, 1881.*

Proctor (Martin). See Willow Valley.

Proctorsville (Crawford). See Marengo.

Progress [PRAH-gres] (Delaware). A post office was established on April 4, 1900; closed on January 15, 1901. The name is commendatory.

Prophets Town (Tippecanoe). See Battle Ground.

Prospect [PRAH-spekt] (Orange). This village was laid out by Nathan Pinnick on September 4, 1836, and called New Prospect, probably for its commendatory value. A post office called New Prospect was established on April 8, 1851; closed on October 17, 1853. The Lick Creek post office serving this area was established on February 13, 1872; closed on January 14, 1889. The post office name, Lick Creek, comes from the stream of the same name, which was named for French Lick, a spring on one of its branches.

Prosperity [prahs-PEHR-uh-tee] (Madison). A post office was established on December 2, 1853; closed on August 6, 1875.* During the canal boom, the village was founded by John Beal, who came to this area around 1838, and Hiram Louder.

Providence [PRAHV-uh-dents; PRAHV-uh-duhnts] (Johnson). This village was platted on October 31, 1837, and first called Union Village, as it is located in Union Township. A post office called Providence was established on June 17, 1880; closed on August 15, 1908.*

Prowsville [PROWZ-vil] (Washington). A post office, named for a local family, was established on February 27, 1855; closed on October 12, 1868. Christian Prow was the first postmaster.

Pucker (Grant). See Fairmount.

Pucker Brush (Wabash). See Pioneer.

Pueblo [PWEB-lo] (Spencer). A post office was established here on January 17, 1898; closed on September 15, 1906.

Pulaski [pu-LAS-keye] (Pulaski). A post office, named for the county in which it was located, was established on June 25, 1852; closed on October 31, 1927. The village was laid out in November 1855 by David Short, proprietor. The village developed around a mill built by J. H. Gillespie in 1853 and opened for business in 1854.

Pulaski County [pu-LAS-keye; pu-LAS-kee]. This county was created in 1835, organized in 1839, and named in honor of Count Casimir Pulaski, a Polish general killed in the attack on Savannah in 1779 while fighting with the Americans in the Revolution. Tippecanoe River State Park and the Winamac State Fish and Wildlife Area are located in this county. Seat: Winamac.

Pulltight [PUL-teyet] (Clark). This settlement appears on Baskin, Forster's 1876 map as a post office located in the southwestern corner of Wood Township, though the name does not appear on 1871 or 1881 postal route maps or in post office records. A variant spelling is Pull Tight.

Pumpkin Center [puhmp-kin SEN-ter] (Orange). The name of this settlement probably celebrates the large pumpkin crops grown here when the village was founded. According to local legend, the name is for a local farmer's pumpkin patch, supposedly the largest in the state. The farmer grew enormous pumpkins, too: "One year he grew a pumpkin that weighed 107 pounds. I know 'cause my uncle told me about it when I was little. Well, anyway, this old guy was so proud of his pumpkins that one day he put this sign up that said 'Duncan's Pumpkin Center of the World.' Well, folks thought this was real funny, and they started just calling his place Pumpkin Center, and that's what people call it to this day, and that's all I'm saying" (ISUFA).

Pumpkin Center [puhnk-uhn SEN-ter; puhmp-kin SEN-ter] (Washington). This name is found in nearby Orange county, too, as well as in South Dakota, where the name was humorously applied "to denote a place excessively rural and isolated." A section of another Hoosier town, Cayuga, also was known as Pumpkin Center, according to the following oral narrative: "It is a little cluster of about 30 or 40 small houses in a scooped-out place by the railroad tracks in Cayuga. It was probably called this [Pumpkin Center] because the houses resemble the seeds in a pumpkin because they are all close together" (ISUFA).

Purcell [PER-suhl] (Knox). This village, earlier called Purcell Station, was named for Andrew Purcell, on whose farm a railroad station was located. A post office called Purcells was established on February 7, 1871; closed on July 31, 1901.*

Purdy Hill [per-dee HIL] (Clay). Some Clay Countians pronounce the name of this locale on the old National Road (now State Road 340) "Pretty Hill" because the houses along the highway were extravagantly decorated during the Christmas season. Purdy is a family name in Clay County, but Purdy appears as a place name in Missouri, New York, Washington, and Wisconsin There also is a nearby Purdy Run.

Putnam County [PUHT-nuhm; PUHT-muhn]. This county was formed in 1821, organized in 1822, and named for General Israel Putnam, officer in the American Revolution. DePauw University is located in this county. Seat: Greencastle.

Putnamville [PUHT-nuhm-vil; PUHT-muhn-vil] (Putnam). This village was laid out in 1830 by James Townsend on land purchased from Edward Heath and named for the county in which it is located. A post office was established on December 4, 1832; closed on November 30, 1935. Putnamville rivaled Greencastle for the location of the county seat.

Pyrmont [PEER-mownt] (Carroll). This village earlier was called Wildcat Corner and Featherhuffs Mills. A post office called Featherhuffs Mills, with John Featherhuff as postmaster, was established on December 3, 1851; changed to Pyrmont, apparently for the German principality, Waldeck-Pyrmont, on June 5, 1866; closed on June 29, 1935.

Q

Quaker [KWAY-ker] (Vermillion). This village was first called Quaker Point for Quakers who settled here. When a post office was established on September 7, 1866, the name became Quaker Hill; and on July 9, 1894, the post office name was changed to Quaker. The post office was closed on February 28, 1914. According to local legend, "Quaker is a small community west of Cayuga, Indiana. It was so named because it was settled by a group of Quakers in the early 19th century. The name was given by the people who lived in the surrounding area because the Quakers did not associate with the other people" (ISUFA).

Quakertown [KWAY-ker-town] (Union). This village originally was called Millboro for local grist and woolen mills. A post office called Quakertown was established on April 6, 1866; closed on October 14, 1903. The first settler was Nathan Henderson, a Quaker who came here before 1826, and the present name honors Quakers who settled here.

Queensville [KWEENZ-vil] (Jennings). A post office named Queensville was established on February 23, 1847; closed on September 30, 1927.* The village was laid out on March 16, 1848.

Quercus Grove [kwerk-uhs GROV; kerk-uhs GROV] (Switzerland). Sometimes called Bark Works, this village was settled in 1816 by Daniel D. Smith and others, who ground and packed oak bark to send to England for dyes, hence the name, *Quercus* being the Latin name for oaks. A post office was established on September 19, 1822; closed on June 30, 1905.*

Quincy (Jay). See Dunkirk.

Quincy (Madison). See Elwood.

Quincy [KWIN-see] (Owen). This village was laid out in June 1853, and a post office was established on July 19, 1854.

Quincy (Putnam). See Clinton Falls.

R

Rabbitville [RAB-uht-vil] (Lawrence). A post office was established here on October 8, 1895; closed on December 21, 1897.*

Raber [RAY-ber] (Whitley). This village, never platted, was named for the local Raber family. Samuel Raber was an early resident. A post office was established on April 1, 1884; closed on March 31, 1902.

Raccoon [ra-KOON] (Putnam). This village was laid out in 1880 and called Lockridge for R. Z. Lockridge, local landowner. The present name comes from the railroad station here, named by railroad officials for nearby Big Raccoon Creek. A post office was established on June 21, 1880; closed on August 15, 1934.

Radioville [RAY-dee-o-vil] (Pulaski). This village was founded in 1934 by Margaret Loughlin. The origin of the name is unknown. A variant name is Anthonys Location.

Radley [RAD-lee] (Grant). This village first was called Elliotville for a local family. A post office called Radley was established on February 2, 1899; closed on July 31, 1911. William S. Elliot was the first postmaster. According to the WPA files, Radley was the name of Elliot's father-in-law.

Radnor [RAD-ner] (Carroll). A post office was established here on July 16, 1883. Locally the name was thought to be Native American of unknown meaning, but more likely it is for the county in Wales, perhaps via Pennsylvania.

Raglesville [RAG-uhlz-vil; RAY-guhlz-vil] (Daviess). This village, first called Stanford, was laid out on June 21, 1837, and named for the local Ragle family. A post office, with John Ragle as postmaster, was established on July 14, 1849; closed on April 30, 1923.*

Ragsdale [RAGZ-dayl] (Knox). A post office was established on August 1, 1917; closed on November 15, 1919. The name honors the local Ragsdale family. Some say Ragsdale was the name of a local preacher, and others say that Ragsdale was the name of the person who owned the property on which the post office was built. Aliceville is a variant name.

Rainsville [RAYNZ-vil] (Warren). This village was platted on April 16, 1833, by Isaac Rains and named for him. Rains settled here in 1832 and built a mill. A post office was established on February 5, 1836; closed on September 15, 1904.*

Raintown [RAYN-town] (Hendricks). This village was founded about 1870 and named for Hiram Rain, who had a sawmill here. A post office called Rainstown was established on May 6, 1872; closed on June 15, 1914. Another variant name is Rainstorm Station.

Raleigh [RAHL-ee] (Rush). This village was platted on November 7, 1847, and named for Raleigh, North Carolina, former home of some of the settlers. A post office was established on May 13, 1840, as McCanns, for William McCann, who built the first house and opened a general store here about 1841. The post office was changed to Raleigh on December 16, 1847; closed on January 31, 1902.

Ramelton [RAY-muhl-tuhn] (Brown). A post office was established here on June 22, 1874; closed on March 31, 1903.

Ramsey [RAM-zee] (Harrison). A post office established as Barren on March 21, 1837, was changed to Ramsey, for a local family, on March 25, 1884. The village was laid out by H. C. Ramsey on March 14, 1883. Samuel Ramsey served as the fifth postmaster of the Barren post office, and William H., Samuel, and Howard Ramsey were postmasters of the Ramsey post office.

Ramseys Mills (Jefferson). See Kent.

Randall [RAN-duhl] (Vermillion). Also called Randall Crossing, for the local Randall family, this village was the site of a grain elevator operated by Dan Randall.

Randolph [RAN-dawf; RAN-dawlf] (Randolph). Formerly called Randolph Station, this village was laid out first in 1836 and named for the county in which it is located. A post office was established on May 27, 1837; closed on September 14, 1852.* Another post office was moved here from Deerfield, q.v., on October 8, 1869; closed on August 15, 1900.

Randolph County [RAN-dawf; RAN-dawlf]. This county was organized in 1818 and, depending on the source, named for Thomas Randolph (1771–1811), territorial attorney general and officer, who was killed in the Battle of Tippecanoe; Thomas Mann Randolph (1768–1828), Virginia statesman, who was Thomas Jefferson's son-in-law; or Randolph County, North Carolina. Seat: Winchester.

Range Line [raynj leyen] (Lake). This village was named for its location on a survey line: "It is on the government survey line dividing range 7 and 8 west of the third principal meridian and gets its name from this fact" (WPA).

Ranger [RAYN-jer] (Perry). A post office was established here on November 27, 1866; closed on February 24, 1856.

Rapture [RAP-cher] (Posey). This village was laid out by John Cox in 1838 and called Winfield. A post office called Rapture was established on August 10, 1893; closed on July 14, 1902. According to the WPA files, the village may have been named for Dr. James Copper's horse, Rapture. The village also has been called Bugtown.

Raub [rahb] (Benton). This village was laid out on April 8, 1872, by A. D. Raub, for whom it was named. A post office was established on July 26, 1872; closed on July 14, 1967.

Ravenswood [RAYV-uhnz-wud] (Marion). This community was platted and incorporated in 1923.

Ray [ray] (Steuben). This village was laid out by Alexander McNaughton on May 26, 1873. A post office was established on July 12, 1872; closed on January 1, 1960.* Cf. Clear Lake.

Raymond [RAY-muhnd; RAY-muhn] (Franklin). This village was platted on July 27, 1903.

Rays Crossing [RAYZ KRAWS-ing] (Shelby). This village, named for the local Ray family, developed as a railroad station in the early 1870s. A post office was established on March 25, 1870; closed on April 30, 1943.

Rays Tavern (Parke). See Rockville.

Raysville [RAYZ-vil] (Henry). This village was laid out on April 10, 1832, and named for James B. Ray (1794–1848), fourth governor of Indiana (1825–1831). A post office was established on October 11, 1830; closed on January 3, 1907.*

Reagan [REE-guhn] (Clinton). This village was named for a local family, perhaps via Reagan Run. R. Reagan settled in this area in 1830.

Red Bridge [red brij] (Wabash). A post office called Red Bridge, for a local bridge that was painted red, was established on April 7, 1879. On November 22, 1894, the spelling was changed to Redbridge, and on January 11, 1905, the post office was closed. This small settlement was never platted, but there was a mill with a store here as well as the post office. Red Bridge State Recreation Area is located about a half mile southeast of the original bridge.

Red Bush [RED bush] (Warrick). A post office was established here on October 6, 1871; closed on April 27, 1875.

Red Cloud [red klowd] (Knox). A post office called Red Cloud was established on August 13, 1874; changed to Redcloud on March 5, 1895; closed on October 14, 1903.* The name possibly comes from the famous Sioux chief Red Cloud (1822–1909), for whom other settlements in the United States were named.

Red Cross Park (Lawrence). See Tarry Park.

Redding [RED-ing] (Lawrence). This village was laid out by Robert Porter and John R. Nugent on August 25, 1842. Nugent was postmaster of the Sinking Springs post office, established on April 20, 1837; closed on July 20, 1852. Apparently the name first was spelled Reading.

Reddington [RED-ing-tuhn] (Jackson). This village was laid out on June 10, 1837, by John Prather and named for Redding Township, in which it is located. A post office was established on January 14, 1837; closed on May 31, 1902.*

Red Hill [red hil] (Lawrence). This village was named for the nearby summit of the same name.

Redkey [RED-kee] (Jay). A post office called Half Way, for a nearby stream, was established on September 19, 1853; changed to Redkey, first spelled Red Key, on January 14, 1870.* The town, originally laid out in September 1854, was platted as Mount Vernon. James Redkey, a pioneer preacher, platted an addition on November 13, 1867, and it was renamed for him. Locally it has been called Lick Skillet, Grab All, and Buzzards Roost, allegedly for the scanty meals served sawmill hands at a local boarding house. Red Key Town is another variant name.

Redsdale (Lake). See Lottaville.

Reed Station [reed STAY-shuhn] (Delaware). A post office called Reeds Station, for the local Reed family, was established on August 22, 1876; changed to Reed on November 28, 1882; closed on April 15, 1901. This village was platted as Reeds Station on February 6, 1877, by William Reed, who served as the first postmaster.

Reedville Station (Hancock). See Carrollton (Hancock).

Reelsville [REELZ-vil] (Putnam). This village was named for the local Reel family. A post office was established on May 11, 1852. William A. Reel was the first postmaster, and John Reel was the second postmaster. The village was laid out in 1852 by John Reel, who came here in 1826.

Rego [REE-go] (Orange). A post office was established here on December 24, 1867; closed on May 29, 1937.* Rego also is a Sudanese place name.

Rehoboth [ree-HO-bith] (Harrison). A post office was established on March 7,

1873; closed on April 30, 1907. This biblical name, literally meaning "enlargement," also is a settlement name in Massachusetts, New Mexico, and Delaware. Indiana churches called Rehoboth are located in Harrison, Putnam, and Randolph counties.

Rei (Ripley). See Delaware.

Reiffsburg [REYEFS-berg] (Wells). This village was platted by John Reiff on August 7, 1851, and named for him. A post office established as Reiffsburgh on September 11, 1854, was changed to Reiffsburg on March 30, 1893; closed on February 15, 1905.

Remington [REM-ing-tuhn] (Jasper). This town, laid out on July 27, 1860, by Jesse H. Fordice, formerly was called Carpenters Creek and Carpenters Station for a nearby stream named for a local family. A post office called Carpenters Creek established on February 12, 1851, was changed to Remington on December 1, 1862. The present name is for a merchant who opened a general store here in 1861.

Reno [REE-no] (Hendricks). This village was platted on December 10, 1870. The name is found in several states and usually honors the American general Jesse Lee Reno, who was killed in the battle of South Mountain, Maryland, in 1862. A post office was established on November 1, 1870; closed on September 30, 1912.

Rensselaer [rents-uh-LEER; ren-suh-LEER] (county seat, Jasper). This city was named for James Van Rensselaer, a merchant from New York who arrived here in 1838 and built a gristmill. The following year, Van Rensselaer laid out the town and called it Newton, sup-

posedly for Sir Isaac Newton. A post office established as Fez in Newton County on August 9, 1837, was changed to Fez in Jasper County on June 19, 1839, to Newton on July 17, 1839, and to Rensselaer on August 9, 1841. Songwriter James F. Hanley, who wrote "Back Home Again in Indiana," was born here in 1892.

Reserve (Miami). See Peoria (Miami).

Reserve (Tippecanoe). See Westpoint.

Retreat [ree-TREET] (Jackson). This village was founded around 1850 when a sawmill was built here. A post office was established on June 19, 1854; closed on February 29, 1904.* The name, suggesting seclusion and tranquillity, may be commendatory.

Rexville [REKS-vil] (Ripley). A post office, named for the local Rex family, was established on June 9, 1870; closed on January 31, 1907.

Reynolds [REN-uhldz] (White). A post office was established on September 19, 1853. The town, settled around 1839, was laid out on January 10, 1854, by George S. Rose, Christian Carroll, William M. Kenton, and Benjamin Reynolds. The name is for the Reynolds family.

Rhodes [rodz] (Vermillion). This village was platted in 1903 by the Brazil Block Coal Company.

Riceville [REYES-vil] (Crawford). This village was founded around 1882 and named for Wash Rice, a local businessman. A post office was established on October 3, 1882; closed on September 15, 1942.* A variant name is Newton Station.

Richards (Brown). See Trevlac.

Richland (Knox). See Fritchton.

Richland [RICH-land] (Rush). A post office was established on March 15, 1827; closed on January 15, 1903.* The village was platted on December 14, 1854. The name is for the township in which the post office was located. The township supposedly was named for the quality of the soil here.

Richland Center [rich-luhnd SEN-ter] (Fulton). A post office called Richland Centre was established in Richland Township, for which it was named, on March 8, 1878; changed to Richland Center on November 12, 1887; closed on November 18, 1902.*

Richland Center (Steuben). See Alvarado.

Richland City [rich-luhnd SID-ee] (Spencer). A post office established on August 15, 1862, and called Lake was changed to Richland on March 19, 1921. The village was laid out in April 1861. Supposedly the present name is for rich farmland in the area.

Richland Furnace (Greene). See Furnace.

Richmond [RICH-muhnd] (county seat, Wayne). David Hoover came here from North Carolina in 1806 and referred to the settlement as "the promised land." The city was platted in 1816 and named Smithville, for the proprietor, John Smith, who arrived in May 1807. An adjoining town was laid out in 1818 by Jeremiah Cox and called Coxborough for him. Later in 1818 the two towns were incorporated together as Richmond. Supposedly Thomas Roberts, James Pegg, and David Hoover, trustees,

were chosen to select a name. Roberts suggested Waterford, Pegg proposed Plainfield, and Hoover offered Richmond, which was accepted by the lot holders. According to the WPA files, the name was selected from several suggested names for its commendatory idea of richness of soil. A post office was established on April 20, 1818.

Richvalley [RICH-val-ee] (Wabash). According to the WPA files, this community was settled around 1827 by Jonathan Keller and his family and first called Kellers Settlement for them. After the railroad was completed through here, the settlement was called Kellers Station. A post office called Rich Valley, descriptive of fertile farmland, was established on February 2, 1861,* and the village, named for the post office, was platted on December 14, 1861, by John H. Keller and Isaac Keller. The spelling of the post office name was changed to Richvalley on January 27, 1896.

Riddle [RID-uhl] (Crawford). A post office, named for Civil War veteran Colonel Riddle, was established on June 28, 1892; closed on June 30, 1951.

Ridertown [REYE-der-town] (Jay). A post office, named for the local Rider family, was established on April 18, 1891; closed on May 31, 1904. Miles Rider was the first postmaster.

Ridgeport [RIJ-pawrt] (Greene). This village was named for its location on a ridge. A post office called Heaton, for the local Heaton family, was established on June 21, 1889; closed on July 14, 1906. Wallace Heaton was a local storekeeper, and David W. Heaton was the first postmaster.

Ridgeview [RIJ-vyoo] (Miami). Now part of Peru, this settlement was platted on May 8, 1884, by Daniel Bearss. The name is descriptive. Peru High School is now located on the ridge, earlier the site of the Wabash Railroad Employees Hospital.

Ridgeville [RIJ-vil] (Randolph). This town originally was platted in 1837 and replatted in 1853, when for a short time it was called Newtown. A post office was established on April 16, 1851. The name is descriptive of the slightly elevated land of the townsite (WPA), as the town was established on the north bank of the Mississinewa River.

Ridgeway [RIJ-way] (Howard). A post office, named for the Ridgeway family, local store owners, was located here on April 7, 1879; closed on August 30, 1902.

Rigdon [RIG-duhn] (Madison). This village, located on the Madison-Grant county line, was laid out in February 1851 and named Independence. A post office named Rigdon was established on August 1, 1855, in Grant County; changed to Madison County on April 26, 1875; changed back to Grant County on April 7, 1876; changed back to Madison County on December 9, 1886; changed back to Grant County on July 15, 1889; closed on September 30, 1912. The name honors Dr. Prior Rigdon, an early settler.

Riley [REYE-lee; REYE-lay] (Vigo). This town was platted in 1836 as Lockport because of its location near three locks on the Wabash and Erie Canal. The post office, established on January 7, 1840,* was named Riley, for the township it is in, by the Post Office Department because there was another post office called Lockport, in Carroll County. Riley is the subject of several legends, including the following three:

1. "Riley, Indiana, used to be called Lockport, Indiana. The old Wabash and Erie Canal came through here, and the city was named for the locks in the canal that were used to move the boats along. The old Lockport Road, which goes from Terre Haute to Riley, was named in the same way" (ISUFA).

2. "Riley was once called Hazelgreen, and the Indians used to live there, the Delawares, I think. Every so often a lone Indian would wander into town when us palefaces had took over and turn around and walk back to the woods. Several of the old Indians were friendly to the villagers, and within a month, four of them were killed, and the Delawares, or whoever they were, threatened a massacre. But the people in Hazelgreen tried to find the killer on their own, and they finally found a new person in town who said when he saw an Indian he shut one eye and they never met again. He was turned over to the Indians and never seen again" (ISUFA).

3. "Riley started with one shanty and a man and a woman. They were joint owners of a barrel of whiskey and a milk cow. The woman managed the whiskey, and the man managed the cow so the man wouldn't drink up all the whiskey. It grew up a whiskey town, and it died a whiskey town before it became Riley today" (ISUFA).

Rileysburg [REYE-leez-berg] (Vermillion). A post office called Rileysburgh was established on February 8, 1887; changed to Rileysburg on May 11, 1893; closed on June 15, 1934. The village, formerly called Riley, was platted on June 4, 1904.

Ringville (Wells). See Domestic.

Ripley [RIP-lee] (Pulaski). This village was laid out in 1900 by Moses A. Dilts.

Ripley (Ripley). See Osgood.

Ripley County [RIP-lee]. This county, noted for its furniture and casket industries, was created in 1816, organized in 1818, and named for Major General Eleazar Wheelock Ripley, officer in the War of 1812. Seat: Versailles.

Ripple (Marion). See Broad Ripple.

Rising Sun [reye-zing SUHN] (county seat, Ohio). An Indiana Territory post office called Rising Sun was established on September 15, 1815; changed to Dearborn County on December 11, 1816; changed to Ohio County on January 4, 1844. The city was founded in 1814 by John James, who came here from Maryland. Since there is a Rising Sun in Maryland, as well as in Delaware and Ohio, possibly the name is a transfer, most likely from Maryland. Some accounts, however, say that James named the settlement for a beautiful sunrise or for a flatboat named Rising Sun. Other histories say the settlement was named by John Fulton, who was inspired by the sunrise when he landed here on the west bank of the Ohio River on a flatboat in 1798 or 1814, depending on the source. According to a printed account in the WPA guide, "The name was suggested by the grandeur of the sunrise over the Kentucky hills above the town of Rabbit Hash, across the river." Local legend offers another explanation: "That's how Rising Sun got its name. They was going down the river, and the sun was a-comin' up, an' they said, 'Look at the rising sun.' And that's right about along

where Rising Sun is, an' that's how they named it. The Indians give Rising Sun its name" (ISUFA).

Ritchie [RICH-ee] (Spencer). This village, founded before 1869, earlier was called Ritchies Station and Ritchies for the local Ritchie family. The station was located on land belonging to R. Ritchie (WPA).

Rivare [ri-VEHR] (Adams). This village was platted in 1883. The railroad name was Rivare, from Antoine Rivare, a Native American who was awarded the only reservation, Rivare Reserve, in the county. A post office named Bobo, for a circuit judge, was established on July 16, 1883; closed on February 28, 1930.

River (Huntington). See Lancaster.

River (Starke). See San Pierre.

Riverside [RIV-er-seyed] (Fountain). This village, first called Fountain City, was platted on October 26, 1857, and named for its location on the Wabash River. A post office was established on February 15, 1872; closed on February 28, 1946.

Riverside [RIV-er-seyed] (Wells). This village was platted on April 12, 1912, by Edwin Neuhauser and named for its location on the Wabash River.

Riverton [RIV-er-tuhn] (Sullivan). This village was laid out in November 1887 and so named because of its location on the Wabash River. A post office was established on December 28, 1887; closed on June 30, 1905.*

Rivervale [RIV-er-vayl] (Lawrence). A post office established at Lawrenceport, q.v., on January 16, 1851, was moved to

Rivervale on April 16, 1859; closed on June 15, 1931. The location of this village on the East Fork of White River influenced its naming.

Riverview [RIV-er-vyoo] (Sullivan). This village was named for its location on the Wabash River.

Riverwood [RIV-er-wud] (Hamilton). This community probably was named for its proximity to White River. The name sometimes is considered a variant of a nearby village, Clare, q.v. (WPA).

Roachdale [ROCH-dayl] (Putnam). This town was laid out in the fall of 1879 by Elijah Graham. A post office established as Langsdale on February 3, 1880, was changed to Roachdale on February 24, 1880. Langsdale was named for the editor of the Greencastle *Banner*. Roachdale was the name of the local railroad station, which was named for Judge Roach of Indianapolis, director of the Monon Railroad.

Roann [ro-AN] (Wabash). This town was platted on September 14, 1853, by Joseph Beckner, who settled here from Virginia in 1836 and opened a tavern. A post office was established on June 12, 1866. Possibly the town was named for Roanne, France; however, only legends explain the origin of the name. One version from the WPA files goes: "During a time of high water, a girl by the name of Ann was in a boat on the river. As she was attempting to get back to shore, the current was swiftly carrying her downstream. Suddenly she was whirled into a place where the current was not so strong, and her father, who had been watching, helpless to aid, called, 'Row, Ann, row, Ann!' So from this the town is said to have received the name." In other versions of this legend, Ann, sometimes identified as Ann Beckner, is chased by Indians rather than carried by a swift current, and in another legend she is an Indian named Ann who, when called upon, rows white settlers across the river. Another local legend says that two women, Ann Roe and Ann Beckner, cooked for the surveyor when he stayed at the nearby Beckner's Tavern, and he named the town for them.

Roanoke [RO-nok; RO-uhn-ok] (Huntington). A sawmill built here in 1845 was named Roanoke Mills. A post office established on June 4, 1846, was called Roanoke. The town was laid out in September 1850. As a place name, Roanoke is found in at least nine states and ultimately comes from the Virginia Indians' word for their shell money.

Roanoke Station [ro-nok STAY-shuhn] (Huntington). This settlement was established as a railroad station about a mile southeast of Roanoke, for which it was named.

Roberts [RAH-berts] (Fountain). This village, originally called Fido (WPA), was founded in 1883 and named for the local Roberts family. A post office was established on February 27, 1890; closed on June 15, 1901.

Robertsdale [RAH-berts-dayl] (Lake). This community was named for an early Whiting resident named Roberts (WPA).

Robinsons Prairie (Lake). See Crown Point.

Robison [RAHB-uh-suhn] (Greene). A post office, named for a local family, was established here on March 22, 1883; closed on August 31, 1926.

Rob Roy [RAHB roy] (Fountain). This village was platted on July 24, 1826, and named for the Scottish outlaw Rob Roy, immortalized by Sir Walter Scott. The name was chosen by John Foster, the proprietor, an avid reader who was especially fond of Scott's novels. A post office was established on June 8, 1832; closed on January 15, 1906.*

Roches Station (Huntington). See Simpson.

Rochester (Franklin). See Cedar Grove.

Rochester [RAH-ches-ter] (county seat, Fulton). This city was laid out in 1835 by Alexander Chamberlain, a local mill owner who came here from the area around Rochester, New York, so the name probably was borrowed from New York. Local legends claim that the name is for Rochester, England, or for a local mill owner named Rochester (WPA). A post office was established on September 17, 1836.

Rock Creek Center [rahk kreek SEN-ter] (Huntington). This village was named for its location in the center of Rock Creek Township, which was established in 1842 and named for Rock Creek, a nearby stream with a rocky bed. A post office called Rock Creek was established on April 27, 1874; closed on December 31, 1902.

Rockdale [RAHK-dayl] (Franklin). A post office, with Conrad Wissel as postmaster, was established as Wissel on September 3, 1886; changed to Rockdale on May 9, 1891; closed on September 14, 1903.

Rockfield [RAHK-feeld] (Carroll). This village, platted on August 11, 1856, is located in Rock Creek Township, so possibly there was a transfer of part of the name; however, it is commonly held that the town was so named because of the rocky soil. A post office was established on May 14, 1857.

Rockford [RAHK-ferd] (Jackson). This village, once a thriving riverfront commercial center, was laid out on March 10, 1830, and so named because it is located "at a point where the bed of the White River is composed of slate rock, forming a good ford" (WPA). A post office, earlier called Fischlies (or Fichlies) Mills, was established as Rockford on December 13, 1831; closed on May 14, 1906.

Rockford [RAHK-ferd] (Wells). This village was platted on September 21, 1849, and formerly called Barbers Mills, as Hallett Barber had a sawmill here. The present name is descriptive of a local ford on Rock Creek.

Rock Hill [rahk hil] (Spencer). This village was named for an outcrop of rock at the site of a local elementary school (WPA).

Rock Island [RAHK EYE-luhnd] (Perry). A post office was established on January 11, 1867; closed on October 29, 1875. The village was named for its location near an island of the same name in the Ohio River. The island, according to an oral account, was so named because "a big rock fell off of the hillside, and it's out in the water" (ISUFA).

Rocklane [rahk-layn] (Johnson). This village, settled around 1843 when a general store was opened, originally was called Clarksburg. A post office called Rocklane was established on April 4, 1873; closed on November 29, 1902. Locally it is thought that the present name is for rocky soil here.

Rock Lick (Harrison). See Bridgeport.

Rockport [RAHK-pawrt] (Parke). A mill was established here near a rocky gorge, which inspired the name of the settlement. Locally the gorge is called Devils Den. Variant names of the village have been Copeland, Rockport Mills, and Wrights Mills.

Rockport [RAHK-pawrt] (county seat, Spencer). Settled in 1802, this city first was called Hanging Rock, for local projecting rock formations, which also gave the city its present name. Around 1807 Daniel Grass changed the name to Mount Duvall, for Colonel William Duvall, his Kentucky friend. When the city became the county seat in 1818, the name was changed to Rockport. A post office called Rock Port was established on May 9, 1823. On March 31, 1854, the spelling of the post office name was changed to Rockport. According to an oral narrative, "It is set on the banks of the Ohio River. Rockport received its name because of its natural setting. In its earlier days, there was a port located there. Also there are some rocky bluffs rising up from the river which the town is built upon. This is where Rockport gets its name. It should be noted that the one-way road which passes by these bluffs is noted as a popular place for young couples to go parking" (ISUFA).

Rockport Junction [rahk-pawrt JUHNK-shuhn] (Spencer). This community, now considered part of Rockport, q.v., was established as a railroad station just east of Rockport, for which it was named.

Rockville [RAHK-vil] (county seat, Parke). This town was laid out in 1823 and selected as the county seat in 1824. A post office was established on July 13, 1824. The name is for a large rock, now on the courthouse lawn. Allegedly part of the rock was used in the foundation of Persius Harris's store, located on the north side of the square, so originally the rock, a glacial boulder, was larger. According to a local legend, "In the late 1700s and early 1800s, the federal government passed a law for every county to have a county seat. Well, three men were appointed in Parke County to find a suitable place for our county seat. The sites chosen were one in Rosedale and one in Rockville. Well, they had to make a decision, so they surveyed both places. Before making the commitment, they went to Ray's Tavern to discuss the sites. Well, after an evening of drinking and eating, they decided to look over the Rockville site once more. Once out there, they agreed that it should be the spot, but they needed a name. Well, the men argued over who it should be named after for hours, when a bystander said they should name it after the one who has been there the longest. Then he pointed at a boulder and said, 'Let's name her Rockville,' so Rockville it is" (ISUFA). Apparently a variant name, Park, is for a local post office established in 1820 or 1821 and closed in 1824. Wallace Rea, the postmaster of the Park post office, also served as the third postmaster of the Rockville post office. Another variant name was Rays Tavern.

Rocky Ripple [rahk-ee RIP-uhl] (Marion). This community was laid out and incorporated in 1928.

Rocky Run (Parke). See Coloma.

Rodmans (Boone). See Royalton.

Rogersville [RAHJ-erz-vil] (Henry). This village was platted on January 16, 1837, by Joseph G. Rogers and John B.

Colburn and named for Rogers. A post office was established on November 19, 1849; closed on June 15, 1901.*

Roland [RO-luhnd; RO-luhn] (Orange). A post office was established on June 30, 1892; closed on July 31, 1906. The name is for the local Roland family. The only postmasters here were Miles, Harry, and George Roland. Rollins is a variant name.

Roll [rahl; rol] (Blackford). A post office called Roll was established on June 6, 1881; closed on March 31, 1955. The name is for Mathias Roll, an early settler (WPA). Dundee was an earlier name of the community, as a post office called Dundee was established in this area on August 4, 1854; closed on May 11, 1865.

Rolling Prairie [RO-ling PREHR-ee] (La Porte). Ezekiel Provolt built a cabin here in the spring of 1831, and the cluster of cabins built up around his was called Nauvoo. On November 26, 1853, W. J. Walker platted the village and called it Portland. A nearby post office called Byron, q.v., was moved here, a mile and a half north of Byron, on April 23, 1857. The present name, descriptive of the undulating terrain, was adopted by the railroad.

Rome [rom] (Perry). Once the county seat, this village was laid out in 1818 and originally called Washington, for President George Washington, but since there were other towns of that name, the name was changed to Franklin, for Benjamin Franklin, the same year. A post office named Rome, for the classical city perhaps via New York, was established on July 17, 1819.

Rome City [ROM SIT-ee; ROM SID-ee] (Noble). This town developed around

1837, when Sylvan Lake was made, and first was called Rome. It was laid out in June 1839. The proprietors were John C. Mather and Ebenezer Pierce. A post office established at nearby Northport on January 14, 1846, was changed to Rome City on January 21, 1868. According to one anecdote, Irish workers on the Northport feeder canal named the place. Both French and Irish workers were employed on the dam, and the French foreman gave the French the best quarters. When the Irish complained, the foreman led the French against the Irish. The Irish were told to "do as the Romans do" and called their camp Rome. When the town was platted in 1839 on the campsite, it was called Rome, then Rome City (WPA).

Romney [RAHM-nee] (Tippecanoe). Founded about 1831, this village was named for Romney, West Virginia, former home of some of the settlers. A post office was established on August 16, 1842.*

Romona [ruh-MO-nuh] (Owen). This village was laid out in 1819 by Adam Brinton and called Brintonville. The present name is for Helen Hunt Jackson's popular novel, *Ramona,* and was adopted, though misspelled, following publication of the book in 1884. A post office was established on March 29, 1886; closed on September 15, 1936. A nearby railroad station and post office was called Mundy, q.v.

Rono (Perry). See Magnet.

Roods Corner (Grant). See Van Buren.

Rosebud [ROZ-buhd] (Washington). A post office was established on June 21, 1898; closed on May 31, 1901. This place name also is found in Jasper and Warrick counties.

Roseburg [ROZ-berg] (Grant). A post office called Roseburgh was established on January 14, 1854; closed on September 30, 1902.*

Roseburg [ROZ-berg] (Union). This village was named for the local Rose family. General John B. Rose, who came here in 1817, helped organize Union County. A variant spelling is Roseburgh.

Rose Creek [roz kreek] (Monroe). A post office was established on August 4, 1874, with Warren R. Roseberry as the first postmaster; closed on January 3, 1881. The name is for the stream of the same name, on which the community was established. The stream also is called Indian Creek.

Rosedale [ROZ-dayl] (Parke). This town was named in 1860 by railroad officials for Chauncey Rose, early settler and promoter and stockholder of the railroad. Rose came here about 1819 and built a gristmill. A post office was established on January 31, 1861. According to an oral account, "Rosedale got its start some time in the 1800s when a man named Chauncey Rose built a mill along Raccoon Creek. Water back then was the principal means of power and transportation. So Chauncey built his mill along Little Raccoon because the water would power his mill and because the creek connects with the Wabash, which was a part of the Erie Canal, which would provide easy transport. Thus, Rosedale became a trade center for Parke County and grew rapidly" (ISUFA). Variant names have been Blacks, Darsyville, and Dotyville.

Rosedale (Pulaski). See Thornhope.

Roseland [ROZ-luhnd] (Saint Joseph). According to local tradition, this town was named for "thousands of wild rose bushes on the farms in the vicinity" (WPA), but the name may honor the local Rose family. David Rose, a Civil War veteran, settled in the township in 1870 on a 110-acre estate called Rose Hill.

Roselawn [ROZ-lawn; ROZ-lahn] (Newton). This village was platted in January 1882. A post office called Rose Lawn was established on December 5, 1881, and about 1882 Jacob Keller of North Judson, Lon Craig of Winamac, and Orlando Rose of Missouri opened a store along the proposed Monon Railroad. According to one account, the village was named for Orlando and Bell Rose, who laid out the village (WPA). According to a county history, the name, originally Rose Lon, was coined from Orlando Rose's last name and Lon Craig's first name. Craig was the first postmaster. The spelling of the post office name was changed to Roselawn on June 17, 1893.

Roselle (La Porte). See Wanatah.

Roseville (Parke). See Coxville.

Rosewood [ROZ-wud] (Harrison). A post office was established here on June 16, 1854; closed on June 30, 1905.

Ross [raws; rahs] (Lake). A post office was established on March 21, 1857; closed on September 15, 1914. The name is for the local Ross family. William Ross was an early settler, perhaps the first permanent settler in Lake County. Ross Township, established in 1848, is named for him (WPA).

Rossburg [RAWS-berg] (Decatur). This village, formerly called Rossville, was laid out in March 1836. Rossburgh is a variant spelling, but the Rossburgh post office in this county was located south of here at New Point, q.v.

Rosston [RAWS-tuhn] (Boone). A post office was established on January 5, 1886; closed on February 28, 1918. The village was named for the Ross brothers, whose farm adjoined the settlement.

Rossville [RAWS-vil] (Clinton). This town was platted in 1834 and named for John Ross, an early county associate judge, probably via Ross Township, which was organized on May 15, 1830. A post office was established on September 30, 1835.

Round Grove [rown grov; rownd grov] (White). A post office named Round Grove was established on December 27, 1878. On February 19, 1895, the spelling of the post office name was changed to Roundgrove, and on November 11, 1900, the post office was closed. The post office was named for Round Grove Township, in which it is located. The township, established on December 31, 1858, was named for a large, circular grove of trees in the southern part of the township.

Royal Center [ROY-uhl SEN-ter] (Cass). A post office named Royal Centre was established on October 26, 1841,* and the town was laid out in April 1846. The name is for Royal Center, New York.

Royalton [ROYL-tuhn] (Boone). A post office called Rodmans, for the local Rodman family, was established on December 15, 1832. An early merchant was John Rodman, and William Rodman was the first postmaster. On September 20, 1838, the post office was changed to Royalton, and on July 31, 1900, the post office closed.

Royerton [ROY-er-tuhn; ROY-yer-tuhn] (Delaware). A post office named Royerton, for the local Royer family, was established on February 15, 1869; closed on June 15, 1915.* John Royer, the first postmaster, laid out the village on December 17, 1870.

Rugby [RUHG-bee] (Bartholomew). According to the WPA files, this village was never platted. A post office was established on August 18, 1884; closed on August 31, 1935. Apparently the name comes from the English town name, which means "Hroca's fortified place." Rugby is also found as a place name in Australia and North Dakota.

Rumble [RUHM-buhl] (Pike). Though this village apparently was settled earlier, a post office was established on June 22, 1888; closed on September 30, 1902. The name is for the local Rumble family, early settlers. Storekeeper Eli F. Rumble was the second postmaster. A variant name is Rumble Town.

Runnymede [RUHN-ee-meed] (La Porte). This village probably was named for the meadow in England where the Magna Carta was granted in 1215.

Runyantown [RUHN-yuhn-town] (Clark). A post office called Runyan, for a local family, was established on November 20, 1897; closed on April 15, 1902. The first postmaster was G. Hesse Runyan.

Rural [RUR-uhl; RUR-awl] (Randolph). This village, earlier called Woods Station for a local family, was founded around 1870. A post office called Rural was established on June 22, 1874; closed on March 30, 1907.

Rush County [ruhsh]. This county, noted for furniture making and rich farmland, was formed in 1821, organized in April 1822, and named for Dr. Benjamin F. Rush, physician, soldier in the Revolution, and a signer of the Declaration of Independence. Seat: Rushville.

Rush Creek Valley [RUHSH kreek VAL-ee] (Washington). A post office, named for a nearby stream, was established here on February 27, 1871; closed on December 31, 1901.

Rushville [RUHSH-vil] (county seat, Rush County). This city was laid out on June 18, 1822, as the seat of Rush County, q.v., and like the county, was named for Dr. Benjamin F. Rush. A post office was located here on October 9, 1822.

Rusk [ruhsk] (Martin). This village was settled in 1836. A post office was established on January 13, 1892; closed on April 30, 1954. According to the WPA files, the village was named for two Rusk brothers, doctors in the Civil War, who were born here, or for Jeremiah McLain Rusk, congressman and U.S. secretary of agriculture.

Russell Lake [ruhs-uhl LAYK] (Boone). This village was named for the lake of the same name.

Russellville [RUHS-uhl-vil] (Parke). A post office called Russells Mills was established on June 28, 1847. On May 12, 1893, the post office name was changed to Russell Mills, and on May 31, 1905, the post office was closed. The name honors the local Russell family. Joseph Russell was the first postmaster. Variant names, Wards Mills and Wards Town, also are for a local family. James C. Ward became the eighth postmaster.

Russellville [RUHS-uhl-vil] (Putnam). This town was laid out in 1828 by Jacob Durham and named for Russell Township, in which it is located. A post office, with Durham as postmaster, was established on March 9, 1832. From December 5, 1882, to September 3, 1885, the post office was called Darter, for a local family. William Darter was postmaster during most of this period.

Russiaville [ROO-shuh-vil] (Howard). This town was laid out in 1845. A post office was established as Russiaville in Clinton County on December 23, 1847. On October 14, 1869, the post office was changed to Howard County. The name is a form of Richardville, for Jean Baptiste Richardville. It generally was pronounced as if it were spelled Rusherville and sometimes written accordingly. Cf. Howard County.

Rutland [RUHT-luhnd] (Marshall). A post office named Cavender, for the local Cavender family, was established on February 27, 1883. Edward Cavender was the first postmaster, and other members of the family also served as postmaster. On March 24, 1884, the post office was changed to Rutland, probably for the English county via an eastern state, and on January 31, 1918, the post office was closed.

Ryders Mill (Noble). See Wilmot.

Rye (Starke). See Toto.

Sabaria (Perry). See Siberia.

Sabine [suh-BEEN; SAY-beyen] (Marion). A post office named Sabine was established on December 30, 1870. The local railroad station was called Sunnyside Station. The name more likely is from the river, lake, and pass in eastern Texas and western Louisiana than from the ancient people or branch of the Italic language.

Saffaras (Perry). See Sassafras.

Saint Anthony [SAYNT AN-thuh-nee] (Dubois). First called Saint Joseph, this village was platted on April 10, 1860 (WPA). A post office was established on February 20, 1874.

Saint Bernard (Harrison). See Frenchtown.

Saint Bernice [saynt ber-NEES] (Vermillion). A nearby post office named Jones (cf. Jonestown), was moved here and called Saint Bernice on March 26, 1867.* The village was platted as Saint Bernice on August 18, 1905.

Saint Croix [saynt kroy; saynt krahks] (Perry). This village was founded in 1855 by Father Dion, who named it Saint Croix. The local parish church was called l'Eglise de la Sainte Croix. A post office called Saint Cross was established on April 8, 1880; changed to Saint Croix on June 28, 1880.

Saint Henry [SAYNT HEN-ree] (Dubois). A post office was established as Saint Henry on October 19, 1870; closed on August 31, 1933. The village was platted in 1874. The name may be for a congregation organized at Henryville in 1862 or for Henry Hogg, a local Benedictine priest.

Saint James [saynt jaymz] (Gibson). A post office, named for the local Saint James Roman Catholic Church, was established on September 30, 1878; closed on September 15, 1902. Apparently the church was named for the fourth bishop of Vincennes, the Right Reverend James Maurice de Long d'Aussac de Saint Palais, though the bishop used the name Maurice. Cf. Saint Maurice. A variant name is Saint James Station.

Saint Joe [saynt jo] (DeKalb). A post office named Blair, for early settler John Blair, was established on April 14, 1875. On June 16, 1886, the post office name was changed to Saint Joe Station, for the local railroad station, which was named for nearby Saint Joseph River; and on January 27, 1906, the name was changed to Saint Joe. The town was laid out by John and Jacob D. Leighty on April 20, 1875.

Saint John [saynt jahn] (Lake). This town was settled in the 1830s and earlier called Western Prairie and Prairie West. The town was platted on December 17, 1881, and like the township it is in, was named for John Hack, a devout

Catholic, who settled in the township in September 1837. Locally the town has been called Saint Johns. A post office, with John Hack as postmaster, was established on January 20, 1846.

Saint John [saynt jahn] (Warrick). This village was named for the local Saint Johns Church.

Saint Johns [saynt jahnz] (DeKalb). A variant name, DeKalb, for the county, was given to a post office established here on September 9, 1840; closed after 1882.

Saint Joseph (Dubois). See Saint Anthony.

Saint Joseph [SAYNT JO-zuhf] (Floyd). Located near the Clark-Floyd county line, this German Catholic community was settled around 1846, and the first church was built in 1853. The settlement first was called Saint Josephs Hill, for devotional reasons and for the hilly countryside. The post office, also called Saint Josephs Hill, was established in Floyd County around 1865, but moved to Clark County on February 10, 1868, and closed on March 31, 1905.*

Saint Joseph [SAYNT JO-zuhf] (Vanderburgh). Nicholas Long settled here around 1830 and built a store, smithy, school, and church. A post office was established on August 7, 1867; closed on February 28, 1903. The village was named for the local Saint Joseph's Catholic Church.

Saint Joseph County [SAYNT JO-zuhf]. This county, home of the University of Notre Dame, was organized in 1830 and named for the Saint Joseph River. The Potawatomi name of the

stream was Sahg-wah-se-be, "Mystery River." The present name of the river, for the Virgin Mary's husband, was applied by Catholic explorers. Seat: South Bend.

Saint Josephs (Saint Joseph). See South Bend.

Saint Leon [SAYNT LEE-ahn] (Dearborn). A post office was established here on October 6, 1852; closed on January 31, 1955.

Saint Louis (Bartholomew). See Old Saint Louis.

Saint Louis Crossing [SAYNT loo-us KRAWS-ing] (Bartholomew). A post office was established on June 24, 1862. The village was laid out on January 30, 1864, by Isaac White on the railroad west of Saint Louis (now Old Saint Louis, q.v.), for which it was named.

Saint Magdalen [SAYNT MAG-duh-luhn] (Ripley). A post office called Saint Magdalene, for Mary Magdalene, was established on April 6, 1871; closed on November 30, 1905. Composed largely of German Catholic settlers, the community locally was called the Dutch Settlement.

Saint Marks [saynt mahrks] (Dubois). This village was platted on February 26, 1872, by M. E. Cox.

Saint Mary-of-the-Woods [SAYNT MEHR-ee-uh-*th*uh-WUDZ] (Vigo). Originally this village, locally called Saint Marys or Saint Marys-of-the-Woods, was called Thralls Station for a local family, but it was renamed in 1837 when Saint Mary of the Woods parish was established here. A post office, with Jacob Thralls as postmaster, was established as Saint Marys on August 15, 1846; changed to Saint Mary-of-the-Woods on March 15, 1912. Saint Mary-of-the-Woods College, founded in 1840 by the Sisters of Providence, is located here.

Saint Marys [SAYNT MEHR-eez] (Floyd). This village earlier was called Saint Marys of the Knobs.

Saint Marys [SAYNT MEHR-eez] (Franklin). A post office established here on October 17, 1861, was called Haymond; closed on November 15, 1907.* The name of the village, Saint Marys, is for a local Catholic church, which was organized in 1837 and called Saint Marys of the Rock.

Saint Maurice [SAYNT MAWR-uhs] (Decatur). This village was laid out on August 12, 1859, around a Catholic church, for which it was named. The church was named for the fourth bishop of Vincennes, the Right Reverend James Maurice de Long d'Aussac de Saint Palais (cf. Saint James). A post office was established on December 23, 1863.

Saint Meinrad [SAYNT MEYEN-rad; SAYNT MEYEN-ruhd; SAYNT MEYEN-erd] (Spencer). This village was settled in 1836, laid out in February 1861, and named for the local Catholic monastery. Saint Meinrad College also is located here. A post office was established on June 27, 1862. Saint Meinrad, murdered in 861, was a Swiss Benedictine monk. According to an oral account: "Saint Meinrad was named after the school and church which were there before the town was actually begun" (ISUFA).

Saint Omer [SAYNT O-mer] (Decatur). This village, possibly named for Saint-Omer in France, was first laid out on January 19, 1831, by John Griffin and A. Major.

Saint Paul [saynt pawl] (Shelby). This town first was called Paul Town, for Jonathan Paul, an early settler from Jefferson County who bought land here in 1820 and built the first mill in this area. The part of the town in Decatur County was laid out in 1854, and the part of the town in Shelby County was platted on April 4, 1856. The post office was established in Decatur County on February 13, 1854.* Locally the town was called Bull Town. Cf. Germantown and Slabtown (Decatur).

Saint Peter [SAYNT PEE-der] (Franklin). A post office called Saint Peters was established on December 4, 1849; closed on April 2, 1906. The village was laid out in August 1853 by Reverend Maurice de St. Palais. German Catholics settled here in 1833 and built a log church on the site of the present church, which was built in 1852. The name of the post office and village comes from the church. Francis Bauer, who became postmaster, opened the first store here in 1848 or 1849.

Saint Phillip [SANT FIL-uhps; SAYNT FIL-uhps; SAYNT FIL-uhp] (Posey). German Catholics settled this village that developed around their church, which was built in 1870. A post office was established as Saint Philip in 1872. Other variant spellings have been Saint Philips and Saint Phillips.

Saint Thomas [SAYNT TAHM-uhs] (Knox). A post office was established on May 4, 1896; closed on September 30, 1901. The name is for the Saint Thomas Church, one of the oldest churches in Knox County.

Saint Wendel [SANT WEN-duhl; SAYNT WEN-duhl] (Vanderburgh). A post office called Saint Wendel was established on May 12, 1852; closed on March 30, 1907. Supposedly the village, located on the Posey-Vanderburgh county line, was named for Wendel Wasman, early settler who was the principal donor for the construction of a Catholic church here. The name also has appeared as Saint Wendells.

Salamonia [SAL-uh-MO-nee; SAL-uh-MON-yuh] (Jay). This town was platted in January 1839 and called Lancaster. The post office, which moved here from Randolph County on February 13, 1838, was called Salamonia, sometimes spelled Salamonie, for the Salamonie River. When the town was incorporated on October 6, 1876, the citizens voted to change the name of the town to Salamonia to agree with the post office name. The stream name is a form of the Miami name, *On-sah-la-mo-nee*, meaning "bloodroot" and "yellow paint," which the Indians made with a dye from bloodroot. The Miami chief nicknamed Le Gros, who lived opposite the mouth of the river, had the same name, so the stream may have been named for him.or he for the stream.

Salem [SAY-luhm] (Adams). This village was platted in 1866 by George W. Syphens, proprietor, and named for Salem, Massachusetts. The alternate name, Steele, was the name of the local post office, which was established on February 3, 1888; closed on December 31, 1904. The post office was named by postal officials for Major George W. Steele, an Indiana congressman, because there already was a post office named Salem in Washington County.

Salem (Elkhart). See Wakarusa.

Salem [SAY-luhm] (Jay). This village was laid out on June 4, 1837, by E. G. Campbell and J. G. Campbell. The post office—established in Randolph County on September 20, 1856; moved to Jay County on April 30, 1857; and closed on May 31, 1904—was called Jordan.

Salem (Randolph). See South Salem.

Salem [SAY-luhm] (county seat, Washington). This city was laid out in 1814 by John DePauw and named for Salem, North Carolina. An Indiana Territory post office was established on January 22, 1815.

Salem Center [SAY-luhm SEN-ter] (Steuben). This village was founded in 1843 and named for the township in which it is located. A post office called Salem Centre was established on April 26, 1852; closed on October 31, 1903.

Salem Crossing (La Porte). See Otis.

Salina [suh-LEE-nuh] (Harrison). A post office was established on October 13, 1869. A variant name is Knob Creek.

Saline City [SAY-leen SID-ee; suh-LEEN SID-ee] (Clay). This village was founded in 1870 by Henry Jamison and called Saline, supposedly for a salt lick here in pioneer days. A post office named Saline City was established on October 4, 1872; closed on August 31, 1951.

Salisbury (Greene). See Solsberry.

Saltillo [sal-TIL-o] (Washington). This town was laid out in 1849 by Madison Bowles and named Saltillo for the Mexican city occupied by United States troops during the Mexican War. When a post office was established on June 15, 1854, the name was changed to Saltilloville because there was already a post office called Saltillo in Jasper County. On July 7, 1897, the post office name was changed to Saltillo, and on October 15, 1938, the post office was closed.

Saluda [suh-LOO-duh] (Jefferson). A post office named for Saluda Township, in which it was located, was established on August 19, 1828; closed on June 6, 1889. This place name appears in other states and originally was a Native American stream name meaning "river of corn." In this county the name was applied to a stream, too—Big Saluda Creek, also called Saluda Creek.

Samaria [suh-MEHR-ee-uh] (Johnson). This village was platted on December 3, 1852, by Singleton Hunter and first called Newburg. On March 5, 1869, the county board changed the name to Samaria. The post office established on July 6, 1857,* was called Musselman, for a local family. Henry Musselman was the first merchant, and Fielding Musselman was the first postmaster. The post office name was changed to Samaria on May 27, 1870. The present name, some-. times applied to churches, comes from the biblical city. Churches in Greene and Morgan counties are named Samaria.

Sandborn [SAN-bawrn] (Knox). This town was laid out on October 7, 1868, by George Halstead and named for a civil engineer on the Indianapolis and Vincennes Railroad. A post office was established on September 2, 1869.*

Sand Creek Station [sand kreek STAY-shuhn] (Parke). This settlement developed as a railroad station east of Rockville and was named for nearby Sand Creek, also called Strangers Brook.

Sandcut [SAN-kuht; SAND-kuht] (Vigo). This village was founded about 1927 and apparently named for sandy soil here. According to the WPA files, the name is "very fitting because the soil is very sandy. During windy months the air is full of sand, and the sand is blown everywhere." Variant names and spellings have been Meltonville, Sand Cut, Sandcute, and Sandcut Farms.

Sanders [SAN-derz] (Monroe). This village was platted on July 14, 1892, and named for the local Sanders family. One of the oldest residents was Billy Sanders (WPA). A post office was established on January 14, 1893.

Sandersville (Vanderburgh). See Inglefield.

Sandford [SAN-ferd; SAND-ferd] (Vigo). A post office established as New Market on April 15, 1840, was changed to Sandford, on March 7, 1855. The village was laid out in 1854 by Hiram Sandford, for whom it was named. Sandford came to this area from Long Island, New York, via Cincinnati around 1820, settling across the state line and also platting West Sandford, Illinois, in 1856.

Sand Ridge [sand rij] (Spencer). This settlement was named for the nearby ridge of the same name.

Sandusky [SAN-duhs-kee; san-DUHS-kee] (Decatur). A post office was established on January 26, 1882; closed on May 15, 1905. The village was laid out on October 7, 1882. The name probably comes from the city, county, river, and bay in Ohio.

Sandy Hook [SAN-dee huk] (Daviess). A post office called Sandyhook, supposedly for sand hills here (WPA), was established on December 4, 1899; closed on February 19, 1900.

Sandytown [SAN-dee-town] (Vermillion). This village was named for extremely sandy soil, in which settlers grew watermelons (WPA). There was a sandstone quarry nearby.

San Jacinto [san juh-SIN-to] (Jennings). A post office was established on April 12, 1852; closed on June 30, 1906.* Probably the name is for the San Jacinto River in Texas, site of the famous battle in which Sam Houston defeated Santa Anna in 1836; the battle decided the independence of Texas.

San Pierre [san pier; san pee-EHR] (Starke). A post office established as River on December 2, 1853, was changed to San Pierre on December 21, 1855, to Pierre on June 21, 1894, and back to San Pierre on March 15, 1899. The village was laid out in 1854 and originally called Culvertown. Supposedly San Pierre comes from a French-Canadian named Pierre who owned a saloon here. According to a local tradition, "a French Canadian, Pierre, made his appearance in the village. His desire was to induce the residents of the community to build homes farther south of Culvertown, so with a barrel of whiskey, in a shack 400 feet south of the village he started a saloon. In this way the site of the town was shifted to the new location, and the name changed to San Pierre" (WPA).

Santa Claus [SAN-tuh klawz] (Spencer). This town was platted in 1846 and incorporated in 1967. The settlement name was Santa Fe; however, there already was a Santa Fe in Indiana, so Santa Claus was suggested as an alternative post office name. A post office called Santa Claus was established on May 21, 1856; changed to Santaclaus on June 25, 1895; changed back to Santa Claus at a later date.* The name has given rise to several local legends that attempt to explain it. Three of these stories go:

1. "Santa Claus Land is located at Highway 162 and 245 in southern Indiana. It was founded by German pioneers on Christmas Eve in 1852 during a village meeting to find a name for their settlement. Snow was very deep, and travel was almost impossible. When all of the settlers arrived, they began proposing names, but none suited them, when all of a sudden the door was swung open, and there stood a man dressed in a Santa Claus costume. They were all pretty drunk and ready for anything, so one of them suggested it be named Santa Claus, and thus it was named Santa Claus, Indiana" (ISUFA).

2. "It is located six miles east of Gentryville on State Road 245. Before receiving the name Santa Claus, this village was named Santa Fe. Due to the fact that there is a Santa Fe in New Mexico, the U.S. Post Office told the people of this area to choose another name. So legend tells it that a group of the citizens were discussing a name for the town near Christmas when a small child came into the room and mentioned the name 'Santa Claus,' which the citizens decided to adopt" (ISUFA).

3. "Several families settled in the area and decided that they should have a name for their community. They decided on Santa Fe. They applied for a post office to make it official. On Christmas of 1855, everyone was greatly excited at the thought of going to their own brand new post office for their Christmas cards and gifts instead of having to ride to Dale. Unfortunately, a large white envelope with important seals arrived the day before Christmas to

reveal that a town in Indiana already was named Santa Fe. Determined to get their post office just as quickly as possible, the citizens of Santa Fe decided to discuss the matter that very night, Christmas Eve. While they were singing, the whole world outdoors became filled with an intense, blinding light, and a little boy came rushing in. 'The star, the Christmas star is falling!' Everyone rushed out just in time to see a flaming mass shooting down from the heavens and crash into a low distant hill. They considered it an omen of good fortune. Returning to the meeting, it seemed a most natural thing for all the folk to agree that the name Santa Fe should be changed to Santa Claus" (ISUFA).

Santa Fe [SAN-tuh FAY] (Miami). This village was laid out by Ebenezer Fenimore on January 22, 1849, though the plat was not recorded until June 1, 1850. Sometimes it is referred to locally as Old Santa Fe to distinguish it from New Santa Fe, q.v., in the same county. Apparently the name is a transfer, probably from Santa Fe, New Mexico, taken by U.S. troops in 1846. A post office was established on August 16, 1849; closed on April 15, 1917.

Santa Fe (Spencer). See Santa Claus.

Sante Fe (Owen). See Cuba.

Saratoga [sehr-uh-TO-guh] (Randolph). A post office was established on October 29, 1867, and the town was platted in 1875 by John C. Albright. The name probably is for Saratoga, New York, perhaps suggested by the name on a railroad car. Several local legends have arisen to explain the name. One story goes: "While looking for a name the postmaster was in Albright's general store when in bounced a beautiful red-headed girl. Her name was Sara Loller. When asked if she would like to have a town named after her she said yes, whereupon Mr. Albright suggested toga be added to her name and the town called Saratoga" (WPA).

Sardinia [sahr-DEEN-yuh] (Decatur). A post office called Sardinia was established on May 11, 1850. The village was laid out in 1865. The name apparently comes from the Mediterranean island, but according to local anecdote, "Sardinia was so named because old Frank Gaston gave a big sardine supper, free, one time in order to get people to trade at his store. After that, everyone called the town Sardinia. It was called Big Creek at one time, but I don't know at what period in history that was. While there was a post office still here some lady wrote and wanted to know if Sardinia was connected in any way to Sardinia Island in the Mediterranean Sea. Em Sherman and I were appointed to do the research to find out, and though we tried and tried, we could not find any connections" (ISUFA).

Sassafras [SAS-uh-fras] (Perry). A post office established on January 19, 1916, was called Saffaras, apparently the postmaster's misspelling of Sassafras, for the trees here, on the application for a post office. On June 15, 1957, the name was changed to Sassafras. According to an oral account, however, Sassafras, not Saffaras, is the mistake name: "It used to be Saffaras. They misspelled it and made it Sassafras" (ISUFA).

Saturn [SAT-ern] (Whitley). A post office was established on January 21, 1857; closed on November 15, 1900. The name probably is for the planet, since James Clerk Maxwell's theory about its rings was in the news at that time. There are other local traditions concerning the name, though. According to an oral account, "the post office was so called because it was a traveling one. It was kept in two or three log cabins run by different individuals, notably William T. Jefferies" (ISUFA). According to a county history, the name came from the planet about 1850 when someone in Jefferson Township built a makeshift telescope and claimed he could distinguish the various planets. He seemed most interested in Saturn and talked about it so much that he became the laughing stock of the community. Allegedly this encouraged William Jefferies, the first postmaster, to send the name Saturn to the Post Office Department, and it was accepted.

Saundersville (Vanderburgh). See Inglefield.

Savah [su-vah] (Posey). A post office was established here on April 26, 1892; closed in 1902.

Sawdust Mill (Whitley). See Luther.

Scalesville [SKAYLZ-vil] (Warrick). A post office, named for the local Scales family, was established on January 13, 1879; closed on December 31, 1903. William Scales was the first postmaster. An earlier name of the village was Stevensport.

Scarboro (Pulaski). See Star City.

Scarlet [SKAHR-luht] (Orange). A post office was established here on May 26, 1898; closed on November 30, 1915. The name is for a local family. Otho C. Scarlet was the first postmaster, and Alvis Scarlet was the second postmaster.

Schererville [SHEER-uh-vil] (Lake). This town was named for Nicholas

Scherer, who arrived in 1865 and laid out the town in 1866. A post office was established on December 20, 1866.

Schley [shleye] (Spencer). A post office was established on June 16, 1899; closed on October 31, 1905. The name probably honors the American admiral Winfield Scott Schley (1839–1909). Another post office named Schley was established in Sullivan County on November 19, 1898; closed on April 1, 1899.

Schneider [SNEYE-der] (Lake). A post office called Schneider, for a local family, was established on March 15, 1902. The Schneiders were landowners in this area.

Schnellville [SHNEL-vil] (Dubois). This village was platted on November 25, 1865, by Henry Schnell, for whom it was named. A post office was established on July 7, 1869.

Schrock (Lagrange). See Honeyville.

Scipio [SIP-ee-o] (Franklin). This village was platted on December 29, 1826, by Paul Clover and Joseph Alyers. The post office serving this locale from December 22, 1836, to May 29, 1839, was called Philanthropy, apparently a commendatory name. Scipio is for one of the classical Roman generals, perhaps via New York.

Scipio [SIP-ee-o] (Jennings). This village was laid out in 1817 and named by William Klapp for the noted Roman generals. A post office established as Geneva on September 23, 1820, was changed to Scipio on November 22, 1834.

Scircleville [SER-kuhl-vil] (Clinton). This village was laid out in 1873 and named for the local Scircle family. John

Scircle opened the first drugstore here, and a member of the Scircle family platted the village. A post office was established on September 21, 1875.* The name has been spelled Circleville.

Scotland [SKAHT-luhnd; SKAHT-luhn] (Greene). This village was platted in 1835 and named by Scots David Wallace and Jimmy Haig for their homeland. The Wallaces, Haigs, Andersons, and other families from Scotland settled near one another here. A post office was established on April 13, 1837.*

Scott [skaht] (Lagrange). A post office was established on November 21, 1837; closed on August 31, 1905.*

Scott County [skaht]. This county was organized in 1820 and named for Major General Charles Scott, officer in the Revolution and governor of Kentucky. Seat: Scottsburg.

Scottsburg [SKAHTS-berg] (county seat, Scott). This city was laid out on March 27, 1871. It was named not for the county in which it is located but for Colonel Horace Scott, general superintendent of the Jeffersonville, Madison, and Indianapolis Railroad. A post office called Scottsburgh was established on June 10, 1873. The spelling was changed to Scottsburg on June 30, 1892.

Scottsville [SKAHTS-vil] (Floyd). This village was laid out on March 23, 1853, and a post office was established on July 9, 1856; closed on April 30, 1904. The name is for the local Scott family. Moses and John Scott settled here in 1812, and Wesley G. Scott was the third postmaster.

Screamerville (Greene). See Hobbieville.

Seafield [SEE-feeld] (White). A post office was established on June 26, 1861; closed on November 30, 1939. The village was platted in June 1863 as a grain market. The name is for a local storekeeper named Sea, whose store was near the site of the village.

Sedalia [suh-DAYL-yuh] (Clinton). This village was laid out in 1872 by J. B. McCune and James A. Campbell. A post office was established on December 6, 1872. Supposedly the name had been coined in 1857 from the nickname, Sed, of the daughter of the founder of Sedalia, Missouri, and spread eastward to several states. The name also is found in Alberta, as well as in five other states, including Ohio and Kentucky.

Sedan [si-DAN] (DeKalb). On September 28, 1854, a post office called Iba (or Ida) was established here. On January 5, 1861, the name was changed to Sedan, apparently for the French city, and on May 3, 1908, the post office was closed. The village, first called Lawrence, was laid out by H. S. Hines and D. N. Hines.

Sedley [SED-lee] (Porter). A post office was established here on March 27, 1883; closed on April 15, 1910.*

Seelyville [SEE-lee-vil] (Vigo). A post office was established on October 2, 1867, and named for Jonas Seely, first postmaster. Seely also laid out the town in 1871. Henry C. Dickerson, who opened the first store, became the second postmaster in 1876. The opening of the McKeen coal shaft, one of the earliest mines in the county, contributed to the growth of the town.

Sellersburg [SEL-erz-berg] (Clark). This town was laid out in 1846 by John

Hill and Moses W. Sellers and named for the Sellers family. A post office named Sellersburgh, with Moses W. Sellers as postmaster, was established on January 16, 1854. Absalom L. Sellers was the second postmaster.

Selma [SEL-muh] (Delaware). This town, built along the line of a railroad survey, was platted on February 9, 1852, and a post office was established on January 15, 1853.

Selvin [SEL-vuhn] (Warrick). This village was laid out on July 13, 1839, and originally called Taylorsville, for the proprietor, George Taylor. A post office established as Polk Patch, sometimes appearing as Poke Patch, on January 15, 1853, was changed to Selvin on February 17, 1881; closed on June 15, 1951.

Sentinel (Franklin). See Mount Carmel.

Servia [SER-vee-uh] (Wabash). A post office established as New Madison on July 17, 1866, was changed to Servia on November 21, 1883. The village was platted on December 18, 1856, and named for the former European kingdom, now Serbia.

Sevastopol [suh-VAS-tuh-pool; suh-VAS-tuh-pul] (Kosciusko). According to the WPA files, this village was settled around 1838, platted in 1855, and named for the Russian city and port. The original proprietor was John Tucker. A post office was established on May 27, 1858, in the home of the first postmaster, William Dunlop; closed on March 31, 1902. A variant spelling is Sevastapol.

Sexton [SEKS-tuhn] (Rush). This village was laid out on May 25, 1882, by Martha J., Francis M., and Rebecca Ham-ilton and named Hamilton for the Hamilton family. Marion Hamilton was one of the earliest residents. The post office established on May 4, 1882, and closed on July 14, 1903, was named Sexton, apparently because there was another post office named Hamilton in Steuben County. The present name is for the Sexton family. Leonidas Sexton of this county was a state representative in 1856 and lieutenant governor of Indiana.

Seyberts [SEE-berts] (Lagrange). A post office named Seybert, for a local family, was established on August 24, 1889; closed on February 28, 1914. Charles Seybert was the first postmaster.

Seymour [SEE-mawr] (Jackson). This city was platted on April 27, 1852, and named for Henry C. Seymour, superintendent of construction of the Ohio and Mississippi Railroad. A post office was established on December 21, 1852.

Shadeland [SHAYD-luhnd] (Tippecanoe). This village was platted in 1824. A post office was established on February 9, 1887; closed on August 31, 1915.

Shady Lane [shay-dee LAYN] (Clay). Located east of Harmony on U.S. 40, this locale received its name from the rows of sycamore trees that once lined both sides of the highway and the median strip here. According to a local superstition, your wish would come true if you held your breath while driving through Shady Lane. The locale is the subject of several legends, including these three:

1. "Before the road was ever paved or anything, it was just a mud road. They cut down trees, saplings they called them, small young trees, and laid them across the road to drive on so they wouldn't mire down in the mud. And

there was dirt over the trees and they started growing; those trees would start growing over the ends, you know, and the trees grew up from each end. That's why there was a row of trees on each side of the road" (ISUFA).

2. "Shady Lane was in a swamp area, so in that day when they came to these soft places in the earth where water came to the top there, it was hard for them to build a road through it, so as a base for it, they put logs across it. They called it corduroy. Those were supposed to be sycamore logs, and as those logs were laid there, seeds from these trees, possibly brush that they trimmed off of them, laid along the edge of the road there. And that's how Shady Lane got its start because they are all sycamore trees" (ISUFA).

3. "When the National Road was laid . . . it was called the National Road because it began in Washington, D.C. . . . it was laid upon a bed of green, freshly cut timber that had been plowed under with an oxen-drawn plow. These seedlings made a soft, spongy road bed. The wagon wheels made big ruts and pushed the road bed off along side the road. After a number of years, these seedlings sprouted, and it wasn't long before an almost perfectly formed row of sycamore trees grew to form a lane. That is how Shady Lane came to be" (ISUFA).

Shakespeare (Kosciusko). See Milford Junction.

Shanghai [SHANG-heye] (Howard). A post office was established on July 13, 1858; closed on December 15, 1900. According to a local anecdote, the village was named for Shanghai chickens owned by a resident here.

Shannondale [SHAN-uhn-dayl; SHAN-nuhn-dayl] (Montgomery). This town

was platted on May 10, 1851, by David A. Shannon and named for the Shannon family. A post office was established on January 17, 1852; closed on February 27, 1909. Several members of the Shannon family served as postmaster.

Sharon [SHEHR-uhn] (Carroll). This village was laid out in 1868 by Benjamin Duncan.

Sharpsville [SHAHRPS-vil] (Tipton). This town was platted in May 1850 with the expectation that it would become the county seat and named for its founder, E. M. Sharp, who came here in 1831. A post office established as Wild Cat on April 6, 1848, was changed to Ballengers, for a local family, on May 31, 1848, and to Sharpsville on October 13, 1851.

Sharptown [SHAHRP-town] (Franklin). A post office called Sharpstown was established here on the Mount Carmel and Johnson's Fort Turnpike on April 10, 1878; closed on April 2, 1906.

Shave Town (Clinton). See Geetingsville.

Shawswick [SHAWZ-wik] (Lawrence). A post office was established on January 29, 1891; closed on May 18, 1896. The name is for the township in which the village is located. According to local legend, the name was coined: "There had been an early judge in that portion of the state named Wick, who had in his county a lot of admirers and who thought that the township should be named in his honor. There was a man named Shaw, who was killed in the battle of Tippecanoe, and a lot of his friends thought that the township should be named after him. Anyway, the two sides compromised and it was called

Shawswick" (ISUFA). According to another traditional account, the name is for "Judge William W. Wick, an eminent jurist of that day and William Shaw, a greatly beloved personal friend of county agent Robert Carlton, who had been killed by Indians at the Battle of Tippecanoe" (WPA).

Sheasville (Owen). See Alaska.

Shedville (Randolph). See Brinckley.

Shelburn [SHEL-bern] (Sullivan). This town was laid out in 1855 by Paschal Shelburn, who settled here in 1818, and named for him. A post office established at nearby Currysville, q.v., on April 24, 1840, was moved to Shelburn on October 9, 1861.*

Shelby [SHEL-bee] (Lake). A post office was established on August 25, 1882. The village was platted in July 1886 by William R. Shelby, president of the Lake Agricultural Company, for whom it was named.

Shelby County [SHEL-bee]. This county, famous for its corn, was formed in 1821 and named for Isaac Shelby, officer in both the Revolution and the War of 1812 and governor of Kentucky, 1792–1796 and 1812–1816. Seat: Shelbyville.

Shelbyville [SHEL-bee-vil] (county seat, Shelby). This city was platted on September 1, 1822, and named for Shelby County, q.v. A post office was established on October 7, 1824.

Shepardsville [SHEP-erdz-vil] (Vigo). This village was settled in 1920 and named for a local mine owner. A post office was established on January 24, 1923. Variant spellings have been Shephardsville and Sheperdsville.

Shepherd [SHEP-erd] (Boone). A post office was established here on September 17, 1886; closed on November 30, 1901.

Sheridan [SHEHR-uh-duhn] (Hamilton). This town, first called Millwood, was laid out in 1860 by Egbert Higbee. A post office named Sheridan was established on January 30, 1871. The present name supposedly honors General Philip Henry Sheridan (1831–1888), Union officer during the Civil War.

Shideler [SHEYED-ler] (Delaware). This village was platted by Isaac Shideler on December 15, 1871, and named for the Shideler family. A post office was established on September 20, 1871. William Shideler was the third postmaster.

Shields [sheeldz] (Jackson). A post office was established as Shields, for the local Shields family, on January 10, 1866; closed on December 31, 1904. The village was laid out by L. L. Shields and William H. Shields on April 29, 1866.

Shielville (Hamilton). See Atlanta.

Shiloh [SHEYE-lo] (Sullivan). Shiloh, a biblical name, is a common church name in Indiana as well as throughout the United States, and the name of this village comes from the local Shiloh Church. Post offices named Shiloh were located in Grant County (April 7, 1868–November 9, 1868) and Howard County (February 7, 1876–October 30, 1876).

Shipshewana [SHIP-shee-WAH-nuh] (Lagrange). This town was platted in 1888 and named for Shipshewana Lake. The lake was named for a Potawatomi chief, Cup-ci-wa-no, "Vision of a Lion." A post office was established on May 22, 1889.

Shirkieville [SHER-kee-vil] (Vigo). This village was founded in 1921 and named for a local mine owner.

Shirley [SHER-lee] (Henry). This town, located on the Hancock-Henry county line, was platted in the fall of 1890 and named for Joseph A. Shirley, division superintendent of the Ohio, Indiana, and Western Railway. A post office was established in Hancock County on May 28, 1891; changed to Henry County on October 19, 1948.

Shirley City (Allen). See Woodburn.

Shoals [sholz] (county seat, Martin). This town, settled in 1816, formerly was called Daughertys Shoals, for William Daugherty, an early settler, and for a shallow ford on White River. The present name is for the town's location at a shoals, a ford or shallow place, in White River. A post office named Halberts Bluff for Joel Halbert, who purchased 1,305 acres here, was changed to Shoals on November 9, 1868.* The town was platted around 1844 as Memphis. According to local legend, "As I used to hear it, there was a man by the name of Halbert, originally from Tennessee, who owned all of this land in and around Shoals. But at that time he called his land 'Memphis,' and, so it went, he had a horse named Memphis. People started settling down in his new town and across the river where Shoals is now. Pretty soon the railroad was to be put in right across the river from Memphis, so it goes that this Halbert guy was real happy because he wanted to see it get a good start. Well, as soon as the railroad was built, the railroad started calling the station 'Shoals,' because it was built right at the shoals of the White River. Sure enough, this name became more familiar with people, and it wasn't long at all before the folks wanted it called Shoals" (ISUFA). The high

school nickname here is Jug Rox, which the following oral account explains: "At Shoals, Indiana, there is a large rock which sits on the side of a hill. This rock has the name of Jug Rock because it is shaped like a jug. It is about ten to twelve feet high and about six to eight feet wide. No one is sure how it was formed. There is one very unusual thing about it, however; it grows. Over the years it has been measured and the measurements recorded. These marks show that it has grown. This high school has adopted the jug rock as its mascot, and in the town of Shoals, the rock has become a legend. Many people come every year to see the unusual rock" (ISUFA).

Shooters Hill [shoo-terz HIL] (Marion). This community was platted and incorporated in 1925.

Shrock (Lagrange). See Honeyville.

Siberia [seye-BEER-ee-uh; seye-BEER-yuh] (Perry). This village was named Sabaria in 1869 by Father Isidore Hobi in honor of the birthplace of Saint Martin of Tours, for whom a local church was named. Apparently the Post Office Department thought the name had been misspelled and changed it to Siberia when a post office was established on August 3, 1883.* Locally some people believe the name comes from the Asian region: "Siberia was named after Russia" (ISUFA).

Sidney [SID-nee] (Kosciusko). According to the WPA files, this town was settled in 1834 and, according to tradition, named for Sidney, Ohio, home of early settlers or named by railroad officials for the Sidney family, from whom land was purchased. It was platted in the fall of 1881 by Daniel Snell, John Mowan, and Aaron Stumpff. A post office was established on July 6, 1882.

Sidney (Marshall). See Argos.

Silver Hills [SIL-ver HILZ] (Floyd). This settlement was named for a nearby range, Silver Hills, usually called The Knobs. Silver Hill is a variant spelling.

Silver Lake [SIL-ver LAYK] (Kosciusko). This town was platted by Jacob Paulus on March 8, 1859, and first named Silver Lakeville for nearby Silver Lake. Jacob and Daniel Paulus were the first merchants, and a post office called Silver Lake, with Jacob Paulus as postmaster, was established in their log store on May 10, 1854; changed to Silverlake on July 25, 1894. A variant name is Silver Lake Junction.

Silverville [SIL-ver-vil] (Lawrence). A post office was established on May 28, 1851; closed on May 31, 1906. The village was platted on July 26, 1855. Apparently the name comes from the belief that silver ore could be found here. One local tradition, though, is that the town was so named because early settlers bought the land with silver dollars. Other local accounts of the name are (1) "Silverville was named for a man named Silvers" (ISUFA); (2) "Silverville's name had something to do with Indians burying silver and gold in a cave in that vicinity" (ISUFA); (3) Silverville "derived its name from the belief that silver ore existed in its vicinity. This proved to be a fallacy" (WPA).

Silverwood [SIL-ver-wud] (Fountain). This village was platted on September 7, 1881, by Cale W. Waterman and apparently named for nearby Silver Island. The Wabash and Erie Canal passed through the county forming, with the Wabash River, an island called Silver Island because Indians supposedly had

hidden silver at this spot. A post office established as Lodi (cf. Lodi [Parke]) on March 24, 1888, was changed to Silverwood on June 22, 1891; closed on December 30, 1933. A variant spelling is Silver Wood.

Simons Corners (Noble). See Laotto.

Simonton Lake [SEYE-muhn-tuhn LAYK] (Elkhart). This village was named for the nearby lake of the same name.

Simonville (Noble). See Laotto.

Simpson [SIMP-suhn] (Huntington). This village was surveyed by Henry H. Wagoner, county surveyor, for George Bippus, trustee, and the plat was filed on May 23, 1885. Originally the village was called Roches Station, but the post office established on December 4, 1886, was called Simpson. The post office was closed on December 15, 1902.

Sims [simz] (Grant). A post office named for Sims Township, in which it is located, was established on December 22, 1881.

Sinking Springs (Lawrence). See Redding.

Sitka [SIT-kuh] (White). A post office named Sitka, apparently for Sitka, Alaska, was established on July 15, 1869; closed on October 14, 1903.*

Six Mile (Jennings). See Hayden.

Six Points [SIKS poynts] (Clay). This community was so named because four county roads converged here with State Road 46.

Six Points [SIKS poynts] (Hendricks). This village was so named because a railroad and two roads intersected here.

Skelton [SKELT-uhn] (Gibson). This village was laid out on July 26, 1911, by William T. Watson and named for J. W. Skelton, an early settler.

Skipperville (Madison). See Summitville (Madison).

Slabtown (Boone). See Waugh.

Slabtown [SLAB-town] (Decatur). The Layton brothers established a mill here in 1855; hence, a variant name is Layton Mills, which is the preferred name on recent maps. Slabs, some of them used to build roads, were cut at the local sawmill, so the village was called Slabtown.

Slabtown (Rush). See Homer.

Slabtown (Whitley). See Collamer.

Slash (Grant). See Normal.

Slate [slayt] (Jennings). A post office named Slate, for its location near Slate Creek, was established on September 27, 1852; closed on February 29, 1904.*

Slatecut [SLAYT-kuht] (Clark). A post office called Slate Cut was established here on September 1, 1858; closed on October 15, 1891.*

Slawson (Switzerland). See Bennington.

Sleeth [sleeth] (Carroll). A post office, named for the local Sleeth family, was established on April 15, 1880; closed on June 15, 1907.* W. H. Sleeth donated land to the village.

Slick Rock Ford (Lawrence). See Guthrie.

Slinkards Mills (Greene). See Newberry.

Sloan [slon] (Warren). A post office, named for the local Sloan family, was established on June 18, 1914; closed on November 29, 1941.

Smartsburg [SMAHRTS-berg] (Montgomery). A post office called Smartsburgh was established on February 26, 1886. The spelling was changed to Smartsburg on September 15, 1892. One source says the village was named "after the smartweed along the creek" (WPA), but it may have been named for a local family, perhaps for Dr. Smart, a pioneer physician.

Smedley [SMED-lee] (Washington). This village was established as a railroad station and earlier called Smedleys Station. A post office called Smedley was established on March 18, 1884. The name honors a local family. Morgan Smedley was the first merchant, and Henry Smedley was the first postmaster. Other members of the Smedley family also served as postmasters. A variant name has been Heffren, sometimes spelled Heffron, for the Heffren post office located just south of the railroad station. Morgan Smedley was the first postmaster of the Heffren post office. Cf. Hitchcock.

Smithfield [SMITH-feeld] (Delaware). A post office was established on November 11, 1830; closed on September 9, 1856. The name, apparently for a local family, was applied to a small collection of houses already here before the village was laid out by David Stout and William Duncan on March 12, 1830.

Smithfield (Gibson). See Patoka.

Smithland [SMITH-luhnd] (Shelby). A post office named Smithland, for the local Smith family, was established on December 2, 1853; closed on October 31,

1901.* Jesse Smith was the first postmaster, and other members of the Smith family also served as postmaster. The village, an early trading center, was laid out by Hezekiah Smith on October 28, 1851.

Smiths Crossing [SMITHS KRAWS-ing] (Decatur). This village was laid out on January 2, 1859, by R. S. Ward and named for William Stewart Smith, who lived here for several years. Wintersville is a variant name for a post office established on December 6, 1850.

Smithson [SMITH-suhn] (White). A post office, named for the local Smith family, was established on August 2, 1880; closed on May 15, 1931. Abel T. Smith came here in 1846, and his son, Lieutenant Bernard G. Smith, for whom the village is said to have been named, was a Civil War veteran. Wheeler, sometimes Wheeler Location, the alternate name, was the name of a flag station on the railroad and honors Hiram Wheeler, who built a tile factory here in 1879.

Smith Valley [SMITH VAL-ee] (Johnson). According to the WPA files, this village was settled in 1869 and originally called Smiths Valley for one of the early settlers, William K. Smith. A post office established as Smiths Valley on June 29, 1870, was changed to Smith Valley on April 18, 1893; closed on August 30, 1904.

Smithville (Gibson). See Patoka.

Smithville [SMITH-vil] (Monroe). This village was laid out on November 26, 1851, by Mansfield Bennett and George Smith and named for Smith, who probably opened the first store and owned some of the land on which the village is located. A post office was established on February 27, 1854.

Smithville (Wayne). See Richmond.

Smocktown (Johnson). See Greenwood (Johnson).

Smockville [SMAHK-vil] (Parke). This village was established as a coal mining community and named for a local family.

Smoky Row (Parke). See Klondyke (Parke).

Smootsdell (Hendricks). See Avon.

Smyrna [SMER-nuh] (Decatur). A post office was established here on June 30, 1846.* This place name, fairly popular in the United States, comes from the seaport in Asia Minor, supposedly the birthplace of Homer. Probably the influence here was biblical, though, since Smyrna was one of the seven cities addressed by John in Revelation.

Smyrna (Jefferson). See Creswell.

Smythe [smeyeth] (Vanderburgh). This village was named for the local Smythe family. Thomas E. Smythe and Henry Smythe, cousins, were the first settlers. A variant name is Burkehart Station, also spelled Burkhart Station.

Snacks [snaks] (Marion). A post office was established on February 20, 1890; closed on May 31, 1901. According to the WPA files, the name is for a settler named Snacks or from an occasion when travelers stopped at a local grocery store and asked for snacks. The community also has been called Glen Eden.

Snake Hollow (Greene). See Doans.

Snoddys Mills (Fountain). See Coal Creek.

Snow Hill [sno hil] (Randolph). Formerly this village was called Mount Pleasant and Vinegar Hill. A post office was established as Snow Hill on February 4, 1859; closed on March 30, 1907.* Allegedly the present name is descriptive of "the snow which gathered on the mound in winter" (WPA), but the place name also is found in England and in other states.

Soapville (Switzerland). See Avonburg.

Sodom (Parke). See Bridgeton.

Solitude [SAHL-uh-tood] (Posey). A post office was established on April 14, 1858; closed on March 15, 1917.* Supposedly, the name, applied by a railroad official, is descriptive of the desolate area here, with only the Evansville and Terre Haute Railroad crossing the New Harmony Road, before the establishment of the post office.

Solon (Clark). See Hibernia.

Solsberry [SAHLZ-behr-ee] (Greene). This village first was laid out in March 1848, and a post office called Solsberry was established on October 22, 1851. According to one oral account, the settlement was named for Solomon Wilkerson, village organizer and builder of the first house (ISUFA). According to another local legend, the village first was called Sol's Berry Patch, but "Patch" was dropped from the name. A likely origin is that Solsberry is a phonetic spelling of Salisbury, an English town name common as a place name in the United States and other English-speaking countries. In fact, on the 1876 Baskin, Forster map the name is spelled Salisbury. The local tradition that the village was named for Solomon Wilkerson is strong, though.

Somerset (Franklin). See Laurel.

Somerset [SUHM-er-set] (Wabash). According to the WPA files this settlement was founded in 1816; however, apparently the village was not platted until January 17, 1844. Originally it was called Twin Springs, descriptive of two nearby springs, and later it was called Springfield, a name probably borrowed from an eastern city but suggested by the twin springs. A post office called Hill Grove, descriptive of prominent hills here, was established on November 19; 1845, and on March 6, 1848, the post office name was changed to Somerset. A local tradition says the present name is for an Indian chief; however, probably it is for the English county of the same name, perhaps via New England. Sometimes the original village is referred to as Old Somerset because in the 1960s, when the Mississinewa Reservoir project was developed, the village was moved a mile east of the original site. The new village, sometimes called New Somerset, was first platted on March 9, 1963.

Somerville [SUHM-er-vil] (Gibson). This town was laid out in 1853 by John E. Smith and originally named Summitville because it is on high ground. A post office was established as Somerville on October 6, 1854.* The present name was applied by the Post Office Department, probably to avoid confusion with a post office named Summitville in Madison County.

South Bend [sowth bend] (county seat, Saint Joseph). Alexis Coquillard established a fur trading post here around 1823 and named the locale the Big Saint Joseph Station, but other settlers called it The Bend or South Bend for its location on the Saint Joseph River, where the river turns north from a westward course. Colonel Lathrop M. Taylor opened a trading post in 1827 and renamed the settlement Saint Josephs. In

1829 the name was changed to Southold, supposedly for its location on the south bend of the Saint Joseph River (WPA), though the name also is found in New York. A post office called South Bend was established on October 30, 1830, and the city was laid out on May 28, 1831.

South Bethany [SOWTH BETH-uh-nee] (Bartholomew). This village was laid out on May 22, 1849, by Jesse Spriggs and called Bethany, for the village in the New Testament, perhaps via a local church. A post office called South Bethany was established on March 9, 1861; closed on March 31, 1903.

South Boston [SOWTH BAW-stuhn] (Washington). Never platted, this village originally was called Boston for the city in Massachusetts. South was added to the name to distinguish it from another Boston in Wayne County (WPA). A store was opened by Bravilian Wood as early as 1834, and a post office called South Boston was established on January 24, 1850.*

South Gate [SOWTH gayt] (Franklin). A post office was established on February 18, 1839,* and the village was laid out in September 1850 by Richard Wood.

South Hanover (Jefferson). See Hanover.

South Haven [SOWTH HAY-vuhn] (Wabash). This housing development was begun in 1950 by Edward Mirante. It is located south of the Wabash River in South Wabash, so the name is partly descriptive and partly commendatory.

South Laketon (Wabash). See Ijamsville.

South La Porte [SOWTH luh-PAWRT] (La Porte). The name of this village is locational, as it is located south of the city of La Porte.

South Martin [SOWTH MAHRT-uhn] (Martin). A post office was established on January 11, 1861; closed on March 14, 1903. The name is locational, for the village is located in the southern part of Martin County.

South Milan (Ripley). See Milan.

South Milford [SOWTH MIL-ferd] (Lagrange). A post office was established on May 31, 1848, and in 1856 the village was laid out by John A. Bartlett and Francis Henry, proprietors. The name is locational, since the village is located in southern Milford Township.

Southold (Saint Joseph). See South Bend.

South Peru [SOWTH PEE-roo; SOWTH pu-ROO] (Miami). This village was platted on September 12, 1873, by Laban, Elizabeth, Maria, and Rachel Armstrong and William Erwin. On March 10, 1914, it became part of Peru. The name is locational, as it is located south of Peru on the south side of the Wabash River.

Southport [SOWTH-pawrt] (Marion). A post office was established on August 16, 1849; closed on April 30, 1960. This city was platted on April 5, 1852. According to local legend, Southport is an incident name. An old sailor riding through here in a stagecoach around 1835 said, as the coach slowed down, "She's laying to—she can't weather the first port south. Run up the sails, boys" (WPA). Since there was also a Northport (see Valley Mills) in Marion County when Southport was platted, the name, perhaps suggested by Northport, is probably locational, as, according to an oral account, it was located about four miles south of the first settlement in Marion County (ISUFA). A variant spelling is South Port.

South Raub [sowth rahb; sowth rawb] (Tippecanoe). This village was platted in 1822 and named for the local Raub family. A post office was established on February 6, 1878. Edward Raub was the second postmaster. Apparently South was added to the name to distinguish it from the village named Raub in Benton County.

South Salem [SOWTH SAY-luhm] (Randolph). This village, which also has been called Salem, was platted on December 25, 1849, by David Polly, and it once was called Pollytown for his family. A post office called Balaka, with David Polly as postmaster, was established on August 20, 1857; closed on June 29, 1885.*

South Union (Monroe). See Victor.

South Wanatah [SOWTH WAH-nuh-tah] (La Porte). This village, earlier called Roselle (cf. Wanatah) for a local post office and Joprice, for local landowner Joseph Price, was founded in 1859. The name is locational, as the village was established along the railroad just south of Wanatah.

South Washington [SOWTH WAWR-shing-tuhn; SOWTH WAW-shing-tuhn] (Daviess). This village was laid out in 1874 by Levi D. Colbert one mile south of Washington, for which it was named. Locally the village has been called Lickskillet.

South Waveland (Parke). See Milligan.

Southwest [sowth-west] (Elkhart). A post office called South West was established on April 21, 1854.* The name of this village is locational, for it is located southwest of Goshen, the county seat.

South Whitley [SOWTH WIT-lee] (Whitley). A post office established as Whitley, for the county, on February 25, 1837, was changed to South Whitley on May 14, 1842; closed on January 16, 1854. The town, first called Springfield, was platted on May 1, 1837. South Whitley is a locational name, as the town is located in the southern part of the county.

Spades [spaydz] (Ripley). A post office called Spades Depot, for the local Spade family, was established at a railroad station here on September 13, 1855; changed to Spades on March 26, 1883; closed on March 31, 1950. The village was laid out in 1855. Jacob Spade was an early settler.

Spanglerville (Ripley). See Cross Roads (Ripley).

Sparksville [SPAHRKS-vil] (Jackson). This village, platted on June 18, 1857, was settled around 1812 by and named for Stephen Sparks, who established a ferry, called "Sparks' Ferry," here. A post office was established on November 25, 1856; closed on January 27, 1956.

Sparta [SPAHR-duh; SPAHR-dee] (Dearborn). A post office, named for the township in which it was located, was established on March 26, 1846; closed on September 14, 1904.

Spartanburg [SPAHRT-uhn-berg] (Randolph). This village, originally called Newberg, first was laid out in 1832, and the plat was recorded on February 18, 1833. A post office named Spartanburg was established on February 10, 1842; closed on January 15, 1907. A variant spelling is Spartanburgh.

Spearsville [SPEERZ-vil] (Brown). This village was founded around 1835 by William Spears and named for him. A post office was established on May 19, 1855; closed on May 15, 1907.*

Speed [speed] (Clark). A post office named Speed was established on July 5, 1922; closed on October 25, 1963. The name honors W. S. Speed, who owned a local cement plant. The village was laid out around 1854 as Petersburg, for Peter McKossky, who lived nearby, but apparently the plat was not recorded.

Speedway [SPEED-way] (Marion). This city was laid out in 1912. It is the home of the Indianapolis Motor Speedway, for which it was named. According to the WPA files, when Carl Fisher, James Allison, and Frank Wheeler laid out and named the city for "Speedway Course," they said the racetrack was horseless, and the city should be horseless. When residents with horses complained, they said the word *speed* meant to hurry, to move forward.

Speicherville [SPEYE-ker-vil] (Wabash). This village was platted on October 21, 1881, by the proprietor and first postmaster, Christian W. Speicher (also spelled Spiker), and named for him. The post office, established on December 30, 1881, and closed on August 31, 1913, was called Spiker because Speicher ap-

parently preferred the anglicized spelling of his name.

Spelterville [SPEL-ter-vil] (Vigo). A post office was established on May 26, 1920; closed on June 31, 1934. The village was named for spelter (zinc), once manufactured here.

Spencer [SPEN-ser] (county seat, Owen). This town was founded in 1820 and named for Captain Spier Spencer of Kentucky, who was killed in the Battle of Tippecanoe. A post office was established on April 7, 1821. The high school nickname was Cops, for COP, as Spencer once was the center of population in the United States.

Spencer County [SPEN-ser]. This county, where Abraham Lincoln spent his formative years (1816–1830), was organized in 1818 and named for Captain Spier Spencer, who was killed in the Battle of Tippecanoe. Seat: Rockport.

Spencerville [SPEN-ser-vil] (DeKalb). This village was settled around 1828 and named for John Spencer, brother-in-law of Reuben J. Dawson, who platted the town in 1842. A post office was established on November 14, 1839.

Spiceland [SPEYES-luhnd] (Henry). This town was settled in the 1820s by Quakers from North Carolina who formed the Spiceland Meeting. A post office was established on April 10, 1838, and the town was platted on January 22, 1850. The name, first applied to the mission and also the name of the township organized in 1842, is for the abundance of spicebush growing in this area. Early settlers in central Indiana made tea from the spicebush: "When I was seven years old and all my brothers and sisters had the measles, I helped my mother collect spicewood branches to cook to make the tea to cure the measles" (ISUFA).

Spien Kopj (Lawrence). See East Oolitic.

Spiker (Wabash). See Speicherville.

Sponsler [SPAHN-sler] (Greene). This village was founded in 1889 and named for William Sponsler, who owned land here when a railroad stop was established.

Spraytown [SPRAY-town] (Jackson). A post office established as White Creek on April 16, 1860, was changed to Spraytown on April 24, 1878; closed on December 31, 1909. The name honors the local Spray family, who operated a store here.

Spring (Spencer). See Chrisney.

Springboro [SPRING-ber-o] (White). This village, founded around 1830, was named for a nearby stream, Spring Creek. A post office called Spring Borough was established on May 28, 1851; closed on September 13, 1853.*

Spring Dale (Harrison). See New Middletown.

Springdale (Ripley). See Morris.

Springersville [SPRING-erz-vil] (Fayette). This village was laid out in 1840 by Thomas Simpson, Jr., who built a frame house here in 1838. A post office, with Simpson as postmaster, was established on May 16, 1840; closed on March 5, 1853.* Springerville is a variant spelling.

Springfield [SPRING-feeld] (Franklin). A post office called Springfield, for the township in which it was located, was established on December 8, 1818; closed on November 15, 1902.* A town called Springfield was platted in 1816 by William Snodgrass, but county records do not locate the plat. Springfield Township was established on May 12, 1817. Some say the township was named for a large spring here, and others say it was named for an eastern town from which the pioneers came.

Springfield [SPRING-feeld] (La Porte). This village was surveyed in 1833 by Daniel M. Leaming, who laid it out for Judah Leaming, the original proprietor, and the plat was recorded on August 19, 1835. Supposedly the name is for a spring of pure, cold water in the area.

Springfield (Noble). See Cosperville.

Springfield [SPRING-feeld] (Posey). This village, intended for the county seat, was platted in 1817 on land donated by George Rapp, and a post office was established on March 10, 1818. The post office was closed in 1828.

Springfield (Wabash). See Somerset (Wabash).

Springfield (Whitley). See South Whitley.

Spring Grove [spring grov] (Wayne). According to the WPA files, this suburb of Richmond was separately incorporated to avoid taxes, and the name is for local springs in a grove of trees.

Springhill [spring-HIL; SPRING-hil] (Decatur). A post office called Spring Hill was established on November 6, 1827; closed on December 30, 1901. James Brison, the first postmaster, ran the post office out of James Conwell's store.

Spring Lake [spring layk] (Hancock). William Dye made a spring-fed lake here in 1884–1885, and the area, a picnic grounds, was called Dyes Grove. Later the site became known as Spring Lake, sometimes called Spring Lake Park, for the artificial lake. The town was platted in 1912.

Spring Mill Village [spring mil VIL-ij] (Lawrence). Spring Mill Village dates from 1815, when Samuel Jackson, Jr., a Canadian, built a small gristmill here. In 1816 Jackson sold his land to two brothers, Thomas and Cuthbert Bullitt, who built a three-story limestone mill building still standing and still working in Spring Mill State Park, established in 1927. A post office called Spring Mill was established on January 17, 1831; closed on April 16, 1859. The village was so named for the spring-fed stream that powered the mill.

Springport [SPRING-pawrt] (Henry). This town was laid out in July 1868 and named for springs located near the local railway depot. A post office was established on June 29, 1869.

Springs (Miami). See Chili.

Spring Station (Spencer). See Chrisney.

Spring Town (Crawford). See Marengo.

Springtown [SPRING-town] (Hendricks). A post office was established here on December 21, 1843; closed on November 23, 1865.

Springville [SPRING-vil] (Clark). This old village was Clark County's first seat of government. It is said that a French-man kept a store here as early as 1799, and the locale was called Tullytown for one of the traders. Supposedly the official name is for a nearby spring.

Springville [SPRING-vil] (La Porte). This village, settled by Germans in the 1830s, was laid out in 1833 or 1834 and named for a large spring here.

Springville [SPRING-vil] (Lawrence). A post office was established on February 8, 1827, and the village was laid out by Samuel Owens on July 11, 1832. The name is for a nearby stream, Spring Creek. According to an oral account, "Springville consisted of 26 lots along Spring Creek, from which the name of the town is derived" (ISUFA).

Sprinklesburg (Warrick). See Newburg.

Spurgeon [SPER-juhn] (Pike). A post office was established on August 2, 1867. The village was laid out as Pleasantville in 1860 by Reverend J. W. Richardson. Since there already was a post office named Pleasantville in Sullivan County, Richardson changed the name to Spurgeon, for Reverend Charles H. Spurgeon, an English preacher.

Squirrels Village (Wabash). See Stockdale.

Stacer [STAY-ser] (Vanderburgh). A post office called Staser, for the local Staser family, was established on June 28, 1892. Frederick Staser was one of the earliest settlers. Other variant names and spellings have been Nash Depot, Stacers, Stacer Station, Stasers, and Steers.

Stalcup Corner [stahl-kuhp KAWR-ner] (Greene). This village was named for the local Stalcup family. William

Thatcher Stalcup was a landowner here in the 1820s (ISUFA).

Stampers Creek (Orange). See Millersburg.

Stanford (Daviess). See Raglesville.

Stanford [STAN-ferd] (Monroe). This village was platted on July 29, 1838, and is said to have been named for the home of early settlers, Stanford, North Carolina (WPA); however, current maps and gazetteers do not show such a place name there. Apparently the name is a transfer, though, perhaps from England or Kentucky. A post office was established on July 12, 1839.

Stanley [STAN-lee] (Warrick). A post office was established here on October 1, 1890; closed on June 29, 1907.

Stapleton (Dubois). See Millersport.

Star (Rush). See Gings.

Star City [STAHR SID-ee] (Pulaski). This village was laid out in August 1859 by John Nickles and Andrew Wirick and called Scarboro, also spelled Scarborough, but the citizens apparently did not like the name and petitioned to change the name to Star City in 1861. A post office called Two Mile Prairie, with Wirick as the first postmaster and Nickles as the second postmaster, was established on February 5, 1850, and changed to Star City on March 3, 1862.

Starke County [stahrk]. This county, notable for its several attractive lakes and fields of mint, was organized in 1850 and named for General John Stark, who served with Rogers' Rangers in the French and Indian War and was a distinguished officer in the Revolution. Seat: Knox.

Starlight [STAHR-leyet] (Clark). A post office was established on March 19, 1892; closed on July 15, 1902. Allegedly, the village received its name for a bright lamp in a local general store. Everyone called the lamp a new star in the settlement, so the story goes, and they named the village Starlight.

Staser (Vanderburgh). See Stacer.

State Line (Lake). See Hammond.

State Line (Newton). See Effner.

State Line [stayt leyen] (Warren). This town, first called State Line City, was platted on June 29, 1857, by Robert Casement and so named because the Indiana-Illinois state line intersects the town. Established as a railroad town, it was the junction point of two branches of the Wabash Railroad. A post office was established on July 14, 1857. This boundary name also appears in Lake, Newton, Saint Joseph, and Vigo counties.

Staunton [STAWNT-uhn] (Clay). This town, founded in 1851 by Michael Combs and Lewis Bailey, first was called Highland, for its alleged elevation, but when a post office was established on July 26, 1853, the name was changed to Staunton, for Staunton, Virginia, Bailey's hometown.

Steam Corner [STEEM KAWR-ner] (Fountain). A post office was established on December 31, 1851; closed on February 13, 1904. A local steam sawmill gave the village its name.

Steam Corners (Whitley). See Lorane.

Stearleyville [STER-lee-vil] (Clay). This village, named for the local Stearley family, was founded in 1891 on land owned by George Stearley. A post office was established on March 3, 1893; closed on January 31, 1902. George Stearley was the fourth postmaster. A variant name is Stearleys.

Steele (Adams). See Salem (Adams).

Steeles (Rush). See Glenwood.

Stemm [stem] (Lawrence). This village was established as a switching station on the Monon Railroad.

Stendal [STAN-dayl; STEN-duhl] (Pike). This village was laid out first in 1867 and later in 1869 by Frederick H. Poetker, who was born in Germany, and named by Reverend W. Baumeister, who also was born in Germany, for his native city. A post office was established on August 13, 1873.

Sterling (Crawford). See Grantsburg.

Steuben County [STOO-buhn]. This county, home of Tri-State University and Pokagon State Park, was formed in 1835, organized in 1837, and named for Baron Friedrich Wilhelm August Heinrich Ferdinand von Steuben, a Prussian general who served with the Americans in the Revolution. Seat: Angola.

Steubenville [STOO-buhn-vil] (Steuben). A post office, named for the county in which it was located, was established on May 15, 1839; closed on August 31, 1932.* The village was laid out on March 10, 1873, by Daniel Till and Samuel Teters.

Stevensburgh (Hamilton). See Strawtown.

Stevenson [STEE-vuhn-suhn] (Warrick). This village originally was called Armery for Francis Armery, who, with

George Goddard, platted it in 1886. The present name apparently comes from an addition, first called Stephens, for the proprietor, and later Stevenson Station, "the spelling and pronunciation being easier" (WPA). A post office established as Fuquay, with William Fuquay as postmaster, on August 30, 1881, was changed to Stephenson on February 12, 1890, and to Stephenton on January 17, 1896. The post office was still operating in 1902 but apparently closed soon after that. The name also has appeared as Stephenston, Stevans, and Stevens.

Stevensport (Warrick). See Scalesville.

Stewartsville [STOO-erts-vil] (Posey). This village, earlier called Paris, was laid out on October 29, 1838, by James Stewart and named for his family. A post office named Stewartsville was established on April 3, 1852.*

Stilesville [STEYELZ-vil] (Hendricks). This town was laid out in 1828 and named for the proprietor, Jeremiah Stiles, who settled here in 1823. A post office was established on July 6, 1832.

Stillwell [STIL-wel] (La Porte). This village was named for an early settler, who gave his name to the prairie on which he settled. According to the WPA files, his name was Thomas Stillwell, and he settled here about 1831. A post office called Stillwell was established on May 25, 1870; closed on March 15, 1963.* The original village site was located about a mile northwest of a railroad station, called Stillwell Station, and the village developed along the railroad.

Stinesville [STEYENZ-vil] (Monroe). This town, once noted for its limestone production, was platted on April 5, 1855, by Eusebius Stine, proprietor, and named for him. Stine built the first gristmill and sawmill here. A post office established at nearby Mount Tabor, q.v., on October 20, 1831, was moved to this site on January 23, 1860.

Stipps Hill (Franklin). See Buena Vista (Franklin).

Stockdale [STAHK-dayl] (Wabash). Originally a Potawatomi village called Squirrels Village for Potawatomi chief Niconga, "Squirrel," Stockdale was platted on October 26, 1839, and is thought to be named for a local family, though the name also is found in Ohio and may be a transfer. Thomas Goudy built the first mill in 1839, but it was washed away in 1856 and rebuilt by Baker and Ranck in 1858. Still standing, this mill was operated by the Decks until 1964. The village is located on the Wabash-Miami county line, with a larger part of the original plat in Wabash County. The Stockdale post office, established in Wabash County, was moved to Miami County on August 1, 1855; closed on March 13, 1883.

Stockport [STAHK-pawrt] (Delaware). A post office was established on November 18, 1892. The village may have received its name "because it was a livestock shipping point" (WPA).

Stockton [STAHK-tuhn] (Owen). This village was laid out in 1852 by David Bush and John Ridge, proprietors, and first called Davidsburg, apparently for David Bush. The name of the village was changed to Stockton when a post office was established on January 17, 1855. The post office was closed on November 23, 1877. Cf. Coal City.

Stockwell [STAHK-wel] (Tippecanoe). This village was platted in 1850 and origi-

nally called Bakers Corner for Reuben Baker, the original landowner. The present name honors Robert Stockwell, who, with others, bought the site from Baker. A post office established as Bakers Corners, with Reuben Baker as postmaster, on June 21, 1853, was changed to Stockwell on December 8, 1859.

Stone [ston] (Randolph). This village, also called Stone Station, was founded around 1870 as a railroad station. The post office serving this area from October 6, 1871, to March 30, 1907, was called Clark, for the local Clark family. Thomas Clark was the first postmaster.

Stone Bluff [ston bluhf] (Fountain). A post office called Stone Bluffs was established on March 26, 1869; changed to Stonebluffs on February 26, 1895; closed on February 24, 1956. The village was platted on August 7, 1873. The name is descriptive of the village's location. A variant spelling is Stonebluff.

Stone Head [STON hed] (Brown). A post office established at nearby Pikes Peak, q.v., was moved here on February 12, 1890; closed on January 14, 1891. Frank A. Hoffman, in *Midwest Folklore* (Spring 1961), reports that a man used to carve large stone heads that were set up along the road as mileage markers, and the village received its name for one of these markers located within the community.

Stones Crossing [STONZ KRAWS-ing] (Johnson). This village, settled in the early 1830s, was named for the local Stone family. A post office was established as Stones Crossing on November 23, 1874; closed on August 15, 1905.* Frank A. Stone was the fourth postmaster.

Stonington [STON-ing-tuhn] (Lawrence). Settled around 1901, this village was named for nearby Stone Mill.

Stony Creek [STON-ee kreek] (Lagrange). This village was established as a railroad station and named for nearby Stony Creek.

Stony Lonesome [ston-ee LON-suhm] (Bartholomew). Apparently the name of this village, sometimes spelled Stoney Lonesome, is descriptive, as the locale was "both stony and lonesome" (WPA). According to one oral account, "It was named this because it is a valley and a hill of stone. Many years ago people were afraid to live there because of the lonely feeling" (ISUFA). Another traditional account says eight people settled here in Civil War times along a stony creek, while still another account says the name comes from the hollow, lonesome sound that steel wagon wheels made as they came through the place. The picturesque name has inspired a number of tales, such as the following oral narrative: "Some of my ancestors settled in Brown County, Nashville, Indiana. It has intrigued me as a town because it is so rural. Names like Stony Lonesome, Needmore, and Weed Patch Hill are just some of the place names. In fact, one of my own ancestors owned land on Weed Patch Hill. Stony Lonesome, my dad said, when he was a little boy, the road went right up to the creek. With these rather steep banks on either side he was told that it was a place where highwaymen would hold up the traveler because you couldn't see down around the bend, but now the highway misses it completely. So he was always scared when he had to go through Stony Lonesome because there might be a holdup, but I don't think that they have had one in several years" (ISUFA).

Story [STAWR-ee] (Brown). Once known locally as Storyville, this village supposedly was named for one of its first settlers, Dr. Story (WPA). Story was, in fact, a family name in this county, as the postmaster at nearby Valley Hill (cf. Christianburg) in 1860 was George P. Story. According to a local anecdote, however, the name is for storytelling at a local store: "There's only a general store where men used to sit and tell stories, lies." A post office called Story was established on May 25, 1882.

Stout (Delaware). See Bethel.

Stoutsburg [STOWTS-berg] (Jasper). A post office was established as Stoutsberg on September 5, 1890. The name honors George W. Stout, founder of the village (WPA).

Strains Mills (Parke). See Mansfield.

Straughn [strawn] (Henry). Originally this town was called Straughns Station, sometimes spelled Straughn Station, for the local Straughn family. Merriman Straughn, a veteran of the War of 1812, came here in the fall of 1820. The town was platted by John L. Starr in 1868. A post office called Straughns Station was established on July 15, 1869; changed to Straughn on November 28, 1882. The name also has been spelled Strawns.

Strawtown [STRAW-town] (Hamilton). This village was named for Chief Straw, a Delaware chief whose village was here, although one printed account says that "its name is derived from a house in it thatched with straw." Bicknell Cole and Jerry K. Leaming kept stores nearby as early as 1821, and Jesse Wood entered the township around 1822 and laid out a village called Woodville on his land; however, Wood's village didn't prosper and lost its identity to

Strawtown. A post office established as Stevensburgh, with Isaac Stevens as postmaster, on October 17, 1829, was changed to Strawtown on April 8, 1834; closed on January 31, 1902.

Stremler (Martin). See Whitfield.

Stringtown [STRING-town] (Boone). The origin of this name is unknown; however, Stringtown is a common derogatory name or nickname in the United States generally applied to a row of houses or buildings strung along a road without a real center. For example, in Miami County there once was a settlement called Stringtown about two and a half miles southeast of Mexico, and it was so named because a number of houses were strung along both sides of the Peru and Mexico Road. Supposedly this village in Boone County was first called Keys Ferry because it was founded by a man named Keys, and when the weather was bad, extra horses had to be used to pull buggies and wagons through here. In addition to the five Hoosier communities named Stringtown that follow, there are also communities called Stringtown in Hancock and Sullivan counties.

Stringtown (Grant). See Van Buren.

Stringtown (Parke). See Armiesburg.

Stringtown [STRING-town] (Ripley). A post office was established here on April 17, 1848; closed on January 10, 1865. Cf. Stringtown (Boone).

Stringtown (Vanderburgh). See Zipp.

Stringtown (Vigo). See North Terre Haute.

Stroh [stro] (Lagrange). A post office was established here on January 26, 1900.

Stroupville (Shelby). See Waldron.

Strouse (Noble). See Burr Oak.

Stumpke Corner [stuhm-kee KAWR-ner; stuhmp-kee KAWR-ner] (Ripley). A post office called Stumkes Corners, for the local Stumke family, was established on January 24, 1876; closed on October 4, 1895.* Henry Stumke was the first postmaster.

Stump Town (Daviess). See Plainville.

Sturdevants Store (Washington). See Chestnut Hill (Washington).

Sugar Branch (Switzerland). See Fairview.

Sugar Creek (Hancock). See New Palestine.

Sugar Creek [SHU-ger kreek] (Shelby). This village was named for the nearby stream of the same name. The stream supposedly was named for the large forests of sugar trees that grew along its banks.

Sugar Grove [SHU-ger grov] (Harrison). A post office called Sugargrove was established here on December 20, 1899; closed on August 31, 1901.

Sullivan [SUHL-uh-vuhn] (county seat, Sullivan). This city was laid out on May 25, 1842, and named for Sullivan County. Apparently the plan was to call the town Benton for Senator Thomas H. Benton of Missouri, but when it was found that there already was a Hoosier town called Benton, the surveyor, William Baker, left the name of the town blank and wrote "Sullivan County" on the map that he sent to Indianapolis with the papers of incorporation. According to local history, when the map was received, Sullivan also was used as the name of the city. A post office was established on September 30, 1843.

Sullivan County [SUHL-uh-vuhn]. This county was formed in 1816, organized in 1817, and named for General Daniel Sullivan, who was killed by Indians while carrying messages from Vincennes to Louisville during the Revolution. Parts of Shakamak State Park and the Greene-Sullivan State Forest are in this county. Seat: Sullivan.

Sulphur [SUHL-fer] (Crawford). This village was named for nearby sulphur springs, probably via the Sulphur Wells post office that was relocated here and called Sulphur on March 16, 1895. Cf. Sulphur Springs (Crawford).

Sulphur Hill (Shelby). See Geneva.

Sulphur Springs [SUHL-fer SPRINGZ] (Crawford). A post office called Sulphur Wells, for nearby sulphur springs, was established on April 18, 1873; moved to Sulphur, q.v., on March 16, 1895.* A popular spa once was here, and local mineral water was marketed regionally. According to one account, "It's just a spring, and the water tastes like rotten eggs. It's healthy, though. I know people that used to go and get jugfuls of water from it" (ISUFA).

Sulphur Springs [SUHL-fer SPRINGZ] (Henry). This town, named for local sulphur springs, was platted on January 7, 1853, by William S. Yost, who opened a store here around 1841. A post office, with Yost as postmaster, was established on February 13, 1844.

Sulphur Wells (Crawford). See Sulphur Springs (Crawford).

Suman [SOO-muhn] (Porter). This village, originally called Sumanville for the local Suman family, was laid out in June 1875 by Isaac C. Suman. A post office called Sumanville, with Suman as postmaster, was established on January 21, 1876; closed on November 17, 1894. Suman came here from Maryland in 1853.

Sumava Resorts [suh-MAH-vuh ri-ZAWRTS] (Newton). This village, established as a summer resort, was founded in 1926 and officially opened on July 1, 1927, as a recreational area. A post office was established on April 14, 1928; closed on March 22, 1957. According to the WPA files, *sumava* is a Native American word meaning "progress" or "success," but it resembles a Czechoslovakian place name, Sumavske Hostice.

Summit [SUHM-uht] (DeKalb). A post office was established on February 8, 1871; closed on October 31, 1908. The village supposedly was so named because the site is the highest elevation along a road here (WPA).

Summit [SUHM-ut; SUHM-uht] (Greene). This village was platted in 1889 and named for the nearby Summit coal mine, so named because it was surrounded by hills.

Summit [SUHM-ut; SUHM-uht] (Hendricks). According to the WPA files, this village was named Summit because it's the highest point on the Pennsylvania Railroad between Indianapolis and Saint Louis.

Summit [SUHM-ut; SUHM-uht] (La Porte). This locale "is probably the highest place in northern Indiana, and therefore given its present name" (WPA).

Summit Grove [SUHM-uht GROV] (Vermillion). This village was surveyed by A. Fitch on March 14, 1871, and the plat was recorded on December 23, 1871. A post office was established on October 11, 1871; closed on March 31, 1911. A variant name is Summit Grove Station.

Summitville (Gibson). See Somerville.

Summitville [SUHM-uht-vil] (Madison). A post office was established on April 28, 1847.* Earlier called Skipperville, the town was laid out around 1867 by Aaron M. Williams on part of his farm. According to one source, the village is called Summitville because it is said to be located about two miles south of the summit of the state. According to another source, the village is so named because railroad surveyors designated it the highest point between Fort Wayne and Indianapolis. According to the WPA files, the town formerly was called Wrinkle "in derision of its diminutive size" and Skipperville "because of the tale of two travellers who had stopped there one night and to whom the storekeeper had sold bad cheese and stale crackers. These travellers quickly spread the word that they had been served skipper cheese [cheese with maggots in it] at Skipperville. The word went 'round and the town became known as such." The name has appeared as Summit Hill and Summitsville.

Sunman [SUHN-muhn] (Ripley). A post office called Sunman, for the local Sunman family, was established on September 27, 1833.* John Sunman was the first postmaster, and Thomas W. Sunman was the second postmaster. The village was laid out in April 1856.

Sunnymede [SUHN-ee-meed] (Wabash). Also called Sunnymeade Addition, this community was first platted by Edward R. and Lois J. Mirante on July 29, 1955.

Sunnyside [SUHN-ee-seyed] (Marion). A post office was established on the National Road here on June 15, 1869; closed on May 14, 1878.

Sunnyside Station (Marion). See Sabine.

Surprise [suh-PREYEZ] (Jackson). A traditional account is that acting postmaster Doc Isaacs said he was surprised the village got a railroad through it and was surprised the village got a post office, so it was called Surprise. Jesse Isaacs was postmaster at the Acme post office, established on January 22, 1884; changed to Surprise on March 21, 1891; closed on September 14, 1905. The village was platted in 1897.

Surrey [SER-ee] (Jasper). A post office, named for the English county, was established here on March 1, 1882.

Survant [SER-vuhnt] (Pike). A post office, named for the local Survant family, was established here on September 10, 1883; closed on October 21, 1903.* George T. Survant was the fifth postmaster.

Swains Hill (Randolph). See Modoc.

Swalls [swawlz] (Vigo). A post office was established on July 3, 1891; closed on September 29, 1900. The name honors the local Swalls (earlier spelled Swall) family, who were among the early settlers of Vigo County. David Swall, Sr., was the first landowner here.

Swan [swahn] (Noble). A post office was established on June 7, 1838; closed on January 31, 1918. The village was laid out in July 1870 by Samuel Broughton, Orville Broughton, and Franklin Hilkert. The name is for Swan Township, in which the village is located.

Swanington [SWAHN-ing-tuhn] (Benton). A post office called Wyndam was established on May 27, 1884; changed to Swanington, for the local Swan family, on April 24, 1886; closed on June 30, 1937. William Swan, a local landowner, was the only postmaster at Wyndam and remained postmaster when the post office name was changed.

Swanville [SWAHN-vil] (Jefferson). A post office was established here on June 10, 1847; closed on January 15, 1907.*

Swayzee [SWAY-zee] (Grant). A post office, named for the local Swayzee family, was established on August 3, 1881. James Swayzee owned land here.

Sweet Home (Saint Joseph). See Lydick.

Sweetser [SWEET-ser] (Grant). A post office called Sweetsers, for the local Sweetser family, was established on February 28, 1870. The town was laid out in September 1871. James Sweetser was a local landowner.

Sweetwater Lake [SWEET-wah-der LAYK] (Brown). This community was named for a nearby reservoir, Sweetwater Lake.

Swinehart (Rush). See Homer.

Switz City [SWIT SID-ee; SWITS SID-ee] (Greene). A post office, named for the local Switz family, was established

on June 15, 1869. John Switz was a local landowner. The name has been spelled Swits City.

Switzerland County [SWITS-er-luhnd]. Noted for its historic architecture, this picturesque county, still largely rural, was organized in 1814 and named for Switzerland by Swiss settlers who came here in 1802. Seat: Vevay.

Sycamore [SIK-uh-mawr] (Howard). This village, an outgrowth of the railroad completed through here, was founded in 1881 by O. Hollingsworth. A post office was established on March 23, 1881; closed on October 31, 1912. According to the WPA files, the name is for a large sycamore tree on the site of the village.

Sylvan Grove [sil-vuhn GROV] (Clark). A post office was established here on September 5, 1849; closed on June 27, 1862.

Sylvania [sil-VAYN-yuh; sil-VAY-nee-uh] (Parke). This village was platted in 1836. A post office was established on March 19, 1850; closed on January 14, 1905.* The Latinized name supposedly is descriptive of the wooded area here but may have been chosen, as well, for its commendatory value.

Syndicate [SIN-duh-kuht] (Vermillion). This village developed as a mining community and apparently was named for a local coal mine.

Syracuse [SEHR-uh-kyooz; SEER-uh-kyooz] (Kosciusko). A post office was established here on July 24, 1837.* The town was laid out by Samuel Crawson and Henry Ward on August 11, 1837.

According to the WPA files, it was settled about 1834 and probably named for Syracuse, New York.

Syria [SAHR-ee] (Orange). A post office, apparently named for the Asian country, was established on March 3, 1880; closed on April 14, 1904. According to oral tradition, two sisters named the village Syria because they wanted a biblical name. Only outsiders pronounce the name SEER-ee-uh.

Tab [tab] (Warren). This village was platted on November 25, 1905, by Harrison "Tab" Goodwin and named for him. A post office was established on April 8, 1907; closed on April 30, 1955.

Tabortown [TAY-ber-town] (Vigo). This locale, located just east of Seelyville, was named for the local Tabor family.

Tailholt (Clinton). See Pickard.

Tailholt (Hancock). See Carrollton (Hancock).

Tail Holt (Rush). See Occident.

Talbot [TAL-buht] (Benton). This village was laid out on February 18, 1873, by Ezekiel M. Talbot and named for him. A post office was established on March 7, 1873.

Talma [TAL-muh] (Fulton). A post office established as Bloomingsburgh on January 13, 1851, was changed to Talma on January 25, 1896; closed on January 2, 1907. According to the WPA files,

Talma is from a local personal name; however, it also is claimed that William Roundtree Cubley (also spelled Kubley) found the word *Talma* in a crossword puzzle at the time the Post Office Department wanted a shorter name for the local post office.

Tamarack Grange [TAM-er-ak GRAYNJ] (Saint Joseph). A post office established as Tamarack on March 21, 1837, was changed to Carmel on July 5, 1838; closed on December 16, 1843. Tamarack, Algonquian for the larch of the pine family, is the name of four lakes, three cemeteries, a church, and a school in northern Indiana.

Tampico (Howard). See Center (Howard).

Tampico [tam-PEE-ko] (Jackson). This village was founded about 1840 when William McConnell and William Morgan built a blacksmith shop here. A post office was established on July 26, 1852; closed on November 30, 1909. The name probably is for the Mexican seaport.

Tangier [tan-jeer; tan-JEER] (Parke). This village was platted on March 13, 1886. A post office was established as Woodys Corner, for the local Woody family, on May 15, 1876. Mary C. Woody was postmaster. The post office was changed to Tangier on August 19, 1886. County surveyor J. T. Campbell suggested naming the village for Tangier, Morocco. Another variant name is Long Siding.

Tanglewood [TANG-guhl-wud] (Ripley). A post office was established on July 6, 1874; closed on July 2, 1877. Supposedly the village "was situated in a tangled thicket of woods, hence the name" (ISUFA).

Tanner [TAN-er] (Greene). A post office, named for John Riley Tanner, Republican governor of Illinois, was established on November 20, 1889; closed on July 14, 1906.

Tarkeo Corner [TAHR-kee-o KAWR-ner] (Decatur). A post office called Tarkeo was established on February 6, 1871; closed on April 27, 1881.*

Tarry Park [TEHR-ee PAHRK] (Lawrence). This village was platted in 1850 as Juliett. The nearby post office, established on January 20, 1880, and closed on November 16, 1886,* was called Yocky, for a local family, and the village also was called Yocky, or Yockey, as well as Red Cross Park because Joseph Gardner donated land near here to the International Red Cross Society. The present name is for Gardner's home.

Taswell [TAZ-wel] (Crawford). This village was platted around 1882 and named Laswell for the local Laswell family, but through a clerical error when a post office was established on September 12, 1882, the name became Taswell. James R. Laswell was the sixth postmaster, and James U. Laswell was the seventh postmaster.

Taylor [TAY-ler] (Tippecanoe). This village, earlier called Taylor Station, was named for a local family.

Taylor Corner [tay-ler KAWR-ner] (DeKalb). A post office called Taylors Corners, for a local family, was established on December 26, 1850; closed on August 5, 1863. Edward H. Taylor was the second postmaster, and John Taylor, Sr., was the sixth postmaster.

Taylorsville [TAY-lerz-vil] (Bartholomew). A post office established as Herod, for a local family, on July 14, 1849, was changed to Taylorsville on April 26, 1852. The village, also first called Herod, was platted on October 11, 1849. The name was changed to Taylorsville, for Zachary Taylor, twelfth president of the United States (1849–1850), because Herod became associated with the biblical Herod.

Taylorsville (Warrick). See Selvin.

Taylorville [TAY-ler-vil] (Vigo). According to the WPA files, this village was named in 1908 for "a farmer called Captain Taylor." Supposedly Taylor defended Fort Harrison from a Shawnee attack in 1812. According to an oral account, though, Taylor was the name of a worker or contractor who assisted in building the Wabash River bridge west of Terre Haute: "Either a worker or the contractor who built the present-day bridge, which replaced the wooden, covered two-lane bridge, lived in what is known as Dresser. . . . As the bridge was finished and the workers moved out, people moved in" (ISUFA). Variant names are Dresser and Taylorsville.

Taw Taw (Allen). See Arcola (Allen).

Tecumseh [tuh-KUHM-suh] (Tippecanoe). This locale was named for the Shawnee chief. Cf. Tecumseh (Vigo).

Tecumseh [tuh-KUHM-see] (Vigo). This village, once a ferry landing, earlier was called Durkees Ferry for John Durkee, who ran the ferry. A post office was established on July 17, 1882; closed on March 30, 1907. The name is for the famous Shawnee chief who attempted to unite the western Indian tribes. Tecumseh's name means "going across" or "crossing over," apparently indicating a meteor crossing the sky. According to local legend, though, the chief's name was "Tee": "There was this band of Indians that had a powwow where the town is now. The chief's name was Tee. A couple of warriors went through the woods and found this huge river. They ran back shouting, 'Tee, come see! Tee, come see!' So that's how Tecumseh got its name" (ISUFA). According to the WPA files, "it was near here that William Henry Harrison held one of his conferences with the Indian chief Tecumseh."

Teegarden [TEE-gahr-duhn] (Marshall). This village was platted on November 18, 1873, and named for the local Teegarden family or for Dr. Teegarden of La Paz. A post office was established on January 30, 1874; closed on December 30, 1966.

Tee Lake [tee layk] (La Porte). This community was named for the nearby lake of the same name.

Tefft [teft] (Jasper). A post office called Tefft was established on October 23,

1883, and the village was laid out on March 15, 1884, by Nancy and Isaac Dunn. The settlement earlier was called Dunnville, for the local Dunn family; however, the name was confused with Danville, so the village was renamed for Isaac Dunn's brother-in-law, Dr. Tefft.

Tell City [TEL SID-ee] (county seat, Perry). This city was founded in 1857 by Swiss settlers, who named it for William Tell, the Swiss legendary hero. A post office was established on August 16, 1858. A variant name is Helvetia.

Temple [TEM-puhl] (Crawford). A post office, named for the local Temple family, was established on June 2, 1884; closed on November 25, 1940. James Temple was an early landowner here.

Templeton [TEM-puhl-tuhn] (Benton). A post office, named for the local Templeton family, was established on May 16, 1873; closed on December 31, 1931. The village was laid out on December 23, 1873, by William J. Templeton.

Tennyson [TEN-uh-suhn] (Warrick). A post office was established on May 4, 1881, and the town was platted about 1882. Possibly the name is for Alfred, Lord Tennyson, then poet laureate of England. Earlier the community was called Tiger for a local tavern called The Tiger where illegal whiskey was sold.

Terhune [TEHR-hoon; tehr-HOON] (Boone). A post office established as Kimberlin on April 17, 1879, was changed to Terhune on July 2, 1883; closed on December 15, 1947.

Terrace Bay [tehr-uhs BAY] (Carroll). This locale was named for the nearby bay of the same name.

Terre Coupee (Saint Joseph). See Hamilton (Saint Joseph).

Terre Hall (Howard). See Hemlock.

Terre Haute [TEHR-uh HOT; tehr hot; TEHR-ee HOT; TEHR-uh HUHT; TEHR-ee HUHT] (county seat, Vigo). There was a French settlement here from about 1720 to 1763, and French explorers entering from the Wabash River named the settlement Terre Haute, "high land," not for its elevation but because the only high banks along the Wabash for a stretch of several miles were here. The city was platted in the fall of 1816 by the Terre Haute Land Company, which held patents to thirteen tracts of land in the area of Fort Harrison. A local pronunciation, TEHR-ee HUHT, has given rise to a legend that the city was named for Terry's Hut, a popular tavern in early days. According to another local legend, Henry Ford gave Terre Haute its nickname, Sin City: "Henry Ford and Paul Fischer once came to Terre Haute and stayed in the Prairie House, which is now the Terre Haute House. This was back before World War I. While Ford was here, he said that Terre Haute was just like a little Chicago and called it ' Sin City.' That is where Indianapolis picked up the name it now uses when talking about Terre Haute" (ISUFA). The post office, established in Sullivan County on February 11, 1818, was changed to Vigo County on January 17, 1828.

Terre Town [TEHR-ee TOWN] (Vigo). This subdivision is located north of Terre Haute, from which it derived its name. Locally the name is pronounced as if it were spelled Terry Town.

Terry [TEHR-ee] (Perry). A post office, probably named for the Terry family, who came to this county from Virginia in 1815, was established on March 3, 1892; closed on September 30, 1943.

Tetersburg [TEE-terz-berg] (Tipton). A post office called Indian Prairie, established on July 1, 1847, was changed to Tetersburg, for the local Teter family, on September 29, 1849; closed on October 20, 1879. The village was established around 1848 on the farm of Mahlon and Asa Teter. About 1840, George Teter, father of Asa Teter, moved here with his family from Virginia, and it is said that he brought with him $900, which he buried near his cabin until he dug it up to purchase land.

Thales [thaylz; taylz] (Dubois). A post office called Thales, possibly for the ancient Greek philosopher, was established on January 9, 1895; closed on June 15, 1909. The community also has been called Hickory Grove, for a nearby post office established on April 24, 1879, and closed on August 5, 1887. The Hickory Grove Church is located just north of Thales.

Thayer [THAY-er] (Newton). This village, once a hunting and fishing resort, was laid out by M. A. Asherton and J. P. Stratton on September 21, 1882. A post office named Kenney, with William M. Kenney as postmaster, was established on September 7, 1880; changed to Thayer on November 18, 1881. According to the WPA files, Thayer was the name of an early resident.

The Bend (Saint Joseph). See South Bend.

The Center (Noble). See Albion.

The Corners (Porter). See Hebron.

The Corners (Posey). See Farmersville.

The Crossing (Lawrence). See Mitchell.

The Mills (Elkhart). See Bainter Town.

The Summit (Benton). See Gravel Hill.

The Vermont Settlement (Steuben). See Orland.

The Vineyard (Switzerland). See Vevay.

Thomas [TAHM-uhs] (Daviess). This village was established in 1855 and named for the local Thomas family (WPA).

Thompsons Mills (Steuben). See Flint.

Thornhope [THAWRN-hop] (Pulaski). This village, earlier called Parisville and Rosedale, was laid out in 1853 by R. L. Parkhurst. A post office called Oak was established on May 29, 1856; closed on September 23, 1966.

Thornton [THAWRN-tuhn] (Lawrence). This village was named for a nearby quarry.

Thorntown [THAWRN-town] (Boone). There was a French trading post here as early as 1720. A post office was established on May 17, 1830,* and the town was laid out by Cornelius Westfall in 1831. The name is a translation of the name of an Indian village here: Ka-wi-a-ki-un-gi, "Place of Thorns," or Ka-win-ja-kiun-gi, "Thorn Tree Place." Several legends attempt to explain the name. Typical versions go:

1. "There is a legend about the way Thorntown got its name. It is said that an Indian princess once fell in love with a brave who was not the one that she had been promised to at birth. She and her father, the chief, had an argument, and she ran away. The two braves had a fight over her, and she ran into the forest of thorn bushes, tripped, and fell. A thorn pierced her heart, and she died on a hill where the Presbyterian Church now stands. That's how Thorntown got its name" (ISUFA).

2. "Thorntown was an Indian town. There was this Indian princess, and she was in love with a warrior. They both lived there. She was unable to marry him, though, because he was either killed in battle or her father had promised her to someone else. Anyway, she was heartbroken about the whole thing. So she went running through a woods full of thorns and briers and thick bushes that hadn't been cleared away. Somehow she got tangled up in the briers and fell, and a thorn went through her heart and killed her. Since she was so pretty and everything the people around there were broke up about it and named the place Thorntown. The name stuck and that's what it's called today" (ISUFA).

3. "Thorntown was all filled up with Indians at one time, and the Indian princess . . . they were being attacked by the white man, and she was afraid. So she climbed up inside a hollow tree. It was dead. And when she got to the top, she pricked her thumb on a thorn, and that's why they called it Thorntown. I don't remember her name though" (ISUFA).

4. "The town's surrounded on all four sides by different little creeks, and the Indians thought that it could never be destroyed by wind because it was surrounded by water. I think that something . . . that Thorntown was supposed to mean an island. There's been about five tornadoes gone through, and it'd hardly done any damage at all" (ISUFA).

Thralls Station (Vigo). See Saint Mary-of-the-Woods.

Thunderbird Mine Dam (Franklin). See Yellow Bank.

Thurman [THER-muhn] (Allen). A post office, named for a local family, was established here on July 9, 1888; closed on September 8, 1899.

Tiger (Warrick). See Tennyson.

Tilden [TIL-duhn] (Hendricks). A post office was established on April 13, 1880; closed on January 31, 1913. The name is for the American statesman and lawyer Samuel Jones Tilden (1814–1886), candidate for president in 1876.

Tillman [TIL-muhn; TIL-muhnz] (Allen). This village, founded in 1898, was named for a local family. John Tillman was an early settler. Variant spellings are Tillmann and Tillmans.

Tiosa [teye-O-suh] (Fulton). This village was founded around 1869 and supposedly named for a Potawatomi chief, Tiosa, "Beaver." A post office was established on June 12, 1872; closed on August 15, 1932.

Tipicanuck (Kosciusko). See Palestine (Kosciusko).

Tippecanoe [tip-ee-kuh-NOO] (Marshall). This village was laid out on January 8, 1882, about a mile south of Tippecanoe Town (Cf. Old Tip Town) along the railroad and called Tippecanoe Town Station. A post office established as Ilion on January 16, 1883, was changed to Tippecanoe on February 12, 1896. Cf. Tippecanoe County.

Tippecanoe County [tip-ee-kuh-NOO]. This county, home of Purdue University, was organized in 1826 and named for the Tippecanoe River. The stream name is a form of the Potawatomi Ke-tap-e-kon-nong, "Ketapekon town or place," an Indian town at the mouth of the stream. The Miami name of the river was Ke-tap-kwon, "buffalo fish," which are common in the river. Some people, though, think the name recalls an incident in which an Indian tipped a canoe. Seat: Lafayette.

Tipton [TIP-tuhn] (county seat, Tipton). This city was laid out on April 16, 1839, by Samuel King, who named it Kingston. When the county was organized in 1844 and King donated the site for the establishment of the county seat here, the name was changed to Canton, for Canton, Ohio. The name was suggested by John D. Smith, member of the Board of Commissioners and a former resident of Ohio. When a post office was established on November 28, 1845, the name was changed to Tipton, for the county in which the city is located, because there already was a post office named Canton in Washington County.

Tipton County [TIP-tuhn]. This county, one of the state's leading producers of corn, was organized in 1844 and named for General John Tipton, Hoosier soldier and United States senator, 1832–1839. Seat: Tipton.

Tiptonia (Bartholomew). See Columbus.

Titus [TEYE-tuhs] (Harrison). A post office was established here on August 22, 1898; closed on August 31, 1905.

Titusville [TEYE-tuhs-vil] (Ripley). A post office, named for the local Titus family, was established on May 22, 1862; closed on November 30, 1904. John Titus was the first postmaster.

Toad Hop [tod hahp] (Vigo). Only legends attempt to explain the colorful name of this village. Some representative examples:

1. "About forty years ago a man by the name of May built two houses down along the road beside of what is now U.S. 40. Well, this here fella was quite a drinker. Well, this went on for a couple years, and finally some of his relatives begin a-buildin' some homes down in there where he was at. Well, after a while some more people started buildin' down there till there was a pretty good bunch of houses down in there. Well, one night there in the summer he come a-trudgin' home all drunk and fell down right in the middle of one of the dirt roads that ran through there. Just as he fell down a toad hopped by right in front of him. He got up and says to himself, 'Toad Hop, yep, that's where I live, Toad Hop'" (ISUFA).

2. "They was something about a little boy that . . . they never decided on a name for Toad Hop, and he was great to catch toads. He'd call 'em toad hops, toad hops, and they . . . I can't remember who the boy was or anything, but that's how Toad Hop got its name" (ISUFA).

3. "It got its name from a family by the name of Harris early in the 1800s . . . above the hill, above Toad Hop to the west and a little south. There were regular floods in the area. Old man Harris would look down from atop the hill where his house was located during the floods and say, 'The toads are hopping,' referring to the Indians" (ISUFA).

4. "Bob's grandmother told me that some people in West Terre Haute set up a mushroom factory over there and that the mushrooms drew all the toads from around here, so they called the place Toad Hop" (ISUFA).

5. "This is how the town of Toad Hop got its name. . . . They got this name because the settlers could tell the weather by the way the toads hopped" (ISUFA).

6. "It is told that at one time the section on which Toad Hop is located was a swampy piece of ground, and that every way one looked one could see toads hopping and frogs jumping, and hence the name Toad Hop" (ISUFA).

Tobinsport [TO-buhnz-pawrt] (Perry). This village, named for the local Tobin family, was settled in 1827. A post office was established on May 11, 1865.* Members of the Tobin family were among the early settlers, and Robert Tobin was the fourth postmaster. A variant spelling is Tobins Port.

Tocsin [TAHK-suhn] (Wells). A post office was established on July 27, 1882; closed on December 2, 1966. The village was platted on August 19, 1884, though it may have been laid out first in 1882. The name means "alarm bell," and allegedly the founder, Michael Blue, thought the fame of the new town would resound through the countryside.

Toledo (Huntington). See Browns Corner.

Tolleston [TOL-stuhn] (Lake). This village was founded around 1857 by George Tolle, for whom it was named. A post office was established as Tolleston on May 31, 1860; closed on December 6, 1864; reestablished as Toleston on February 14, 1865; changed to Tolleston on May 14, 1909; closed on September 30, 1912. Another variant spelling is Tollestone.

Topeka [tuh-PEE-kuh] (Lagrange). A post office established as Haw Patch, for abundant hawthorn trees or haw bushes (WPA), on May 27, 1837, was changed to Topeka on August 11, 1893.* The village was platted in 1843. Although commonly Topeka is said to mean "potatoes," it is the Shawnee word for the Jerusalem artichoke. According to the WPA files, railroad officials applied the name because the surrounding country resembled Topeka, Kansas.

Toronto [ter-AHN-to] (Vermillion). A post office was established here on April 5, 1838; closed on June 15, 1912.*

Toto [TO-do] (Starke). A post office called Toto was established on May 23, 1855; closed on March 30, 1907.* The village, which developed as a railroad station, was platted on March 20, 1891, by Isaac and Martha Short. Allegedly, the name was adopted by railroad officials from an Indian word meaning "bullfrog," according to some sources, or "frog pond," according to others. An alternate name, Rye, is perhaps for the English borough.

Tower [TOW-er] (Crawford). A post office, named for a local family, was established here on October 17, 1890; closed on May 31, 1945.

Tracewell (Gibson). See Warrenton.

Tracy [TRAY-see] (La Porte). A post office established as Tracy Station on March 20, 1879, was changed to Tracy on November 28, 1882, and closed on January 15, 1912. The station was named for the foreman of a railroad crew (WPA).

Tracy (Wells). See Markle.

Traders Point [TRAY-derz POYNT] (Marion). This village was platted in 1864. A post office established on July 9, 1867, was closed on February 14, 1902. The name is for an Indian trading post that was located nearby.

Trafalgar [truh-FAL-ger] (Johnson). First a town called Liberty was platted

by A. M. Buckner and Elijah Moore on September 30, 1850. Then a town called Hensley Town, for the township, which was named for a local family, was platted about a half mile west of Liberty by George Bridges on February 16, 1853. In June 1866 the name of Hensely Town was changed to Trafalgar, and soon after that, Liberty was included within the limits of Trafalgar. The present name comes from the British naval victory over the French and Spanish fleets in 1805. A post office called Hensley, with Richard Hensley as postmaster, was established in this county on December 4, 1832; closed on September 16, 1850.* The Trafalgar post office was established on January 17, 1852.

Trail Creek [trayl krik; trayl kreek] (La Porte). This town was incorporated in 1923 and named for a nearby stream, Trail Creek. The French name of the stream was Rivière du Chemin, which, like the English name, is a translation of the Potawatomi name, Mi-e-we-si-bi-we. Dishmaw, a form of the French name, appears on early maps.

Transitville (Tippecanoe). See Buck Creek.

Travisville [TRAV-uhs-vil] (Wells). This village was named for John Travis, who settled here in 1865 and platted the village on January 21, 1871. A post office called Travis was established on September 15, 1873; closed on January 8, 1877.

Treaty [TREE-dee] (Wabash). This village, which dates from the mid-1870s, when George Wolgamuth opened a store, was named for nearby Treaty Creek. A variant name was Treaty Station when the railroad was completed through here. The stream received its name from the treaty with the Miamis made near its mouth in 1826. A post office was established on June 22, 1874; closed on June 29, 1935.

Treaty Grounds (Wabash). See Wabash.

Tree Spring [tree spring] (Vermillion). This community north of Perrysville was named for a local spring that flowed through a large tree and emptied into a trough along the road.

Tremont [TREE-mahnt] (Porter). This village was founded about 1845 and named for three large sand dunes called Three Mountains or Tremont (WPA).

Trenton [TRENT-uhn] (Blackford). This village dates from around 1840 (WPA) and was laid out on January 20, 1845, by Robert H. Lanning, Ezekiel Lanning, Basel Anderson, and William Cortright. Supposedly the name is for Trenton, New Jersey. The post office established on July 25, 1856, and closed on August 31, 1907, was called Priam because there already was a post office in Randolph County called Trenton.

Trenton (Randolph). See Huntsville.

Trevlac [TREV-lak] (Brown). Earlier this village was called Bear Creek, for a nearby stream. John Richards, who was born in Tennessee in 1808, settled with others on Bear Creek about 1823. Richards owned 940 acres on Bear Creek and served as justice of the peace, constable, and county commissioner. A post office called Richards, for the local Richards family, was established on December 22, 1881. Marion Richards and Stephen A. Richards were postmasters. On December 26, 1907, the post office name was changed to Trevlac, the name of the local Calvert family spelled backwards.

Tri Lakes [treye layks] (Whitley). This community was named for nearby lakes, alternately called Tri-Lakes and Shriner Lake.

Trinity [TRIN-uh-tee] (Jay). This village was named for the Holy Trinity Church, which was built here in 1861.

Trinity Springs [TRIN-uh-tee SPRINGZ] (Martin). This village was platted on August 3, 1837, as Harrisonville. The present name is for three local mineral springs, which are also called Trinity Springs. A post office called Trinity Springs was established on January 24, 1848; changed to Trinity on May 11, 1895; closed on January 31, 1943.

Tripton (Jennings). See North Vernon.

Troy [troy] (Perry). This town, once the county seat, was thought to have been named for the Homeric city; however, it probably was named for Judge Alexander Troy of Salisbury, North Carolina, by settlers from there. It was laid out in 1815, though settled earlier. A post office was established on December 13, 1818.

Troy (Switzerland). See Patriot.

Tuckerville (Crawford). See Marengo.

Tulip [TOO-lup] (Greene). A post office established on January 14, 1884, was closed on July 14, 1906. The name may be for the tulip, or yellow poplar, tree rather than for the flower, but according to local legend, "The main flower that grew around those parts was the tulip, and that's why the town was called Tulip" (ISUFA). The original village named Tulip was located a short distance from this site and was called Old Tulip after the post office was moved here.

Tullytown (Clark). See Springville.

Tunker [TUHNK-er] (Whitley). This village was settled in 1839 by Dunkers (i.e., Dunkards), sometimes spelled Tunkers, and named for them. A post office was established on September 3, 1886; closed on February 29, 1904.

Tunnelton [TUHN-uhl-tuhn] (Lawrence). This village was platted on April 28, 1859, and named for two nearby railroad tunnels, especially for the Big Tunnel, constructed in 1857. The second tunnel was dug about two miles west of here. A post office was established on May 23, 1860.

Turkey Creek (Kosciusko). See Leesburg.

Turkey Creek [ter-kee KREEK] (Steuben). A post office, named for its location on Turkey Creek, was established on May 18, 1852; closed on May 31, 1900.* The village was platted by Porter Johnson in March 1857.

Turkey Creek Meadows [ter-kee kreek MED-oz] (Lake). This community was named for nearby Turkey Creek. A village called Turkey Creek was established in this county in the middle 1830s (WPA).

Turner [TER-ner] (Clay). This village was founded in 1854 and first called Newburg, although the first post office in this area was called Sherman (established on October 20, 1864; closed on February 1, 1867). When a post office was reestablished on March 7, 1870, it was named Turner, for Reverend Turner of Indianapolis, who was president of the Indianapolis Mining, Coal and Coke Company and had local business interests. The post office was closed on May 31, 1917. Turners is a variant spelling.

Twelve Mile [TWELV meyel] (Cass). A post office named Twelve Mile, for nearby Twelve Mile Creek, was established on January 6, 1851. The village, known locally as Hen Peck, developed around a sawmill built by Daniel Brubaker. A local legend offers another account of the origin of the name Twelve Mile: "About 100 years ago there arose a small community of people who lived in Cass County, Indiana. As this small settlement gradually got bigger in size and population, they realized they had no official name to call their little establishment. Since they had to go into the nearest town, which was Logansport, for practically all their major supplies, they decided to arrive at a reasonable guess as to how far it was to Logansport, and they would name their town that number. Well, as it turned out they estimated it to be about 12 1/2 or 13 miles into Logansport. Being the suspicious bunch of old settlers that they were, they wouldn't think of naming their town Thirteen Mile, so the only logical thing to do was to call it Twelve Mile, meaning that it was 12 miles from Logansport" (ISUFA).

Twelve Points [TWELV poynts] (Vigo). Now part of Terre Haute, this community received its name from several streets converging with old U.S. 41 here: "Twelve Points, a section of North Terre Haute, was named for the twelve corners which are produced by the intersection of Maple Avenue, Lafayette Avenue, and Thirteenth Street" (ISUFA).

Twightwee Village (Allen). See Fort Wayne.

Twin Beach [twin BEECH] (Clay). This community west of Brazil received its name from a former recreation area here on a reservoir, Twin Beach Lake.

Twin Lakes [twin layks] (Lagrange). This village was named for nearby Twin Lakes, two lakes of about equal size.

Twin Lakes [twin layks] (Marshall). A post office called Twin Lake was established on September 27, 1887; changed to Twinlake on May 4, 1895; closed on January 2, 1907. The name is for two nearby lakes that resemble each other.

Twin Springs (Wabash). See Somerset (Wabash).

Two Mile Prairie (Pulaski). See Star City.

Tyner [TEYE-ner] (Marshall). This village, first called Tyner City, was platted on June 18, 1855, and named for the local Tyner family. Thomas Tyner was one of the founders of the village, and Francis M. Tyner was the fifth postmaster. A post office established as Tyner City on September 11, 1856, was changed to Tyner on July 10, 1894.

U

U Know (Carroll). See Bringhurst.

Ulen [YOO-luhn] (Boone). This community, incorporated in 1929, was developed and named for Henry C. Ulen, corporate director of the Ulen Construction Company, who moved the main offices of that company from New York and Paris to nearby Lebanon in 1929.

Uncle Otts Town (Henry). See Cadiz.

Underwood [UHN-der-wud] (Clark). This village is located on the Clark-Scott county line. A post office called Underwood was established in Scott County on September 2, 1878, but it was moved back and forth across the county line five times, finally ending with a move to Clark County on August 17, 1900. The post office closed on December 30, 1966.* Supposedly the suggested names for this village were Dallas Town and Underbrush, and Underwood was a compromise (WPA).

Union (Franklin). See Whitcomb.

Union (Parke). See West Union.

Union [YOON-yuhn] (Pike). Allegedly James Oliphant named this village for his hometown, Unionville, Pennsylvania. A post office established as Union in Gibson County on February 9, 1842, was moved to Pike County on October 24, 1845; closed on March 31, 1955. The village, first laid out in 1867, apparently was platted again on May 9, 1883.

Union (Whitley). See Churubusco.

Union Center [YOON-yuhn SEN-ter] (La Porte). This village was settled before 1835 and named for Union Township, in which it is located. A post office called Union Centre was established on May 19, 1884; changed to Union Center on April 29, 1892; closed on June 14, 1924.

Union City [YOON-yuhn SIT-ee; YOON-yuhn SID-ee] (Randolph). This city was platted in Ohio in 1838 and in Indiana in 1849. A post office was established on June 25, 1852. The location of this city in Ohio as well as in Indiana may have influenced the name, though the Indiana and Ohio sections remain separate corporations.

Union County [YOON-yuhn]. This county, the state's third smallest in area, was organized in 1821. The name is inspirational, suggesting a feeling of patriotism. Seat: Liberty.

Uniondale [YOON-yuhn-dayl] (Wells). This town was platted on April 10, 1883, and named for Union Township, in which it is located. A post office was established on January 25, 1886.

Union Mills [YOON-yuhn MILZ] (La Porte). A post office established as Bacon on October 15, 1842, was changed to Union Mills on March 14, 1845. The village was platted on December 7, 1849; however, it was settled as early as 1832

when Joseph Wheaton built the first house here. The village was named for the first gristmill, which was chartered as Union Mills in 1837 and opened in 1838.

Unionport [YOON-yuhn-pawrt] (Randolph). This village was platted on March 30, 1837, in the center of a proposed township, Union, that was never organized, and apparently named for it. A post office was established on May 13, 1878; closed on April 15, 1902.

Uniontown [YOON-yuhn-town] (Jackson). This village was laid out on March 1, 1859, by George King and Cornelius Conway. According to the WPA files, it was "called Uniontown because it was founded by two men."

Union Town (Marshall). See Culver.

Uniontown [YOON-yuhn-town] (Perry). A post office called Fosters Ridge, for the local Foster family, was established on June 7, 1858. Alexander Foster was the first postmaster, and several other members of the Foster family were postmasters. The post office changed to Uniontown on May 28, 1890; closed on April 12, 1974.

Uniontown [YOON-yuhn-town] (Wells). A post office, named for Union Township, in which it was located, was established on September 21, 1848; closed on October 30, 1855.

Union Valley (Dubois). See Cuzco.

Union Village (Johnson). See Providence.

Unionville [YOON-yuhn-vil] (Monroe). J. J. Alexander opened a store here in 1836. The village, platted on June 5, 1837, has been called Youngs Ridge, Buzzards Roost, Fleenersburg or Flenersburg, Union, and Old Unionville, to distinguish it from New Unionville, q.v. The present name comes from a Baptist congregation called Little Union, which was organized in 1832. A post office was established on June 22, 1848.

Unionville (Orange). See Youngs Creek.

Universal [yoon-uh-VER-suhl] (Vermillion). This town was platted in March 1911 and formerly called Bunsen, for the Bunsen Coal Company, which operated Universal mines no. 4 and no. 5 here. On August 8, 1912, a post office was established and named Universal for the local mines.

University Heights [yoon-uh-VER-suh-dee HEYETS] (Marion). This community was established around 1902–1903 and incorporated in 1907. Probably the name was influenced by the location here of Indiana Central College, now the University of Indianapolis.

Upland [UHP-luhnd] (Grant). This town was platted in 1867 with the coming of the railroad and believed to have been named by railroad officials because they thought it was the highest point between Union City and Logansport. A post office was established on December 30, 1867.

Upper Raccoon (Putnam). See Portland Mills.

Upton [UHP-tuhn] (Posey). This village was established as a railroad station and was named for the Upton family, who lived near the station. A post office named Uptons was established on May 20, 1878; closed on March 24, 1879. Another post office named Upton was established on February 20, 1886; closed on July 15, 1904.

Urbana (Miami). See Denver.

Urbana [er-BAN-uh] (Wabash). This village was platted on March 13, 1854, by Samuel Wellman, William Richards, and Isaac Wright. Urbana is a common commendatory name in the United States, but according to a local tradition reported in the WPA files, the name was drawn from a hat in which the proprietors had put several names. It's also said that George Wellman, son of one of the proprietors, suggested the name. A post office was established on February 9, 1858.

Urmeyville [ER-mee-vil] (Johnson). This village was platted on March 29, 1866, by Henry Fisher. A post office was established on December 20, 1866; closed on August 8, 1898.

Utah [YOO-taw] (Dearborn). This name ultimately comes from the Ute tribe and for some reason was moderately popular in Indiana as a place name after 1850, when Utah was being organized as a territory. For example, post offices named Utah were located in both Lagrange and Harrison counties.

Utica [YOO-di-kuh] (Clark). This village was platted on August 9, 1816, and probably named for Utica, New York. A post office was established on September 25, 1817; closed on March 15, 1919.

 **V**

Valeene [val-LEEN] (Orange). This village was laid out by John Hollowell, Sr., and John Hollowell, Jr., on April 10, 1837, and a post office was established on February 26, 1838; closed on November 27, 1853.*

Valentine [VAL-uhn-teyen] (Lagrange). A post office named Valentine was established on February 15, 1869. William Painter opened a hotel called Valentine House in 1874. In April 1879 James McKibben laid out the village.

Valley Brook [VAL-ee BRUK] (Wabash). Also called Valley Brook Addition, this housing development was platted on May 5, 1958, by J. W. Lewis. Like many real-estate names, this name is commendatory.

Valley City [VAL-ee SID-ee] (Harrison). This village was surveyed in November 1859, and the plat was recorded on January 11, 1860. A post office was established on April 15, 1863; closed on November 30, 1911.* According to the WPA files, the village was named for its location in a valley.

Valley City (Montgomery). See New Ross.

Valley Hill (Brown). See Christiansburg.

Valley Mills [VAL-ee MILZ] (Marion). This village was platted in 1839 as Northport and changed to Fremont in 1856. A post office was established as Valley Mills on June 27, 1861; closed on March 15, 1917. The present name is for the local Mills family and for the town's location in a small valley (WPA). Abner Mills was the second postmaster, and Thornton A. Mills was the tenth postmaster.

Vallonia [vuh-LON-yuh] (Jackson). This village, the county's oldest, was founded in 1810 on the site of Fort Vallonia, which was built in 1805 and so named because of its location in a valley. There was a French settlement here in the 1700s, and the name suggests a French influence. An Indiana Territory post office was established as Vallonia on April 4, 1815. Apparently the plat wasn't recorded until October 7, 1856.

Valparaiso [val-puh-RAY-zo] (Porter). This city was laid out by Benjamin McCarty in 1836 as Portersville. A post office established as Portersville on March 14, 1836, was changed to Valparaiso on January 19, 1837. The present name is for the city in Chile, off the coast of which Captain David Porter, for whom the county was named, fought the British in the War of 1812. According to local legend, "The story of how Valparaiso got its name was related to me this way. There were three sailors back in the 1800s; [they] were in this area, and they were at the point where the Northern Indiana Bank is now—one of the geographical highest points in the area. And they could look over the whole countryside, and one remarked that it reminded him of Valparaiso, Chile, which means Valley of Paradise. According to the story, that's how Valparaiso got its name" (ISUFA).

Van (Jay). See Bluff Point.

Van Buren [van BYUR-uhn] (Grant). This town was settled in 1843 by G. H. Rood and formerly called Roods Corner, Roods School House, Roods Crossroads, and Stringtown. A post office called Van Buren, for the township in which it is located, was established on July 10, 1872.* The town was laid out in 1880.

Vandalia [van-DAYL-yuh] (Owen). This village was laid out in February 1839 by Joseph Cochran and Jacob Hicks. A post office was established on July 6, 1846. Probably the name is a transfer, perhaps from New York or Ohio. The name is found in other states, too, including Michigan and Illinois, where it is the name of the former capital.

Vandalia (Wayne). See Cambridge City.

Vanderburgh County [VAN-der-berg]. This county, relatively small in area but ranking high in population, was organized in 1818 and named for Judge Henry Vanderburgh, officer in the Revolution and judge of the first court in the Indiana Territory. Seat: Evansville.

Van Ness Town (Parke). See Piattsville.

Van Weddings Station (Dearborn). See Weisburg.

Vawter Park [VAW-der PAHRK] (Kosciusko). A post office called Vawters Park, for the local Vawter family, was established on June 22, 1888; changed to Vawter Park on September 22, 1893; closed October 31, 1911. John T. Vawter was the second postmaster.

Veedersburg [VEE-derz-berg] (Fountain). This town was platted on May 2, 1872, by Peter S. Veeder, Christopher Keeling, W. L. D. Cochran, and Franklin Yerkes and named for Veeder, a local businessman who opened the first warehouse and lumberyard and sold the first agricultural implements here in 1872. A post office was established on June 12, 1872.*

Velpen [VEL-puhn] (Pike). A post office was established on December 30, 1881. The name may come from the Belgium River, Velpe, or from the Dutch place name, Velp, though it is said that Herman Hollenberg named the village for his hometown in Bavaria.

Vera Cruz [vehr-uh KROOZ] (Wells). This town was laid out on September 21, 1848, and named for the Mexican city taken by American soldiers in 1847. A post office was established on March 14, 1850; closed on April 3, 1942.

Vermillion County [ver-MIL-yuhn]. This county, thirty-seven miles long but only seven miles wide, was organized in 1824 and named for the Vermilion River, also called the Big Vermilion River, which passes through the county to the Wabash River near Eugene. The French name of the stream, Vermillon Jaune, is a literal translation of its Algonquian name, Osanamon, "yellow-red," i.e., vermilion paint. Seat: Newport.

Vermont [ver-MAHNT] (Howard). Milton Hadley, a native of Ohio, came here in 1845 and laid out this village in 1849. Apparently he named it for the state. A post office was established on June 14, 1849; closed on June 15, 1904.* In 1880 a railroad station was established near the village.

Verne [vern] (Knox). A post office was established here on May 6, 1892; closed on May 31, 1907.

Vernon [VER-nuhn] (county seat, Jennings). This town was platted in 1815 and named for Mount Vernon, the home of George Washington. It became the county seat in 1817, and a post office was established on December 21, 1817.

Vernon (Wabash). See Mount Vernon.

Versailles [ver-SAYLZ] (county seat, Ripley). This city was selected as the county seat in 1818, officially laid out in September 1819, and named for the French city and palace near Paris, perhaps via Kentucky. A post office was established as Versailles on February 3, 1823.*

Vesta [VES-tuh] (Clark). A post office was established here on July 10, 1884; closed on April 15, 1902.

Vevay [VEE-vee] (county seat, Switzerland). This town was settled in 1802 by Swiss immigrants and called New Switzerland. It also was called The Vineyard because settlers terraced the hills, grew grapes, and produced and sold wine as well as beer, whiskey, and brandy. The Vineyard post office (1880–1887), however, was located east of here near Long Run. An Indiana Territory post office, with Jean F. Dufour as postmaster, was established as Vevay on March 23, 1810, and the town was laid out in the spring of 1813 by Dufour and his brother. The present name is for the district in Switzerland, home of the settlers.

Vicksburg [VIKS-berg] (Greene). A post office was established on March 13, 1901; closed on April 15, 1935. According to the WPA files, the village was named for Victoria Hanna, whose father was a local landowner.

Victor [VIK-ter] (Monroe). A post office established as South Union on December 22, 1887, was changed to Victor on March 31, 1891; closed on January 14, 1905.

Victoria [vik-TAWR-ee-uh] (Greene). This community, established around 1905, was named for the nearby Old Victoria coal mine.

Vienna (DeKalb). See Newville.

Vienna (Rush). See Glenwood.

Vienna [veye-IN-uh; veye-EN-uh] (Scott). A post office, named for the capital of Austria, was established on January 12, 1832; closed on May 15, 1942. The village, apparently platted first in 1815, was platted again on March 24, 1849.

Vigo [VEYE-go; VEE-go] (Vigo). A post office, named for Vigo County, in which it was located, was established here on May 17, 1844; closed on November 15, 1905.*

Vigo County [VEYE-go; VEE-go]. This county, home of Indiana State University, was organized in 1818 and named for Colonel Francis Vigo, a Sardinian merchant who came to Vincennes about 1777 and assisted George Rogers Clark's army. Seat: Terre Haute.

Vilas [VEYE-luhs] (Owen). A post office was established on June 25, 1885; closed on April 30, 1912. It was named for William Freeman Vilas, postmaster-general, 1885–1888, and secretary of the interior, 1888–1889. Arcola is a variant name.

Vincennes [vin-SINZ; vin-SENZ] (county seat, Knox). The capital of the Old

Northwest Territory, this is the oldest continuously inhabited city in Indiana. Some say a French trading post was established here as early as 1683. Settlers arrived before 1727, and a fort was built about 1732 under the command of François-Marie Bissot, Sieur de Vincennes, for whom it was named about 1736 when he was captured and burned at the stake by Chickasaw Indians. The settlement went by several names, including Au Poste, Post Saint Ange, Post Ouabache, Post Saint Vincent, and Post Vincennes. A Northwest Territory post office was established on February 17, 1799.

Vine [veyen] (Fountain). A post office was established on March 1, 1895. According to the WPA files, the Post Office Department wanted a short name, so Vine was selected simply because it's short.

Vinegar Hill (Randolph). See Snow Hill.

Vine Springs [veyen SPRINGZ] (Ripley). A post office named Vines Springs, for the local Vines family, was established on May 22, 1868; closed on August 27, 1887. Abraham Vines was the first and only postmaster.

Virgie [VER-jee] (Jasper). A post office was established on September 19, 1890; closed on May 31, 1913.* The village was platted on May 11, 1893. According to the WPA files, the name is for Virgie Warner, daughter of one of the founders.

Virginia (Henry). See Luray.

Vistula [VIS-chuhl-uh; vis-CHOOL-uh] (Elkhart). A post office named Vistula, probably for the river in northern Europe via the old Vistula Road, was established on February 27, 1854. The village was laid out in 1865 and originally called Middlebury Station, as it was a railroad depot for the town of Middlebury.

Vivalia [veye-VAYL-yuh] (Putnam). This village was settled as early as 1828. A post office was established on December 26, 1882; closed on February 28, 1905. Vivalia appears to be a unique place name in the United States.

Volga [VOL-guh] (Jefferson). A post office, apparently named for the Volga River in Russia (WPA), was established on May 29, 1856.

Voltz (Pulaski). See Beardstown.

Vulcan (Randolph). See Huntsville (Randolph).

Wabash [WAW-bash] (county seat, Wabash). A post office established as Treaty Grounds on March 31, 1829, was changed to Wabash on February 18, 1839. This city was platted first in April 1834 by Hugh Hanna and David Burr.

Burr was the first postmaster of the Treaty Grounds post office, and Hanna was postmaster when the post office name was changed to Wabash. The settlement, dating from 1827, earlier was called Wabash Town, sometimes written Wabashtown, and was named for the Wabash River, on which it is located. Cf. Wabash County.

Wabash County [WAW-bash]. This county, still mainly farmland, was organized on March 1, 1834, and named for the Wabash River, the principal Indiana river, which flows through the county. The stream name is a contraction of the Miami name for the stream, Wah-bah-shik-ki, or Wah-pah-shik-ki, "b" and "p" being convertible in most Algonquian languages. The name suggests that the object named is pure white, or bright, inanimate, and natural. It refers to a limestone bed in the upper part of the river. The French spelled the name of the stream Ouabache. Seat: Wabash.

Waco [WAY-ko](Daviess). A post office, named for the Texas city, was established on November 11, 1891; closed on November 29, 1902. Ultimately the name comes from We-ko, "heron," a subtribe of the Wichitas.

Wadena [wuh-DEE-nuh] (Benton). A post office was established on June 25, 1883, and the village was platted in 1884. The name, also the name of a county and town in Minnesota, may come from an Ojibwa word meaning "little round hill."

Wadesville [WAYDZ-vil] (Posey). This village, formerly called Cross Roads, was laid out on February 16, 1852, and named for the local Wade family. Zachariah and Abner Wade were storekeepers

here. A post office was established on March 2, 1855.

Wagne Station [wag-nee STAY-shuhn] (Knox). This community, apparently first called Wagners Station and also called Wagner, developed as a station on the Indianapolis and Vincennes Railroad before 1876. The present name is a form of the earlier name, Wagners Station.

Wagoner [WAG-ner] (Fulton). Located on the Fulton-Miami county line, this village was established as a railroad station and formerly was called Wagoners Station, for the local Wagoner family. For a time it served as a major shipping and receiving point for the large farming area in southern Fulton County and northwestern Miami County. The post office established on February 23, 1872, was called Wagoners Station. On November 28, 1882, the name was changed to Wagoner. J. F. Wagoner was the first postmaster, and Samuel D. Wagoner was the second postmaster. The post office was closed on April 30, 1921.*

Wakarusa [wah-kuh-ROO-suh] (Elkhart). This town was platted in 1852 and first called Salem. A post office established two and a half miles north of here as Mount Olive on August 31, 1852, was moved to this location and the name changed to Wakarusa on March 15, 1860, because there already was a post office called Salem in Washington County. According to local history, Mahlon Woolverton suggested changing the name to Wakarusa for a stream or a place in Kansas, where he had once lived. Oral tradition claims that "the city of Wakarusa, Indiana, is so named because of its Indian name meaning 'knee deep in mud'" (ISUFA). Allegedly, the townsfolk accepted Woolverton's suggestion because the name appropriately described the boggy soil here.

Wakefield [WAYK-feeld] (Jefferson). A post office, named for Robert Wakefield (WPA), was established on July 8, 1899; closed on February 15, 1905.

Wakeland [WAYK-luhn] (Morgan). A post office was established here on December 29, 1884; closed on June 15, 1904.

Waldron [WAWL-druhn] (Shelby). This village was laid out on March 27, 1854, by George Stroup and originally called Stroupville. A post office called Conns Creek, for a nearby stream, was established on March 3, 1832. The stream was named for a local family. Samuel Conn was the second postmaster. The post office was changed to Waldron on January 31, 1876. Apparently the name was changed to Waldron by petition of the citizens.

Walesboro [WAYLZ-ber-o] (Bartholomew). This village was laid out on June 26, 1851, by John P. Wales and named for his family.

Walkers Bluff (Parke). See Numa.

Walkerton [WAWK-er-tuhn] (Saint Joseph). This town first was platted on June 20, 1856, and named for John Walker, who promoted building the railroad through here. Another town platted on December 14, 1854, as West Troy was absorbed by Walkerton. A post office established as West York on June 21, 1852, was changed to Walkerton on May 24, 1860.

Walkertown (Parke). See Numa.

Wallace [WAWL-uhs] (Fountain). This town was platted on September 25, 1832, as Jacksonville, supposedly for Andrew Jackson. The present name is for Governor David Wallace, who was one of the first merchants in Covington. A post office was established as Wallace on November 13, 1837.

Wallen [WAWL-uhn] (Allen). This village was platted in 1870 by Joseph K. Edgerton. He named it for a railroad superintendent named Wallen who worked for the Grand Rapids and Indiana Railway. A post office was established on January 10, 1871; closed on August 15, 1924.*

Walnut [WAWL-nuht] (Marshall). This village was platted on April 16, 1866, in Walnut Township and called Fredericksburg, for the founder, Frederick Stair; however, the railroad named it Walnut for the township in which it is located. A post office named Walnut was established on January 6, 1869; closed on March 15, 1906.

Walnut Grove [WAWL-nuht GROV] (Hamilton). The name of this village appears to be commendatory as well as descriptive.

Walnut Hill (Daviess). See Odon.

Walnut Ridge (Washington). See Plattsburg.

Walpole (Hancock). See Fortville.

Walton [WAWL-tuhn] (Cass). This town, named for the local Wall family, was laid out in August 1852 by Gilbert Wall. A post office was established on July 1, 1856.

Wanamaker [WAH-nuh-may-ker] (Marion). This village, once called New Bethel, was platted on March 24, 1834.

The first name probably was for the New Bethel Baptist Church, which was organized on April 7, 1827. A post office called Wanamaker was established on August 21, 1889; closed on April 30, 1960. The present name honors John Wanamaker, postmaster-general.

Wanatah [WAH-nuh-tah] (La Porte). A post office established as Roselle on May 31, 1856, was changed to Wanatah on October 28, 1862. The Roselle post office was located about a mile south of Wanatah at the point where the New York, Chicago, and St. Louis Railroad crossed the Monon, and the village that developed there was called Joprice (cf. South Wanatah). Joseph Unruh kept a store there before he moved to Wanatah, which was laid out by Joseph Unruh, T. A. E. Campbell, Ruel Starr, and William Unruh on September 7, 1865. Wanatah, for an Indian chief, means "he who charges his enemies."

Wards Mills (Parke). See Russellville.

Warnock Station (Henry). See Honey Creek.

Warren [WAWR-uhn] (Huntington). This town was platted on December 11, 1836, by Samuel Jones, who came here in 1833. First it was named Jonesboro for him. The post office established on August 12, 1839, was called Warren. According to the WPA files, it is believed that the present name is for General Joseph Warren of the Revolution.

Warren Center (Warrick). See Lydick.

Warren County [WAWR-uhn]. This county was organized in 1827 and named for General Joseph Warren, Massachusetts physician and soldier who was killed in the Battle of Bunker Hill in 1775. Seat: Williamsport.

Warren Park [wawr-uhn PAHRK] (Marion). This community was laid out and incorporated in 1928.

Warrenton [WAWR-uhn-tuhn; WAHR-uhn-tuhn] (Gibson). This village was platted in 1840 and named for General Joseph Warren of the American Revolution. A post office established on October 26, 1841, was closed on January 8, 1856.* Variant names have been Greeley, Tracewell, and Warrentown.

Warrick County [WAWR-ik]. This county, a major producer of coal, was organized in 1813 and named for Captain Jacob Warrick, who was killed in the Battle of Tippecanoe. Seat: Boonville.

Warrington [WAWR-ing-tuhn] (Hancock). This village was laid out on October 6, 1834, by John Oldham. A post office was established on September 14, 1849; closed on October 15, 1919. The name is found in England and Pennsylvania and may be a transfer.

Warsaw [WAWR-saw] (county seat, Kosciusko). This city was platted on October 21, 1836, by W. H. Knott, proprietor, and named by John B. Chapman for the capital of Poland. A post office was established on February 1, 1837.

Washington [WAWR-shing-tuhn; WAW-shing-tuhn] (county seat, Daviess). This city was platted in 1815 and was called Liverpool until 1817. A post office was established as Washington on October 9, 1817. The present name is for Washington Township, apparently named for George Washington.

Washington (Perry). See Rome.

Washington (Wayne). See Greens Fork.

Washington Center [WAW-shing-tuhn SEN-ter] (Whitley). A post office named Washington Centre was established on June 27, 1855; closed on December 22, 1874. The name is for its location near the center of Washington Township, which was named for George Washington.

Washington County [WAWR-shing-tuhn; WAW-shing-tuhn]. This predominantly agricultural county was formed in 1813, organized in 1814, and named in honor of George Washington. Seat: Salem.

Waterford [WAH-der-ferd] (La Porte). A post office was established on July 16, 1850; closed on September 15, 1900.* According to a local legend, the village was named Waterford because settlers forded a stream here (WPA).

Waterford Mills [WAH-der-ferd MILZ] (Elkhart). In 1833 Judge Elias Baker built a log house and a gristmill here. Supposedly Baker built the gristmill near a ford over the Elkhart River (WPA); if so, the name is descriptive. Cephas Hawks, Sr., bought the mill from Baker in June 1836 and the following year turned the operation of it over to his son, Cephas, Jr. In 1838 the village, also called Waterford, was laid out by Cephas Hawks, Sr., Cephas Hawks, Jr., and David Ballentine, who also had an interest in the mill. A post office was established on September 19, 1853; closed on January 14, 1904.*

Waterloo [WAH-der-loo] (DeKalb). This town was laid out on March 14, 1856, by Miles Waterman and John Hornberger and apparently named for the Belgian village (WPA), site of the famous battle of 1815, though perhaps suggested by the name of the cofounder, Waterman, who served as a state representative for several terms. Earlier the town was called Waterloo City to distinguish it from the other Waterloo in Fayette County. A post office established as Waterloo City on February 20, 1862, was changed to Waterloo on May 2, 1870.*

Waterloo [WAH-der-loo] (Fayette). A post office, named for Waterloo Township, in which it was located, was established on February 2, 1818; closed on May 18, 1868. William Port, who kept a tavern here as early as 1825, became the third postmaster on May 4, 1825. The village was platted on October 28, 1841. According to a local legend, the name is for an incident. When two drunks were brawling in a saloon, someone said that the bloody fight was worse than the Battle of Waterloo, and the town was named for that remark (WPA).

Waterman (Parke). See Lodi (Parke).

Watson [WAHT-suhn] (Clark). A post office was established here on February 29, 1872; closed on February 15, 1928. The village apparently was laid out in 1876 by J. B. Speed, but the plat wasn't recorded. A variant name is New Watson.

Waugh [waw] (Boone). A post office called Waugh was established on July 3, 1891; closed on December 14, 1900. Slabtown is a variant name.

Waveland [WAYV-luhnd] (Montgomery). A post office named Waveland was established on January 18, 1832.* The town was platted in 1835 by John Milligan, the first merchant, who named it for the post office. According to the WPA files and other sources, the post office was named for Waveland, Kentucky, but current maps and gazetteers do not show a town with this name in Kentucky. Both local history and oral tradition (ISUFA), though, say the post office and subsequently the town were named for "a Kentucky gentleman's home." Thus it appears that the name is for the home of a Kentucky family rather than for a settlement. See Hambleton Tapp's eleven-page typescript, "Waveland: Home of the Bryans," in the University of Kentucky library.

Waverly [WAY-ver-lee] (Morgan). This village was established about 1837, when work began on the proposed Central Canal, and it was platted in 1841 by M. H. Brown, O. G. Kershner, and D. W. Howe. The name, from Sir Walter Scott's popular *Waverley* novels, is spelled Waverley in Australia, New Zealand, Nova Scotia, and South Africa. In the United States, where the name is found in at least twenty states, it generally is spelled Waverly. A post office was moved here from nearby Johnson County on March 16, 1859; closed on June 30, 1927.

Waverly Woods [WAY-ver-lee WUDZ] (Morgan). This community is located on the south edge of Waverly, q.v., for which it was named. Jacob Whetzel, who blazed the sixty-mile Whetzel Trace with his son, Cyrus, through Delaware country in 1818, lived here.

Wawaka [wuh-WAH-kuh] (Noble). This village was laid out in February 1857 by Isaac Tibbot, proprietor, who built the first house here in 1834. A post office was established on September 14, 1857. According to the WPA files, this Native American name means "big heron."

Wawasee [WAH-wah-see] (Kosciusko). A post office established as Cedar Beach (or Cedar Branch) on August 21, 1879, was changed to Wawasee, for Wawasee Lake, on May 6, 1893, and was closed on September 15, 1938. The lake was named for a Potawatomi chief, Wah-we-as-see, "full moon," or literally, "the round one."

Wawpecong [WAH-puh-KAHNG] (Miami). A post office established as Mishwah on February 15, 1847, was changed to Wawpecong on November 27, 1849; closed on June 15, 1907. The village, first called White Hall, was laid out on April 13, 1849, by James Hiland, Jacob Hight, and Andrew Petty, but the plat was not recorded until July 4, 1849. On June 16, 1851, Hiland and Petty platted an addition north of White Hall and renamed the original plat and the addition Wawpecong, apparently spelled Waupecong, for the post office. The name comes from the Miami name of the place, Wa-pi-pa-ka-na, "shell-bark hickories," for the large number of these trees growing here.

Waymansville [WAY-muhnz-vil] (Bartholomew). This village, named for the local Wayman family, was laid out on November 24, 1849, by Charles L. Wayman. An oral account says that "there once was a family who lived here by the name of Wayman in the 1830s, and I think it was named after them" (ISUFA). A post office was established on June 22, 1860; closed on October 15, 1940.*

Wayne County [wayn]. This county, home of Earlham College and the Indiana Football Hall of Fame, was formed in 1810, organized in 1811, and named for General Anthony Wayne, officer in the Revolution but noted here mainly for his defeat of Little Turtle at the Battle of Fallen Timbers in 1794. Seat: Richmond.

Waynedale [WAYN-dayl] (Allen). This village was platted in 1922 by Abner W. Elzey.

Waynesburg [WAYNZ-berg] (Decatur). This village was laid out on November 4, 1844, by George Lough. A post office called Waynesburgh was established on April 4, 1854; changed to Waynesburg on September 28, 1894; closed on August 30, 1902.

Waynesville [WAYNZ-vil] (Bartholomew). This village was laid out on October 9, 1851, by James C. Thompson. It was built on the railroad about a mile north of the original settlement, Augusta, an unplatted village soon abandoned in favor of Waynesville. A post office established as Bannersville on August 6, 1851, was changed to Waynesville on July 6, 1853; closed on June 27, 1907.

Waynetown [WAYN-town] (Montgomery). Originally called Middletown, this town was platted on July 28, 1830, by Samuel Mann. A post office named Waynetown was established on July 27, 1835. The name is for Wayne Township, in which the town is located. The township was named for General Anthony Wayne.

Wayport [WAY-pawrt] (Monroe). This village was laid out on April 21, 1851, by Isaac Gillaspy, Thomas Gillaspy, and G. W. Smith, proprietors. A post office was established on August 9, 1877; closed on May 26, 1879.

Weaver [WEE-ver] (Grant). A post office, named for the local Weaver family, was established on December 23, 1880; closed on August 14, 1902. Henry Weaver owned the first store here, and John H. Weaver was the second postmaster.

Weaver City (Benton). See Ambia.

Webster [WEBZ-ster; WEB-ster] (Wayne). This village earlier was called Dover for Dover Meeting, a Friends' meeting that was organized here in 1821. A Friends' school was established here about the same time. Another early name was Fairfax. The village was laid out about 1850, and the present name is for the township in which the village is located. A post office called Webster was established on January 6, 1851.

Weddleville [WED-uhl-vil] (Jackson). This village, named for the local Weddle family, was laid out on August 15, 1855, by local miller John Weddle, Claiborne Weddle, and Gabriel Osborne. A variant spelling is Weddlesville.

Wegan [WEE-guhn] (Jackson). A post office was established on October 28, 1892; closed on August 18, 1896. Locally it is thought that the name is for the local Wegand family, who owned land in this area (ISUFA).

Weisburg [WEYES-berg] (Dearborn). Jacob Van Wedding came to this area from Belgium in 1831. A post office established as Cork, probably named by Irish settlers for the Irish county, on November 17, 1851, was changed to Van Weddings Station, for the local Van Wedding family, on November 29, 1855, and to Weisburgh, for the local Weis family, on June 25, 1859. On August 4, 1889, the spelling was changed to Weisburg, and on March 20, 1933, the post office was closed. The village was laid out on January 7, 1858. Philip Weis settled near here in 1832 and built a sawmill and gristmill on the West Fork of Tanners Creek. His son, also named Philip, moved the mill to Weisburg in 1881.

Wellington (Marion). See Broad Ripple.

Wells [welz] (Miami). This community was named for James Oscar Wells, Dolly Wells, and Eugene Wells, who developed it. It is now called Forest Hills, a more commendatory name for a subdivision.

Wellsboro [WELZ-ber-o] (La Porte). This village was laid out on April 8, 1875, and named for the local Wells family—two brothers, Charles F. and Theodore H. Wells, according to some sources. A post office called Wellsborough was established on November 6, 1877. On June 7, 1883, the spelling was changed to Wellsboro, and on January 31, 1954, the post office was closed.

Wellsburg [WELZ-berg] (Wells). This village was platted on March 16, 1855, and named for Wells County. A post office called Wellsburgh was established on December 20, 1870; closed on January 9, 1873.

Wells County [welz]. This county, one of the state's major producers of wheat and soybeans, was created in 1835, organized in 1837, and named for Captain William H. Wells, who was killed by Indians in 1812 while escorting a garrison from Fort Dearborn to Fort Wayne. Seat: Bluffton.

Wesley (Fulton). See Akron.

Wesley [WES-lee] (Montgomery). A post office was established on March 16, 1860; closed on March 31, 1902. A flag station and the short-lived Wesley Academy also were located in this village.

West Atherton [WEST ATH-er-tuhn] (Parke). A post office called Atherton was established on February 27, 1872; closed on June 21, 1881. The village was platted in 1904. The name is locational, as the village is located just west of Atherton, q.v.

West Baden Springs [WEST BAYD-uhn SPRINGZ] (Orange). Dr. John A. Lane, an itinerant medicine peddler, purchased 770 acres and built the first resort here in 1851, naming it West Baden for the famous spa in Germany. It was first known as Mile Lick, since it was one mile from French Lick. A post office established as West Baden on December 30, 1861, was changed to West Baden Springs on September 1, 1935. John A. Lane was the first postmaster.

West Bloomfield (Greene). See Elliston.

Westchester [WEST-ches-ter] (Jay). A post office was established here on April 29, 1854; closed on May 31, 1904.

West Clinton [WEST KLINT-uhn] (Vermillion). This village, also called West Clinton Junction, developed because a railroad roundhouse was built here. It was platted on May 31, 1911, and named for its location west of Clinton.

West College Corner [WEST KAHL-ij KAWR-ner] (Union). This town was platted in 1859. The name is locational, as the town was established west of College Corner, Ohio, founded about 1837. College Corner Station is a variant name.

Western Prairie (Lake). See Saint John.

Westfield [WEST-feeld] (Hamilton). This town, settled by Quakers, was laid out on May 6, 1834. A post office was established on April 20, 1837. The name is common in other states and may be a transfer name, though formerly the village was called Westville.

West Fork [WEST fawrk] (Crawford). This village, earlier called West Fork Post, was named for the West Fork of Little Blue River, on which it is located. A post office called West Fork was established on February 8, 1871. A variant name is Marietta.

West Franklin [WEST FRANK-luhn] (Posey). This village was laid out in January 1837 by John B. Stinson, although settled by Jacob Weinmiller around 1807. A post office was established on March 22, 1837.* According to an anecdote published in a county history, "The town was named West Franklin, it is said, to distinguish it from a man living near called East Franklin." Since Franklin is nearly as popular as Washington as a place name, this account is dubious. In the early days, this locale was called Diamond Island Ferry, and settlers from Tennessee, North Carolina, and Georgia crossed here from Kentucky.

West Gary (Lake). See Ivanhoe.

West Harrison [WEST HEHR-uh-suhn] (Dearborn). An Indiana Territory post office called Allens Ferry, for the local Allen family, was established on February 5, 1812. John Allen was one of the postmasters, apparently the first. This post office was changed to Harrison on April 17, 1813. On June 30, 1817, the post office was moved to Hamilton County, Ohio. Jamie Harrison was the second postmaster of the Harrison post office, so the name may be for a local family. The town of West Harrison is located in western Harrison Township, though, so the name may be locational.

The Ohio side of the town, first called Harrison, was platted on December 8, 1813, by Jonas Crane, and the Indiana side was laid out the same year by John Allen and Peter Hannan.

West Lafayeffe [WEST lahf-ee-ET; WEST laf-ee-ET; WEST layf-ee-ET] (Tippecanoe). This city was founded in 1845 on land owned by Jesse B. Lutz and called Kingston. Subsequently, the Chauncey family from Philadelphia founded a settlement called Chauncey adjoining Kingston, and on December 21, 1865, a post office called Chauncey was established. The two towns united, and on January 2, 1866, they were incorporated as Chauncey. On November 15, 1873, the Chauncey post office was closed. The town of Chauncey virtually became a part of Lafayette, and by 1888 it was called West Lafayette, a locational name. The West Lafayette post office was established in 1909.

Westland [WEST-land] (Hancock). The first store in this unplatted village, a log house, was built in 1852 by Samuel Heavenridge. The Westland post office was established on January 17, 1852; closed on August 31, 1905.* The name may be for Henry West, the first postmaster.

Westland [WEST-land] (Putnam). A post office was established here on March 8, 1845; closed on April 28, 1847.

West Lebanon [WEST LEB-uh-nuhn] (Warren). This town was platted in 1830 by Ebenezer Purviance, John G. Jamison, and Andrew Fleming and first called Lebanon, probably for the biblical mountains. The post office established on December 26, 1832, was called West Lebanon to distinguish it from the city and post office called Lebanon in Boone County.

West Liberty (Henry). See Knightstown.

West Liberty [WEST LIB-er-dee] (Howard). Israel Zentmyer came here in 1847 and a year later built a house and a blacksmith shop. In the spring of 1849, Moses Jones bought Zentmyer's land, built a mill northeast of the village, earlier called Mills Corner, and had the village surveyed in the latter part of 1849. A post office was established on August 20, 1855; closed on August 30, 1902.*

West Liberty [WEST LIB-er-dee] (Jay). A post office called West Liberty was moved here from nearby Bear Creek on July 14, 1851, but it was moved back to Bear Creek on January 29, 1852. Another post office called Mills Corners was established here on June 18, 1869; closed on May 31, 1904. According to the WPA files, the variant name, Mills Corners, is for a local flour mill, but possibly the name is for the local Mills family, as the third postmaster was Elizabeth Mills. There was a mill here, though, for James Marquis built a gristmill on Bear Creek in 1838 and another mill in 1839. The village was laid out first on August 20, 1851, by James Marquis, May Marquis, and William Bateman.

West Middleton [WEST MID-uhl-tuhn] (Howard). A post office was established on November 23, 1874. About the same time the village, earlier called Middletons Station, for the local Middleton family, was laid out along the railroad by William Middleton.

West Muncie [WEST MUHN-see] (Delaware). This village was platted on January 4, 1892, and named for its location west of Muncie. A post office was established on February 3, 1893; closed on August 15, 1902.

West Newton [WEST NOOT-uhn] (Marion). This village was platted in April 1851 and first called Easton, then Newton. West was added to the name to distinguish it from other towns named Newton. A post office was established on June 21, 1854.

West Noblesville [WEST NO-buhlz-vil] (Hamilton). The name of this village is locational. Cf. Noblesville.

Westphalia [wes-FAYL-yuh] (Knox). This village was laid out in December 1881 by Frederick Pohlmeir and named for the German region and former province. A post office was established on December 7, 1881.*

West Point (Lake). See Gibson (Lake).

West Point (Huntington). See Bippus.

Westpoint [WEST-poynt] (Tippecanoe). This village was platted in 1833 by Samuel Kiser and called Middleton, sometimes spelled Middletown, because it was the middle point between Lafayette and Attica. A post office established as Reserve on September 23, 1833, was changed to West Point on July 21, 1836. On December 4, 1894, the spelling was changed to Westpoint. Apparently postal authorities influenced changing the name from Middleton to West Point, as there already was a post office named Middletown in Henry County.

Westport [WEST-pawrt] (Decatur). This town was laid out on March 23, 1836. A post office was established as West Port on February 20, 1839.

Westport (Parke). See Howard.

West Salem (Morgan). See Alaska.

West Saratoga Springs (Pike). See Coats Springs.

West Sonora (Carroll). See Deer Creek.

West Terre Haute [WES tehr-uh HOT; WES tehr HOT] (Vigo). This town was platted on November 23, 1836, and originally called Macksville, for the founder, Samuel McQuilkin. The Macksville post office, first spelled Macsville, was established on March 19, 1840, with McQuilkin as postmaster. The post office name was changed to West Terre Haute on September 21, 1899.* The present name is locational, as the town is west of Terre Haute, q.v.

West Union (Fayette). See Everton.

West Union (Madison). See Chesterfield.

West Union [WEST YOON-yuhn] (Parke). This village was settled in 1822 and platted in 1837. Apparently the first post office serving this area was Union—established on January 3, 1838; closed on January 31, 1840. The Delta post office—established on January 1, 1840; closed on October 31, 1891—also served this area, but it was located north of here. The West Union post office was established on November 3, 1886; closed on May 31, 1932. Supposedly the name was suggested by the village's location at the junction of roads, a railroad, Sugar Creek, and the Wabash and Erie Canal feeder canal.

West Union Station (Marion). See Camby.

Westville (Hamilton). See Westfield.

Westville [WEST-vil] (La Porte). Settled in 1836, this town was platted on May 1, 1851, by W. Cattron and J. A. Cattron. A post office established at nearby New Durham (cf. Pinhook [La Porte]) on May 10, 1842, was moved here and called Westville on March 1, 1852.

Westwood [WEST-wud] (Henry). This village was platted in August 1923 (WPA).

Wheatfield [WEET-feeld] (Jasper). This town was laid out in 1858 and apparently named for the good wheat-growing land here, though one source says the town was so named because it was built on the site of the first wheat field in the county. A post office was established on August 29, 1882.

Wheatland [WEET-luhnd] (Knox). This town was laid out on December 29, 1858. A post office established as Berryville (or Berrysville), for the local Berry family, on August 14, 1830, was changed to Wheatland on December 7, 1858. Andrew Berry was the first postmaster at Berryville, and William Long, sometimes credited as the town's founder, was postmaster when the name was changed to Wheatland. The name is descriptive of the surrounding territory, which produced large yields of wheat.

Wheatonville [WEET-uhn-vil] (Warrick). A post office was established here on June 20, 1860; closed on June 12, 1872.

Wheeler [WEE-ler] (Porter). This village was laid out by T. A. E. Campbell, who owned the land, on September, 29, 1858, and named for Captain Wheeler, a fur trader who had a trading post here in the 1820s (WPA), or for an engineer on the railroad built through here. A post office established as City West on June 23, 1838, was changed to Fillmore, for Millard Fillmore, thirteenth president of the United States (1850–1853), on November 5, 1849, and to Wheeler on December 11, 1858.

Wheeler (White). See Smithson.

Wheeling [WEE-ling] (Carroll). This village was platted in 1837 and first called Carroll, for Carroll County. A post office called Carroll was established on February 26, 1839; closed on November 15, 1905. The present name may be a transfer, although allegedly it honors an expert wheelwright who had a shop here (WPA). A variant name of the village is Carrollton Location, probably for its location in Carrollton Township.

Wheeling [WEE-ling] (Delaware). A post office established here as Cranberry on January 17, 1834, was changed to Wheeling on December 14, 1838; closed on December 15, 1933. The village was laid out by William McCormick, Cranberry postmaster, in September 1837.

Wheeling [WEE-ling] (Gibson). This village was platted on July 4, 1856, and first called Kirksville, sometimes spelled Kirkville, probably for Robert Kirk, an early judge. Locally it also was called Bovine, as a post office called Bovine was established here on April 4, 1854; closed on July 14, 1902.*

Whitaker [WID-uh-ker; WID-ee-ker] (Morgan). A post office was established on July 11, 1883; closed on October 30, 1937.* The name is for the local Whitaker family. John Whitaker built the first store here (WPA).

Whitcomb [WIT-kuhm] (Franklin). First called Union, this village was platted on September 14, 1816. The post office was established as Whitcomb on June 12, 1846; closed on April 2, 1906.

White Cloud [weyet klowd] (Harrison). This village was settled about 1879 in a valley between two ranges of hills. According to traditional accounts, the name was suggested by fog that often hangs over the village: "[It is] located between the lofty hills of Blue River, and on a foggy day clouds of fog hang over the place for a long time, and this suggested the name of White Cloud" (WPA). A post office was established on August 1, 1884; closed on May 15, 1934.

White County [weyet]. This county was organized in 1834 and named for Colonel Isaac White, who was killed in the Battle of Tippecanoe. White County is noted for its rich farmlands as well as two major recreational areas, Lake Freeman and Lake Shafer. Seat: Monticello.

White Creek (Bartholomew). See Mount Healthy.

White Creek (Jackson). See Spraytown.

Whitehall [WEYET-hawl] (Owen). This village was laid out in 1838 by James Brown, who named it for White Hall, North Carolina, a town in his native state. A post office was established as White Hall on April 28, 1848; changed to Whitehall on July 20, 1894; and closed on November 30, 1907.

White Hall (Miami). See Wawpecong.

Whiteland [WEYET-luhnd] (Johnson). A post office, named for the local White family, was established on June 26, 1861. Joel B. White was the first postmaster, and Jacob B. White was the second postmaster. The town was laid out on March 11, 1863.

Whitelick [WEYET-lik] (Hendricks). A post office named White Lick, for a nearby stream, was established on September 19, 1853; closed on December 7, 1853. The stream name supposedly is a translation of the Native American Wa-pa-ke-way, "white salt." Cf. Avon.

White Oak Grove (Pike). See Otwell.

White Post (Pulaski). See Medaryville.

White River [WEYET riv-er] (Gibson). This village was named for the stream of the same name, perhaps via White River Township. The Miami name of the stream was Wah-pi-kah-me-ki, "white waters." The Delawares at first used a variant of the same name, although later they called the stream Wah-pi-ha-ni, "white river."

White Rose [weyet roz] (Greene). This village was founded in 1903 when the White Rose mine, for which it was named, began operations here. The mine allegedly received its name because a white rosebush was found on the spot where the shaft was sunk (WPA). A variant name is Whites Crossing.

Whitestown [WEYETS-town] (Boone). This town was laid out in 1851 and first called New Germantown; however, there was difficulty in securing a post office under that name, so the name was changed to Whitestown, probably for Albert S. White, first president of the I. C. and L. Railroad and congressman from this district. Joseph White, though, was among the first settlers in 1833 and may have influenced the naming. The post office was established on August 18, 1853.

White Sulphur Springs [WEYET SUHL-fer SPRINGZ] (Pike). A variant name of this village is Fidelity for a post office established on July 24, 1871; closed on December 26, 1884.*

Whitesville [WEYETS-vil] (Montgomery). A post office, named for the local White family, was established on September 27, 1852. Joseph S. White was the first postmaster, and Thomas E. White was the second postmaster. The village was platted in 1862.

Whitewater [WEYET-wah-der] (Wayne). First called Hillsborough, this town was platted on November 12, 1828. A post office called White Water was established on July 10, 1832; closed on April 15, 1914. The present name is for Whitewater River, the principal stream in southeastern Indiana. The stream name is a translation of the Native American name, Wapinepay, "white, clear water," descriptive of its bed of white sand, gravel, and limestone.

Whitfield [WIT-feeld] (Martin). A post office established as Stremler on April 19, 1892, was changed to Whitfield (also given as Whitefield) on May 25, 1892. An oral account says the village was named for Whitfield Force, a resident (ISUFA), but Whitfield is an English place name that also is found in Alabama and Mississippi. According to an oral account, "About the same time they started Hindostan, they started Whitfield. Named after Whitfield Force. Used to be some Forces around here. I remember my dad telling me about 'em. I guessed they all died off or moved away" (ISUFA).

Whiting [WEYE-ding] (Lake). A post office was established on January 10, 1871, and the city was laid out in 1889. The settlement developed around a railroad crossing and earlier was called Whitings Crossing, Whitings Station, and Whitings, supposedly for a railroad conductor involved in a train wreck here (WPA).

Whitley County [WIT-lee]. This county, noted for its lakes and once famous for its onions, was formed in 1835, organized in 1838, and named for Colonel William Whitley, Kentucky soldier who was killed in the Battle of the Thames in 1813. Seat: Columbia City.

Wickliffe [WIK-lif] (Crawford). A post office was established on August 26, 1842; closed on July 31, 1952.* According to the WPA files, the name is for John Wickliffe (or Wycliffe), English religious reformer and translator of the Bible.

Wilbur [WIL-ber] (Morgan). This village was founded in the 1830s. A post office was established on September 15, 1873; closed on November 30, 1906. Lickskillet is a variant name.

Wild Cat (Carroll). See Adams Mill. Cf. Burlington.

Wild Cat (Tipton). See Sharpsville.

Wildcat Corner (Carroll). See Pyrmont.

Wilders [WEYEL-derz] (La Porte). A post office established as Wilders Station on May 18, 1889, was changed to Wilder on May 17, 1894. Formerly the village was called Wilders Crossing, Wilders Junction, and Wilders Station, as well as Wilder and Wilders. According to a local anecdote, it was named Wilders because it was located in the wilderness (WPA), but the settlement may have been named for a family name.

Wilfred [WUL-fruhd; WIL-fruhd] (Sullivan). This village, though settled earlier, developed around 1902 because of local coal mining operations. The name was coined from the names of two mine operators, Wilford and Fredman (WPA).

Wilkinson [WIL-kuhn-suhn] (Hancock). This town was platted on January 16, 1883, by Elnathan and Thomas B. Wilkinson and named for them. A post office was established on April 2, 1883.

Williams [WIL-yuhmz] (Adams). This village was platted in 1871 by David Crabbs and Benjamin Rice. A post office called Bingen was established on November 22, 1871; closed on February 28, 1914.

Williams [WIL-yuhmz] (Lawrence). A post office was established on October 31, 1876, and the village was platted on May 20, 1889, by Henry Cox. The name is for the local Isaac Williams family, who settled here from Tennessee around 1816. According to oral tradition, "Williams was named by a man named Williams" (ISUFA). Byrd E. Williams became postmaster in 1900. Greenville, for the Green brothers, is a variant name.

Williamsburg (Johnson). See Ninevah.

Williamsburg [WIL-yuhmz-berg] (Wayne). This village was platted in March 1830 by William Johnson and probably named for him. A post office was established on July 22, 1830.

Williams Creek [WIL-yuhmz KREEK] (Marion). This community, laid out and incorporated in 1932, was named for the nearby stream of the same name.

Williamson (Parke). See Lyford.

Williamsport (Allen). See Poe.

Williamsport [WIL-yuhmz-pawrt] (county seat, Warren). This town, a port on the Wabash River, was platted in November 1828 and named for the proprietor, William Harrison. A post office was established on September 28, 1829. According to a local legend, "Williamsport is located on the Wabash River, and before it was a settled town, it was a stop off for river boats. A man by the name of Williams ran the port the boats stopped at, so it was called William's port. Later, when the town began to become settled, the name Williamsport was given to it" (ISUFA). The Side-Cut Canal was finished here about 1852, and the town was commonly called the Side-Cut City. When the canal was abandoned, the business center shifted from the riverfront, called Old Town, to an area called New Town closer to the Wabash Railroad, completed through here in 1856. Williamsport also has been called the "City of Rocks" because of a rocky ledge on which part of the town stands and because of the lime rock through which Little Dry Creek runs.

Williamstown (Clay). See Billtown.

Williamstown [WIL-yuhmz-town] (Decatur). William Knox and Hugh Montgomery laid out this village in September 1830, and it may have been named for Knox. A post office called Williamstown was established in Rush County on January 13, 1834, and moved across the county line on February 19, 1835. According to the WPA files, the village, located on the Decatur-Rush county line, was named for an early trader.

Willis [WIL-uhs] (Knox). A post office called Willis Grove was established on May 6, 1878; changed to Willis on November 16, 1894; closed on June 15, 1907. A variant spelling is Wills.

Willow Branch [WIL-o BRANCH; WIL-uh BRANCH] (Hancock). A post office called Willow Branch, for the nearby stream, was established near here on August 8, 1855; closed on August 29, 1992. On December 7, 1894, the post office name was changed to Willow; however, apparently the village, platted on April 21, 1882, retained Willow Branch as its name, and in 1914 the original post office name was restored. The post office was established in Green Township, with Jonathan Smith, farmer and merchant, as postmaster. In 1874 A. B. Thomas opened a store across the township line in Brown Township, and on June 22, 1874 the post office was moved there, with Thomas as postmaster.

Willow Creek [WIL-o KREEK; WIL-uh KREEK] (Porter). This village was named for the stream of the same name.

Willow Prairie (Steuben). See Fremont.

Willow Valley [WIL-o VAL-ee; WIL-uh VAL-ee] (Martin). This village originally was called Proctor, probably for County Agent George R. Proctor. A post office called Willow Valley was established on July 13, 1828; closed on January 5, 1864. Supposedly the name is descriptive of willows that were abundant in a valley here (WPA).

Wilmington [WIL-ming-tuhn] (Dearborn). This village was laid out on May 30, 1815, by William C. Chamberlain, Michael Flake, and Robert Moore. A post office was established on July 16, 1817; closed on May 31, 1907.* The name probably was borrowed from an eastern state.

Wilmington (Rush). See Manilla.

Wilmot [WIL-maht] (Noble). According to the WPA files, this village originally was called Ryders Mill, for John Ryder, who had a sawmill here in 1848. A post office called Wilmot, for early settlers, was established on October 30, 1850; closed on April 20, 1911.

Wilson Corner [WIL-suhn KAWR-ner] (Shelby). Also called Wilson, this un-platted community was established around a country store owned by the Wilson family, for whom it was named. A post office called Wilson was established on July 2, 1883; closed on January 31, 1905.*

Winamac [WIN-uh-mak] (county seat, Pulaski). This town was laid out in April 1839. A post office was established as Winnimack on September 7, 1839. The spelling was changed to Winamac in 1861. The name is for the Potawatomi chief Wi-na-mak, literally "mudfish," i.e., "catfish."

Winchester [WIN-ches-ter] (county seat, Randolph). This city was established as the county seat in 1818. A post office was established on May 27, 1820. The name may be for the English town via an eastern state, though it is said that the name honors Brigadier General James Winchester, War of 1812 officer.

Windfall [WIN-fawl] (Tipton). This town was laid out by James B. Fouch in 1853, the same year that he built a sawmill here. A post office was established on June 21, 1855. Fouch platted the town because he wanted to secure a railroad station to ship his lumber. A local explanation is that the town was so named because of a local windstorm, but the origin is uncertain. A more positive explanation, but still a guess, is that the name is commendatory, suggesting an expected gain when the railroad came through town. A variant name is Windfall City.

Windom [WIN-duhm] (Martin). A post office was established here on April 8, 1892; closed on November 15, 1906. The name is for William Windom, secretary of the treasury under James Garfield and Benjamin Harrison.

Windsor [WIN-zer] (Randolph). A post office was established on June 10, 1831; closed on December 5, 1898.* The village was platted on January 30, 1832. Supposedly the name is for the castle in England (WPA).

Winfield [WIN-feeld] (Lake). A post office called Winfield, for the township in which it was located, was established on April 11, 1848; closed on May 22, 1882. The village formerly was called Bibler. The township was named for General Winfield Scott by the first settler, Jeremy Hixson.

Winfield (Posey). See Rapture.

Wingate [WIN-gayt] (Montgomery). This town was laid out around 1831 and originally called Pleasant Hill, subjectively descriptive of its location. A post office established as Pleasant Hill on September 26, 1833, was changed to Wingate on January 20, 1882.* The name honors John Wingate, who assisted in getting a railway through town.

Winnington (Clay). See Hoosierville.

Winona (Jay). See Fiat.

Winona [wuh-NO-nuh; wi-NO-nuh] (Starke). This village was laid out in 1891, and a post office was established on

March 20, 1891. Supposedly the name was picked by the government from several suggested names because there was no other post office named Winona in Indiana (WPA). Cf. Winona Lake.

Winona Lake [wuh-NO-nuh LAYK] (Kosciusko). A post office established as Eagle Lake on December 31, 1889, was changed to Winona Lake, for the lake of the same name, on January 20, 1898. The name of the lake comes from Wi-no-nah, a Sioux proper name given to a firstborn child if it is female. Wenonah of Longfellow's *Hiawatha* is the same name.

Winships Mill (Clinton). See Mulberry.

Winslow [WINZ-lo] (Pike). This town was laid out in November 1837 by John Hathaway, a local mill owner, and a post office was established on December 23, 1839. The name is for Hathaway's son, William Winslow Hathaway, who was then seven months old. According to a local family legend, "Winslow, Indiana, is supposed to have gotten its name in the following manner. Many years ago on the banks of the Patoka, there sprang up a community based around a mill on the river. When enough people had settled around there, it was decided that they should name the town. My great-great-great-grandfather was the owner of the mill, and his name was Old Man Winslow. He said that the town should be named after the first child that was born in the settlement. Everyone agreed, but Old Man Winslow knew full well that his son's wife was already overdue. The baby was born, and it was a boy, and the proud parents named it after the old man; thus, Winslow got its name" (ISUFA).

Winterrow [WINT-er-rod] (Shelby). A post office called Winterroud, of which the present name is a form, was estab-lished on December 5, 1853; closed on April 30, 1902. The name is for the local Winterroud family. William P. Winter-roud was the first postmaster.

Wintersville (Decatur). See Smiths Crossing.

Winthrop [WIN-thruhp] (Warren). A post office was established on September 11, 1883. The village was platted by Jacob M. Rhode on March 3, 1884.

Wirt [wert] (Jefferson). A post office was established on December 22, 1834; closed on June 30, 1950.* The village was laid out on July 18, 1837, by John W. Parsons and James Burns. The name is for an early settler, William Wirt.

Wirt Station [WERT STAY-shuhn] (Jefferson). This community sprang up along the railroad just west of Wirt, q.v., for which it was named.

Wissel (Franklin). See Rockdale.

Wittigton (Clay). See Hoosierville.

Witts Station [WITS STAY-shuhn; WIT STAY-shuhn] (Union). This village was named for a local family. The Witts were among the early settlers in this area. There's also a Witts Run nearby.

Woinona (Jay). See Fiat.

Wolcott [WAWL-kuht; WUL-kuht] (White). This town, named for the local Wolcott family, was laid out in 1861 by Ebenezer and Maria Wolcott, according to some sources, or by Anson Wolcott, according to other sources. Anson Wolcott, a New Yorker, purchased land in this area in 1858. A post office was established on June 13, 1861. Chauncy S. Wolcott was the second postmaster.

Wolcottville [WUL-kuht-vil; WAWL-kuht-vil] (Noble). Located on the Lagrange and Noble county line, this town, first called Wolcotts Mills, was named for George Wolcott, a native of Connecticut, who settled here in June 1837 and established a gristmill, sawmill, carding mill, and distillery. It is said that Wolcott built fifteen buildings in this town and that at one time he was engaged in seven different occupations: milling, sawing, blacksmithing, merchandising, coopering, farming, and manufacturing potash. In addition, in 1852, after becoming dissatisfied with the local schools, Wolcott established the Wolcottville Seminary. A post office called Wolcotts Mills was established on April 20, 1848, and the post office name was changed to Wolcottsville on July 24, 1864. George Wolcott also was the second postmaster. The town was laid out in October 1849.

Wolf Lake [wulf layk] (Noble). According to some accounts, this village was settled in 1827, but officially it was laid out by Patrick C. Miller and Andrew Stewart in April 1836. A post office called Wolf Lake was established on June 12, 1834, and the spelling was changed to Wolflake on May 1, 1894, though the preferred local spelling still appears to be Wolf Lake. The name comes from Wolf Lake, on which the village is located. According to the WPA files, wolves roamed around the lake in the early days.

Wood (Kosciusko). See Atwood.

Woodburn [WUD-bern] (Allen). This city was platted in 1865 as Woodburn, sometimes called Woodburn City, probably for John Woodburn, although a variant name has been Shirley City, for Indiana Senator Robert B. Shirley. A post office established as Phelps on October 10, 1863, was changed to Woodburn on October 10, 1865.*

Woodbury [WUD-behr-ee] (Hancock). One local history says that this town was laid out on December 12, 1851, by Ellen Wood; other sources say the town was laid out on December 12, 1857, by Francis Ellingwood. In either case, the name may have been coined from the name of the founder, most likely Ellingwood, which someone rendered Ellen Wood. A post office called Woodbury was established on May 30, 1858; closed on August 15, 1903.

Woodland [WUD-luhnd] (Saint Joseph). A post office was established on April 25, 1856; closed on January 15, 1907. The village, dating from around 1855, was not laid out until August 7, 1899. The name possibly is for the extensive forests and lumber business once here. At one time there were at least eight sawmills in the area.

Woodlawn (Delaware). See Desoto.

Woodruff [WUD-ruhf] (Lagrange). A post office established as Marcy on September 30, 1835, was changed to Woodruff, for local merchants, on May 6, 1880.* Allen Woodruff was postmaster when the post office name was changed. Earlier the village was called Wrights Corners, for the local Wright family.

Woodruff Place [WUD-ruhf PLAYS] (Marion). Also called Woodruff, this community, located in the heart of Indianapolis, was platted on October 2, 1872, by J. O. Woodruff, for whom it was named, and incorporated in 1876.

Woodruffs (Johnson). See Nineveh.

Woods Station (Randolph). See Rural.

Woodstock [WUD-stahk] (Marion). This community was platted and incorporated in 1920.

Woodville (Hamilton). See Strawtown.

Woodville [WUD-vil] [(Henry). This village was platted by James Atkinson on May 30, 1836, and probably was named for the dense forests surrounding it.

Woodville [WUD-vil] (Lawrence). This village was laid out on December 10, 1849, by Edwin Wood, for whom it was named.

Woodville [WUD-vil] (Porter). A post office was established here on April 21, 1882; closed on July 31, 1914.

Woodys Corner (Parke). See Tangier.

Wooster [WOOS-ter] (Kosciusko). A post office was established here on April 4, 1854; closed on June 30, 1903.

Wooster [WOOS-ter] (Scott). This village was platted on January 23, 1847. A post office called Woostertown was established here on April 25, 1865; closed on September 13, 1875. According to the WPA files, the village was named "after Worchester of the American Revolution. Localisms have brought about the present spelling of the town." Cf. New Frankfort.

Worthington [WER-*th*ing-tuhn] (Greene). This town was laid out in April 1849 and named for Worthington, Ohio, former home of one of the founders. A post office was established on July 16, 1850.

Worthington (Wells). See Poneto.

Wright (Greene). See Midland.

Wright Corner [REYET KAWR-ner] (Dearborn). A post office called Wrights Corners, for the local Wright family, was established on May 12, 1853; closed on December 14, 1903.* Washington Wright opened a store about 1825, and Milton Wright was the second postmaster.

Wrights (Shelby). See Pleasant View.

Wrights Corners (Lagrange). See Woodruff.

Wrights Mills (Parke). See Rockport.

Wrinkle (Madison). See Summitville.

Wyandot [WEYEN-daht] (Tippecanoe). Around 1828 William Heaton bought 1,400 acres of the Richardsville Reserve and about a year later platted the village. A post office named Wyandotte was established on January 27, 1849. The name is for an Indian village, which was located about a mile north of here.

Wyandotte [WEYEN-daht] (Crawford). A post office was established on August 1, 1884, and named for the nearby Wyandotte caves. The caves were named for the Indian tribe, whose name probably means "people of one speech." Though Big Wyandotte Cave was inhabited by humans at least 3,000 years ago, the Wyandottes probably never lived here. The Wyandotte caves have some of the largest underground rooms and mountains in the world. The caves have inspired several legends, including the following:

1. "The Wyandotte Cave was discovered by an old coon hunter when his dog fell into a sink hole. Since it was one of his best dogs, the old hunter tried to get him out. When the old man got down in the sink hole, he found that it was a cave instead. It turned out to be a pretty good sized one after he explored it" (ISUFA).

2. "Back in the cowboy days, two men were goin' to try to make their fortune

from selling onion sets. Since people used onions for so many cures, they thought they could do it. So these two men bought all the onion sets that they could get hold of between Evansville and Louisville. Well, they needed some place to store these sets, so they used the Wyandotte Cave. Well, the men put the sets in the cave and left them there until plantin' season was about here. They went to the cave, and all their sets had dehydrated because the cave was so dry. So the men didn't have any use for them and left them in the cave, and those onion sets are still there" (ISUFA).

Wyatt [WEYE-uht] (Saint Joseph). A post office called Wyatt was established on May 11, 1893. The village, first called Littleton, was platted on March 27, 1894.

Supposedly Wyatt is for a place in Pennsylvania, but maps and gazetteers do not show this name in Pennsylvania. The name may have been borrowed from Wyatt, West Virginia, which is located only about twenty miles from Pennsylvania.

Wylands Mills (Elkhart). See Bainter Town.

Wyncoop (Decatur). See Horace.

Wyndam (Benton). See Swanington.

Wynn (Franklin). See Palestine.

Wynnsboro [WINZ-ber-o] (Harrison). This village was laid out on April 25, 1820, by John R. Wynn, for whom it was named.

Xenia (Carroll). See Prince William.

Xenia (Miami). See Converse.

Yankee Settlement (Posey). See Farmersville.

Yankeetown (Fayette). See Bentonville.

Yankeetown (Posey). See Farmersville.

Yankeetown [YANK-ee-town] (Warrick). A post office established as Frisbies Mills, for the local Frisbie family, on December 5, 1835, was changed to Yankeetown on February 2, 1853. Alpha Frisbie was the first postmaster at Frisbies Mills. The village was laid out on April 9, 1858, by Thomas Day. According to traditional accounts, Yankeetown is for Yankee settlers from New England (WPA) or for Union sympathizers from Kentucky. It also is said that Ralph Waldo Emerson's relatives named the village.

Yearbyville (Spencer). See Bloomfield.

Yeddo [YED-o] (Fountain). A post office was established on March 31, 1881; closed on April 10, 1964. The village was platted on April 15, 1881. Yeddo, or Jeddo, was the former name of Tokyo. Supposedly, the Post Office Department named the post office because it wanted a short, uncommon name, but according to another account, the name was chosen from a geography book: "My father, James Stuart, was requested to engineer the legal process to procure [a post office]. . . . So one evening Father came in the room where I was . . . reviewing some school books and it so happened that there was a Geography lying on the table. The Geography happened to be open at a page that contained the map of Asia. I glanced at the map and noticed the word Yeddo in bold type and spoke up and said 'name her Yeddo.' Which I had not the least idea he would do but he did. . . . Regardless of all other claims, you may put the above down as the true story of how Yeddo received its name" (undated letter in ISUFA).

Yellow Bank [YEL-o bank] (Franklin). This community was named for nearby Yellow Bank Creek. A variant name is Thunderbird Mine Dam.

Yellowbanks [YEL-o-banks] (Kosciusko). This village possibly was named for Yellow Creek. A post office, with Job Meredith as postmaster, was established as Merediths Mills in Fulton County on December 28, 1846; moved to Kosciusko County on October 16, 1855; changed to Yellow Creek on January 28, 1856; and closed on December 6, 1882.

Yellowstone [YEL-o-ston] (Monroe). A post office was established on May 18, 1887, and probably closed in the 1920s. The village originally was called Hunters Creek, for the nearby stream of the same name. The stream was named for a local family. David Hunter was an early settler (WPA).

Yenne [YEN-ee] (Martin). A post office, named for the local Yenne family, was established on May 27, 1897; closed on October 31, 1906. Samuel P. Yenne was postmaster at Shoals when this post office was established, and some sources claim this village was named for him.

Yeoman [YO-muhn] (Carroll). A post office was established on September 26, 1879, and the town was platted on September 29, 1880. The name is for Colonel Yeoman, a railroad official.

Yockey (Lawrence). See Tarry Park.

York [yawrk] (Steuben). A post office called York was established in York Township on March 25, 1839; closed on July 28, 1841. Another post office called York Centre, sometimes spelled York Center, was established on November 6, 1855; changed to York on December 14, 1894. Another variant name has been Hathaway.

Yorktown [YAWRK-town] (Delaware). This town was laid out by Oliver H.

Smith on November 5, 1836, and named for the York tribe of the Delawares. A post office was established on September 22, 1836; closed on January 31, 1964.

Yorkville [YAWRK-vil] (Dearborn). A post office established as York Ridge on November 12, 1833, was changed to Yorkville on December 9, 1845; closed on May 15, 1955.* The name is for York Township, in which the village is located.

Young America [YUHNG uh-MEHR-uh-kuh] (Cass). This village was platted on December 30, 1863, and a post office was established on February 8, 1876. The name preserves a phrase that was a political catchword of expansionists. According to a local anecdote, Thomas Henry bought a steam boiler for his sawmill about 1855. Someone wrote "Young America," indicating enterprise, on the boiler, and Henry named the village Young America.

Youngs Creek [YUHNGZ kreek] (Orange). This village, laid out about 1864, formerly was called Unionville, al-legedly as a result of two political parties uniting. A post office was established as Youngs Creek, for the stream of the same name, on April 3, 1867.* The stream was named for William Young, who settled here in 1816.

Youngstown [YUHNGZ-town] (Vigo). This village was established in 1865, subdivided on March 31, 1868, by Chauncey Carr, and named for a local family. Samuel Young was an early settler. A post office was established on November 19, 1867; closed on September 15, 1912.

Yountsville [YAHNTS-vil] (Montgomery). This village was named for the Younts family, Daniel and his brother, Allen, who established a woolen mill here around 1840. The town grew up around Younts Mill, which at one time employed nearly 300 workers. A three-story brick and stone mill built in 1864 is still standing. A post office, with Allen Yount as postmaster, was established on August 19, 1844; closed on December 31, 1909.*

 **Z**

Zanesville (Daviess). See Maysville.

Zanesville [ZAYNZ-vil] (Wells). Located on the Allen-Wells county line, this village was platted first on February 22, 1848, and named for Zanesville, Ohio, by early settlers from Ohio. A post office established as Choppeen on April 9, 1850, was changed to Zanesville on August 23, 1854.*

Zard (Jasper). See McCoysburg.

Zelma [ZEL-muh] (Lawrence). This village was platted on May 23, 1890, by Stephen and James Fountain and named for Zelma Fountain, one of Stephen Fountain's daughters. A post office was established on April 3, 1890; closed on January 31, 1913.

Zenas [ZEE-nuhs] (Jennings). This village was founded in 1826. A post office established as Ely on May 7, 1830, was changed to Zenas on August 30, 1839; closed on July 15, 1911.

Zionsville [ZEYE-uhnz-vil] (Boone). This town, settled around 1830, was laid out in 1852 and named for surveyor William Zion, one of the founders. A post office was established on September 3, 1853.

Zipp [zip] (Vanderburgh). This village formerly was called Mechanicsville, probably because a blacksmith shop and wagon shop were located here. Locally it was called Stringtown because the houses here were strung along the road. A post office called Mechanicsville was established on December 25, 1829; closed on September 17, 1879.* A post office called Zipps, for the local Zipp family, was established on March 10, 1881, with Frank Zipp, Jr., as the first postmaster. On May 16, 1894, the post office name was changed to Zipp.

Zoar [zawr] (Pike). A post office was established on June 11, 1900; closed on June 15, 1907. The name Zoar generally is associated with the Zoar community, a nineteenth-century communal sect of German Protestant separatists founded at Zoar, Ohio, in 1817. Hoosier churches named Zoar are located in Harrison, Jay, Jefferson, Posey, Vanderburgh, and Warrick counties.

Zulu [ZOO-loo] (Allen). A post office was established on January 21, 1880. Allegedly the name had to be changed from Four Corners when a post office was established, and the present name was selected from a geography book. A pin stuck in the book fell on the word *Zulu* on a page about Africa.

Bibliography

Alvord, Samuel E. *Alvord's History of Noble County, Indiana.* Logansport, 1902.
American Atlas Company. *Atlas and Directory of Madison County, Indiana.* Cleveland, 1901.
American Map and Atlas Company. *Descriptive Atlas of Jackson County, Indiana.* Chicago, 1900.
American Publishing Company. *Living Leaders: An Encyclopedia of Biography. Special Edition for Daviess and Martin Counties.* N.p., 1897.
Andreas, Alfred Theodore. *Atlas Map of Parke County, Indiana.* Chicago, 1874.
Andreas, Alfred Theodore. *Atlas Map of Vigo County, Indiana.* Chicago, 1874.
Andreas, Alfred Theodore. *Illustrated Historical Atlas of the State of Indiana.* Chicago, 1876.
Andreas and Baskin. *An Illustrated Historical Atlas of La Grange County, Indiana.* Chicago, 1874.
Andreas and Baskin. *An Illustrated Historical Atlas of Noble County, Indiana.* Chicago, 1874.
Baber, Jack. *The Early History of Greene County, Indiana.* Worthington, 1875.
Bailey, John C. W., and Company. *Floyd County Gazetteer.* Chicago, 1868.
Baird, Lewis C. *Baird's History of Clark County, Indiana.* Indianapolis, 1909.
Baker, J. David. *The Postal History of Indiana.* 2 vols. Louisville, 1976.
Baker, Ronald L. "Brown County Place Names," *Midwestern Journal of Language and Folklore,* 2 (Fall 1976), 64–70.
Baker, Ronald L. "County Names in Indiana," *Indiana Names,* 2 (Fall 1971), 39–54.
Baker, Ronald L. *Hoosier Folk Legends.* Bloomington, 1982.
Baker, Ronald L. *Jokelore: Humorous Folktales from Indiana.* Bloomington, 1986.
Baker, Ronald L. "The Role of Folk Legends in Place-Name Research," *Journal of American Folklore,* 85 (1972), 367–373.
Baker, Ronald L., ed. *The Study of Place Names.* Terre Haute, 1991.
Baker, Ronald L., and Marvin Carmony. *Indiana Place Names.* Bloomington, 1975.

Ball, Timothy Horton. *Lake County, Indiana, from 1834 to 1872*. Chicago, 1873.

Ball, Timothy Horton. *The Lake of the Red: A Record of the First Thirty Years of Baptist Labors in the County of Lake*. Crown Point, 1880.

Ball, Timothy Horton. *Northwestern Indiana from 1800 to 1900*. [Chicago], 1900.

Ball, Timothy Horton, ed. *Encyclopedia of Genealogy and Biography of Lake County, Indiana*. Chicago and New York, 1904.

Banta, David Demaree. *A Historical Sketch of Johnson County, Indiana*. Chicago, 1881.

Barrows, Frederick Irving. *History of Fayette County, Indiana*. Indianapolis, 1917.

Bartlett, Charles Henry. *Tales of Kankakee Land*. New York, 1904.

Bash, Frank Sumner, ed. *History of Huntington County, Indiana*. 2 vols. Chicago, 1914.

Baskin, O. L., and Company. *An Illustrated Historical Atlas of Carroll County, Indiana*. Chicago, 1874.

Battey, F. A. [Printing Company]. *Counties of La Grange and Noble, Indiana: Historical and Biographical*. Chicago, 1882.

Battey, F. A. [Printing Company]. *Counties of Warren, Benton, Jasper and Newton, Indiana: Historical and Biographical*. Chicago, 1883.

Battey, F. A. [Printing Company]. *Counties of White and Pulaski, Indiana: Historical and Biographical*. Chicago, 1883.

Beckwith, Hiram Williams. *History of Fountain County, Together with Historic Notes on the Wabash Valley*. Chicago, 1881.

Beckwith, Hiram Williams. *History of Montgomery County, Together with Historic Notes on the Wabash Valley*. Chicago, 1881.

Beckwith, Hiram Williams. *History of Vigo and Parke Counties, Together with Historic Notes on the Wabash Valley*. Chicago, 1880.

Beckwith, H. W. "Indian Names of Water Courses in the State of Indiana." In *Annual Report of the Indiana Department of Geography and Natural History*. Indianapolis, 1883.

Beers, J. H., and Company. *Atlas of Bartholomew County, Indiana*. Chicago, 1879.

Beers, J. H., and Company. *Atlas of Decatur County, Indiana*. Chicago, 1882.

Beers, J. H., and Company. *Atlas of DeKalb County, Indiana*. Chicago 1880.

Beers, J. H., and Company. *Atlas of Franklin County, Indiana*. Chicago, 1882.

Beers, J. H., and Company. *Atlas of Hendricks County, Indiana*. Chicago, 1878.

Beers, J. H., and Company. *Atlas of Johnson County, Indiana*. Chicago, 1881.

Beers, J. H., and Company. *Atlas of Montgomery County, Indiana*. Chicago, 1878.

Beers, J. H., and Company. *Atlas of Putnam County, Indiana*. Chicago, 1879.

Beers, J. H., and Company. *Atlas of Shelby County, Indiana*. Chicago 1880.

Beers, J. H., and Company. *Atlas of Steuben County, Indiana*. Chicago, 1880.

Beers, J. H., and Company. *Atlas of Union County, Indiana*. Chicago, 1884.

Beers, J. H., and Company. *Commemorative Biographical Record of Prominent and Representative Men of Indianapolis and Vicinity*. Chicago, 1908.

Binford, John H. *History of Hancock County, Indiana*. Greenfield, 1882.

Biographical Publishing Company. *Portrait and Biographical Record of Madison and Hamilton Counties, Indiana*. Chicago, 1893.

Birch, Jesse S. *History of Benton County and Historic Oxford*. Oxford, Indiana, 1928.

Blair, Don. *Harmonist Construction*. Indianapolis, 1964.

Blanchard, Charles, ed. *Counties of Clay and Owen, Indiana*. Chicago, 1884.

Blanchard, Charles, ed. *Counties of Howard and Tipton, Indiana*. Chicago, 1883.

Blanchard, Charles, ed. *Counties of Morgan, Monroe and Brown, Indiana*. Chicago, 1884.

Blane, William. *An Excursion through the United States and Canada during the Years 1822–1823*. London, 1824.

Bodurtha, Arthur Lawrence, ed. *History of Miami County, Indiana.* 2 vols. Chicago, 1914.

Bogardus, Carl R. *The Centennial History of Austin, Scott County, Indiana.* Paoli, Indiana, 1953.

Bolton, Nathaniel. *Early History of Indianapolis and Central Indiana.* Indianapolis, 1897.

Booth, Norborne M. *Gleanings.* Evansville, 1896.

Bowen, A. W., and Company. *History of Montgomery County, Indiana.* 2 vols. Indianapolis, [1913].

Bowen, A. W., and Company. *Portrait and Biographical Record of Boone and Clinton Counties, Indiana.* Chicago, 1895.

Bowen, A. W., and Company. *A Portrait and Biographical Record of Delaware County, Indiana.* Chicago, 1894.

Bowen, B. F., and Company. *Biographical Memoirs of Grant County, Indiana.* Chicago, 1901.

Bowen, B. F., and Company. *Biographical Memoirs of Greene County, Indiana.* 3 vols. Indianapolis, 1908.

Bowen, B. F., and Company. *Biographical Memoirs of Hancock County, Indiana.* Logansport, 1902.

Bowen, B. F., and Company. *Biographical Memoirs of Henry County, Indiana.* Logansport, 1902.

Bowen, B. F., and Company. *Biographical Memoirs of Huntington County, Indiana.* Chicago, 1901.

Bowen, B. F., and Company. *Biographical Memoirs of Jay County, Indiana.* Chicago, 1901.

Bowen, B. F., and Company. *Biographical Memoirs of Wabash County, Indiana.* Chicago, 1901.

Bowen, B. F., and Company. *Biographical Memoirs of Wells County, Indiana.* Logansport, 1903.

Bowen, B. F., and Company. *Biographical Record and Portrait Album of Tippecanoe County, Indiana.* Chicago, 1888.

Bowen, B. F., and Company. *Biographical Record of Bartholomew and Jackson Counties, Indiana.* [Indianapolis], 1904.

Bowen, B. F., and Company. *Biographical Record of Bartholomew County, Indiana.* [Indianapolis], 1904.

Bowen, B. F., and Company. *History of DeKalb County, Indiana.* Indianapolis, 1914.

Bowen, B. F., and Company. *History of Lawrence and Monroe Counties, Indiana.* Indianapolis, 1914.

Bowen, B. F., and Company. *History of Parke and Vermillion Counties, Indiana.* Indianapolis, 1913.

Bowen, B. F., and Company. *Progressive Men and Women of Kosciusko County, Indiana.* Logansport, 1902.

Bradsby, Henry C. *History of Vigo County, Indiana.* Chicago, 1891.

Branigin, Elba L. *History of Johnson County Indiana.* Indianapolis, 1913.

Brant and Fuller Publishing Company. *History of Bartholomew County, Indiana.* Chicago, 1888.

Brant and Fuller Publishing Company. *History of Grant County, Indiana.* Chicago, 1886.

Brant and Fuller Publishing Company. *History of Huntington County, Indiana.* Chicago, 1887.

Brant and Fuller Publishing Company. *History of Jackson County, Indiana.* Chicago, 1886.

Brant and Fuller Publishing Company. *History of Johnson County, Indiana.* Chicago, 1888.

Brant and Fuller Publishing Company. *History of Miami County, Indiana.* Chicago, 1887.

Brant and Fuller Publishing Company. *History of Rush County, Indiana.* Chicago, 1888.

Brant and Fuller Publishing Company. *History of Shelby County, Indiana: from the Earliest Time to the Present.* Chicago, 1887.

Brant and Fuller Publishing Company. *History of Vanderburgh County, Indiana.* [Madison, Wisc.], 1889.

Brant and Fuller Publishing Company. *Valley of the Upper Maumee River, with Historical Account of Allen County and the City of Fort Wayne, Indiana.* 2 vols. Madison, Wisc., 1889.

Brewster, Paul G. "Additional Observations on Indiana Place-Names," *Hoosier Folklore Bulletin,* 3 (December 1944), 74–76.

Brewster, Paul G. "A Glance at Some Indiana Place-Names," *Hoosier Folklore Bulletin,* 6 (June 1943), 14–16.

Brice, Wallace A. *History of Fort Wayne.* Fort Wayne, 1868.

Brunvand, Jan H. "Some Indiana Place-Name Legends," *Midwest Folklore,* 9 (Winter 1959), 245–248.

Buley, R. Carlyle. *The Old Northwest: Pioneer Period, 1815–1840.* Bloomington, 1950.

Bulleit, F. A. *Illustrated Atlas and History of Harrison County, Indiana.* Corydon, 1906.

Burke, Kenneth. "Literature as Equipment for Living." In *The Philosophy of Literary Form.* New York, 1961, pp. 253–262.

Campbell, Frank S. *The Story of Hamilton County, Indiana.* N.p., 1962.

Carmony, Marvin. "The Place-Name Correspondence of Chester Arthur Brown," *Names,* 33 (1985), 6–20.

Cauthorne, Henry Sullivan. *A Brief Sketch of the Past, Present and Prospects of Vincennes.* Vincennes, 1884.

Cauthorne, Henry Sullivan. *A History of the City of Vincennes, Indiana, from 1702 to 1901.* [Vincennes, 1902].

Chadwick, Edward H. *Chadwick's History of Shelby County, Indiana.* Indianapolis, 1909.

Chamberlain, E. *The Indiana Gazetteer, or Topographical Dictionary of the State of Indiana.* Indianapolis, 1849.

Chambers, Doris M. *Ghost Towns of Huntington County.* Huntington, Indiana, 1971.

Chapman, Charles C., and Company. *History of Elkhart County, Indiana.* Chicago, 1881.

Chapman, Charles C., and Company. *History of La Porte County, Indiana.* Chicago, 1880.

Chapman, Charles C., and Company. *History of St. Joseph County, Indiana.* Chicago 1880.

Chapman Brothers. *Portrait and Biographical Record of Montgomery, Parke and Fountain Counties, Indiana.* Chicago, 1893.

Chicago Printing Company. *Biographical and Historical Souvenir for the Counties of Clark, Crawford, Harrison, Floyd, Jefferson, Jennings, Scott and Washington, Indiana.* Chicago, 1889.

Child, Francis J. *The English and Scottish Popular Ballads.* 5 vols. New York, 1965.

Clifton, Thomas A., ed. *Past and Present of Fountain and Warren Counties Indiana.* Indianapolis, 1913.

Cline and McHaffie. *The People's Guide: A Business, Political and Religious Directory of Bartholomew County, Indiana.* Indianapolis, 1874.

Cline and McHaffie. *The People's Guide: A Business, Political and Religious Directory of Hamilton County, Indiana.* Indianapolis, 1874.

Cline and McHaffie. *The People's Guide: A Business, Political and Religious Directory of Hendricks County, Indiana.* Indianapolis, 1874.

Cline and McHaffie. *The People's Guide: A Business, Political and Religious Directory of Henry County, Indiana.* Indianapolis, 1874.

Cline and McHaffie. *The People's Guide: A Business, Political and Religious Directory of Marion County, Indiana.* Indianapolis, 1874.

Cline and McHaffie. *The People's Guide: A Business, Political and Religious Directory of Montgomery County, Indiana.* Indianapolis, 1874.

Cline and McHaffie. *The People's Guide: A Business, Political and Religious Directory of Morgan County, Indiana.* Indianapolis, 1874.

Cline and McHaffie. *The People's Guide: A Business, Political and Religious Directory of Vermillion County, Indiana.* Indianapolis, 1874.

Clodd, Edward. *Tom Tit Tot, an Essay on Savage Philosophy in Folk-tale.* London, 1897.

Condit, Blackford. *The History of Early Terre Haute.* New York, 1900.

Cox, Sandford C. *Recollections of the Early Settlement of the Wabash Valley.* Lafayette, 1860.

Crist, L. M. *History of Boone County, Indiana.* 2 vols. Indianapolis, 1914.

Daggett, Rowan K. "The Place-Names of Chester Township, Wabash County, Indiana," *Indiana Names,* 4 (Spring 1973), 4–30.

Daggett, Rowan Keim. "Upper Wabash Valley Place Names: Wabash and Miami Counties, Indiana." Ph.D. dissertation, Indiana University, 1978.

Dalbey, Ed F., ed. *Dalbey's Souvenir: Pictorial History of the City of Richmond, Indiana.* Richmond, Indiana, 1896.

Daniels, E. D. *A Twentieth Century History and Biographical Record of Laporte County, Indiana.* Chicago and New York, 1904.

Deahl, Anthony, ed. *A Twentieth Century History and Biographical Record of Elkhart County, Indiana.* Chicago and New York, 1905.

Dégh, Linda. "Importance of Collecting Place-Name Legends in Indiana." In *The Study of Place Names,* ed. Ronald L. Baker. Terre Haute, 1991.

De Hart, Richard P., ed. *Past and Present of Tippecanoe County, Indiana.* 2 vols. Indianapolis, 1909.

De la Hunt, Thomas James. "History Lessons from Indiana Names," *Indiana History Bulletin,* 3 (March 1926), 43–49.

De la Hunt, Thomas James. *Perry County: A History.* Indianapolis, 1916.

Dorson, Richard M. *American Folklore and the Historian.* Chicago, 1971.

Dorson, Richard M. *Davy Crockett: American Comic Legend.* New York, 1977.

Dorson, Richard M. "Interpretation of Research." In *Handbook of American Folklore,* ed. Richard M. Dorson. Bloomington, 1983, pp. 323–325.

Dorson, Richard M. "Oral Tradition and Written History: The Case for the United States," *Journal of the Folklore Institute,* 1 (1964), 220–238.

Dunn, Jacob Piatt. "Glossary of Indian Names, and Supposed Indian Names, in Indiana." *Indiana and Indianans,* vol. 1, pp. 86–97. Chicago, 1919.

Dunn, Jacob Piatt. "Indiana Geographical Nomenclature," *Indiana Magazine of History,* 8 (September 1912), 109–114.

Dunn, Jacob Piatt. Notes on Indiana Place Names in the Indiana Historical Society Library, Indianapolis, Indiana.

Dunn, Jacob Piatt. *True Indian Stories with Glossary of Indiana Indian Names.* Indianapolis, 1909.

Dunn, Jacob Piatt. *The Word Hoosier.* Indiana Historical Society Publications, vol. 7, no. 2. Indianapolis, 1907.

Elliot, Joseph Peter. *A History of Evansville and Vanderburgh County, Indiana.* Evansville, 1897.

Ellis, John Seymour. *Our County: Its History and Early Settlement by Townships.* [Muncie, 1898].

Esarey, Logan. *History of Indiana: An Account of Fulton County,* ed. H. A. Barnhart. Vol. 3. Dayton, Ohio, 1923.

Esarey, Logan. *History of Indiana: An Account of St. Joseph County,* ed. John B. Stoll. 3 vols. Dayton, Ohio, 1922.

Esarey, Logan. *A History of Indiana from Its Exploration to 1850.* Indianapolis, 1970.

Forkner, John La Rue. *Historical Sketches and Reminiscences of Madison County, Indiana.* Anderson, Indiana, 1897.

Forkner, John La Rue. *History of Madison County, Indiana.* 2 vols. Chicago and New York, 1914.

Fortune, Will, ed. *Warrick and Its Prominent People: A History of Warrick County, Indiana.* [Evansville], 1981.

Fox, Henry Clay, ed. *Memoirs of Wayne County and the City of Richmond, Indiana.* 2 vols. Madison, Wisc., 1912.

[Gannett, Henry.] "Indiana Geographical Nomenclature," *Indiana Magazine of History,* 8 (June 1912), 70–83.

Gerould, Gordon. *The Ballad of Tradition.* Oxford, 1957.

Gilbert, Frank M. *History of the City of Evansville and Vanderburgh County, Indiana.* 2 vols. Chicago, 1910.

Glassie, Henry. "Folklore and History," *Minnesota History,* 50 (1987), 188–192.

Gomme, George Laurence. *Folklore as an Historical Science.* London, 1908.

Goodspeed, Weston Arthur, ed. *Counties of Porter and Lake, Indiana.* Chicago, 1882.

Goodspeed, Weston Arthur, ed. *Counties of Whitley and Noble, Indiana.* Chicago, 1882.

Goodspeed Publishing Company. *History of Greene and Sullivan Counties, State of Indiana.* Chicago, 1884.

Goodspeed Publishing Company. *History of Knox and Daviess Counties, Indiana.* Chicago, 1886.

Goodspeed Publishing Company. *History of Lawrence, Orange and Washington Counties, Indiana.* Chicago, 1884.

Goodspeed Publishing Company. *History of Pike and Dubois Counties, Indiana.* Chicago, 1885.

Goodspeed Publishing Company. *History of Posey County, Indiana.* Chicago, 1886.

Goodspeed Publishing Company. *History of Warrick, Spencer, and Perry Counties, Indiana.* Chicago, 1885.

Goodspeed Publishing Company. *Pictorial and Biographical Memoirs of Elkhart and St. Joseph Counties, Indiana.* Chicago, 1893.

Goodspeed Publishing Company. *Pictorial and Biographical Memoirs of Indianapolis and Marion County.* Chicago, 1893.

Goodspeed Publishing Company. *Pictorial and Biographical Record of La Porte, Porter, Lake and Starke Counties, Indiana.* Chicago, 1894.

Gratzer, Florence Elise. "A Study of the Place Names in Lawrence County, Indiana." M.A. thesis, Indiana State University, 1957.

Green, George E. *History of Old Vincennes and Knox County, Indiana.* 2 vols. Chicago, 1911.

Griffing, Gordon, and Company. *Atlas of Daviess County, Indiana.* Philadelphia, 1888.

Griffing, Gordon, and Company. *Atlas of Hancock County, Indiana*. Philadelphia, 1887.

Griffing, Gordon, and Company. *Atlas of Indianapolis and Marion County, Indiana*. Philadelphia, 1889.

Griffing, Gordon, and Company. *Atlas of Jay County, Indiana*. Philadelphia, 1887.

Griffing, Gordon, and Company. *Atlas of Scott County, Indiana*. Philadelphia, 1889.

Griffing, Stevenson, and Company. *Atlas of Randolph County, Indiana*. Philadelphia, 1874.

Griffing, Stevenson, and Company. *Atlas of Wayne County, Indiana*. Philadelphia, 1874.

Guernsey, E. Y. *Indiana, the Influence of the Indian upon its History*. Publication [map] of the Indiana Department of Conservation, no. 122. [1970].

Gunckel, John Elstner. *The Early History of the Maumee Valley*. Toledo, 1902.

Guthrie, James M. *Thirty-three Years in the History of Lawrence County, 1884–1917*. Greenfield, 1958.

Hadley, John V., ed. *History of Hendricks County, Indiana*. Indianapolis, 1914.

Hahn, Holly Jane. "The Place-Names of Brown Township, Montgomery County, Indiana," *Indiana Names*, 5 (Spring 1974), 19–36.

Haimbaugh, Frank D. *History of Delaware County, Indiana*. 2 vols. Indianapolis, 1924.

Hamilton, Louis H., and William Darroch. *A Standard History of Jasper and Newton Counties, Indiana*. Chicago and New York, 1916.

Hardacre, F. C. *Historical Atlas of Knox County, Indiana*, Vincennes, 1903.

Harden, Samuel, comp. *Early Life and Times in Boone County, Indiana*. [Indianapolis], 1887.

Harden, Samuel, comp. *History of Madison County, Indiana*. Markleville, 1874.

Harden, Samuel, comp. *The Pioneer: An Account of Madison and Hancock Counties*. Greenfield, 1895.

Hardesty, A. G. *Illustrated Historical Atlas of Porter County, Indiana*. Valparaiso, 1876.

Hardesty, H. H. *Historical Hand Atlas Illustrated . . . and History of Jay County*. Chicago, 1881.

Harding, Lewis Albert, ed. *History of Decatur County, Indiana*. Indianapolis, 1915.

Harrison, John W. *Some Early History: A Boy's Experience* [in Montgomery County]. [Ladoga, 1909].

Hassam, Loren. *A Historical Sketch of Lafayette, Indiana*. Lafayette, 1872.

Hassam, Loren. *A Historical Sketch of Terre Haute, Indiana*. Terre Haute, 1873.

Hazzard, George. *History of Henry County, Indiana*. 2 vols. New Castle, 1906.

Helm, Thomas B., ed. *History of Allen County, Indiana*. Chicago, 1880.

Helm, Thomas B., ed. *History of Carroll County, Indiana*. Chicago, 1882.

Helm, Thomas B., ed. *History of Cass County, Indiana*. Chicago, 1886.

Helm, Thomas B., ed. *History of Delaware County, Indiana*. Chicago, 1881.

Helm, Thomas B., ed. *History of Hamilton County, Indiana*. Chicago, 1880.

Helm, Thomas B., ed. *History of Madison County, Indiana*. Chicago, 1880.

Helm, Thomas B., ed. *History of Wabash County, Indiana*. Chicago, 1884.

Herald Print Company. *Historical Sketch of Huntington County, Indiana*. Huntington, 1877.

Higgins, Belden, and Company. *An Illustrated Historical Atlas of Elkhart County, Indiana*. Chicago, 1874.

Higgins, Belden, and Company. *An Illustrated Historical Atlas of Fayette County, Indiana*. Chicago, 1875

Higgins, Belden, and Company. *An Illustrated Historical Atlas of Henry County, Indiana*. Chicago, 1875.

Higgins, Belden, and Company. *An Illustrated Historical Atlas of La Porte County, Indiana*. Chicago, 1874.

Higgins, Belden, and Company. *An Illustrated Historical Atlas of St. Joseph County, Indiana*. Chicago, 1875.

Hixson, Jerome C. "Some Approaches to Indiana Place Names," *Indiana Names*, 1 (Spring 1970), 11–19.

Hodges, Laura Fletcher. *Early Indianapolis*. Indianapolis, [1919].

Hoffman, Frank A. "Place Names in Brown County," *Midwest Folklore*, 11 (Spring 1961), 57–62.

Hollar, Jean. "Place Names of Fayette County, Indiana," *Indiana Names*, 5 (Fall 1974), 43–70.

Holloway, William Robeson. *Indianapolis: A Historical and Statistical Sketch of the Railroad City*. Indianapolis, 1870.

Holt, J. C. *Robin Hood*. London, 1982.

Hovey, Alvin P. *Centennial Historical Sketch of Posey County, Indiana*. N.p., [1876].

Howard, Timothy Edward. *A History of St. Joseph County, Indiana*. 2 vols. Chicago, 1907.

Howat, William Frederick, ed. *A Standard History of Lake County, Indiana*. 2 vols. Chicago, 1915.

Hyman, Max Robinson, ed. *Hyman's Handbook of Indianapolis*. Indianapolis, 1909.

Imperial Publishing Company. *The County of Steuben, Indiana: An Atlas*. Angola, 1898.

Indiana Board on Geographic Names. *Findings*. 3 vols. May 1961–June 1965.

Indiana Broadcasters Association. *A Guide to the Pronunciation of Indiana Cities and Towns*. [West Lafayette], n.d.

Indiana Historical Society Library, Indianapolis. Indiana Place-Names Card File.

Indiana State Chamber of Commerce. *Here Is Your Indiana Government*. Indianapolis, 1973.

Indiana State Library, Indiana Section, Indianapolis. Card File of Indiana Post Offices.

Indiana State Library, Indiana Section, Indianapolis. Place-Name Files, Mainly from Newspapers.

Indiana State University Folklore Archives, Manuscript Files.

Inter-state Publishing Company. *History of Clinton County, Indiana*. Chicago, 1886.

Inter-state Publishing Company. *History of DeKalb County, Indiana*. Chicago, 1885.

Inter-state Publishing Company. *History of Hendricks County, Indiana*. Chicago, 1885.

Inter-state Publishing Company. *History of Henry, County, Indiana*. Chicago, 1884.

Inter-state Publishing Company. *History of Steuben County, Indiana*. Chicago, 1885.

Inter-state Publishing Company. *History of Wayne County, Indiana*. 2 vols. Chicago, 1884.

Jansen, Wm. Hugh. "Reality the Non-Story and Realism the Story," *Midwestern Journal of Language and Folklore*, 1 (1975), 52–59.

Jay, Milton T. *History of Jay County, Indiana*. 2 vols. Indianapolis, 1922.

Jerman, Ed C. *History and Directory of Ripley County*. [Versailles, 1888].

Kaler, Samuel P. *History of Whitley County, Indiana*. [Indianapolis], 1907.

Keller [Printing Company]. *Biographical Cyclopedia of Vanderburgh County, Indiana.* Evansville, 1897.

Keller and Fuller. *Illustrated Atlas of Posey County, Indiana.* Evansville, 1900.

Kelley, J. Will. *The New Atlas of Jay County, Indiana.* [Portland], 1901.

Kemper, General William Harrison, ed. *A Twentieth Century History of Delaware County, Indiana.* 2 vols. Chicago, 1908.

Kingman, A. L. *Combination Atlas Map of Fulton County, Indiana.* N.p., 1883.

Kingman Brothers. *Combination Atlas Map of Boone County, Indiana.* [Chicago], 1878.

Kingman Brothers. *Combination Atlas Map of Clinton County, Indiana.* Chicago, 1878.

Kingman Brothers. *Combination Atlas Map of Grant County, Indiana.* [Chicago], 1877.

Kingman Brothers. *Combination Atlas Map of Howard County, Indiana.* [Chicago], 1877.

Kingman Brothers. *Combination Atlas Map of Kosciusko County, Indiana.* [Chicago], 1879.

Kingman Brothers. *Combination Atlas Map of Miami County,* Indiana. [Chicago], 1877.

Kingman Brothers. *Combination Atlas Map of Tippecanoe County, Indiana.* [Chicago], 1878.

Knapp, Horace S. *History of the Maumee Valley.* Toledo, 1872.

Krappe, Alexander. *The Science of Folklore.* New York, 1964.

Kreitzer, Alves John. *A History of Northeast County.* Dubois, 1970.

La Grange Publishing Company. *Illustrated Atlas and Columbian Souvenir of La Grange County, Indiana.* Lagrange, 1893.

Lake, D. J., and Company. *An Atlas of Gibson and Pike Counties, Indiana.* Philadelphia, 1881.

Lake, D. J., and Company. *An Atlas of Greene County, Indiana.* Philadelphia, 1879.

Lake, D. J., and Company. *An Atlas of Harrison County, Indiana.* Philadelphia, 1882.

Lake, D. J., and Company. *An Atlas of Jennings County, Indiana.* Chicago, 1884.

Lake, D. J., and Company. *An Atlas of Ripley County, Indiana.* Philadelphia, 1883.

Lake, D. J., and Company. *An Atlas of Switzerland and Ohio Counties, Indiana.* Philadelphia, 1888.

Lake, D. J., and Company. *An Atlas of Washington County, Indiana.* Philadelphia, 1878.

Lake, D. J., and Company. *An Illustrated Historical Atlas of Knox County, Indiana.* Philadelphia, 1880.

Lake, D. J., and Company. *An Illustrated Historical Atlas of Spencer County, Indiana.* Philadelphia, 1879.

Lake, D. J., and Company. *An Illustrated Historical Atlas of Warrick County, Indiana.* Philadelphia, 1880.

Lake, D. J., and Company. *Griffing's Atlas of Vanderburgh County, Indiana.* Philadelphia, 1880.

Lake, Griffing, and Stevenson. *Atlas of Dearborn County, Indiana.* Philadelphia, 1875.

Leffel, John C., ed. *History of Posey County, Indiana.* Evansville, 1978.

Leonard, William P. *History and Directory of Posey County.* Evansville, 1882.

Levine, Lawrence W. "How to Interpret American Folklore Historically." In *Handbook of American Folklore,* ed. Richard M. Dorson. Bloomington, 1983, pp. 338–344.

Lewis Publishing Company. *Biographical and Genealogical History of Cass, Miami, Howard and Tipton Counties, Indiana.* 2 vols. Chicago, 1898.

Lewis Publishing Company. *Biographical and Genealogical History of Wayne, Fayette, Union and Franklin Counties, Indiana.* 2 vols. Chicago, 1899.

Lewis Publishing Company. *Biographical and Historical Record of Adams and Wells Counties, Indiana.* Chicago, 1887.

Lewis Publishing Company. *Biographical and Historical Record of Jay and Blackford Counties, Indiana.* Chicago, 1887.

Lewis Publishing Company. *Biographical and Historical Record of Kosciusko County, Indiana.* Chicago, 1887.

Lewis Publishing Company. *Biographical and Historical Record of Putnam County, Indiana.* Chicago, 1887.

Lewis Publishing Company. *Biographical and Historical Record of Vermillion County, Indiana.* Chicago, 1888.

Lewis Publishing Company. *Biographical History of Tippecanoe, White, Jasper, Newton, Benton, Warren and Pulaski Counties, Indiana.* 2 vols. Chicago, 1899.

Lewis Publishing Company. *A Genealogical and Biographical Record of Decatur County, Indiana.* Chicago, 1900.

Lynch, Martha C. [Martin]. *Reminiscences of Adams, Jay and Randolph Counties.* [Fort Wayne, 1897].

McClennan, Ruth Miley. *Our People of Pike County.* Evansville, 1978.

McCormick, Chester A. *McCormick's Guide to Starke County.* [Knox], 1902.

McDavid, Raven. "Word Magic, or Would You Want Your Daughter to Marry a Hoosier?" In *Dialects in Culture: Essays in General Dialectology by Raven McDavid, Jr.,* ed. William A. Kretzschmar, Jr. University, Alabama, 1979, pp. 254–257.

McDonald, Daniel. *History of Marshall County, Indiana.* Chicago, 1881.

McDonald, Daniel. *A Twentieth Century History of Marshall County, Indiana.* 2 vols. Chicago, 1908.

McDowell, John R., ed. *The History of Hendricks County, 1914–1976.* Danville, Indiana, 1976.

McPherson, Alan. *Indian Names in Indiana.* Monticello, Indiana, 1993.

Madison, James H. *The Indiana Way: A State History.* Bloomington, 1986.

Madison, James H., ed. *Heartland: Comparative Histories of Midwestern States.* Bloomington, 1988.

Mencken, H. L. *The American Language.* New York, 1962.

Mencken, H. L. *The American Language: Supplement II.* New York, 1962.

Montgomery, M. W. *History of Jay County, Indiana.* Chicago, [1864].

Morrow, Jackson. *History of Howard County, Indiana.* Indianapolis, [1909].

The National Gazetteer of the United States of America—Indiana, 1988. U.S. Geological Survey Professional Paper 1200-IN. Reston, Va., 1988.

Nicholson, Meredith. *The Hoosiers.* New York, 1915.

Nicolaisen, W. F. H. *Scottish Place Names: Their Study and Significance.* London, 1976.

Normal Publishing House. *History of Valparaiso.* Valparaiso, Indiana, 1876.

Nowland, John H. B. *Early Reminiscences of Indianapolis.* Indianapolis, 1870.

Nowland, John H. B. *Sketches of Prominent Citizens of 1876.* Indianapolis, 1877.

Oakey, Charles Cochran. *Greater Terre Haute and Vigo County.* 2 vols. Chicago and New York, 1908.

O'Donnell, Harold L. *Newport and Vermillion Township: The First 100 Years, 1824–1924.* Danville, Illinois, 1969

Ogle, George A., and Company. *Plat Book of La Porte County, Indiana.* Chicago, 1892.

Ogle, George A., and Company. *Standard Atlas of Benton County, Indiana.* Chicago, 1909.

Ogle, George A., and Company. *Standard Atlas of Hendricks County, Indiana.* Chicago, 1904.

Ogle, George A., and Company. *Standard Atlas of Jasper County, Indiana.* Chicago, 1900.

Ogle, George A., and Company. *Standard Atlas of Marshall County, Indiana.* Chicago, 1908.

Ogle, George A., and Company. *Standard Atlas of Parke County, Indiana.* Chicago, 1908.

Ogle, George A., and Company. *Standard Atlas of St. Joseph County, Indiana.* Chicago, 1895.

Packard, Jasper. *History of La Porte County, Indiana.* La Porte, 1876.

Paul, Hosea. *Atlas of Wabash County, Indiana.* Philadelphia, 1875.

Pegee, O. W. *Atlas of Ripley County, Indiana.* New York, 1900.

Pleas, Elwood. *Henry County: A Brief History of the County from 1821 to 1871.* New Castle, Indiana, 1871.

Pleasant, Hazen Hayes. *A History of Crawford County, Indiana.* Greenfield, Indiana, 1926.

Plummer, John T. *A Directory to the City of Richmond, Together with a Historical Sketch by John T. Plummer.* Richmond, Indiana, 1857.

Powell, Jehu Z., ed. *History of Cass County, Indiana.* 2 vols. Chicago and New York, 1913.

Power, Richard Lyle. "The Hoosier as an American Folk-Type," *Indiana Magazine of History,* 38 (1942), 108–122.

Pulaski County Centennial Association. *Souvenir Program and History, Pulaski County, Indiana.* Winamac, 1939.

Putnam County Sesquicentennial Committee. *A Journey through Putnam County History.* N.p., 1966.

Quinn, French. *A Short, Short Story of Adams County, Indiana.* Berne, Indiana, n.d.

Randall, G. A. *An Illustrated Historical Atlas of Jackson County, Indiana.* N.p., 1878.

Reifel, August J. *History of Franklin County, Indiana.* Indianapolis, 1915.

Rennick, Robert M. "Cecil Charles as an East Central Indiana Place Names Tradition Bearer," *Midwestern Folklore,* 17 (Spring 1991), 14–22.

Rennick, Robert M. "The Folklore of Place-Naming in Indiana," *Indiana Folklore,* 3, No. 1 (1970), 35–94.

Rennick, Robert M. *Kentucky Place Names.* Lexington, 1984.

Rennick, Robert M. "Place-Name Derivations Are Not Always What They Seem," *Indiana Names,* 2 (Spring 1971), 19–28.

Rennick, Robert M. "Research in Placenames, a Cautionary Note," *Names,* 40 (1992), 229–234.

Rennick, Robert M. "The Role of Oral History in Place-Name Research." In *The Study of Place Names,* ed. Ronald L. Baker. Terre Haute, 1991, pp. 65–72.

Rerick Brothers. *The County of Henry, Indiana; Topography, History, Art Folio.* N.p., n.d.

Rerick Brothers. *The County of Wayne, Indiana: An Imperial Atlas and Art Folio.* Richmond, Indiana, 1893.

Richman, George J. *History of Hancock County, Indiana.* Indianapolis, 1916.

Roberts, Warren E. *Viewpoints on Folklife: Looking at the Overlooked.* Ann Arbor, 1988.

Roose, William H. *Indiana's Birthplace: A History of Harrison County, Indiana*. New Albany, 1911.

Royalty, James H. *History of the Town of Remington and Vicinity, Jasper County, Indiana*. Logansport, 1894.

Rudolph, Robert S. *Wood County Place Names*. Madison, Wisc., 1970.

Rushville Publishing Company. *Atlas and Directory of Rush County, Indiana*. Rushville, 1908.

Sanders, Scott Russell. *Staying Put*. Boston, 1993.

Scott, John. *The Indiana Gazetteer or Topographical Dictionary, 1826*. Indiana Historical Society Publications, vol. 18, no. 1. Indianapolis, 1954.

Seits, Laurence E. "Place Names of Parke County, Indiana," M.A. thesis, Indiana State University, 1970.

Shinn, Benjamin G. *Biographical Memoirs of Blackford County, Indiana*. Chicago, 1900.

Shinn, Benjamin G. *Blackford and Grant Counties, Indiana: A Chronicle of Their People*. 2 vols. Chicago, 1914.

Shirts, August Finch. *A History of the Formation, Settlement and Development of Hamilton County, Indiana*. [Noblesville], 1901.

Shumaker, Arthur W. *A History of Indiana Literature*. Indianapolis, 1962.

Slocum, Charles Elihu. *History of the Maumee River Basin*. 3 vols. Toledo, 1905.

Smith, Hubbard Madison. *Historical Sketches of Old Vincennes*. Vincennes, 1902.

Smith, John L. *Past and Present of Randolph County, Indiana*. Indianapolis, 1914.

Snow, J. F. *Snow's History of Adams County, Indiana*. Indianapolis, 1907.

Snowden, Juliet. *Legends and Lore of Parke County, Indiana*. Rockville, Indiana, 1981.

Spicer, R. [Printing Company]. *History of Shelby County, Indiana: from 1822 to 1876*. Shelbyville, Indiana, 1876.

Stephens, John H. *History of Miami County*. Peru, Indiana, 1896.

Stewart, George S. *American Place-Names*. New York, 1970.

Stewart, James Hervey. *Recollections of the Early Settlement of Carroll County, Indiana*. Cincinnati, 1872.

Stormont, Gilbert R. *History of Gibson County, Indiana*. Indianapolis, 1914.

Sullivan Times Company. *Art Souvenir of Leading Citizens and Farmers' Directory of Sullivan County, Indiana*. [Sullivan], 1896.

Tartt, James T., and Company. *History of Gibson County, Indiana*. Edwardsville, Illinois, 1884.

Taylor, Robert M., Jr., et al. *Indiana: A New Historical Guide*. Indianapolis, 1980.

Tillman and Fuller Publishing Company. *An Illustrated Plat Book of Vanderburgh and Warrick Counties, Indiana*. Evansville, [1899].

Tillman and Fuller Publishing Company. *An Illustrated Standard Atlas of Warrick County, Indiana*. Evansville, [1899].

Travis, William. *A History of Clay County, Indiana*. 2 vols. New York and Chicago, 1909.

Tucker, E. *History of Randolph County, Indiana*. Chicago, 1882.

Vansina, Jan. *The Oral Tradition*. Chicago, 1961.

The Wall Street Journal, January 27, 1987, p. 1; February 9, 1987, p. 19; February 24, 1987, p. 33; March 18, 1987, p. 31; March 26, 1987, p. 37; April 27, 1987, p. 25.

Warner, Beers and Company. *History of Fayette County, Indiana*. Chicago, 1885.

Warren County Historical Society. *A History of Warren County, Indiana*. N.p., 1966.

Wasson, John Macamy. *Annals of Pioneer Settlers on the Whitewater and its Tributaries*. Richmond, Indiana, 1875.

Weakley, F. E., and Company. *History of Dearborn and Ohio Counties, Indiana*. Chicago, 1885.

Weakley, Harraman and Company. *History of Dearborn, Ohio and Switzerland Counties, Indiana*. Chicago, 1885.

Webster's New World Dictionary of the American Language. Cleveland and New York, 1964.

Webster's Ninth New Collegiate Dictionary. Springfield, Mass., 1983.

Weik, Jesse William. *Weik's History of Putnam County, Indiana*. Indianapolis, 1910.

Western Publishing Company. *Holland's Plymouth City Directory for 1876–7, Containing a Historical Sketch of the City and History of Marshall County, Indiana*. Chicago, 1876.

White, Edward, ed. *Evansville and Its Men of Mark*. Evansville, 1873.

Whitson, Rolland Lewis, ed. *Centennial History of Grant County, Indiana*. 2 vols. Chicago and New York, 1914.

Wilgus, D. K., and Lynwood Montell. "Beanie Short: A Civil War Chronicle in Legend and Song." In *The American Folk Legend*, ed. Wayland D. Hand. Berkeley, 1971, pp. 133–156.

Williams, L. A., and Company. *History of the Ohio Falls Cities and Their Counties*. 2 vols. Cleveland, 1882.

Wilson, Fuller and Company. *An Illustrated Standard Atlas of Sullivan County, Indiana*. [Evansville, 1899].

Wilson, George R. *History and Art Souvenir of Dubois County*. [Jasper], 1896.

Wilson, William E. *Indiana: A History*. Bloomington, 1966.

Wolfe, Thomas Jefferson, ed. *A History of Sullivan County, Indiana*. 2 vols. New York and Chicago, 1909.

Wood, Mary Elizabeth. *The French Imprint on the Heart of America*. Knightstown, Indiana, 1977.

Woollen, William Wesley. *Biographical and Historical Sketches of Early Indiana*. Indianapolis, 1883.

Works Progress Administration. *Indiana: A Guide to the Hoosier State*. American Guide Series. New York, 1941.

Works Progress Administration. Indiana Manuscript Files of the Federal Writers' Project, Cunningham Memorial Library, Indiana State University, Terre Haute.

Wright, Joseph. *The English Dialect Dictionary*. 6 vols. London, 1898–1905.

Wright, Williamson Swift. *Pastime Sketches, with Papers Read before the Cass County, Indiana, Historical Society*. [Logansport], 1907.

Young, Andrew White. *History of Wayne County, Indiana*. Cincinnati, 1872.

RONALD L. BAKER, Chairperson and Professor of English at Indiana State University, is the author of *Folklore in the Writings of Rowland E. Robinson, Hoosier Folk Legends, Jokelore: Humorous Folktales from Indiana, French Folklife in Old Vincennes,* and numerous articles in folklore journals. He is coauthor of *Indiana Place Names.*